options
markets

John C. Cox

Massachusetts Institute of Technology

Mark Rubinstein

University of California, Berkeley

PRENTICE-HALL, INC., *Englewood Cliffs, New Jersey 07632*

Library of Congress Cataloging in Publication Data

Cox, John C.
  Options markets.

  Bibliography: p.
  Includes index.
  1. Put and call transactions. I. Rubinstein,
Mark. II. Title.
HG6042.C69 1985   332.64'52   84-24764
ISBN 0-13-638205-3

HG 6042
.C 69
1985

To
Maria and James
and to
Nancee, Judd, and Maisie

Editorial/production supervision: Greg Hubit
Cover design: Edsal Enterprises
Manufacturing buyer: Ed O'Dougherty

Printed in the United States of America

10

ISBN 0-13-638205-3 01

Prentice-Hall International, Inc., *London*
Prentice-Hall of Australia Pty. Limited, *Sydney*
Editora Prentice-Hall do Brasil, Ltda., *Rio de Janeiro*
Prentice-Hall Canada Inc., *Toronto*
Prentice-Hall Hispanoamericana, S.A., *Mexico*
Prentice-Hall of India Private Limited, *New Delhi*
Prentice-Hall of Japan, Inc., *Tokyo*
Prentice-Hall of Southeast Asia Pte. Ltd., *Singapore*
Whitehall Books Limited, *Wellington, New Zealand*

contents

preface

The trading of options and the scientific study of options both have long histories, yet both underwent revolutionary changes at virtually the same time in the early 1970s. These changes, and the subsequent events to which they led, have greatly increased the practical value of a thorough understanding of options.

Although options have been traded for centuries, they were, until recently, relatively obscure and unimportant financial instruments. Options markets were fragmented, and transactions were both costly and difficult to arrange. All of this changed in 1973 with the creation of the Chicago Board Options Exchange, the first registered securities exchange for the purpose of trading in options. The exchange began modestly, with trading only in call options on sixteen common stocks, but it soon became a tremendous success. This success, in turn, led to a series of innovations in options trading. In 1975 and 1976, the American, Philadelphia, and Pacific Stock Exchanges began trading call options on common stocks. In 1977, put options were also listed on all of the exchanges. Within ten years of the establishment of the first options exchanges, the volume of trading in stock options grew to a level often exceeding, in terms of share equivalents, that of the New York Stock Exchange, and the number of stocks on which exchange-listed options were available rose from sixteen to nearly four hundred. In the early 1980s, listed options trading has also expanded into financial instruments other than common stocks, including options on stock indexes, foreign currencies, U.S. Treasury securities, stock index futures, commodity futures, U.S. Treasury bond futures, and foreign currency futures. It certainly seems reasonable to predict that options will play an increasingly important role in financial markets in the future.

The study of options has an illustrious history dating back to the late nineteenth century, and some of the early works in the field made pioneering contributions to the theory of stochastic processes. Nevertheless, a completely satisfactory theory of option valuation was not developed until the early 1970s. Since that time, option pricing theory has been refined and expanded in many ways and has proven to be extremely useful. Indeed, its implications have extended well beyond exchange-traded options. Quite generally, an option contract can be thought of as any security whose returns are contractually related to the returns on some other security or group of securities. From this perspective, the principles of option valuation can be applied to a broad range of financial instruments. Included in this range are not only securities that have obvious option-like features, such as warrants and convertible bonds, but also securities that do not seem to be like options at all, such as common stocks and ordinary bonds.

The purpose of our book is to provide a detailed discussion of these academic and institutional developments. Rather than give superficial coverage of many different kinds of options, we have chosen to concentrate on the oldest and largest segment of the options markets, options on common stocks. As will be evident, most of our conclusions reached in the context of stock options can be easily modified to apply to other types of options.

Chapter 1 gives a basic introduction to put and call contracts and the market structure in which they are traded. This chapter also shows the profit-and-loss consequences of some elementary option trading strategies. In Chapter 2, we examine the fundamental variables that affect option value and discuss why investors use options. Chapter 3 continues the introduction to market structure given in Chapter 1 and provides a detailed description of the environment in which stock options are traded.

Chapter 4 begins our material on option valuation. Here we derive certain basic properties that option prices must satisfy if there are to be no arbitrage opportunities. These methods require virtually no knowledge of stock price movements, and are consequently quite general. In Chapter 5, we describe how additional information about stock price movements can be used to derive the exact value of an option. In Chapter 6, we show how to modify and implement the theory developed in Chapter 5 for practical investment purposes. Chapter 7 provides some further extensions of option valuation and shows how the theory can be applied to corporate securities. Chapter 8 discusses the social role of options and gives suggestions for improving options markets, some of which have already been implemented.

We owe a substantial debt to our academic colleagues who have contributed to the strong theoretical basis for option valuation now available. For each subject, we have usually given only one or two primary references, but many additional references can be found in the bibliography. Special thanks go to Fischer Black and Myron Scholes, who developed the first completely satisfactory theory of option valuation; to Robert Merton, who extended the theory in fundamental ways and provided many other insights into option pricing; and to William Sharpe, who discovered a way to derive the basic principles of option valuation using only elementary mathematics. We have also benefited greatly from the comments and suggestions of a number of other individuals, including Michael Brennan, George Constantinides, Kenneth Dunn, John Ezell, Gary Gastineau, Robert Geske, Steven Givot, Blair Hull, Jonathan Ingersoll, Hayne Leland, Louis Morgan, Krishna

Ramaswamy, Scott Richard, Stephen Ross, Harry Roth, Andrew Rudd, Eduardo Schwartz, David Shukovsky, Richard Stitt, and Hans Stoll. We also appreciate the secretarial assistance of Ellen McGibbon, Edie Vranjes, and June Wong. Last, but by no means least, we are grateful to our families for their help and encouragement.

John C. Cox

Mark Rubinstein

introduction

1

1-1. WHAT ARE PUTS AND CALLS?

Every field has its own special vocabulary. Since options trading is no exception, we will begin with some basic definitions. Options markets exist or are planned for a wide variety of instruments, so to avoid needless repetition we will focus on the oldest and largest of these markets, options on common stocks.

> A *call* option is a contract giving its owner the right to
> *buy* a fixed number of shares of a specified common
> stock at a fixed price at any time on or before a given
> date.

The act of making this transaction is referred to as *exercising* the option. The specified stock is known as the *underlying security*. The fixed price is termed the exercise price or *striking price*, and the given date, the maturity date or *expiration date*. The individual who creates or issues a call is termed the seller or *writer*,[1] and the individual who purchases a call is termed the holder or *buyer*. The market price of the call is termed the premium or *call*

---

[1] The term *writer* is preferred to *seller* to emphasize the fact that, unlike stock which originates with a corporation, a call is literally issued on behalf of a single individual investor.

1

price. In other words, if a call is exercised, the complete transaction involves an exchange of

call price from buyer
for
call from writer

and a subsequent exchange of

striking price + call from buyer
for
common stock from writer.

The buyer has the right, but not the obligation, to make this subsequent exchange, so it will take place only if he feels it is in his best interest.[2]

For example, an ALCOA/JAN/50 call bought on the Chicago Board Options Exchange at the close of trading on August 20, 1979, would have cost $750, exclusive of commissions. This call gave the buyer the right to purchase 100 common shares of Alcoa stock for $50 per share at any time until January 18, 1980. On any trading day until the expiration date, the buyer can do one of three things:

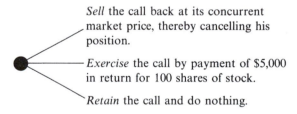

Sell the call back at its concurrent market price, thereby cancelling his position.

Exercise the call by payment of $5,000 in return for 100 shares of stock.

Retain the call and do nothing.

On the expiration date itself, the third alternative is equivalent to permitting the call to *expire*. On this date, ignoring the sell alternative, it is easy to see which of the other two alternatives is in the best interest of the buyer. This depends on the concurrent price of Alcoa's common stock. If the stock price is greater than $50 per share, then (neglecting commissions), it will pay the call buyer to exercise the call, since by doing so he can buy the stock for $50 and, if he desires, immediately resell it on the market at a profit. On the other hand, if the stock price is less than $50, then the call buyer should let the call expire. Of course, after the expiration date, the call will be worthless, since the first two alternatives will have lapsed.

---

[2] A call should not be confused with a forward contract. At its maturity, a forward contract *must* be exercised. For a more detailed comparison of options with forward contracts, see the appendix to Chapter 2.

To represent the contractual implications of a call on its expiration date in symbols, let

K = the striking price,

$S*$ = the market price of the underlying security on the expiration date, and

$C*$ = the value of the call (to one share) on its expiration date.

Then

$$C* = \begin{cases} S* - K & \text{if } S* > K \\ 0 & \text{if } S* \leq K \end{cases}$$

or, alternatively, $C* = \max[0, S* - K]$. Some race-track terms have slipped into the options vocabulary: if $S* > K$, the call is said to "finish in-the-money"; if $S* < K$, the call is said to "finish out-of-the-money."

In contrast to a call,

> A *put* option is a contract giving its owner the right to *sell* a fixed number of shares of a specified common stock at a fixed price at any time on or before a given date.

If a put is exercised, the complete transaction involves an exchange of

put price from buyer

for

put from writer

and a subsequent exchange of

common stock + put from buyer

for

striking price from writer.

Again, this subsequent exchange will take place only at the choice of the buyer. If $P*$ is the value of a put (to one share) on its expiration date, then

$$P* = \begin{cases} 0 & \text{if } S* \geq K \\ K - S* & \text{if } S* < K \end{cases}$$

or, alternatively, $P* = \max[0, K - S*]$. In this case, if $S* < K$, the put finishes in-the-money.

There are thus two *types* of options—puts and calls. All option contracts of the same type written on the same underlying stock constitute a
class of options. Call and put options on the same underlying security are
considered separate classes. Within a given class, all option contracts with
the same expiration date and striking price constitute an option *series*.

Puts and calls are the basic forms of options. However, many other
securities, such as corporate bonds and stocks, have similar characteristics.
Thus much of what we have to say about puts and calls applies also to
other types of securities. In Chapter 7 we will take advantage of this correspondence and develop relative pricing relationships among differing claims
against the assets of a corporation.

It is easy to determine the value of a put or call on its expiration date.
Finding its value at any time prior to expiration is much more difficult. We
will provide an informal analysis in Chapter 2 and some precise answers in
Chapters 4, 5 and 7. Taking a first cut now, it should be obvious that a put
or call, since it can be exercised at any time until its expiration date, must
be worth at least its current exercise value. Let

S = the current market price of the underlying security,

C = the current value of an associated call, and

P = the current value of an associated put.

The current value C of a call must then at least equal $\max[0, S - K]$, and
the current value P of a put must at least equal $\max[0, K - S]$. We will
refer to $\max[0, S - K]$ and $\max[0, K - S]$ as the exercise value or *parity
value* of a call and a put, respectively. Since an option may be more valuable retained than exercised, its price may exceed its parity value.[3] We term
this difference, $C - \max[0, S - K]$ for a call and $P - \max[0, K - S]$ for a
put, the *premium over parity* of an option. The market price of an option is
then equal to the sum of its parity value and premium over parity.[4]

The race-track terms mentioned earlier are applied before expiration
as well: If $S > K$, a call is *in-the-money*; if $S = K$, it is *at-the-money*; if
$S < K$, it is *out-of-the-money*. For a put, the definitions are reversed; a put is
in-the-money if $S < K$. Thus, an option is in-the-money if its parity value is
positive. If S is much greater than K, then a call is said to be *deep-in-the-*

---

[3] We will refer to exercise before the expiration date as *early exercise*; this does not imply that
such exercising is inappropriate or untimely.

[4] The use of the term "premium" to refer to the total price of an option is a carryover from
former times when options were almost always sold at-the-money (that is, $K = S$). Consequently, at the time of sale the "premium" and "premium over parity" were the same thing. To
prevent possible confusion, we will always use the term "price" in place of premium, and
reserve the term "premium over parity" to refer to the excess of the option price over the
difference between the stock price and the striking price.

money and a put *deep-out-of-the-money*. If S is much less than K, then a call is *deep-out-of-the-money* and a put is *deep-in-the-money*.

The profit and loss implications of an option position are often confusing at first. *Payoff diagrams*, relating the profit from a position *if held to expiration* to the underlying stock price *at expiration*, are a useful aid. The most elementary payoff diagram (Fig. 1-1) describes a long position in stock. This relates the net profit realized on a given date in the future to the stock price on that date.

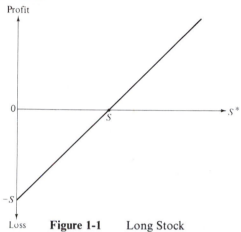

Figure 1-1   Long Stock

If the stock price on the final date is zero (that is, $S^* = 0$), then a long stock position will have experienced a net loss of S, where S is the current stock price. If $S^* = S$, the position will result in no profit or loss. In general, net profit will equal $S^* - S$. A \$1 increase in S^* is exactly matched by a \$1 increase in net profit. In brief, the *payoff line* for this position is a 45° line with positive slope, with a zero profit point at S. For simplicity, we have so far ignored complications that may be created by commissions, margin, taxes, and dividends. Similarly, a short position[5] in the stock is described by Figure 1-2. With a long position in the stock, the possible loss is limited to S, while the possible gain is unlimited. With a short position, just the reverse is true. Here the possible gain is limited to S, while the possible loss is unlimited.

---

[5] A short position involves selling stock one does not own. This is accomplished by borrowing the stock from an investor who has purchased it. At some subsequent date, the short seller is obligated to buy the stock to pay back the lender of the shares. Since this repayment requires *equal shares rather than equal dollars*, the short seller benefits from a decline in the stock price.

If cash dividends are paid on the stock while a short position is maintained, these are paid to the buying party of the short sale. The short seller must also compensate the investor from whom the stock was borrowed by matching the cash dividends from his own resources. In brief, not only does the short seller not receive cash dividends, but he must also make matching payments.

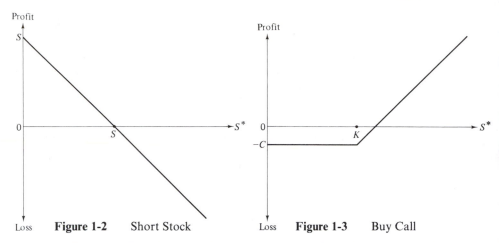

Profit

S

0 S S^*

Loss   **Figure 1-2**   Short Stock

Profit

0 K S^*

$-C$

Loss   **Figure 1-3**   Buy Call

Figures 1-3, 1-4, 1-5, and 1-6 show the profit-and-loss implications of the four basic positions in options. Evidently, a purchased call is like a long position in the underlying security, except that it has the advantage of insurance against extreme downside movements in the stock price. Similarly, a purchased put is like a short position in the underlying security, except that it affords protection against extreme upside movements in the stock. However, both puts and calls have an important disadvantage: The insurance they provide costs money in the form of the premium over parity. To emphasize this point, suppose the current stock price S is equal to the striking price K and by the expiration date the stock price remains unchanged, so that $S^* = S$. While a long or short position in the stock would show a zero net profit, a purchase of a put or a call would result in the loss of the entire investment, the current option price.

At first glance, it seems that a stop-loss order would provide the same kind of insurance as a call. Suppose that we purchase a share of the stock

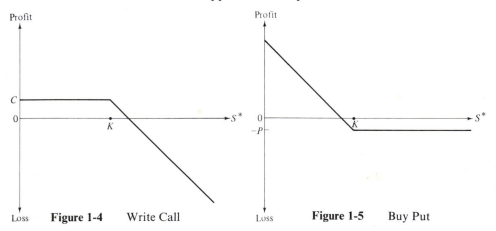

Profit

C

0 K S^*

Loss   **Figure 1-4**   Write Call

Profit

0 K S^*

$-P$

Loss   **Figure 1-5**   Buy Put

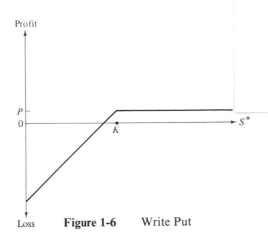

Figure 1-6   Write Put

by investing $S - K$ and borrowing the remainder, K. At the same time we tell our broker to sell the stock if its price drops to K and place the proceeds in default-free bonds. To make things simpler, suppose interest rates and dividends are zero. The value of our position on any specified expiration date is, after repayment of the borrowing, apparently exactly the same as a call—0 if $S^* \leq K$ and $S^* - K$ if $S^* > K$. Furthermore, the net investment required was only $S - K$. But this argument has a fatal flaw. A call will indeed receive $S^* - K$ whenever $S^* > K$, but we will receive this amount only if $S^* > K$ *and* the stock price never goes below K before the expiration date. Furthermore, it may not be possible to execute the stop-loss order exactly at K. If the stock price can take sudden jumps, we may end up being sold out at a price below K. In that event, we would not receive enough from the sale to cover our borrowing. Not only would we lose our initial investment, but also we would have to put up more money to close out the position. This can never happen with a call. Consequently, the owner of a call may receive some gains that we will miss, and he will avoid some losses that we may have to bear. These advantages make a call worth more than its parity value. As we will see in the next chapter, when dividends and interest rates are not zero, they will also influence the premium over parity. Hence, we can conclude that an option gives a kind of insurance that cannot be obtained with a stop-loss order (or, in the case of a put, with a contingent buy order).

The payoff diagrams clearly illustrate an important point: *the options market is a zero-sum game.* That is, what the option buyer profits, the option writer loses, and vice versa. Ignoring the impact of taxes, any claim that the options market is typically profitable for both buyers and writers cannot be correct. Indeed, considering commissions, it could, on average, be simultaneously unprofitable for both groups and must be unprofitable for both groups taken together. Nevertheless, the welfare of both groups can be

...proved by trading in options. Other forms of insurance, for example, are also zero-sum games, but no one would argue that they do not have an important economic function.

The great flexibility afforded by puts and calls only becomes evident when combined positions are considered, such as writing a call against a long position in the stock, or simultaneously writing and buying different calls on the same underlying stock. In the next section, payoff diagrams are used to analyze these more complex "covered" positions. In Chapter 6, these diagrams are further generalized to analyze the potential profit from a position prior to expiration.

1-2. PAYOFF DIAGRAMS FOR ELEMENTARY STRATEGIES

If the only securities to be bought or sold are puts and calls on the same underlying security and the underlying security itself, then there are four elementary types of positions that can be taken:

1. Uncovered
2. Hedge
3. Spread
4. Combination

The six *uncovered* or "naked" *positions*—long stock, short stock, buy call, write call, buy put, write put—have already been examined. These were shown to give rise to relatively simple payoff lines. Hedges, spreads, and combinations are types of *covered positions*, in which one or more securities protect the returns of one or more other securities, all related to the same underlying stock.

> A *hedge* combines an option with its underlying stock in
> such a way that either the stock protects the option
> against loss or the option protects the stock against loss.

In other words, a hedge combines a long position in the stock with a written position in calls or a purchased position in puts; a "reverse hedge" combines a short position in the stock with a purchased position in calls or a written position in puts. The most popular hedge consists of writing one call against each share owned of the underlying stock. To analyze this, as for all covered positions, we superimpose the relevant separate payoff diagrams—long stock and write call. The payoff line for the combined position is determined, for each value S^* of the stock at expiration, by adding together the vertical distances of the two separate payoff lines from the horizontal axes. A comparison of Figures 1-6 and 1-7 shows that the payoff diagram for writing a call and buying the stock has the same shape as the payoff diagram for writing a put. We might now suspect that this result could be used to find a relationship between put and call values, and we will soon see that this is indeed true.

Slight variations of the one-to-one hedge produce new payoff patterns. A "ratio" hedge might involve two calls written against each share of stock. As shown in Figure 1-8, this combined position creates a "payoff triangle" that produces a profit as long as the stock price does not experience an extreme change in either direction. However, suppose you, as a potential investor, believe some important news is about to be made public (such as the results of a merger negotiation) that would have a significant impact on the market price of a stock. But you do not know in advance whether the news will be favorable or unfavorable. The "reverse hedge" (Figure 1-9)— buy two calls against each shorted share of the stock—might be an appropriate position. In this case, you show a profit only if the stock price makes a strong move—and it does not matter in which direction! Without options it may be difficult for you to take proper advantage of your beliefs. This is a clear example, among many others, where the availability of options adds flexibility to investment decisions.

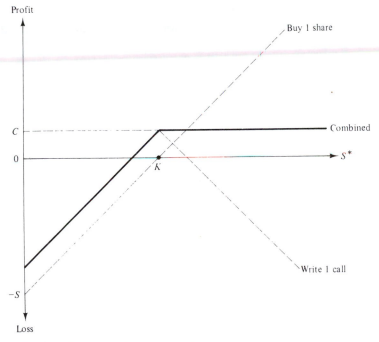

Figure 1-7   1 : 1 Hedge ($S = K$)

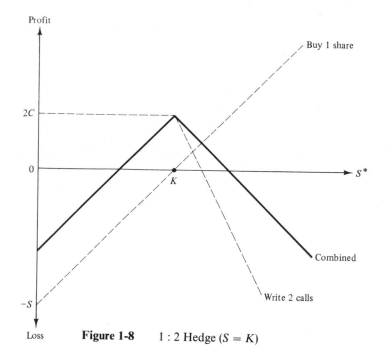

Figure 1-8   1 : 2 Hedge $(S = K)$

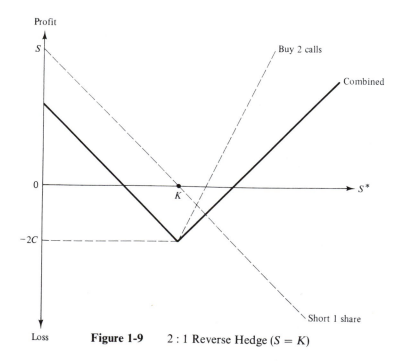

Figure 1-9   2 : 1 Reverse Hedge $(S = K)$

Figures 1-10, 1-11, and 1-12 show some similar hedges using puts.

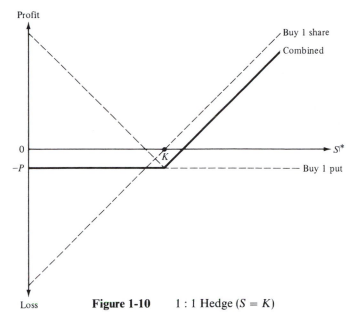

Figure 1-10   1 : 1 Hedge ($S = K$)

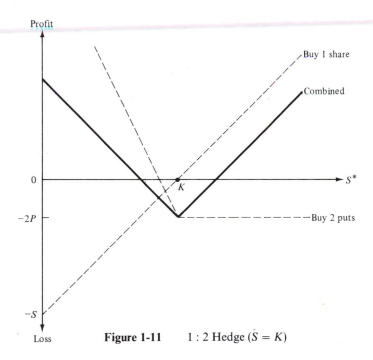

Figure 1-11   1 : 2 Hedge ($\acute{S} = K$)

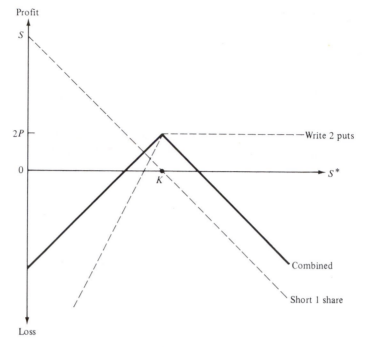

Figure 1-12   2 : 1 Reverse Hedge $(S = K)$

**A *spread* combines options of different series but of the
same class, where some are bought and others are
written.**

Two common spreads are the *vertical spread* (also termed "money," "price,"
or "perpendicular" spread) and the *horizontal spread* (also termed "time" or
"calendar" spread). As shown in Table 1-1, in a vertical spread, one option
is bought and another sold, both on the same underlying stock and with the
same expiration date, but with *different striking prices*.

Table 1-1
VERTICAL SPREAD (CALLS)

| Striking Price | *Expiration Month* | | | Stock Price |
	JAN	*APR*	*(JUL)*	
XYZ ⑳30	11	$12\frac{3}{8}$	$13\frac{1}{2}$	40
XYZ 40	$4\frac{1}{2}$	$6\frac{1}{4}$	$7\frac{7}{8}$	40
XYZ ㊿50	$1\frac{1}{4}$	$2\frac{7}{8}$	$4\frac{3}{8}$	40

Table 1-2
HORIZONTAL SPREAD (CALLS)

Striking Price	Expiration Month			Stock Price
	JAN	APR	JUL	
XYZ 30	11	$12\frac{3}{8}$	$13\frac{1}{2}$	40
XYZ 40	$4\frac{1}{2}$	$6\frac{1}{4}$	$7\frac{7}{8}$	40
XYZ 50	$1\frac{1}{4}$	$2\frac{7}{8}$	$4\frac{3}{8}$	40

As shown in Table 1-2, in a horizontal spread, one option is bought and another sold, both on the same underlying stock and with the same striking price, but with *different expiration dates.*

Note that horizontal spreads cannot be represented by a standard payoff diagram. Later, when we develop exact formulas for pricing options, it will be possible to represent horizontal spreads by payoff diagrams, since we will know the value of the long-maturity option on the expiration date of the short-maturity option for each level of the stock price on that expiration date.

In a *diagonal spread*, one option is bought and another sold, both on the same underlying stock, but with *different striking prices* and *different expiration dates.* By extension, there are four types of diagonal spreads. Again, these cannot be graphed in the usual payoff diagram because they involve options of different maturity. The terms vertical, horizontal, and diagonal arise from the format for listing put and call prices in the newspaper.

Each of the spreads has its *bullish* and *bearish* versions. In a bullish vertical spread, the option purchased has the lower striking price. For a bullish horizontal spread, the option with the longer time to expiration is purchased. Finally, with a bullish diagonal spread, the purchased option has both a lower striking price and a longer time to expiration than the written option. For the corresponding bearish spreads, the positions are reversed. Although these terms are frequently used, they can be quite misleading. The names imply that a bullish spread should benefit from an increase in the stock price and that a bearish spread should benefit from a decrease. Unfortunately, as we will see in Chapter 6, this is not always true for horizontal and diagonal spreads. The implication is correct only for vertical spreads.

Figure 1-13 is the payoff diagram for a bullish vertical spread. The call with the lower striking price has been purchased and the call with the higher striking price has been written. In Table 1-1 we would have bought the XYZ/30 for $13\frac{1}{2}$ and sold the XYZ/50 for $4\frac{3}{8}$. Our spread requires an

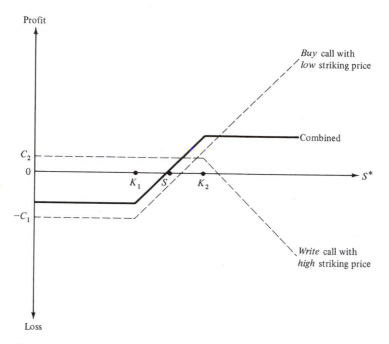

Figure 1-13   Bullish Vertical Spread

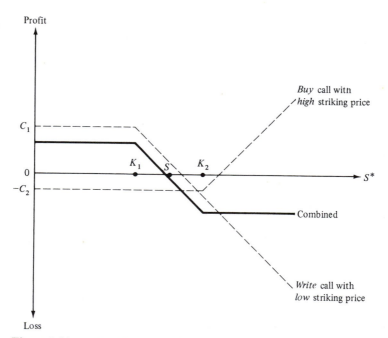

Figure 1-14   Bearish Vertical Spread

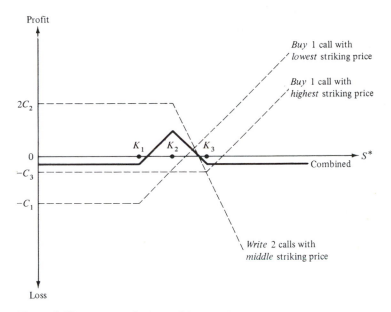

Figure 1-15   Butterfly Spread $(S = K_2)$

initial cash outlay. This suggests why a bullish spread is alternatively termed a *purchased spread*. We would be said to have "bought the spread."

On the other hand, had the XYZ/30 been sold and the XYZ/50 bought, we would have a bearish or *written spread*. These designations are actually more appropriate than the terms bullish and bearish. As we will see in Chapter 4, neglecting margin, all of the spreads described as bullish should, for calls, indeed require initial cash outlays. Similarly, the bearish positions should produce an initial cash inflow. The terms *purchased* and *written* are descriptively accurate, while the terms *bullish* and *bearish* are not. One disadvantage is that the labels must be reversed for puts. A bullish spread using puts will be a written spread; the corresponding bearish spread will be a purchased spread.

In a *butterfly spread*, two options in the middle, with respect to striking price or expiration date, are purchased (written) against writing (buying) one option on each side, all on the same underlying stock. Figure 1-15 illustrates a butterfly vertical spread, where the middle calls have been written and the end calls purchased. A small profit would be realized only if the stock price stays near the striking price of the written calls. A butterfly spread does not qualify as an "elementary" position because it can be interpreted as a portfolio of a bearish and bullish vertical spread, or a portfolio of a bearish and bullish horizontal spread.

Figures 1-16, 1-17, and 1-18 show some similar spreads using puts.

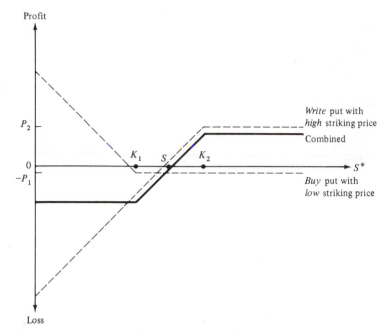

Figure 1-16   Bullish Vertical Spread

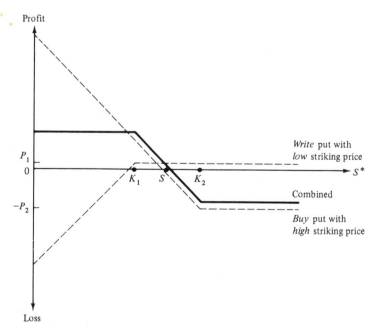

Figure 1-17   Bearish Vertical Spread

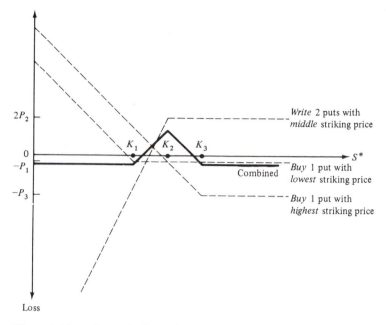

Figure 1-18   Butterfly Spread $(S = K_2)$

A *combination* combines options of different types on the
same underlying stock so that they are either both bought
or both written.

The most popular combination combines a put and a call on the same
underlying stock, with the same striking price and the same expiration date.
This is termed a *straddle*. An example is shown in Table 1-3. If written at-the-
money, this straddle profits only if the stock price remains near the common
striking price. In contrast to a butterfly vertical spread with calls, where the
middle calls are written, this straddle has greater potential for profit and loss,
while the butterfly has less maximum profit and a limited loss. In a written vertical combination around-the-money, the written call is out-of-the-money, and
the written put is in-the-money. While having the same range of profit as a
straddle, the profit triangle is flattened.

As Figures 1-19 through 1-24 suggest, combinations have *bottom* and
top versions, depending on whether the options are bought or written. This
same terminology may be applied to the more complex forms of hedges in
Figures 1-8, 1-9, 1-11, and 1-12. In general, top positions are described by

Table 1-3
STRADDLE

Striking Price	Type	Expiration Month			Stock Price
		JAN	*APR*	(*JUL*)	
XYZ 30	C	11	$12\frac{3}{8}$	$13\frac{1}{2}$	40
XYZ 30	P	$\frac{7}{16}$	$1\frac{1}{8}$	$1\frac{3}{4}$	40
XYZ (40)	C	$4\frac{1}{2}$	$6\frac{1}{4}$	($7\frac{7}{8}$)	40
XYZ (40)	P	$3\frac{1}{2}$	$4\frac{3}{4}$	($5\frac{1}{2}$)	40
XYZ 50	C	$1\frac{1}{4}$	$2\frac{7}{8}$	$4\frac{3}{8}$	40
XYZ 50	P	$10\frac{1}{4}$	11	$11\frac{1}{2}$	40

upward pointing triangles, and bottom positions by downward pointing triangles. "Top" indicates a maximum profit limit, and "bottom" a maximum loss limit.

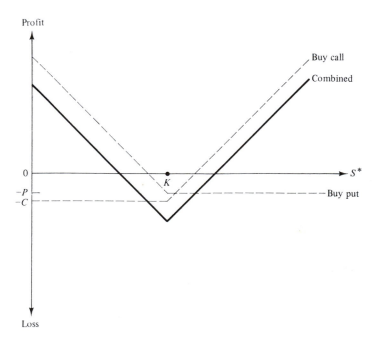

Figure 1-19   Bottom Straddle ($S = K$)

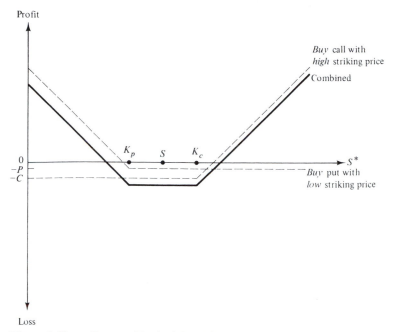

Figure 1-20 Bottom Vertical Combination

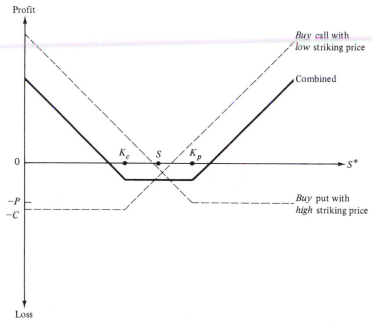

Figure 1-21 Bottom Vertical Combination

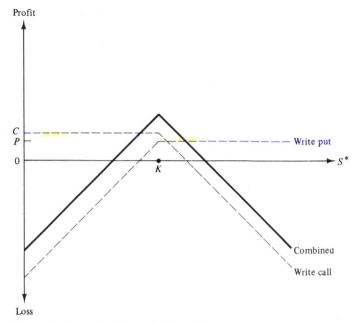

Figure 1-22   Top Straddle $(S = K)$

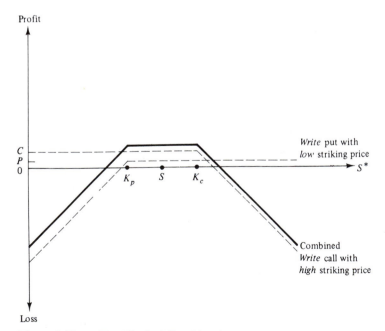

Figure 1-23   Top Vertical Combination

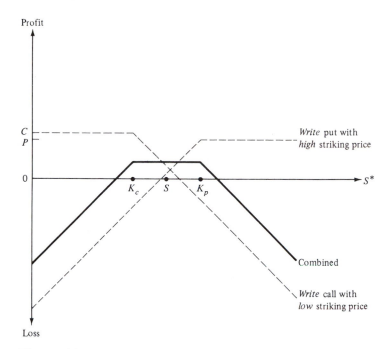

Figure 1-24   Top Vertical Combination

These payoff diagrams provide a good way to become familiar with various investment strategies. However, to interpret them correctly it is important to remember their limitations. They are valid only if all parts of the position are held until expiration. Since most of them involve selling as well as buying options, one could not be sure that they would be held until expiration unless the options could be exercised only at that time. In this case, the options are popularly termed *European*, in contrast to their *American* counterparts, which can be exercised at any time on or before the expiration date.[6] Although these labels do have some historical justification, nearly all options now traded in Europe, as well as in the United States, are of the American type. Nevertheless, we will often find it useful to consider European options.

A few additional qualifications should be kept in mind. If a strategy involves holding a long or short position in the stock, as in Figures 1-7 through 1-12, then the corresponding diagram is valid only if the stock does not pay a dividend during the life of the position. One could informally adjust for this by adding in an amount for dividends received by the stock,

---

[6] A European option obviously cannot be worth more than an otherwise identical American option. However, this does not imply that it will always be worth less. We will discuss this more fully in Chapter 4.

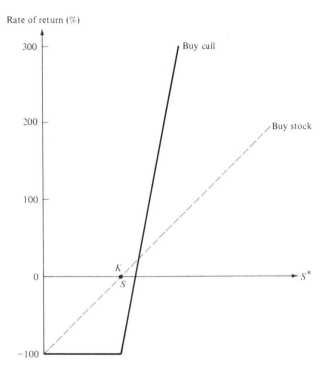

Figure 1-25   Rate of Return Diagram

or subtracting it if the stock is sold short. Also, the vertical placement of each diagram, and the corresponding profit or loss, of course depends on the initial price specified for the options.[7] An alternative that avoids this dependence is the final value diagram, which gives the value of the position at the expiration date for each possible final stock price. Finally, the profit and loss shown do not include the time value of the money invested in the position. The investment must be made now, but the final value is not received until the expiration date. For some purposes it might be helpful to adjust for this by calculating profit and loss relative to the amount to which the initial investment would have grown if it had been invested in default-free bonds.

Another way to illustrate the implications of options positions requiring a positive net investment is with a rate of return diagram. In this case, the profit on the vertical axis is replaced by the corresponding rate of return earned on the net investment in the position. Figure 1-25 compares the rate of return on a long position in one share of stock with the rate of

---

[7] Figures 1-1 through 1-24 correspond to the July option prices shown in Tables 1-1, 1-2, and 1-3.

return on a purchased call option. It shows the considerable difference in risk of equal dollar investments in stock and options.

1-3. A BRIEF SURVEY OF THE WAY OPTIONS ARE TRADED

In the United States, puts and calls have had a history of sporadic acceptability since their first appearance in 1790. The popular misconception equating options with gambling has resulted in extensive government regulation, with puts and calls at times considered illegal. The Securities Act of 1934 empowered the Securities and Exchange Commission (SEC) to regulate options trading, and the Put and Call Brokers and Dealers Association was formed to represent option dealers. Although very small during the 1940s, options volume increased considerably during the next two decades. However, even by 1968, annual contract volume reached only 302,860, representing about 1% of New York Stock Exchange (NYSE) volume, measured in terms of share equivalents.

In retrospect, it is easy to see why the over-the-counter (OTC) market fared so poorly. First, transactions costs were very high. Purchase or sale of an *OTC call* generated three types of direct transactions costs: endorsement fees (to guarantee performance of an option in the event of exercise), the dealer spread, and, typically, a further commission paid by the buyer. Indirect transactions costs resulted from subsequent equity sales or purchases in the event of exercise.

For example, on a call contract (rights to 100 shares) for which the public writer received $200, the public buyer would typically have paid $250. The $50 difference was split among the writer's share of the endorsement fee ($12.50), the buyer's share of the endorsement fee ($12.50), and the dealer bid-ask spread ($25). In addition, the buyer usually paid a $6.25 commission, so the call would actually cost him $256.25. In the event of exercise, the writer of a call would pay a regular stock commission on the forced sale of stock to the call buyer. If he had not already purchased the stock, he would pay another commission. Finally, after receiving payment for the stock sold due to exercise, the writer would usually reinvest the proceeds, generating another commission.

Transactions costs on *OTC puts* were even greater. Since the supply of written puts was usually larger than the demand from put buyers, an intermediary, called a "converter," would buy the put from the writer, and through a series of arbitrage transactions in the underlying stock and default-free instruments, would transform the purchased put into a call, for which there was the requisite demand. Just how this was done need not concern us now; it will become apparent later in Chapter 2. It was,

however, a costly process, adding approximately $20 to the total trans-
actions cost. In effect, the difference in the price paid and received for a put
contract would typically be $70, not including the buyer's commission.

A second reason for the low volume of the OTC options market was
that no convenient secondary market was available for puts and calls.
Buyers and writers were essentially committed to their positions until the
expiration date. Not only did this force equity commissions on options
finishing in-the-money, but also considerably increased a writer's exposure
to risk.

The recent and most significant change in the options market was a
response to these and other deficiencies in the OTC market. On April 26,
1973, the Chicago Board Options Exchange (CBOE) became the first registered exchange for trading listed call contracts. At the time, a total of 48
option series were traded to 16 underlying securities for three different
maturities. Initially, 305 seats were sold for $10,000 each. Average daily
contract volume during May, the first full month of operation, equaled
1,584, with an average of 1.7 contracts per trade. In a short time, interest in
listed options trading has far surpassed initial projections. The CBOE,
given its short tenure, has been the most successful securities exchange in
the history of U.S. capital markets. By March 1974, monthly contract
volume on the CBOE exceeded the entire 1972 annual volume of the earlier
over-the-counter market. By the end of 1974, in terms of share equivalents,
volume exceeded shares traded on the American Stock Exchange. In
December 1983, calls and puts on 145 underlying securities were listed on
the CBOE for an average daily contract volume of 364,977, with an average
of 13.5 contracts per trade. In many cases, daily volume in underlying
stocks was typically exceeded by daily volume in their associated options.
CBOE open interest, the number of outstanding option contracts at any
point in time, had grown 421 times, from 16,222 at the end of May 1973 to
6,840,625 at the end of December 1983. Membership in the CBOE had
expanded to 1,753 by December 1983, with the last sale seat price for the
year of $212,000.

Since the opening of the CBOE, calls have been listed on the American Stock Exchange (AMEX) commencing January 13, 1975, on the Philadelphia Stock Exchange (PHLX) commencing June 25, 1975, on the Pacific
Stock Exchange (PSE) commencing April 9, 1976, and on the Midwest
Stock Exchange (MSE) commencing December 10, 1976.[8] Listed put option
trading was initiated on all five exchanges on June 3, 1977. For the year
1983, average daily option contract volume totaled across all exchanges
equaled 536,201. The market shares for the year were 52.8% for the CBOE,
26.7% for the AMEX, 12.3% for the PHLX, 8.2% for the PSE. Under-

---

[8] The options market of the MSE was combined with the CBOE on June 2, 1980.

standably, OTC contract volume has fallen off, and many OTC dealers have stopped trading. The remaining interest in the OTC market derives principally from longer-than-one-year option maturities on underlying stocks with listed options and options on active and volatile stocks that fail to meet listing requirements.

The success of the organized options exchanges can be attributed to several innovations.

1.   The creation of a *central marketplace*, with its attendant regulatory, surveillance, and price-dissemination capabilities. The exchanges distribute pamphlets on trading in options (on tax aspects or spreading strategies, for example) and make their annual reports and the prospectus of the Options Clearing Corporation available to the public.[9]

2.   The introduction of the *Options Clearing Corporation* as the single guarantor of every CBOE, AMEX, PHLX, and PSE option affords greater protection to option buyers than arrangements provided by the over-the-counter market. The buyer of a contract looks directly to the Clearing Corporation, and not to any particular writer, for performance in the event of exercise.

3.   In creating a *secondary market*, the Clearing Corporation stands as the opposite party to every trade, making it possible for buyers and sellers to terminate their positions at any time by an offsetting transaction. Prior to the CBOE, buyers and writers of options in the over-the-counter market were essentially committed to their positions until the expiration date.

4.   On the CBOE and PSE (but not on the AMEX or PHLX), the *broker/dealer functions of the specialist are separated*. For example, on the CBOE, the broker function is handled by *Floor Brokers* and *Order Book Officials*, who may not trade for their own account; and the dealer function is performed by *Market Makers*, who may only trade for their own account. Public orders are therefore filled exclusively by Floor Brokers and Order Book Officials, while Market Makers, trading from their own capital and inventory, provide liquidity to the market. To reduce further the potential for conflict of interest and to increase liquidity, the CBOE, as well as the PSE, has instituted a competitive Market Maker system. With the exception of certain limited memberships, any Market Maker can trade in any option at any time. In addition, for each underlying security, a number of

---

[9] Materials prepared by the AMEX may be ordered from the Publications Department, American Stock Exchange, 86 Trinity Place, New York, New York 10006. CBOE publications can be obtained by writing to the Marketing Services Coordinator, The Chicago Board Options Exchange, LaSalle at Jackson, Chicago, Illinois 60604. The CBOE also provides a seminar kit for brokers certified to deal in options and makes available on loan a film describing trading on the exchange floor.

Market Makers are assigned the responsibility of trading in the options on a regular basis.

5.   Unlike the over-the-counter markets, the exchanges employ *certificate-less trading.* The ownership of an option is evidenced by confirmations and monthly statements received by customers from their brokers. This facilitates one-day business settlement on option sales and purchases and reduces costs.

6.   *Standardization* of the terms of option contracts has also served to decrease transaction costs.

Options on the same underlying stock have either a January/April/July/October *expiration cycle*, a February/May/August/November cycle, or a March/June/September/December cycle. At any time, options are available with the three expiration dates of the cycle nearest to the present. Therefore, the longest maturity an option can have is nine months. In its expiration month, an option expires at 10 : 59 P.M. Central Time (11 : 59 P.M. Eastern Time) on the Saturday immediately following the third Friday of the month.[10] This is the final time an option can be tendered to the Clearing Corporation. However, secondary market trading of the option ceases at 3 : 00 P.M. Central Time on the business day immediately preceding the expiration date. Furthermore, to exercise an option, a customer must instruct his broker no later than 4 : 30 P.M. Central Time on the business day immediately preceding the expiration date.[11] The calendar in Table 1-4, supplied by the CBOE, marks the expiration dates for 1981 and the Quotron Option Retrieval Code.

Striking prices are chosen by the exchanges from among those permitted by the SEC. As of 1984, the allowable prices were integers evenly divisible by 5, in 5-point intervals for striking prices up to $100 and in 10-point intervals for striking prices over $100. Striking prices that violate this rule are allowed if they arise from adjustments for stock splits or stock dividends, as described below. If an exchange chooses to do so, it may use larger intervals for at least some stocks, and thus omit some possible striking prices. For example, an exchange could choose to use 5-point intervals for striking prices up to $50, 10-point intervals for striking prices between $50 and $200, and 20-point intervals for striking prices over $200.[12] When options with a new expiration date are to be introduced, an exchange will

---

[10] Prior to July 1974, listed options expired on the last business day of their expiration month. From July 1974 to January 1976, the expiration date was the last Monday of the expiration month.

[11] Each brokerage firm has its own rules regarding the deadline for receiving exercise instructions, which may be prior to the 4 : 30 deadline set by the exchanges.

[12] These were the striking price intervals that were allowed by the SEC prior to October 31, 1980.

Table 1-4
EXPIRATION CALENDAR

3OE Expiration Calendar—1981

The Chicago Board **Options Exchange**

UARY, 1981	APRIL, 1981	JULY, 1981	OCTOBER, 1381	JANUARY, 1982	APRIL, 1982	JULY, 1982
M T W T F S	S M T W T F S	S M T W T F S	S M T W T F S	S M T W T F S	S M T W T F S	S M T W T F S
1 2 3	1 2 3 4	1 2 3 4	1 2 3	1 2	1 2 3	1 2 3
5 6 7 8 9 10	5 6 7 8 9 10 11	5 6 7 8 9 10 11	4 5 6 7 8 9 10	3 4 5 6 7 8 9	4 5 6 7 8 9 10	4 5 6 7 8 9 10
2 13 14 15 16 17	12 13 14 15 16 17 18	12 13 14 15 16 17 18	11 12 13 14 15 16 17	10 11 12 13 14 15 16	11 12 13 14 15 16 17	11 12 13 14 15 16 17
9 20 21 22 23 24	19 20 21 22 23 24 25	19 20 21 22 23 24 25	18 19 20 21 22 23 24	17 18 19 20 21 22 23	28 19 20 21 22 23 24	18 19 20 21 22 23 24
6 27 28 29 30 31	26 27 28 29 30	26 27 28 29 30 31	25 26 27 28 29 30 31	24 25 26 27 28 29 30	25 26 27 28 29 30	25 26 27 28 29 30 31
				31		

THE FOLLOWING CBOE UNDERLYING STOCKS EXPIRE DURING THE ABOVE CYCLE

AA	● ARC	BS	FNC	DIS	● XON	● FLR	● HM	● IBM	IP	MRK	MTC	PEP	SQB	● TDY	WY
AXP	● AVP	● BNI	DAL	● DD	● FDX	GWF	● HOI	● HR	JNJ	● MER	NWA	● PRD	● STK	● TXN	● XRX
T	BAM	BGH	DEC	● EK	FNM	● HAL	INA	IGL	● KMG	MMM	PZL	SY	TAN	UPJ	

RUARY, 1981	MAY, 1981	AUGUST, 1981	NOVEMBER, 1981	FEBRUARY, 1982	MAY, 1982	AUGUST, 1982
M T W T F S	S M T W T F S	S M T W T F S	S M T W T F S	S M T W T F S	S M T W T F S	S M T W T F S
2 3 4 5 6 7	1 2	1	1 2 3 4 5 6 7	1 2 3 4 5 6	1	1 2 3 4 5 6 7
9 10 11 12 13 14	3 4 5 6 7 8 9	2 3 4 5 6 7 8	8 9 10 11 12 13 14	7 8 9 10 11 12 13	2 3 4 5 6 7 8	8 9 10 11 12 13 14
6 17 18 19 20 21	10 11 12 13 14 15 16	9 10 11 12 13 14 15	15 16 17 18 19 20 21	14 15 16 17 18 19 20	9 10 11 12 13 14 15	15 16 17 18 19 20 21
3 24 25 26 27 28	17 18 19 20 21 22 23	16 17 18 19 20 21 22	22 23 24 25 26 27 28	21 22 23 24 25 26 27	16 17 18 19 20 21 22	22 23 24 25 26 27 28
	24 25 26 27 28 29 30	23 24 25 26 27 28 29	29 30	28	23 24 25 26 27 28 29	29 30 31
	31	30 31			30 31	

THE FOLLOWING CBOE UNDERLYING STOCKS EXPIRE DURING THE ABOVE CYCLE

AEP	● BLY	● BA	CEA	CWE	GF	● HIA	● JM	● NSM	RJR	SO	UAL	JWC
AHS	BAX	BCC	KO	● CDA	HRS	● HON	MGI	● OXY	● SLB	● SN	UNC	● WCI
AMP	BDK	CBS	CL	● GD	● HWP	IFF	● MOB	RTN	SKY	TG	UTX	● WMB

CH, 1981	JUNE, 1981	SEPTEMBER, 1981	DECEMBER, 1981	MARCH, 1982	JUNE, 1982	SEPTEMBER, 1982
M T W T F S	S M T W T F S	S M T W T F S	S M T W T F S	S M T W T F S	S M T W T F S	S M T W T F S
2 3 4 5 6 7	1 2 3 4 5 6	1 2 3 4 5	1 2 3 4 5	1 2 3 4 5 6	1 2 3 4 5	1 2 3 4
6 17 18 19 20 21	14 15 16 17 18 19 20	6 7 8 9 10 11 12	6 7 8 9 10 11 12	7 8 9 10 11 12 13	6 7 8 9 10 11 12	5 6 7 8 9 10 11
3 24 25 26 27 28	21 22 23 24 25 26 27	13 14 15 16 17 18 19	13 14 15 16 17 18 19	14 15 16 17 18 19 20	13 14 15 16 17 18 19	12 13 14 15 16 17 18
0 31	28 29 30	20 21 22 23 24 25 26	20 21 22 23 24 25 26	21 22 23 24 25 26 27	20 21 22 23 24 25 26	19 20 21 22 23 24 25
		27 28 29 30	27 28 29 30 31	28 29 30 31	27 28 29 30	26 27 28 29 30

THE FOLLOWING CBOE UNDERLYING STOCKS EXPIRE DURING THE ABOVE CYCLE

APA	CHA	● GLW	EVY	● GE	● HT	● KN	MSU	● OI	● REV	S	● TEK
● BMY	CGP	● DOW	F	● GM	ITT	● LIT	● NCR	● RAL	● ROK	● SOC	
BC	CSC	● ESM	● FT	● GW	KM	MCD	● NWT	RCA	SA	● SYN	

OPTION PRICE RETRIEVAL CODES

To retrieve option prices, first key in stock symbol. Then add appropriate expiration month code (put or call) and striking price code.

Expiration Month Codes

Months	Calls	Puts	Month	Calls	Puts	Month	Calls	Puts
anuary	A	M	February	B	N	March	C	O
april	D	P	May	E	Q	June	F	R
uly	G	S	August	H	T	September	I	U
October	J	V	November	K	W	December	L	X

Striking Price Codes

Striking Prices		Code	Striking Prices		Code	Striking Prices		Code
5	105	205	A	35	135	235	G	70	170	270	N
10	110	210	B	40	140	240	H	75	175	275	O
15	115	215	C	45	145	245	I	80	180	280	P
20	120	220	D	50	150	250	J	85	185	285	Q
25	125	225	E	55	155	255	K	90	190	290	R
30	130	230	F	60	160	260	L	95	195	295	S
				65	165	265	M	100	200	300	T

xamples: Alcoa Jan/50/Call—AAAJ
General Motors April/70/Call—GMDN
Control Data Feb/60/Put—CDANL
Hewlett Packard Nov/80/Put—HWPWP

◯ Expiring option classes cease trading today

◇ Expiration date   ☐ Exchange holiday   ● Puts traded

NOTE: New nine-month options are ordinarily introduced on the first business day (usually Monday) following an expiration date.

CBOE EXPIRATION CALENDAR published with the permission of the Chicago Board of Options Exchange.

usually select, for the interval size chosen, the two striking prices closest to the current stock price. If the stock price is very close to one of these striking prices, then often that striking price and the surrounding two will be selected. If the stock price subsequently reaches or moves beyond the highest or lowest existing striking price, then ordinarily trading will be opened two days later in a new striking price, the end point of the new interval. However, without special permission from the SEC, an option cannot be opened with less than 45 days remaining until its expiration or while the underlying stock trades below $6.

With the exception of certain adjustments, described below, *contract units* of options are in "round lots" of 100; that is, one option contract represents rights to 100 shares of the underlying stock. Unlike OTC options, *no adjustments are made for cash dividends.*[13] However, adjustments are made for stock splits and stock dividends by proportionately increasing the number of shares of the underlying stock covered by the option and by decreasing the striking price. For example, consider a single option covering 100 shares of stock with a striking price of $50 per share. Suppose that the stock splits 5 for 4 or, equivalently, issues a 25% stock dividend. Then, after the adjustment, the option will cover 125 ($100 \times \frac{5}{4}$) shares of stock with a striking price of $40 ($50 \times \frac{4}{5}$) per share. However, if a stock split is 1 for 1 or more whole shares, the number of shares covered by an option is not adjusted. Instead, the number of outstanding options is proportionately increased and the striking price is proportionately decreased. Thus if the split were 2 for 1 rather than 5 for 4, after the adjustment the single option would be replaced by two options, each covering 100 shares and having a striking price of $25 per share. In any case, at the time of the adjustment, additional new options with standard terms are usually introduced. These new options have contract units of 100 shares and striking prices chosen according to the rules given in the previous paragraph. Consequently, options that differ in contract units but are identical in every other way may sometimes be traded simultaneously. In the event of recapitalizations, reorganizations, or other distributions, the Clearing Corporation will attempt to adjust the terms of outstanding options in a way that will be fair to both buyers and sellers.

The *underlying securities* chosen for listing must meet a number of requirements. They must be registered and listed on a national securities exchange; be widely held (at least 7,000,000 outstanding shares held by at least 6,000 shareholders); meet a minimum trading volume requirement

---

[13] For this purpose, cash dividends are specified as cash distributions from "earnings and profits" as defined in the Federal Internal Revenue Code. Note that a call buyer would have to exercise the call on the business day *just prior* to the ex-dividend date or earlier to receive the dividend. On the other hand, a put buyer who also holds the underlying stock must wait until the ex-dividend date or after to exercise the put and still receive the dividend.

(2,400,000 shares per year); have a closing market price of at least $10 per share for the prior three-month period; have a record of not defaulting on sinking fund installments, interest, principal and preferred dividend payments during the prior three years; and have a minimum after-tax net income of $1,000,000 for the prior eight quarters. Securities can be voluntarily withdrawn from listing by any exchange, or they are mandatorily withdrawn if they fail to meet certain similar but less stringent requirements. If a security is withdrawn, options trading will continue in all outstanding striking prices and expiration dates, but no new options will be introduced. If a delisted security subsequently satisfies the requirements, it can be listed again. Many underlying securities that would be attractive for listing in terms of their anticipated option trading volume fail to meet one or more of the requirements. It has not been uncommon for an exchange to request permission of the Securities and Exchange Commission to list a new underlying security within a short time after it first qualifies for listing. At the time of this writing, all underlying securities are traded on either the NYSE or the AMEX.

Table 1-5 illustrates how option price information is presented in the *Wall Street Journal*. The particular figures shown are an excerpt from the quotations for December 6, 1983. Each row contains the prices for all options on a given stock with a given striking price. Along each row, the call and put prices are shown for each expiration month. The prices are quoted on a per-share basis, so that the cost of an option contract is given by multiplying the option price by the number of shares covered. Options trading under $3, in terms of rights to one share, trade in sixteenths of a point, while those over $3 trade in eighths.

The recorded prices for options represent the last trade of the day. The closing stock prices reported in the *Wall Street Journal* on the options page may differ from the corresponding stock prices reported on the stock pages. Since January 26, 1976, the high, low, and close reported on the stock pages are composite prices drawn from a pooled ticker tape from all U.S. exchanges. In particular, for NYSE stocks dually listed on the Pacific Stock Exchange, which remains open after the NYSE close, the composite close is likely to represent the last trade on the PSE. However, to value an option at any point in time, we need to know the simultaneous stock price. Since all U.S. options exchanges, as of this writing, close with the NYSE, the NYSE closing stock price is more relevant to value an option at the close of trading than is the composite price.[14] Consequently, the *Wall Street Journal* is careful to record the NYSE closing stock price on the options page. Unfortunately, if all the option quotes for a particular stock

---

[14] To allow a more orderly closing, during 1979 the CBOE, MSE, and PSE initiated the practice of closing at 3 : 10 P.M. Central Time, ten minutes after the NYSE close.

Table 1-5

OPTIONS QUOTATIONS FROM THE *WALL STREET JOURNAL**

Philadelphia Exchange

Option & NY Close	Strike Price	Calls–Last			Puts–Last		
		Dec	Mar	Jun	Dec	Mar	Jun
AirPd	... 40	r	6¼	r	r	r	r
46⅛	... 45	1⅛	3¼	r	½	2¼	r
46⅛	... 50	1-16	1⅛	r	r	r	r
AnheusB	60	4⅝	6⅜	r	1-16	1	1¾
64⅜	... 65	⅝	3½	5¼	1	2½	3¼
64⅜	... 70	⅛	1⅝	3½	r	5⅞	6½
64⅜	... 75	r	½	r	r	10½	r
ArchDM	.20	2⅛	r	r	r	r	r
22	 25	r	½	1⅛	r	r	r
Arch o	.23¾	1-16	1¼	s	r	r	s
Avco	 30	4¼	5¼	r	r	9-16	¾
34⅜	... 35	¼	r	r	1⅛	r	r
BecDic	..35	2¼	r	4⅛	¼	⅞	r
36¾	... 40	⅛	1½	2	3½	3¾	4¼
36¾	... 45	r	¼	1	r	r	8¼
36¾	... 50	r	r	s	13¾	r	s
Chartr	...10	3-16	15-16	1 5-16	½	1⅜	1⅝
9¾	 15	r	3-16	5-16	r	r	r
ChFC o	26⅝	2	s	s	r	s	s
ChFChk	. 25	3⅝	5⅛	r	1-16	⅞	r
28½	... 30	½	2 11-16	3½	1¾	3	r
28½	... 35	⅛	1	1⅞	6¾	r	r
DonLJ	...15	1¼	r	r	⅛	¾	r
16⅛	... 20	r	⅝	1⅛	r	r	r
EGG	 35	¾	2⅜	3½	⅞	2⅛	r
34⅝	... 40	r	⅝	r	r	r	r
E D S	.37½	1	s	s	1¼	s	s
36½	... 30	r	r	r	1-16	¾	r
36½	... 35	2⅜	5	7	r	2⅝	3½
36½	... 40	⅜	2¾	4½	3⅜	5¼	r
36½	... 45	1-16	1⅝	3¼	r	r	9½
Emery	.. 20	r	7	r	r	½	r
26¼	... 25	r	3¾	4¼	½	1¾	r
26¼	... 30	s	1¼	2¼	s	r	r
FinC o	...20	r	3	s	⅜	r	s
20⅞	. 23⅜	⅛	1¾	r	2⅝	3⅝	r
20⅞	. 26⅝	r	⅞	r	5⅞	6⅛	r
20⅞	... 30	1-16	r	1⅜	9⅜	r	r
FinCp	... 20	1⅛	3¼	4¼	3-16	2	r
20⅞	... 25	⅛	1½	2⅝	r	5	r
GnInst	...30	2⅜	4⅜	5¾	¼	1 9-16	r
32⅛	... 35	¼	2¼	3⅜	2¾	4¼	5⅛
32⅛	... 40	1-16	1 1-16	2	8	8⅜	r
32⅛	... 45	r	⅝	s	r	r	s

Option & NY Close	Strike Price	Calls–Last			Puts–Last		
		Dec	Mar	Jun	Dec	Mar	Jun
Getty	55	22½	s	s	r	s	s
77¾	... 60	17⅝	18⅛	r	r	½	r
77¾	... 65	12⅞	r	15⅝	1-16	1	1⅝
77¾	... 70	7¾	10⅜	11¼	⅛	1¾	3⅛
77¾	... 75	3⅝	7½	r	13-16	3½	r
77¾	... 80	s	5	7⅜	s	6¼	7
LearSg	..40	6¼	6¾	r	r	r	r
46⅝	... 45	2	3½	5¼	½	r	r
46⅝	... 50	3-16	1¼	2¼	3¼	r	r
MartnM	35	r	3¼	r	r	1¼	r
36¾	... 40	¼	1	2¼	r	r	r
MrtM o	..40	3-16	r	r	r	r	r
36¾	. 43⅜	1-16	r	r	r	r	r
Morgan	..65	r	7⅛	r	r	1	r
70¾	 70	1⅛	r	r	¾	r	3½
70¾	... 75	1-16	1⅜	r	4¾	r	6
NMedCr	15	¼	1¼	1⅝	r	r	r
Newmnt	45	9⅜	r	11¼	r	r	r
54⅛	... 50	4⅛	r	r	r	r	r
54⅛	... 55	¾	3½	r	1⅛	r	r
54⅛	... 60	1-16	r	r	r	r	r
OwensC	35	1¼	2⅞	r	r	r	2⅝
36	 40	r	r	1¾	4¼	r	r
PennC	...30	9	9⅝	s	r	r	s
38⅞	... 35	3⅞	r	6½	r	r	r
38⅞	... 40	⅜	2⅛	r	r	2⅜	r
38⅞	... 45	r	¾	r	r	r	r
TexOG	.. 40	r	r	r	r	1⅛	r
43¼	... 45	⅜	2⅞	r	r	3	r
43¼	... 50	r	1 5-16	r	6⅝	6⅜	r
43¼	... 55	1-16	r	r	r	r	r
Textrn	...35	r	1½	r	1⅜	r	r
33⅞	... 40	r	⅜	r	r	r	r
Time	 60	3¼	5½	r	⅛	2⅜	r
63⅝	... 65	¾	3½	r	2¾	3¾	r
63⅝	... 70	1-16	r	r	r	r	r
TriCtl	... 25	3⅞	r	r	r	r	r
28⅝	... 30	1-16	½	r	r	r	r
WmsEl	..10	⅛	13-16	1	1⅛	1⅝	1⅞
9⅛	 15	r	3-16	7-16	r	5¾	r
9⅛	 20	1-16	r	s	r	r	s

are for the same striking price, then everything is listed on one line and no NYSE closing stock price is given. For example, no stock price is quoted for National Medical Care in Table 1-5. In such cases, only the composite close from the stock pages will be available.

The letter "r" means a particular option is available for trading but did not trade during that day. The letter "s" means no option of the corresponding type, underlying stock, expiration date, and striking price has been opened by the exchange. Moreover, if no options for a given underlying stock and striking price have traded during the day, no reference to them will appear in the listing, even though at least some of them are available for trading. For example, on this particular day, there were no trades in any Avco options with a striking price of 40. Consequently, they are not mentioned in Table 1-5, even though options were available for trading in all three expiration months.

The letter "o" indicates certain options that have nonstandard contractual terms as a result of a stock split, stock dividend, spinoff, or special circumstances. This designation is customarily used in situations where the identities of some of the options might otherwise be unclear. The options on Martin Marietta provide an example. Martin Marietta stock split 3 for 2 on October 18, 1983. Subsequently, the outstanding options were adjusted according to the rules given above; each old contract now covered 150 shares, with a striking price equal to $\frac{2}{3}$ of the former amount. For the options whose original striking price was $60, the adjusted striking price was $40; these are the options listed as MrtM o 40. The quotes designated as MartnM are for the new options with standard contract sizes that were introduced after the split. The contracts of the same type and expiration date listed as MartnM 40 and MrtM o 40 are thus identical except that one covers 100 shares and the other covers 150 shares. Their last trades, however, could have occurred at quite different times during the day. Consequently, it is not surprising that Table 1-5 shows different prices for the two December 40 calls.

Usually no special identification is given when the adjustment for a stock split or stock dividend results in a standard contract size. In that case, adjusted and new options with the same striking price would be identical in every way and no distinction would be needed. For example, this was the situation when Electronic Data Systems split 2 for 1 on June 8, 1983, and no special designation for its options appears in Table 1-5. Also, normally no special identification is given when the terms of an adjustment are such that none of the adjusted options has a standard price. Occasionally, a stock with a special designation from a split will split a second time during the life of a listed option. In that event, the original options, which will then have been adjusted twice, are denoted by the symbol "oo," while the options introduced after the first split but before the second will be indicated with an "o."

Mergers, acquisitions, and spinoffs often result in the options of one company being adjusted to cover a certain number of shares of one or more other companies. In such instances, the *Wall Street Journal* policy is to give no quotation for the closing stock price, even when all of the securities concerned are publicly traded. On some occasions, however, the *Journal* has followed the confusing practice of quoting the closing price of only one of the securities in the package underlying the option.

The *Wall Street Journal* also gives, for each exchange, total volume and open interest figures for both puts and calls. The total volume figures tell the number of contracts traded during the day.[15] The open interest figures show the total number of contracts outstanding as of the end of the day. Unfortunately, the *Wall Street Journal* gives separate volume figures for each option only for the most actively traded options. However, *Barron's*, a financial weekly, does quote the weekly volume and open interest at the end of the week for most individual options. *Barron's* also gives the high, low, and closing prices for the week for each option.

The brief institutional description of organized option markets provided in this section is supplemented by Chapter 3, which describes in considerable detail the placement of a public order to buy or sell an option, the role of the Options Clearing Corporation, floor trading procedures, margin requirements, listed option commissions, and tax aspects of option trading.

---

[15] These figures are the *reported* volume for the day. For a number of reasons they may differ from *cleared* volume, which is the actual number of contracts for which payment is subsequently made. For example, reported trades may be cancelled due to a misunderstanding between the buying and selling parties that is not reconciled until the next day. More frequently, cleared volume exceeds reported volume since some trades are not reported, particularly during very active trading periods. However, as a general rule, reported and cleared volume will not be significantly different.

some fundamental aspects of options

2

2-1. DETERMINANTS OF OPTION VALUE

In Chapter 1, we looked at the values of various options positions on the expiration date. At that time, an option's value depended on only two variables—the stock price and the striking price. However, at any time before expiration, a number of other variables will also be important. In fact, the differences among the option prices that we see in Table 1-5 are the result of the interaction of a number of different forces.

The only way we can hope to sort out their effects is to take them one at a time, so that is what we will do. We will always make the following comparison: If two options are alike in every way except for a single variable, how will their values differ? If we find some difference, we will call that variable a direct determinant of option value. If we find no effect, then we will have to conclude that if this variable influences option values at all, it must do so *indirectly* through its effect on the direct determinants.

The same set of variables matters for both puts and calls, but not always in the same way, so we will talk about calls first and then come back to puts. Here is our list of the six fundamental direct determinants of option value:

1. **Current stock price** (S)
2. **Striking price** (K)

3. **Time to expiration** (t)
4. **Stock volatility**
5. **Interest rates**
6. **Cash dividends**

The first candidates for the list are easy to agree upon. The *stock price* S and the *striking price K* will certainly matter before expiration as well as on the expiration date. The higher the stock price, the higher the call value. Similarly, the higher the striking price, the lower the call value.

Another important determinant is the stock's *volatility*. For the moment, we can think of the volatility as a measure of the dispersion of possible future stock prices.[1] The higher the volatility, the greater the likelihood that the stock will do either very well or very poorly. These are offsetting effects for the owner of the stock, but not for the owner of a call. He will get the full dollar benefit from the favorable outcomes, but will avoid most of the dollar loss from the unfavorable outcomes, since in those cases he will not exercise the call. Consequently, the higher the volatility over the lifetime of a call, the higher is its value relative to the stock.[2]

If time is measured in years, then *time to expiration t* measures the fraction of a year remaining in the life of the option. For currently listed puts and calls, t is $\frac{3}{4}$ (that is, nine months) or less. One effect of a longer time to expiration works in the same way as a higher volatility. Over a long period of time, a lot can happen to even a very low volatility stock. The call premium over parity therefore tends to be higher the more time remaining

---

[1] Volatility is not the same thing as a stock's "beta." Volatility is a measure of the variability of the stock price, while beta is a measure of the stock's sensitivity to overall market movements. Beta is thus a measure of the component of risk which cannot be diversified away (nondiversifiable risk). Empirically, high volatilities and high betas often go together, but not always. Gold stocks, for example, are very volatile, but they tend to have low betas. For a discussion of beta coefficients, and modern portfolio theory in general, see William F. Sharpe, *Investments*, 2nd Ed. (Englewood Cliffs, N.J.: Prentice-Hall, Inc., 1981).

[2] Note that volatility is a measure of the total risk of a stock. If you have studied modern portfolio theory, this may seem puzzling. You have probably heard again and again: Total risk is irrelevant, only nondiversifiable risk matters. It turns out that option valuation and portfolio theory are completely consistent, but it will not be clear why this is so until much later in the book.

In the meantime, here is an example that will show that if we measure volatility by nondiversifiable rather than total risk, we will get results that are obviously wrong. Suppose that we wish to value two options with identical terms on two different companies. The current stock price of each company is the same and is below the present value of the striking price. Suppose also that interest rates are constant. The first company invests only in government bonds; it has neither nondiversifiable risk nor total risk. The second company also has no nondiversifiable risk (a zero beta), but it has substantial total risk. The option on the first company has a zero value, since with certainty the stock price will never be above the striking price. If volatility were measured by nondiversifiable risk, the option on the second company would also have zero value. But this is ridiculous, since there is a positive probability that it will finish in-the-money.

before expiration. Since this premium shrinks to zero as the expiration date approaches, a call is sometimes interpreted as a "wasting asset."

The higher the *interest rate*, the lower the present value of the striking price the call buyer has contracted to pay in the event of exercise. From this effect, a higher interest rate will have the same influence as a lower striking price.[3] Consequently, higher interest rates tend to imply higher call values.[4]

The present value of the striking price decreases as t increases, so time to expiration has a second way of influencing the call value: first, by providing more time for changes to occur in the stock price, and second, through its effect via the rate of interest. For a call, these effects reinforce each other.

One other fundamental determinant of call values remains. Listed options are protected against stock splits and stock dividends. However, unlike over-the-counter options, they provide no protection for *cash dividends*.[5] This affects the values of listed calls in *two* ways. To understand why, we must first analyze how cash dividends affect the price of shares.

To a first approximation, the average stock price change on an ex-dividend date will be lower than the average change on other days by the amount of the dividend.[6] For any given current stock price, higher future dividends come at the expense of lower future price appreciation. In the extreme case, a final liquidating dividend would drive the stock price to zero. Ordinary dividends can be interpreted as partial liquidation of the firm with a resulting lowering of the stock price. To examine this more carefully, let S be the stock price just before the stock goes ex-dividend and S^x be its expected price just after. Let D be the amount of the dividend. Suppose $S^x > S - D$, so that the stock price falls by less than the dividend. Leaving aside taxes, margin requirements, and transactions costs, a good strategy would be to buy the stock just before it goes ex-dividend, then sell it just after the ex-dividend date. Since we are then entitled to the dividend, we pay S and receive $S^x + D$.[7] Since we assumed $S^x + D > S$, we will expect

---

[3] At first it might seem that the present value of both the cost of exercising *and its benefit* (receiving the stock) will be lower, so that the overall effect is ambiguous. But the present value of a random future sum is simply the amount you would have to pay today to secure the ownership of that sum. No matter what the interest rate, to secure today the ownership of a random future stock price, you have to pay the current stock price, S. But we are changing only one variable at a time, so S, and therefore the present value of the benefit, remains constant.

[4] The full influence of interest rates will also depend on, among other things, their own volatility and their correlation with the stock price.

[5] With over-the-counter options, the striking price is typically reduced by the amount of the dividend on each ex-dividend date. This provides partial but not complete payout protection.

[6] If you sell a stock prior to its ex-dividend date, you transfer the right to receive the dividend to the buyer. If, instead, you sell a stock *on or after* its ex-dividend date, then you retain the right to receive the dividend.

[7] To avoid trivial details, we will assume throughout the book that cash dividends are received on the ex-dividend date.

to earn a profit. If this were not possible, we must instead require $S^x \leq S - D$. A similar argument shows that if $S^x < S - D$, we could short the stock, then buy it back and expect to earn a profit.[8] Therefore, if such strategies permitting expected profit are not available, we must expect $S^x = S - D$: The stock price is expected to fall by the amount of the dividend.[9]

The owners of the stock get both components of total return, cash dividends and price changes. The holders of unprotected calls can receive no benefit from cash dividends, only from price changes. Hence, it stands to reason that the larger the fraction of total return made up by cash dividends to be paid *with ex-dividend dates prior to the expiration date*, the lower the call value. The second influence of cash dividends is related to the first, but is more complex. It concerns the optimal timing of exercise, and will be treated later in Chapter 4. The basic idea is very intuitive, however. The time remaining in the life of the option now has a third effect, which works in the opposite direction from the previous two: The longer the time to expiration, the more the stock price will be reduced by cash dividends. If this effect becomes dominant, it will be advantageous for the owner of a call to end its life voluntarily by exercising it.

These same six factors listed on pp. 33 and 34 also influence put values. Other things equal, puts should be more valuable the lower the stock price, the higher the striking price, and the lower the interest rate— just the reverse of a call. However, increased stock volatility, by raising the probability of extreme outcomes, increases both put and call values.

These effects are straightforward, but the influence of dividends merits some discussion. A long position in a put can be compared to a short position in a stock. Anyone who is short the stock does not benefit from price declines due to a dividend being paid, because he or she is required to make restitution for the dividend to the person from whom the stock was borrowed. On the other hand, the owner of a put does get the full benefit of price declines due to dividends as well as price declines due to other factors. Hence, as dividends increase, a put becomes more attractive relative to the stock itself as a vehicle for going short. The higher the cash dividends prior to expiration, the higher the value of a put. In addition, as explained in Chapter 4, cash dividends will affect the optimal exercise strategy for puts as well as calls.

---

[8] Of course, at best we could actually only initiate the position at the close of trading on the business day just prior to the ex-dividend date and close out the position at the opening on the ex-dividend date. In the interim, we would be exposed to other factors besides the dividend affecting the stock price, but, with so little time between the transactions, this risk would be quite minor. In addition, the transactions costs to market professionals are very small.

[9] As an institutional practice, open orders for stock are automatically reduced by the dividend on the ex-dividend date.

The only surprise is the influence of time to expiration. Even with no dividends, this variable has separate contrary effects: Greater time to expiration tends to decrease put values by reducing the present value of the net proceeds from exercise of the put, and it tends to increase put values by widening the dispersion of possible future stock prices. At low stock prices (relative to K), the former effect dominates, since increased dispersion then has a relatively small influence on put values. Moreover, exercise at or before expiration is likely, and the present value of the net proceeds is more sensitive to the time of their receipt. For opposite reasons, the latter effect dominates at high stock prices. In brief, if it were not for the possibility of early exercise, at a sufficiently low current stock price, put values would decrease with a longer time to expiration, and at a higher stock price, put values would increase with a longer time to expiration. However, as shown in Chapter 4, the possibility of early exercise insures that put values never decrease when time to expiration increases.

Table 2-1 summarizes our analysis of option values to this point.

Table 2-1
SOME DETERMINANTS OF OPTION VALUE

	Effect of Increase	
Determining Factors	*P*	*C*
1. Current stock price (S)	↓	↑
2. Striking price (K)	↑	↓
3. Time to expiration (t)	↑	↑
4. Stock volatility	↑	↑
5. Interest rates	↓	↑
6. Cash dividends	↑	↓

NOTE: An arrow pointing in one direction means that the effect cannot be in the opposite direction.

Are there any other significant factors that can affect option values? There are, but they differ in essential ways from the ones we have just listed. Those six variables are fundamental determinants of option values. They will always matter. The following four additional variables appear to be equally basic. In some circumstances they would be, but not always. We will find, most surprisingly, that in many very important situations they have no direct influence at all:

7. **Expected rate of growth of the stock price**
8. **Additional properties of stock price movements**
9. **Investors' attitudes toward risk**
10. **Characteristics of other assets**

The expected rate of growth of the stock price would seem to be one of the most obvious determinants of option value. Since call values are higher the greater the current stock price, intuition would strongly suggest that, *other things equal*, the current value of a call would be higher the greater the stock price is expected to be in the future. On the other hand, the same intuition implies that put values, *other things equal*, should be lower the greater the expected growth rate of the stock price. However, with the development of the put-call parity relationship in the next section, it will be easy to see this intuition must be incorrect! As incredible as it may seem, the expected rate of growth of the stock price may not be a direct determinant of option value.

The importance of additional properties of stock price movements really depends on what is included in the volatility variable. If we allow it to be a multidimensional measure, then it is possible for it to encompass all of the relevant information about the probability distribution of future stock prices, so further variables may be unnecessary.

Modern financial theory suggests that investors' attitudes toward risk and the characteristics of other assets should play a critical role in determining the value of any asset, including an option. However, this does not mean that these variables must be direct determinants of option value. Indeed, they may affect option values only indirectly, through their influence on the stock price, stock volatility, and interest rates.

In summary, the seventh through tenth variables are all ones that could conceivably influence option values. When they do, their effects will be relatively complex. Fortunately, many results of great practical value can be obtained without having to deal with these complications.

Four more variables, related to the institutional environment, may also affect option values. These are:

11. **Tax rules**
12. **Margin requirements**
13. **Transactions costs**
14. **Market structure**

In principle, these variables will always matter, but their significance may be small. Chapter 3 describes the current structure of options markets and discusses prevailing tax rules, margin requirements and transactions costs. A detailed analysis of the effects on option values of every facet of these rules and regulations would be very tedious, since they are so involved, and unrewarding, since they frequently change. Instead, in the subsequent chapters, we will show general ways for examining the effects of these variables.

We do not mean to imply that the market price of options will never be affected by yet other additional factors. Rather, we are saying that these other factors should influence option values only through their effect on the variables we have mentioned. If they have a direct influence, then market prices will differ from underlying values, and this may provide especially attractive investment opportunities.

In this section, we have discussed option valuation only on an informal basis. This discussion serves as an introduction to Chapters 4 and 5, which present a considerably more detailed and precise treatment of option valuation. In Chapter 4, under the assumption that no riskless profitable arbitrage opportunities are available in the options market, we develop general properties which the values of puts and calls must possess. In Chapter 5, by additionally characterizing the path of the stock price as it moves through time, we derive an *exact* formula relating the value of a given put or call to the six fundamental factors: the current stock price, the striking price, time to expiration, stock volatility, interest rates, and cash dividends.

2-2. THE RELATIONSHIP BETWEEN PUTS AND CALLS

An important and surprising relationship exists between the values of puts and calls with the same expiration date and striking price and written on the same underlying stock. We are introducing this relationship now for several reasons. Comparison of Figures 1-5 and 1-7 alerts us to the fact that a strategy of buying the stock, writing a call, and buying a corresponding put will produce a constant profit (or loss), no matter what the final stock price turns out to be. Surely this implies something about put and call values. Furthermore, the relationship between puts and calls provides a good illustration of some parts of our discussion in the previous section. We could pursue these questions using payoff diagrams. Instead, as a prelude to Chapter 4, we will use an *arbitrage table*. This table describes the returns of a specially constructed portfolio of securities associated with the same underlying stock. The future value of the portfolio is calculated for each possible level of the stock price at the expiration date. By applying the simple principle that a portfolio yielding zero returns in every possible situation must have zero current value to prevent riskless profitable arbitrage, we can derive the relationship between put and call values.

To focus on the basic issues, we assume that there are no transactions costs, margin requirements, or taxes. We believe that for examining arbitrage relationships, these simplifications are as appropriate as they are convenient. In the long run, we would expect recurring arbitrage opportunities to be whittled away to the point where there is no longer a profit to even the most advantageously situated traders. These persons will undoubtedly be market professionals with extremely low transactions costs and margin requirements. Also, if all sources of income are taxed at the same rate, which approximates the situation for a professional trader, then the relationship remains unchanged when taxes are included. We also assume that it is possible to borrow and lend at the same rate. Again, that is not unreasonable in this context. The main reasons private borrowing rates exceed lending rates are transactions costs and differences in default risk. Transactions costs per dollar decline rapidly as the scale increases, so they are of secondary importance in a large operation. And if the arbitrage operation in which we are using the borrowed funds is indeed riskless, it should be possible to collateralize the loan so that the lender will bear no possibility of default. Furthermore, interested readers can easily modify the relationship between put and call values to include all of the things we have left out.

Before proceeding, we need to introduce one more symbol related to interest rates. We define r^{-t} to be the number of dollars that would have to be paid today in order to obtain one dollar with certainty at time t from now. Thus, in return for the loan of one dollar now, we will receive r^t dollars at time t from now. In other words, r^{-t} is a *present value* factor. If the payment of the striking price K will be made at time t from now, then Kr^{-t} is its present value. In terms of bond prices, r^{-t} dollars is the current price of a default-free bond[10] with time t until maturity, paying one dollar on its maturity date and nothing before then; in general, r will depend on the time to maturity. If t is measured in years, then for each maturity date the corresponding annualized interest rate is $r - 1$. For example, suppose that the current price of a bond paying \$1 three months from now is \$0.96. Then an investment of \$1 now will give \$1/.96 = \$1.042 at the end of three months. If we could reinvest the principal and accumulated interest on the same terms every three months for a year, then we would have $\$(1.042)^4 = \$1.1789$ at the end of the year for each \$1 initially invested. Hence, we can refer to 17.89% as the annualized interest rate corresponding to the quarterly rate of 4.2%. (Sometimes the corresponding annualized rate is quoted as simply four times the quarterly rate, $4(4.2\%) = 16.8\%$, but this understates the true return because it ignores the fact that the accumulated interest can be reinvested.)

Table 2-2 reviews all of the symbols and their definitions.

---

[10] Strictly speaking, no bond can be default-free. Here we refer to bonds whose value is negligibly affected by the possibility of default. For example, we regard bonds issued by the U.S. government as "default-free." By the same token, any arbitrage operation can at best be virtually riskless. For example, there is always the remote possibility of government action nullifying some contracts.

Table 2-2
SYMBOLS

S = current market price of underlying stock
C = current value of an associated call
P = current value of an associated put
K = striking price
S^* = market price of underlying stock on expiration date
t = time to expiration
r = one plus the rate of interest on a default-free loan over a
    given period

We will first consider European puts and calls on a stock which will pay no dividends during the life of the options. All results derived assuming no dividends will also hold with dividends if the options are *payout-protected*. An option is payout-protected if its contractual terms are adjusted in a way that will make its value insensitive to cash dividends. Subsequently, we will see what happens for unprotected options on stocks that do pay cash dividends.

Consider taking the following simultaneous position in a *European put and call* on the same underlying stock with the same striking price K and time to maturity t: write one call, buy one put, buy one share of stock, and borrow Kr^{-t} by selling zero-coupon bonds with time t to maturity. As shown in Table 2-3, this gives you the amount $C - P - S + Kr^{-t}$ now. On the expiration date, if $S^* \leq K$, the put you bought will be worth $K - S^*$ and the call you wrote will expire worthless. On the other hand, if $S^* > K$, then the call will be worth $S^* - K$, and you will let your put expire unexercised. In either case, you will own the stock, worth S^*, and will owe K to

Table 2-3
ARBITRAGE TABLE ILLUSTRATING
PUT-CALL PARITY RELATIONSHIP FOR
PAYOUT-PROTECTED EUROPEAN
OPTIONS

	Current Date	Expiration Date	
		$S^* \leq K$	$K < S^*$
Write call	C	—	$K - S^*$
Buy put	$-P$	$K - S^*$	—
Buy stock	$-S$	S^*	S^*
Borrow	Kr^{-t}	$-K$	$-K$
Total		—	—

repay your borrowing. Hence, the future cash flow will be zero in all possible circumstances. The reverse position obtained by buying one call, writing one put, shorting one share of stock, and lending will also give a future cash flow of zero in all possible circumstances. Consequently, if there are to be no arbitrage opportunities, it must be true that the initial investment required to set up either of these positions is also zero:

$$C - P - S + Kr^{-t} = 0,$$

which can be rewritten as

$$\boxed{C = P + S - Kr^{-t}.}$$

This equation is known as the *put-call parity relationship* for European options on stocks that pay no dividends.

   If this relationship were violated in actual markets and we ignored transaction costs, margin, and taxes, we could make a certain profit on zero investment by selling the relatively overpriced option and using the proceeds to buy the relatively underpriced option, together with an appropriate position in the stock and borrowing or lending. The remaining proceeds would be our sure profit, since the portfolio would require no cash outflow (or inflow) on the expiration date of the options.

   To see how this might work, suppose we can invest in two four-month ($t = \frac{1}{3}$) options, both with striking price $K = \$40$. Their underlying stock price is $S = \$40$, and the annualized interest rate on a four-month loan is 5% ($r = 1.05$). Suppose, further, the put and call were available at $2 and $3, respectively. Since $Kr^{-t} = \$39.35$, with the call selling at $3, we know from the put-call parity relationship that the put should be worth $2.35. Since the put is then underpriced relative to the call, we can be sure of a profit if we

- Write one call at $3
- Buy one put at $2
- Buy one share at $40
- Borrow $39.35 at 5% annual rate to be paid back in four months.

This nets us $0.35 immediately, representing the extent of relative underpricing of the put. On the expiration date, no further gain or loss results. To see this, if the stock price remains at $40, both the put and call expire unexercised, and proceeds from the sale of the stock will exactly retire the loan. If the put finishes in-the-money, the call would expire unexercised, we can deliver the stock upon exercise of the put, and the $40 proceeds from exercise will exactly retire the loan. If, instead, the call finishes in-the-money, the put would expire unexercised, we can deliver the stock when the call is exercised against us, and the $40 proceeds from exercise will exactly retire the loan. In any event, no net cash outflow is required at the expiration date. We therefore net an immediate profit of $0.35. Had we expanded the position to 10 option contracts for 100 shares each on both sides, our profit would have been $350.[11]

What effect do cash dividends have on the put-call parity relationship? If we can predict the cash dividends with certainty prior to expiration of an option, we can make an exact correction in this relationship. As we concluded earlier, on its ex-dividend date, a stock has a tendency to experience a decline in price roughly equal to the amount of the cash dividend per share. This causes puts to be worth more and calls to be worth less than their payout-protected values. Let D be the sum of the present values of all cash dividends to be paid with *ex-dividend dates prior to the expiration date* of an option. The European put-call parity relationship for unprotected options then becomes

$$C = P + S - D - Kr^{-t}.$$

In other words, the stock price is replaced by the difference between itself and the present value of the dividends. The reader should assure himself or herself that violation of this relationship presents an opportunity for profitable riskless arbitrage. In Chapter 4, we will expand this relationship to allow for uncertain cash dividends.

To summarize, for European puts and calls, knowing only

1. The put price
2. The underlying stock price
3. Interest rates
4. Anticipated cash dividends

fully determines the value of an associated call with the same expiration date and striking price as the put. This implies there is *basically only one type of European option*—the put; all other positions (calls, spreads, combinations) can be created by an investor on his own account. Moreover, regarding the put as an insurance contract against the risk of a long position in stock, a call is a combination of insurance and a levered long position in the stock. Alternatively, of course, we can regard the call as basic and the put as derived from its associated call.

---

[11] In this example, the borrowed funds are simply a bookkeeping item which permits us to realize immediately a profit equal to the underpricing of the put. They are unnecessary to the arbitrage transaction. Without them, we would show a certain rate of return on our investment greater than the interest rate.

The formula, with certain dividends, can also be rearranged as $S = C - P + D + Kr^{-t}$, implying that a long position in the stock can be replicated by a portfolio containing a purchased call, a written put, and lending of the amount $D + Kr^{-t}$.

Finally, we can use the formula to shed some light on an issue raised in Section 2-1: the effect on option values, other things equal, of the expected rate of growth of the underlying stock price. The put-call parity relationship says that $C = P + S - D - Kr^{-t}$. On the left side we have the call value; on the right side we have the put value plus five of the fundamental determinants of option value: S, K, D, r, and t. This means that if we change *any other variable* that may affect option value while holding these five constant, then the change must affect put and call values in exactly the same way. For example, an increase in volatility must increase both the put and call values by the same amount. This squares with our intuition. Likewise, if a higher expected rate of growth of the stock price, other things equal, were to increase the call value, then it must also increase the put value. Since this contradicts our intuitive arguments in Section 2-1, our intuition must be wrong.

At first, the explanation seems to be that we have made a comparison that could never occur. But this is a red herring; such a situation could definitely happen.[12] We must conclude that the expected rate of growth affects option values in a more subtle manner than initially contemplated. This in turn makes it much easier to believe that the expected rate of growth may have no direct influence at all on option values. As a practical matter, we believe this is at least very close to being the case. It is not a logical necessity, however. In Section 7-1 we give an example where an increase in the expected rate of growth increases both put and call values.

Finally, we want to emphasize once again that all parity relationships developed thus far apply to *European options* only. Listed options are American. In Chapter 4, these relationships will be extended to encompass American puts and calls.

2-3. WHY INVESTORS USE OPTIONS

There are many reasons why investors may find options useful. Some of them are obvious, but others will require some reading in subsequent chapters to be fully appreciated. Here we can give only a broad overview.

---

[12] Here is an example. Modern portfolio theory suggests that for a given dividend policy the equilibrium expected rate of growth of a stock will be determined by its degree of non-diversifiable risk. Even the theory's severest critics admit that there must be some truth to this. But nondiversifiable risk is only one component of volatility. So it is perfectly possible for two stocks to have the same current value, the same dividend policy, the same volatility, but different degrees of nondiversifiable risk and hence different expected rates of growth.

We will not try to provide a general framework for making investment decisions. Such an attempt would take us far off track, and there are many other books offering this information. We will instead take it for granted that everyone interested in options is making decisions in a careful, intelligent way, has considered both his or her long-run objectives and the range of available alternatives, and wants no further general advice. Our goal is to show that options can offer investors a somewhat wider range of alternatives than they may have realized. The question we wish to ask is thus, What can options do for you that stocks and bonds cannot? However, we cannot resist quoting one of the most important messages of modern work on investments, mainly because it is so relevant to many of the reasons we give for using options. The message is not surprising, for it is really just good common sense: *Diversification offers many advantages; in a highly competitive environment, it is very difficult to obtain information not already reflected in market prices; consequently, one should be very cautious about giving up diversification in an attempt to use special information, especially when significant transactions costs will be incurred as well.*

Some of the additional opportunities provided by options will exist only in certain circumstances. Many of them may be valid for some investors but not for others. Nevertheless, the rapid growth of the exchange-traded options indicates that many investors have found that at least one of the following reasons applies to them.

1. OPTIONS MAY OFFER A PATTERN OF RETURNS THAT COULD NOT BE OBTAINED WITH THE STOCK. This is probably the most often mentioned reason for using options. After all, Figures 1-1 and 1-2 look quite different from Figures 1-3 and 1-4. However, this comparison can be very misleading because it takes into account only *fixed buy-and-hold* positions in stock and default-free bonds. It overlooks the possibilities provided by dynamic strategies that make subsequent adjustments in the amount of stock and bonds held. To find out what options offer over and above stock and bonds, we will have to examine these additional opportunities very carefully.

With this in mind, suppose we set out to find a dynamic strategy for a stock and bond portfolio which will make it as much like a call (on one share of stock) as possible. A brief study of daily or weekly call prices will show that they tend to have the following features:

1. Call prices and stock prices change in the same direction.
2. A $1 change in the stock price causes a change of less than $1 in the call price.
3. A 1% change in the stock price causes a change of more than 1% in the call price.

Hence, at a minimum we would want the value of our stock and bond portfolio to have these same three features. This will be very easy. To satisfy the first two conditions, we will want to have a long position in less than one share of stock. We can meet the third condition by financing our stock position partly through borrowing (that is, by selling bonds). For example, suppose that we buy $\frac{1}{2}$ share of a stock selling for $100 per share by investing $10 and borrowing $40. The current value of our portfolio is $10—$50 worth of stock minus the $40 owed on the borrowing. If the stock price now goes up by $1, then the value of our portfolio will go up by only $0.50. However, this will be a 5% increase for the portfolio, compared to only 1% for the stock.

Some further observation of call prices will show that they have additional important properties which we will want to match. When a call is deep-out-of-the-money, a $1 change in the stock price has little effect on the call price. If the stock price rises so that the call becomes at-the-money, then as a rough rule of thumb, a $1 change in the stock price produces a $0.50 change in the call price. If the stock rises further so that the call becomes deep-in-the-money, then a $1 move in the stock price produces nearly a $1 change in the call price.

Here is where the opportunity to use a dynamic strategy becomes essential. We want to be holding almost no shares when the stock price is low, and we want to be buying more shares as the stock price rises. In particular, when the call is at-the-money, we want to be holding about $\frac{1}{2}$ share. As the stock price rises further and the call becomes deep-in-the-money, we want to have gradually bought in to the point where we are now holding almost one share. Similarly, whenever the stock price falls, we will want to reduce the number of shares held.

We will also want the adjustments we are making to depend on the passage of time. On the expiration date, we want to hold one share of stock if the call is in-the-money or no shares at all if it is out-of-the-money. We could do this by gradually increasing the number of shares we hold at any given stock price as time passes for stock prices greater than the striking price, and gradually reducing the number of shares held at each stock price less than the striking price.

There is one more very important property we would want the portfolio to have. After a call is purchased, no subsequent out-of-pocket expenditures are ever required, nor are any funds ever received until the position is closed out. The same should be true for our portfolio. To meet this condition, we will finance new purchases of stock by selling more bonds (that is, by borrowing more), and we will use any proceeds from the sale of stock or from dividends to buy bonds (that is, to repay part of the borrowing).

Strategies having all these features will obviously get much closer to the returns of a call than any buy-and-hold strategy. But could we find one which would duplicate a call *exactly*? In some circumstances of great interest, the answer turns out to be yes. In Chapter 5, we will show precisely how this can be done and examine its profound implication for option pricing. You may have already guessed what that will be. If we can indeed find some dynamic stock and bond portfolio which will require no subsequent investment and will be worth exactly $\max[0, S^* - K]$ on the expiration date, then the current value of that portfolio must be the fair value of the call.[13]

Furthermore, if we can duplicate a call, then we can duplicate any other type of option position as well. Table 2-4 shows some of the properties of the corresponding equivalent portfolios for several basic positions.

Table 2-4
STOCK-BOND PORTFOLIOS EQUIVALENT TO OPTIONS

		Long Stock (less than one share)		Short Stock (less than one share)			
		+ Long bonds (lending)	+ Short bonds (borrowing)	+ Long bonds (lending)	+ Short bonds (borrowing)		
As Stock Price Rises	Buy stock and sell bonds	Long stock (one share) + Long one put	Long one call	Long one put	Short stock (one share) + Long one call	Sell stock and buy bonds	As Stock Price Falls
	Sell stock and buy bonds	Long stock (one share) + Short one call	Short one put	Short one call	Short stock (one share) + Short one put	Buy stock and sell bonds	

For each option position, the corresponding stock and bond portfolio is given at the top of its column and the appropriate revision strategy is given at the ends of its row. For example, the table says that buying a put is equivalent to a short position in the stock combined with lending, which

---

[13] In that case, it is really proper to say that call prices have the features we have listed *because* the equivalent portfolio has them, rather than the other way around.

will be revised by buying more bonds and shorting more stock when the stock price falls and by selling back bonds and buying back stock to reduce the short position as the stock price rises.

Can we then conclude that we can always duplicate a call using only stock and bonds and that options can therefore never offer a new and different pattern of returns? No, this is not the case at all. To see what could go wrong with a duplication strategy, let us return to Section 2-1. Our arguments there imply that an unanticipated increase in volatility will increase the value of a call. It is certainly conceivable that such a change could occur without affecting the price of the underlying stock (or of bonds). Consequently, the value of the call would change but the value of our portfolio would not, no matter what dynamic strategy we were using. An unanticipated change in a firm's dividend policy would cause the same problem. Once again, the value of the call could change without any corresponding change in the value of a stock and bond portfolio.

One further circumstance could also derail an attempt to duplicate a call exactly. It involves the possibility of a sudden large jump in the stock price.[14] Here is an example. Suppose a company has as its only assets a group of copper mines in a foreign country. The price of the company's stock will normally fluctuate with the price of copper and general economic conditions. However, there is a small, but continual, probability that a coup will occur. If this happens, the mines will be nationalized and the stock will be worthless. A coup could succeed only if it were completely secret, so there will be no advance warning and the news will be available to many people simultaneously. In such a catastrophe, stop-loss orders or portfolio revision strategies will be of no help in limiting losses—there will be no buyers at any price. Now a call could provide something that a levered position in the stock cannot—a way to insure that the losses do not exceed the value of the call.

It seems that in some circumstances we will be able to duplicate an option and in other circumstances we will not. Which of these situations is of practical relevance? In our opinion, they both are. Certainly, we are unlikely to find a stock which will never have an unanticipated change in volatility or dividend policy and will never make a sudden jump. However, it is also unlikely that we will find a stock for which these factors are so important that we cannot construct a portfolio which will be very similar to an option. For this reason, we strongly feel that the concept of an option being equivalent to a carefully adjusted portfolio of stock and bonds is close enough to being true in most situations of practical interest to make it an

---

[14] When we say that the stock price makes no sudden jumps, we mean that even though the stock price may move very quickly from, say, 50 to 51, it will still be possible, if we wish to do so, to execute trades at $50\frac{1}{8}$, $50\frac{1}{4}$, $50\frac{3}{8}$, and so on.

invaluable tool for understanding options. Accordingly, we will use it as the context for explaining our next four reasons for using options. On the other hand, we feel that these factors are important enough for us to conclude that options can in fact give a pattern of returns that could not be obtained with stock and bonds. Indeed, it is the possible significance of these factors that leads to our sixth, seventh, and eighth reasons for using options.

Furthermore, even when there is a duplicating strategy, it will typically involve a considerable amount of trading. Thus it may happen that a market professional with very low transactions costs can effectively duplicate an option by trading in stock and bonds, while it would be very impractical for an individual investor to do so. For the individual investor, the option and the equivalent portfolio of stock and bonds may offer identical returns before transactions costs are included, but not afterward. If such an individual would in fact like to have a portfolio that is continually readjusted in a way equivalent to some option position, then he would be better off achieving it indirectly but automatically with the option rather than directly with stock and bonds.

In any case, the automatic readjustment feature of options would still not make them useful if there were no investors who would like to change their mix of stocks and bonds as stock prices change. But it is probably self-evident that many people would like to do this. Two categories immediately come to mind. First, there are those whose degree of risk aversion changes as their wealth changes. Some people prefer to reduce their total exposure to risk when their wealth decreases. Similarly, when their wealth increases, they feel that they can then afford to take more chances. Others react in just the opposite way. When their wealth increases, their inclination is to protect their higher standard of living by taking less risk. Accordingly, when their wealth decreases, they would be willing to accept more risk to try to recoup their losses. Although all of this could be done directly by adjusting a portfolio of stocks and bonds, each group might benefit from having a way to make the desired adjustments automatically. Options can provide this. A portfolio of calls and bonds would exhibit the behavior wanted by the first group. A portfolio of stock and written calls would meet the requirements of the second group. Option funds now make it easier for individual investors to hold diversified portfolios of options. However, in either case, an investor would ideally like to use options on his total portfolio, or perhaps on a market index, for this purpose. A portfolio of options would be the next best thing, but, as we will see in Chapter 8, it is not the same as an option on a portfolio.

In the second category are those who feel that the sequence of past price movements conveys information about future price movements. For example, an investor may have some rather questionable information indicating that a stock is a good buy. A common way of reacting to this is as follows: If the stock moves upward, this is a good sign that the information was right, and consequently I would like to increase my holdings; if the stock goes down, then I will assume that it was a mistake and reduce my holdings. A call will make the necessary adjustments automatically. Of course, many more examples like this could be given, and in each case the desired portfolio revision strategy could often be accomplished directly with the stock. But usually an investor will also have available as an alternative an option position which will provide the same pattern of returns automatically.

2.   OPTIONS MAY OFFER YOU AN OPPORTUNITY TO BORROW OR LEND AT MORE FAVORABLE RATES THAN YOU CAN OBTAIN ELSEWHERE. We have just discussed how in many situations options may be equivalent to a portfolio containing a long or short position in a stock and some amount of borrowing or lending. But at what interest rates are this borrowing and lending implicit in options being done? The answer is, usually at the rates available to large market participants. For many individuals, these rates will be more favorable than they can obtain on their own. They may thus find it advantageous to borrow or lend indirectly in options markets rather than combining stock positions with direct borrowing or lending.

3.   OPTIONS MAY IN EFFECT ALLOW YOU TO TAKE A POSITION IN A STOCK UNDER MORE FAVORABLE MARGIN RESTRICTIONS THAN WOULD BE AVAILABLE DIRECTLY IN THE STOCK MARKET.   Margin requirements really involve three separate things: limits on borrowing against long positions, limits on the use of the proceeds from short sales, and requirements for collateral to guarantee performance on short sales. Current regulations limit the amount of borrowing that can be done using the stock as collateral to 50% of the stock's value; no borrowing at all is allowed against options. The remaining two requirements concern short sales. A short sale of borrowed stock generates funds equal to the price of the stock. Who gets the use of the money? Large investors are often able to negotiate a rental fee directly with the lender of the stock. In effect, the short seller and the lender divide the use of the money. Small investors are less fortunate. They have little choice but to arrange their short sales through brokerage firms, which typically use stock held in street name[15] to make the sale. Neither the short seller nor the actual owner of the loaned stock receive the use of any of the money. The funds are kept by the brokerage firm and the interest they earn is at least partly passed along to all customers in the form of reduced charges. Furthermore, an individual will typically have to put up more funds, in addition to those generated by the short sale, as a performance bond to

---

[15] When an individual finances a stock purchase partly by a loan from a brokerage firm, the stock must be left with the firm and registered in its name; that is, the stock is held in street name.

guarantee his ability to cover the short sale. But now there is an important difference. The individual can receive the interest on these additional funds, so this requirement imposes no economic loss on individuals with sufficient capital. In summary, more favorable margin requirements are always desirable. Any investor would benefit from having the use of the funds from a short sale, and investors with insufficient capital may also benefit from less stringent borrowing limits and collateral requirements. Although all margin requirements fall into the broad categories given here, their actual computation can be very complicated, particularly with combined positions. We will discuss these calculations in much more detail in an appendix to Chapter 3.

Options may allow individuals to obtain more favorable margin requirements than would be available directly in the stock market. Again, the easiest way to see this is to consider the situations where an option is equivalent to a portfolio of stock and bonds. We have seen that a put is then equivalent to a portfolio combining a short position in the stock with lending. The total amount loaned can be broken into two parts: an amount equal to the value of the stock sold short and an amount equal to the value of the put. Brokerage firms and certain other institutions would have no difficulty accomplishing this; they have the full use of the proceeds from a short sale. However, if an individual sets up such a portfolio directly, margin requirements would prevent him from receiving the proceeds of the short sale and lending them. He would only receive the interest from the second component of the loan, which was equal to the value of the put. By taking a position in the options market instead, he may be able to obtain much more favorable margin requirements. In effect, he may be able to obtain full use of the proceeds from the short sale of stock implicit in the purchase of a put.

A similar argument applies to written calls. They would be equivalent to a short position in the stock combined with lending, but now the total amount of lending is less than the value of the stock sold short. The difference is the value of the call. So we could think of this as a short sale equal to the amount of the lending, plus another short sale equal to the amount of the call. Margin regulations normally allow the writer to receive the use of the proceeds from the sale of the call. In effect, he too has received complete use of the proceeds from the short sale of stock implicit in the sale of a call. Of course, if the written call is uncovered, some collateral will also be required, but even this may be less than would be necessary with a direct short sale of stock.

So far we have looked at options positions that give a short position in the stock—buying puts and writing calls. Long positions—buying calls or writing puts—may also offer margin advantages. Margin requirements limit the amount of borrowing that can be done using the stock as collateral to a fixed percentage of the stock's value. We have seen that a call may be equivalent to a long position in the stock combined with borrowing. For some calls, especially those out-of-the-money, this implicit borrowing is a much higher percentage of the stock's value than would be allowed if the position were taken directly in the stock market. This is true even though no borrowing is allowed on the purchase of the call. For individuals wanting a highly levered position in a stock, the options market may offer the best, or even only, way of obtaining it.

The writer of a put may be able to obtain a long position in the stock with even greater leverage. We have said that buying a put is equivalent to a short position in the stock combined with lending an amount greater than the value of the short sale. So the sale of a put is equivalent to buying the stock by borrowing its entire value, and then borrowing some more. The amount of this additional borrowing is equal to the value of the put. If you are an uncovered writer, some collateral will be necessary. This requirement can be met with interest-bearing securities, so it will cause no actual loss of interest. However, it will reduce the borrowing potential. In effect, you will be forced to loan back part of the borrowing. But the remaining borrowing may still be more than you could obtain directly in the stock market.

4. OPTIONS MAY OFFER TAX ADVANTAGES UNAVAILABLE WITH STOCK AND BONDS. No one has ever accused our tax laws of being too simple. Indeed, we will need to devote an appendix to Chapter 3 just to a survey of the parts concerning options. Nevertheless, we can get some idea of the effects of taxes without going into specific details. Anyone who is completely unfamiliar with the tax laws may wish to read this appendix before reading the next few paragraphs.

Earlier we argued that the borrowing and lending rates implicit in option prices will tend to be those applicable to professional market participants. Much the same is true for tax rates. Although these professionals do have the opportunity to place some securities in special accounts taxed at capital gains rates, most of their gains and losses are taxed as ordinary business income regardless of the source. When they consider a portfolio of stock and bonds that is equivalent to an option, they are looking at a portfolio that will provide the same *after-tax* returns as an option when both the call and all of the components of the portfolio are taxed at the rates for ordinary business income. The trading activities of these professionals will tend to make the market price of the option fairly close to the current cost of *their* equivalent portfolio. This is not necessarily to the detriment of individual investors; in fact, it may work in their favor. As an individual investor, you will consider *your* equivalent portfolio—the portfolio of stock and bonds that will give the same after-tax returns as an option when all of the securities involved are taxed at the rates applicable to you. Will the resulting portfolio always be different from that of the market professional? Not necessarily. It turns out that if your income from all sources is somehow taxed at a constant multiple of the rate applying to market professionals, then your portfolio will be the same. This would be the case, for example, for tax-exempt investors. But if some of your sources of income from securities transactions are taxed at a rate different from others, your equivalent portfolio will be different, as we will show in Chapter 6. You can then compare its cost with the market price of the option and take your position in the more favorable alternative. For example, suppose that you found that the market price of calls was consistently above that of your equivalent portfolio. Then you may be able to make consistently better after-tax returns with a strategy including some covered writing than you could using stock and bonds alone. At the same time, someone in a completely different tax situation might be able to achieve better after-tax returns by selling some calls. You would both gain at the expense of the government.[16]

So far we have looked at options and stocks and bonds as alternative investment vehicles and found that one or the other may be preferable for tax purposes. Options may also have tax advantages that are completely unrelated to any position we might want to take in the underlying stock. These advantages have survived a number of tax changes. Typically, it will be to our advantage to have the tax consequences of gains (not the gains themselves) postponed as long as possible and the tax consequences of losses taken as soon as possible. For example, suppose we have a current gain from, say, a real estate transaction. If we could delay the tax on this until next year or later, we will have the use of the tax money in the meantime. One way to do this would be to generate a comparable loss in the current tax year followed by an offsetting gain in the next tax year. Option spreads may provide a completely legal way of accomplishing this. Basically, you would want to take a long position in some option and a short position in another option on the same stock but with a different striking price or expiration date. By carefully choosing the proportions, you can keep the position as close to perfectly hedged as is permissible for tax purposes. You can then close out the unprofitable side of the spread just before the end of the current tax year and close out the profitable side just after the beginning of the next tax year. The main difficulty is that you cannot be sure how much the stock will move. If it stays put, the unprofit-

---

[16] If the Tax Reform Bill of 1984 becomes law, stock and stock options traded by options professionals will be treated as capital assets and any gain or loss will be taxed as if it were 60% long-term and 40% short-term. However, it appears that some of the transactions of options professionals who are also classified as dealers in stock may continue to be treated as generating ordinary income or loss. Our main conclusions would still hold: For stock options, professional traders will be taxed differently from individuals and will have different equivalent portfolios, thus providing the possibility that options will offer tax advantages.

able side may not generate much of a loss. But you can compensate for this by picking a volatile stock and taking a large position.[17]

5. OPTIONS MAY ALLOW LOWER TRANSACTIONS COSTS THAN THE STOCK.   As was the case with borrowing and lending rates and with taxes, there are good reasons for thinking that it is the transactions costs faced by market professionals rather than by individual investors that are relevant in determining the market price of options. These costs are fairly low, so option prices may be very close to those that would prevail if there were no transactions costs at all.

At the same time, individual investors may face substantial transactions costs. These are described in Appendix 3B. Proper consideration of these costs will be essential in any investment decision. Once again, options markets may offer favorable opportunities. An investor would wish to compare the costs of obtaining a particular kind of portfolio for a particular length of time for the two alternatives: stock and bonds or options (and bonds, if necessary). All costs must be considered: those of setting up the position, maintaining it, and liquidating it; the explicit brokerage fee and the costs implicit in the bid-ask spread.

Typically we would find the following: If the position is to be held for a short period of time and will require frequent switching between stock and bonds if taken in that way, it will be cheaper to use options and bonds. On the other hand, if the position is to be held for a long time and would require only infrequent adjustment between stock and bonds, it will be cheaper to use the stock and bonds. This may, in part, explain the comparative popularity of shorter-term over the longest-term listed options.

6. OPTIONS MAY PROVIDE AN OPPORTUNITY TO USE CERTAIN KINDS OF SPECIAL KNOWLEDGE TO OBTAIN A PORTFOLIO WITH SUPERIOR PERFORMANCE—ONE THAT OFFERS A HIGHER EXPECTED RETURN THAN OTHER PORTFOLIOS WITH THE SAME DEGREE OF RISK.   If an option is fairly priced, it will offer you an expected return appropriate for its degree of risk. If you are able to identify options that are undervalued or overvalued relative to the underlying stock, then you will have found superior investment opportunities—ones that offer a higher expected return than is justified by their risk. By combining these opportunities with fairly priced ones you can obtain an overall portfolio that has the amount of total risk you wish to bear while still providing superior performance. This is true even if you have no ability to identify undervalued or overvalued stocks. Of course, if you are able to do this as well, then you could obtain superior performance without using options.

---

[17] If the proposed law mentioned in footnote 16 is enacted, the opportunities for deferring taxes with spreads and hedges will be limited to certain covered writing positions. These positions would entail substantially more risk than the positions allowed under previous law.

But you could do even better by combining the two. For example, you could pick undervalued calls on undervalued stocks.

The essential requirement is the ability to pick options that are undervalued or overvalued relative to the stock. To do this, you need to have special information. You need to know something that is not already widely known and reflected in current market prices. One way to achieve this would be to have a special insight into how the fundamental variables we discussed fit together to determine exact option values. Alternatively, you might value options by widely known techniques, but have special knowledge about some of the determining factors. Certainly the striking price, the time to expiration, and the current stock price are available to everyone, but the other variables may offer better opportunities. The most promising of these is undoubtedly the volatility variable. What you want is an accurate prediction of the volatility of the underlying stock during the life of the option. Any special information about changes in the firm's investment or financing policies could lead to a better prediction than that being made by the market. For example, suppose that you are confident that a paper company will soon unexpectedly change its plans to sell the mineral rights on part of its land for a fixed fee and will instead take a large participatory interest in their development. You have no ideas about the likely success of this venture, but you do know that as a result the stock will be much more volatile in the future than the market had anticipated. You know that as soon as this becomes known, options will rise in price, relative to the stock. But you do not know how the stock price will respond. You could not take advantage of your information in the stock market, but you could in the options market. You could obtain superior performance, as we have defined it, by buying options. However, if you simply bought calls, you might lose money if the stock price fell, even though your analysis was correct. Similarly, if you only bought puts you might lose money if the stock price increased. So a better plan might be to buy both puts and calls with the same striking price. Or you could buy calls and sell some stock, or buy puts and buy some stock. Indeed, as suggested above, you might be able to adjust your portfolio to keep a neutral position in the stock, while still getting full benefit of your insights about volatility.

Another possibility is that you may be able to use publicly available information in a unique way to produce volatility forecasts that are better than those of the market. You may have a more efficient statistical method of extracting information from a series of past stock prices, or you may have a superior understanding of the relationship between future volatility and published accounting data. Such insights would be more valuable than information about a specific company, since they could potentially be used on all listed stocks simultaneously. This same advantage would accrue, to a lesser extent, to a special ability to forecast the volatility of the market. This would be useful information, since we would expect the volatilities of listed stocks as a group to move in the same way. It would be less useful than information about individual stocks, however, since we would need to form a diversified portfolio of options to take advantage of it. The volatility of any given stock might decrease, even though the volatility of the market as a whole increased.

Options may also offer the best opportunity to benefit from superior predictive ability about a firm's dividend policy. For example, suppose your analysis indicates that a firm will soon declare a completely unexpected sizeable cash dividend. It is not clear whether the market will interpret this as good news or bad news, so there is no sure way to make a profit with the stock. But you do know that when the announcement is made, the price of puts will rise relative to the underlying stock price, and the price of calls will fall. If you simply bought puts and wrote calls, you could lose money if the stock price rose in response to the news. But you could offset this by simultaneously taking an appropriate long position in the stock. The combined position would be hedged against stock price movements but would get full benefit from your information about dividends.

Since an unanticipated rise in interest rates will in general cause call prices to increase and put prices to decrease, it seems that you could also use options markets to profit from predictive ability about interest rates. This is true, but it would almost certainly be better to use this information directly in the bond markets or the financial futures markets.

Finally, you may have some special information about option values that does not require knowledge of valuation formulas or the inputs into such formulas. Various forms of technical analysis based on past price movements would be an example. For instance, your analysis might indicate that options are properly priced on average but tend to be overvalued after a large rise in the stock market and undervalued after a large fall. Naturally, such information could be used profitably in the options markets but not in the stock market.

In conclusion, it may be useful to recall that not all special information about the stock will favor the use of options. In deciding that a stock is undervalued or overvalued, you may feel that you have special information about its expected rate of return, or its volatility, or both. As we have just discussed, the latter may give you the ability to pick undervalued or overvalued options as well. But since the stock's expected rate of return may not be a separate determinant of option value, special information about it may be of no help whatsoever in spotting mispriced options. Of course, this information would influence the size of the total position you would want to take in the stock, but it would not in itself provide any reason for preferring any one way of taking that position to another.

7. OPTIONS MAY PROVIDE A MEANS OF HEDGING AGAINST UNANTICIPATED CHANGES IN STOCK VOLATILITY. Imagine the following situation. You feel that a particular stock is an excellent buy, so you have taken a substantial position in the stock. Nevertheless, you realize that its future price is uncertain, and that its volatility may unexpectedly increase. If this happens, your position will have more risk than you can afford to bear, so you will have to cut back and forego much of your potential profit. For protection, you might very well like to buy insurance against such an unexpected increase in volatility.

Options markets give you a way to do this. In this case, you might want to take the position in calls rather than directly in the stock. An unexpected increase in volatility will increase the value of the calls, and this will at least partly offset the foregone profits. More generally, by carefully selecting long positions in some options and short positions in others, you may be able to find a portfolio of options whose total value will be very sensitive to changes in volatility but relatively immune to changes in the stock price and other uncertainties. Such a portfolio would thus offer a pure opportunity to buy or sell insurance on volatility changes.

Of course, this strategy is very similar to the one we discussed earlier for taking advantage of special information about future volatility, but the motivation is different. A desire to hedge against certain kinds of risk does not imply, nor is it implied by, possession of special information.

8. OPTIONS MAY PROVIDE A WAY TO HEDGE AGAINST UNANTICIPATED CHANGES IN A FIRM'S DIVIDEND POLICY AND A WAY TO DIVIDE A STOCK'S TOTAL RETURN INTO SEPARATE DIVIDEND AND PRICE CHANGE COMPONENTS. Unexpected changes in a firm's dividend policy inevitably impose some costs on investors. For most people, there are only the small costs of minor portfolio adjustments to regain their preferred mix of capital gains income and dividend income. For others, the costs may be more severe. These individuals may well be interested in hedging against unexpected changes in dividend policy. Options provide a way to do this. For example, suppose an individual is the beneficiary of a trust fund that gives him the dividend income from large holdings in a few stocks. As is often the case, the stocks cannot be sold and the residual ownership will pass to another beneficiary. For this individual, a firm's decision to decrease dividends in favor of more price appreciation would be a major disaster, one he would like to insure himself against. To do this, he would like to find a portfolio whose total value is sensitive to dividend changes but is immune to other sources of risk. He could do this by taking a long position in calls combined with a properly chosen short position in stock and perhaps a few other calls. An unanticipated decrease in dividends will increase the value of

the purchased calls and provide the individual some compensation for his lost income. The remaining securities will make the value of the portfolio relatively insensitive to other sources of risk, including any changes in the stock price caused by the dividend announcement.

It might be argued that anyone with a large stake in dividends would be better advised to reduce his risk by selling off part of his position. This may be very difficult, but in principle options can give a way to do this as well. They can provide a way to separate the two parts of total return—dividends and price changes—into individual marketable components. Consider a covered writer of a European call with a zero striking price. He in fact owns only the dividends to be paid during the life of the option. In turn, the buyer of the call owns the entire price change component, but has no claim on the dividends. This latter division might be particularly attractive for an individual in a high tax bracket who would like to take a position in a stock paying large dividends. Another portfolio could also accomplish this same division. Suppose an individual buys a European call, sells a European put with the same striking price and expiration date, and makes a loan that will pay the amount of the striking price on the expiration date. A reexamination of the put-call parity relationship shows that he has purchased the entire price change component but owns no part of the dividend component. Of course, the difficulty is that European options are required to completely separate the two components. Because of the possibility of early exercise, American options will not do. Since European options are not currently traded on any exchange, the transaction would require a special arrangement in the over-the-counter market.

9.   Options offer the opportunity to avoid certain impediments to the short sale of stock.   We have already discussed ways in which options may provide advantages over a direct short sale: They may offer more favorable margin requirements and they may allow gains to be taxed at the long-term capital gains rate. There are two further advantages. Under current regulations, a stock can be sold short only after an up-tick in its price or after one or more zero-ticks preceded by an up-tick. In other words, the trade can take place only at a price higher than that of the last trade at a different price. In a declining market, some time may pass before an order can be filled. No such rule applies in the options market. An order to buy a put or sell a call can be filled immediately. Finally, for a stock to be sold short, it must be borrowed from its owner or a brokerage firm holding it in street name. The lender has the right to recall the stock at any time unless specific arrangements to the contrary have been made. In certain situations, it may be difficult to find the borrowed stock necessary to open the short position or maintain it after a recall. No such problems occur in the options market.

We conclude that options have much to offer. The success of the options exchanges is no accident; indeed, the puzzling thing is why it did not happen earlier. Similarly, the popularity of options on stock market indexes is exactly what economic arguments would have predicted. In fact, the reasons we gave suggest that there would be demand for an even broader menu of options than is currently available. Options with more frequent expiration dates and with longer maturities would be particularly useful. So would European options, in spite of lingering but questionable worries about their vulnerability to stock manipulation.

Also, individuals and firms may benefit from the existence of an options market even though they are not active participants. Publicly available price quotations on options may provide information that will be useful in other activities, and options may have other indirect beneficial effects on the allocation of resources. We will discuss this more fully in Chapter 8.

Finally, we must note that we have not yet mentioned a potential source of competition for options—convertible securities. These securities, such as convertible bonds, convertible preferred stock, and warrants, have many optionlike features. Indeed, we will show in Chapter 7 that nearly all corporate securities can be considered as packages of options on the assets of the firm. Consequently, convertible securities may offer many of the same advantages as options. But they are sufficiently different that the two are really complements rather than competitors. Although our discussion of convertible securities in Chapter 7 will be brief, we hope the analogies with options will show the possibilities they may provide.

APPENDIX 2A
The Relationship Between Options and Forward and Futures Contracts

Forward contracts are often confused with options. A *forward contract* is an arrangement whereby the seller currently agrees to deliver to the buyer a specified asset on a specified future date at a fixed price, to be paid on the *delivery date*. A long position in a forward contract and a European call are thus somewhat similar: both involve exchanging the underlying asset for a specified amount of money on a specified future date. However, there is a critical difference. The owner of a forward contract is committed to make this exchange; the owner of a call has the right, but not the obligation, to do so.

If the fixed price to be paid on the delivery date were sufficiently low, the buyer would have to pay a positive amount for the contract. If it were set high enough, the seller would have to pay the buyer to take the contract. Clearly, there is an intermediate price, known as the *forward price*, at which the current value of the contract would be zero. This is the fixed price that is customarily used for newly-written forward contracts. Consequently, a forward contract will have a value of zero when the contract is initiated. Of course, the value of an outstanding contract will subsequently change as the value of the underlying asset changes. On the delivery date, the value of the contract will be $S^* - F$, where S^* is the value of the underlying asset on the delivery date and F is the forward price at the time the contract was initiated. In contrast, the value of a call expiring on the same date would be $\max[0, S^* - K]$, where K is the striking price.

Although options and forward contracts have quite different payoffs, there is an interesting connection between them. To focus on the main issues, we will ignore the effects of transactions costs, margin requirements, and taxes. Table 2A-1 shows that under these conditions, *a newly-written forward contract is equivalent to a portfolio consisting of one purchased European call option on the underlying asset and one written European put option on the underlying asset, both with a common expiration date equal to the delivery date, and both with a common striking price equal to the forward price.*

Consequently, if there are to be no arbitrage opportunities, *the forward price must be the striking price that equates the value of the put and the call.* If C were less than P, we could lock in a sure profit by buying the call, selling the put, and selling a forward contract. This position would give an immediate cash inflow of $P - C$ and would never require any subsequent cash outflows. If C were greater than P, we could lock in a sure profit by selling the call, buying the put, and buying a forward contract.

Note that none of these results requires any information about the characteristics of the underlying asset. The conclusions are equally valid for

Table 2A-1
THE RELATIONSHIP BETWEEN OPTIONS AND FORWARD CONTRACTS

		Delivery Date and Expiration Date	
	Current Date	$S^* \leq F$	$S^* > F$
Buy forward contract	0	$S^* - F$	$S^* - F$
Buy call with $K = F$	$-C$	—	$S^* - F$
Sell put with $K = F$	P	$S^* - F$	—
Total	$P - C$	$S^* - F$	$S^* - F$

a common stock whose owner receives dividends and a commodity whose owner must pay storage costs. In fact, the same arguments would apply even if the underlying asset does not currently exist, as might be the case with a perishable commodity before the next harvest.

If the underlying asset is a common stock that does not pay dividends, then we can use the put-call parity relationship for European options to determine the forward price F. From Section 2-2, we know that

$$C - P = S - Kr^{-t}.$$

From our arbitrage analysis, we know that the forward price F is that value of the striking price K for which the put and call have the same value. Hence, $C = P$ and

$$F = K = Sr^t.$$

Now consider the case where the stock is paying cash dividends. In Section 2-2, we found that the put-call parity relationship would then be

$$C - P = S - D - Kr^{-t},$$

where D is the sum of the present values of all anticipated cash dividends with ex-dividend dates prior to the expiration date of the options. Our previous analysis then implies

$$F = (S - D)r^t.$$

In Section 2-2, we argued in the following way: If we know the market value of the dividends, then in the absence of arbitrage opportunities we can find the relative market prices of the options. Of course, we could have reversed this argument: If we know the market prices of the options, we can find the market price of the dividends,

$$D = P - C + S - Kr^{-t}.$$

As mentioned in our eighth reason for using options, we could purchase the right to receive all dividends paid during the life of the options by buying the stock, buying the put, selling the call, and borrowing Kr^{-t}. By applying our previous conclusions, we can infer the same information and accomplish the same result with a forward contract. The market value of the dividends can be written as

$$D = S - Fr^{-t}$$

and the ownership of the dividends can be obtained by buying the stock, selling a forward contract, and borrowing Fr^{-t}.

A futures contract is similar to a forward contract in many ways, but there is an important difference. An individual who takes a long position in a futures contract nominally agrees to buy a designated good or asset on the delivery date for the futures price prevailing at the time the contract is initiated. Hence, the futures price must also equal the spot price on the delivery date. Again, no money changes hands initially. Subsequently, however, as the futures price changes, the party in whose favor the price change occurred must immediately be paid the full amount of the change by the losing party. As a result, the payment required on the delivery date to buy the underlying good or asset is simply its spot price at that time. The difference between that amount and the initial futures price has been paid (or received) in installments throughout the life of the contract. Like the forward price, the equilibrium futures price must also continually change over time. It must do so in such a way that the remaining stream of future payments described above always has a value of zero.

In general, the continual resettlement feature of futures contracts makes it a difficult matter to determine an equilibrium futures price in terms of its underlying variables. However, if interest rates are non-stochastic and there are no arbitrage opportunities, it can be shown that futures prices are equal to forward prices. Consequently, the valuation formulas given for forward prices will then also hold for futures prices.

To see this, consider simultaneous forward and futures contracts on the same underlying asset with the same delivery date. Suppose that interest rates are nonstochastic and that the forward price is greater than the futures price. Then it would be possible to make an arbitrage profit with the following strategy. On the initial date, take a short position in a number of forward contracts equal to the total return that will be received from holding until its maturity a zero-coupon bond having the same maturity date as the contracts. With nonstochastic interest rates, this total return is the same as that which would be received from continually reinvesting in one-period bonds from the initial date until the delivery date. On each trading date, take a long position in a number of futures contracts equal to the total return received from continually reinvesting in one-period bonds from the initial date to the following trading date. Liquidate each of these futures positions on the following trading date and continually reinvest the (possibly negative) proceeds in one-period bonds until the delivery date.

By adding up the returns and remembering that the forward and futures prices must be equal on the delivery date, we would find that this strategy would produce an arbitrage profit proportional to the difference in the forward and futures prices. If the futures price were greater than the forward price, then an arbitrage profit could be obtained by reversing this strategy, so we can conclude that the two prices must be equal.

the structure
of the market
for puts and calls

3

3-1. PUBLIC ORDERS

The first chapter dealt briefly with the marketplace for listed puts and calls. In this chapter, we will examine the internal mechanism of the market in considerably more detail.

When a customer places an order with a broker to buy or sell an option, the order requires the following information:

1. Buy/sell
2. Put/call
3. Number of contracts
4. Underlying security
5. Expiration month
6. Striking price
7. Market/limit
8. Opening/closing
9. Day/good-until-cancelled
10. Special instructions

For example, a customer might instruct his broker to buy 10 ALCOA/JAN/ 50 calls in an opening transaction at $5\frac{1}{8}$ or better to be good-until-cancelled.

This order is one of four possible transactions:

1. Opening purchase transaction
2. Opening sale transaction
3. Closing purchase transaction
4. Closing sale transaction

In an *opening purchase transaction,* a customer buys an option he does not already hold as a writer in his portfolio. This transaction tends to increase the number of options outstanding (that is, the open interest). In contrast, a *closing purchase transaction* cancels his position as a writer of some options and tends to reduce the open interest.

In either case, the broker directly transmits the order to a communications booth on the exchange floor. From there, a "runner" conveys the order to a Floor Broker. He or she is a member of the exchange and may or may not be an employee of the brokerage house. The Floor Broker moves to the post where the particular option is traded, and acts as the customer's representative on the floor, attempting to obtain the best price he can. In a typical transaction, through a process of open outcry, the Floor Broker makes a matching trade with an Order Book Official, Market Maker, or another Floor Broker. Order Book Officials perform a function similar to a specialist on a stock exchange except they only trade on behalf of public customers, not for their own account. A Market Maker is a member of the exchange who trades for his or her own personal account, partnership, or corporation, and does not represent another customer. Immediately following their verbal agreement, they both independently write up the transaction.[1] When the exchange checks this later that day, if they agree, a *matched trade* is said to have occurred. The Clearing Corporation then receives a report of the matched trade from the exchange. On the next business day following the trade, the option is issued by the Clearing Corporation at 10 : 00 A.M. Central Time. The Clearing Member (usually the brokerage house representing the buyer) must pay the option price before 9 : 00 A.M. Central Time that same day. A similar procedure is followed for *opening* and *closing sale transactions.* Note that, in contrast to the procedure of stock exchanges, where a transaction is settled on the fifth business day after the agreement, only one business day is required for options.

A customer desiring to *exercise* an option he has purchased, notifies his broker who, in turn, notifies the Clearing Corporation.[2] When the

---

[1] Somewhat different procedures are followed on the AMEX and PHLX.

[2] Despite the one-day settlement, options can now be exercised the same day they are bought. Moreover, since the Clearing Corporation updates its open position records at the end of the day before it assigns exercise notices, an option may be exercised against a writer the same day it is written.

Clearing Corporation has received exercise instructions, it assigns an exercise notice to a Market Maker, an exchange member firm representing itself, or a Clearing Member representing a public customer, selected at random from those who represent writers of the appropriate option, on the following business day.[3] For public customers, the Clearing Member, in turn, allocates the exercise notice to a customer maintaining a written position. Regardless of how this allocation is made—for example, by random selection, or on a first-in, first-out basis—the method chosen must be fair and equitable to the Clearing Member's customers, who may request that their brokers inform them of this method. The Clearing Member is then required to deliver the underlying security, in the case of call, or the striking price, in the case of a put, by 12 : 00 noon Central Time directly to the exercising Clearing Member on the "exercise settlement date" in return for the striking price. This date is the fifth business day following the date when the exercise notice is properly tendered to the Clearing Corporation.[4]

Orders fall into two general classes: market and limit orders. A *market order* instructs the Floor Broker to fill the order immediately at the best possible price. A *limit order* instructs the Floor Broker to fill the order only if he can transact at a specified price or better. A market or limit order contingent upon additional conditions being satisfied is called a *contingency order*. Such an order may specify execution contingent upon the underlying stock price or the prices of other related options. For example, a "stop-limit order" instructs the Floor Broker to execute at a given limit if the option trades at or through a specified price. A "stop-loss order" becomes a market order if the option trades at or through a specified price. A "not-held order" gives the Floor Broker discretion as to the price and time an order may be executed.

A *spread order* instructs the Floor Broker to buy a given number of option contracts and to sell the same number of option contracts of the same class of options at the same time. The order is to be filled only if the difference in prices of the two options is greater, or perhaps lower, than a prespecified number. For example, suppose the midday quotations for two XYZ July calls are currently described by Table 3-1. If we want to sell 5 JUL/40s and buy 5 JUL/45s, the best indication of the market is usually the bid-ask quote rather than the price of the last sale. This is particularly true for spreads, since the last prices are apt to represent trades at different times. Placing an order to sell 5 JUL/40s at 3 and to buy 5 JUL/45s at $1\frac{3}{8}$

---

[3] Prior to 1980, for "block" exercises of 25 contracts or more in the same series an attempt was made to match the exercise with writers with a similar number of contracts.

[4] Options closing with parity value of $\frac{3}{4}$ of a point or more on their expiration date are automatically exercised by the Clearing Corporation for public customers. Automatic exercise occurs at $\frac{1}{4}$ of a point parity value or more for Market Maker or exchange member firm proprietary positions.

creates a cash inflow per matched option of $\$3 - \$1\frac{3}{8} = \$1\frac{5}{8}$ (credit). Since the market prices of the calls can easily change before the order is executed, a spread order is not placed at specific prices, but rather as: "Sell 5 JUL/40s and buy 5 JUL/45s at a $1\frac{5}{8}$ 'credit'." Had the 40s been bought and the 45s written, the order would be placed at a $1\frac{5}{8}$ "debit."

Table 3-1
DATA FOR VERTICAL SPREAD

Call Identification	Last	Bid	Ask
XYZ/JUL/40	$3\frac{1}{8}$	(3)	$3\frac{1}{8}$
XYZ/JUL/45	$1\frac{1}{4}$	$1\frac{1}{4}$	$(1\frac{3}{8})$

A *straddle order* is similar to a spread order except it instructs the Floor Broker to buy or sell a straddle. If the straddle is bought (sold), the prices of both sides of the position are added to determine the debit (credit).[5]

All orders are day or good-until-cancelled (GTC). A *day order* results in cancellation of the order at the end of the day if it has not already been filled. In contrast, a *GTC order* remains in effect until notification from the customer or until expiration. A *one-cancels-the-other* order treats two or more orders as a unit, where execution of any one of the orders causes the others to be cancelled. A *market-on-close* order requires that an order be executed during, or just prior to, the close of trading for the day. An *all-or-none* order requires that it be executed in entirety or not at all. A *fill-or-kill* order is similar to an all-or-none order, but in addition requires that the order is to be cancelled if it cannot be executed in entirety as soon as it is introduced into the trading crowd.

The exchanges, to provide financial protection and to prevent manipulative practices, have established *position limits* on the maximum number of options relating to the same underlying security that can be held by a single investor or group of investors acting in concert. As of May 1984, stocks having a trading volume in the past six months of at least 20,000,000 shares or having 60,000,000 or more shares outstanding and a six-month trading volume of at least 15,000,000 shares have the following limits:

1. The total number of purchased calls and written puts cannot exceed 4,000 contracts.

---

[5] Because options and their underlying stocks are not traded at the same post (indeed, usually not even at the same exchange), the simultaneity of price insured for spreads and combinations cannot be guaranteed for hedges.

2. The total number of written calls and purchased puts cannot exceed 4,000 contracts.

Each part is calculated separately; positions in one category cannot be offset against those in the other. For example, a total position of 4,100 purchased calls and 3,900 written calls would not be allowed. However, a total position of 4,000 purchased calls and 4,000 written calls would be acceptable. For stocks not meeting the above requirements on volume and number of shares, the 4,000 contract limit is lowered to 2,500 contracts. The SEC may change these limits from time to time; for example, prior to October 31, 1980, the limits were only 1,000 contracts in each category.[6]

Exercise limits have also been established by the exchanges. The largest number of contracts for a single option class that can be exercised within any five consecutive business days by a single investor, or group of investors acting in concert, is the same as the position limits described above. In parallel with the position limits, puts and calls are considered separately and are not aggregated. For example, for a stock meeting the higher requirements on volume and number of shares, at most 4,000 puts and 4,000 calls could be exercised within a five-day period.

However, in the event of a stock split or stock dividend, the exercise and position limits on outstanding options are adjusted accordingly. For example, if a 2-for-1 stock split leads to each old contract being replaced with two new ones, each on 100 shares, then the exercise and position limits for those options would be changed from 4,000 to 8,000 contracts, or from 2,500 to 5,000 contracts.

Initial and maintenance *margin requirements* for public customers are described in detail in Appendix 3A. For uncovered option purchases, the entire option price must be put up by the investor. This contrasts with purchased stock for which a maximum of 50% may be borrowed from the brokerage house. However, because a call typically sells for much less than its underlying stock, less equity is usually required to purchase stock indirectly through its associated options than directly by purchase of the stock. For example, consider the purchase of a call with a striking price of 30 when the stock price is 40. Since the call is deep-in-the-money, it will sell for close to its parity value and should experience a dollar profit or loss similar to the stock. Yet, the net equity[7] required to purchase the option is $10, half

---

[6] Also, prior to November 1, 1980, with the exception of all Market Maker and certain public trades, opening transactions were prohibited in options which were both more than $5.00 out-of-the-money and priced less than $0.50. This "restricted option" rule was also dropped on October 31, 1980.

[7] The net equity equals the net cash outflow experienced by an investor to establish a position. This depends on the cost of purchased securities, the proceeds of sales of written and short securities, and the required margin.

the $20 minimum net equity to purchase the stock. In a similar manner, buying a put requires less net equity than shorting the stock. Moreover, in a short stock position, the investor foregoes interest on the proceeds from the sale. Purchase of a put does not suffer from this disadvantage.[8]

Uncovered written positions require a margin deposit from the writer to guarantee performance. Not only is the required amount considerably less than the stock price itself, but the proceeds from the sale of the option may be applied to reduce the deposit, and T-bills may be deposited as margin, accruing interest to the investor. Again, this contrasts with short sales of stock, where the proceeds are not available for reinvestment.

If a written option is covered by an opposing position in the same underlying stock, the margin required for the same option written uncovered may be considerably reduced. For example, if at-the-money calls are written against an equal number of underlying shares (one-for-one hedge), not only is no margin required for the call, but the call proceeds can be used to reduce the equity required to purchase the stock.

Calculation of margin for covered positions first entails pairing of opposing securities on the same underlying stock on a one-for-one basis. Each pair is then margined separately. Written or short securities remaining after all possible pairings are considered uncovered for margin purposes. Hence, ratio-covered positions require more net equity than one-for-one positions. Table 3A-3 demonstrates that the net equity required to back hedges is usually greater than the net equity required for written combinations and spreads. For spreads, net equity is usually least for purchased horizontal spreads, next lowest for purchased vertical spreads, and highest for written horizontal spreads.

Commissions for public customers are described in detail in Appendix 3B. Option buyers pay commissions when they buy options and when they close out their positions by sale or exercise. Similarly, writers pay commissions at each of these events. No commissions are paid if a position is closed out by letting an option expire. Since May 1, 1975, commissions have been determined by negotiation between a customer and his broker. In practice, commissions have usually been quoted as a percentage discount from the pre-May Day fixed rate schedule.

Commissions per dollar of investment for both stock and options decrease as the value of the order and the price of each round lot or contract increases. In an extreme case, prior to negotiated commissions, on an order to buy or sell one option contract at a sixteenth, commissions equalled the value of the order. On the other hand, an order to buy ten option contracts at $30 per option cost $322 in commissions, about 1% of the value of the order.

---

[8]However, we argue in Section 4-4 that the unavailability for reinvestment of the proceeds of a short sale may cause the prices of puts to be higher than they otherwise would be.

A comparison of stock and option commissions reveals that option contracts typically have higher commissions per dollar of investment than an equal number of round lots of their underlying stock. However, since a lower-priced option can provide an investor with a similar opportunity for dollar profit and loss as its higher-priced stock, this commission comparison may not be relevant. As demonstrated by Tables 3B-3 and 3B-4, commissions on stock are almost always greater than commissions on options, where the number of options is adjusted to provide comparable "action." By this comparison, option commissions tend to be lower, relative to stock commissions, the higher the price of the underlying stock, the shorter the time to expiration, the nearer the option is to the money, and the lower the volatility of the underlying stock. Commissions on option positions adjusted relative to single and multiple round lot stock orders tend to be relatively more favorable for multiple than single orders.

In summary, if we think of options as another way to buy or short stock, options frequently prove superior to stock, both in terms of margin and commissions. Appendix 3C also shows that, under certain circumstances, options may provide a tax advantage. As we discussed in Chapter 2, these margin, commission, and tax advantages help explain the justifiable popularity of options among public investors. The relative commission and tax advantages of options are particularly significant for short-term positions. However, if it is desired to hold stock for several years, direct purchase of stock is almost invariably preferable. This avoids the intermediate commissions from rolling over the position every nine months and allows gains to qualify as long term for tax purposes.

3-2. THE OPTIONS CLEARING CORPORATION

Clearing should not be confused with execution. Simply stated, execution is the transacting of an order on an exchange floor, while clearing is the subsequent recognition of the transaction by the Options Clearing Corporation (OCC) and the actual cash settlement.

To clear option trades, a firm must become a member of the Clearing Corporation. To qualify for membership, an applicant must be a member of an exchange trading listed options and must intend to clear option contracts. In addition, the applicant must have a prescribed minimum amount of net capital. Initial payments to the Clearing Corporation include a nonrefundable qualification fee of $2,000 and a refundable $10,000 deposit with the Clearing Fund, used to insure performance of option contracts issued by the Clearing Corporation. Subsequently, the deposit is adjusted quarterly so that it equals the greater of $10,000 and the daily average number of the member's open option positions during the preceding quarter multiplied by $10. All Clearing Fund deposits must be made in cash or in securities issued by the U.S. government with a maturity of five years or less. Any interest earned on these securities accrues to the Clearing Member.

In day-to-day operation, a Clearing Member receives a number of reports from the Clearing Corporation each morning, including the Daily Position Report, Depository Report, Exercise Assignment Summary, and Daily Margin Report. For each contract transacted through a Clearing Member, the Clearing Member must pay a fee to the OCC, the size of which depends on the nature of the transaction. For regular trades, the fee is $0.075 per contract; for "scratch trades" of Market Makers guaranteed by the Clearing Member, $0.015; for each exercise notice tendered, $1.00. A scratch trade occurs when the same contract is bought and sold the same day at the same price by the same Market Maker. In addition, the Clearing Member must pay an exchange fee for each contract; on the CBOE, the fee is $0.30 per customer contract with a price of $1.00 or more per share, $0.15 per customer contract with a price per share of less than $1.00, and $0.03 per contract for Market Makers and Clearing Member firms. In short, excluding back office work (such as trade comparisons, cash settlements, margin checks, and security movements) and floor operations (such as runners, employed Floor Brokers, and phone clerks), and with the exception of some exercises, each transaction costs a Clearing Member at most $0.375 per contract.

A Clearing Member must also deposit margin with the Clearing Corporation for options for which it represents the writer, by 9 : 00 A.M. Central Time of the business day following the day on which the option was written. In the case of a call, the Clearing Member can deposit the underlying security in lieu of margin. Otherwise, appropriate margin must be deposited in the form of cash, U.S. government securities, or a bank letter of credit.

Clearing Members are required to deposit with the OCC 100% of the purchase price of every option for which they represent a buyer and (if not covered by the underlying security) 130% of the price of the closing ask quotation for every option for which they represent a writer.[9] This is an OCC requirement and should not be confused with the margin requirements that the exchange imposes on Clearing Member customers (see Appendix 3A).

These margin deposits and the Clearing Fund maintained by the Clearing Corporation serve as part of an elaborate back-up system that insures purchased option contracts will be honored. When an option is

---

[9] In addition, by the current practice, whenever the Dow Jones Industrial Average increases by 10 points during any day, at the discretion of the OCC, an additional amount may be required to be immediately deposited, equal to 10% of the otherwise total margin.

presented to the buyer's broker for exercise, the Clearing Corporation randomly selects a writing Clearing Member to deliver the shares (in the case of a call) or deliver the striking price (in the case of a put). The Clearing Member then assigns the exercise notice to one of its customers. If the customer cannot deliver, then the customer's margin on deposit with the Clearing Corporation is tapped. If this is insufficient, the Clearing Member must use its own net capital. If this proves inadequate, then the member's contribution to the Clearing Fund is used and, following this, the entire Clearing Fund on a pro rata basis. In the exceedingly unlikely event that this were to exhaust the Clearing Fund, each Clearing Member would then be assessed an amount up to 100% of its prescribed Clearing Fund deposit. Any remaining deficiency would then be made up by the Clearing Corporation's own assets. If further assessment of Clearing Members is required, they have the alternative of paying or terminating their membership in the Clearing Corporation. The exchanges themselves are not held liable.

The back-up system makes it highly improbable that any properly negotiated option contract will not be honored. Indeed, it would appear that the collapse of the entire listed options market would be required. The only event that could conceivably create this debacle would be a very sudden and strong movement in stock prices, one considerably more extreme than any on record.[10]

3-3. HOW THE EXCHANGES WORK

Each of the four exchanges trading puts and calls in the United States uses somewhat different rules and procedures. Perhaps the most important difference is the use of Specialists and Registered Options Traders by the AMEX and PHLX in place of Order Book Officials and competing Market Makers on the CBOE and PSE. The Specialist system more closely resembles procedures used on stock exchanges, while the competing Market Maker system is more similar to floor trading on commodity exchanges. Rather than survey the rules and procedures followed on each exchange, we will instead provide a very detailed description of only one exchange: the Chicago Board Options Exchange.[11] The CBOE pioneered the concept of

---

[10] Even a large movement over an hour during the day should not be a problem since Market Makers have time to adjust their positions. However, a "gap" opening, where stock prices were to change by an unprecedented amount from the previous day's close, might force a collapse of the market.

[11] A comparison of many institutional practices across all four options exchanges, as well as the New York Stock Exchange, can be found in *Report of the Special Study of the Options Markets to the Securities and Exchange Commission*, December 1978.

exchange-traded options and is responsible for the principal features of today's options market. Even with aggressive competition from other exchanges, it still accounts for well over half of the volume of listed option contracts in the United States.

In February 1984, the Chicago Board Options Exchange moved from its original facilities into a new building to accommodate increased trading volume.[12] The trading floor covers approximately 50,000 square feet and takes up the entire third floor of the building. Over 600 communications booths—most equipped with phones, Teletype machines, and Quotron price display screens—line the perimeter of the floor. These are rented exclusively to Clearing Firm members for the primary purpose of handling incoming public and Market Maker orders. Six trading posts for stock options occupy more than half of the center of the trading floor. Trading in all options on the same underlying stock occurs at an Order Book Official's station. Each post has nine or ten of these stations. A typical station will have three or four stocks.[13] The remainder of the trading floor is reserved for trading in index and bond options and for future expansion. On the fourth floor overlooking the trading floor are a lounge and restaurant for exchange members and a gallery for visitors.

At 7 : 00 A.M. Central Time on a trading day, the Exchange floor is quiet. By 7 : 30, members and trade checkers begin to arrive to rectify any clerical errors from the previous day and to resolve trades that have not yet been matched ("out-trades"). By 9 : 00, the floor is crowded with more than 250 Floor Brokers, 40 Order Book Officials, and 600 Market Makers, all Exchange members, and more than 1,000 employees of the exchange and member firms. Only Exchange members—Floor Brokers and Market Makers—can trade options on the floor. One Order Book Official (OBO) governs each station and takes his position behind a raised counter, together with his team of assistants.[14] Floor Brokers and Market Makers stand on two or three semicircular stairs in front of each station.

---

[12] Prior to November 1977, the record daily cleared volume on the CBOE of 211,008 contracts occurred on Friday, July 15, 1977. The expiration for the July series coincidentally followed the New York City blackout of July 14, when the closing of the NYSE necessitated the closing of the CBOE. Since then, successive cleared volume records have been set of 223,781 contracts on November 11, 1977, 284,900 contracts on April 14, 1978; and an extreme peak of 425,930 contracts on April 17, 1978, the same day the NYSE experienced a record reported volume of 63,510,000 shares. Reported CBOE volume for April 17 was 402,440 contracts, representing an unprecedented difference between cleared and reported trades. In 1982, a record high occurred of 666,457 cleared trades.

[13] The configuration of stations on the floor changes from time to time depending on the activity of various option classes, and the introduction of new underlying stocks.

[14] The CBOE has phased out its original Board Broker system and replaced it with Order Book Officials, a system first used on the PSE. Board Brokers were Exchange members while OBOs are employees of the Exchange. Otherwise they perform the same function.

Some stations may have many more Market Makers present than others. Each trading "crowd" follows different psychological and economic rules; some are very competitive within, while others are cooperative within but unfriendly to strangers; some are well capitalized and able to handle large trades, while others are cautious and inactive; some are quiet and have a well-defined price leader, while others are noisy with competing quotes.

Floor Brokers who usually fill market orders are apt to be employees of a Clearing Member and are prepared to trade at several posts, while those who specialize in limit orders are usually self-employed and do most of their trading in a very few underlying securities. In either case, orders come to the respective Floor Brokers, usually by a teletype machine located in a communications booth, which imprints the order on individual order cards. A Floor Broker either tears off the order card and walks the order to the appropriate post or a runner delivers the order to a Floor Broker already standing at a post. Floor Brokers who fill limit orders may hold a "deck" of different orders in their hand. In contrast, Market Makers hold buy and sell forms, and possibly a record of their current positions and option value estimates.

At each post, in front of the Floor Brokers and Market Makers and above and behind the Order Book Official, is a line of Quotron price display screens. For each underlying security, one screen contains price-volume information relating to the underlying stock and its call options, and, if puts are available, a second screen contains similar information for puts. Another screen contains recent news as reported by the Dow Jones and Reuters News Services, general market indices, and prices of key stocks. If options to the same underlying security are dually listed on another exchange, another screen relays the most recent pricing information from that exchange. Floor Brokers and Market Makers spend most of their time at the post watching the screens displaying CBOE price-volume information for the underlying securities traded at that post. An example of the type of information available on this screen is provided in Table 3-2.

The first column lists all Polaroid calls available for trading, listed in order of time to expiration. The second column is the price of the previous business day's closing transaction. Prices under 3 may appear with a plus sign, signifying sixteenths. For example, "7 + " means $\frac{7}{16}$, and "2 11 + " means $2\frac{11}{16}$. The third column contains prices of the most recent trades. Nothing appears in this column for PRD/JAN/45, since this call has not yet traded for the day.

The next two columns are price-volume information on the best quotes contained in the book of limit orders managed by the Order Book Official. While the entire contents of the book are only known to the OBO

Table 3-2
POST SCREEN FOR POLAROID CALLS

Polar 1	*Close*	*Last*	*B-Bid A-Ask*	*Size*	*Mkt-Quote*
A JAN 30	$8\frac{1}{2}$	$7\frac{5}{8}$	$7\frac{3}{8}$–$7\frac{3}{4}$	2×5	$7\frac{1}{2}$–$7\frac{3}{4}$
B JAN 35	$3\frac{3}{4}$	2 13 +	$2\frac{3}{4}$–3	1×2	2 13 + –2 15 +
C JAN 40	11 +	. 7 +	$\frac{3}{8}\frac{1}{2}$	3×2	$\frac{3}{8}\frac{1}{2}$
D JAN 45	1 +		–3 +	$\times 2$	–1 +
E APR 35	$5\frac{1}{2}$	$4\frac{3}{4}$	$4\frac{1}{2}$–5	3×6	$4\frac{5}{8}$–$4\frac{3}{4}$
F APR 40	2 11 +	$2\frac{1}{4}$	$2\frac{1}{8}$–2 7 +	2×1	2 3 + –2 5 +
G APR 45	$1\frac{1}{8}$	$\frac{3}{4}$	$\frac{1}{2}$–1 1 +	3×2	$\frac{3}{4}\frac{7}{8}$
H JUL 35	$6\frac{1}{2}$	$5\frac{5}{8}$	$5\frac{1}{4}$–6	1×1	$5\frac{5}{8}$–$5\frac{7}{8}$
I JUL 40	4	$3\frac{1}{4}$	3–$3\frac{5}{8}$	2×2	$3\frac{1}{4}$–$3\frac{3}{8}$
J					
K					
L					
M					
N					
O					
P					

PRD $-37\frac{1}{2}$–1   B $37\frac{3}{8}$ A $37\frac{5}{8}$ O $38\frac{3}{8}$ H $38\frac{1}{2}$ L $37\frac{1}{2}$ V 96,000   AT 1 : 12

PRD $37\frac{5}{8}$ PRD 2s $37\frac{1}{2}$ PRD 800s $37\frac{1}{2}$

and his assistants, Market Makers and Floor Brokers are informed of the bid-ask quotes in the book which are closest to the market. For example, for PRD/JAN/35, the highest order to buy in the book is for one contract at $2\frac{3}{4}$, and the lowest order to sell in the book is for two contracts at 3. These quotes are continuously updated by the Order Book Official terminal operator, a member of the OBO's staff, as limit orders are received into the book. Although this partial glimpse at the book is not disseminated to the public, the public interest is nonetheless served by making this information available to Market Makers and Floor Brokers. According to the rules of the exchange:

1. Only public market or public limit orders may be placed in the book.[15]
2. These orders have priority over all other orders.[16]

---

[15] In particular, Market Makers and Exchange member firms trading for their own account through Floor Brokers may not place orders in the book.

[16] Public market orders may be placed in the book prior to the initiation of trading for the day to assure priority at the opening.

For example, in PRD/JAN/40, before a Floor Broker, representing an exchange member or a public customer, or a Market Maker representing himself, can buy at $\frac{3}{8}$ or less, the customer's limit order of three contracts at $\frac{3}{8}$ in the book must first be filled.[17] Only if Floor Brokers and Market Makers are aware of the best bid and ask quotes in the book can they check that transactions among themselves do not violate these rules. In PRD/JAN/40, if a Floor Broker has a market order to sell two contracts, and the best bid from the trading crowd is $\frac{3}{8}$ or lower, the Floor Broker is obligated to say, "Sell 2 JAN/40s to the book." He thus executes a transaction between himself and the Order Book Official, who always represents a public customer.

The last column is the best bid-ask quotes from the trading crowd at the moment. For example, for PRD/APR/35, $4\frac{5}{8}$ is the highest bid price and $4\frac{3}{4}$ the lowest ask price at which a member of the trading crowd (that is, a Floor Broker, a Market Maker, or the OBO) is willing to transact. Each side may be represented by different individuals and no information is given as to size. These are the bid-ask quotes available in brokerage offices throughout the country. Properly updated, these quotes are the relevant short description of the "market" at any point in time. Note that no positive quote is available for bid PRD/JAN/45, either in the book or in the trading crowd. Presumably, no one is willing to buy at $\frac{1}{16}$, the lowest allowable transaction price.

The two lines of data at the bottom of the screen contain information about the underlying stock. "$-37\frac{1}{2}$" indicates that the last transaction in New York during the day was at $37\frac{1}{2}$, down from the previous different price (which, as we will see, was $37\frac{5}{8}$). It is this number more than any other on the screen that absorbs the attention of the trading crowd. An up-tick or a down-tick is apt to generate a flurry of trading and revisions of market quotes, particularly if the stock price moves more than $\pm\frac{1}{4}$. The "-1" indicates $37\frac{1}{2}$ is down one point from yesterday's close, which therefore must have been $38\frac{1}{2}$. The stock prices following are, respectively, the current bid, current ask, opening price for the day, high for the day, and low for the day. Evidently, the stock is currently at its low for the day. So far, 96,000 shares or 960 round lots of stock have traded during the day, with the last trade registered at 1 : 12 P.M. Eastern Time. If a news bulletin on Polaroid has recently come across the Dow Jones or Reuter's News Service, this will

---

[17] Spread orders made on the basis of a price difference, or straddle orders made on the basis of a total bid or ask, are exceptions. In these cases, both sides of the order may be placed with the trading crowd, even though the book displays an equal price for at most one side of the order. To qualify for this privilege, the spread or straddle order must involve an equal number of options on the buy side and the sell side.

be indicated by "DJ" or "RN" on the screen just before the time of the last trade. The data below give the ticker tape for the most recent trades in Polaroid stock—100 shares at $37\frac{5}{8}$, followed by 200 shares at $37\frac{1}{2}$, with the last trade of 800 shares at $37\frac{1}{2}$.

The time of the last trade, in conjunction with the current time and the bid-ask stock quote, may be used to update the price of the last trade. If the last trade took place a few minutes earlier, the bid-ask quote may be a better indicator than the last price of the price of the next stock transaction. Among other things, this depends on how frequently the specialist in New York updates his bid-ask quotes. In this case, since the last transaction took place midway between the bid-ask spread, the bid-ask prices simply confirm the last price. However, in analyzing transactions data on stock prices, empiricists have discovered that price reversals, transaction to transaction, are somewhat more likely than price continuations. This is due to the way a specialist manages his book. In this case, particularly if the bid-ask quote is out of date, we are somewhat more likely to see the next print at $37\frac{5}{8}$ than at $37\frac{3}{8}$, but probably most likely to see no change at $37\frac{1}{2}$. The trading activity given by the bottom line may also influence our prediction. Many traders believe that a large block coming across the tape at the bid (ask) price indicates selling (buying) pressure and they expect the stock price to fall (rise) in subsequent transactions.[18] A print of a large block, even if at a price unchanged from the previous transaction, often generates sudden activity in the associated options.

At the opening at 9:00 A.M. Central Time, option trading at each station awaits the first print of the underlying stock. As soon as the stock trades,[19] the Order Book Official opens each associated option series, one at a time, calls before puts, by calling for bid and ask prices from the Market Makers. After all the options to an underlying stock have been opened, then for the remainder of the day any option on that security can be traded at any time. A similar closing rotation occurs for expiring series at 3 : 00 P.M. on their last day of trading.[20]

A typical trade begins with a runner delivering a public order to a Floor Broker already stationed in the crowd at an Order Book Official station. The Floor Broker then asks out loud, so that all in the crowd can hear, "What's the market in PRD/JUL/40?" Since calls are traded in a continuous auction, both Market Makers and Floor Brokers will vie to be

---

[18] We hasten to add that we know of no empirical verification of this theory.

[19] If a bid-ask stock quote has been sent from the stock exchange by 9:15 or 9:30, the OBO will usually open the associated options for trading, even if a stock transaction has not yet occurred.

[20] In the past, closing rotations were used routinely for all series at the close of trading every day. This practice has been discontinued.

the first to give the best quote. For example, if the book, as given on the Quotron display for PRD/JUL/40, shows the current bid-ask for the call at $3-3\frac{5}{8}$, the Market Makers and Floor Brokers must quote a market within the book, where at most one side can coincide with the book, to have any hope of getting the trade. In addition, Market Makers must always quote a two-sided market and, depending on the option price level, their spread must lie within a given interval. For options trading at 3, the maximum spread[21] a Market Maker can quote is $\frac{1}{2}$. Therefore, ignoring the book, if he simply says, "$\frac{1}{8}$ bid," he is implicitly quoting a $3\frac{1}{8}-3\frac{5}{8}$ market; if he says, "at $\frac{3}{8}$," he is implicitly quoting a $2\frac{7}{8}-3\frac{3}{8}$ market. In this case, we suppose many Market Makers and Floor Brokers shout out quotes almost simultaneously. Suppose the first two Market Makers give the best markets, with one saying, "$\frac{1}{4}$ to $\frac{1}{2}$," and the other saying, "$\frac{1}{8}$ to $\frac{3}{8}$." The market is then $\frac{1}{4}$ to $\frac{3}{8}$, with the first Market Maker willing to buy at $3\frac{1}{4}$, and the second Market Maker willing to sell at $3\frac{3}{8}$. The Market Makers together have quoted a spread of $\frac{1}{8}$, which is the narrowest possible market, since options trading over 3 trade in intervals of eighths. If this market supersedes the market given on the Quotron display, a QRTO (quote reporting terminal operator) sitting at the station immediately updates the market quotes available on the display. This same information simultaneously becomes available on computer terminals in brokerage houses across the country.

If the Floor Broker is holding a limit order to sell at $3\frac{3}{8}$, he returns the order to his deck and it goes temporarily unfilled. Alternatively, if he feels the market will take considerable time coming to a $3\frac{3}{8}$ bid, he may "book the order" by placing the ticket in a sell-order box on the counter in front of the Order Book Official. The OBO's staff then picks up the ticket and enters it in the book. For each option, the book is simply a stack of buy and sell tickets of limit orders, arranged by price, with priority of execution given to price and then time of entry, irrespective of the size of the order. By booking the order, the Floor Broker sacrifices the floor brokerage to the Exchange, as represented by the Order Book Official. For a $3 price level, the floor brokerage charged by the OBO is about $1 per contract. A Floor Broker negotiates the floor brokerage he receives with the Exchange member for whom he is transacting. Although a Floor Broker sacrifices the floor brokerage, he will book an order when the firm whose orders he holds requires him to do so in order to afford its customers the priority that only the book can offer. A Floor Broker will also be motivated to book the order if his deck of limit orders is becoming large and complicated to follow, or if

---

[21] A maximum spread of $\frac{1}{4}$ is allowed for options trading at less than $\frac{1}{2}$, $\frac{1}{2}$ for options trading between $\frac{1}{2}$ and 10, $\frac{3}{4}$ for options between 10 and 20, and 1 point for options over 20. Market Makers are restricted to bids (asks) within one point, plus the movement in the underlying stock, below (above) the last option transaction.

he wishes to move to another post. If a Floor Broker fails to fill properly orders left in his trust, he, or the firm that employs him, is personally liable for his errors. For example, suppose the Floor Broker decided not to book his $3\frac{3}{8}$ sell limit order. If the market subsequently moves to $3\frac{1}{2}$–$3\frac{5}{8}$, then falls to 3–$3\frac{1}{8}$, and he neglects to fill the order, he then can be held responsible to fill the order at $3\frac{3}{8}$. He may be required to sell contracts at 3 and then liquidate his position by buying the same number of contracts from his customer at $3\frac{3}{8}$. The loss he incurs is charged to his error account, for which he or his employer is liable. With the exception of correcting errors, Floor Brokers are not allowed to trade for their own account. It follows that a Floor Broker holding a deck of several limit orders on a variety of options will, depending on his skill in juggling his deck, book the orders that are farthest away from the market.

If, instead, the Floor Broker receives a market order (or a limit order at the market—that is, to sell at $3\frac{1}{4}$), then he will fill the order immediately. If he delays and the market moves up, he will be a hero to his customer and may attract future business from him. On the other hand, if the market moves down, he may be held accountable for the lost opportunity. Since the market is "$\frac{1}{4}$–$\frac{3}{8}$," with a sell market order, he usually first offers to sell at $3\frac{3}{8}$. If the crowd shows no interest, he turns to the Market Maker quoting "$\frac{1}{4}$–$\frac{1}{2}$" and says, "Sold at $\frac{1}{4}$; I have five." Any delay on the Floor Broker's part may cause him to lose the market, since a Market Maker or another Floor Broker is only held to his quote for the moment after he announces it. Since the Market Maker's quote only commits him to one contract, he can then reply, "I'll buy one," or any larger number. If, in this case, the Market Maker says, "I'll buy three," the Floor Broker has a partial fill and turns to other Market Makers and Floor Brokers in the crowd to fill the remainder of the order.

To keep it simple, suppose, instead, that the Market Maker says, "Done," which commits him to the entire order. The Market Maker then fills out a buy ticket and the Floor Broker fills out a sell ticket. A properly marked buy ticket is shown in Figure 3-1. RAP is the personal identifying symbol of the selling Floor Broker. B is the symbol of the Clearing Member represented by the Floor Broker. DVD is the symbol identifying the Clearing Member guaranteeing the Market Maker, and SIG is the Market Maker's personal identifying symbol.

The seller time stamps his ticket and deposits a copy of the sell ticket in a conveyor belt attached to the counter at the post. The process of filling out and filing the sell ticket usually takes from five to forty seconds, depending on the number of traders involved, how fast they write, and how far they are from the belt. The sell ticket is then automatically conveyed to a small bin at one end of the post. Here a PRTO (price reporting terminal

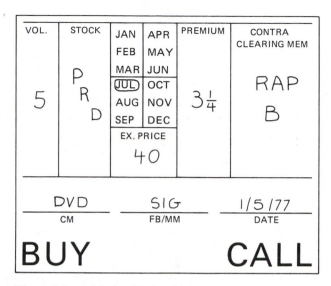

Figure 3-1   Market Maker Ticket

operator) immediately removes the ticket from the bin, with a single key stroke simultaneously enters the stock symbol, expiration month, and striking price, and then separately enters the number of contracts traded, the option transaction price, and the identifying symbols of the selling and buying Floor Traders (that is, RAP and SIG). The computer completes the record of the transaction by automatically registering the time of day to the second and the price of the last transaction in the underlying stock. Market Maker selling tickets for puts are blue and for calls are red, permitting immediate visual differentiation. The PRTO will also enter a "transaction prefix" code under unusual circumstances—if, for example, a transaction is known to be recorded out of sequence. The time that elapses between filing the order and the appearance of the transaction on the ticker tape is typically less than one minute. However, tape delays on very active days can result in a much longer time lapse. The Market Maker simply keeps his own copy of the trade and prepares for his next quote. The Floor Broker hands one of his copies of the trade to a runner, who delivers it back to its originating communications booth, and the result is teletyped to the brokerage office where the order originated. If no runner is available, the Floor Broker drops the ticket in the conveyor belt at the post. For a market order, the whole process to and from the booth usually takes from one-half to two and one-half minutes, primarily depending on how far the booth is from the particular post, the availability of runners, and whether or not the Floor Broker is walking multiple orders.

Although typical, a given execution may not follow this description exactly. Market Makers may trade with other Market Makers, Floor Brokers may trade with other Floor Brokers, and both may trade with the Order Book Official. As we have noted, the book takes precedence over Market Makers and orders held by Floor Brokers if they compete at the same price. In the example above, if 3 were the best bid from the crowd, the Floor Broker must fill his order by "selling to the book." He and the OBO are then on opposite sides of the transaction. A Floor Broker, if he is fortunate, can even trade with himself (that is, "cross" orders) by announcing (so that, in principle, the entire crowd can hear) that he has orders to buy and sell at the same price and announcing the price. If no one in the crowd intervenes, he is allowed to cross the orders.

There are probably as many Market Maker trading strategies as there are Market Makers. It would be futile to attempt a detailed enumeration here, even if we knew what they were. However, most short-run strategies can be classified either as "scalping" or "spreading." A scalper tries to earn the bid-ask spread for himself through a succession of quick in and out trades. He hopes to pick up $\frac{1}{8}$ more often than he loses $\frac{1}{8}$. A spreader tends only to take a position on one side if he can match it by an appropriately offsetting position in another associated option on the other side. He may follow price estimates he has prepared or has purchased from an option pricing service to buy the temporarily underpriced options and write the overpriced options. Some Market Makers, after months of experience in options on the same underlying stock, will tell you they simply "know" when the relative prices are out of line. Many subscribe to "technical" theories, which claim to predict future movements in the associated stock. For example, some follow price trends of a few stocks that are supposed to lead the market. Virtually all published academic work in finance heavily discounts the validity of technical theories; however, almost all of the research concerns the behavior of stock prices over intervals of one day or longer. In contrast, Market Makers employ technical theories over much shorter time intervals, measured in terms of transactions and minutes rather than days. It is quite possible—particularly given the additional and more timely information about the state of the market available on the floor of the Exchange and the imbalances between supply and demand that may exist over short intervals but are dispelled over longer periods—that a few of these technical theories may work.

Market Makers, both individually and as a group, try to protect themselves against "information traders." Based on information not yet in the public domain, Exchange member firms trading for large public investors or for their own account, may buy or sell options anticipating a subsequent move in the underlying stock price. By an Exchange rule, Floor Brokers are obligated to "give up" to the other party to a transaction the name of the member firm initiating an order. From perhaps bitter past experience, Market Makers learn to identify likely information traders and protect themselves by giving more conservative quotes in response.

Needless to say, like public investors, Market Makers also assume long-run positions based on long-term predictions about stock price movements, and they may put on covered positions designed to take advantage of the relative mispricing of associated securities that will only be eliminated after many days or weeks. These positions are likely to be freely placed across the range of underlying securities available on the floor. To assume positions outside options he customarily trades, a Market Maker may place his order through a Floor Broker rather than execute the order himself.

Whatever long-term positions he assumes, a Market Maker must not impair his primary obligation to make a fair and orderly market in the option classes to which he is assigned. According to the rules of the Exchange, as interpreted by the Floor Procedures Committee, no more than 25% to 50% of a Market Maker's trades (measured in number of contracts) can be outside his principal assignment—usually options on three underlying stocks—in any given quarter (for example, January 1 to March 31).[22]

Despite our previous assertions, the same individual can be both a Market Maker and a Floor Broker, provided he is appropriately authorized to perform both these functions by his associated Clearing Member. *However, on the same day, in the same underlying security, he can act only as a Market Maker or a Floor Broker but not both.* This rule probably eliminates most opportunities for a conflict of interest to arise.

Before he can trade on the floor, a Market Maker must buy or lease a seat, or be the agent of a firm that buys or leases a seat for him. He must fill out a number of forms, which are submitted to the Securities and Exchange Commission and to the Exchange, and he must be approved by these agencies. He must pass an examination on options given by the Exchange. He must associate himself with a Clearing Member, who must file a Letter of Guarantee with the Options Clearing Corporation on his behalf. This document certifies that the Clearing Member accepts full financial responsibility for all Exchange transactions of the Market Maker. The Clearing Member receives the benefit of commissions on the Market Maker's trades, since all of his trades are cleared through the associated Clearing Member.

Commissions are negotiated on a basis mutually satisfactory to the Market Maker and his Clearing Member. Commissions typically vary with the contract price and the volume of trading in the Market Maker's

---

[22] This rule has been modified to provide more freedom for Market Makers with assignments in relatively inactive option classes.

account during the year. A typical one-way schedule is $1.00 per contract for options over $1.00, $0.75 per contract for options less than $1.00, and $0.25 for scratch trades (that is, the same option bought and sold on the same day at the same price). These rates are usually reduced if a Market Maker generates sufficient volume during the year. While these commissions are quite low relative to those faced by the public, they benefit the public, since Market Makers can afford to quote tighter spreads. As previously noted, Clearing Members, in turn, pay a fee per contract to the Clearing Corporation and to the Exchange. In addition, the Clearing Member bears overhead costs and costs associated with providing special services for Market Makers. For example, one large Clearing Member supplies Market Makers with an off-the-floor lounge and private desks, on-line computer option price estimates, as well as an accounting package monitoring Market Maker accounts.

The rules regarding Market Maker capital requirements are complex. Their general effect is to provide Market Makers with substantially more flexibility than a public customer with the same capital.

3-4. THE PERFORMANCE OF OPTIONS MARKETS

The performance of a securities market may be judged on several grounds, including:

1. Size and profitability
2. Liquidity
3. Transactions speed
4. Fairness
5. Effects on other financial markets

In this section, we will again restrict our attention to the CBOE.

Size and Profitability. Table 3-3, taken from the CBOE publication "Market Statistics," gives the history of the extraordinary expansion of the Exchange for calendar years beginning April 1973 through 1983 in terms of contract trading volume, listings, and memberships. The Exchange's success is clearly indicated by the price of a membership. A seat on the CBOE was one of the best investments one could have made over this period.

Table 3-4 shows the underlying stocks with the highest daily average cleared contract volume on the CBOE during 1983. Options trading in these ten stocks accounted for over 41% of the total CBOE volume for the year. As one might guess from this figure, many stocks had a much lower volume; in some cases, a daily average of less than a hundred contracts.

Table 3-3
CBOE VOLUME, LISTED STOCKS, AND MEMBERSHIP

	Cleared Contract Volume				Stocks Listed at Year End	Membership Profile at Year End	
Year	For Year	Daily Average	Daily High	Market Share		Total Membership	Last Sale ($000's)
1973	1,119,117	6,469	17,319	100.0%	32	520	25
1974	5,682,907	22,462	63,929	100.0%	40	684	39
1975	14,431,023	57,040	124,528	79.7%	79	1,281	64
1976	21,498,027	84,972	168,555	66.4%	86	1,337	62
1977	24,838,632	98,566	223,781	62.7%	95	1,293	45
1978	34,277,350	136,021	425,930	59.9%	95	1,253	75
1979	35,379,600	139,840	342,334	55.1%	95	1,240	99
1980	52,916,921	209,158	432,639	54.7%	120	1,640	152
1981	57,584,175	227,605	426,780	52.6%	120	1,666	180
1982	75,721,605	299,295	666,457	55.2%	140	1,697	174
1983	71,695,563	283,382	592,890	52.8%	145	1,753	212

Liquidity. The average number of contracts per trade has increased eight-fold from the first few months of the Exchange to the end of 1983. This increase, in large part, reflects greater institutional participation in the marketplace and the willingness of Market Makers to accept more substantial commitments. Both the capital of Clearing Members doing Market Maker business and the equity in Market Maker accounts have grown considerably since 1973.

The distribution of bid-ask spreads and the price changes between successive trades are other important measures of liquidity. In many cases,

Table 3-4
CBOE UNDERLYING SECURITIES WITH HIGHEST DAILY AVERAGE CLEARED CONTRACT VOLUME DURING 1983

Security	Volume
International Business Machines	31,572
Teledyne	14,743
Superior Oil	11,537
General Motors	10,282
Federal Express	8,947
Eastman Kodak	8,900
American Telephone and Telegraph	8,643
Texas Instruments	7,993
Honeywell	7,127
Homestake Mining	6,973

price continuity will be justifiably interrupted if the underlying security ticks up or down. Other interruptions can be attributed to unexpected surges in buy or sell orders which tax the capital of available Market Makers, lack of competition among Market Makers, and the attempt of Market Makers to earn the bid-ask spread for themselves as compensation for their service of providing depth and continuity to the market. From the point of view of a trading crowd quoting $5\frac{1}{4}$–$5\frac{3}{8}$, for example, nothing could be better than a flood of market orders, as many to sell as to buy. Without accumulating inventory, the Market Makers in the crowd are able to reap the $\frac{1}{8}$ spread on every contract, buying from the public at $5\frac{1}{4}$ and selling to other public traders at $5\frac{3}{8}$. The greater the extent to which the public is spared this spread, the more liquid the market.

Evidence available in the CBOE publication "Market Statistics" indicates that bid-ask spreads quoted by Market Makers are typically $\frac{1}{4}$ or less, reflecting competition from an average of more than fifteen Market Makers per OBO station. About 62% of the total trades occur at no price change from the previous trade, and about 32% at a price change of $\frac{1}{8}$ or $\frac{1}{16}$.

Transaction Speed. Three time intervals are important to public customers:

1. Execution
2. Price and quote dissemination
3. Settlement

Based on a sample reported in the Securities Industry Association's 1976 study of the options market,[23] trade-execution time for market orders on the CBOE averaged 3.4 minutes for 1975. The Exchange now claims substantial improvement over this figure. For a given market order, execution time varies primarily with the distance of the receiving communications booth to the post where the option is traded. Since October 1975, the installation of high-speed communication equipment and an increase in the quote-reporting staff has meant almost instantaneous dissemination of quotes. In the absence of "tape lates," following the procedure described in Section 3-3, prices of trades usually reach the ticker tape within one minute after the representatives of the two parties to the trade have made a verbal agreement on the Exchange floor, and news of the trade usually reaches the executing broker in less than 90 seconds after execution. A "tape late" is defined as a delay in a single class of options from execution to public dissemination of more than two minutes. During January 1976, the heaviest month of trading prior to 1978, 214 periods of "tape lates" occurred, but in no instance did they exceed ten minutes. The most extreme form of delay is

---

[23] See the Securities Industry Association, *The State of the Options Sector of the Securities Industry*, May 1976.

a trading halt in a particular class of options, either initiated in the market for the underlying security or initiated at the CBOE. During January 1976, seven trading halts were initiated at the CBOE, and in other months there have typically been fewer.

To facilitate the entry of orders into the book, Phase I of the Exchange's new electronic Order Support System (OSS) became operative in 1981. This system allows brokerage firms to enter, cancel, or check electronically the status of public customer orders placed in the book. Moreover, notice of execution of booked limit orders is to be automatically reported back through the firm's wire system. The CBOE will be the first securities exchange to computerize its limit order book.

Fairness. The competing Market Maker system and the priority of public orders in the limit order book are the primary features of the Exchange that support fair dealing for the public. Other provisions, such as position and exercise limits and the back-up system described in Section 3-2 for honoring purchased option contracts, are also obvious examples of mechanisms for customer protection.

Less visible, but equally important, are a host of special rules and routine self-regulatory surveillance practices. Securities and Exchange Commission Release No. 34-14056, which proposed to formalize the listed options market "moratorium" on October 17, 1977, provides a natural format for addressing this subject.[24] Quoting from the release:

> The Commission announced today the initiation of an investigation and study, pursuant to ... the Securities Act of 1934, to determine what action is necessary to aid in the enforcement of the Act, and whether additional rules thereunder should be proposed to protect investors and the public interest and to maintain fair and orderly markets in connection with the trading of standardized options and underlying securities.

The release proposed Temporary Rule 9b-1(T), which would make it unlawful for any national securities exchange by any means

> to permit expansion of existing programs for the trading of standardized options, to alter such programs in any material respect not expressly approved by order of the Commission, or to permit the initiation of new programs designed to expand the trading of options.

This phrase, "expansion of existing programs," was interpreted to include, among other things, the listing of options on additional new underlying securities and the listing of puts on existing underlying securities which, thus far, only had listed calls.

---

[24] The October 17, 1977, release was a step toward formalizing the previous "voluntary" moratorium requested by the SEC on July 18, 1977. Although the proposal was subsequently withdrawn, through exchange cooperation, its provisions were effectively enforced over two and one-half years.

Underlying this unusually strong action taken by the Commission was the general concern that incentives for fraudulent investor behavior may be significantly greater in the listed options market, as contrasted with the listed stock market. Moreover, listed options in the United States had only been available for a short time, yet the new market had expanded extremely rapidly to the point where trading, measured in terms of share equivalents, rivaled the New York Stock Exchange.

At the same time, a number of Exchange proposals were pending before the Commission, including proposals to change striking price intervals, to multiply existing expiration cycles, to expand the number of authorized call option classes, to open the listing of puts on all underlying securities with currently listed calls, to increase the number of dually listed option classes (that is, the same options traded on two exchanges), to modify position limits, to initiate trading of options on debt instruments of the federal government, to list options on underlying securities traded in the over-the-counter market, to list options on a broad-based stock market index, and to initiate trading of options at the New York Stock Exchange.

Perhaps the most troublesome issue was whether options and their underlying stock should be traded together at the same post. This proposal arises naturally from the close contractual relationship between options and common stock and the consequent parallelism of changes in their prices. With the exceptions that stock is originally issued by a corporation and conveys the power of control over corporate activities, stock is economically equivalent to a perpetual American call with zero striking price and protection against cash dividends. Trading options and stock together would improve the efficiency of both markets in many ways. For example, hedged positions would be easier to execute, economies of scale and reduction of information trading should reduce transactions costs, and illegal trading practices would be more easily detected. The trading of options and stock together would necessitate a major restructuring of those markets and force a confrontation between the NYSE and the CBOE.

Faced with the responsibility to rule on these proposals and uncertain about the adequacy of listed options market surveillance, the Commission felt it needed time to develop a consistent approach to these issues that would be in the public interest. To support its action, the Commission raised a number of regulatory concerns directed specifically at the options exchanges. These concerns included:

1. Adequacy of Exchange audit trails[25]
2. Fictitious trades to influence Market Maker capital requirements

---

[25] An audit trail is the information in available records for reconstructing a transaction from its inception to its completion. A complete audit trail makes it possible to identify all parties to, and the timing of steps in, a transaction.

3. Market Maker wash sales for tax purposes
4. Proprietary trading to attract order flow
5. Intermarket price manipulation
6. Front running of block trades

For each of these, we will examine the procedures used by the CBOE.

1. ADEQUACY OF EXCHANGE AUDIT TRAILS. The primary surveillance tool of the CBOE is its Market Data Report (MDR), a computer-readable, time-stamped record of every reported transaction and bid-ask quote on its trading floor. For example, for the Polaroid quote change and transaction described in Section 3-3, the MDR would contain the following two computer-coded records:[26]

$$01/05/77 \quad 12{:}13{:}01 \quad \text{PRD JUL} \quad 40 \quad \text{C} \quad 3\tfrac{1}{4} \quad 3\tfrac{3}{8} \quad 37\tfrac{1}{2}$$
$$01/05/77 \quad 12{:}13{:}41 \quad \text{PRD JUL} \quad 40 \quad \text{C} \quad 5 \quad 3\tfrac{1}{4} \quad 37\tfrac{1}{2} \quad \text{RAP SIG}$$

The first record says that on January 5, 1977, at twelve thirteen and one second Central Time, a bid-ask quote of $3\tfrac{1}{4}$–$3\tfrac{3}{8}$ occurred for PRD/JUL/40 calls and at that time the last stock transaction price was $37\tfrac{1}{2}$. From the second record we learn that on the same date, 40 seconds later, 5 PRD/JUL/40 calls traded at $3\tfrac{1}{4}$, for which the seller was RAP and the buyer SIG, and, at that time, the last stock transaction price was $37\tfrac{1}{2}$. The Exchange confirms the transaction information by subsequently compiling a Matched Trade Listing (MTL) from the information on matched trades received from Clearing Members. These trades are then reported by the Exchange to the Clearing Corporation. These two independently constructed versions of transactions on the floor are compared by computer, which produces the daily MDR-MTL Comparison Report. All Market Maker stock transactions cleared through OCC Clearing Members are also reported to the CBOE.

In contrast, while the NYSE generates a computer-readable listing of stock transactions as they occur on the floor, this listing does not include the identification symbols of the floor traders.[27] Moreover, its record of cleared stock trades does not include about one quarter of the transactions. The omitted trades are those for which both sides are cleared by the same brokerage house because it represented both the buyer and the seller or

---

[26] For ease in reading, the information in each record has been somewhat reorganized. "Transaction prefixes" indicating a record that is out of sequence, part of a spread order, etc., may also appear on each record.

[27] The NYSE record also only time stamps the trade to the minute.

those cleared through a regional exchange. It would appear that the CBOE audit trail is superior to the audit trail at the NYSE, despite the more complex organization of the options market (for example, many different options on the same underlying stock and the competitive Market Maker system).

2. FICTITIOUS TRADES TO INFLUENCE MARKET MAKER CAPITAL REQUIRE-MENTS. Market Maker capital requirements have been based on the final ask prices for the day. If the Market Makers as a group tend to be on one side of the market in an option series, there may be an incentive to insert a closing ask quote considerably above or below the last trade. This may force the trade of a token single contract at a high price, if these Market Makers tend to be buyers, or at a low price if they tend to be writers. Although it is unusual for all Market Makers to be on one side of the market, to meet this potential problem, the CBOE has changed its marking system to use the last transaction if it lies between the closing bid and ask, the closing bid if the last transaction lies above the bid and ask, and the closing ask if the last transaction lies below the bid and ask. Using its daily MDR, the CBOE also routinely checks the end-of-day Market Maker trades.

3. MARKET MAKER WASH SALES FOR TAX PURPOSES. Market Makers may engage in prearranged trades, resulting in reported trades on the tape, which are agreed to be reversed after the tax year. To identify this illegal behavior, on a daily, weekly, monthly, and quarterly basis, the CBOE creates computer-generated reports, constructed from the daily MTL, grouping all trades by each Market Maker together. Special attention is paid to Market Maker–to–Market Maker trades and to trades executed by a Floor Broker on behalf of a Market Maker. These reports allow the Exchange to detect reversals at the same price and volume, reversals at the same volume with a price differential, and other unusual trading patterns. Other reports with different formats are also used to enforce the rule requiring a Market Maker to complete at least 50% of his trades in his principal assignment and to detect violation of position limits almost imme-diately after they occur. The Exchange has several employees whose prin-cipal task is to provide a continuous monitoring of Market Maker transactions utilizing these reports.

4. PROPRIETARY TRADING TO ATTRACT ORDER FLOW. The dual listing of some options has created intensive competition among options exchanges. For each option class, brokerage firms typically designate a single exchange as the "primary market." Unless a broker specifically indicates otherwise, the house's computer system automatically routes all orders in an option

class to the designated exchange. For example, although at one time both the CBOE and PSE listed BankAmerica options, Merrill Lynch sent virtually all of its BankAmerica orders to the CBOE, since that was the designated primary market.[28] No attempt was made to check whether a better execution was possible on another exchange. Moreover, other brokerage firms tend to follow Merrill Lynch's lead. To earn designation as the primary market, the exchange usually selected is the one providing the greatest liquidity, often imperfectly measured by volume. Under these circumstances, members of an exchange have a strong incentive to trade solely for the purpose of creating the appearance of liquidity. This trading practice is known as "chumming." When the CBOE became aware of this behavior, it took several steps to end it, including improved surveillance of Market Maker–to–Market Maker transactions, and published volume data separating public from proprietary trades.

5. INTERMARKET PRICE MANIPULATION. It is frequently suggested that Exchange members, with substantial written option positions, manipulate the price of the underlying security near the expiration date to prevent profitable exercise. This procedure is known as "capping."[29] However, attempted capping is fraught with risk, and success, particularly in very active stocks, is probably rare if not impossible. Nonetheless, on a daily basis, the Exchange checks Market Makers with both substantial option positions and stock transactions in the same underlying stock.

6. FRONT RUNNING OF BLOCK TRADES. "Front running" occurs when a firm or individual, knowing in advance that a large block of stock is about to be traded, buys or sells options to profit from this information. When the CBOE first became aware of this practice, it filed a proposed new rule with the SEC, which would prevent Exchange members from executing proprietary orders in options when they possess nonpublic information concerning an agreed-to block transaction (that is, 10,000 shares or more) in underlying securities. This prohibition would also apply to an Exchange member who passes on nonpublic information concerning block transactions to a customer, who then trades on the basis of the information. The CBOE audit trail provides the capability for enforcement. A similar strategy, "tape racing," occurs when a firm or individual knows of a price change in an underlying stock before it prints on the tape. To a great extent, this problem was eliminated when, at the request of the CBOE, the NYSE installed a high-speed tape.

---

[28] Subsequently, the PSE has found it economically advisable to delist its BankAmerica options.

[29] The opposite procedure, effecting transactions to prevent a decline in the stock price, is called "pegging."

The surveillance procedures of the CBOE are considerably more extensive than our brief survey can cover. Indeed, some aspects of these procedures are, for obvious reasons, confidential. The Exchange assigns more than 50 employees and budgets several million dollars annually to surveillance, compliance, investigation of customer and member complaints, and enforcement through Exchange committees or legal remedies. Of course, all violations of OCC and Exchange rules cannot be completely eliminated or detected, and the rules themselves can no doubt be improved. Nonetheless, if judged by comparison with current practices across the entire organized market for securities in the United States, it appears that the Exchange has developed very sophisticated procedures for dealing with these problems and has been very sensitive to the peculiar aspects of option trading.

A final area of concern was directed at the brokerage industry. In its release, the Commission claimed it was aware of broker conduct in selling listed options involving communication of deceptive sales literature, churning of customer accounts, and recommendation of transactions unsuited to customers' financial means and investment objectives.

To reduce deceptive sales practices, each Exchange member firm doing option business with public customers must appoint a *Registered Options Principal* (ROP), who must be an officer or partner in the firm, and who must qualify by passing a written examination on options. Before a *Registered Representative* (a broker) of the firm can trade listed options for public customers, he must also pass an examination. Moreover, for each public customer, the Registered Representative must receive specific approval for listed option trading from his firm's Registered Options Principal, and written approval by the firm's ROP is required for each discretionary option order.[30] Each public customer must submit a written agreement, acknowledging that his account will be handled in accordance with the rules of the OCC and the options exchanges. In particular, he must agree not to violate the position and exercise limits.

Before commencement of trading, the Registered Representative is required to deliver the prospectus of the Options Clearing Corporation to his customer, and the prospectus must accompany any distribution of option sales literature, market letters, research reports, or exchange educational materials. Moreover, all distributed information generated by the firm must first be approved by the firm's ROP and then by the options exchanges.

---

[30] In a discretionary account, the Registered Representative can place orders without prior approval of the customer. However, the customer is required to provide prior written authorization for any discretionary power he delegates.

Unfortunately, none of these precautions can assure a customer will read the prospectus, let alone understand the risk-return implications of option trading. Even after more than ten years since the opening of the CBOE and extensive Exchange efforts to educate the public, options remain, to most investors, an arcane and complex subject. The high commissions per dollar invested, the ability to generate more transactions through covered positions that conserve margin, and the forced turnover due to the relatively short maturities of options can, without careful management, lead to excessive transactions costs and little hope of profit commensurate with the risk borne. These conditions, together with the high risk potential of indiscriminately selected option positions, can make investment in options dangerous for uninformed investors.

Because of the potential of options to generate high commissions, an uninformed investor becomes particularly vulnerable if he permits his broker to trade his account on a discretionary basis. To be sure, the customer is sent a record of every transaction, but this information is often incomplete or difficult to summarize. Brokerage firms are charged with policing the suitability of option transactions, particularly for discretionary accounts. Nonetheless, there have been several instances of intentional churning of discretionary option accounts, which, for various reasons, have been permitted to continue for two or three years before reaching the customer's attention.

As these improper brokerage practices meet with judicial remedy, new standards will be needed to gauge excessive turnover in options-oriented accounts. For equity accounts, a turnover rate of more than six times per year has been regarded as prima facie evidence of churning.[31] From an economist's point of view, this standard is unfortunate. Since different types of securities, or even the same security traded under different conditions, have different commission rates, turnover does not adequately reflect the level of commissions in the account. It would be better if the courts focused on the ratio of annual commissions to the average market value of the account during the year. This measure indicates the rate of return required in the account simply to break even (that is, to cover commissions). With a 1% one-way commission rate on stock, an annual turnover of six times is equivalent to a 12% annual commission cost–to–value ratio. Since option commissions per invested dollar are about two and one-half times stock commissions, the turnover standard for an options-oriented account should

---

[31] N. Wolfson, R. Phillips, and T. Russo, *Regulation of Brokers, Dealers, and Securities Markets* (Boston: Warren, Gorham, and Lamont, 1977), Sec. 2.11. Turnover is the dollar value of purchases during a period, divided by the average net market value (net equity) of an account. This measure would be improved, particularly for options-oriented accounts, if purchases were replaced with half of purchases plus sales.

be *lower* than for a pure equity account. For example, if equity and optic
transacted dollars are split two-thirds and one-third, respectively, then
annual turnover of only about three and one-third times would be need
to produce a 12% annual commission cost–to–value ratio. In this case,
be consistent with the treatment of equity accounts, a turnover of three a
one-third times per year would be prima facie evidence of churning.

Effects on Other Financial Markets.   For a number of reasons, one mig
suspect options trading should influence the price and volume behavior
the underlying stocks. In particular, trading activity might be diverted fro
underlying stocks to their associated options, and the resulting decreased
liquidity in the stock might increase stock price volatility. Another hypothesis contends that the options market draws speculative capital away from
the new-issue market and low-priced stocks. Finally, abnormal stock price
behavior might be observed near expiration dates for underlying stocks
with a large open interest in in-the-money options. In response to these
criticisms, the CBOE has completed its own internal studies and commissioned Robert R. Nathan Associates and, more recently, Management
Analysis Center to investigate these issues by statistical procedures.[32] Both
groups have concluded the new listed options market has had little effect on
other capital markets. Quoting from a Summary of the 1974 Nathan
Report:

> The Chicago Board Options Exchange has been a useful and promising
> addition to the capital markets. Our study has not found any evidence
> that the CBOE has had an adverse effect on the market for underlying
> stocks or on the markets for low-priced stocks or new issues. Rather,
> during a period of great uncertainty in the capital markets generally,
> the CBOE has attracted a number of investors to return to equity-type
> risks through the risk redistribution, risk limitation, and various
> hedging strategies it makes possible. We believe this has helped improve
> the efficiency and fairness of the stock market itself.

However, until these findings have been confirmed by investigators wholly
independent of Exchange support, they cannot be viewed as definitive.[33]

---

[32] See Robert R. Nathan Associates, Inc., *Review of Initial Trading Experience at the Chicago Board Options Exchange*, December 1974; and Management Analysis Center, *The Impact of Exchange-Traded Options on the Market for New Issues of Common Stock of Small Companies*, June 1977. Summaries, as well as the studies themselves, are available on request from the CBOE.

[33] The SEC itself conducted a study of these matters but did not release its findings for public scrutiny. However, reports in the press indicate the study more or less confirms CBOE-supported studies.

3-5. INSTITUTIONAL PARTICIPATION IN OPTIONS MARKETS

All of the reasons we gave in Chapter 2 for trading in options apply to institutional investors as well as individuals. Yet as of this writing, financial institutions (banks, pension funds, insurance companies, and mutual funds) play a very limited role in the listed options market. This stands in marked contrast to their extensive activity in stock and bond markets. But options are an alternative to direct investment in stocks and bonds, and it would seem that the reasons listed would often cause them to be the preferred way. Of course, the relative importance of the reasons may differ for individuals and institutions. The large scale of institutional investors already gives them access to favorable borrowing and lending rates, transactions costs, and margin requirements. Furthermore, many institutions are tax exempt or have all sources of income taxed at the same rate, so options may offer fewer tax advantages. On the other hand, institutional investors are more likely to have the kinds of special information that can best, or only, be used in the options market. Nevertheless, it is conceivable that a careful examination of all of the factors given, some favoring the use of options and some favoring direct investment in stocks and bonds, leads most institutional investors to favor the latter alternative most of the time. Indeed, if this is not the explanation, then why has their use of options remained so limited? Possible answers to this question fall into two categories: (1) legal restrictions pertaining to financial institutions, and (2) deficiencies in the current market structure for puts and calls.

Prudent Man Rule. A common thread underlying the specific regulations of financial institutions is the Prudent Man Rule. This rule requires that portfolios be managed in accordance with the principles that would be followed by an idealized "prudent man." Such an individual would: (1) make his own investigation of suitable investments, (2) use reasonable skill in evaluating these investments, and (3) act in the best interests of the portfolio beneficiaries. For most portfolios these needs are usually expressed in terms of the preservation of capital and the provision of a reasonable lifetime income. By implication, investments of high risk and return, or high turnover, are usually considered imprudent.

Several objections have been made to the use of options under the Prudent Man Rule. The first conflict arises from the speculative nature of certain option positions. For example, if the stock price remains unchanged, at-the-money purchased calls or puts lose 100% of their initial value. Even more extreme, written calls and puts can result in losses which are several times the initial price received. Consequently, options have been held to be inconsistent with the goal of preservation of capital. Since purchased options pay no dividends, they have also been seen as contrary to the goal of provision of income. Finally, as we know from our earlier discussion, if other things are kept constant, a call will decrease in value as the time until expiration decreases. For this reason, calls are termed "wasting assets" and hence are judged not proper as prudent investments.

Here it is worthwhile to take a brief detour to explain a troubling point. If an option is equivalent to a portfolio of stock and default-free bonds, how can it possibly be a "wasting asset"? First, consider a call. We have argued that a call may be equivalent to a particular continually adjusted portfolio containing the underlying stock financed partially by borrowing. The adjustments are made by buying more stock when the stock price increases and selling stock when the stock price decreases. Now let us see what happens if the stock price returns to its initial value by the expiration date. In this case, the equivalent stock/borrowing portfolio will have sustained a loss due to the interest payments on the borrowing. What is more, even if the interest rate were zero, the equivalent portfolio would still have shown a loss since it is always "chasing" the stock. If the stock price at first rises (falls), to mimic a call, we will have bought (sold) stock but then have subsequently sold (bought) it back at a loss when the stock price falls (rises) back to its initial value. Thus, there is a sense in which calls are "wasting assets," but by this same criterion, so are many portfolios containing only stocks and bonds.

On the other hand, a purchased put is similar to a portfolio containing lending partially financed by the proceeds from a short position in the underlying stock. Here the interest rate and volatility effects work in opposite directions, and depending upon which is stronger, a European put may or may not decay in value as the expiration date approaches. However, for American puts, whenever the interest rate effect would otherwise have proved stronger, it will be optimal to exercise the put. Thus, optimally exercised American puts are also "wasting assets."

These objections made to options on the basis of the Prudent Man Rule are misleading because they adopt a myopic perspective. For example, the income requirement ignores two important considerations. In Chapter 2, we have already argued that for common stock, dividend income is only received at the sacrifice of capital gains. Thus, there is an intrinsic contradiction between the goals of preservation of capital and provision of income. Second, tax advantages may favor capital gains over income. Therefore, a portfolio manager may be more prudent investing in low dividend yield stocks and realizing income by selling portions of the portfolio over time. And in any case, writing options can provide current income, although of course it will come at the expense of foregoing possible capital gains. However, it must be admitted that the preference for high-yield investments shown in enforcement of the Prudent Man Rule is at least partly designed to encourage the choice of low-risk investments, since high yield and low risk are often found together in many types of investments. We now turn to the issue of risk.

An even more important problem with the application of the Prudent Man Rule to options is its failure to evaluate individual investments in the context of the overall portfolio. Many investments that would be foolish or inappropriate if held in isolation are nevertheless very sensible when combined with other investments. To take an extreme case, it may be prudent to purchase a stock with a negative expected return if its performance is sufficiently inversely correlated with the returns of other securities in a portfolio. The reduction in portfolio expected return may be more than compensated by the reduction in *portfolio* risk. By using the wrong concept of risk, the Prudent Man Rule may actually discourage or prevent investments that would lead to both a lower total risk and higher expected rate of return than the ones it allows.

If it makes little sense to look at individual stock positions apart from the overall portfolio, it makes even less sense to isolate the separate components of the total position in an individual stock. If it is agreed that the stock itself is not a speculative investment, then it seems reasonable to say that any combination of options, stock, and bonds that is always less volatile than the stock should also be a nonspeculative investment. Many combinations involving options will have this property. For example, our earlier discussions about stock and bond portfolios equivalent to options imply that the investment of a given amount in the following fixed combinations (that is, ones which are not subsequently readjusted) will be less volatile than the same amount invested only in the stock:

1. Buy stock and buy puts in a one-to-one ratio.
2. Buy one call and place the remainder in bonds.
3. Buy stock and write calls in a one-to-one ratio.
4. Write one put and place the proceeds and the given amount in bonds.

Any legal arguments based solely on specific results from option pricing theory are not likely to carry the day in court in the near future. However, the case for the conservative nature of certain option combinations can be supported by the actual historical results obtained with these combinations. Moreover, as we have seen in Chapter 1, these conclusions are intuitively reasonable. When held to maturity, the combinations in the examples do more poorly than the stock when the final stock price is high, but they fare better than the stock when the final stock price is low. This is just what one would expect from a safer investment. Hence, it is not surprising that the same results tend to hold if the position is liquidated before the expiration date.

A particularly persuasive argument can be made for the first example. An investor with an uncovered stock position can be likened to a man who fails to insure his home against fire. The home insurance provided by fire and casualty insurance companies is similar to the stock insurance through purchased puts provided by the options market. This analogy also shows how misleading the "wasting assets" criterion can be. If the market value of the house remains unchanged, then the continual drain of insurance premiums will cause the total investment to be a "wasting asset." If this is not allowed, the home owner can behave like a "prudent man" only by foregoing insurance on his house. Furthermore, the put-call parity relationship shows that the second example, buying one call and placing the remaining funds in bonds, is very similar to owning the stock and insuring it with a put.

Specific Legal Restrictions.   Trust accounts of *commercial banks* are subject to the rules of the Comptroller of the Currency for banks chartered by the federal government, and to the rules of state banking departments for banks chartered by the state in which they reside. In addition, pension trusts are also governed by the Employment Retirement Income Security Act of 1974, charitable foundations by the Internal Revenue Service, and investment advisory accounts by common law fiduciary standards. As of 1979, the Comptroller of the Currency and several state banking departments specifically permitted the writing of call options, provided these transactions were authorized by the trust department. However, this approval may be unnecessary since, according to trust law, express authorization in the trust instrument is sufficient to make any investment appropriate. Moreover, most state banking departments had no rules or regulations relating to option transactions.[34]

Pension and profit sharing plans are subject to ERISA, the Employment Retirement Income Security Act of 1974. Under ERISA, the Prudent Man Rule has been given a liberal interpretation, shifting fiduciary concern away from the conservation of principal to a strategy more closely tailored to more general stated investment objectives. Although the Department of Labor has primary authority for enforcing ERISA, it has only stated broad policies and not recommended or objected to specific types of investments. However, the Department has clearly announced that individual invest-

---

[34] In a circular dated December 19, 1979, the Office of the Comptroller of the Currency states that it now views options as "investment tools which are neither prudent nor imprudent. Once it has been determined that the use of options is legally permissible for a specific account, the question of appropriateness is applied to *how* the option is utilized and what specific strategy is being implemented in the overall portfolio."

ments are not to be judged in isolation but rather in the context of the overall portfolio. The writing of covered calls and, especially, the purchase of covered puts should be appropriate under ERISA. The latter strategy may even be advisable in view of the language of ERISA which places an affirmative fiduciary duty "to minimize the risk of large losses."

Whether or not *insurance companies* can deal in options depends on the regulation in the states in which they are incorporated and licensed to do business. As of 1979, covered call writing was expressly permissible in Arkansas, Connecticut, Delaware, Idaho, Illinois, Indiana, Kansas, Kentucky, Massachusetts, Minnesota, Missouri, Nebraska, New York, Ohio, Tennessee, Texas, and Utah. Three of these states had also approved the opening purchase of calls—Illinois, Missouri, and Tennessee. However, several states did not at that time permit options transactions—Alaska, Arizona, California, Iowa, Louisiana, Nevada, North Dakota, and Wyoming. A number of other states had no specific regulations.

Mutual funds are regulated by the Investment Company Act of 1940, the Internal Revenue Code, and state "Blue Sky" laws. The 1940 Act does not prohibit any type of option strategy provided complete information of its implications for risk, return, taxes, and portfolio turnover are made available to shareholders. According to Subchapter M of the Internal Revenue Code, for net capital gains to be distributed to shareholders without a tax at the fund level, no more than 30% of the fund's realized gross income can be derived from securities held less than three months. This regulation reduces the incentive for mutual funds to deal in short-term options. "Blue Sky" laws permit mutual funds to write covered call options in all states. However, various states place limitations on the extent of covered call writing and some prohibit uncovered positions. For example, California limited covered written call positions to 25% of the net assets of the fund, unless a special exemption has been approved. Indiana, Michigan, Minnesota, Missouri, and Wisconsin prohibited a mutual fund from investing more than 5% of its net assets in options. Illinois, Iowa, North Carolina, and Texas expressly prohibited certain uncovered option positions.

For the most part, the main restriction on option trading by mutual funds has been the language contained in their prospectuses, which often specifically exclude option positions. A number of funds have obtained shareholder approval to remove these restrictions. Since 1976, new option-oriented funds have been marketed, most of which rely on a systematic program of covered call writing to increase portfolio yield. One fund holds 90% of its assets in money market instruments and invests the remaining 10% in uncovered call options. This strategy is similar to buying puts against individual stocks held long in a portfolio. Thus far, these option-oriented funds have accounted for a very small share of all assets managed by mutual funds.

Deficiencies of the Current Market. As of this writing, there are *position limits* on the maximum number of option contracts on the same underlying security that can be held by any investor or group of investors acting in concert. These limits make it difficult for large institutional investors to write calls or buy puts on even a significant part of their total position in stocks with listed options.

Furthermore, institutional investors would undoubtedly find the options market more appealing if a wider range of contracts were offered. Earlier we mentioned that individuals would find longer-maturity options and options on portfolios or indexes to be useful. The same is true for institutional investors. The introduction of listed options on stock market indexes is an important step in this direction.

Concluding Comments. The relative unpopularity of options among financial institutions is explained largely by naive legal restrictions and structural deficiencies in the current listed options market. In principle, options should be very attractive to institutional investors. As some of these legal restrictions and structural deficiencies are removed, we can expect to see a much broader participation of financial institutions in the options market.

APPENDIX 3A
Margin

3A-1. RULES

Together, the Federal Reserve Board's Regulation T, the New York Stock Exchange, and the options exchanges determine *minimum* initial and maintenance margin requirements for options. Even though options are not currently traded on the NYSE, all member firms must adhere to the NYSE margin rules on *all* of their public security transactions, even those off the exchange. Since most brokerage houses that do customer business in options are also members of the NYSE, the NYSE option margin regulations, in effect, apply to options. However, it should be stressed that almost all brokerage houses have more restrictive margin requirements than the required minimum.

At first, margin requirements for stock and option positions may seem confusing. To make things easier, we will describe these requirements in three different ways. First, we state the requirements in words as five rules, one each for

---

NOTE: This appendix relates only to public customer margin requirements.

1. Uncovered stock
2. Uncovered options
3. Hedges
4. Spreads
5. Combinations

Following each rule, we explain the logic behind it and illustrate it with an example. Second, in Tables 3A-1 and 3A-2 we show the application of these rules for every possible stock/option position in terms of algebraic symbols.

Table 3A-1
UNCOVERED POSITION MARGINS

Position	Cash Inflow in Absence of Margin	Additional Cash Inflow as a Result of Margin	
1. Long stock	$-S$	initial	at most .5S
		maintenance	at most .75S
2. Short stock[a]	S	initial	$-1.5S$
		maintenance	$-1.3S$
3. Buy call	$-C$		$-$
4. Write call	C	$-\max(1.3S - K, 2.50)$	
5. Buy put	$-P$		$-$
6. Write put	P	$-\max(K - .7S, 2.50)$	

[a] See footnote 3 for an exception.

Then, in Table 3A-3, we illustrate the margin requirements for each of these positions by an extended numerical example. Rather than read through the five rules first, the reader may instead find it easier to take each rule one at a time, looking to the tables to see the applications of the rule before proceeding to the next rule.

The set of five rules given below provides a description of the *minimum initial and maintenance* margin requirements for *nonsuperrestricted accounts* and, in each case, a rationale for the requirement is given.[1] Initial requirements are based on stock prices at the time a position is first taken. Subsequently, if the stock price moves favorably, based on the updated stock

---

[1] As defined by the Federal Reserve Board, an account becomes *restricted* whenever it is margined at less than 50%. In this case, the proceeds from the sale of securities must generally be applied to increase the margin in the account and cannot be used to back subsequent purchases or short sales. However, by the "same-day substitution privilege," an exception is made if these purchases or short sales occur on the same day the securities are sold. An account is defined as *superrestricted* whenever it is margined at less than 30%. In this case, the same-day-substitution privilege is not allowed and more complex margin rules are applied.

Table 3A-2

COVERED POSITION MARGINS

	Long Stock $-S$	Buy Call				Write Put			
S		$-C(t_1, K_1)$	$-C(t_1, K_2)$	$-C(t_2, K_1)$	$-C(t_2, K_2)$	$P(t_1, K_1)$	$P(t_1, K_2)$	$P(t_2, K_1)$	$P(t_2, K_2)$
Short Stock	*Box* $-.1S$	*Reverse Hedge (calls)* Initial: $-1.5S$ Maintenance: $-1.3S$				*Hedge (puts)* Initial: $-1.5S - \max(0, K_P - S)$ Maintenance: $-1.3S - \max(0, K_P - S)$			
$C(t_1, K_1)$	*Hedge (calls)* Initial: At most $\min(.5S, .5K)$ Maintenance: At most $\min(.75S, .75K)$	—	Bearish Vertical Spread $-\min[\max(1.3S - K_w, \$2.50), K_b - K_w]$	*Spread (calls)* 0	Diagonal Spread $-\min[\max(1.3S - K_w, \$2.50), K_b - K_w]$	*Write Combination*			
$C(t_1, K_2)$		0	—	0	0	If $S \geq (K_C + K_P)/2$, then $-\max(1.3S - K_C, \$2.50) - \max(0, K_P - S)$			
$C(t_2, K_1)$		Write Horizontal or Diagonal Spread	—	—	Bearish Vertical Spread $-\min[\max(1.3S - K_w, \$2.50), K_b - K_w]$				
$C(t_2, K_2)$		$-\max(1.3S - K_w, \$2.50)$	0	0	—	If $S < (K_C + K_P)/2$, then $-\max(K_P - .7S, \$2.50) - \max(0, S - K_C)$			

	Reverse Hedge (puts) Initial: At most .5S Maintenance: At most .75S	Buy Combination	Spread (puts)		
					Write Horizontal or Diagonal Spread
$-P(t_1, K_1)$			—	Bullish Vertical Spread $-\min[\max(K_w - .7S, \$2.50), K_w - K_b]$	
$-P(t_1, K_2)$			0	—	$-\max(K_w - .7S, \$2.50)$
$-P(t_2, K_1)$			0	Diagonal Spread $-\min[\max(K_w - .7S, \$2.50), K_w - K_b]$	Bullish Vertical Spread $-\min[\max(K_w - .7S, \$2.50), K_w - K_b]$
$-P(t_2, K_2)$			0	0	—

Buy Put

NOTE: All positions are on a one-for-one basis and margins are scaled to one share. See footnote 3 for an exception involving short positions in stock.

Table 3A-3
NET EQUITY REQUIRED FOR COVERED POSITIONS: EXAMPLE

$S = 40$

	Long Stock	Buy Call				Write Put			
	$-S$	$-C(1, 35)$	$-C(1, 45)$	$-C(7, 35)$	$-C(7, 45)$	$P(1, 35)$	$P(1, 45)$	$P(7, 35)$	$P(7, 45)$
Short Stock S	Box	Reverse Hedge (Calls)							
	400	2522	2016	2717	2224	1992	1994	1878	1896
Write Call (Calls) — Hedge		Spread (Calls)				Hedge (Puts)			
$C(1, 35)$	1728	–	494	[195]	702	1170	1172	1156	1054
$C(1, 45)$	1984	[506]ᵃ	–	[701]	[206]	676	1178	562	1160
$C(7, 35)$	1533	1505	999	–	507	975	977	861	859
$C(7, 45)$	1776	998	494	[493]	–	468	970	354	852
Buy Put (Puts) — Reverse Hedge		Buy Combination				Spread (Puts)			
$-P(1, 35)$	2008	[530]	[24]	[725]	[232]	–	502	586	1084
$-P(1, 45)$	2506	[1028]	[522]	[1223]	[730]	[408]	–	1084	1582
$-P(7, 35)$	2122	[644]	[138]	[839]	[346]	[114]	316	–	498
$-P(7, 45)$	2624	[1146]	[640]	[1341]	[848]	[616]	[118]	[502]	–

$C(1, 35) = 522$ $P(1, 35) = 8$
$C(1, 45) = 16$ $P(1, 45) = 506$
$C(7, 35) = 717$ $P(7, 35) = 122$
$C(7, 45) = 224$ $P(7, 45) = 624$

NOTE: All positions are on a one-for-one basis and margins are scaled to one contract. For $C(t, K)$ and $P(t, K)$, t is in units of months and K is in dollars. Put and call values are taken from Tables 5-2 and 5-5. Specifically, per contract:

ᵃBracketed numbers require no margin; only the net cost of the securities is required as equity.

price, funds are freed to support other investments. That is, the initial margin requirement is "marked-to-the-market." For all option positions not involving stock, initial margin requirements are also marked-to-the-market for unfavorable moves in the stock price. In this case, additional funds will be required to support stock option positions. However, for positions involving stock, as the stock moves unfavorably, no additional margin is required until a lower maintenance margin requirement is breached. From this point on, the position is marked-to-the-market at the maintenance margin requirements for further unfavorable stock price moves. And, for favorable stock price moves, margins cannot be reduced until the initial margin requirement is again satisfied.

In each case below, it is assumed that securities purchased have been paid for, and revenue has been received for those short or written. Consequently, the rules below describe any *additional* cash requirements.[2] All covered positions are assumed to be one-for-one. Ratio positions must be decomposed into one-for-one covered positions and uncovered positions. Exchange and Federal Reserve Board rules permit the pairings of options and stock which would produce the lowest total margin for the account. The rules below are based on current regulations and are therefore subject to change at future dates.

Rule 1 (Uncovered Stock): Up to 50% of a long position can be borrowed (at interest), and the proceeds of a short sale must be deposited (in a noninterest-bearing account), plus 50% of the short sale (in cash or interest-bearing securities). These must be maintained at 75% for long positions and 30% for short positions.[3]

For long positions, the brokerage house is protected against a 50% decline in the stock price and, for short positions, against a 50% increase.

For example, for a short sale of one share worth $40, the $40 proceeds are held as collateral by the broker, earning no interest for the investor. In addition, the investor must deposit $20 which can be invested in Treasury-Bills. No further margin is required unless the stock price rises to $46\frac{1}{4}$.

---

[2] For a description of initial margin for restricted or superrestricted accounts, see the "Margin Manual," published by the Chicago Board Options Exchange.

[3] Except for the proceeds of a short sale of stock, margin may be deposited in the form of T-bills, with interest accruing to the account. For short positions, if the stock price is less than $16\frac{3}{4}$ but greater than $5, maintenance margin is $5 per share. If the stock price is less than $5, the maintenance margin is $2.50 or 100% of the stock price, whichever is greater.

> *Rule 2* (Uncovered Options): No borrowing is allowed on pur-
> chased options. Written options require a deposit of 30% of the
> stock price, plus the in-the-money amount or less the out-of-the-
> money amount, with a $2.50 minimum deposit per share.
> Written option margin is marked-to-the-market.

A purchased option is already a highly levered security. Unlike purchased
stock, investors cannot borrow against purchased options to support positions in other securities. If the stock price equals the striking price, the
brokerage house is protected against a 30% rise in the stock price in the
case of a written call and a 30% fall in the price in the case of a written put.
The difference between the stock price and the striking price must be added
in the case of a call to reflect the fact that, even if the stock price remains
unchanged, an in-the-money call, when exercised, will obligate the writer to
greater cash payments than receipts. The $2.50 requirement (that is, $250
per contract) is difficult to rationalize.

For example, a written call worth $7\frac{1}{4}$ with a striking price of $35 on a
stock priced at $40 requires a margin deposit of

$$(40 \times .3) + (40 - 35) = \$17.$$

But this deposit can be reduced by the proceeds from the sale of the option
to $17 - \$7\frac{1}{4} = \$9\frac{3}{4}$. If the stock price then rises to $42, the margin required
would then be

$$(42 \times .3) + (42 - 35) = \$19.60$$

so that it would be necessary to deposit an additional $2.60. On the other
hand, should the stock price fall to $38, then $2.60 could be withdrawn.

> *Rule 3* (Hedges): Hedges are margined like uncovered long or
> short positions in the stock, depending on whether the stock has
> been bought or sold short, with two exceptions: If a written call
> is in-the-money, only 50% of its *striking price*, not 50% of the
> stock price, can be borrowed; if a written put is in-the-money,
> the in-the-money amount must also be deposited.

Since a long position in the stock protects a written call, no margin is
required for the call. However, if the call is in-the-money, this protection is
inadequate, since the writer can be expected to owe on the call the difference between the stock price and the striking price. Since a short position in

the stock can be held after the expiration of a call purchased against it, the brokerage house will then face the exposure of an uncovered short. It therefore requires the margin on an uncovered short to begin with.

For example, consider a call worth $7\frac{1}{4}$ with a striking price of $35 written against a long position in a stock priced at $40. An investor can then borrow only $0.5 \times 35 = \$17\frac{1}{2}$; but, in addition, he can use the $7\frac{1}{4}$ proceeds from the call. As a result, he need only deposit $40 - 17\frac{1}{2} - 7\frac{1}{4} = \$15\frac{1}{4}$ to assume the hedge.

Rule 4 (Spreads): The general rule is that margin is required on written spreads (that is, where the spread begins with a net receipt) and margin is not required on bought spreads (that is, where the spread begins with net cash payments). Specifically, written horizontal spreads or diagonal spreads (the far maturity option is written and the near maturity option is purchased) are margined like an uncovered written option at the striking price of the written option. All other spreads are margined at the lesser of:

1. The margin required on the written option if it were uncovered
2. For calls (puts), the greater of zero or the difference between the striking price of the purchased (written) option and the striking price of the written (purchased) option

Spread margin is marked-to-the-market.

For a purchased horizontal spread, the far maturity option protects the written near maturity option, and even after expiration or exercise of the near maturity option, the position is never uncovered short. However, for a written horizontal spread, since the written option matures after the purchased option, the position can be exposed as an uncovered short. From the payoff diagram for a bullish vertical spread (Fig. 1-13), while the position can only lose money if the stock price falls, it is easy to see that the brokerage house is nonetheless protected, since the difference in call prices covers the loss to the position. However, for a bearish vertical spread, the difference in call prices does not cover the loss sustained by a rise in the stock price, but a deposit of the difference in the striking prices is always sufficient to cover the loss. In any case, it would be unreasonable for the margin required on the written leg of the spread to be more restrictive than the margin required on an uncovered written option.

For example, consider a bullish vertical spread in calls where the stock price is $40, the striking price of the written call is $35, and the striking price of the purchased call is $40. Suppose the calls are selling for $7\frac{1}{4}$ and $3\frac{3}{8}$, respectively. If the written call were uncovered, the required margin would be $17. However, since the difference between their striking prices is $5, only $5 is required as margin for the spread. This can be reduced further to a $5 - (7\frac{1}{4} - 3\frac{3}{8}) = \$8\frac{7}{8}$ net deposit by application of the proceeds from the spread.

> *Rule 5* (Combinations): No borrowing is allowed on purchased combinations. Written combinations require a deposit of the margin on an uncovered written put (at the striking price of the put) or the margin on an uncovered written call (at the striking price of the call), whichever is greater, plus the in-the-money amount, if any, on the other side. Written combination margin is marked-to-the-market.

No borrowing can be allowed on a purchased combination, since 100% of the position is lost if the stock price remains unchanged. For a written combination, protection is needed, whether the stock price moves up or down, but the protection will be needed for only one leg of the combination, provided the other leg is at- or out-of-the-money. Otherwise, additional margin is needed for the unrealized loss (that is, $K_P - S$ or $S - K_C$) on the other (that is, unmargined) option.

For example, consider a written straddle with a striking price of $35 on a stock priced at $40, where the call and the put are worth $7\frac{1}{4}$ and $1\frac{1}{4}$, respectively. If the call (put) was written uncovered, it would require margin of $17 ($7). Therefore, the margin required is $17, but this can be reduced by the proceeds of the straddle so that the position only requires a net deposit of $17 - 8\frac{1}{2} = \$8\frac{1}{2}$.

Tables 3A-1 and 3A-2 provide an alternative description of minimum margin requirements for stock and/or options. Every position can be first considered as if every security were "uncovered" and, second, analyzed for reduction in margin from favorable pairings (that is, offsetting positions). The minimum margin then resulting is the total margin required. For example, a particular diagonal spread in calls first involves the receipt of cash from a written call $C(t_1, K_1)$ and the payment of cash to purchase a call $-C(t_2, K_2)$, where $K_2 = K_b > K_1 = K_w$ and $t_2 > t_1$. Second, margin per share is required equal to the minimum of either the maximum of 1.3 times the stock price minus K_w, the striking price of the written call, and $2.50, or the difference between the striking prices $K_b - K_w$ of the purchased and written calls. In other words,

Net cash flow
$$= C(t_1, K_1) - C(t_2, K_2) - \min[\max(1.3S - K_w, 2.50), K_b - K_w].$$

Of these three terms, the last is termed the required margin deposit, and the negative of the three taken together, the "net equity" in the account required to back the position. In other words, net equity is equal to the value of the account (ignoring transactions costs) if all positions were immediately liquidated.

Table 3A-3 illustrates the net equity required for all basic covered positions. Suppose that the current underlying stock price is $40, a call with one month to go and a striking price of $35 is worth $5.22, and a call with seven months to go and a striking price of $45 is worth $2.24.[4] A one-for-one written diagonal spread in these two options requires $-$10 margin per share, so that the net equity required to back the position is $-(5.22 - 2.24 - 10.00) = 7.02, or, equivalently, $702 per contract.

3A-2. ALGORITHMS FOR DETERMINING LEAST MARGIN

Complex stock/option positions, possibly involving several different options on the same underlying security, make the calculation of margin difficult. In particular, depending upon which options are paired with other options, the required margin may be higher than necessary. However, the following algorithm for pairing associated options and stock results in approximately the least margin.

STEP 1:   Pair each share of short stock with one share of long stock.

STEP 2:   Pair each purchased call with one written call, and pair each purchased put with one written put, to form the following spreads in the order given:

1. Bullish horizontal spreads (pairing options with nearest maturities)
2. Bullish vertical spreads
3. Diagonal spreads, where the long option not only matures after the short option, but also is more in-the-money
4. Bearish vertical spreads
5. Diagonal spreads, where the long option not only matures after the short option, but also is more out-of-the-money

---

[4] These option values are calculated from an exact option pricing formula to be developed in Chapter 5.

STEP 3:   Pair each remaining written call with remaining long stock, and pair each remaining written put with remaining short stock.

STEP 4:   Pair each remaining written call with one remaining written put.

STEP 5:   Regard all remaining unpaired short stock, written calls, and written puts as uncovered.

STEP 6:   Total margin is the sum of the margin deposits on these paired and uncovered positions minus, at most, 50% of the long position in the stock.

Observe that spreads (Step 2), hedges (Step 3), and combinations (Step 4) are formed in that order.

   Under certain circumstances, this algorithm does not produce the least possible margin. Fortunately, there is a cost-efficient optimal linear programming algorithm for computing minimum margin, which can result in significantly lower margin than the simple heuristic given here.[5]

   Suppose we let $i = 1, 2, \ldots, I - 1$ index short stock, written calls and bought puts, and let $j = 1, 2, \ldots, J - 1$ index long stock, bought calls and written puts. Then m_{ij} can represent the margin required for a position involving one share or option of security i paired with one share or option of security j. If $m_{ij} > 0$, then additional funds, beyond the net costs of the paired position, are required as margin. If $m_{ij} < 0$, then the paired position has loan value. The m_{ij} correspond to the negative of the cell values of the matrix in Table 3A-2. To incorporate uncovered positions, let indices I and J represent a "null" security, so that m_{iJ} and m_{Ij} are the required margin on uncovered short and long positions, respectively. Let $m_{IJ} = 0$. Let x_{ij} indexed over $i = 1, 2, \ldots, I$ and $j = 1, 2, \ldots, J$ be the number of contracts paired between securities i and j; then

$$\text{Required margin} = \sum_{i=1}^{I} \sum_{j=1}^{J} x_{ij} m_{ij}, \qquad (1)$$

where by convention

$$x_{ij} \geq 0 \qquad \text{for} \quad i = 1, 2, \ldots, I \quad \text{and} \quad j = 1, 2, \ldots, J. \qquad (2)$$

   Our problem is to select the x_{ij} in such a way that the required margin is minimized. Whatever we do, we must include all securities bought or sold. Let $Y_i \geq 0$ for $i = 1, 2, \ldots, I - 1$ be the number of shares or options

---

[5] See Andrew Rudd and Mark Schroeder, "The Calculation of Minimum Margin," *Management Science,* 28 (December 1982), 1368–1379.

held of type i, and $Z_j \geq 0$ for $j = 1, 2, \ldots, J - 1$ be the number of shares or options held of type j. To allow for the possibility that all securities are held uncovered, define

$$Y_I \equiv \sum_{j=1}^{J-1} Z_j, \qquad Z_J \equiv \sum_{i=1}^{I-1} Y_i$$

and

$$x_{IJ} \equiv Y_I - \sum_{j=1}^{J-1} x_{Ij} = Z_J - \sum_{i=1}^{I-1} x_{iJ}.$$

Then, however we chose to pair the securities,

$$\sum_{j=1}^{J} x_{ij} = Y_i \qquad \text{for} \quad i = 1, 2, \ldots, I, \tag{3}$$

$$\sum_{i=1}^{I} x_{ij} = Z_j \qquad \text{for} \quad j = 1, 2, \ldots, J. \tag{4}$$

In summary, the linear program that produces minimum margin selects the x_{ij} that minimizes (1) subject to the constraints of Equations (2), (3) and (4).

The number of different associated securities in present day security markets is sufficiently small to permit a very inexpensive computer solution for any brokerage account. Moreover, the same matrix containing the m_{ij} can be applied to every customer account and is easily revised to cope with foreseeable changes in margin regulation. As a bonus, the algorithm can be used to determine the order to liquidate positions to meet a margin call in the optimal manner. In this case, maintenance margin requirements can be used to supply the cells of the margin matrix.

APPENDIX 3B
Commissions

3B-1. RATES

Since May 1, 1975, commissions have been negotiable. Prior to that time, they were fixed by the exchange on which a security was traded. However, except for large block trades, these fixed commissions give an approximation to the negotiated commissions the public can now expect, although discounts, occasionally as large as 70%, are sometimes available through some brokerage houses.

NOTE: This appendix relates only to public customer commissions.

Option buyers pay commissions when they buy options, when they close out their position by sale, and upon exercise. Similarly, writers pay commissions at each of these events. No commission is paid if a position is closed out by letting an option expire.

Commissions are usually quoted in terms of a percentage discount from the pre-May Day rates. Since options and stock are often held together, and we will want to compare option and stock commissions, we will describe the pre-May Day commission schedule for both NYSE round-lot transactions and CBOE contracts.

Commission schedules differ for single and multiple trading unit orders (see Tables 3B-1 and 3B-2). For both single and multiple orders of *stock*, add 10% to the commission calculated from the schedules if the order is less than $5,000 and 24.2% if the order is $5,000 or more.

Table 3B-1

SINGLE TRADING UNIT ORDER		
Order Value ($)	*Stock Commission*	*Option Commission*
0–12.50	8.4%	Order value
12.50–100	8.4%	12.50
100–800	2.0% + 6.40	25
800–1,000	1.3% + 12	25
1,000–2,500	1.3% + 12	1.3% + 12
2,500–4,777	0.9% + 22	0.9% + 22
4,777 and above	65	65

Table 3B-2

MULTIPLE TRADING UNIT ORDER		
Order Value ($)	*Stock Commission*	*Option Commission*
0–12.50	8.4%	Order value
12.50–100	8.4%	12.50
100–1,000	1.3% + 12	25
1,000–2,500	1.3% + 12	1.3% + 12
2,500–20,000	0.9% + 22	0.9% + 22
20,000–30,000	0.6% + 82	0.6% + 82
30,000–300,000	0.4% + 142	(negotiable)
300,000 and above	(negotiable)	(negotiable)

Add $6 per trading unit for 1st to 10th; $4 per trading unit for 11th and above.

In no case may the commission per trading unit be greater than the commission on a single trading unit order.

An exception occurs for option contracts priced at less than $100 but where the order value is greater than $100. in this case, the commission is the maximum of $25, or 4% plus $2 per contract. Commissions on stock priced less than $1 per share are also an exception.

3B-2. COMPARISON OF OPTIONS AND STOCKS

These schedules imply that, per dollar of investment, option commissions will tend to be higher than stock commissions. This occurs because options usually have much lower prices than their underlying shares and, hence, for the same order value, will tend to incur more $6 and $4 charges per trading unit. However, this comparison of stock and option commissions may not be appropriate since it presupposes that *equal dollar* positions in stock and options are similar investments. Following our discussion in Section 2-3, an option provides a return over a short period, similar to a particular portfolio of stocks and bonds. Therefore, it is perhaps more meaningful to compare the commissions on an option to the commissions on its equivalent portfolio. For example, deep-in-the-money calls have equivalent portfolios which contain almost one share of stock. For these options, then, it may be more appropriate to compare the commissions *per share*, rather than the commissions *per dollar* invested.

Table 3B-3 provides this comparison. The column entitled "Option Commission Per Share" shows the movement in the option price required for an investor to break even on commissions. For example, if he buys two contracts at $\frac{1}{2}$, the total commission will be $12.50, and the option must rise by at least $\frac{1}{16}$ (0.063) for him to break even (not counting exit commissions). As a percentage of the stock price (assumed equal to $40 per share), the option commission is a negligible 0.2%. Finally, the option commission is only 9% of the commission on two round lots of stock. In every instance, if we think of the option as an alternative way to buy the stock, option commissions are smaller.

However, this interpretation of Table 3B-3 makes the unwarranted assumption that the equivalent portfolio of a single option contains one share of stock. More generally, for one call, this portfolio can contain anywhere from zero to one share of stock. To consider this, Table 3B-4 compares option and stock commissions for options which are in-, at-, and out-of-the-money and near, middle, and far in maturity, at different stock price levels. In this table, the equivalent position is standardized to contain one share of stock in each case and, instead, the number of options is adjusted to provide the same short-run return. For example, when the underlying stock price is 40, for a JAN/40 call, on a single round-lot stock order ($n = 1$), the ratio of call to stock commission for equivalent positions is .42. To make the positions equivalent, it is necessary to purchase 1.9 call contracts.[1] Again, in almost every case, it is cheaper, in terms of commis-

---

[1] The price of the JAN/40 call, used to determine the order value, is based on the exact option pricing formula developed in Chapter 5. This same formula also indicates the number of calls per share that must be purchased to make the option and stock positions equivalent. This same formula is used to develop the remainder of the table.

Table 3B-3
COMPARISON OF OPTION AND STOCK COMMISSIONS

Option Price	Number of Contracts	Total Option Commission ($)	Option Commission Per Share ($)	Option Commission/ Stock Price Ratio	Option Commission/ Stock Commission Ratio
$\frac{1}{8}$	1	12.50	0.125	.003	.20
	2	12.50	0.063	.002	.09
	5	12.50	0.025	.001	.04
	10	25.00	0.025	.001	.06
	50	125.00	0.025	.001	.09
$\frac{1}{2}$	1	12.50	0.125	.003	.20
	2	12.50	0.063	.002	.09
	5	25.00	0.05	.001	.09
	10	40.00	0.04	.001	.09
	50	200.00	0.04	.001	.14
1	1	25.00	0.25	.006	.39
	2	26.60	0.133	.003	.20
	5	48.50	0.097	.002	.17
	10	85.00	0.085	.002	.19
	50	287.00	0.057	.001	.20
2	1	25.00	0.25	.006	.39
	2	29.20	0.146	.004	.22
	5	55.00	0.11	.003	.19
	10	98.00	0.098	.002	.22
	50	332.00	0.066	.002	.23
4	1	25.00	0.25	.006	.39
	2	34.40	0.172	.004	.26
	5	68.00	0.136	.003	.24
	10	118.00	0.118	.003	.26
	50	442.00	0.084	.002	.29
8	1	25.00	0.25	.006	.39
	2	44.80	0.224	.006	.34
	5	88.00	0.176	.004	.31
	10	154.00	0.154	.004	.34
	50	negotiable	–	–	–

NOTE: The stock used for comparison is assumed to be priced at $40 per share.

Table 3B-4

CALL-STOCK COMMISSION RATIO FOR EQUIVALENT POSITIONS

S	K	$n = 1$			$n = 5$			$n = 25$		
		Expiration Month[a]								
		JAN	APR	JUL	JAN	APR	JUL	JAN	APR	JUL
	15	.59	.61	.63	.42	.44	.46	.45	.47	.49
		(1.0)	(1.0)	(1.1)						
20	20	.60	.62	.63	.26	.46	.48	.40	.48	.50
		(1.9)	(1.7)	(1.7)						
	25	—b	.60	.60	—b	.61	.52	—b	.93	.79
			(7.5)	(4.3)						
	35	.40	.46	.49	.27	.32	.35	.32	.40	.44
		(1.1)	(1.2)	(1.3)						
40	40	.42	.46	.49	.30	.34	.36	.35	.41	.45
		(1.9)	(1.7)	(1.7)						
	45	.41	.58	.55	.45	.43	.41	.79	.56	.52
		(9.8)	(3.2)	(2.6)						
	50	.32	.37	.41	.27	.31	.34	.33	—	—
		(1.0)	(1.1)	(1.2)						
60	60	.35	.41	.44	.26	.31	.33	.30	.37	.40
		(1.9)	(1.7)	(1.7)						
	70	.65	.55	.50	.72	.42	.38	1.22	.55	.49
		(22.0)	(4.2)	(3.0)						

NOTE: Option values and the size of equivalent positions are calculated from an exact option pricing formula to be developed in Chapter 5. The variable n is the number of round lots of stock bought or sold.

[a] The January options have one month to expiration, the Aprils four months, and the Julys seven months.

[b] Option value less than $\frac{1}{16}$.

sions, to buy the stock indirectly through options than to buy the stock itself.[2]

Three complications to this analysis must be considered to give a complete picture. First, the comparison in Table 3B-4 only applies strictly to the short run. Over a longer period, as we have argued, an option is only equivalent to a position in stock and bonds which is appropriately adjusted over time. Still, if we insist on comparing an option with a *fixed* position in stock of roughly *comparable dollar return and risk*, our short-run comparison also usually gives us a good approximation of what we can expect over

[2] This conclusion is not sensitive to the particular level used for the underlying variables in calculating the option values and equivalent positions.

the intermediate term through the life of the option.[3] Of course, over the longer term, given the short duration of currently listed options, it is necessary to roll an option over. If it is desired to obtain the risk and return of stock over several years, then direct purchase of the stock will invariably be cheaper than a sequence of nine-month option positions. If, on the other hand, in addition to these static features, the automatic dynamic stock-bond portfolio adjustments implicit in a sequence of option positions are desired, then options will be the cheaper alternative.

Second, we have only considered one-way commissions. Unlike stock, options may expire worthless, requiring no exit commission. Options can also be exercised by paying the commission on the stock, evaluated at the striking price. These commissions on in-the-money expiring options can make the difference between exercising or selling as the optimal strategy. A call buyer must pay *two* commissions upon exercise—one to exercise and buy the stock and a second when he later sells the stock—but only one if he sells the call. Although selling the call usually produces lower commissions, it may nonetheless be better to exercise. The higher cost of exercise often causes the call to sell slightly below its parity value near expiration. This occurs when the commissions to floor traders are greater than the premium over parity in the absence of commissions. Under these conditions, the call is likely to be priced so that the buyer is almost indifferent to exercising or selling. He will tend to favor exercising if he desires to hold the stock in his portfolio; otherwise, he will typically favor selling.

Third, total transactions costs consist of a dealer bid-ask spread, as well as a commission. If the Order Book Official and Floor Brokers match trades among themselves, then their customers, taken together, do not lose the option spread. However, if matching requires the intervention of a Market Maker, the customer tends to give up the spread to the Market Maker. If the bid-ask spread is $\frac{1}{8}$, he will lose $\frac{1}{16}$ when he opens his position, and another $\frac{1}{16}$ when he closes it out. Evidence is scant on the average spread actually sacrificed by stock and option public customers.[4] Casual observation indicates the average bid-ask spread sacrificed for both options and stock is less than $\frac{1}{8}$. That is, on average, a public customer gives up less than $\frac{1}{16}$ of a point when he buys and less than $\frac{1}{16}$ of a point when he sells.

The spread per contract for options is likely to be no less than the spread per round lot for stocks. This is because the higher leverage provided by options should attract more information trading. However, option

---

[3] This is suggested by Tables 6-20 and 6-22 in Section 6-5. To convert to dollar return and risk, multiply the numbers in the tables by the corresponding current option values. That is, not only are the dollar return and risk similar for an option and the amount of stock in its equivalent portfolio held fixed over the short run, but they are also usually expected to be roughly similar if held fixed even through the life of the option.

[4] However, see Section 3-4.

position limits may dampen this behavior. Even if we suppose the dealer spread is the same, since more options than the stock need to be bought or written to obtain action-equivalent positions, as in Table 3B-4, the spread tends to even up the total transactions costs for comparable option and stock positions.

APPENDIX 3C
Taxes

In this appendix we summarize the most important tax rules relevant to options. The rules that we cite are those in effect at the beginning of 1984. The tax laws have changed repeatedly in the past and will undoubtedly continue to do so. Consequently, no one should make investment decisions solely on the basis of the information given here. On the other hand, the changes tend to be evolutionary, so the rules presented below may nevertheless provide a useful general frame of reference about the tax environment for options.

Several changes in the tax code under consideration at the beginning of 1984 deserve special mention. If passed into law, as seems likely, these changes would reduce the holding period for long-term capital gains from one year to six months and would limit the extent to which options can be used to defer taxes from one year to the next. The proposed changes would also substantially alter the tax treatment of options on financial instruments other than common stocks and some stock indexes. Such options would be taxed in a way analogous to futures contracts, and most parts of our subsequent discussion would no longer apply to them.

3C-1. CAPITAL GAINS AND LOSSES

Before examining the federal tax regulations governing puts and calls, it is useful to review the rules relating to capital gains and losses and some investment strategies that may arise from them, using the more familiar common stock transactions as illustrative examples. Unless otherwise stated, the discussion applies only to an individual investor who is a resident of the United States and is not a dealer or considered to be in the business of trading securities for his own account.

For income tax purposes, a key distinction is made between *ordinary income* and *capital gains*. In contrast to ordinary income (i.e., wages, interest, dividends, etc.), capital gains arise from the sale or exchange of *capital assets*. Stock and options are examples of capital assets. This distinction is important, since ordinary gains are usually included in full in taxable income and ordinary losses deducted in full from taxable income, while special rules exist to limit the tax liability on capital gains and the tax deductibility of capital losses.

These special rules depend on the classification of gains and losses as *short term* or *long term*. The general rule, as of January 1, 1978, is that gains and losses on capital assets (except commodity futures) held for *one year or less* are considered short term. In the case of common stock, the day the stock is acquired is excluded and the day the stock is sold is included for the purpose of this calculation. Furthermore, trade dates, not settlement dates, are used. For example, the holding period for stock purchased on 3/6/80 and sold on 3/6/81 is from 3/7/80 to 3/6/81, and gains or losses are regarded as short term. To be treated as long term, the stock must be sold on or after 3/7/81. In the case of several lots of the same stock purchased and sold over a period of time, the first-in, first-out method is used to determine the holding period, unless the stock to be sold is properly identified.[1]

The main complications in this classification arise from short sales and wash sales. The general principle for short sales is that gains and losses are short term or long term depending on the holding period of the capital asset delivered to close out the short position. *This is true regardless of the length of time for which the short position has been maintained.* For example, suppose an investor sells a certain number of shares of some stock he does not own by borrowing them from his broker. After 13 months he purchases a like quantity of shares of identical stock and instructs his broker to close out the short sale. In spite of the fact that the investor maintained the short position for more than one year, the resulting gain or loss is considered short term, since the delivered stock has been held less than one year. There are, however, two major exceptions to this principle contained in the so-called *short sale rule*.

First, if on the date of the short sale the underlying capital asset has been held long *for more than one year* (i.e., short selling against the box), any loss on the short sale is considered long term, irrespective of whether that particular asset or substantially identical property, actually held short term, is used to close out the short position. This first part of the short sale rule prevents an investor from realizing a short-term loss on a short sale of stock, while holding identical stock for a long-term gain.

Second, if on the date of the short sale the short seller has held the underlying capital asset *for one year or less*, or acquired it during the time he maintained the short position, any gain on the short sale is considered short term, regardless of the actual holding period of the asset delivered to close out the short position. Moreover, the holding period of the asset

---

[1] Proper identification requires that an investor instruct his broker to sell the shares, identified as to cost, purchase date, or both, in a particular sequence, and receive written confirmation of this specification.

triggering the short sale rule is assumed to date not from its purchase, *but from the date the short sale is closed out.* This second part of the rule prevents an investor from locking in a short-term gain on long stock by assuming a short position in that stock while continuing to hold it for long-term capital gains treatment. The elimination of the holding period of the long stock is necessary to remove the incentive to close out the short sale with new stock and realize a long-term gain on the old stock. The number of shares affected by this rule is determined by the number of shares sold short. Although any gain on a short sale is long term only if the delivered stock has been held for more than one year on the date of the short sale, a short sale can be used to hedge an unrealized gain and defer it into a future tax period.

A wash sale occurs when securities are purchased within 30 days before or after the sale of substantially identical securities.[2] According to the *wash sale rule*, while gains on wash sales are taxed in the usual manner, losses are not deductible when they are incurred. Instead, they are deferred until the final sale of the securities whose purchase triggered the wash sale. The holding period in this case is determined by the total number of days the securities have been held. For example, suppose an investor purchased shares of some stock on 3/1/80 and sold them on 6/30/80, then repurchased the same number of shares of the same stock on 7/14/80, and finally sold them on 3/30/81. If the 6/30/80 sale resulted in a profit, it would be treated as a short-term capital gain, and any loss on the 3/30/81 sale would be considered short term. If, on the other hand, the 6/30/80 sale took place at a loss, this loss would be added to the cost basis of the shares bought on 7/14/80. On 3/30/81 these shares would be treated as if they had been held for $12\frac{1}{2}$ months, and any gain or loss would be long term.[3] In this particular example, the wash sale rule deferred the deductibility of the short-term loss incurred on 6/30/80 into 1981 and transformed this loss as well as the otherwise short-term capital gain or loss on the 3/30/81 sale into a long-term gain or loss. The wash sale rule thus prevents the recognition of a short-term loss (though not that of a long-term gain) when the investor intends to continue holding the stock, possibly for a preferentially treated larger long-term capital gain. Exempt from the wash sale rule are "traders" who, because of the frequency of their trades, classify as being in the business of buying and selling securities for their own account.

Having classified gains and losses as short or long term, it remains to calculate the taxable capital gain. All short-term gains and losses are aggregated, and the resulting figure is called *net short-term capital gain or loss* (*S*).

---

[2] In case of a short sale, the relevant date is the date of the short sale, not the date it is closed out, if stock held at the former date is delivered to terminate the short position.

[3] If the number of shares repurchased is less than the number originally sold, the matching for purposes of the wash sale rule is based on the first-in, first-out principle.

Table 3C-1
CALCULATION OF NET TAXABLE GAIN OR LOSS

Condition	Amount Added to or Subtracted from TI
Net Gain ($N > 0$)	
1. $L \leq 0$	N
2. $S \leq 0$	$.4N$
3. $S > 0$	$S + .4L$
$\quad L > 0$	
Net Loss[a] ($N < 0$)	
1. $L \geq 0$	$-\min[TI, -N, \$3{,}000]$
2. $S \geq 0$	$-\min[TI, -.5N, \$3{,}000]$
3. $L < 0$	$-\min[TI, -(S + .5L), \$3{,}000]$
$\quad S < 0$	

[a] To the extent the net loss is not exhausted by this deduction from taxable income, the excess may be carried forward to subsequent tax periods. This carryover will not affect the long-term and/or short-term character of the excess losses. They will be treated as specified in the table, that is, as if they had been realized in that future tax period. To determine which losses are carried forward, short-term losses are always deducted first, even if they were incurred after the long-term losses. For married individuals filing separately, the loss deduction is limited to $1,500 rather than $3,000 for each return.

In a similar fashion, the *net long-term capital gain or loss* (L) is determined. The sum of S and L is called the *net gain or loss* (N). Under each possible situation, Table 3C-1 shows the amount of the net gain by which taxable income from other sources (TI) is increased or reduced.[4]

There are two amendments to the treatment of capital gains as summarized above. First, an individual investor is subject to a minimum tax which replaces the regular income tax (including any add-on tax, if applicable), if the former exceeds the latter. Under the alternative minimum tax, an individual pays at most 25% of the sum of his taxable income plus 60% of the excess of net long-term capital gains over net short-term capital losses and adjusted itemized deductions.[5] Second, the alternative of five-year income averaging, when there are substantial changes in taxable

---

[4] Table 3C-1 conforms to the Revenue Act of 1978. It increased the deductible part of the excess of net long-term gains over net short-term losses from 50% to 60% for transactions taking place after October 31, 1978, but disallowed the pre-1979 alternative treatment of net gains which placed a 25% ceiling rate on the first $50,000 of long-term gains.

[5] This alternative minimum tax became effective January 1, 1979. It was introduced by the Revenue Act of 1978 which removed the deductible part of long-term capital gains and adjusted itemized deductions from the category of so-called tax preference income. Tax preference income, reduced by the greater of $10,000 ($5,000 if married filing separately) and one-half of the regular income tax imposed for the year, is taxed at an added-on 15% flat rate and reduces the amount of earned income eligible for the 50% maximum tax dollar for dollar. Under certain conditions, the treatment of long-term capital gains as preference income could lead to marginal tax rates of almost 50%.

income between tax years, can affect the portion of capital gains and losses allocated to a given year.

The rules governing the taxation of capital gains and losses as stated in Table 3C-1 give rise to several strategies an investor can use to reduce his tax liability. The first two strategies assume that the investor has some discretion concerning the term character of capital gains and losses, but not with regard to the tax period in which they are realized. As a rough approximation, long-term capital gains are taxed at 40% of the rate applicable to short-term gains. Short-term capital losses are fully deductible, while only 50% of long-term capital losses are deductible. More specifically, if he has either only net gains or only net losses in both term categories, each dollar converted from a short-term into a long-term gain reduces taxable income by 60¢ and each dollar converted from a long-term into a short-term loss reduces it by 50¢. Therefore, an investor is motivated to take his gains long term, his losses short term. *On the other hand, if he has net gains in one term category and net losses in the other, such conversion has no effect on his tax liability.* This is an important caveat to these commonly propounded strategies, since conversion is likely to involve some cost. It should be kept in mind, especially in view of the limited deductibility of net losses of any one tax period and their carryover into a future period, where they may have to be offset against long-term gains.

The next strategies take the term character of capital gains and losses as given, but the investor has some leeway regarding the timing of their realization. It should be noted that this group of strategies only indicates a tendency that may be modified by two interacting factors. First, any reallocation of gains and losses may change the overall tax liability, since marginal tax rates vary with taxable income. Second, other things equal, deferring the realization of gains and accelerating the deductibility of losses postpones the tax liability and reduces its burden. The following two strategies arise from the fact that the difference between net short-term gains (losses) and net long-term losses (gains) is treated differently depending on whether there is an overall net gain or loss. If an investor has net short-term gains and net long-term losses, he should time their realization to minimize the difference between them in each tax period. The reason is that an overall net gain adds to taxable income dollar for dollar, while only 50% of an overall net loss is deductible. On the other hand, an investor with net long-term gains and net short-term losses should try to maximize the difference between them in each tax period, since only 40% of an overall net gain is added to taxable income, while an overall net loss reduces it dollar for dollar. This is not the same as advising the investor to sell losing stocks at the end of the year for a short-term loss and to retain gaining stocks for long-term treatment in the next year. Such a strategy is likely to run into the pitfall discussed in connection with the conversion strategies.

Finally, of much less importance, the asymmetric treatment of long-term gains and long-term losses, introduced by the Revenue Act of 1978, gives some incentive to realize these gains and losses in different periods.

As we will see in the following section, options have at present only limited effectiveness in changing the term character of capital gains, but provide excellent opportunities to defer or accelerate their realization and to generate offsetting short-term gains when needed.

3C-2. THE TAX TREATMENT OF OPTIONS

The Internal Revenue Code,[6] as amended by the Tax Reform Act of 1976, contains two important provisions for puts and calls. First, for options written on or after September 2, 1976, an option writer realizes a capital, rather than ordinary, gain or loss on a closing purchase transaction or if the option expires unexercised.[7] Previously, it was possible to assume covered positions where the profits on the long side were treated as capital gains and the losses on the short side as ordinary losses. Second, to qualify as a long-term capital gain, options (as well as other securities) sold subsequent to December 31, 1977, must be held long for more than one year. Since, as of the beginning of 1984, all *listed* puts and calls expire in less than one year, all gains and losses through sale or expiration are considered short term. Prior to 1977 a holding period of more than six months gave rise to long-term treatment, and an option buyer could take his losses short term and his profits long term by closing out unprofitable positions before six months while retaining his profitable options. As a consequence, prior to both of these changes it was possible for covered positions involving options to produce long-term capital gains on one side and ordinary losses on the other. These reforms, designed to eliminate the more blatantly tax-

---

[6] The tax code regarding options is complex, and certain issues have not yet been decided definitively by the IRS or the courts. Furthermore, changes are likely to occur in the future, since the treatment of some option transactions lacks consistency and violates the intent, if not the letter of the law in its present form. The reader is, therefore, cautioned to consult his broker or a tax authority before investing. A more extensive treatment of the issues covered here, and additional material relating to institutional investors, security dealers and other special taxpayers, as well as some more sophisticated tax-oriented strategies can be found in Jack Crestol and Herman M. Schneider, *Tax Planning for Investors* (Homewood, Illinois: Dow Jones-Irwin, 1983).

[7] Prior to this date the only case where a short-term capital gain rather than an ordinary gain was realized on an unexercised written option was the expired side of a written straddle. Consequently, an investor with long-term capital gains and short-term capital losses (realized or carried forward) could in effect achieve long-term treatment for the short-term capital gain on the expired side of a written straddle. This gain would offset short-term losses that would otherwise reduce long-term gains, while any loss on the other side of the straddle, if repurchased, would be treated as a reduction in ordinary income. It should be noted that the closing of this loophole preceded the listing of puts.

motivated option transactions, have had the effect of simplifying the tax treatment of options substantially.

The following brief description of the tax code, as it relates to puts and calls on common stocks, again applies only to an individual investor who is not a dealer or considered to be in the business of trading options for his own account. Other rules apply to corporations, regulated investment companies, tax-exempt organizations, and nonresident aliens. Transactions costs are neglected. Their treatment as a cost component of options is straightforward, although their existence may outweigh the benefit from tax-motivated strategies involving a number of transactions.

For *buyers* of puts and calls, the deductibility of the cost of the option is deferred until termination of the whole transaction. The purchased option can be closed out in one of three ways with the following tax consequences:

Sale:	Capital gain or loss equal to the difference between the sale price and the original purchase price; short term or long term, depending on the length of time the option is held; recognized at the time of sale.
Expiration:	Capital loss equal to the original purchase price; short term or long term, depending on the length of time the option is held; recognized at the time of expiration.
Exercise:	For a *call*: Basis for the purchased stock is the striking price plus the purchase price of the call; holding period of the stock starts on the day after the acquisition of the stock—it does not include the holding period of the call; recognition of the capital gain or loss on the call is, in effect, deferred until the stock is sold—it will then be long-term or short-term, depending on the length of time the stock is held.
	For a *put*: Proceeds from the sale of the stock are based on the striking price minus the purchase price of the put; resulting capital gain or loss is recognized at the time of exercise and is long-term or short-term, depending on the holding period of the stock delivered.

Exercise provides the only complication. In this case the purchased option is considered part of the resulting stock transaction, except that the holding period of the option is disregarded.

For *writers* of listed puts and calls,[8] the price received is not recognized until termination of the whole transaction. The writers' obligation can

---

[8] In keeping with the treatment of short positions in stock, the length of time for which an option writer has actually been obligated is immaterial for tax purposes. The gain or loss realized on the date of repurchase or expiration is short term even for long-term written positions.

end in one of three ways:

Repurchase: Short-term capital gain or loss equal to the difference between the original sale price and the closing purchase price; recognized at the time of repurchase.

Expiration: Short-term capital gain equal to the original sale price; recognized at the time of expiration.

Exercise: For a *call:*   Proceeds from the sale of stock are based on the striking price plus the sale price of the call; resulting capital gain or loss is recognized at the time of exercise and is long-term or short-term, depending on the holding period of the stock delivered.

For a *put:*   Basis for the purchased stock is the striking price minus the sale price of the put; holding period of the stock starts on the day after acquisition of the stock—it does not include the holding period of the put; recognition of the capital gain or loss on the put is, in effect, deferred until the stock is sold—it will then be long-term or short-term, depending on the length of time the stock is held.

As of the beginning of 1984, the only way short-term capital gains on uncovered listed options can be converted into long-term gains is to exercise a purchased call or have a written put exercised and hold the acquired stock for more than one year from the exercise date. On the other hand, even uncovered options offer some leeway with respect to the timing of the short-term gains or losses.

But the real tax strategic advantages of option transactions emerge only when we consider covered positions, either involving options alone or, more importantly, options and stock. For covered positions or a sequence of positions involving options, the main complications arise from the question to what extent the wash sale and short sale rules are applicable.

The general principle governing the taxation of *positions involving only options* (that is, spreads and combinations) is that each side of the position is treated separately, such that the rules for uncovered options apply. Since listed options cannot be held long term, the short sale rule is immaterial and the only exceptions may be created by the wash sale rule. It is unclear whether or not options are "securities" under that rule. But even if they are, so that their sale at a loss and the purchase of identical options within the wash sale period would trigger the rule, options of different types and series are not considered "substantially identical securities." Furthermore, closing a written position coupled with the opening of an identical written position is not regarded as a sale combined with a reacquisition. There are, thus, ample opportunities to circumvent the intent of the wash sale rule and to manipulate the timing of gains and losses for tax purposes without incurring the risks associated with uncovered positions.

For purchased options, losses are recognized on the trade date, and gains on the settlement date, one business day later. Gains and losses of written options are realized on the settlement date. If, for example, an option spread shows a gain on the written side, it can be closed out on the last business day of the tax year. This allocates the short-term loss on the long side to the present year, while postponing the realization of the gain into the next. Due to the limited applicability of the wash sale rule, this strategy may be generalized to liquidating the losing side of a spread just before the end of the year, retaining the other side, and reconstituting the spread by the purchase or sale of an option in a *different series* but same class. This, furthermore, provides the opportunity to continue deferment of the gain by rolling the position over year after year. In the meantime, the realized short-term losses may be used to offset capital gains elsewhere in the portfolio.[9]

Although the wash sale rule may be circumvented with impunity for virtually all positions involving only options, the IRS may challenge transactions with no possibility of positive return were it not for tax savings. But there are many ways of utilizing combinations of options without even violating the intent of the tax laws. For example, if an investor holds a profitable call (put) he can hedge and defer the short-term capital gain by writing a call (put) of a different series.

Joint *option-stock positions* offer an even wider array of advantageous strategies, due to the haphazard manner the wash sale and short sale rules have been interpreted up to the present time. Not only can options in this context defer or accelerate gains and losses, but they can transform their term character in ways impossible to achieve through pure stock transactions. Of course, the effect, if any, of an option on the holding period and tax basis of the underlying stock is limited to the number of shares represented by that option.

The *wash sale rule* applies only to the *purchase* of a *call* within the critical period 30 days before or after the sale of the underlying security at a loss. That is, if a call is bought within the wash sale period and is subsequently exercised, the holding period of the stock acquired through exercise is increased by the number of days the stock sold previously has been held. The loss sustained on the sale of the old stock, as well as any gain or loss on the call and on the acquired stock, is recognized on the date the new stock is sold. Alternatively, if the call is sold or expires, the wash sale loss is realized at that time.

---

[9] Changes in the tax laws under consideration at the beginning of 1984 would limit the opportunities for affecting the timing of gains and losses with options to certain near-the-money and out-of-the-money covered call writing positions.

On the other hand, there is a way to realize a loss, about to go long term, on long stock immediately, while maintaining an equivalent long position in that stock for future gain, without interference from the wash sale rule. The investor simply combines the sale of the stock with the writing of an appropriate number of puts. Unless the puts move so far in-the-money that they are exercised prior to the end of the wash sale period, the loss on the stock is recognized at the date of its sale.

In the same vein, the sale of a call at a loss coupled with the purchase of the underlying stock is not considered a wash sale. Nor does the rule apply to the purchase of the underlying stock within the wash sale period around the purchase of a put. But, as the following shows, the short sale provision comes into play in the latter case.

The *short sale rule* is restricted to the *purchase* of a *put*, if the underlying security has been acquired prior to or during the time the put position is maintained. Moreover, it applies only with respect to short sale gains (that is, the second part of the rule). In particular, any loss on the short sale is short term or long term depending on the actual holding period of the delivered stock (that is, the first part of the rule does not apply). This means that a purchased put can accomplish (at the price of the put) what the short sale of stock could not. An investor can realize a short-term loss on stock held long term by exercising the put and delivering new stock at a loss, while the long stock has appreciated in the meantime. It should be noted that the short-term character of the loss on a listed put at expiration and of the gain or loss at its sale is not affected by the long position in the underlying stock. And furthermore, since the wash sale rule does not apply to purchased puts, this treatment of losses remains unaltered even if the underlying stock was acquired within 30 days before or after this put. On the other hand, any gain on the sale of the covering stock is long term only if the stock has been held for more than one year, either prior to the purchase of the put or after its sale, expiration, or exercise. Consequently, a short-term profit (minus the put price) on a long stock can only be hedged and deferred through the purchase of a put, but it cannot be locked in and converted into a long-term gain, if the put is exercised, or into a short-term loss combined with a larger long-term gain, if the put expires or is sold.

An exception to the short sale rule is made in case of a so-called "married put." To qualify as a married put, the underlying stock must be purchased on the same day as the put, and must be explicitly identified as the stock to be delivered in the event of exercise. If the identified stock is delivered at exercise or if the put expires unexercised, the actual holding period of the stock determines the term character of a capital gain. Since the life of a listed option is less than one year, a long-term capital gain can only be realized if the put expires, in which case the recognition of the loss on the put is deferred until the stock is sold. If the put initially married to the stock is sold, its holding period begins on the date of that sale.

Unlike purchased puts, calls written against long stock are not considered a short sale. Thus, while the written call provides a hedge for the long stock, the two transactions are almost completely independent for tax purposes. If the call is exercised, and the writer holds a profitable position in the underlying stock which is long-term at the expiration date, he can deliver that stock for a long-term capital gain (including the call price), or he may purchase additional stock and deliver it. This latter strategy converts a long-term gain on the combined position into a greater long-term gain on the long stock and an immediate short-term loss (reduced by the call price) on the option transaction, which may offset short-term gains elsewhere in the portfolio. This course of action may be especially advantageous, if the covering stock is still short term at the time the call is exercised. It avoids the realization of a short-term capital gain by transforming it into the combination of a short-term loss and a possibly greater future long-term gain. In addition, the written call position can be rolled over without causing wash sale problems, even if it is desirable to open an identical position.

The preceding discussion highlighted some ways in which *listed* options can be used to influence the term character of capital gains and losses, without incurring the risks associated with uncovered positions. Although there were few positions that could accomplish this particular task, the variety of joint option-stock transactions suitable to accelerate or postpone the recognition of gains and losses, without regard to their term character, is very large indeed. The simplest strategies involve only one option and one stock position. Suppose an investor wants to hedge and defer a gain on a stock or option position. If he has a profit on a long (short) stock, he can purchase (write) a put or write (purchase) a call on that stock. Conversely, he can hedge and postpone the gain from an in-the-money purchased (written) put or an in-the-money written (purchased) call by purchasing the underlying stock (selling it short). It should be noted that a hedge involving purchased options is established at the cost of the option, while a hedge with written options offers only protection to the extent of the option price received.[10] There are also more complex strategies to hedge and defer unrealized gains. Suppose, for instance, that an investor holds a profitable stock for which no puts are available, and he now wants to hedge the stock without limiting his future profit possibilities by writing

---

[10] Remember that transactions costs were disregarded throughout this Appendix, although they may play a substantial role in determining the benefits from transactions undertaken for tax purposes.

a call. In this case, he can simultaneously sell the stock short and purchase a call. This strategy will, for the price of the call, hedge his present profit, if the stock price declines, and generate additional profits, if the stock price increases.

Finally, an investor can use options in conjunction with stock to avoid the dilemma, mentioned at the end of the preceding section, of having to offset short-term capital losses against long-term capital gains. A carefully designed options portfolio can complement a stock portfolio in a way that the short-term losses generated by the latter are closely matched by short-term gains on the former, without changing the risk exposure to a major extent or impairing the long-term character of the stock gains.

general arbitrage
relationships

4

In Chapter 2, we showed that the value of a European call is completely determined by the price of an otherwise identical put, the price of its underlying stock, the value of the cash dividends paid by the stock, and the prices of default-free bonds. In this chapter, we will find the similar relationships that must hold for each of the following: (1) among the price of an option, the price and cash dividends of its underlying stock, and the prices of default-free zero-coupon bonds, (2) between the prices of two (and three) options differing only in their striking prices, and (3) between the prices of two options differing only in their times to expiration. These relationships are developed for American as well as European options and allow for uncertain dividends. In addition, we give some results about the optimal exercise strategy for American options. Finally, we extend the previous put-call parity relationship to include American options.

Our conclusions take the form of properties that option values must possess if there are to be no riskless arbitrage opportunities.[1] Riskless arbitrage opportunities in this context are situations that require no initial investment but that yield a positive amount immediately and only nonnegative amounts in the future under all possible circumstances. Hence, the

---

[1] Many of these results were first developed, in a somewhat different form, by Robert C. Merton in "Theory of Rational Option Pricing," *Bell Journal of Economics and Management Science,* 4 (Spring 1973), 141–183.

results provide a set of conditions that must be satisfied by any reasonable option pricing theory.

We also give constructive recipes for realizing these riskless profits if market prices violate the arbitrage restrictions. The procedures given do not depend on knowledge of stock price movements or knowledge of the optimal exercise policy for an option. They also do not depend on assumptions about the subsequent behavior of option prices, once a position is initiated. It is important to remember that if you have information about any of these things, you could earn even more money from an arbitrage violation, and you would not necessarily follow the exact steps given in these recipes. Of course, violations of the arbitrage conditions will rarely, if ever, persist, precisely because they are so easy to exploit.

Even if you cannot sell securities short, as required by most of the recipes, the results will still be useful. They can be rearranged to show the following conclusion: If an arbitrage restriction were violated, it would be possible to form a portfolio that would give higher returns in all possible circumstances than a second portfolio with the same initial cost. In that event, you would never want to buy the combination of securities given by the second portfolio. Furthermore, those who already own the second portfolio would have an incentive to sell it and use the proceeds to buy the first portfolio. For example, consider the European put-call parity relationship given in Chapter 2, $C = P + S - Kr^{-t}$. Even if you cannot sell securities short, it is still true that if $C > P + S - Kr^{-t}$, you should not be willing to buy a call; instead, it would always be better to buy a put, buy the stock, and borrow Kr^{-t}. Similarly, if $C < P + S - Kr^{-t}$, buying the call would always be preferable to taking a levered long position in the stock hedged by a long position in the put.

For the reasons discussed in Chapter 2, we continue to ignore margin requirements, transactions costs, taxes, and differences between borrowing and lending rates unless it is stated otherwise. Although we will comment only briefly on the implications of these factors, readers interested in including them will find it relatively simple to do so. Furthermore, we assume that all of the transactions necessary to set up or close out a position can be accomplished simultaneously and without affecting market prices. We also assume that interest rates are always positive; that is, r is always greater than one. All of the results are valid for interest rates that change randomly over time.

In Chapter 2, we assumed that the cash dividends to be paid during the life of the option were known with certainty, but this is often not the case. To allow for the possibility of uncertain cash dividends, we need to introduce two new symbols, D^+ and D^-. As discussed earlier, anyone who takes a short position in the stock over some period must make restitution for all cash dividends paid during that period. Suppose the individual wishes to purchase a portfolio, containing bonds and perhaps some of the stock, which can be liquidated during the period in a way sufficient to cover this obligation under all possible circumstances. The smallest amount necessary to set up such a portfolio for a period equal to the remaining life of the option is defined as D^+, which we will refer to as the present value of the maximum dividends to be paid during the remaining life of the option. When an individual purchases this portfolio, we will say that he buys D^+. The present value of the minimum dividends to be paid during the remaining life of the option, D^-, is defined in a similar way. Suppose that an individual who owns the stock wishes to obtain some cash now, by borrowing and possibly selling some of the stock short, and be sure that he can repay the borrowing and buy back the stock under all possible circumstances with cash dividends he will receive over some period. The largest amount he can obtain for a period equal to the remaining life of the option is D^-. We will refer to this as selling D^-. Of course, if dividends are known with certainty, then $D^+ = D^-$. The appendix to this chapter gives some further information about D^+ and D^-.

4-1. ARBITRAGE RESTRICTIONS ON CALL VALUES

As an aid to reading this section, we will follow a fixed pattern. For each of the five propositions, we first state it, then prove it by showing how riskless arbitrage profits could be earned if it were violated. Finally, we comment on the proposition or illustrate it with a numerical example. A reader who wishes to skip the proofs should read the proposition, then skip to the paragraph following the italicized words, "*End of proof.*"

Proposition 1 (boundaries): The value of a call is never *less than* the larger of

a. zero

b. the stock price minus the striking price

c. the stock price minus the present value of the striking price minus the present value of the maximum dividends that will be paid during the remaining life of the option,

and the value of a call is never *greater than* the price of its underlying stock:

$$S \geq C \geq \max[0, S - K, S - Kr^{-t} - D^+].$$

Proof: We break the proof of this proposition into four parts. First, we show $C \geq 0$; second, that $C \geq S - K$; third, that $C \geq S - Kr^{-t} - D^{+}$; and fourth, that $S \geq C$.

If C is negative, you can earn a riskless profit by buying the call and holding it to expiration. This gives you a positive amount now and a nonnegative amount later.

If $C < S - K$, buy the call and exercise it immediately. Note that you could not do this with a European call, so its value could be less than $S - K$.

If $C < S - Kr^{-t} - D^{+}$, lock in a sure profit by forming the following portfolio: short one share, buy one call, buy D^{+}, and place Kr^{-t} in default-free bonds maturing on the expiration date. This produces the positive amount $S - Kr^{-t} - D^{+} - C$ now. Hold this portfolio until the expiration date. Liquidate D^{+} as required to cover the cash dividends due from the short position in the stock. If the dividends actually paid are less than the maximum amount, then you will have some money left over. Table 4-1 shows the value of the remainder of the portfolio on the expiration date. Since the loan of Kr^{-t} will have grown to $Kr^{-t} \times r^{t} = K$, the portfolio will at worst be worth zero (if $S^{*} \geq K$) and at best will return the positive amount $K - S^{*}$ (if $S^{*} < K$).

Table 4-1
ARBITRAGE TABLE ILLUSTRATING THE
LOWER BOUNDARY CONDITION

	Current Date	Expiration Date	
		$S^{*} \leq K$	$K < S^{*}$
Short stock	S	$-S^{*}$	$-S^{*}$
Buy call	$-C$	—	$S^{*} - K$
Buy bonds	$-Kr^{-t}$	K	K
Total		$K - S^{*}$	—

If $C > S$, buy the stock and sell the call, receiving a positive amount now. If the call you sold is exercised on or before the expiration date, deliver the stock and receive the amount K. If it expires unexercised, you still have the stock, which cannot have a negative price. *End of proof.*

The conditions given in Proposition 1 are hardly surprising. The owner of the stock is like someone who owns a car outright, while the owner of a call is like someone who still owes a payment on the car and does not get to drive it (receives no dividends) until the payment is made.

So certainly a call should never be worth more than the stock itself. Since a call has limited liability, it should never be worth less than zero, and since it can be traded for its exercise value at any time, it should never be worth less than $S - K$. The last condition is almost as intuitive. A contract that must be exercised on the expiration date and cannot be exercised before then should be worth at least $S - Kr^{-t} - D^+$, since its payoffs could be at least duplicated with an investment of $S - Kr^{-t} - D^+$ by buying the stock, borrowing Kr^{-t}, and selling D^+. Since a call option offers everything that this contract does and more, it should never be worth less.

Proposition 1 also gives some information about the extreme values of a call. If $S = 0$, then the proposition says that $0 \geq C \geq 0$, which implies that $C = 0$. If $K = 0$, then it says that $S \geq C \geq S$, which in turn implies that $C = S$. In other words,

1. If $S = 0$, then $C = 0$.
2. If $K = 0$, then $C = S$.

Figure 4-1 summarizes Proposition 1 graphically for the case where the striking price is greater than the present value of the striking price plus the present value of the maximum dividends to be paid during the life of the option. The figure shows that the graph of the value of a call as a function

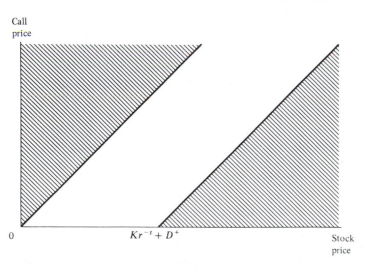

Figure 4-1   Arbitrage Restrictions on the Value of a Call as a Function of the Current Stock Price

of the current stock price cannot lie in the shaded areas. The condition $S \geq C$ rules out the area on the left, and the condition $C \geq S - Kr^{-t} - D^+$ rules out the area on the right.

Table 4-2 shows some option prices that could make you rich in a hurry: They violate Proposition 1 and all of our following propositions. As we will see, all but one of the options shown could potentially play a role in a profitable arbitrage operation. To find how this would work for Proposition 1, consider the JAN/35. You could buy this call for $1 and then immediately exercise it, for a total cost of $36. You could then immediately sell the stock acquired through exercise for $40, for a net profit of $4.

Table 4-2
NINE CALLS ON *XYZ*

Striking Price	*Expiration Month*			Stock Price
	JAN	*APR*	*JUL*	
XYZ 35	1	6	14	40
XYZ 40	2	5	7	40
XYZ 45	4	3	5	40

NOTE: Assume the January expiration date is three months from now, the annualized interest rate for all expiration dates is 15%, and the stock pays no cash dividend prior to the July expiration date.

Suppose the stock will pay no cash dividends during the lives of the options. Then the APR/35 provides another opportunity. It is not selling for less than its exercise value, but it is selling for less than the current stock price, $40, minus the present value of the striking price, $35 $(1.15)^{-1/2} = \$32.64$. To take advantage of this, you could buy the call, short one share of stock, and lend $32.64 at an annualized interest rate of 15% to be paid back in six months. This portfolio nets an immediate cash inflow of $40 - \$32.64 - \$6 = \$1.36$. If you hold the portfolio until the expiration date and the call finishes in-the-money, you will have no further gain or loss. The $35 received from the loan will exactly cover the striking price payment required to exercise the call, which in turn provides the stock needed to cover the short sale. If the call finishes out-of-the-money, you not only have the original $1.36, but an additional profit as well. For example, if the stock price at expiration is $30, then you make an additional $35 - \$30 = \$5$.

Proposition 2 (striking price): Three arbitrage restrictions relate to striking price:

a. The value of a call can never be less than the value of an otherwise identical call with a higher striking price:

$$C(K_1) \geq C(K_2) \qquad \text{if} \quad K_2 > K_1.$$

b. The difference in the values of two otherwise identical calls is never greater than the difference in their striking prices:

$$K_2 - K_1 \geq C(K_1) - C(K_2) \qquad \text{if} \quad K_2 > K_1.$$

c. Of three otherwise identical calls with striking prices $K_3 > K_2 > K_1$, the value of the middle call is never greater than a weighted average of the values of the extreme calls, where the weights are $(K_3 - K_2)/(K_3 - K_1)$ for the first call and $(K_2 - K_1)/(K_3 - K_1)$ for the third call:

$$C(K_2) \leq \left(\frac{K_3 - K_2}{K_3 - K_1}\right)C(K_1) + \left(\frac{K_2 - K_1}{K_3 - K_1}\right)C(K_3).$$

Proof: To show restriction (a), suppose $C(K_2) > C(K_1)$. Then the appropriate strategy is a vertical spread. Buy the lower-priced call and write the higher-priced one. This produces a positive amount now. If the owner of the call you wrote exercises it before expiration, then exercise the purchased call at the same time and net the positive amount $K_2 - K_1$. Otherwise, hold the purchased call until the expiration date. Then there are three possible outcomes: either $S^* \leq K_1$, $K_1 < S^* < K_2$, or $K_2 \leq S^*$. In each case, it is easy to see that you will receive a nonnegative amount.

Turning to restriction (b), suppose, to the contrary, that $C(K_1) - C(K_2) > K_2 - K_1$. Again the appropriate strategy is a vertical spread. To obtain a positive amount now, write $C(K_1)$, buy $C(K_2)$, and place $K_2 - K_1$ in a savings account (or, alternatively, continually reinvest it at the default-free spot interest rate). If the call you sold is not exercised early, hold the entire position until the expiration date and receive the payoff shown in Table 4-3. There r^* stands for the (possibly random) number of dollars received for each dollar invested in the savings account. Regardless of the outcome, you will receive a nonnegative amount. Suppose, instead, that the written option is exercised with, say, time t' remaining until expiration when the stock price is S'. If at this time $C(S', t', K_2) > S' - K_2$, then

Table 4-3
ARBITRAGE TABLE ILLUSTRATING
THE SECOND STRIKING PRICE CONDITION

	Current Date	Expiration Date		
		$S^* \leq K_1$	$K_1 < S^* < K_2$	$K_2 \leq S^*$
Write call at K_1	$C(K_1)$	—	$K_1 - S^*$	$K_1 - S^*$
Buy call at K_2	$-C(K_2)$	—	—	$S^* - K_2$
Place $K_2 - K_1$ in savings account	$-(K_2 - K_1)$	$(K_2 - K_1)r^*$	$(K_2 - K_1)r^*$	$(K_2 - K_1)r^*$
Total		$(K_2 - K_1)r^*$	$(K_2 - K_1)(r^* - 1) + K_2 - S^*$	$(K_2 - K_1)(r^* - 1)$

sell it; if not, then exercise it. In either case, withdraw $K_2 - K_1$ from the savings account to close the position. You keep the accumulated interest plus, if you sold your call, $C(S', t', K_2) - (S' - K_2)$.

Finally, consider restriction (c). Let λ be defined such that

$$K_2 = \lambda K_1 + (1 - \lambda)K_3,$$

so $\lambda = (K_3 - K_2)/(K_3 - K_1)$ and $(1 - \lambda) = (K_2 - K_1)/(K_3 - K_1)$.   If $C(K_2) > \lambda C(K_1) + (1 - \lambda)C(K_3)$ in violation of (c), write $C(K_2)$ and buy $\lambda C(K_1) + (1 - \lambda)C(K_3)$. This gives you a positive amount now. If the written call is not exercised prior to the expiration date, hold the calls you bought until the expiration date and receive the payoffs shown in Table 4-4.

To see that $\lambda(S^* - K_1) + (K_2 - S^*) > 0$ when $K_2 < S^* < K_3$, observe, first, that $K_3 > S^*$, so that $(1 - \lambda)K_3 > (1 - \lambda)S^*$. This implies that $\lambda S^* > S^* - (1 - \lambda)K_3$. Therefore,

$$\lambda S^* - \lambda K_1 > S^* - \lambda K_1 - (1 - \lambda)K_3,$$

which, in turn, implies $\lambda(S^* - K_1) + (K_2 - S^*) > 0$. Thus you could never lose money at the end, and you would make money if $K_1 < S^* < K_3$. On the other hand, suppose the call you sold is exercised when the time to expiration is, say, t' and the stock price is S'. If $C(S', t', K_1) > S' - K_1$, sell it; if not, exercise it. If you exercise both calls, you will exactly break even, since $\lambda(S' - K_1) + (1 - \lambda)(S' - K_3) = S' - K_2$. If you choose to sell the call with striking price K_1, you receive an additional positive amount. *End of proof.*

Table 4-4

ARBITRAGE TABLE ILLUSTRATING THE THIRD STRIKING PRICE CONDITION

	Current Date	*Expiration Date*			
		$S^* \leq K_1$	$K_1 < S^* \leq K_2$	$K_2 < S^* < K_3$	$K_3 \leq S^*$
Write 1 call at K_2	$C(K_2)$	—	—	$K_2 - S^*$	$K_2 - S^*$
Buy λ calls at K_1	$-\lambda C(K_1)$	—	$\lambda(S^* - K_1)$	$\lambda(S^* - K_1)$	$\lambda(S^* - K_1)$
Buy $1 - \lambda$ calls at K_3	$-(1 - \lambda)C(K_3)$	—	—	—	$(1 - \lambda)(S^* - K_3)$
Total		—	$\lambda(S^* - K_1)$	$\lambda(S^* - K_1) + (K_2 - S^*)$	—

The first two parts of Proposition 2 are quite reasonable, but the third part may appear to have little intuitive content. However, it is also a very sensible result. If the striking price is very low relative to the stock price, then a call is typically very likely to be exercised and we would expect a one-dollar increase in the striking price to have a significant effect on the call price. As we look at higher and higher striking prices, the likelihood of exercise becomes lower and lower, so each dollar increase should have a smaller and smaller effect on the price of a call. Indeed, for extremely high striking prices, a typical call will be almost worthless, so an extra dollar added on to the striking price could not possibly decrease its value by very much. The behavior of call prices just described is exactly what is implied by restriction (c) of Proposition 2.

Figure 4-2 illustrates Proposition 2. It shows a graph of the value of a call as a function of its striking price. Restriction (a), combined with the fact that $C = S$ when $K = 0$, implies that the graph cannot lie in the upper shaded area. Restriction (b) says that the slope of the graph can never be less than -1, so this rules out the lower shaded area. Finally, restrictions (a) and (c) together indicate that the graph should have the general shape shown. Note that Proposition 1 also says that the graph cannot lie in the shaded areas: The condition $S \geq C$ implies that the upper area is out of bounds, while the condition $C \geq S - K$ implies the same for the lower area.

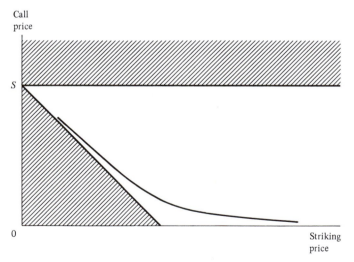

Figure 4-2   Arbitrage Restrictions on the Value of a Call as a
Function of the Striking Price

Proposition 2 provides additional recipes for profiting from the option prices shown in Table 4-2. All parts of the proposition are violated by at least some of the prices. For example, all the January calls violate restriction (a): The call prices increase as the striking price increases. One way to profit from this is the following vertical spread: Buy one JAN/40 for $2 and sell one JAN/45 for $4. This nets an immediate cash inflow of $2. And certainly you could never lose money later; if the call you sold is exercised, you could exercise the call you own and make an additional $5.

Restriction (b) is violated by the JUL/35 and JUL/40 calls: The difference in call prices is greater than the difference in striking prices. A vertical spread is again the appropriate strategy: Write one JUL/35 and buy one JUL/40. This produces an immediate cash inflow of $14 − $7 = $7. If the JUL/35 is held to expiration, the maximum cash outflow at expiration occurs if the stock price $S*$ is $40 or more. In that case, the position loses $5, the difference in the striking prices. However, this is less than the initial cash inflow (plus the accumulated interest), so overall the spread is sure to net a profit. If instead the JUL/35 is exercised before expiration, then you can simultaneously either sell or exercise the JUL/40, whichever is most profitable. At a maximum, the cash outflow at this time will again be $5, the difference between the striking prices. However, since this is less than the initial cash inflow of $7, the spread is sure to net a profit.

Note that with European calls you could be assured of getting the interest on the initial cash inflow of $7 for the entire lifetime of the options. Therefore, for European calls, the second arbitrage restriction can be strengthened to:

$$(K_2 - K_1)r^{-t} \geq C(K_1) - C(K_2).$$

The April calls provide the opportunity to benefit from the strategy described in the proof of restriction (c): For this maturity the XYZ 40 has a price greater than half the sum of the corresponding XYZ 35 and XYZ 45. Consider the following butterfly spread: Write two APR/40 calls at $5 each, buy one APR/35 call at $6, and buy one APR/45 call at $3. This portfolio nets an immediate cash inflow of $1. If you can hold the portfolio until the expiration date, four things can happen. First, suppose the stock price at that time is less than $35. Since none of the calls finishes in-the-money, no further gain or loss results. Second, suppose the stock price is between $35 and $40, so that only the APR/35 finishes in-the-money. Then you make a profit on the APR/35. Third, suppose the stock finishes between $40 and $45. In this case both the APR/35 and APR/40 calls finish in-the-money. Again, the portfolio has a net profit, since the profit from the one APR/35 is greater than the loss from the two APR/40 calls. Finally, if the stock price is greater than $45, no further gain or loss results. A similar argument shows that you could not lose money if the written calls are exercised before the expiration date. Once again, the quoted prices allow a strategy giving an initial cash inflow that in the future, at worst, breaks even and may yield an additional profit.

Proposition 3 (time to expiration): The value of a call can never be less than the value of an otherwise identical call with a shorter time to expiration:

$$C(t_2) \geq C(t_1) \qquad \text{if} \quad t_2 > t_1.$$

Proof: To show this, suppose, to the contrary, $C(t_2) < C(t_1)$. Buy $C(t_2)$ and write $C(t_1)$, receiving a positive amount now. Suppose the shorter maturity call expires or is exercised when the time to expiration of the purchased call is t' and the stock price is S'. At this time, your position is worth $C(t') - \max[0, S' - K]$. If this is positive, then sell your call and close out the position at a profit. If it is not positive, then exercise your call immediately and receive $\max[0, S' - K]$, so that no further gain or loss results. *End of proof.*

Note that this proposition compares the values on a given calendar date of two calls with different expiration dates. It does not say anything about how the value of a single call will change as time passes. Also, the proposition does not necessarily hold for European calls, since we cannot exercise them before the expiration date as required by the above strategy.

It might seem that, analogous to restriction (c) of Proposition 2, we could use a horizontal "butterfly spread" to show that, for calls with the same striking price, middle-maturity calls should sell for *more* than half the sum of the shortest and longest maturity calls. Although, as an empirical matter, this is usually true, violation of this condition does *not* give rise to a riskless arbitrage opportunity.

However, the option prices shown in Table 4-2 do offer yet another arbitrage opportunity: The APR/45 is selling for $3, while the JAN/45 is selling for $4. The appropriate strategy is a horizontal spread: Buy one APR/45 and write one JAN/45. This produces an immediate cash inflow of $4 − $3 = $1. If the call you wrote is exercised on or before its expiration date, you can always close out the position with no further gain or loss by simultaneously exercising the call you own. If, instead, you can sell your call for more than its exercise value, you will make an additional profit as well.

> *Proposition 4:* The value of a call must be greater than $S - K$ at any time other than the expiration date or just before an ex-dividend date.

Proof: Suppose that $C = S - K$ at some time between ex-dividend dates. Then you could lock in an arbitrage profit by buying the call, shorting the stock, lending the striking price, and subsequently closing out the entire position just before the next ex-dividend date. The profit on your position would be at least the interest earned on the striking price and could be even more.

Note that if you did not close out the position then, but instead held it through the ex-dividend date, you could no longer be sure of making a profit. You would have to make restitution for the dividend to the person from whom the stock was borrowed, and the required payment could, in general, be more than the value of the interest that you would earn on the striking price even if you subsequently held the position until just before the following ex-dividend date. (The case in which the present value of the dividends is less than the present value of the interest leads to restriction (c) of Proposition 5 below.) *End of proof.*

We conclude this section with a proposition that gives some results about the optimal exercise of calls. These results are consequences of our previous propositions. They are all based on the fact that the owner of a call should never exercise it if he can sell it for more than its exercise value, $S - K$, on the secondary market. If he does not wish to own the stock, he would certainly be better off selling the call than exercising it and selling the stock. Even if he does wish to own the stock, he would still be better off selling the call because he could then take the proceeds plus the striking price, buy the stock, and still have some money left over. Accordingly, if a call is selling for its exercise value, then exercising it would be neither better nor worse than selling it. (Of course, exercising would be preferable to selling if the market price were less than the exercise value, but we know from Proposition 1 that this would imply immediate arbitrage opportunities.)

Under the conditions described in Proposition 5, the price of a call must always be greater than $S - K$ if there are to be no arbitrage opportunities. Consequently, these conditions also state circumstances in which a call *should not* be exercised early. After proving the proposition, we discuss it in detail. In doing so, we also examine some important related questions: When and why *should* a call sell for exactly its exercise value? If a call is properly selling for its exercise value, should it be exercised (or sold) immediately?

Proposition 5 (optimal exercise): Three arbitrage restrictions relate to the optimal timing of exercise:

a. A call should never be exercised at any time other than the expiration date or just before an ex-dividend date.

b. If the present value of the maximum dividends to be paid during the remaining life of a call will at all times be less than the concurrent present value of the interest that can be earned on the striking price during the remaining life of the call, then the call should not be exercised before the expiration date.

c. If at any time it is optimal to exercise a call, then it is never optimal to leave unexercised an otherwise identical call that has either a lower striking price or a shorter time to expiration.

Proof: The rationale for restriction (a) is very simple. Proposition 4 says that under the stated condition, the value of a call must be greater than its exercise value. Hence, between ex-dividend dates it would always be better to sell the call rather than exercise it.

The reasoning behind restriction (b) is very similar. Under the condition described, the market price of a call prior to the expiration date must always be greater than its exercise value if there are no arbitrage opportunities. This is a direct consequence of Proposition 1. Since a loan of K today will be worth Kr^t on the expiration date, the present value of the interest that can be earned will be $r^{-t}[Kr^t - K] = K - Kr^{-t}$. Now note that if $D^+ < K - Kr^{-t}$, then $S - Kr^{-t} - D^+ > S - K$. Furthermore, Proposition 1 tells us that $C \geq S - Kr^{-t} - D^+$, so as of today, $C > S - K$. Under the assumed conditions, exactly the same argument will be valid not only today, but also at all times before the expiration date as well.

Now consider the first part of restriction (c). If the market prices did not embody this conversion policy, there would not necessarily be any immediate arbitrage opportunities, but there would be a possibility for them to arise later. Suppose that, at some time in the future, when the stock price is S', calls with time to expiration t' and striking price K_2 are optimally being exercised, while those with the same expiration date and a lower striking price K_1 are not. That is, $C(S', t', K_2) = S' - K_2$, while $C(S', t', K_1) > S' - K_1$. However, together this implies $C(S', t', K_1) - C(S', t', K_2) > K_2 - K_1$. Therefore, by Proposition 2, contrary to what we have assumed, you could then make arbitrage profits by applying the recipe accompanying the proof of the second part of the proposition.

Finally, consider the second part of restriction (c). As before, if market prices did not embody this conversion policy, there would not necessarily be any immediate arbitrage opportunities, but there would be a possibility for them to arise later. Suppose that, at some time in the future, when the stock price is S', calls with striking price K and time to expiration t_2 are optimally being exercised, while those with the same striking price and a shorter time to expiration t_1 are not. That is, $C(S', t_2, K) = S' - K$, while $C(S', t_1, K) > S' - K$. However, together this implies $C(S', t_1, K) > C(S', t_2, K)$, which would violate Proposition 2. *End of proof.*

Restriction (a) is a very sensible result. Suppose, for example, that you are considering exercising at some time between ex-dividend dates. If instead you wait until just before the next ex-dividend date, you have lost nothing, have gained the interest earned on the striking price in the meantime, and have retained the right to change your mind about exercising. Consequently, it would never be to your advantage to exercise between ex-dividend dates. Restriction (b) is also quite reasonable. Suppose that under the stated conditions you are nevertheless considering early exercise. If instead you wait until the expiration date and exercise then, you will have lost the dividends paid by the stock in the meantime, but this loss will be more than offset by the interest earned on the striking price. The intuitive content of restriction (c) is not quite so clear. However, this proposition is simply a consequence of our earlier very plausible conclusions that a call with a longer maturity cannot sell for less than an otherwise identical one with a shorter maturity, and that the difference in the prices of two otherwise identical calls cannot be greater than the difference in their striking prices.

Proposition 5 has several important implications. One is that *an American call on a stock paying no dividends should never be exercised prior to the expiration date.* Under these circumstances, otherwise identical American and European calls will have the same value.[2] However, *if the underlying stock has an ex-dividend date prior to the expiration date, then early exercise of an unprotected American call may be optimal.* To see why this could be true, think of the extreme case of a firm that plans to liquidate and pay out all of its assets as a cash dividend. The stock will no longer have any value after the ex-dividend date, so any in-the-money call should certainly be exercised before then. Hence, it is reasonable to conclude that a normal cash dividend, which is like a partial liquidation of the firm's assets, might also lead to optimal early exercise.

---

[2] By definition, payout-protected options have the same value for any dividend policy that they would have if the stock pays no dividends. Consequently, this result also implies that a payout-protected American call should never be exercised prior to the expiration date.

To examine this more closely, suppose that we are now at the last trading time before an ex-dividend date that will occur when there is, say, time τ remaining until expiration. If the owner of a call exercises now, he foregoes both the interest that he could have earned on the striking price and the right to subsequently change his mind about exercising. But in return he receives the dividend, D, or, if he chooses, he can sell the stock before it goes ex-dividend. In making his decision, he will choose between his best available portfolio containing the call and his best available portfolio without the call but with an additional $S - K$ to invest.

The easiest way to understand the choice is to suppose that the last trading time and the ex-dividend date are effectively simultaneous and that the ex-dividend stock price will be its current value minus the dividend, $S - D$. If the owner exercises just before the stock goes ex-dividend, then just afterward his holdings will be worth $(S - D) - K + D = S - K$. If he does not exercise, his holdings will be worth $C(S - D, \tau, K)$. Thus, the value of the call just before the stock goes ex-dividend will be $\max[S - K, C(S - D, \tau, K)]$. As long as an owner prefers more wealth to less, he will find it advantageous to exercise (or sell at the exercise value) if $S - K > C(S - D, \tau, K)$. In other words, if a call is properly priced at $S - K$, it should immediately be either exercised or sold.[3,4,5]

Let us pursue this a little further. Suppose that we make the entirely reasonable assumption that a one-dollar increase in the stock price just before an ex-dividend date will always increase the value of a call on the ex-dividend date by less than one dollar. This means that if there is a value of S, say $\underline{S}$, such that $\underline{S} - K = C(\underline{S} - D, \tau, K)$, then for any larger value of S, $S - K > C(S - D, \tau, K)$, and for any smaller value of S, $C(S - D, \tau, K) > S - K$. Hence, $\underline{S}$ will be the minimum stock price at which the call should be exercised, and immediate exercise will be optimal for all

---

[3] This concurs with an often mentioned rule: If a call is selling at or near its exercise value shortly before an ex-dividend date, then a writer who does not close out his position with a covering purchase should expect to receive an exercise notice in the near future. Of course, this does not mean that the call's selling for nearly its exercise value causes the possibility of optimal early exercise. Instead, just the opposite is true: it is the possibility of optimal early exercise that is causing the call to sell for nearly its exercise value.

[4] However, it should be remembered that an individual's particular tax or transactions costs situation may lead him to continue to hold a call that he would have otherwise exercised or sold.

[5] If there is a significant amount of time between the close of trading with the dividend and the opening of trading without the dividend, then the choice may be more complicated. For example, if there is no close substitute for the call, then an individual who particularly desired the call's unique pattern of returns over the period might find it advantageous to hold it through the ex-dividend date even if it is properly priced at $S - K$ and some other owners are exercising it or selling it. In our opinion, the short interval between one day's close and the next day's open is not significant enough for this case to merit further discussion.

$S \geq \underline{S}.$[6] This minimum stock price, the *optimal exercise boundary*, is thus a function of all of the variables that affect the value of a call except the current stock price. Any change in the underlying variables, except K, that increases (decreases) the value of $C(\underline{S} - D, \tau, K)$ will increase (decrease) the optimal exercise boundary. This is a sensible result. For example, compare your current decision with one that you would make in a situation identical in every way except for a higher volatility. Then our statement simply says that if one of the things you will have to give up by exercising—the right to change your mind later—were more valuable, then you would no longer be willing to exercise at the old $\underline{S}$. However, this right would be worth less and less as the call gets deeper and deeper in-the-money, so there would ultimately be some higher level at which you would again be willing to exercise. Similar reasoning, combined with Proposition 2(b), shows that $\underline{S}$ is a nondecreasing function of K. These conclusions agree with the findings of Proposition 5(c), which imply that $\underline{S}(t, K_2) \geq \underline{S}(t, K_1)$ if $K_2 > K_1$ and that $\underline{S}(t_2, K) \geq \underline{S}(t_1, K)$ if $t_2 > t_1$. They also give certain other properties of optimal exercise that cannot be established directly by arbitrage principles.

If the stock price just before an ex-dividend date is above the optimal exercise boundary, but a call is nevertheless not exercised, then its value will drop from $S - K$ to $C(S - D, \tau, K)$ when the stock goes ex-dividend and its owner will suffer an unnecessary loss. The amount of the loss could conceivably be as large as the value of the dividend. However, if the stock price at that time is below the optimal exercise boundary, then the value of the call will *not* drop when the stock goes ex-dividend. The effect of all anticipated future dividends (and the optimal exercise strategy) will be fully reflected in a lower current value of the call, so as long as the optimal strategy is followed, no further decline in value should occur when they are actually paid. Indeed, if in this case the call price did drop when the stock went ex-dividend, we could expect to earn a profit by selling the call just before then and buying it back just afterward.

In any event, Proposition 5(a) tells us that *the only time to consider early exercise is just before an ex-dividend date.*[7] In other words, the optimal exercise policy for a call will typically have the following form: Just before

---

[6] If a one-dollar increase in the stock price just before an ex-dividend date can decrease the value of a call on the ex-dividend date, or can increase it by more than a dollar, then the optimal exercise policy may not have this simple form. Such a situation is possible, but it is most unlikely to be encountered in practice. Here is an example. Suppose that we are now just before an ex-dividend date on which the firm will have the following policy: If $S > \$60$ or $S < \$50$, no dividend will be paid, but if $\$50 \leq S \leq \$60$, then the firm will liquidate and pay out all of its assets as a cash dividend. Clearly, if $K < \$50$, we would exercise immediately if $\$50 \leq S \leq \$60$, but we would not exercise if S is above or below this region.

[7] If the striking price of a call changes over time, then a similar argument can be used to show that early exercise may also be optimal just before an increase in the striking price.

each ex-dividend date, we compare the current stock price, S, with the current $\underline{S}$ for the call; if $S > \underline{S}$, then we should exercise immediately, and if $S < \underline{S}$, we should hold the call at least until just before the next ex-dividend date. If, for any reason, we wish to close out the position in the meantime, and if there are no arbitrage opportunities, we would always be better off selling the call rather than exercising it and selling the stock. We will postpone giving an explicit example of determining $\underline{S}$ until Chapter 5. There we will develop an exact option pricing model and provide a recipe for finding the corresponding optimal exercise strategy.

Proposition 5(b) says that under some circumstances early exercise will never be optimal even just before an ex-dividend date. Under the stated conditions, we would always find that $C(S - D, \tau, K)$ is greater than $S - K$ no matter how high the stock price becomes. This is because only one of the disadvantages of early exercise—losing the interest on the striking price—would then be more than sufficient to offset the advantage of receiving the dividend. For example, suppose the underlying stock pays a maximum quarterly dividend of $0.20, $K = \$40$, r is a constant 1.08, and the last ex-dividend date occurs one month before the expiration date. Would we ever exercise just before this ex-dividend date? No, since at that time $D^+ = \$0.20$ and $K - Kr^{-t} = 40[1 - (1.08)^{-1/12}] = \$0.28$, so early exercise is not optimal. On the other hand, if $D^+ > K - Kr^{-t}$, then early exercise *may* be optimal. Whether or not it is depends on whether or not the stock price at that time is above the optimal exercise boundary. In practice, it usually does not pay to exercise a listed call early, and if it does pay, the optimal time is almost always just before the last ex-dividend date.

Note that Proposition 5(c) provides a comparison of the minimum stock price at which immediate exercise would be optimal (the optimal exercise boundary) for calls with different times to expiration on a given calendar date. It does not imply that, for any given call, the optimal exercise boundary cannot increase as its time to expiration decreases through changes in the calendar date. This is obviously not true; you should never exercise between ex-dividend dates. So, in effect, the optimal exercise boundary is infinite at all times other than the expiration date and just before ex-dividend dates. In practice, for any given call, it is usually true that the optimal exercise boundary just before any ex-dividend date will be lower than it was just before the previous ex-dividend date. This is not a logical necessity, however. The optimal exercise boundary depends on more than just the time remaining until expiration. For example, if the current dividend will be much less than the previous one, or if there has been a significant unanticipated increase in volatility or interest rates since the last ex-dividend date, the current level of the optimal exercise boundary may actually be higher than its previous level.

4-2. ARBITRAGE RESTRICTIONS ON PUT VALUES

In this section, we state and discuss arbitrage restrictions on *unprotected American puts*. In view of the considerable overlap with Section 4-1, we will omit the proofs of these propositions.

Proposition 1 (boundaries): The value of a put is never *less than* the larger of

a.   zero

b.   the striking price minus the stock price

c.   the present value of the striking price, plus the present value of the minimum dividends that will be paid during the remaining life of the option, minus the stock price,

and the value of a put is never *greater than* its striking price:

$$K \geq P \geq \max[0, K - S, D^- + Kr^{-t} - S].$$

Proposition 2 (striking price): Three arbitrage restrictions relate to striking price:

a.   The value of a put can never be less than the value of an otherwise identical put with a lower striking price:

$$P(K_2) \geq P(K_1) \qquad \text{if} \quad K_2 > K_1.$$

b.   The difference in the values of two otherwise identical puts is never greater than the difference in their striking prices:[8]

$$K_2 - K_1 \geq P(K_2) - P(K_1) \qquad \text{if} \quad K_2 > K_1.$$

c.   Of three otherwise identical puts with striking prices $K_3 > K_2 > K_1$, the value of the middle put is never greater than a weighted average of the values of the extreme puts, where the weights are $(K_3 - K_2)/(K_3 - K_1)$ for the first put and $(K_2 - K_1)/(K_3 - K_1)$ for the third put:

$$P(K_2) \leq \left(\frac{K_3 - K_2}{K_3 - K_1}\right)P(K_1) + \left(\frac{K_2 - K_1}{K_3 - K_1}\right)P(K_3).$$

---

[8] As in the case of calls, this part of the proposition can be strengthened to $(K_2 - K_1)r^{-t} \geq P(K_2) - P(K_1)$ for European puts.

Proposition 3 (time to expiration): The value of a put can never be less than the value of an otherwise identical put with a shorter time to expiration:[9]

$$P(t_2) \geq P(t_1) \qquad \text{if} \quad t_2 > t_1.$$

The intuitive rationale for Propositions 1, 2, and 3 is very similar to that for the corresponding propositions about calls. A put can be exchanged for its exercise value, $K - S$, at any time, so it should never be worth less than that. A put has limited liability, so it should never be worth less than zero. Since the stock itself also has limited liability, a put should never be worth more than its striking price. The remaining part of Proposition 1 is also very sensible. A contract that must be exercised on the expiration date and cannot be exercised before then should be worth at least $D^- + Kr^{-t} - S$, since its payoffs could be at least duplicated by buying D^-, lending Kr^{-t}, and shorting the stock. Since a put option offers everything this contract does and more, it should never be worth less. Proposition 3 follows for the same reason: A longer maturity put offers everything a shorter maturity one does and more, so it should never be worth less.

The first two parts of Proposition 2 are obvious, just as they were for calls. Here is an intuitive explanation of the third part. If the striking price is very low relative to the stock price, then a put is very likely to expire worthless and a one-dollar increase in the striking price should have only a small effect on the put price. But as we look at higher and higher striking prices, each dollar added will have a higher likelihood of being received than the one before it and hence should have a greater effect on the price of the put. This is exactly the relationship implied by Proposition 2(c).

Figures 4-3 and 4-4 illustrate Propositions 1 and 2. Figure 4-3 shows that the graph of the value of a put as a function of the current stock price cannot lie in the shaded areas. The condition $K \geq P$ rules out the upper area, and the condition $P \geq K - S$ rules out the lower triangular area. These same conditions imply that the graph of the value of a put as a function of its striking price cannot lie in the shaded areas of Figure 4-4. Furthermore, restriction (c) of Proposition 2 indicates that this graph should have the general shape shown in the figure.

Proposition 4 merits more extensive discussion. Earlier we found that under some conditions, it would never be optimal to exercise a call before the expiration date. Proposition 4(a) gives a sufficient condition for a put not to be exercised if the time remaining until expiration is greater than t'.

---

[9] As discussed in Section 2-1, this proposition does not hold for European puts.

Proposition 4 (optimal exercise): Two arbitrage restrictions relate to the optimal timing of exercise:

a. If, throughout a period ending with time t' until expiration, the present value of the minimum dividends to be paid during the remainder of this period will at all times be greater than the concurrent present value of the interest that can be earned on the striking price during the remainder of the period, then the put should never be exercised before the end of the period.

b. If at any time it is optimal to exercise a put, then it is never optimal to leave unexercised an otherwise identical put that has either a higher striking price or a shorter time to expiration.

However, at best, this condition can only guarantee that early exercise will not be optimal until just after the last ex-dividend date, since the present value of the remaining dividends will of course be zero after that time. Furthermore, the results are weaker than those for calls in another way. A firm can always maintain an upper limit on the dividends it will pay in a given period, but it can maintain a lower limit only if it follows a compatible investment policy. Since the present value of the minimum dividends to

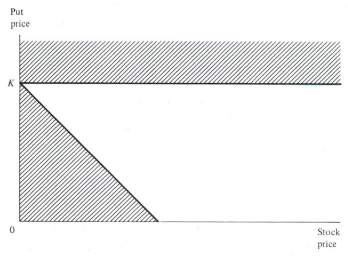

Figure 4-3   Arbitrage Restrictions on the Value of a Put as a Function of the Current Stock Price

Put
price

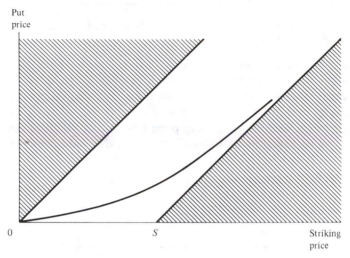

0   S   Striking
                                                                   price

Figure 4-4   Arbitrage Restrictions on the Value of a Put as a
                    Function of the Striking Price

be paid during any period can never be greater than S, to keep their present value above a given level, the investment policy must be such that the stock price can never drop below that level. Nevertheless, Proposition 4(a) can give additional information of practical value. For example, suppose that $K = \$40$, r is a constant 1.08, the underlying stock has a promised quarterly dividend of \$0.52, and t' is the time remaining until expiration on a given ex-dividend date. If we regard the dividend as certain, then Proposition 4(a) tells us that we would not exercise at any τ for which $\$0.52[1.08^{-(\tau-t')}] >$ $\$40[1 - 1.08^{-(\tau-t')}]$. This inequality will hold for any $\tau < t' + \frac{2}{12}$, so this implies that we would never exercise if an ex-dividend date is less than two months away. We can then conclude that optimal early exercise will occur during this period only if the firm suffers misfortunes severe enough to endanger the full payment of the dividend.

Note that we cannot use Proposition 4(a) to say, as we did for a call, that early exercise of a put should be considered only at a few specific times. In fact, it turns out that such a conclusion is not true at all. Given our discussions in Sections 2-1 and 4-1, this does not come as a complete surprise. The owner of a call faced one consideration that encouraged early exercise (receiving the dividend) and two that discouraged it (losing the interest that could have been earned on the striking price and losing the opportunity to change his mind later about exercising). Since exercise just before an ex-dividend date is always sufficient to receive the dividend, he had no reason even to consider incurring the losses at any other time. The owner of a put faces similar considerations, but their effects are quite different. It is perhaps easiest to think in terms of someone who already owns the stock to be delivered. If he exercises early, he gains the interest that can be earned on the striking price, but he foregoes both the opportunity to subsequently change his mind about exercising and the dividends that he would receive if he waited. The owner of the put will, of course, weigh all of these factors in making his decision. The important thing to note here is that the factor encouraging early exercise is in effect at all times, not just on a few specific dates. As we have seen, the countervailing influence of dividends may be sufficiently large to offset it during some periods, but when it is not, early exercise of a put may in general be optimal at any time.[10,11]

In most relevant situations, the optimal exercise policy for a put will have the following form. At each instant there will be a critical stock price, $\overline{S}$, such that if $S \le \overline{S}$, the put should be exercised immediately. Hence $\overline{S}$ is the maximum stock price at which immediate exercise would be optimal (the optimal exercise boundary). Like the corresponding boundary for calls, it will depend on all of the variables that affect the value of a put except the current stock price. Proposition 4(b) then implies that $\overline{S}(t, K_2) \ge \overline{S}(t, K_1)$ if $K_2 > K_1$ and that $\overline{S}(t_2, K) \ge \overline{S}(t_1, K)$ if $t_2 > t_1$. Note that this compares the optimal exercise boundary of puts with different times to expiration on a given calendar date. It does not say that, for any given put, the optimal exercise boundary cannot decrease as its time to expiration decreases through changes in the calendar date.

In fact, in many situations of practical importance, the optimal exercise boundary for a given put will behave in the following way as time passes. The boundary drops to zero just before an ex-dividend date and then, immediately after the ex-dividend date, it jumps upward to a level greater than it had just after the previous ex-dividend date. If this is not the last ex-dividend date, the boundary then starts declining again toward zero. If it is the last one, the boundary begins to increase, and actually rises to K as the time to expiration goes to zero. The put should be exercised immediately if the current stock price ever drops below this boundary. In this

---

[10] On the other hand, the potential loss from missing the optimal exercise time will be much smaller with a put than with a call. To see this, compare someone who owns a put and has a long position in the stock with someone who owns a call and has a short position in the stock. If both miss the optimal exercise time by one day, the call owner could lose up to the entire amount of the dividend, while the put owner could lose at most only one day's interest on the striking price.

[11] The important role of interest rates in all of these propositions can be appreciated by noting that if interest rates were always negative, rather than always positive as we have assumed, our conclusions about optimal early exercise would be completely different. In that case, the owner of a call would prefer to pay the striking price sooner rather than later, and the owner of a put would prefer to receive the striking price later rather than sooner. Then it would never be optimal to exercise a put before the expiration date, and early exercise for a call could in general be optimal at any time, rather than only just before ex-dividend dates. If the real rate of interest is negative, then these conclusions would be relevant for an option contract with a payoff indexed for inflation.

case, an American put should either be exercised before expiration or not at all. However, if commissions are included, they will often more than offset the slight advantage from exercising near the expiration date. In Chapter 5 we will give an explicit example of the optimal exercise strategy for puts as well as calls.

4-3. FURTHER RESULTS ON THE RELATIONSHIP BETWEEN PUTS AND CALLS

In Chapter 2, we developed the put-call parity relationship for payout-protected and unprotected European options with certain dividends. Here we extend this analysis to American options and uncertain dividends.

Proposition 1 restates one of our previous results.

Proposition 1 (payout-protected European options): The value of a payout-protected European put equals

1. the price of an otherwise identical call
2. minus the stock price
3. plus the present value of the common striking price:

$$P = C - S + Kr^{-t}.$$

Proposition 2 generalizes the result of Chapter 2 for certain dividends to include uncertain dividends. The steps used to profit from a violation of this condition are very similar to those given in that chapter.

Proposition 2 (unprotected European options): The value of an unprotected European put is never *less than*

1. the price of an otherwise identical call
2. minus the stock price
3. plus the present value of the common striking price
4. plus the present value of the *minimum* dividends that will be paid during the remaining life of the option,

and the value of the put is never *greater than* the sum of (1), (2), (3), and

4'. plus the present value of the *maximum* dividends that will be paid during the remaining life of the option:

$$C - S + Kr^{-t} + D^+ \geq P \geq C - S + Kr^{-t} + D^-.$$

Next we state the new proposition for payout-protected American options.

Proposition 3 (payout-protected American options): The value of a payout-protected American put is never *less than*

1. the price of an otherwise identical call
2. minus the stock price
3. plus the *present value* of the common striking price,

and the value of the put is never *greater than* the sum of (1), (2), and

3'. plus the common striking price:

$$C - S + K \geq P \geq C - S + Kr^{-t}.$$

Proof: First, we prove the lower boundary restriction $P > C - S + Kr^{-t}$ and, second, we prove the upper boundary restriction $P < C - S + K$. Suppose initially that the stock will pay no dividends during the life of the options. If $P < C - S + Kr^{-t}$, buy the put, write the call, buy the stock, and borrow Kr^{-t} by selling default-free zero-coupon bonds with time t until maturity. This nets a positive amount now. If the written call is not exercised against you before expiration, hold the put until expiration and experience no further gain or loss. If, instead, the call is exercised with time t' remaining, deliver the stock and receive K. Use this to pay off the loan and have amount $K - Kr^{-t'}$ left over. Moreover, you still own the put, which has a positive value.

If $P > C - S + K$, then write the put, buy the call, sell the stock short, and place the amount K in a savings account. This gives you a positive amount now. If the put you sold is exercised on or before the expiration date, withdraw the amount K from the loan and pay that in return for the stock. Use the stock received to close out the short sale. You then still have the call and the accumulated interest from the savings account. Hence, if there are no arbitrage opportunities, $C - S + K \geq P \geq C - S + Kr^{-t}$. Since payout-protected options have the same value for any dividend policy as they would have if the stock paid no dividends, this conclusion holds for them as well. *End of proof.*

The lower boundary restriction for payout-protected American options follows immediately from Proposition 1 and our earlier result that an American option is at least as valuable as an otherwise identical European option. However, while the upper and lower boundaries (in terms of a call) for payout-protected European puts are the same, the upper boundary is higher for American puts. This results from the loss in accumulated interest from the arbitrage strategy if the written put is exercised before the expiration date.

Finally, our most general proposition gives boundaries for unprotected American options.

Proposition 4 (unprotected American options): The value of an unprotected American put is never *less than*

1. the price of an otherwise identical call
2. minus the stock price
3. plus the present value of the striking price,

and the value of the put is never *greater than* the sum of (1), (2), and

3'. plus the common striking price
4'. plus the present value of the *maximum* dividends that will be paid during the remaining life of the option:

$$C - S + K + D^+ \geq P \geq C - S + Kr^{-t}.$$

Proof: First, we prove the upper boundary restriction $P < C - S + K + D^+$ and, second, we prove the lower boundary restriction $P > C - S + Kr^{-t}$. If $P > C - S + K + D^+$, write the put, buy the call, sell the stock short, buy D^+, and place K in a savings account. This nets a positive amount now. As you hold this position, liquidate D^+ as required to make restitution for dividends paid to the stock while it is held short. If the short position is closed before expiration or if less than the maximum dividends is actually paid, you will have some money left over from this source. If the put is not exercised early, continue to hold the call and the short stock position and close the entire position without loss at the expiration date. On the other hand, if the put is exercised before the expiration date, withdraw the amount K from the savings account and pay for the stock. Use the stock received to close out the short sale. You still have the call, the accumulated interest on K, and the unused portion of D^+.

If $P < C - S + Kr^{-t}$, buy the put, write the call, buy the stock, and borrow Kr^{-t} by selling zero-coupon bonds with time t until maturity. This gives you a positive amount now. If the call you sold is not exercised early, hold your entire position until the expiration date and invest the dividends you receive in a savings account. At the expiration date you can close out the position with no further gain or loss, and you still have the dividends and the interest they have accumulated.

On the other hand, if the call is exercised before the expiration date, then deliver the stock and receive K. Use K to buy back the bonds. Since interest rates are always positive, there will always be enough to do this, and there may be a positive amount left over. In addition, you still have the put as well as the dividends received in the meantime and their accumulated interest. *End of proof.*

If we had additional information about interest rate movements, over and above what we have assumed so far, then we could strengthen Proposition 4 to:

$$C - S + X \geq P \geq C - S + Y.$$

Here X is the largest amount which could be obtained by selling a portfolio that could always be repurchased with the funds received from two sources: (1) the amount K, received at any time τ before the expiration date, and (2) the dividends paid to the stock before time τ. Y is the smallest amount necessary to purchase a portfolio which will always be sufficient to meet these two obligations: (1) the amount K, demanded at any time τ before the expiration date, and (2) restitution for any dividends paid to the stock before time τ. If we know only that all future interest rates must be positive, then this is equivalent to the conditions stated in Proposition 4.

It is not difficult to generalize the arbitrage restrictions in this chapter to incorporate transactions costs, differences between borrowing and lending rates, margin requirements, and taxes. Transactions costs and borrowing and lending rate differentials widen the band within which a put option can trade relative to a call, without creating a riskless arbitrage opportunity. For example, since enforcement of the lower (upper) boundary requires borrowing (lending), it may be restated in terms of the borrowing (lending) rate of interest.

For any given investor, the relevance of these amendments will depend on the portfolio she is already holding. For example, if she is already lending, to take advantage of a violation of the lower boundary it will be unnecessary to borrow at a higher rate, since she can simply reduce her lending. If she is already holding stock in her portfolio, she can save the transactions costs involved in buying stock to initiate an arbitrage position enforcing the lower boundary. These considerations imply that puts and calls will typically trade within the boundaries of Proposition 4, since if they stray outside these boundaries, arbitrage opportunities will exist for many individual investors as well as professional traders.

Margin requirements, by themselves, will not alter Propositions 1–4 if an investor is allowed to earn interest on margin deposits. However, as we have discussed before, public investors usually lose the interest from the proceeds of short sales. Although this convention affects the upper boundary for European options, it will not affect the boundaries for American options. The lower boundary is not affected because its enforcement does not require short selling. The American upper boundary is not affected even though its enforcement entails shorting stock against a written put. This is because the investor must be prepared to have the written put exercised against her immediately, in which case she could not count on earning any interest from the proceeds of the short sale, even if she were allowed to do so.

Since early exercise is not possible for European options, their upper boundary would be affected. However, if shorting stock is particularly disadvantageous, there may be other strategies to profit from relative put-call mispricing. One possibility is a "box combination" in which a put and a call are written and a different put and call are bought, all on the same underlying stock.

For American options, the net effect of the short sale convention may reduce the incentive for investors to sell puts near the upper boundary, particularly when early put exercise seems unlikely.[12] As a result, it should be easier for American puts to trade nearer their upper boundary than their lower boundary.

4-4. SOME RESTRICTIONS ON OPTION VALUES AS A FUNCTION OF THE STOCK PRICE

In this section we cover several topics related to the way option values depend on the price of the underlying stock. First, we give a representative graph of this relationship and analyze its properties. This leads to a discussion of payout-protected options. We mentioned such options a number of times earlier, but we never said exactly how this protection could be achieved; when you read this part of the section, you will see why. Finally, we return to the graph and show how it can be used to indicate the potential profit from a hedged position in the stock.

Many of the relationships between an option price and its major determining variables can be represented by an *option-stock price diagram*. This graphs the option price against its concurrent underlying stock price. We will only illustrate the diagram for options on stocks paying no dividends. Several of the arbitrage relationships developed in Sections 4-1 and 4-2 are represented graphically in Figures 4-5 and 4-6. In Figure 4-5, the

---

[12] NYSE member firms, trading for their own accounts, are an exception. If the shorted stock is borrowed from public accounts they handle, the member firms have full use of the proceeds of their own short sales. We therefore suspect that many of these firms will be the first to invest up to their position limits when market prices violate the upper European boundary.

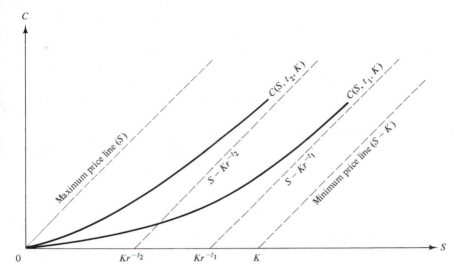

Figure 4-5   Call-Stock Price Diagram

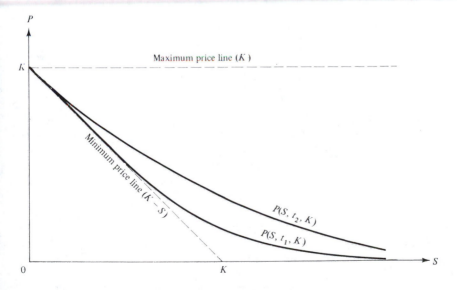

Figure 4-6   Put-Stock Price Diagram

dashed diagonal 45° line labeled S is called the *maximum price line*. The first solid curved line, called an *actual price line*, gives the call value, for varying levels of S, for a call with time to expiration t_2 and striking price K. This is an increasing convex curve starting at $C = 0$ and asymptotically approaching $C = S - Kr^{-t_2}$ as S approaches infinity.[13] Our arbitrage propositions tell us that the curve must always be above the horizontal axis from 0 to Kr^{-t_2} and above the dashed line $S - Kr^{-t_2}$ thereafter. The actual price line to the right illustrates what happens to the call price as time to expiration decreases (that is, $t_2 > t_1$). For every level of stock price S, the call price is lower. Finally, at expiration, when $t = 0$, the call price lies either along the horizontal axis if $S \leq K$, or along the rightmost dashed diagonal line if $S > K$. This is the *minimum price line* for any call. Note that as the expiration date nears, the vertical distance between the actual price line and the minimum price line (the premium over parity) diminishes for each value of S. Figure 4-6 gives the corresponding information for puts.

The option-stock price diagram in Figure 4-5 contains two "arbitrage restrictions" relating to stock price that can be added to those given in Section 4-1:

a. The value of a call can never be less than the value of an *otherwise identical* call with a lower stock price:

$$C(S_2) \geq C(S_1) \qquad \text{if} \quad S_2 > S_1.$$

b. Of three *otherwise identical* calls with stock prices $S_3 > S_2 > S_1$, the value of the middle call is never greater than a weighted average of the values of the extreme calls, where the weights are $(S_3 - S_2)/(S_3 - S_1)$ for the first call and $(S_2 - S_1)/(S_3 - S_1)$ for the third call:

$$C(S_2) \leq \left(\frac{S_3 - S_2}{S_3 - S_1}\right) C(S_1) + \left(\frac{S_2 - S_1}{S_3 - S_1}\right) C(S_3).$$

In comparing calls on different stocks, as we are doing here, the "otherwise identical" condition requires that the relative values of the stocks, one to another, remain constant throughout the life of the options. For example, on the expiration date it must be true that

$$S_1^*/S_1 = S_2^*/S_2 = S_3^*/S_3.$$

For practical purposes, this could occur only if the three underlying stocks were holding companies with identical portfolio composition (for example, index funds on the same index). The proofs of restrictions (a) and (b) are

---

[13] Convex means that a straight line drawn between any two points on the curve never lies below the curve.

very similar to those for the striking price propositions given in Section 4-1, so we will omit them. Restriction (b) also applies to puts, as does restriction (a) when the words "lower stock price" are changed to "higher stock price."

We believe that in any situation of practical importance, the value of a *single* call will also satisfy restrictions (a) and (b) as the stock price is changed, holding other things constant. In other words, except in special circumstances, *the value of a call is an increasing convex function of the stock price*, and hence its graph will have the shape shown in the option-stock price diagram. However, these are not conditions that can be enforced by arbitrage. Restrictions (a) and (b) applied to a single call are true as an empirical fact but not as a logical necessity.[14]

If we wish to compare options with different striking prices, or to continue to examine an option after its striking price has been changed because of a stock split, then we will apparently need more than one option-stock price diagram. However, this is not always true. Sometimes a single diagram will contain all of the necessary information. This simplification is made possible by the following result, which we will state but not prove.

If the stock price, striking price, and cash dividends per share are multiplied by the same positive constant λ, if the distribution of the total rate of return on the stock with the reinvestment of cash dividends is unaffected by this change, and if two otherwise identical options on two stocks having the same distribution of rate of return with reinvestment of cash dividends have the same value, then the value of an option will itself be multiplied by this same constant.[15] Stating this symbolically for calls,

$$C(\lambda S, t, \lambda K) = \lambda C(S, t, K).$$

Care must be taken to ensure that the result is applied correctly. The key point is whether or not the proposed change will affect the distribution of the rate of return on the stock. Let us initially consider two examples where it would not be affected. First, suppose that there is a change in the units in which all monetary values are expressed, say in terms of cents

---

[14] Here is an example that violates both conditions. Assume that $K = \$50$ and, to make things simpler, that interest rates will always be zero. The firm has the following investment policy. As long as the stock price is between $30 and $40, it will invest its assets in a risky project that will give the stock price some probability of doubling in a single jump; however, if the stock price rises above $40 or falls below $30, the firm will invest all of its assets in default-free bonds. When S is in the $30 to $40 range the call obviously has some value, but for $S < \$30$ or $\$40 < S < \$50$ it will be worthless, since there is no way it can finish in-the-money. Consequently, the value of the call is not a convex function of the stock price, and it may decrease as the stock price increases. Some dividend policies can lead to the same result, as can be inferred from footnote 6.

[15] Another way to say this is that the call value is homogeneous of degree one in the stock price, the striking price, and cash dividends per share.

rather than dollars. Then nothing real would change, and all numerical magnitudes, including cash dividends, would be multiplied by 100. After multiplying the numbers on each axis by 100, we could continue to use the same option-stock price diagram.

Now consider a stock split or stock dividend. Again, nothing real about the firm's operations has changed, so if the cash dividend per share is simultaneously adjusted so that the total payout remains the same, as it often would be, the result will be applicable. Suppose, for example, that there is an n for 1 stock split. Then the price per share will change from S to S/n, so $\lambda = 1/n$, and

$$nC(S/n, t, K/n) = C(S, t, K).$$

Thus the standard adjustment correctly protects options from stock splits and dividends. Once again, only a change in the scale of the axes of the diagram is required.

This means that a single diagram will cover these special situations, but what about the more important case of the everyday changes in the stock price arising from real changes in the firm or in the economy? Now there are two problems in applying the result. First, as mentioned earlier, there is no fundamental reason why the distribution of the total rate of return should be unaffected. Second, cash dividends will not necessarily be changed in proportion to the stock price; this would occur only if the firm maintained a constant dividend yield. However, if these conditions are met, the result will apply and the value of an option with any striking price can be obtained from a single option-stock price diagram. In this case, if we let $\lambda = 1/K$, then

$$C(S, t, K) = KC(S/K, t, 1),$$

so all calls can be standardized to options with a striking price of $1 by dividing the option and stock prices by the striking price. In the option-stock price diagram, we could plot C/K or P/K against S/K.

Finally, if the distribution of the rate of return on the stock with reinvestment of cash dividends does not depend on the firm's cash dividend policy, and if two otherwise identical options on stocks having the same distribution have the same value, then these results suggest the way to adjust the terms of an option to protect it against cash dividends. That is, with this adjustment, the value of an option is completely unaffected by the firm's dividend policy. It can be shown that under the hypothesized conditions, the proper adjustment is the following: On each ex-dividend date, replace an option with a striking price of K with $1 + D/S^x$ options, each with a striking price of $K/(1 + D/S^x)$, where D is the dividend and S^x is the ex–dividend stock price. An equivalent adjustment is to multiply the number of shares covered by the option by $1 + D/S^x$ on each ex-dividend date. If the distribution of the rate of return does depend on the firm's dividend policy, then a more complicated adjustment is required. Intuitively, there are two reasons for this. First, changes in dividend policy might then affect the stock price at the time they are announced (not just on the ex-dividend dates) because they convey new information. Second, even with a fixed dividend policy, cash dividend payments would then also affect volatility through their effect on the stock price on ex-dividend dates. Both of these possibilities are ruled out by the hypothesized conditions. To account for them, one would have to know exactly how to value an option in order to determine the proper adjustment. Note that the adjustments described here differ from that made on over-the-counter options, where the striking price is reduced by the amount of the dividend on each ex-dividend date. Consequently, contrary to what is sometimes believed, the over-the-counter adjustment cannot possibly be a universally correct procedure. As a practical matter, however, either the over-the-counter adjustment or the adjustments given here will substantially reduce the impact of cash dividends on option value.

Can we get even more mileage out of a simple option-stock price diagram by using it to compare the values of options on different underlying stocks? No, this is too much to hope for. Option values will also depend at least on the volatility and cash dividends of the stock. The graphs of option price versus stock price for two otherwise identical options on different stocks will not coincide, and there is no way to obtain one from the other.

However, our earlier arguments suggested that if the underlying stocks differ only in their volatilities, then the graph for the option on the more volatile stock should typically be higher than the graph for the option on the less volatile stock. That is, in most situations of practical interest, option values should be nondecreasing functions of volatility. However, like our earlier propositions about the effects of changes in the current stock price, this proposition is true as an empirical fact rather than as a logical necessity, and a violation of the proposition does not provide an arbitrage opportunity.[16]

---

[16] For example, consider a European call option with a zero striking price on a stock that will make one dividend payment before the expiration date. Let $\hat{S}$ be the stock price just before the ex-dividend date and suppose that the amount of the dividend will be $\max[.5(\hat{S} - X), 0]$, where X is a constant. From the appendix to Chapter 2, we know that the current value of the option must be the current stock price minus the current value of the dividends to be paid during the life of the option. But the current value of the dividends is itself one-half of the current value of a call on a stock with a striking price of X and an expiration date just before the ex-dividend date. Consequently, if the current value of this call is an increasing function of the volatility of the stock, then the original call must be a decreasing function of volatility.

Nevertheless, we can obtain some related results with an arbitrage type argument. Suppose that two stocks have the same current value and that options on the two stocks with identical terms also have the same value. Consider now an option, with terms identical to the previous ones, on a portfolio containing one-half share of each of the stocks. Intuition would suggest that because of diversification this portfolio should be less volatile than either of the stocks alone and that the option on the portfolio should not be worth more than either of the options on the individual stocks. In Chapter 8, we show that arbitrage profits are possible if this is not the case.

There is still more information to be obtained from the option-stock price diagrams. In addition to comparing the prices of different calls on the same underlying security, the call-stock price diagram can also be used to indicate the potential profit from a hedged position with the stock. In Figure 4-7, the dashed line, called the *zero-profit line*, indicates the profit for a y/x position ratio (that is, y shares long for x calls written). For example, suppose that $y/x = \frac{1}{3}$, so we start with a position of $y = 1$ share long and $x = 3$ calls written. When the stock price rises by 1 point, if the call moves along the zero-profit line, it would increase by $\frac{1}{3}$ of a point. With 1 share long and 3 calls written, we would break even, since $\$1 \times 1 - \$\frac{1}{3} \times 3 = 0$. Therefore, all points below the zero-profit line represent a profit, and those above, a loss. The intersections of the zero-profit line with the minimum-price line and horizontal axis indicate the stock price range at expiration

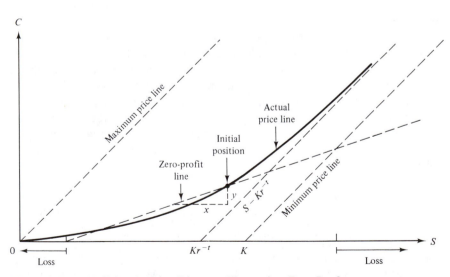

Figure 4-7   Call-Stock Price Diagram Illustrating Zero-Profit Line

over which there is a profit. Of course, this same range can be determined from a payoff diagram.

For the one-to-three hedge, if the stock price moves up (down), then along the actual price line, the hedge shows a loss (profit). If the position ratio is reduced, the zero-profit line will flatten, increasing the sensitivity of the hedge to the stock price. The position ratio which minimizes the loss from small changes in the stock price is described by the zero-profit line tangent to the actual price line (Figure 4-8). We call this a *neutral* hedge.

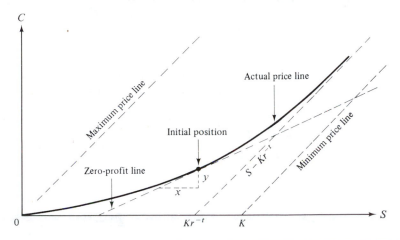

Figure 4-8   Call Stock Price Diagram Illustrating Neutral Hedge

For this hedge, if the stock price moves up or down along the actual price line, the hedge shows a loss in either case. However, in compensation, if the stock price remains unchanged as the expiration date approaches, since the actual price line approaches the minimum-price line, the hedge shows a profit. Neutral positions play a significant role in the development of an exact option pricing formula in Chapter 5, and neutral trading strategies are examined in detail in Chapter 6.

APPENDIX 4A
Arbitrage Restrictions on the Value of Cash Dividends

In this appendix, we will develop some restrictions on $D^+(t, t')$ and $D^-(t, t')$ that must hold if there are to be no arbitrage opportunities. Suppose that there are n ex-dividend dates in the period beginning at time t until expiration and ending at time t' until expiration. Let S_j be the stock price on the jth ex-dividend date and D_j be the corresponding dividend, which may be a function of S_j. If each payment D_j can be bounded above by some constant, then $D^+(t, t')$ is simply the sum of the present values of these constant amounts. The same is true for $D^-(t, t')$ if each payment can be bounded below by some constant.

However, if D_j depends on S_j, which it very well might, it at first appears that these concepts are very imprecise. If S_j can take on arbitrarily high values, it seems that D^+ should also take on arbitrarily high values. Similarly, if S_j could be zero, it seems that D^- should also be zero. However, this is not necessarily the case, and usually very useful bounds can be placed on D^+ and D^- in terms of current stock price, S. This is illustrated in the following proposition.

Dividend Proposition About $D^+(t, t')$: Suppose $D_j \leq a_j S_j$ for all j, where a_j is a positive constant less than or equal to one. Then

$$D^+(t, t') = S\left[1 - \prod_{j=1}^{n}(1 - a_j)\right],$$

where $\prod_{j=1}^{n}(1 - a_j)$ denotes the product

$$(1 - a_1)(1 - a_2) \cdots (1 - a_n).$$

We will demonstrate this by showing that ownership of $[1 - \prod_{j=1}^{n}(1 - a_j)]$ shares of stock is exactly sufficient to duplicate the dividend stream if $D_j = a_j S_j$ for all j. Since D_j is never greater than $a_j S_j$ by assumption, the current value of the dividends cannot then be greater than $S_n[1 - \prod_{j=1}^{n}(1 - a_j)]$. To verify that we could duplicate the dividend stream with $[1 - \prod_{j=1}^{n}(1 - a_j)]$ shares of stock, consider what happens on the first ex-dividend date. For simplicity only, we will assume that the dividend is actually received on this date. Each share of stock will receive a payment of $a_1 S_1$ and the value of each share will drop to $(1 - a_1)S_1$. Your holdings will then be worth $[1 - \prod_{j=1}^{n}(1 - a_j)](1 - a_1)S_1$. You will have received a payment of $[1 - \prod_{j=1}^{n}(1 - a_j)]a_1 S_1$, but to duplicate the payment of $a_1 S_1$, you will have to sell shares worth $a_1 S_1 - [1 - \prod_{j=1}^{n}(1 - a_j)]a_1 S_1$. This leaves you with

$$\left[1 - \prod_{j=1}^{n}(1 - a_j)\right](1 - a_1)S_1 - a_1 S_1 + \left[1 - \prod_{j=1}^{n}(1 - a_j)\right]a_1 S_1$$

$$= (1 - a_1)S_1\left[1 - \prod_{j=2}^{n}(1 - a_j)\right].$$

Continuing in this way verifies the proposition.

A similar argument verifies the corresponding proposition about $D^-(t, t')$.

Dividend Proposition About $D^-(t, t')$: Suppose $D_j \geq b_j S_j$ for all j, where b_j is a positive constant less than or equal to one. Then

$$D^-(t, t') = S\left[1 - \prod_{j=1}^{n}(1 - b_j)\right].$$

---

an exact option pricing formula

5

In the previous chapter, we developed some general propositions about option values. We showed that to prevent profitable riskless arbitrage opportunities, the value of an option must have certain relationships to the following variables:

1. Current stock price
2. Striking price
3. Time to expiration
4. Stock volatility
5. Interest rates
6. Cash dividends

These relationships took the form of inequalities and directional effects of each variable on option value. Only on the expiration date were we able to provide an equality relationship,

$$C = \max[0, S - K] \quad \text{or} \quad P = \max[0, K - S].$$

Prior to expiration, we could only say that the option value must lie within certain boundaries; we were not able to specify an exact formula between C or P and its determining variables.

The purpose of this chapter is to derive and analyze such an exact formula. To get such a precise result, we will now need more information than we did before. The required information characterizes the probability distribution of future stock prices and interest rates. As we will see, obtaining this information is not as formidable a task as it may first seem. It does not require superior forecasting ability, in the sense of being able to beat the market, nor does it require an understanding of the fundamental variables which cause stock prices to change.

Option pricing theory has a long and illustrious history, but it underwent a revolutionary change in 1973. At that time, Fischer Black and Myron Scholes presented the first completely satisfactory equilibrium option pricing model.[1] In the same year, Robert Merton, Professor of Finance at the Massachusetts Institute of Technology, extended their model in several important ways.[2] These path-breaking articles have formed the basis for many subsequent academic studies.

The mathematical tools employed in the Black-Scholes and Merton articles are quite advanced and have tended to obscure the underlying economic principles. Fortunately, William Sharpe, Professor of Finance at Stanford University, discovered a way to derive the same results using only elementary mathematics. His brilliant insight has the additional advantage of clearly showing the basic idea behind the model. In this chapter, we build on Sharpe's method and develop it into a complete model of option pricing.

Although each step in the argument can be easily understood, the length of the derivation may discourage many readers. To provide some motivation, and to illustrate the basic idea, we will first work through a simple numerical example.[3]

5-1. THE BASIC IDEA

Suppose the current price of a stock is $S = \$50$, and at the end of a period of time, its price must be either $S^* = \$25$ or $S^* = \$100$. A call on the stock is available with a striking price of $K = \$50$, expiring at the end of the period. It is also possible to borrow and lend at a 25% rate of interest. The

---

[1] Their celebrated article, "The Pricing of Options and Corporate Liabilities," appeared in the May-June 1973 issue of the *Journal of Political Economy*, pp. 637–659. Fischer Black is now Professor of Finance at the Massachusetts Institute of Technology and Myron Scholes is Professor of Finance at Stanford University.

[2] These results and many others are contained in Robert C. Merton, "Theory of Rational Option Pricing," *Bell Journal of Economics and Management Science*, 4 (Spring 1973), 141–183. Some additional results that are particularly relevant for our approach can be found in Robert C. Merton, "On the Pricing of Contingent Claims and the Modigliani-Miller Theorem," *Journal of Financial Economics*, 5 (November 1977), 241–250.

[3] This chapter draws on an article by John Cox, Stephen Ross, and Mark Rubinstein, "Option Pricing: A Simplified Approach," *Journal of Financial Economics*, 7 (September 1979), 229–263.

one piece of information left unfurnished is the current value of the call, C. However, if profitable riskless arbitrage is not possible, we can deduce from the given information *alone* what the value of the call *must* be!

Consider forming the following levered hedge:

1. Write three calls at C each
2. Buy two shares at $50 each
3. Borrow $40 at 25%, to be paid back at the end of the period

Table 5-1 gives the return from this hedge for each possible level of the stock price at expiration. Regardless of the outcome, the hedge exactly breaks even on the expiration date. Therefore, to prevent profitable riskless arbitrage, the current cash flow from establishing the position must be zero; that is,

$$3C - 100 + 40 = 0.$$

Table 5-1
ARBITRAGE TABLE ILLUSTRATING THE
FORMATION OF A RISKLESS HEDGE

	Current Date	Expiration Date	
		$S^* = 25$	$S^* = 100$
Write 3 calls	$3C$	—	−150
Buy 2 shares	−100	50	200
Borrow	40	−50	−50
Total		—	—

The current value of the call must then be $C = \$20$.

If the call were not priced at $20, a sure profit would be possible. In particular, if $C = \$25$, the hedge in Table 5-1 would yield a current amount of $15 and would experience no further gain or loss in the future. On the other hand, if $C = \$15$, then the same thing could be accomplished by buying three calls, selling short two shares, and lending $40.

Table 5-1 can be interpreted as demonstrating that *an appropriately levered position in stock will replicate the future returns of a call.* That is, if we buy shares and borrow against them in the right proportion, we can, in effect, duplicate a pure position in calls. In view of this, it should seem less surprising that all we needed to determine the *exact* value of the call was its *striking price, underlying stock price, range of movement in the underlying stock price, and the rate of interest.* What may seem more incredible is what we do not need to know: Among other things, *we do not need to know the probability that the stock price will rise or fall.* Bulls and bears must agree on the value of the call, relative to its underlying stock price.[4]

This example is very simple, but it shows several essential features of option pricing. And we will soon see that it is not as unrealistic as it seems.

5-2. BINOMIAL RANDOM WALKS

Before we can derive an exact formula, we will need to develop some elementary statistical concepts. Suppose you play a game of chance in which, on n successive turns, you draw a single ball from an opaque urn containing 100 balls, of which k are black and $100 - k$ are red. After each drawing, you replace the ball drawn, so you always draw from an urn of the same composition. According to the rules, you can bet only at the beginning of the game. Thereafter, for every \$1 initially bet, you receive on each turn \$$u$ for every dollar accumulated up to then if you draw a black ball and \$$d$ if you draw a red ball, where $u > d$. To try it out, you decide to bet \$1.00. For this case, the possible outcomes after each of the first four drawings are represented in the following tree diagram:

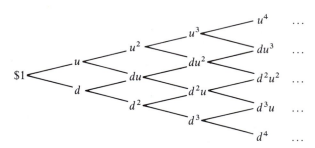

For example, if $u = 1.1$ and $d = .9$, if you were fortunate to draw four black balls in a row, your bet would have grown to $u^4 = (1.1)^4 \approx \$1.46$. On the other hand, had you drawn a black followed by two reds and a black, you would have accumulated $uddu = u^2 d^2 = (1.1)^2(.9)^2 \approx \$0.98$, netting you a 2¢ loss.

A first step in analyzing this game is counting, for a given total number of drawings n, the number of each possible outcome. If $n = 0$ (that is, you decide not to play and keep your dollar), you have one outcome of \$1; if $n = 1$, you have one d outcome and one u outcome; if $n = 2$, you have one d^2, two ud, and one u^2; and so on. A convenient way to represent these

---

[4] This provides an example of our earlier observation that the expected rate of growth of the stock price may not be a direct determinant of option value.

results is in the following array, known as Pascal's Triangle:

j / n	0	1	2	3	4	5	6	...
0	1							
1	1	1						
2	1	2	1					
3	1	3	3	1				
4	1	4	6	4	1			
5	1	5	10	10	5	1		
6	1	6	15	20	15	6	1	...
⋮			⋮					

For example, row $n = 4$ represents one d^4, four ud^3, six u^2d^2, four u^3d, and one u^4. From the tree diagram, it is easily confirmed that this is the correct enumeration. Observe that an interior number in any row can be generated by summing the two numbers above and to the left in the row immediately above it. The sum of the numbers in each row is 2^n. Most important, there is a formula for representing any element in the array in terms of its row and column numbers (n, j):

$$\frac{n!}{j!(n - j)!},$$

where $n! \equiv n \cdot (n - 1) \cdot (n - 2) \cdots 3 \cdot 2 \cdot 1$.[5] The numbers in the triangle are called binomial coefficients because they appear in the algebraic expansion of $(a + b)^n$.

Let us represent the outcome after n drawings as X_n. For example, if $n = 3$, then $X_3 = d^3, ud^2, u^2d$, or u^3. More generally,

$$X_n = d^n, ud^{n-1}, u^2d^{n-2}, \ldots, u^{n-2}d^2, u^{n-1}d, \quad \text{or} \quad u^n,$$

or, equivalently, $X_n = u^jd^{n-j}$ for $j = 0, 1, 2, \ldots, n$. Since we do not know in advance what value X_n will have for each drawing $n > 0$, we call X_n a *stochastic process*.

Since the urn contains exactly k black balls and $100 - k$ red balls at every drawing, the chance of drawing a black ball is $q \equiv k/100$, which we call the *probability* of a black ball. $1 - q \equiv (100 - k)/100$ is the probability of drawing a red ball. The probability q satisfies $0 \leq q \leq 1$ and the sum of the probabilities of each possibility, u and d, equals 1.

---

[5] $0! \equiv 1$.

In general, the probability q at any drawing n can depend on at least two things:

1. The number of previous drawings: $n - 1$
2. The sequence of previous outcomes: $X_0, X_1, ..., X_{n-1}$

For example, (1) would be true if we knew at the start of the game that $q = \frac{1}{2}$ at drawing $n = 10$ and $q = \frac{1}{4}$ at drawing $n = 13$; (1) would be false if $q = \frac{1}{3}$ for every drawing n; (2) would be true if, after a sequence d, d, and d in the first three drawings, the probability of u in the fourth were greater than if it were instead preceded by the sequence u, u, and u. For our game, q does not depend on (1) or (2). In other words, for every drawing, the urn has the same composition. For that reason, the stochastic process X_n is said to follow a *stationary multiplicative random walk*. Equivalently, we say the successive outcomes $(X_1/X_0), (X_2/X_1), ..., (X_n/X_{n-1})$ are independently and identically distributed.

Since successive drawings have this property, the outcomes for $n = 2$ of d^2, du, ud, and u^2 have associated accumulated probabilities of $(1 - q)^2$, $(1 - q)q$, $q(1 - q)$, and q^2. Observe that whatever the value of q, each accumulated probability is between 0 and 1, and their sum $(1 - q)^2 + 2q(1 - q) + q^2 = 1$. In general, the probability of any *one sequence* containing j drawings of black balls and $n - j$ red balls is $q^j(1 - q)^{n-j}$. Since there are exactly $n!/[j!(n - j)!]$ ways of this occurring, the probability of outcome X_n is

$$\left(\frac{n!}{j!(n-j)!} \right) q^j (1 - q)^{n-j}.$$

Moreover,[6]

$$\sum_{j=0}^{n} \left(\frac{n!}{j!(n-j)!} \right) q^j (1 - q)^{n-j} = 1.$$

For a given $j = a$, what is the probability that $X_n \geq u^a d^{n-a}$? Since $u^j d^{n-j}$ increases as j increases, we have

$$\Phi[a; n, q] \equiv \sum_{j=a}^{n} \left(\frac{n!}{j!(n-j)!} \right) q^j (1 - q)^{n-j},$$

the *complementary binomial distribution function*.

---

[6] $\sum$ is a shorthand notation for summation. For example,

$$\sum_{j=0}^{n} x_j \equiv x_0 + x_1 + x_2 + \cdots + x_n.$$

5-3. THE BINOMIAL OPTION PRICING FORMULA

In this section, we will develop the framework illustrated in the example into a complete valuation method. We begin by assuming that the stock price follows a multiplicative binomial process over discrete periods. The movement of the stock price will thus be essentially the same as the simple game described in the previous section. The rate of return on the stock over each period can have two possible values: $u - 1$, with probability q, or $d - 1$, with probability $1 - q$. For the moment, we assume the stock pays no dividends. If the current stock price is S, the stock price at the end of the period will thus be either uS or dS. We can represent this movement with the following diagram:

$$
S \begin{cases} uS & \text{with probability } q \\ \\ dS & \text{with probability } 1 - q. \end{cases}
$$

We also assume that the interest rate is constant and positive. To focus on the basic issues, we will continue to assume that there are no taxes, transaction costs, or margin requirements. Hence, individuals are allowed to sell short any security and receive full use of the proceeds.[7] Furthermore, we assume that markets are competitive: A single individual can buy or sell as much of any security as he wishes without affecting its price.

Letting r denote one plus the interest rate over one period, we require $u > r > d$. If these inequalities did not hold, there would be profitable riskless arbitrage opportunities involving only the stock and riskless borrowing and lending.[8] For example, if $u > d > r$, an investor could make a certain profit on no investment by borrowing at r and buying the stock.

To see how to value a call on this stock, we start with the simplest situation: The expiration date is just one period away. Let C be the current value of the call, C_u be its value at the end of the period if the stock price goes to uS, and C_d be its value at the end of the period if the stock price goes to dS. Since there is now only one period remaining in the life of the call, we know that the terms of its contract and a rational exercise policy imply that $C_u = \max[0, uS - K]$ and $C_d = \max[0, dS - K]$. Therefore,

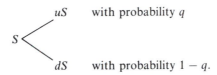

$$
C \begin{cases} C_u = \max[0, uS - K] & \text{with probability } q \\ \\ C_d = \max[0, dS - K] & \text{with probability } 1 - q. \end{cases}
$$

---

[7] Of course, restitution is required for payouts made to securities held short.

[8] We will ignore the uninteresting special case where q is zero or one and $u = d = r$.

Suppose we form a portfolio containing Δ shares of stock and the dollar amount B in riskless bonds.[9] This will cost $S\Delta + B$. At the end of the period, the value of this portfolio will be

$$S\Delta + B \begin{cases} uS\Delta + rB & \text{with probability } q \\ \\ dS\Delta + rB & \text{with probability } 1 - q. \end{cases}$$

Since we can select Δ and B in any way we wish, suppose we choose them to equate the end-of-period values of the portfolio and the call for each possible outcome. This requires that

$$uS\Delta + rB = C_u,$$
$$dS\Delta + rB = C_d.$$

Solving these equations, we find

$$\Delta = \frac{C_u - C_d}{(u - d)S}, \tag{1}$$
$$B = \frac{uC_d - dC_u}{(u - d)r}.$$

With Δ and B chosen in this way, we have what we referred to in Section 2-3 as an *equivalent portfolio*.

If there are to be no riskless arbitrage opportunities, the current value of the call, C, cannot be less than the current value of the equivalent portfolio, $S\Delta + B$. If it were, we could make a riskless profit with no net investment by buying the call and selling the portfolio. It is tempting to say that it also cannot be worth more, since then we would have a riskless arbitrage opportunity by reversing our procedure and selling the call and buying the portfolio. But this overlooks the fact that the person who bought the call we sold has the right to exercise it immediately.

Suppose that $S\Delta + B < S - K$. If we try to make an arbitrage profit by selling calls for more than $S\Delta + B$, but less than $S - K$, then we will soon find that we are the source of arbitrage profits rather than their recipient. Anyone could make an arbitrage profit by buying our calls and exercising them immediately.

We might hope that we will be spared this embarrassment because everyone will somehow find it advantageous to hold the calls for one more period as an investment rather than take a quick profit by exercising them

---

[9] Buying bonds is the same as lending; selling them is the same as borrowing.

immediately. But each person will reason in the following way. If I do not exercise now, I will receive the same payoff as a portfolio of Δ shares of stock and B in bonds. If I do exercise now, I can take the proceeds, $S - K$, buy this same portfolio and some extra bonds as well, and have a higher payoff in every possible circumstance. Consequently, no one would be willing to hold the calls for one more period.

Summing up all of this, we conclude that if there are to be no riskless arbitrage opportunities, it must be true that

$$C = S\Delta + B$$
$$= \frac{C_u - C_d}{u - d} + \frac{uC_d - dC_u}{(u - d)r}$$
$$= \left[\left(\frac{r - d}{u - d} \right)C_u + \left(\frac{u - r}{u - d} \right)C_d \right] \Big/ r \tag{2}$$

if this value is greater than $S - K$, and if not, $C = S - K$.[10]

Equation (2) can be simplified by defining $p \equiv (r - d)/(u - d)$, so that $1 - p = (u - r)/(u - d)$ and we can write

$$C = [pC_u + (1 - p)C_d]/r. \tag{3}$$

It is easy to see that in the present case, with no dividends, this will always be greater than $S - K$ as long as the interest rate is positive.[11] Hence, Equation (3) is the exact formula for the value of a call one period prior to expiration in terms of S, K, u, d, and r.

This formula has a number of notable features. First, the probability q does not appear in the formula. This means, surprisingly, that even if different investors have different subjective probabilities about an upward or downward movement in the stock, they could still agree on the relationship of C to S and r.

Second, the value of the call does not depend on investors' attitudes toward risk. In constructing the formula, the only assumption we made about an individual's behavior was that he prefers more wealth to less wealth and therefore has an incentive to take advantage of profitable riskless arbitrage opportunities. We would obtain the same formula whether investors are risk averse or risk preferring.

---

[10] Our discussion could be easily modified to include European calls. Since immediate exercise is then precluded, their value would always be given by Equation (2), even if this is less than $S - K$.

[11] To confirm this, note that if $uS \leq K$, then $S < K$ and $C = 0$, so $C > S - K$. Also if $dS \geq K$, then $C = S - (K/r) > S - K$. The remaining possibility is $uS > K > dS$. In this case, $C = p(uS - K)/r$. This is greater than $S - K$ if $(1 - p)dS < (r - p)K$, which is certainly true as long as $r > 1$.

Third, the only random variable on which the call value depends is the stock price itself. In particular, it does not depend on the random prices of other securities or portfolios, such as the market portfolio containing all securities in the economy. If another pricing formula involving other variables was submitted as giving equilibrium market prices, we could immediately show that it was incorrect by using our formula to make riskless arbitrage profits while trading at those prices.

It is easier to understand these features if it is remembered that the formula is only a relative pricing relationship giving C in terms of S, u, d, and r. Investors' attitudes toward risk and the characteristics of other assets may indeed influence call values indirectly, through their effect on these variables, but they will not be separate determinants of call value.

Finally, observe that $p \equiv (r - d)/(u - d)$ is always greater than zero and less than one, so it has the properties of a probability. In fact p is the value q would have in equilibrium if investors were risk neutral.[12] To see this, note that the expected rate of return on the stock, which is the sum of each possible rate of return times its probability of occurring, would then be the riskless interest rate, so

$$q(uS) + (1 - q)(dS) = rS$$

and $q = (r - d)/(u - d) = p$. Hence, the value of the call can be interpreted as the expectation of its discounted future value in a risk-neutral world.[13] In light of our earlier observations, this is not surprising. Since the formula does not involve q or any measure of attitudes toward risk, then it must be the same for any set of preferences, including risk neutrality.

It is important to note that this does not imply that the equilibrium expected rate of return on the call is the riskless interest rate. Indeed, our argument has shown that, in equilibrium, holding the call over the period is exactly equivalent to holding the equivalent portfolio. Consequently, the risk and expected rate of return of the call must be the same as that of the equivalent portfolio. As we will show in Section 5-5, $\Delta \geq 0$ and $B \leq 0$, so the equivalent portfolio is a particular levered long position in the stock. In equilibrium, the same is true for the call. Of course, if the call is currently mispriced, its risk and expected return over the period will differ from that of the equivalent portfolio.

A different interpretation of p and the valuation formula may also be helpful. In Chapter 8, we show that p/r is the value of a claim that will pay

---

[12] We define a *risk-neutral investor* to be one who is indifferent between an investment with a certain rate of return and another investment with an uncertain rate of return which has the same expected value. He neither insists on being paid for bearing risk nor is he willing to pay others to let him bear risk.

[13] This property was first noted by John Cox and Stephen Ross in "The Valuation of Options for Alternative Stochastic Processes," *Journal of Financial Economics*, 3 (January–March 1976), 145–166.

one dollar at the end of the period if and only if the stock price moves to uS. Similarly, $(1 - p)/r$ is the value of a claim that will pay one dollar if and only if the stock price moves to dS. The payoff to a call is equivalent to that of a package containing C_u units of the first claim and C_d units of the second claim, so its value should be $[C_u(p/r)] + [C_d(1 - p)/r]$, which is exactly Equation (3).

Now we can consider the next simplest situation: a call with two periods remaining before its expiration date. In keeping with the binomial process, the stock can take on three possible values after two periods:

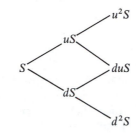

Similarly, for the call,

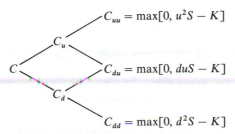

C_{uu} stands for the value of a call two periods from the current time if the stock price moves upward each period; C_{du} and C_{dd} have analogous definitions.

At the end of the current period there will be one period left in the life of the call and we will be faced with a problem identical to the one we just solved. Thus, from our previous analysis, we know that when there are two periods left,

$$C_u = [pC_{uu} + (1 - p)C_{ud}]/r \tag{4a}$$

and

$$C_d = [pC_{du} + (1 - p)C_{dd}]/r. \tag{4b}$$

Again we can select a portfolio of $S\Delta$ in stock and B in bonds whose end-of-period value will be C_u if the stock price goes to uS and C_d if the stock price goes to dS. Indeed, the functional form of Δ and B remains unchanged. To get the new values of Δ and B, we simply use Equation (1) with the new values of C_u and C_d.

Can we now say, as before, that an opportunity for profitable riskless arbitrage will be available if the current price of the call is not equal to the new value of this portfolio or $S - K$, whichever is greater? Yes, but there is an important difference. With one period to go, we could plan to lock in a riskless profit by selling an overpriced call and using part of the proceeds to buy the equivalent portfolio. At the end of the period, we knew that the market price of the call must have been equal to the value of the portfolio, so the entire position could have been safely liquidated at that point. But this was true only because the end of the period was the expiration date. Now we have no such guarantee. At the end of the current period, when there is still one period left, the market price of the call could still be in disequilibrium and be greater than the value of the equivalent portfolio. If we closed out the position then, selling the portfolio and repurchasing the call, we could suffer a loss that would more than offset our original profit. However, we could always avoid this loss by maintaining the portfolio for one more period. The value of the portfolio at the end of the current period will always be exactly sufficient to purchase the portfolio we would want to hold over the last period. In effect, we would have to readjust the proportions in the equivalent portfolio, but we would not have to put up any more money.

Consequently, we conclude that even with two periods to go, there is a strategy we could follow that would guarantee riskless profits with no net investment if the current market price of a call differs from the maximum of $S\Delta + B$ and $S - K$. Hence, the larger of these is the current value of the call.

Since Δ and B have the same functional form in each period, the current value of the call in terms of C_u and C_d will again be $C = [pC_u + (1 - p)C_d]/r$ if this is greater than $S - K$, and $C = S - K$ otherwise. By substituting from Equation (4) into the former expression, and noting that $C_{du} = C_{ud}$, we obtain

$$
\begin{aligned}
C &= [p^2 C_{uu} + 2p(1 - p)C_{ud} + (1 - p)^2 C_{dd}]/r^2 \\
&= \{p^2 \max[0, u^2 S - K] + 2p(1 - p) \max[0, duS - K] \\
&\quad + (1 - p)^2 \max[0, d^2 S - K]\}/r^2.
\end{aligned}
\tag{5}
$$

A little algebra shows that this is always greater than $S - K$ if, as assumed, r is always greater than one, so this expression gives the exact value of the call.[14]

---

[14] In the current situation, with no dividends, we know from Chapter 4 that the call should not be exercised before the expiration date. In the general case, with dividends, this is no longer true, and we must use the procedure of checking every period.

All of the observations made about Equation (3) also apply to Equation (5), except that the number of periods remaining until expiration, n, now emerges clearly as an additional determinant of the call value. For Equation (5), $n = 2$. That is, the full list of variables determining C is S, K, n, u, d, and r.

We now have a recursive procedure for finding the value of a call with any number of periods to go. By starting at the expiration date and working backwards, we can write down the general valuation formula for any n:

$$C = \left\{ \sum_{j=0}^{n} \left(\frac{n!}{j!(n-j)!} \right) p^j (1-p)^{n-j} \max[0, u^j d^{n-j} S - K] \right\} \bigg/ r^n. \qquad (6)$$

This gives us the complete formula, but with a little additional effort we can express it in a more convenient way.

Let a stand for the minimum number of upward moves that the stock must make over the next n periods for the call to finish in-the-money. Thus a will be the smallest nonnegative integer such that $u^a d^{n-a} S > K$. By taking the natural logarithm of both sides of this inequality, we can write a as the smallest nonnegative integer greater than $\log(K/Sd^n)/\log(u/d)$.

For all $j < a$, $\max[0, u^j d^{n-j} S - K] = 0$ and for all $j \geq a$, $\max[0, u^j d^{n-j} S - K] = u^j d^{n-j} S - K$. Therefore,

$$C = \left\{ \sum_{j=a}^{n} \left(\frac{n!}{j!(n-j)!} \right) p^j (1-p)^{n-j} [u^j d^{n-j} S - K] \right\} \bigg/ r^n.$$

Of course, if $a > n$, the call will finish out-of-the-money even if the stock moves upward every period, so its current value must be zero.

By breaking up C into two terms, we can write

$$C = S \left[\sum_{j=a}^{n} \left(\frac{n!}{j!(n-j)!} \right) p^j (1-p)^{n-j} \left(\frac{u^j d^{n-j}}{r^n} \right) \right]$$

$$- Kr^{-n} \left[\sum_{j=a}^{n} \left(\frac{n!}{j!(n-j)!} \right) p^j (1-p)^{n-j} \right].$$

Now, the latter bracketed expression is the complementary binomial distribution function $\Phi[a; n, p]$. The first bracketed expression can also be interpreted as a complementary binomial distribution function $\Phi[a; n, p']$, where

$$p' \equiv (u/r)p \qquad \text{and} \qquad 1 - p' = (d/r)(1-p).$$

p' is a probability, since $0 < p' < 1$. To see this, note that $p < (r/u)$ and

$$p^j(1 - p)^{n-j}\left(\frac{u^j d^{n-j}}{r^n}\right) = [(u/r)p]^j[(d/r)(1 - p)]^{n-j} = p'^j(1 - p')^{n-j}.$$

We can summarize our development of the Sharpe binomial method up to this point in the following formula:

BINOMIAL OPTION PRICING FORMULA

$$C = S\Phi[a; n, p'] - Kr^{-n}\Phi[a; n, p]$$

where

$$p \equiv (r - d)/(u - d) \quad \text{and} \quad p' \equiv (u/r)p$$
$a \equiv$ the smallest nonnegative integer greater than

$$\log(K/Sd^n)/\log(u/d).$$

If $a > n$, $C = 0$.

It is now clear that all of the comments we made about the one-period valuation formula are valid for any number of periods. In particular, the value of a call should be the expectation, in a risk-neutral world, of the discounted value of the payoff it will receive. In fact, that is exactly what Equation (6) says. Why, then, should we waste time with the recursive procedure when we can write down the answer in one direct step? The reason is that while this one-step approach is always technically correct, it is really useful only if we know in advance the circumstances in which a rational individual would prefer to exercise the call before the expiration date. If we do not know this, we have no way to compute the required expectation. In the present example, a call on a stock paying no dividends, it happens that we can determine this information from other sources: The call should never be exercised before the expiration date. As we will see in Section 5-9, with puts or with calls on stocks which pay dividends, we will not be so lucky. Finding the optimal exercise strategy will be an integral part of the valuation problem. The full recursive procedure will then be necessary.

5-4. RISKLESS TRADING STRATEGIES

The following numerical example illustrates how we could use the formula if the current *market price M* ever diverged from its *formula value C*. If

$M > C$, we would hedge, and if $M < C$, "reverse hedge," to try and lock in a profit. Suppose the values of the underlying variables are

$$S = 80, \quad n = 3, \quad K = 80, \quad u = 1.5, \quad d = .5, \quad r = 1.1.$$

In this case, $p = (r - d)/(u - d) = .6$. The relevant values of the discount factor are

$$r^{-1} = .909, \qquad r^{-2} = .826, \qquad r^{-3} = .751.$$

The paths the stock price may follow and their corresponding probabilities (using probability p) are:

When $n = 3$, with $S = 80$,

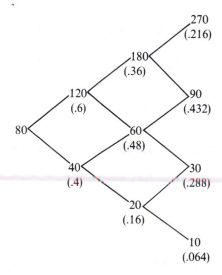

When $n = 2$, if $S = 120$,

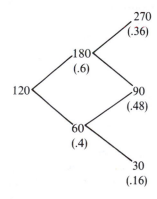

When $n = 2$, if $S = 40$,

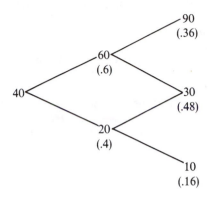

Using the formula, the current value of the call would be

$$C = .751[.064(0) + .288(0) + .432(90 - 80) + .216(270 - 80)] = 34.065.$$

Recall that to form a riskless hedge, for each call we sell, we buy and subsequently keep adjusted a portfolio containing $S\Delta$ in stock and B in bonds, where $\Delta = (C_u - C_d)/(u - d)S$. The following tree diagram gives the paths the call value may follow and the corresponding values of Δ:

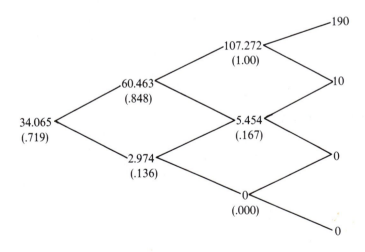

With this preliminary analysis, we are prepared to use the formula to take advantage of mispricing in the market. Suppose that when $n = 3$, the market price of the call is 36. Our formula tells us the call should be worth

34.065. The option is overpriced, so we could plan to sell it and assure ourselves of a profit equal to the mispricing differential. Here are the steps you could take for a typical path the stock might follow.

STEP 1 ($n = 3$): Sell the call for 36. Take 34.065 of this and invest it in a portfolio containing $\Delta = .719$ shares of stock by borrowing $.719(80) - 34.065 = 23.455$. Take the remainder, $36 - 34.065 = 1.935$, and put it in the bank.

STEP 2 ($n = 2$): Suppose the stock goes to 120 so that the new Δ is .848. Buy $.848 - .719 = .129$ more shares of stock at 120 per share for a total expenditure of 15.480. Borrow to pay the bill. With an interest rate of .1, you already owe $23.455(1.1) = 25.801$. Thus, your total current indebtedness is $25.801 + 15.480 = 41.281$.

STEP 3 ($n = 1$): Suppose the stock price now goes to 60. The new Δ is .167. Sell $.848 - .167 = .681$ shares at 60 per share, taking in $.681(60) = 40.860$. Use this to pay back part of your borrowing. Since you now owe $41.281(1.1) = 45.409$, the repayment will reduce this to $45.409 - 40.860 = 4.549$.

STEP 4d ($n = 0$): Suppose the stock price now goes to 30. The call you sold has expired worthless. You own .167 shares of stock selling at 30 per share, for a total value of $.167(30) = 5$. Sell the stock and repay the $4.549(1.1) = 5$ that you now owe on the borrowing. Go back to the bank and withdraw your original deposit, which has now grown to $1.935(1.1)^3 = 2.575$.

STEP 4u ($n = 0$): Suppose, instead, the stock price goes to 90. The call you sold is in the money at the expiration date. Buy back the call, or buy one share of stock and let it be exercised, incurring a loss of $90 - 80 = 10$ either way. Borrow to cover this, bringing your current indebtedness to $5 + 10 = 15$. You own .167 shares of stock selling at 90 per share, for a total value of $.167(90) = 15$. Sell the stock and repay the borrowing. Go back to the bank and withdraw your original deposit, which has now grown to $1.935(1.1)^3 = 2.575$.

In summary, if we were correct in our original analysis about stock price movements (which did not involve the unenviable task of predicting whether the stock price would go up or down), and if we faithfully adjust our portfolio as prescribed by the formula, then we can be assured of walking away in the clear at the expiration date, while still keeping the original differential and the interest it has accumulated. It is true that closing out the position before the expiration date, which involves buying back the option at its then current market price, might produce a loss that would more than offset our profit, but this loss could always be avoided by waiting until the expiration date. Moreover, if the market price comes into line with the formula value before the expiration date, we can close out the position then with no loss and be rid of the concern of keeping the portfolio adjusted.

It still might seem that we are depending on rational behavior by the person who bought the call we sold. If instead he behaves foolishly and exercises at the wrong time, could he make things worse for us as well as for himself? Fortunately, the answer is no. Mistakes on his part can only mean greater profits for us. Suppose that he exercises too soon. In that circumstance, the equivalent portfolio will always be worth more than $S - K$, so we could close out the position then with an extra profit.

Suppose, instead, that he fails to exercise when it would be optimal to do so. Again there is no problem. Since exercise is now optimal, our equivalent portfolio will be worth $S - K$.[15] If he had exercised, this would be exactly sufficient to meet the obligation and close out the position. Since he did not, the call will be held at least one more period, so we calculate the new values of C_u and C_d and revise our equivalent portfolio accordingly. But now the amount required for the portfolio, $S\Delta + B$, is less than the amount we have available, $S - K$. We can withdraw these extra profits now and still maintain the equivalent portfolio. The longer the holder of the call goes on making mistakes, the better off we will be.

Consequently, we can be confident that things will eventually work out right no matter what the other party does. The return on our total position, when evaluated at prevailing market prices at intermediate times, may be negative. But over a period ending no later than the expiration date, it will be positive.

In conducting the hedging operation, the essential thing was to maintain the proper proportional relationship: For each call we are short, we hold Δ shares of stock and the dollar amount B in bonds in the equivalent portfolio. To emphasize this, we will refer to the number of shares held for each call as the *neutral position ratio*. In our example, we kept the number of calls constant and made adjustments by buying or selling stock and bonds. As a result, our profit was independent of the market price of the call between the time we initiated the hedge and the expiration date. If things got worse before they got better, it did not matter to us.

Instead, we could have made the adjustments by keeping the number of shares of stock constant and buying or selling calls and bonds. However, this could be dangerous. Suppose that after initiating the position, we

---

[15] If we were reverse hedging by buying an undervalued call and selling the equivalent portfolio, then we would ourselves want to exercise at this point. Since we will receive $S - K$ from exercising, this will be exactly enough money to buy back the equivalent portfolio.

needed to increase the neutral position ratio to maintain the proper proportions. This can be achieved in two ways: (1) buy more stock, or (2) buy back some of the calls. If we adjust through the stock, there is no problem. If we insist on adjusting through the calls, not only is the hedge no longer riskless, but it could even end up losing money! This can happen if the call has become even more overpriced. We would then be closing out part of our position in calls at a loss. To remain hedged, the number of calls we would need to buy back depends on their value, not their price. Therefore, since we are uncertain about their price, we then become uncertain about the return from the hedge. Worse yet, if the call price gets high enough, the loss on the closed portion of our position could throw the hedge operation into an overall loss.

To see how this could happen, let us rerun the hedging operation, where we adjust the hedge ratio by buying and selling calls.

STEP 1 ($n = 3$):   Same as before.

STEP 2 ($n = 2$):   Suppose the stock goes to 120, so that the new $\Delta = .848$. The call price has gotten further out of line and is now selling for 75. Since its value is 60.463, it is now overpriced by 14.537. With .719 shares, you must buy back $1 - .848 = .152$ calls to produce a hedge ratio of $.848 = .719/.848$. This costs $75(.152) = 11.40$. Borrow to pay the bill. With the interest rate of .1, you already owe $23.455(1.1) = 25.801$. Thus, your total current indebtedness is $25.801 + 11.40 = 37.201$.

STEP 3 ($n = 1$):   Suppose the stock goes to 60 and the call is selling for 5.454. Since the call is now fairly valued, no further excess profits can be made by continuing to hold the position. Therefore, liquidate by selling your .719 shares for $.719(60) = 43.14$ and close out the call position by buying back .848 calls for $.848(5.454) = 4.625$. This nets $43.14 - 4.625 = 38.515$. Use this to pay back part of your borrowing. Since you now owe $37.20(1.1) = 40.921$, after repayment you owe 2.406. Go back to the bank and withdraw your original deposit, which has now grown to $1.935(1.1)^2 = 2.341$. Unfortunately, after using this to repay your remaining borrowing, you still owe .065.

Since we adjusted our position at Step 2 by buying overpriced calls, our profit is reduced. Indeed, since the calls were considerably overpriced, we actually lost money despite apparent profitability of the position at Step 1. We can draw the following adjustment rule from our experiment: *To adjust a hedged position, never buy an overpriced option or sell an underpriced option.* As a corollary, whenever we can adjust a hedged position by buying more of an underpriced option or selling more of an overpriced option, our profit will be enhanced if we do so. For example, at Step 3 in the original hedging illustration, had the call still been overpriced, it would have been better to adjust the position by selling more calls rather than selling stock. In summary, by choosing the right side of the position to adjust at intermediate dates, *at a minimum* we can be assured of earning the original differential and its accumulated interest, and we may earn considerably more.

Is it ever possible to work our way into a position where, to maintain neutrality, we are *forced* to buy an overpriced option or sell an underpriced option? This can never happen with a hedge, since, if necessary, we can always adjust with the stock. However, if we are careless, this can happen with spreads and combinations. To see this, suppose, at the initiation of a neutral purchased straddle, both the put and the call are underpriced. Each side of the straddle is then separately profitable. At a subsequent date, suppose both options remain underpriced and we need to increase the position ratio to maintain neutrality. We can do this without violating our rule by buying more calls. If, instead, the position ratio should be decreased, we can buy more puts. This position has no dangers.

However, suppose, at its initiation, the call is underpriced and the put overpriced. Despite this, the purchased straddle looks profitable since the calls are significantly underpriced, relative to the overpricing of the puts. At a subsequent date, suppose the call remains underpriced and the put overpriced. If we need to increase the position ratio, we can buy more of the underpriced calls—again, no problem. However, if we need to *decrease* the position ratio, we must either (1) sell back some calls, or (2) buy more puts. In either case, we are forced to violate our adjustment rule. Suppose that we did so by selling calls. If the calls are less underpriced than they were originally, then we will be giving up some of our potential profit, but we still will not be risking a loss. However, suppose the calls are more underpriced than they were originally. The potential loss from the sale could then indeed be greater than the original potential profit. However, market prices are now more out of line than ever, so it certainly seems that we could still insure a profit by adding another neutral straddle of large enough size to our original position. In effect, we would be increasing the scale of each side of our position. And we could keep doing this each period if necessary, knowing that market prices must come into line at the end of the last period. The problem is that the scale of our position may become so large that capital limitations or even the smallest mistake in analysis or implementation could lead to disaster.

We can avoid being pushed into this unfortunate position if we *never initiate a covered position where one side of the position is unfavorable.* For example, we should never put on a spread where both sides are overpriced or both are underpriced. We should not put on a combination where one side is overpriced and the other underpriced. As a corollary, *whenever one side of a covered position becomes unfavorable, we should liquidate that side and replace it with another option with a favorable price.* For instance, suppose we buy a straddle in underpriced calls and puts and, at a subsequent date, the puts become overpriced. We should immediately sell the puts and replace them with other underpriced purchased puts or other overpriced written calls. If neither are available, we can always short the stock.

To recapitulate, we have the following rules for initiating and maintaining neutral positions:

1. Never initiate a neutral position where one side of the position is unfavorable.
2. Whenever one side of a neutral position becomes unfavorable, liquidate that side and replace it with another option with a favorable price.
3. Never adjust by buying an overpriced option or selling an underpriced option.
4. If possible, always adjust by buying an underpriced option or selling an overpriced option.

Adhering faithfully to these rules ensures a profit of at least the original pricing differential and eliminates all ambiguity about which side of a position to adjust to maintain neutrality.

5-5. OPTION RISK AND EXPECTED RETURN

In this section, we show how the equilibrium risk and expected return of an option are related to the risk and expected return of the underlying stock. We will also derive the relationship of option pricing to the "capital asset pricing model," which is widely used in portfolio management. In particular, we show how to calculate the "alpha" and "beta" of an option.

It is important to note that this information will be derived from our previous results without additional assumptions (except in the calculation of alpha and beta). If we were interested only in valuing an option in terms of the stock, or in pursuing riskless arbitrage profits if market prices differed from this value, then we would not need the results of this section. However, if we plan to include options as part of an investment portfolio, then the risk and return analysis that follows is of critical importance.

Stock Risk and Expected Return. Over a single period, the total return on a security is its price at the end of the period, plus any cash distribution made at the end of the period, divided by its price at the beginning of the period. In our binomial model, the total return of the stock is either u or d.

Its *expected return*, m_S, is the weighted average of the possible total returns, where the weights are the respective probabilities. That is,

$$m_S \equiv qu + (1 - q)d.$$

One measure of stock risk is the variance of the total return, v_S^2. This is the weighted average of the squared deviations of the possible total returns from their mean, where the weights are the respective probabilities. That is,

$$v_S^2 \equiv q(u - m_S)^2 + (1 - q)(d - m_S)^2.$$

Substituting for the mean m_S from the previous equation, we can simplify this to

$$v_S = [q(1 - q)(u - d)^2]^{1/2},$$

where v_S, the square root of the variance, is called the *standard deviation*, or simply the stock *volatility*. Often these measures are expressed in terms of the rate of return, which is the total return minus one. It is easy to see that the expected rate of return is $m_S - 1$ and that the standard deviation of the rate of return is v_S.

Option Elasticity.   Recall that the neutral hedge ratio is

$$\Delta = \frac{C_u - C_d}{(u - d)S}.$$

Suppose that we think of the stock price as having moved downward and then ask: What would be the change in the value of the call relative to the change in the value of the stock if the stock had instead moved upward? This is exactly what Δ tells us. If we wish to make this comparison in terms of percentage changes, then we would divide the numerator of Δ by the current call value C, and the denominator by the current stock price S. This concept is called the option's *elasticity* and will be denoted by Ω. That is,

$$\Omega \equiv (S/C)\Delta.$$

For a put, $\Delta = (P_u - P_d)/(u - d)S$ and $\Omega = (S/P)\Delta$. Since $P_u \leq P_d$, both Δ and Ω are less than or equal to zero. One further fact, which we will state but not prove, will be useful later: For both puts and calls, Ω increases as K increases.

Option Risk.   We can apply these same measures to an option. The mean m_C and standard deviation v_C of the total return of a call over one period are computed in the same way as the corresponding statistics for the stock:

$$m_C \equiv \frac{qC_u + (1 - q)C_d}{C} \quad \text{and} \quad v_C \equiv \left[q(1 - q) \left(\frac{C_u - C_d}{C} \right)^2 \right]^{1/2}.$$

By combining our equations for v_S and v_C and using the definitions of Δ and Ω, we find that

$$v_C = \Omega v_S.$$

This equation relates the risk of a call to the risk of the underlying stock. The *risk of a call* (the standard deviation of its rate of return) *equals its elasticity times its underlying stock volatility.* The elasticity Ω can be easily computed, since it requires knowing only u, d, C, C_u, and C_d.

   Moreover, it is easy to show that in percentage terms (rates of return), *the call can never be less risky than the stock.* That is, $v_C \geq v_S$. To demonstrate this, we must show that $\Omega \geq 1$. In Section 5-3 we showed that

$$C = \frac{pC_u + (1 - p)C_d}{r} \quad \text{where} \quad p \equiv \frac{r - d}{u - d}.$$

This implies

$$r[C_u - C_d - (u - d)C] + [uC_d - dC_u] = 0.$$

If the second bracketed expression is nonpositive, then the first is nonnegative. By the definition of Ω,

$$C_u - C_d - (u - d)C \geq 0 \quad \text{if and only if} \quad \Omega \geq 1.$$

Therefore, if we can show $uC_d - dC_u$ is nonpositive, then we have proved $\Omega \geq 1$.

   From our earlier development in Section 5-3, we know that one period from the present the call value will be either

$$C_d = \{E \max[0, dSu^j d^{n-1-j} - K]\}/r^{n-1},$$

or

$$C_u = \{E \max[0, uSu^j d^{n-1-j} - K]\}/r^{n-1},$$

where E represents the expected value with respect to the probability distribution for j when $q = p$. After substituting these expressions, it should be clear that $uC_d - dC_u \leq 0$, so that we have confirmed our result.

Note that $\Omega \geq 1$ implies that $C - S\Delta \leq 0$. Since $B = C - S\Delta$, this verifies our earlier comment that $B \leq 0$ and hence our conclusion that over a single period the call is equivalent to a particular levered long position in the stock. This, of course, squares with our result about option risk and stock risk, since in rate of return terms a levered portfolio is more risky than an unlevered one.

The mean m_P and standard deviation v_P of the total return of a put over one period are defined in the same way as for a call:

$$m_P = \frac{qP_u + (1 - q)P_d}{P} \quad \text{and} \quad v_P = \left[q(1 - q)\frac{(P_u - P_d)^2}{P} \right]^{1/2}.$$

The volatility of a put can then be written as

$$v_P = -\Omega v_S.$$

The minus sign is necessary because v_P, the standard deviation of the rate of return, is by definition never negative, while the Ω of a put is never positive. The analogy with a call might lead us to think that the Ω of a put must be less than or equal to -1 but this is not the case; it can be shown that the only restriction we can place on Ω is that it be less than or equal to zero. Consequently, it is possible for the volatility of a put to be less than the volatility of the stock.

Option Expected Return. To find the relationship between m_C and m_S, we need to go back to the derivation of the binomial formula. Recall that the equivalent portfolio has the same end-of-period values as the call for each possible outcome. That is,

$$uS\Delta + rB = C_u \quad \text{and} \quad dS\Delta + rB = C_d.$$

With Δ and B chosen in this way, we found that $C = S\Delta + B$. We can combine these in the following way:

$$uS\Delta - C_u = r(S\Delta - C) \quad \text{and} \quad dS\Delta - C_d = r(S\Delta - C).$$

Multiplying the first equation by q and the second by $1 - q$, then adding the respective left- and right-hand sides, gives

$$q[uS\Delta - C_u] + (1 - q)[dS\Delta - C_d] = r(S\Delta - C).$$

By rearranging terms and substituting for m_S and m_C, we have

$$m_S S\Delta - m_C C = r(S\Delta - C).$$

Finally, rearranging again and using the definition of Ω, we obtain

$$m_C - r = \Omega(m_S - r).$$

That is, the *excess expected rate of return* (over the risk-free rate) *on the call is equal to Ω times the excess expected rate of return on the stock.* Since $\Omega \geq 1$, if the expected rate of return on the stock is greater (less) than the risk-free rate, then the expected rate of return on the call is never less (greater) than the expected rate of return on the stock.

The same relationship holds for puts:

$$m_P - r = \Omega(m_S - r).$$

Now, however, $\Omega \leq 0$. Consequently, we can only say that if the expected rate of return on the stock is greater (less) than the riskless rate, then the expected rate of return on the put is less (greater) than the riskless rate.

Option Beta. In all of this, m_S, the expected total return of the stock, could have been determined in any manner. However, if we also have a theory about how it is determined, we could then incorporate this theory into our results. The capital asset pricing model is an example of just such a theory. It says that, under certain conditions, the expected rate of return of a stock can be written in terms of the expected rate of return on a portfolio containing all available assets in proportion to their market values.[16] This portfolio is usually called the "market portfolio," and its expected total return will be denoted by m_M. Stating this relationship precisely,

$$m_S - r = \beta_S(m_M - r),$$

where β_S is the *beta* of the stock—that is, the covariance[17] of the stock's rate of return with that of the market portfolio, divided by the variance of the rate of return of the market portfolio. If we substitute this expression for $m_S - r$ into our earlier equation for $m_C - r$, we obtain

$$m_C - r = \Omega\beta_S(m_M - r).$$

---

[16] For an introduction to the capital asset pricing model, see William F. Sharpe, *Investments*, 2nd Ed. (Englewood Cliffs, N.J.: Prentice-Hall, Inc., 1981), Chs. 5 and 6.

[17] If the market portfolio also followed a binomial process, with a total return over each period of u_M or d_M, then by definition this covariance would be

$$q_1(u - m_S)(u_M - m_M) + q_2(u - m_S)(d_M - m_M) + q_3(d - m_S)(u_M - m_M) + q_4(d - m_S)(d_M - m_M)$$

where q_1 is the probability that both the stock and the market will go up, q_2 is the probability that the stock will go up and the market will go down, and so on. Note, however, that the results in the text do not require that the *market portfolio* follow a binomial process.

It can be shown that $\Omega\beta_S$ is indeed the covariance of the rate of return on the call with the rate of return on the market divided by the variance of the rate of return on the market, so we can write the beta of a call β_C as

$$\beta_C = \Omega\beta_S.$$

The *option beta equals its elasticity times its underlying stock beta.* Since $\Omega \geq 1$ for a call, in the normal case of $\beta_S \geq 0$, we have $\beta_C \geq \beta_S$. For a put, $\Omega \leq 0$, so if $\beta_S \geq 0$, then $\beta_P \leq 0$. For both puts and calls, Ω will change from period to period due to stock price changes and the passage of time. Therefore, even if the beta of the stock remains constant, the beta of an option will not.

Theories like the capital asset pricing model, which seek to explain the relationships of rates of return on all assets, will imply a particular relationship between option and stock prices. The converse is not true, however. Indeed, we have seen that in deriving an option pricing formula we needed to know only some properties of the underlying stock. We did not need to know whether this stock was fairly priced relative to other stocks or, in fact, anything at all about other stocks. Although the option pricing formula and the capital asset pricing model may both be very useful, the validity of the former does not depend on the latter.[18]

Option Alpha. So far we have presumed that the option is properly valued relative to its associated stock, and that the stock is valued relative to the market portfolio according to the capital asset pricing model. However, suppose that independent estimates of m_C and m_S imply that our expected return and risk relationships are not satisfied. Then, if our predictions and models are correct, we will have isolated mispriced securities.

For example, suppose that our independent estimate of m_S implies that $m_S - r > \beta_S(m_M - r)$. We then believe the stock is underpriced and promises an expected return greater than that justified by its level of risk. This extra expected return is commonly termed the stock *alpha* and is determined by

$$m_S - r = \alpha_S + \beta_S(m_M - r).$$

Of course, α_S can be positive or negative, and is equal to zero only if we believe a stock is properly priced by the market.

---

[18] Indeed, in the limiting case discussed in the next section, the capital asset pricing model implies the option pricing formula, but the option pricing formula itself does not imply the capital asset pricing model. The option pricing theory is therefore more general than the capital asset pricing model. However, this should not be surprising, since the task of the option pricing formula, to explain the pricing relationship between particular contractually related securities, is clearly less ambitious than the task of the capital asset pricing model, which is to explain the pricing relationships among all securities.

The alpha of an option can be broken into two components: the associated stock alpha and the relative pricing relationship between the option and the stock. For a call, we can quantify the latter source by $\hat{\alpha}_C$ in

$$m_C - r = \hat{\alpha}_C + \Omega(m_S - r).$$

If the call is underpriced (overpriced) relative to the stock, then $\hat{\alpha}_C > 0$ (< 0). Putting the above two equations together gives

$$m_C - r = \hat{\alpha}_C + \Omega\alpha_S + \Omega\beta_S(m_M - r),$$

so that the call alpha[19] can be written as

$$\alpha_C = \hat{\alpha}_C + \Omega\alpha_S.$$

Since $\Omega \geq 1$, α_C will tend to be greater in magnitude than α_S unless this difference is fully offset by an opposing relative mispricing between the call and the stock.

For a put, we have a similar relationship, $m_P - r = \hat{\alpha}_P + \Omega\alpha_S + \Omega\beta_S(m_M - r)$, but some of the conclusions are different. Since $\Omega \leq 0$, if $\hat{\alpha}_P = 0$, then α_P and α_S have opposite signs. In other words, if a put is properly priced relative to the stock, and the stock is underpriced (overpriced) relative to the market, then the put must be overpriced (underpriced) relative to the market.

Figure 5-1(a) illustrates the relationship between expected rate of return and beta given by the capital asset pricing model for some representative options that are properly priced relative to the underlying stock. If an option is underpriced (overpriced) relative to the stock, then it will lie above (below) the line shown. If the stock itself is properly priced relative to the market, then all other properly priced securities will lie somewhere along the line shown. If instead the stock is underpriced (overpriced) relative to the market, then all properly priced securities will lie along another straight line which crosses the vertical axis at the same point as the line shown but has a smaller (larger) slope.

Figure 5-1(b) shows the corresponding relationship between expected rate of return and volatility for properly priced options. Note that along the lower section of the graph, expected rate of return decreases as volatility increases. Even though a put has a higher variability of return than a default-free bond, it has a lower expected rate of return. However, this is not surprising. We know from Section 2-3 that a put will be equivalent to a

---

[19] The alpha of either the stock or the option will depend on the length of time before equilibrium is restored. Other things equal, an alpha will be greater the shorter this time period.

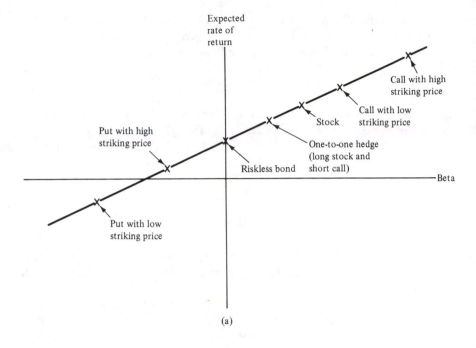

(a)

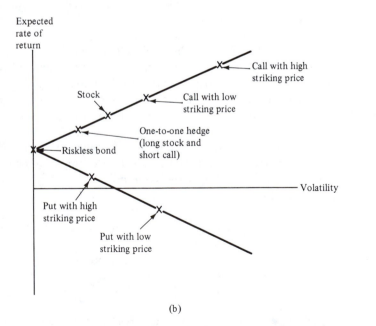

(b)

Figure 5-1   Relationship of Expected Rate of Return to Beta and
Volatility

portfolio containing a long position in default-free bonds and a short position in the stock. If the expected rate of return on the stock is greater than the riskless rate, then the expected rate of return on such a portfolio must be less than the riskless rate. Although this conclusion does not depend on the validity of the capital asset pricing model, the two are completely consistent, since we know that a put has a negative beta.

Risk and Expected Return in Terms of Dollar Changes. Sometimes it is convenient to express risk and expected return in terms of the dollar change, which is the rate of return multiplied by the price at the beginning of the period. Since this price is not a random variable, we are in effect simply multiplying the random rate of return by a constant. Hence, for the stock, the expected dollar change will be $(m_S - 1)S$ and the standard deviation of the dollar change will be $v_S S$. For the call, the corresponding values will be $(m_C - 1)C$ and $v_C C$.

We can now use our previous results to write

$$v_C C = v_S S\Delta,$$
$$m_C C - rC = [m_S S - rS]\Delta.$$

In other words, Δ tells us:

1. The ratio of the standard deviation of the dollar change in the call value to the standard deviation of the dollar change in the stock price.
2. The ratio of the excess expected dollar change (over the risk-free dollar change) in the call price to the excess expected dollar change in the stock price.

If we can show that $\Delta \le 1$, then we can also make the following statements:

1. In absolute terms (standard deviation of dollar changes), the call is never more risky than the stock.
2. If the expected dollar change in the stock is nonnegative, then the expected dollar changes on the call are never greater than the expected dollar changes on the stock.

To see that $\Delta \le 1$, consider the following argument. $\Delta \le 1$ if and only if $C_u - C_d \le (u - d)S$, or $uS - C_u \ge dS - C_d$. From our earlier development, we know that this can be rewritten as

$$r^{-(n-1)}E\{uSu^j d^{n-1-j} - \max[0, uSu^j d^{n-1-j} - K]\}$$
$$\ge r^{-(n-1)}E\{dSu^j d^{n-1-j} - \max[0, dSu^j d^{n-1-j} - K]\},$$

or

$$E \min[uSu^j d^{n-1-j}, K] \ge E \min[dSu^j d^{n-1-j}, K].$$

The last inequality obviously holds, so Δ is indeed less than or equal to one.
The corresponding results for a put are:

$$v_pP = -v_SS\Delta$$
$$m_pP - rP = [m_SS - rS]\Delta.$$

The interpretation of Δ in terms of information about dollar changes is
similar to that for a call. Also, it can be shown that $\Delta \geq -1$, so we can
conclude that in absolute terms (standard deviation of dollar changes), a
put is never more risky than the stock.

Risk and Expected Return Over Many Periods. We have found the risk and
expected return of a call relative to that of the stock over a single period.
The relationships were simple and direct. This is just as we would have
expected, since we had earlier shown that over any single period the call
was equivalent to a particular levered long position in the stock.

Often, we will also want to know about the corresponding measures
for positions that are held over a number of periods. The definitions of risk
and expected return can be easily extended for the stock. If there are no
payouts, we simply substitute the value of the security at the end of the
entire holding interval in place of its value at the end of the current period.
Straightforward calculations show that over k periods, the expected total
return, $m_S(k)$, and variance of total return, $v_S^2(k)$, are

$$m_S(k) = [qu + (1 - q)d]^k = m_S^k,$$
$$v_S^2(k) = [qu^2 + (1 - q)d^2]^k - [qu + (1 - q)d]^{2k}.$$

We might hope that there will again be a simple way to relate the risk
and expected return of the option to that of the stock. However, this is not
the case. The reason is that while the call is equivalent to a portfolio of
stock and bonds that is readjusted every period in a specified way, it is *not*
equivalent to *any* portfolio of stock and bonds whose proportions remain
fixed over the entire interval. It is easy to see why this is true. At the end of
k periods, the stock can take on $k + 1$ possible values. So can the call. With
only two choice variables—the amount of stock and the amount of bonds—
we could not hope to find a portfolio whose end-of-interval value would be
the same as that of the call in each of the $k + 1$ possible outcomes. In other
words, over more than one period, the call offers a pattern of returns that
cannot be duplicated by any fixed portfolio of stock and bonds. Hence, its
risk and expected return cannot be expressed in terms of those of such a
portfolio.

Nevertheless, we have at hand all of the information we need. For any
future date, we know the value of a call as a function of the stock price at

that time. We also know the probability distribution of this future stock price. We can thus in principle calculate the risk and expected return—or any other statistic we might want—for the option over any interval, but the exact results will usually be quite complicated. We will pursue this further in Section 6-5.

If the end of the holding interval is the expiration date, then things will be somewhat simpler. For example, the expected total return on a call will then be the expected total return on the stock times an adjustment factor. This factor is the current value that the call would have if $r = m_s$, divided by the current value of the call.

A Numerical Example. We can illustrate all of this with the numerical example developed in Section 5-4. There we assumed that $S = 80$, $K = 80$, $n = 3$, $u = 1.5$, $d = .5$, and $r = 1.1$. The resulting call values were $C = 34.065$, $C_u = 60.463$, $C_d = 2.974$, $C_{uu} = 107.272$, $C_{du} = 5.454$, and $C_{dd} = 0$. Since we now need to know the actual distribution of the stock price, let us suppose that $q = .7$.

We can calculate the initial values of m_S, v_S, m_C, and v_C directly from their definitions. These values are

$$m_S = .7(1.5) + .3(.5) = 1.2,$$
$$m_S - r = 1.2 - 1.1 = .1,$$
$$v_S^2 = .7(1.5 - 1.2)^2 + .3(.5 - 1.2)^2 = .21,$$

$$v_S = .458,$$
$$m_C = .7\left(\frac{60.463}{34.065}\right) + .3\left(\frac{2.974}{34.065}\right) = .7(1.775) + .3(.087) = 1.269,$$
$$m_C - r = .169,$$
$$v_C^2 = .7(1.775 - 1.269)^2 + .3(.087 - 1.269)^2 = .598,$$
$$v_C = .773.$$

To verify that these values are consistent with our formulas, we first need to evaluate Ω. This gives

$$\Omega = \frac{S\Delta}{C} = \frac{C_u - C_d}{(u - d)C} = \frac{60.463 - 2.974}{34.065} = 1.689.$$

To confirm the formulas, we note that

$$v_C = \Omega v_S = 1.689(.458) = .773,$$
$$m_C - r = \Omega(m_S - r) = 1.689(.1) = .169.$$

If we wished to compute the expected total return over, for instance, two periods, we would find

$$m_S(2) = (1.2)^2 = 1.44,$$

$$m_C(2) = (.7)^2\left(\frac{107.272}{34.065}\right) + 2(.7)(.3)\left(\frac{5.454}{34.065}\right) + (.3)^2\left(\frac{0}{34.065}\right) = 1.61.$$

Some Additional Comments. A few other points are worth emphasizing. Although the value of the call, in terms of the stock (our option pricing formula) did not depend on q, the expected rate of return of the call certainly does depend on q, through its dependence on m_S, the expected rate of return of the stock. The higher the probability of an up movement in the stock, the higher its expected rate of return, and the higher the expected rate of return of the option, just as we would have thought.

Furthermore, the risk and expected rate of return on the call were that which would hold if the call were in equilibrium at the beginning and end of the period. If the call price is currently out of equilibrium, but will move back into line at the end of some interval (possibly one period), then we can calculate the risk and expected return over this interval by substituting the current market price in place of the current formula value, C. If the call price could move even more out of equilibrium, then the risk and expected return on holding a call over the interval could conceivably be almost anything. This squares with our earlier observation that if an arbitrage strategy is liquidated before expiration, it will not necessarily be riskless. We could then make definite statements about risk and expected return over any holding period only if we make some assumption about the disequilibrium behavior of option market prices. However, we know that an investment in an undervalued call will, if held until expiration, have a higher expected rate of return than its equivalent portfolio of stock and bonds.

Finally, all of the results in this section hold for an American option on a stock that pays dividends. There are only two minor differences. First, the total return on holding the stock should include reinvestment of cash dividends. Second, the risk and expected return relationships for holding the option over the next period will not apply if the option should be exercised immediately.

5-6. THE BLACK-SCHOLES FORMULA

The Effect of More Frequent Trading. In reading the previous sections, there is a natural tendency to associate with each period some particular length of calendar time, perhaps a day. With this in mind, you may have had two objections. In the first place, prices a day from now may take on many more than just two possible values. Furthermore, the market is not open for trading only once a day, but, instead, trading takes place almost continuously.

These objections are certainly valid. Fortunately, our option pricing approach has the flexibility to meet them. Although it might have been natural to think of a period as one day, there was nothing that forced us to do so. We could have taken it to be a much shorter interval—say an hour—or even a minute. By doing so we have met both objections simultaneously. Trading would take place far more frequently, and the stock price could take on hundreds of values by the end of the day.

However, if we do this, we have to make some other adjustments to keep the probability small that the stock price will change by a large amount over a minute. We do not want the stock to have the same percentage up and down moves for one minute as it did before for one day. But again there is no need for us to have to use the same values. We could, for example, think of the price as making only a very small percentage change over each minute.

To make this more precise, suppose that h represents the elapsed time between successive stock price changes. That is, if t is the fixed length of calendar time to expiration, and n is the number of periods of length h prior to expiration, then

$$h \equiv t/n.$$

As trading takes place more and more frequently, h gets closer and closer to zero. We must then adjust the interval-dependent variables r, u, and d in such a way that we obtain empirically realistic results as h becomes smaller, or, equivalently, as $n \to \infty$.

When we were thinking of the periods as having a fixed length, r represented both the interest rate over a fixed length of calendar time and the interest rate over one period. Now we need to make a distinction between these two meanings. We will let r continue to mean one plus the interest rate over a fixed length of calendar time. When we have occasion to refer to one plus the interest rate over a period (trading interval) of length h, we will use the symbol $\hat{r}$.

Clearly, the size of $\hat{r}$ depends on the number of subintervals, n, into which t is divided. Over the n periods until expiration, the total return is $\hat{r}^n$, where $n = t/h$. Now not only do we want $\hat{r}$ to depend on n, but we want it to depend on n in a particular way—so that as n changes the total return $\hat{r}^n$ over the fixed time t remains the same. This is because the interest rate obtainable over some fixed length of calendar time should have nothing to do with how we choose to think of the length of the time interval h.

If r (without the "hat") denotes one plus the rate of interest over a *fixed* unit of calendar time, then over elapsed time t, r^t is the total return.[20] Observe that this measure of total return does not depend on n. As we have argued, we want to choose the dependence of $\hat{r}$ on n, so that

$$\hat{r}^n = r^t,$$

for any choice of n. Therefore, $\hat{r} = r^{t/n}$. This last equation shows how $\hat{r}$ must depend on n for the total return over elapsed time t to be independent of n.

We also need to define u and d in terms of n. At this point, there are two significantly different paths we can take. Depending on the definitions we choose, as $n \to \infty$ (or, equivalently, as $h \to 0$), we can have either a continuous or a jump stochastic process. In the first situation, very small random changes in the stock price will be occurring in each very small time interval. The stock price will fluctuate incessantly, but its path can be drawn without lifting pen from paper. In contrast, in the second case, the stock price will usually move in a smooth deterministic way, but will occasionally experience sudden discontinuous changes. Both can be derived from our binomial process simply by choosing how u and d depend on n. In this chapter, we examine only the continuous process which leads to the option pricing formula originally derived by Fischer Black and Myron Scholes. We will postpone discussion of the jump process formula until Chapter 7.

Recall that we supposed that over each period the stock price would experience a one plus rate of return of u with probability q and d with probability $1 - q$. It will be easier and clearer to work, instead, with the natural logarithms of the one plus rate of return, $\log u$ and $\log d$. This gives the continuously compounded rate of return on the stock over each period.[21] It is a random variable which, in each period, will be equal to $\log u$ with probability q and $\log d$ with probability $1 - q$.

---

[20] The scale of this unit (perhaps a day, or a year) is unimportant as long as r and t are expressed in the same scale.

[21] Continuously compounded rates of interest are commonly used by banks on savings accounts. To convert the discrete one plus rate of return u over a single period into a continuously compounded rate, consider what happens as we divide the period into m subperiods of equal length. Suppose we denote by g/m the rate of increase required over each of these subperiods to produce u over the entire period; that is,

$$u = (1 + g/m)^m.$$

g itself depends on m and is the m subperiod compounded rate of increase. Now, as $m \to \infty$, g becomes the continuously compounded rate of increase. In the limit, it can be shown that $u = e^g$, where e is the exponential constant, $e = 2.718 \ldots$, which is the limiting value of $[1 + (1/k)]^k$ as $k \to \infty$. Therefore, the continuously compounded rate of increase $g = \log u$. Similarly, since $r^t = e^{(\log r)t}$, the continuously compounded rate of interest is $\log r$.

Consider a typical sequence of five moves, say u, d, u, u, d. Then, $S^* = uduudS$, $S^*/S = u^3 d^2$, and $\log(S^*/S) = 3 \log u + 2 \log d$. More generally, over n periods,

$$\log(S^*/S) = j \log u + (n - j) \log d = j \log(u/d) + n \log d,$$

where j is the (random) number of upward moves occurring during the n periods to expiration. Therefore, the expected value of $\log(S^*/S)$ is

$$E[\log(S^*/S)] = E(j)[\log(u/d)] + n \log d$$

and its variance is

$$\text{Var}[\log(S^*/S)] = \text{Var}(j)[\log(u/d)]^2.$$

Each of the n possible upward moves has probability q. Thus, $E(j) = nq$. Also, since the variance each period is

$$q(1 - q)^2 + (1 - q)(0 - q)^2 = q(1 - q),$$

then $\text{Var}(j) = nq(1 - q)$. Combining all of this, we have

$$E[\log(S^*/S)] = [q \log(u/d) + \log d]n \equiv \hat{\mu}n$$
$$\text{Var}[\log(S^*/S)] = q(1 - q)[\log(u/d)]^2 n \equiv \hat{\sigma}^2 n.$$

Let us go back to our discussion. We were considering dividing up our original longer time period (a day) into many shorter periods (a minute or even less). Over a fixed length of calendar time t, our procedure calls for making n larger and larger. Now if we held everything else constant while we let n become large, we would be faced with the problem we talked about earlier. In fact, we would certainly not reach a reasonable conclusion if either $\hat{\mu}n$ or $\hat{\sigma}^2 n$ went to zero or infinity as n became large. Since t is a fixed length of time, in searching for a realistic result, we must make the appropriate adjustments in u, d, and q. In doing that, we would at least want the mean and variance of the continuously compounded rate of return of the assumed stock price movement to coincide with that of the actual stock price as $n \to \infty$. Suppose we label the actual empirical values of $\hat{\mu}n$ and $\hat{\sigma}^2 n$ as μt and $\sigma^2 t$, respectively. Then we would want to choose u, d, and q, so that

$$\left. \begin{array}{l} [q \log(u/d) + \log d]n \to \mu t \\ q(1 - q)[\log(u/d)]^2 n \to \sigma^2 t \end{array} \right\} \quad \text{as} \quad n \to \infty.$$

A little algebra shows we can accomplish this by letting

$$u = e^{\sigma\sqrt{t/n}}, \qquad d = e^{-\sigma\sqrt{t/n}}, \qquad \text{and} \qquad q = \tfrac{1}{2} + \tfrac{1}{2}(\mu/\sigma)\sqrt{t/n}.$$

In this case, for any n,

$$\hat{\mu}n = \mu t \qquad \text{and} \qquad \hat{\sigma}^2 n = [\sigma^2 - \mu^2(t/n)]t.$$

Clearly, as $n \to \infty$, $\hat{\sigma}^2 n \to \sigma^2 t$, while $\hat{\mu}n = \mu t$ for all values of n.

Alternatively, we could have chosen u, d, and q so that the mean and variance of the future stock price for the discrete binomial process approach the prespecified mean and variance of the actual stock price as $n \to \infty$. However, just as we would expect, the same values will accomplish this as well. Since this would not change our conclusions, and it is computationally more convenient to work with the continuously compounded rates of return, we will proceed in that way.

This satisfies our initial requirement that the limiting means and variances coincide, but we still need to verify that we are arriving at a sensible limiting probability distribution of the continuously compounded rate of return. The mean and variance only describe certain aspects of that distribution.

For our model, the random continuously compounded rate of return over a period of length t is the sum of n independent random variables, each of which can take the value log u with probability q and log d with probability $1 - q$. We wish to know about the distribution of this sum as n becomes large and q, u, and d are chosen in the way described. We need to remember that as we change n, we are not simply adding one more random variable to the previous sum, but instead are changing the probabilities and possible outcomes for every member of the sum. At this point, we can rely on a form of the central limit theorem which, when applied to our problem, says that as $n \to \infty$, if

$$\frac{q |\log u - \hat{\mu}|^3 + (1 - q)|\log d - \hat{\mu}|^3}{\hat{\sigma}^3 \sqrt{n}} \to 0,$$

then

$$\text{Prob}\left\{\left[\frac{\log(S^*/S) - \hat{\mu}n}{\hat{\sigma}\sqrt{n}}\right] \le z\right\} \to N(z),$$

where $N(z)$ is the standard normal distribution function. Putting this into words, as the number of periods into which the fixed length of time to expiration is divided approaches infinity, the probability that the standardized continuously compounded rate of return of the stock through the

$u = 1.0000 0316$

$d = 0.99999 684$

expiration date is not greater than the number z approaches the probability under a standard normal distribution.

The initial condition says roughly that higher-order properties of the distribution, such as how it is skewed, become less and less important, relative to its standard deviation, as $n \rightarrow \infty$. We can verify that the condition is satisfied by making the appropriate substitutions and finding

$$\frac{q|\log u - \hat{\mu}|^3 + (1 - q)|\log d - \hat{\mu}|^3}{\hat{\sigma}^3 \sqrt{n}} = \frac{(1 - q)^2 + q^2}{\sqrt{nq(1 - q)}},$$

which goes to zero as $n \rightarrow \infty$ since $q = \frac{1}{2} + \frac{1}{2}(\mu/\sigma)\sqrt{t/n}$.

Properties of Normal and Lognormal Random Variables. Since the normal and lognormal distributions are important to our analysis of options, it will be useful to review their properties. The density function of a normally distributed random variable, depicted in Figure 5-2(c), is described by a "bell-shaped" curve, familiar from almost all elementary books on statistics.

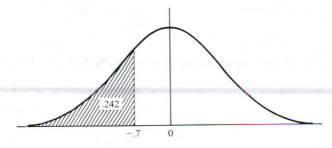

(a) Standard normal density function

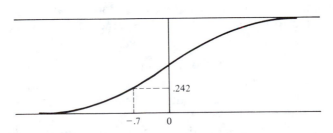

(b) Standard normal distribution function

Figure 5-2   Comparison of Normal and Lognormal
Probability Functions

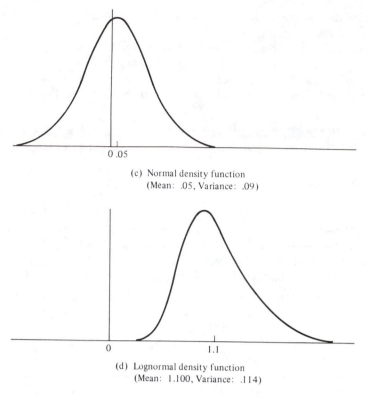

(c) Normal density function
(Mean: .05, Variance: .09)

(d) Lognormal density function
(Mean: 1.100, Variance: .114)

Figure 5-2   Comparison of Normal and Lognormal Probability
Functions (continued)

It is symmetrical about the mean, and the mean, median, and mode are all
equal. About two-thirds of the area under the curve lies within one standard
deviation of the mean. Furthermore, the distribution is completely specified
by its mean and standard deviation.

A standardized normally distributed random variable has a mean of
zero and a standard deviation of one. The standard normal density function,

$$N'(x) \equiv (1/\sqrt{2\pi})e^{-x^2/2},$$

is shown in Figure 5-2(a). The standard normal distribution function, $N(z)$,
gives the area under this density from $-\infty$ to z. That is, it gives the
probability that the random variable will take on a value less than or equal
to z. Therefore,

$$N(-\infty) = 0, \qquad 0 \leq N(z) \leq 1, \qquad \text{and} \qquad N(+\infty) = 1.$$

Furthermore, from the symmetry of the distribution, $N(-z) = 1 - N(z)$. Figure 5-2(a, b) illustrates some of these properties for $z = -.7$.

In our case, it is the variable

$$\frac{\log(S^*/S) - \mu t}{\sigma\sqrt{t}}$$

which has a standardized normal distribution. Consequently, $\log(S^*/S)$ has a normal distribution with mean μt and variance $\sigma^2 t$, and $\log S^*$ has a normal distribution with mean $\mu t + \log S$ and variance $\sigma^2 t$. This is shown in Figure 5-2(c) for $\mu t = .05$ and $\sigma^2 t = .09$. Since it is customary to think in terms of the price relative S^*/S, Figure 5-2(d) shows the implied shape of the density of $x \equiv S^*/S$, given that $\log(S^*/S)$ is normally distributed with mean $\mu t = .05$ and variance $\sigma^2 t = .09$. This distribution is termed lognormal. That is, whenever the random variable $\log x$ is normally distributed, then x itself is lognormally distributed. To clarify this transformation, remember that

$$\log x = \begin{cases} -\infty \\ 0 \\ 1 \\ +\infty \end{cases} \rightarrow x = \begin{cases} 0 \\ 1 \\ e \\ +\infty \end{cases}$$

These properties are illustrated in Figure 5-3, which shows a graph of the log function.

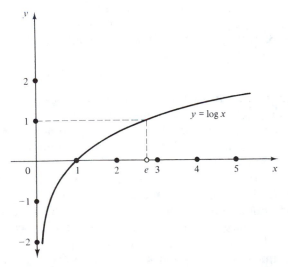

Figure 5-3   The Natural Logarithm

While $\log(S^*/S)$ is symmetric, S^*/S is skewed to the right, and the probability that $S^*/S \leq 0$ is zero. While the mean and variance of $\log(S^*/S)$ are μt and $\sigma^2 t$, the mean and variance of (S^*/S) are

$$e^{\mu t + \sigma^2 t/2} \quad \text{and} \quad e^{2\mu t + \sigma^2 t}(e^{\sigma^2 t} - 1).$$

For $\mu t = .05$ and $\sigma^2 t = .09$, the mean is 1.100 and the variance is .114. The median of (S^*/S) is $e^{\mu t}$ and its mode is $e^{\mu t - \sigma^2 t}$. If we were interested in the corresponding quantities for S^* rather than (S^*/S), we would simply multiply the mean, mode, and median by S and the variance by S^2.

We have shown that the multiplicative binomial model includes the lognormal distribution as a limiting case. This distribution has a number of sensible properties. It implies that stocks have limited liability, since, provided $S > 0$, S^* can never become negative. On the other hand, there is no upper limit on how far the stock price might rise, but very large increases are quite unlikely. Because of the symmetry of the normal distribution, equal up and down movements in $\log(S^*/S)$ about its mean are equally likely. For example, if $S = \$100$ and $E(S^*) = \$100$, then an increase to $S^* = \$133$ is just as likely as a decrease to $S^* = \$75$. This follows since $\log(133/100) = -\log(75/100)$. In other words, equal *relative* changes in S^* about its mean are equally likely. We might compare this with the supposition that equal *absolute* changes in S^* about the mean are equally likely. In this latter case, an increase to $S^* = \$133$ would be just as likely as a decrease to $S^* = \$67$. Taken in the extreme, the absolute hypothesis would imply moves to $S^* = \$0$ and $S^* = \$200$ were equally likely. To be sure, for most stocks the empirical reality may lie somewhere between the relative and absolute hypotheses, and we will consider other possibilities in Chapter 7.

Convergence to the Black-Scholes Option Pricing Formula. Black and Scholes began directly with continuous trading and the assumption of a lognormal distribution for stock prices. Their approach relied on some quite advanced mathematics. However, since our approach contains continuous trading and the lognormal distribution as a limiting case, the two resulting formulas should then coincide. We will see shortly that this is indeed true, and we will have the advantage of using a much simpler method. It is important to remember, however, that the economic arguments we used to link the option value and the stock price are the same as those advanced by Black and Scholes and Merton.

The formula derived by Black and Scholes, rewritten in terms of our notation, is

BLACK-SCHOLES OPTION PRICING FORMULA

where

$$C = SN(x) - Kr^{-t}N(x - \sigma\sqrt{t})$$

$$x \equiv \frac{\log(S/Kr^{-t})}{\sigma\sqrt{t}} + \tfrac{1}{2}\sigma\sqrt{t}$$

Here is one interpretation of the formula. If we exercise the call on the expiration date we will receive the stock, but in return we will have to pay the striking price. Of course, this exchange will not take place unless the call finishes in-the-money. The first term in the formula, $SN(x)$, is the present value of receiving the stock if and only if $S^* > K$, and the second term, $-Kr^{-t}N(x - \sigma\sqrt{t})$, is the present value of paying the striking price if and only if $S^* > K$. Just as we would expect from this interpretation, if S is very large relative to K, then $N(x) \approx N(x - \sigma\sqrt{t}) \approx 1$, and $C \approx S - Kr^{-t}$.

The formula has another interpretation which is particularly useful. Shortly, we will show that $N(x) = \Delta$, the number of shares in the equivalent portfolio. We know from our earlier discussions that $C = S\Delta + B$, where B is the dollar amount invested in default-free bonds in the equivalent portfolio. We can then see that $B = -Kr^{-t}N(x - \sigma\sqrt{t})$ directly from inspection of the Black-Scholes formula. As we stated in Chapter 2, the equivalent portfolio consists of a long position in less than one share of stock financed partly by borrowing. *The first term in the Black-Scholes formula, $SN(x)$, is the amount invested in the stock; the second term, $Kr^{-t}N(x - \sigma\sqrt{t})$, is the amount borrowed.*

We now wish to confirm that our binomial formula converges to the Black-Scholes formula when t is divided into more and more subintervals, and $\hat{r}$, u, d, and q are chosen in the way we described—that is, in a way such that the multiplicative binomial probability distribution of stock prices goes to the lognormal distribution.

For easy reference, let us recall our binomial option pricing formula:

$$C = S\Phi[a; n, p'] - K\hat{r}^{-n}\Phi[a; n, p].$$

The similarities are readily apparent. $\hat{r}^{-n}$ is, of course, always equal to r^{-t}. Therefore, to show the two formulas converge, we need only show that as $n \to \infty$,

$$\Phi[a; n, p'] \to N(x) \qquad \text{and} \qquad \Phi[a; n, p] \to N(x - \sigma\sqrt{t}).$$

We will consider only $\Phi[a; n, p]$, since the argument is exactly the same for $\Phi[a; n, p']$.

The complementary binomial distribution function $\Phi[a; n, p]$ is the probability that the sum of n random variables, each of which can take on the value 1 with probability p and 0 with probability $1 - p$, will be greater than or equal to a. We know that the random value of this sum, j, has mean np and standard deviation $\sqrt{np(1 - p)}$. Therefore,

$$1 - \Phi[a; n, p] = \text{Prob}[j \leq a - 1] = \text{Prob}\left[\frac{j - np}{\sqrt{np(1 - p)}} \leq \frac{a - 1 - np}{\sqrt{np(1 - p)}}\right].$$

Now we can make an analogy with our earlier discussion. If we consider a stock which in each period will move to uS with probability p and dS with probability $1 - p$, then $\log(S^*/S) = j \log(u/d) + n \log d$. The mean and variance of the continuously compounded rate of return of this stock are

$$\hat{\mu}_p = p \log(u/d) + \log d \quad \text{and} \quad \hat{\sigma}_p^2 = p(1 - p)[\log(u/d)]^2.$$

Using these equalities, we find that

$$\frac{j - np}{\sqrt{np(1 - p)}} = \frac{\log(S^*/S) - \hat{\mu}_p n}{\hat{\sigma}_p \sqrt{n}}.$$

Recall from the binomial formula that

$$a - 1 = \log(K/Sd^n)/\log(u/d) - \epsilon = [\log(K/S) - n \log d]/\log(u/d) - \epsilon,$$

where ϵ is a number between zero and one. Using this and the definitions of $\hat{\mu}_p$ and $\hat{\sigma}_p^2$, with a little algebra, we have:

$$\frac{a - 1 - np}{\sqrt{np(1 - p)}} = \frac{\log(K/S) - \hat{\mu}_p n - \epsilon \log(u/d)}{\hat{\sigma}_p \sqrt{n}}.$$

Putting these results together,

$$1 - \Phi[a; n, p] = \text{Prob}\left[\frac{\log(S^*/S) - \hat{\mu}_p n}{\hat{\sigma}_p \sqrt{n}} \leq \frac{\log(K/S) - \hat{\mu}_p n - \epsilon \log(u/d)}{\hat{\sigma}_p \sqrt{n}}\right].$$

We are now in a position to apply the central limit theorem. First, we must check if the initial condition,

$$\frac{p|\log u - \hat{\mu}_p|^3 + (1 - p)|\log d - \hat{\mu}_p|^3}{\hat{\sigma}_p \sqrt{n}} = \frac{(1 - p)^2 + p^2}{\sqrt{np(1 - p)}} \to 0$$

as $n \to \infty$, is satisfied. By first recalling that $p \equiv (\hat{r} - d)/(u - d)$, and then $\hat{r} = r^{t/n}$, $u = e^{\sigma\sqrt{t/n}}$, and $d = e^{-\sigma\sqrt{t/n}}$, it is possible to show that as $n \to \infty$,

$$p \to \frac{1}{2} + \frac{1}{2}\left(\frac{\log r - \frac{1}{2}\sigma^2}{\sigma}\right)\sqrt{\frac{t}{n}}.$$

As a result, the initial condition holds, and we are justified in applying the central limit theorem.

To do so, we need only evaluate $\hat{\mu}_p n$, $\hat{\sigma}_p^2 n$, and $\log(u/d)$ as $n \to \infty$.[22] Examination of our discussion for parameterizing q shows that as $n \to \infty$,

$$\hat{\mu}_p n \to (\log r - \tfrac{1}{2}\sigma^2)t \qquad \text{and} \qquad \hat{\sigma}_p \sqrt{n} \to \sigma\sqrt{t}.$$

Furthermore, $\log(u/d) \to 0$ as $n \to \infty$.

For this application of the central limit theorem, then, since

$$\frac{\log(K/S) - \hat{\mu}_p n - \epsilon \log(u/d)}{\hat{\sigma}_p \sqrt{n}} \to z \equiv \frac{\log(K/S) - (\log r - \frac{1}{2}\sigma^2)t}{\sigma\sqrt{t}},$$

we have

$$1 - \Phi[a; n, p] \to N(z) = N\left[\frac{\log(Kr^{-t}/S)}{\sigma\sqrt{t}} + \tfrac{1}{2}\sigma\sqrt{t}\right].$$

---

[22] A surprising feature of this evaluation is that although $p \neq q$ and thus $\hat{\mu}_p \neq \hat{\mu}$, and $\hat{\sigma}_p \neq \hat{\sigma}$, nonetheless $\hat{\sigma}_p \sqrt{n}$ and $\hat{\sigma}\sqrt{n}$ have the same limiting value as $n \to \infty$. By contrast, since $\mu \neq \log r - \frac{1}{2}\sigma^2$, $\hat{\mu}_p n$ and $\hat{\mu}n$ do not. This results from the way we needed to specify u and d to obtain convergence to a lognormal distribution. Rewriting this as $\sigma\sqrt{t} = (\log u)\sqrt{n}$, it is clear that the limiting value σ of the standard deviation does not depend on p or q, and hence must be the same for either. However, at any point before the limit, since

$$\hat{\sigma}^2 n = [\sigma^2 - \mu^2(t/n)]t \qquad \text{and} \qquad \hat{\sigma}_p^2 n = [\sigma^2 - (\log r - \tfrac{1}{2}\sigma^2)^2(t/n)]t,$$

$\hat{\sigma}$ and $\hat{\sigma}_p$ will generally have different values.

The fact that $\hat{\mu}_p n \to (\log r - \frac{1}{2}\sigma^2)t$ can also be derived from the property of the lognormal distribution that

$$\log E[S^*/S] = \mu_p t + \tfrac{1}{2}\sigma^2 t,$$

where E and μ_p are measured with respect to probability p. Since $p = (\hat{r} - d)/(u-d)$, it follows that $\hat{r} = pu + (1 - p)d$. For independently distributed random variables, the expectation of a product equals the product of their expectations. Therefore,

$$E[S^*/S] = [pu + (1 - p)d]^n = \hat{r}^n = r^t.$$

Substituting r^t for $E[S^*/S]$ in the previous equation, we have

$$\mu_p = \log r - \tfrac{1}{2}\sigma^2.$$

The final step in the argument is to use the symmetry property of the standard normal distribution that $1 - N(z) = N(-z)$. Therefore, as $n \to \infty$,

$$\Phi[a; n, p] \to N(-z) = N\left[\frac{\log(S/Kr^{-t})}{\sigma\sqrt{t}} - \tfrac{1}{2}\sigma\sqrt{t}\right] = N(x - \sigma\sqrt{t}).$$

Since a similar argument holds for $\Phi[a; n, p']$, this completes our demonstration that the binomial option pricing formula contains the Black-Scholes formula as a limiting case.[23]

The Continuous-Trading Valuation Equation.[24] When Black and Scholes originally derived their formula, they followed a different line of argument. However, we can use our simpler binomial model to explain their approach. In our original binomial development, recall that our ability to create an equivalent portfolio led to the following equation (somewhat rewritten)

$$\left[\frac{\hat{r} - d}{u - d}\right]C_u + \left[\frac{u - \hat{r}}{u - d}\right]C_d - \hat{r}C = 0 \qquad (7)$$

relating the value of a call at the beginning of any period to its possible values at the end of the period. For our current purposes, it will be more convenient to write C as $C(S, t)$, C_u as $C(uS, t - h)$, and C_d as $C(dS, t - h)$.

By their more difficult methods, Black and Scholes obtained directly a partial differential equation analogous to our discrete-time difference equation. Their equation is

$$\tfrac{1}{2}\sigma^2 S^2 \frac{\partial^2 C}{\partial S^2} + (\log r)S \frac{\partial C}{\partial S} - \frac{\partial C}{\partial t} - (\log r)C = 0, \qquad (8)$$

where $\partial^2 C/\partial S^2$, $\partial C/\partial S$, and $\partial C/\partial t$ are partial derivatives, and $\log r$ is the continuously compounded rate of interest. The value C of the call was then derived by solving this equation.

Based on our previous analysis, we would now suspect that, as we divide up the time to expiration into more and more intervals with smaller and smaller moves in the way described earlier, our binomial valuation equation would approach the continuous-time valuation equation of Black and Scholes. We will turn now to an intuitive confirmation of this.

---

[23] The only difference is that as $n \to \infty$,

$$p' \to \frac{1}{2} + \frac{1}{2}\left(\frac{\log r + \tfrac{1}{2}\sigma^2}{\sigma}\right)\sqrt{\frac{t}{n}}.$$

[24] The material in this subsection will be used only in Section 7-8.

If we choose $\hat{r}$, u, and d in the way described earlier, and substitute these values into our binomial valuation equation, we obtain

$$\left[\frac{r^h - e^{-\sigma\sqrt{h}}}{e^{\sigma\sqrt{h}} - e^{-\sigma\sqrt{h}}}\right] C(e^{\sigma\sqrt{h}}S, t - h)$$

$$+ \left[\frac{e^{\sigma\sqrt{h}} - r^h}{e^{\sigma\sqrt{h}} - e^{-\sigma\sqrt{h}}}\right] C(e^{-\sigma\sqrt{h}}S, t - h) - r^h C(S, t) = 0.$$

Now let us express $C(e^{\sigma\sqrt{h}}S, t - h)$ and $C(e^{-\sigma\sqrt{h}}S, t - h)$ as a Taylor series around the point (S, t). We will be interested only in terms multiplied by $\sqrt{h}$ or by h, since the remaining terms will become negligible, relative to these, as h becomes small. For an up move, we have

$$C(e^{\sigma\sqrt{h}}S, t - h) = C(S, t) + (e^{\sigma\sqrt{h}} - 1)S \frac{\partial C}{\partial S}$$

$$+ \tfrac{1}{2}(e^{\sigma\sqrt{h}} - 1)^2 \frac{\partial^2 C}{\partial S^2} - h \frac{\partial C}{\partial t},$$

and a similar expression for a down move, except $-\sigma\sqrt{h}$ replaces $\sigma\sqrt{h}$. We can now replace the exponential functions and r^h with their Taylor series expansions. Of course, we could have done that along with the first step, and the separation is only to make the exposition clear. Here we would have, for example,

$$e^{\sigma\sqrt{h}} = 1 + \sigma\sqrt{h} + \tfrac{1}{2}\sigma^2 h + \tfrac{1}{6}\sigma^3(h)^{3/2} + \cdots.$$

By substituting these into the equation, collecting terms, and retaining only terms of order h, we obtain

$$\tfrac{1}{2}\sigma^2 h S^2 \frac{\partial^2 C}{\partial S^2} + (\log r)hS \frac{\partial C}{\partial S} - h \frac{\partial C}{\partial t} - (\log r)hC = 0.$$

This form perhaps makes it easier to see why we did not bother with higher-order terms. If we had, to the above four terms we would have added $R = [\text{terms in } (h)^{3/2}, (h)^2, \ldots]$. If we then divide by h, we get

$$\tfrac{1}{2}\sigma^2 S^2 \frac{\partial^2 C}{\partial S^2} + (\log r)S \frac{\partial C}{\partial S} - \frac{\partial C}{\partial t} - (\log r)C + \frac{R}{h} = 0.$$

Now R/h goes to zero when h goes to zero, but the other terms do not, so we are left with the Black-Scholes equation.

Option Risk and Expected Rate of Return. We have just seen that the Black-Scholes formula is a limiting special case of the binomial formula we developed in Section 5-3. We showed in Section 5-5 how the one-period risk and expected return of an option were related to those of the stock for the binomial model. Since the results derived there did not depend on the length of the period, they must be valid for the Black-Scholes model as well. By pursuing arguments similar to those used earlier in this section, it can be shown that as the length of a period h becomes very small, the expected rate of return on the stock over the period approaches $(\mu + \frac{1}{2}\sigma^2)h$, and the variance of the rate of return over the period approaches $\sigma^2 h$. Naturally, the shorter the period, the smaller the risk and expected rate of return. In the same way, we could find the corresponding measures for a call. The results of Section 5-5 then tell us that these measures will be related to those of the stock in the following way:

> Expected rate of return of a call $-$ riskless interest rate
> $= \Omega$(expected rate of return of the stock
> $-$ riskless interest rate)
>
> Volatility of a call $= \Omega$(volatility of the stock)
>
> Beta of a call $= \Omega$(beta of the stock)

where $\Omega = (S/C)\Delta$. To complete the analysis, we need to find the limiting value of Δ. By applying the Taylor series expansions discussed in the last subsection, we find that as $n \to \infty$ and $h \to 0$,

$$\Delta = \frac{C_u - C_d}{(u - d)S} \to \frac{\partial C}{\partial S},$$

where $\partial C/\partial S$ is the partial derivative of C with respect to S. Using the Black-Scholes formula, it can be shown that $\partial C/\partial S = N(x)$. In other words, a change in the stock price by the very small amount g, other things equal, causes the call value to change by $(\partial C/\partial S)g = N(x)g$. In summary, for the limiting Black-Scholes case, the *delta* and *elasticity* of a call are, respectively,

$$\Delta = N(x)$$
$$\Omega = \frac{SN(x)}{C}.$$

Note once again that the expected rate of return of a call *does* depend on the expected rate of return of the stock, even though the value of a call *does not*.

Two other concepts will prove useful later. The delta of a call clearly depends on the level of the stock price. We will denote the sensitivity of delta to changes in the stock price, as measured by the partial derivative, as the *gamma* of a call:

$$\Gamma \equiv \frac{\partial \Delta}{\partial S}.$$

Similarly, we will refer to the sensitivity of the value of a call to the passage of time as the call's *theta*. Since time to expiration t decreases as time passes, theta will be the negative of the partial derivative of C with respect to t:

$$\Theta \equiv -\frac{\partial C}{\partial t}.$$

Black-Scholes Put Valuation. The Black-Scholes formula for valuing European puts can be derived in a similar manner to the call formula. However, we can shortcut this procedure by combining this latter formula with the European put-call parity relationship for payout-protected options.

From Chapters 2 and 4, we recall that

$$P = C - S + Kr^{-t}.$$

This holds under the very general condition that no profitable riskless arbitrage opportunities exist. Since this assumption is consistent with the assumptions underlying the formula, we know this parity relationship must hold here as well.

Therefore, substituting for the Black-Scholes value of C, we have

$$P = -S[1 - N(x)] + Kr^{-t}[1 - N(x - \sigma\sqrt{t})].$$

Using the symmetry property of the standard normal distribution, we find the Black-Scholes put formula:

$$P = Kr^{-t}N(y + \sigma\sqrt{t}) - SN(y)$$

where

$$y \equiv \frac{\log(Kr^{-t}/S)}{\sigma\sqrt{t}} - \tfrac{1}{2}\sigma\sqrt{t}.$$

For a put, $\Delta \equiv \partial P/\partial S = -N(y)$ and $\Omega = S\Delta/P$. Consequently, $\Delta \leq 0$ and $\Omega \leq 0$, and the volatility of the put, which must be positive, equals the negative of Ω times the volatility of the stock. Except for these changes, we have the same risk and return relationships that hold for calls. Since nothing in our discussion of the continuous-trading valuation equation specifically concerned a call, Equation (8) will also hold for a put.

Some Minor Generalizations.   Thus far we have assumed the interest rate is known and constant over time. If, instead, the interest rate were predictably certain but different for different periods, then we would need to associate a different interest rate $r_k - 1$ with each period k. The same formula could then be derived, except that the discount factor r^{-t} in the formula is replaced by $1/(r_1 r_2 r_3 \cdots r_t)$, which in the continuous limit becomes $\exp(-\int_0^t \log r(v)\, dv)$.[25] Since we could have written r^{-t} as $\exp[-(\log r)t]$, this simply says that the constant interest rate $\log r$ is replaced by the average interest rate which will prevail over the remaining life of the option $\int_0^t \log r(v)\, dv/t$.

Likewise, the volatility could vary predictably with time. This implies the up and down movements u and d will depend on the date. In the limiting case, σ will depend on the date, and the variance of $\log(S^*/S)$ will be $\int_0^t \sigma^2(v)\, dv$ rather than $\sigma^2 t$. The Black-Scholes formula remains valid when $\sigma^2 t$ is replaced by this integral. Once again, this is a very sensible result. It says that the constant volatility σ is replaced by the average volatility which will prevail over the remaining life of the option, $[\int_0^t \sigma^2(v)\, dv/t]^{1/2}$.

Consequently, there is no difficulty including interest rates and volatility that change over time in a predictable way. However, if future interest rates or volatility cannot be predicted with certainty, then our option pricing approach requires more serious modification. We will return to this possibility in Chapter 7.

5-7. AN ALTERNATIVE DERIVATION

This section contains a brief description of an alternative approach to deriving the Black-Scholes formula.[26] It shows how the Black-Scholes formula can be derived directly from the more traditional discrete-time, general equilibrium models used in the theory of finance.

---

[25] The notation $\exp(z)$ means e raised to the power z.

[26] This section is not necessary for understanding subsequent chapters. Also, it presumes some familiarity with the capital asset pricing model. For these reasons, the reader may wish to skip directly to Section 5-8.

The now traditional form of the capital asset pricing model says that, under certain circumstances, the current price X of *any* security is determined by

$$X = \frac{E(X^*) - \lambda \, \text{Cov}(X^*, r_M)}{r},$$

where X^* is its (uncertain) price at the end of the period, λ is a positive constant, $r_M - 1$ is the rate of return on the market portfolio, and $r - 1$ is the rate of interest over the period. E and Cov denote expectation and covariance, respectively.

Since this holds for any security, for an underlying stock and its call option,

$$S = \frac{E(S^*) - \lambda \, \text{Cov}(S^*, r_M)}{r} \quad \text{and} \quad C = \frac{E(C^*) - \lambda \, \text{Cov}(C^*, r_M)}{r},$$

where

$$C^* = \max[0, S^* - K].$$

These equations link the option and stock together. Remembering that S^* and r_M are jointly normally distributed, we can hope to use them to derive an option pricing formula relating C to S.

Although this can be done, the theory has two critical disadvantages. First, the theory assumes the joint distribution of *all* available securities is multivariate normal. However, by the contractual provisions of a call (that is, $C^* = \max[0, S^* - K]$, C^* cannot be normally distributed even if S^* is normally distributed. Moreover, if S^* is normally distributed, among other unfortunate implications, it cannot also have limited liability. Second, the option pricing problem is inherently multiperiod, where the purchaser of an option has many opportunities to sell or exercise it before it expires. The classical capital asset pricing model is essentially a single-period theory and does not conveniently accommodate opportunities for portfolio revision before a terminal date.[27]

To create a satisfactory theory, yet one that does not require continuous trading or binomial outcomes, one can replace the normality restriction on security returns with a logarithmic utility assumption on investor preferences. If this is done,[28] the following multiperiod formula

---

[27] Attempts to place the model in a useful multiperiod context require the further assumption that λ is an intertemporal constant.

[28] See Mark Rubinstein, "The Valuation of Uncertain Income Streams and the Pricing of Options," *Bell Journal of Economics*, 7 (Autumn 1976), 407–425.

replaces the usual capital asset pricing model:

$$X = \sum_{k=1}^{\infty} \frac{E(D_k) - \lambda_k \operatorname{Cov}(D_k, -r_M^{-k})}{r^k},$$

where

$$\lambda_k = \sqrt{(1 + \lambda^2)^k - 1} \quad \text{and} \quad \lambda \equiv [E(r_M^{-1})]^{-1}.$$

D_k represents the (uncertain) cash distribution received on date k from the security.

For non-dividend-paying stock over time t, this formula simplifies to

$$S = \frac{E(S^*) - \lambda_t \operatorname{Cov}(S^*, -r_M^{-t})}{r^t},$$

and for a call with time to expiration t,

$$C = \frac{E(C^*) - \lambda_t \operatorname{Cov}(C^*, -r_M^{-t})}{r^t},$$

where

$$C^* = \max[0, S^* - K].$$

This is quite similar to the three relationships derived from the capital asset pricing model, except we have not imposed the disagreeable stochastic restrictions on S^* and C^*, and have accounted for the multiperiod nature of options markets.[29]

However, without some stochastic assumption governing S^*, we cannot completely solve the problem of finding a formula for C in terms of S. We need to know something about the probability that it will pay to exercise the call. Since we are free to adopt whatever stochastic restriction we wish, we will choose a reasonable one: S^* and r_M are *jointly lognormally* distributed. Although this is a stronger stochastic assumption than that made in our original derivation in Section 5-6, since it implies S^*/S will itself be lognormally distributed, it is consistent with that derivation.

Since the proof is tedious, it is not repeated here. Suffice it to say that the above three equations, together with the joint lognormality assumption, yield a result *identical with the Black-Scholes formula*. At first thought, this is quite surprising, since neither continuous trading nor binomial outcomes have been assumed. Rather, investors are only permitted to trade at discrete points in time and, at each point, the stock price—being lognormal—can have any one of an infinite number of values. Investors are thus unable to

---

[29] Moreover, unlike the capital asset pricing model, investor agreement about the joint probability distribution of security returns is also not required.

construct riskless hedges with the option and the stock, a capability that was crucial to previous proofs. Indeed, it was precisely to circumvent a riskless hedging argument that this alternative model was created.

A simple explanation of this anomaly can be found in portfolio theory: Logarithmic utility is the only utility function for which portfolios are chosen independently of opportunities to revise them in the future. Therefore, the relative pricing relationship between a European option and its underlying stock will be independent of the number of times portfolio revision can occur before the expiration date of an option. In particular, the same relationship will hold even if the investor faces continuous revision opportunities. But we have already shown that assumption leads directly to the Black-Scholes formula.

In summary, the discrete-time logarithmic utility model, by reaching the same option pricing conclusion as a hedging model, indicates the robustness of the Black-Scholes formula to its assumption of continuous trading. To underscore the significance of this result, consider an investor who, for some reason, cannot implement a dynamic riskless hedging strategy similar to that described in Section 5-4. Nonetheless, he may very well *value* an option according to the Black-Scholes formula. Only at the Black-Scholes price will a static position in the option provide fair compensation in terms of expected return for the risk borne.

5-8. HOW CHANGES IN THE VARIABLES AFFECT BLACK-SCHOLES OPTION VALUES

Extreme Values. One way to understand the formula is to examine what happens to the call value C as the variables S, K, t, σ, and r, on which it depends, change in value. To keep the effects clear, we will choose one of these five variables and change its value, while holding the other four fixed. First, we examine extreme changes:

1. Stock price:
   as $S \to 0$, then $C \to 0$
   as $S \to \infty$, then $C \to \infty$
2. Striking price:
   as $K \to 0$, then $C \to S$
   as $K \to \infty$, then $C \to 0$
3. Time to expiration:
   given $S < K$: as $t \to 0$, then $C \to 0$
   given $S > K$: as $t \to 0$, then $C \to S - K$
   as $t \to \infty$, then $C \to S$

4. Volatility:

given $S < Kr^{-t}$: as $\sigma \to 0$, then $C \to 0$
given $S > Kr^{-t}$: as $\sigma \to 0$, then $C \to S - Kr^{-t}$
as $\sigma \to \infty$, then $C \to S$

5. Interest rate:

as $r \to \infty$, then $C \to S$

The reader should try to prove each of these assertions. To take the most difficult case, as $\sigma \to \infty$, then $x = [\log(S/Kr^{-t})/\sigma\sqrt{t}] + \frac{1}{2}\sigma\sqrt{t} \to +\infty$ and $x - \sigma\sqrt{t} \to -\infty$. Since

$$N(x) \to N(+\infty) = 1 \quad \text{and} \quad N(x - \sigma\sqrt{t}) \to N(-\infty) = 0,$$

then $C \to S$.

All these implications of the formula are fully consistent with the general arbitrage relationships developed in Chapter 4. Of course, if they were not, our exact formula would be in error.

Tabular Representation. Table 5-2 gives formula-generated values for nine calls in a typical option class with current stock price of $40. The class includes out-of-, at-, and in-the-money series ranging over near, middle, and far maturities. Values for the nine series cover low, middle, and high volatilities, and low, middle, and high interest rates. As we would expect from Chapter 4, call values increase with lower striking price, longer time to expiration and higher volatility.

Table 5-2

REPRESENTATIVE BLACK-SCHOLES CALL VALUES

		$S = 40$								
		$r = 1.03$			$r = 1.05$			$r = 1.07$		
σ	K	*Expiration Month*								
		JAN	*APR*	*JUL*	*JAN*	*APR*	*JUL*	*JAN*	*APR*	*JUL*
	35	5.09	5.56	6.08	5.15	5.76	6.40	5.20	5.95	6.71
.2	40	.97	2.04	2.77	1.00	2.17	3.00	1.04	2.30	3.24
	45	.02	.46	.98	.02	.51	1.10	.02	.56	1.23
	35	5.17	6.08	6.90	5.22	6.25	7.17	5.27	6.42	7.44
.3	40	1.43	2.95	3.97	1.46	3.07	4.19	1.49	3.20	4.40
	45	.16	1.19	2.09	.16	1.25	2.24	.17	1.33	2.39
	35	5.34	6.74	7.85	5.39	6.89	8.09	5.44	7.05	8.34
.4	40	1.89	3.86	5.16	1.92	3.98	5.37	1.95	4.10	5.58
	45	.41	2.02	3.27	.42	2.10	3.43	.43	2.18	3.59

NOTE: The January options have one month to expiration; the Aprils, four months; and the Julys, seven months. Both r and σ are expressed in annual terms.

An unresolved issue in that chapter was the effect of the interest rate. Although it lacks the status of a general arbitrage relationship, within the context of the Black-Scholes formula, call values appear to increase with higher interest rates. Indeed, this can be directly verified analytically. This result is anticipated, since r enters the formula inversely to K. However, the same percentage change in the interest rate $r - 1$ has a much smaller effect on call values than a percentage change in the striking price, time to expiration, or volatility. For example, for the at-the-money, middle-maturity calls at 5% interest rate, doubling the volatility from .2 to .4 increases the option value from $2.17 to $3.98. In contrast, for the at-the-money, middle-maturity calls at .3 volatility, more than doubling the interest rate from 3% to 7% only raises the option value from $2.95 to $3.20.

Graphical Representation. Figures 5-4 through 5-11 show how the formula values for typical out-of-, at-, and in-the-money calls and puts change as the current stock price, time to expiration, volatility and interest rate change gradually over wide ranges. Figures 5-4 and 5-8 are the option-stock price diagrams for a call and a put, respectively. Just as we would expect, the properties shown in the graphs correspond exactly to those given in Chapter 4. In all the graphs, time is measured in years. Thus σ and r are expressed in annualized terms.

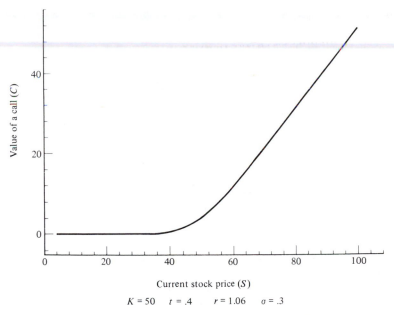

$K = 50 \quad t = .4 \quad r = 1.06 \quad \sigma = .3$

Figure 5-4 The Value of a Call as a Function of the Current Stock Price

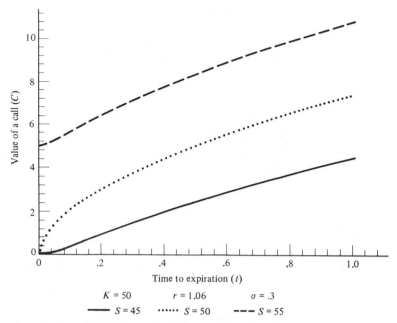

$K = 50$	$r = 1.06$	$\sigma = .3$
—— $S = 45$	⋯⋯ $S = 50$	‑‑‑ $S = 55$

Figure 5-5   The Value of a Call as a Function of the Time to
Expiration

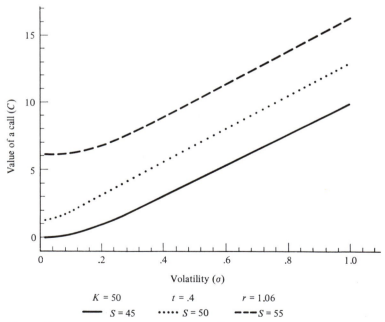

$K = 50$	$t = .4$	$r = 1.06$
—— $S = 45$	⋯⋯ $S = 50$	‑‑‑ $S = 55$

Figure 5-6   The Value of a Call as a Function of the Volatility

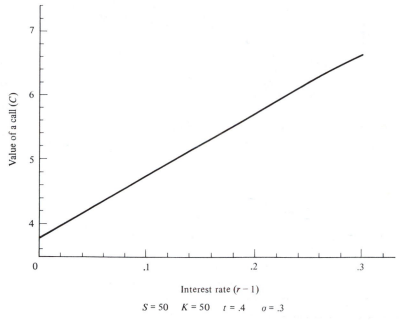

Interest rate $(r - 1)$

$S = 50 \quad K = 50 \quad t = .4 \quad \sigma = .3$

Figure 5-7   The Value of a Call as a Function of the Interest
Rate

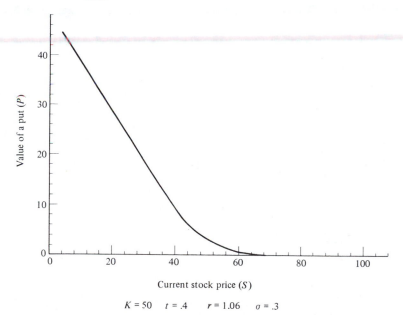

Current stock price (S)

$K = 50 \quad t = .4 \quad r = 1.06 \quad \sigma = .3$

Figure 5-8   The Value of a Put as a Function of the Current
Stock Price

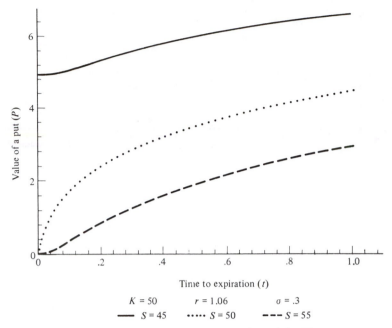

Time to expiration (*t*)

$K = 50$ $r = 1.06$ $\sigma = .3$
—— $S = 45$ •••• $S = 50$ – – $S = 55$

Figure 5-9   The Value of a Put as a Function of the Time to
                   Expiration

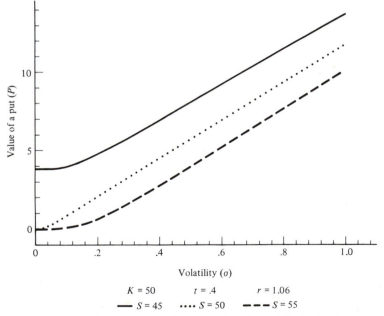

Volatility (*σ*)

$K = 50$ $t = .4$ $r = 1.06$
—— $S = 45$ •••• $S = 50$ – – $S = 55$

Figure 5-10   The Value of a Put as a Function of the Volatility

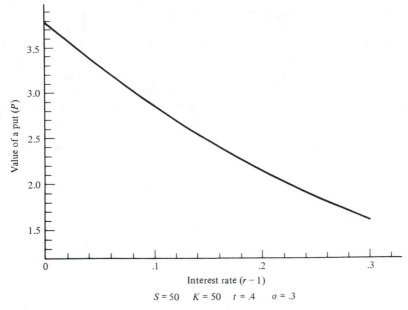

Figure 5-11 The Value of a Put as a Function of the Interest Rate

The *sensitivity* of the formula call value to small changes in each of the five determining variables gives an alternative mathematical representation:[30]

1. Stock price: $\partial C/\partial S = N(x) > 0$
2. Striking price: $\partial C/\partial K = -r^{-t}N(x - \sigma\sqrt{t}) < 0$
3. Time to expiration:
   $\partial C/\partial t = (S\sigma/2\sqrt{t})N'(x) + Kr^{-t}(\log r)N(x - \sigma\sqrt{t}) > 0$
4. Volatility: $\partial C/\partial \sigma = S\sqrt{t}N'(x) > 0$
5. Interest rate: $\partial C/\partial r = tKr^{-(t+1)}N(x - \sigma\sqrt{t}) > 0$

---

[30] Readers familiar with calculus who would like to verify these derivatives should use the fact

$$\frac{\partial N(z)}{\partial v} = N'(z)\frac{\partial z}{\partial v},$$

where $N'(z)$ is the standard normal density function evaluated at z. That is, $N'(z) = (1/\sqrt{2\pi})e^{-z^2/2}$.

In other words, for example, a change in the volatility of the stock by the small amount g causes the call value to change by $(\partial C/\partial \sigma)g = S\sqrt{t}\, N'(x)g$. The sensitivity $\partial C/\partial S$ is, of course, the option delta, and the sensitivity $-\partial C/\partial t$ is the option theta.

Figures 5-12 through 5-19 show how these sensitivities for a call vary with the current stock price and time to expiration.[31] Figure 5-12 shows that the call delta will be near zero for deep-out-of-the-money calls and

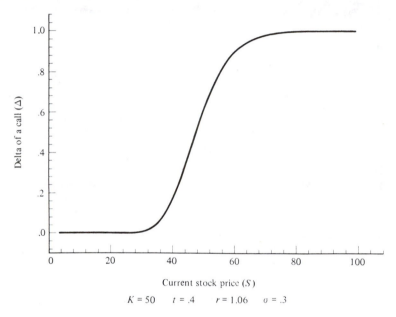

$$K = 50 \qquad t = .4 \qquad r = 1.06 \qquad \sigma = .3$$

Figure 5-12   The Delta of a Call as a Function of the Current Stock Price

near one for deep-in-the-money calls. The delta only changes quickly with the current stock price for calls near-the-money. Figure 5-13 indicates that the call delta falls as the expiration date approaches for out-of-the-money calls but tends to rise for in-the-money calls. From Figure 5-14 we learn that changes in time to expiration have the greatest dollar effect on calls near-the-money. In Chapter 4, from pure arbitrage considerations, we were unable to say if, for three otherwise identical calls, the middle maturity call should sell for more than half the sum of the near- and far-maturity calls.

---

[31] The reader familiar with calculus should recognize the slopes of these figures as representing second and cross-partial derivatives.

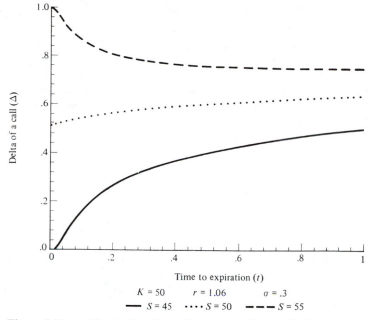

Figure 5-13 The Delta of a Call as a Function of the Time to Expiration

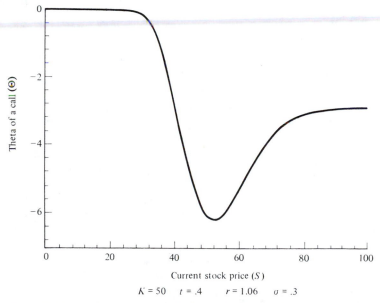

Figure 5-14 The Theta of a Call as a Function of the Current Stock Price

Figure 5-15 gives the answer in the context of the Black-Scholes formula: This relationship will hold except for out-of- or in-the-money calls when the near-maturity call is very close to expiration. Figures 5-16 and 5-17 show that calls with values most sensitive to volatility are near-the-money and of long maturity, while Figures 5-18 and 5-19 show that the values of deep-in-the-money long-maturity calls are the most sensitive to the interest rate.

For the Black-Scholes model, the gamma and elasticity of a call are

$$\Gamma \equiv \frac{\partial \Delta}{\partial S} = \frac{1}{S\sigma\sqrt{t}} N'(x),$$

$$\Omega \equiv \frac{S\Delta}{C} = \frac{SN(x)}{C}.$$

Figures 5-20 through 5-23 show how these values depend on the current stock price and time to expiration.

Figure 5-20 indicates that the delta of a call will be most sensitive to changes in the stock price when the call is slightly out-of-the-money. Further calculations with the formula confirm this and show that gamma

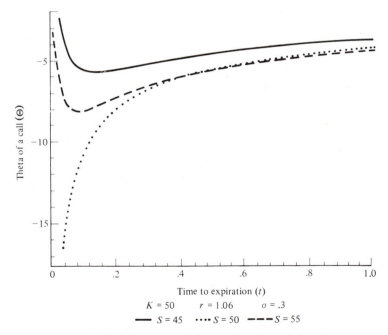

Figure 5-15   The Theta of a Call as a Function of the Time to Expiration

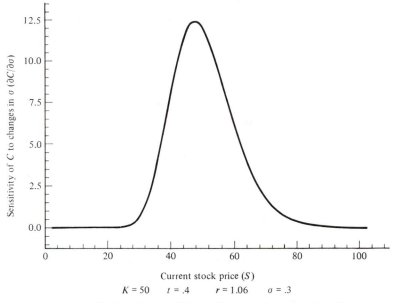

Figure 5-16   The Sensitivity of C to Changes in σ as a Function of the Current Stock Price

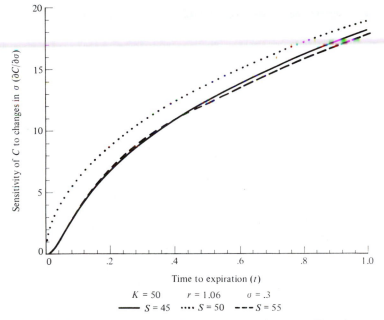

Figure 5-17   The Sensitivity of C to Changes in σ as a Function of the Time to Expiration

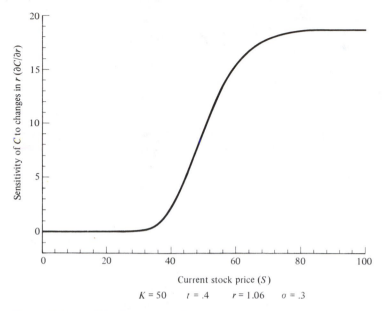

Figure 5-18   The Sensitivity of *C* to Changes in *r* as a Function
of the Current Stock Price

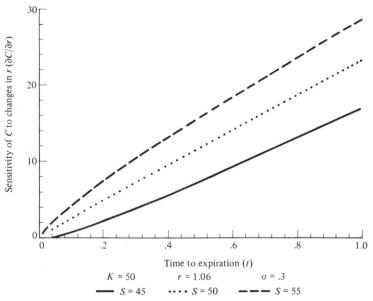

Figure 5-19   The Sensitivity of *C* to Changes in *r* as a Function
of the Time to Expiration

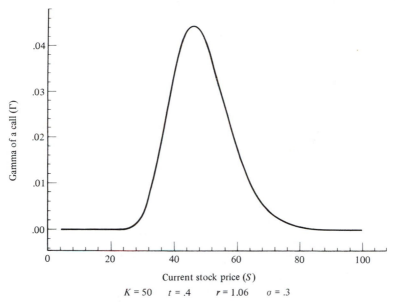

K = 50   t = .4   r = 1.06   σ = .3

Figure 5-20   The Gamma of a Call as a Function of the Current
                    Stock Price

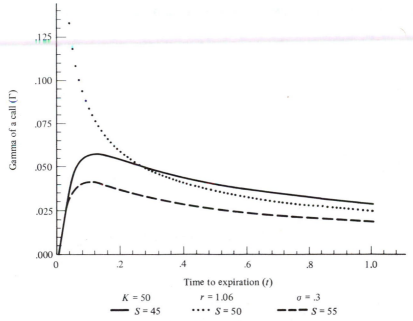

K = 50   r = 1.06   σ = .3
——— S = 45   •••• S = 50   —— S = 55

Figure 5-21   The Gamma of a Call as a Function of the Time to
                    Expiration

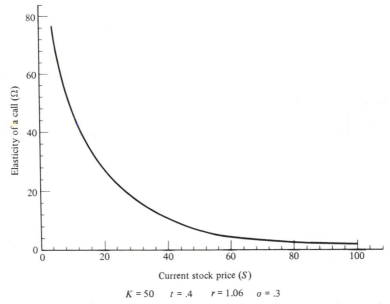

$$K = 50 \quad t = .4 \quad r = 1.06 \quad \sigma = .3$$

Figure 5-22   The Elasticity of a Call as a Function of the Current Stock Price

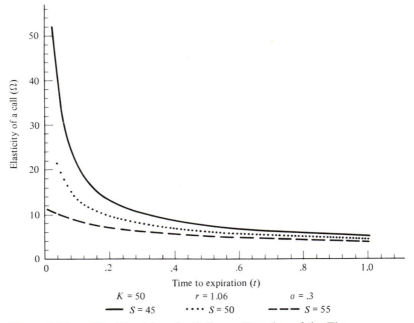

$$K = 50 \qquad r = 1.06 \qquad \sigma = .3$$

—— $S = 45$ •••• $S = 50$ ––– $S = 55$

Figure 5-23   The Elasticity of a Call as a Function of the Time to Expiration

reaches its largest value when $S = Kr^{-t}[\exp(-\frac{3}{2}\sigma^2 t)]$. Figure 5-21 shows that, for a given stock price, gamma will go to zero as the expiration date approaches if the call is in-the-money or out-of-the-money, but will become very large if it is exactly at-the-money. For an at-the-money call with a short lifetime, a very small change in the stock price can lead to a significant change in the composition of the equivalent portfolio.

Remember that the elasticity of an option shows the percentage change in its value that will accompany a small percentage change in the stock price. Figure 5-22 shows that the elasticity increases as the stock price decreases. Taking an extreme case, according to Figure 5-22, a call 30 points out-of-the-money (that is, $S = \$20$) changes about 28% in value for a 1% change in the stock price. It is certainly no overstatement to say that deep-out-of-the-money calls are highly levered securities. Figure 5-23 shows that the elasticity also increases as the time to expiration decreases. Other things equal, a call will be more sensitive to stock price movements *in percentage terms* the shorter the time remaining until expiration.

Figures 5-24 through 5-35 show comparable relationships for puts. The sensitivities for puts are

---

1. Stock price: $\partial P/\partial S = (\partial C/\partial S) - 1 < 0$
2. Striking price: $\partial P/\partial K = (\partial C/\partial K) + r^{-t} > 0$
3. Time to expiration:
$$\partial P/\partial t = (\partial C/\partial t) - (\log r)Kr^{-t} \gtrless 0$$
4. Volatility: $\partial P/\partial \sigma = \partial C/\partial \sigma > 0$
5. Interest rate: $\partial P/\partial r = (\partial C/\partial r) - tKr^{-(t+1)} < 0$

Again $\partial P/\partial S$ is the put delta and $-\partial P/\partial t$ the put theta. As expected, the sign of the theta for European puts is ambiguous. Also, note that the interest rate affects put and call values in opposite directions.

For puts,

$$\Gamma \equiv \frac{\partial \Delta}{\partial S} = \frac{1}{S\sigma\sqrt{t}} N'(x)$$

and

$$\Omega \equiv (S/P)\Delta = \frac{S}{P}[N(x) - 1].$$

Observe that the gammas of puts and calls with identical terms are equal. This is confirmed by comparing Figures 5-20 and 5-21 with Figures 5-32 and 5-33.

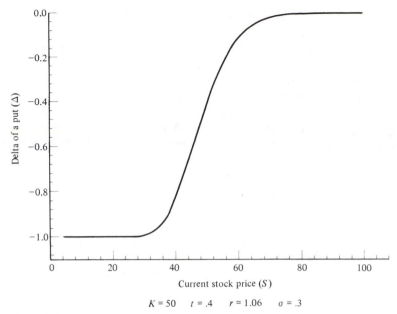

K = 50   t = .4   r = 1.06   σ = .3

Figure 5-24   The Delta of a Put as a Function of the Current
                    Stock Price

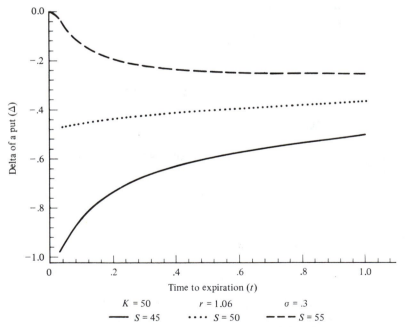

K = 50   r = 1.06   σ = .3
——— S = 45   •••• S = 50   — — — S = 55

Figure 5-25   The Delta of a Put as a Function of the Time to
                    Expiration

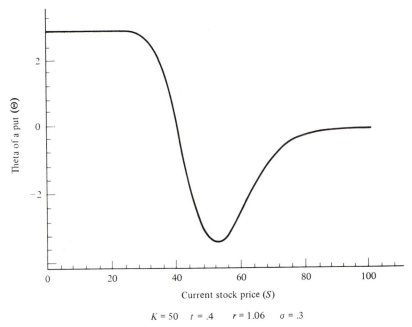

$$K = 50 \quad t = .4 \quad r = 1.06 \quad \sigma = .3$$

Figure 5-26   The Theta of a Put as a Function of the Current Stock Price

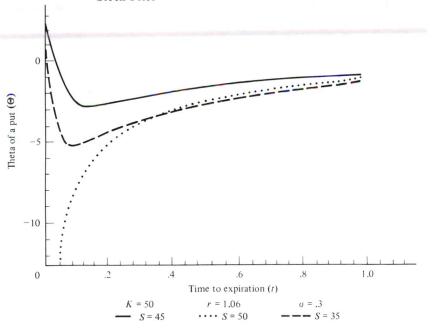

$$K = 50 \qquad r = 1.06 \qquad \sigma = .3$$

——— $S = 45$ •••• $S = 50$ — — — $S = 35$

Figure 5-27   The Theta of a Put as a Function of the Time to Expiration

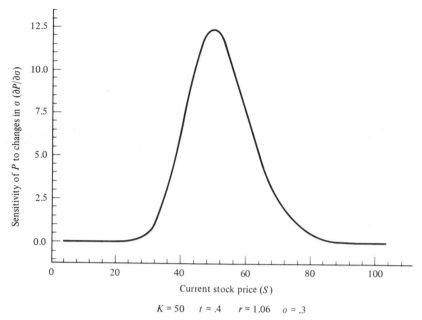

$$K = 50 \qquad t = .4 \qquad r = 1.06 \qquad \sigma = .3$$

Figure 5-28   The Sensitivity of P to Changes in σ as a Function
of the Current Stock Price

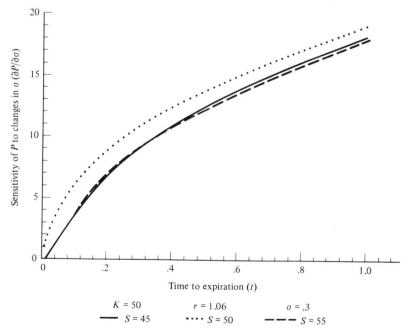

$K = 50$	$r = 1.06$	$\sigma = .3$
—— $S = 45$	•••• $S = 50$	——— $S = 55$

Figure 5-29   The Sensitivity of P to Changes in σ as a Function
of the Time to Expiration

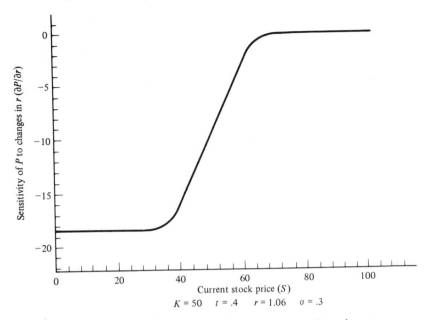

Figure 5-30   The Sensitivity of *P* to Changes in *r* as a Function of the Current Stock Price

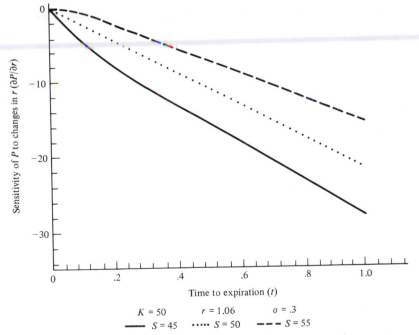

Figure 5-31   The Sensitivity of *P* to Changes in *r* as a Function of the Time to Expiration

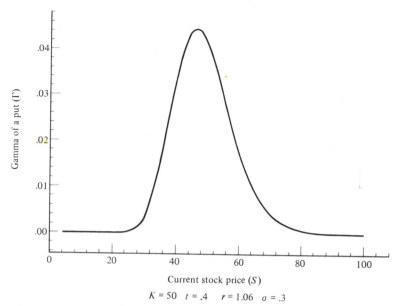

Current stock price (S)

K = 50   t = .4   r = 1.06   σ = .3

Figure 5-32   The Gamma of a Put as a Function of the Current
Stock Price

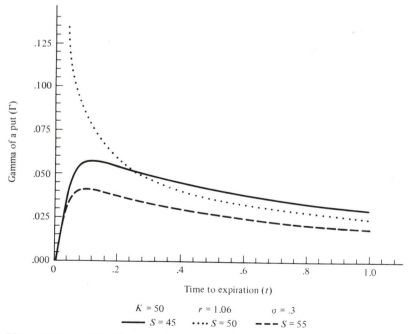

Time to expiration (t)

K = 50   r = 1.06   σ = .3
——— S = 45   •••• S = 50   — — — S = 55

Figure 5-33   The Gamma of a Put as a Function of the Time to
Expiration

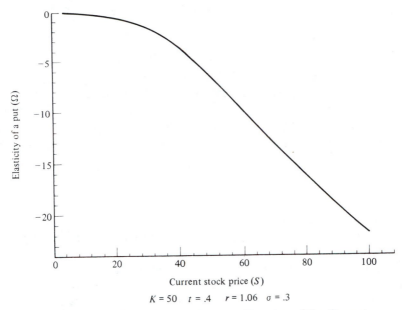

$K = 50 \quad t = .4 \quad r = 1.06 \quad \sigma = .3$

Figure 5-34   The Elasticity of a Put as a Function of the Current Stock Price

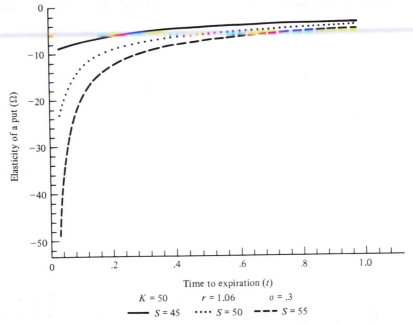

$K = 50 \qquad r = 1.06 \qquad \sigma = .3$

—— $S = 45$ •••• $S = 50$ – – – $S = 55$

Figure 5-35   The Elasticity of a Put as a Function of the Time to Expiration

5-9. HOW TO INCLUDE DIVIDENDS AND THE POSSIBILITY OF EARLY EXERCISE

As we have seen, the value of an option with no payout protection will be affected if the stock pays cash dividends. Furthermore, it may then be optimal to exercise an American call before the expiration date. This possibility causes the value of an American call to exceed the value of an otherwise identical European call. Although cash dividends are not necessary for early exercise to be optimal for an American put, they will nevertheless affect the optimal exercise strategy.

To handle the effects of cash dividends with a riskless hedging argument, we must assume that the dividends that will be paid on any future date are a known function of, at most, the path followed by the stock price up to that date. This condition is actually not very restrictive. It allows sufficient flexibility to represent the dividend behavior of most firms. In particular, current and future dividends could be influenced in a quite general way by the sequence of dividends paid in the past. It requires us to know the dividend policy of the firm, but it certainly does not imply that we must know today exactly what future dividends will actually be, since they may depend on the currently unknown values of future stock prices.

It does, however, rule out random changes in the dividend level which are not perfectly correlated with the stock price. The critical feature was that, in every period, the ex-dividend stock price at the end of the period can take on only two possible values. Suppose, instead, that a dividend D on an ex-dividend date one period from now can either be D' or D'', where $D' < D''$, and that the size of the dividend is independent of the stock price. Then, the stock price could have four possible values one period hence:

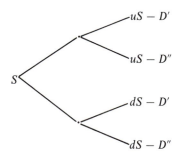

For example, if, in the absence of dividends, the stock price would move up to uS, then the ex-dividend price will be $uS - D'$ or $uS - D''$. This uses the fact that to prevent arbitrage, the stock price must fall by the amount of the dividend. With *four* possible ex-dividend values of the stock price at the end of one period, we cannot set up a riskless arbitrage position using only *three* securities—the stock, a call, and a default-free security. If we try to choose a hedge ratio Δ that will equate the returns in two of the four outcomes, we will still be exposed to risk in the remaining two outcomes.

To make the following discussions more concrete, we will consider as an example a specific and particularly important dividend policy: The stock maintains a constant yield $\delta \equiv D/S$ on each ex-dividend date. Suppose there is one period remaining before expiration and the current stock price is S. If the end of the period is an ex-dividend date, then an individual who owned the stock during the period will receive at that time a dividend of either δuS if the stock price goes up to uS or δdS if the stock price goes down to dS. Hence, the stock price at the end of the period can take on only two possible values: $(1 - \delta)uS$ or $(1 - \delta)dS$.

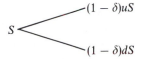

In particular, if $\delta = .05$, then 5% of the value of the stock on an ex-dividend date would be paid out in dividends, leaving $1 - .05$ or 95% of the stock value remaining.

Although we will not pursue it further, a very similar setting can be used to illustrate more complicated policies that depend on past stock prices. For example, suppose that the dividend yield paid at the end of the current period will be 7% if the stock price moved upward in the previous period and 3% if it moved downward. The dividend policy will then depend on both the current stock price and the stock price last period.

Dividends and European Options. An *unprotected European option* written on a stock with a constant dividend yield δ is valued identically to one written on a stock paying no dividends, except that the current stock price S is replaced with $S(1 - \delta)^{\bar{v}}$, where $\bar{v}$ is the number of ex-dividend dates prior to the expiration of an option. To see this, consider any path the stock price may take over time. For instance, suppose, in the absence of dividends, the stock price at expiration $S^* = uudduuududS = u^6d^4S$, implying a down movement was followed by an up movement, which was followed by a down movement, etc. Suppose an ex-dividend date occurs every third period. Then,

$$S^* = u(1 - \delta)udd(1 - \delta)uuu(1 - \delta)dudS = u^6d^4(1 - \delta)^3S.$$

Now consider another path, $S^* = dudddudddu S = u^3 d^7 S$. Again, with an ex-dividend date every third period, this becomes:

$$S^* = d(1 - \delta)udd(1 - \delta)dud(1 - \delta)ddu S = u^3 d^7 (1 - \delta)^3 S.$$

Unlike an American option, the current value of a European option depends only on its possible values at expiration, which in turn depend only on the possible prices of its associated stock at expiration. In particular, given the same ending value, the path the stock price takes over time is irrelevant. As we can see, with a constant dividend yield, the stock price at expiration depends on the *number* $\bar{v}$ of ex-dividend dates, but it does not depend on the *timing* of the dividends. Therefore, *we will obtain identical values for unprotected European options whether we consider the actual path taken by the stock price or regard the dividends as all paid immediately.*

American Calls.   The possible early exercise of unprotected American calls implies their current value depends on the path of the stock price through expiration and thereby on the timing of the ex-dividend dates. We know from Section 4-1 that the only time early exercise of calls should be considered is just prior to their ex-dividend dates. If the call holder exercises his call just prior to the ex-dividend date, he receives the dividend on the stock that he would otherwise forego. Exercise between ex-dividend dates sacrifices premium over parity unnecessarily.

One way to take early exercise into account is to calculate for each listed call several European values, one for early exercise just before each ex-dividend date prior to expiration, and one assuming exercise at expiration. Shortening the life of the call tends to decrease its value, but deducting fewer dividends tends to increase it. The estimated, or "pseudo-American," current call value is then simply the highest of these European values.

Unfortunately, this method of adjusting American calls for dividends understates their actual values. For example, if the highest European value is based on exercising just before the last ex-dividend date prior to expiration, then the method presumes that exercise policy will remain optimal. But, if the stock price experiences a sudden decline, pushing the call out-of-the-money, early exercise may no longer be advisable. The additional flexibility actually afforded by an American call to change our minds about exercise means that an American call will be worth more than its pseudo-American value.

To derive a method for valuing American calls, we return to the binomial argument of Section 5-3. With one period remaining before expiration, we suppose the current stock price S will change either to $d(1 - \delta)^v S$ or $u(1 - \delta)^v S$ by the end of the period; $v = 0$ or 1, depending on whether or not the end of the period is an ex-dividend date. When the call expires, its contract and a rational exercise policy imply that its value must be either $C_u = \max[0, u(1 - \delta)^v S - K]$ or $C_d = \max[0, d(1 - \delta)^v S - K]$. Therefore,

$$C \Big\langle \begin{array}{l} C_u = \max[0, u(1 - \delta)^v S - K] \\[2em] C_d = \max[0, d(1 - \delta)^v S - K] \end{array}$$

Now we can proceed exactly as before. Again we can select a portfolio of Δ shares of stock and the dollar amount B in bonds which will have the same end-of-period value as the call.[32] By retracing our previous steps, we can show that

$$C = [pC_u + (1 - p)C_d]/\hat{r}$$

if this is greater than $S - K$, and $C = S - K$ otherwise. Here, once again, $p = (\hat{r} - d)/(u - d)$ and $\Delta = (C_u - C_d)/(u - d)S$.

Thus far the only change is that $(1 - \delta)^v S$ has replaced S in the values for C_u and C_d. Now we come to the major difference: Early exercise may be optimal. To see this, suppose that $v = 1$ and $d(1 - \delta)S > K$. Since $u > d$, then, also, $u(1 - \delta)S > K$. In this case, $C_u = u(1 - \delta)S - K$ and $C_d = d(1 - \delta)S - K$. Therefore, since $(u/\hat{r})p + (d/\hat{r})(1 - p) = 1$,

$$[pC_u + (1 - p)C_d]/\hat{r} = (1 - \delta)S - (K/\hat{r}).$$

For sufficiently high stock prices, this can obviously be less than $S - K$. Hence, there are definitely some circumstances in which no one would be willing to hold the call for one more period.

In fact, there will always be a critical stock price, $\underline{S}$, such that if $S > \underline{S}$, the call should be exercised immediately. $\underline{S}$ will be the stock price at which $[pC_u + (1 - p)C_d]/\hat{r} = S - K$. That is, it is the lowest stock price at which the value of the equivalent portfolio exactly equals $S - K$. This means $\underline{S}$ will, other things equal, be lower the higher the dividend yield, the lower the interest rate, and the lower the striking price.

We can extend the analysis to an arbitrary number of periods in the same way as before. There is only one additional difference, a minor modification in the hedging operation. Now we will buy bonds with any dividends received, and sell bonds to make restitution for dividends paid while we have a short position in the stock.

---

[32] Remember that if we are long the portfolio, we will receive the dividend at the end of the period; if we are short, we will have to make restitution for the dividend.

Although the possibility of optimal exercise before the expiration date causes no conceptual difficulties, it does seem to prohibit a simple closed-form solution for the value of a call with many periods to go. However, our analysis suggests a sequential numerical procedure that will allow us to calculate the continuous-time value to any desired degree of accuracy.

Let C be the current value of a call with n periods remaining. Define

$$\bar{v}(n, i) \equiv \sum_{k=1}^{n-i} v_k,$$

so that $\bar{v}(n, i)$ is the number of ex-dividend dates occurring during the next $n - i$ periods. Let $C(n, i, j)$ be the value of the call $n - i$ periods from now, given that the current stock price S has changed to $u^j d^{n-i-j}(1 - \delta)^{\bar{v}(n, i)}S$, where $j = 0, 1, 2, \ldots, n - i$.

With this notation, we are prepared to solve for the current value of the call by working backward in time from the expiration date. At expiration, $i = 0$, so that

$$C(n, 0, j) = \max[0, u^j d^{n-j}(1 - \delta)^{\bar{v}(n, 0)}S - K] \quad \text{for} \quad j = 0, 1, \ldots, n.$$

One period before the expiration date, $i = 1$, so that

$$\begin{aligned} C(n, 1, j) = \max\{&u^j d^{n-1-j}(1 - \delta)^{\bar{v}(n, 1)}S - K, \\ &[pC(n, 0, j + 1) + (1 - p)C(n, 0, j)]/\hat{r}\} \\ &\text{for} \quad j = 0, 1, \ldots, n - 1. \end{aligned}$$

More generally, i periods before expiration

$$\begin{aligned} C(n, i, j) = \max\{&u^j d^{n-i-j}(1 - \delta)^{\bar{v}(n, i)}S - K, \\ &[pC(n, i - 1, j + 1) + (1 - p)C(n, i - 1, j)]/\hat{r}\} \\ &\text{for} \quad j = 0, 1, \ldots, n - i. \end{aligned}$$

Observe that each prior step provides the inputs needed to evaluate the right-hand arguments of each succeeding step. The tree diagram in Figure 5-36 illustrates this process. The number of calculations decreases as we move backward in time.

Finally, with n periods before expiration, since $i = n$,

$$C = C(n, n, 0) = \max\{S - K, [pC(n, n - 1, 1) + (1 - p)C(n, n - 1, 0)]/\hat{r}\},$$

and the hedge ratio is

$$\Delta = \frac{C(n, n - 1, 1) - C(n, n - 1, 0)}{(u - d)S}.$$

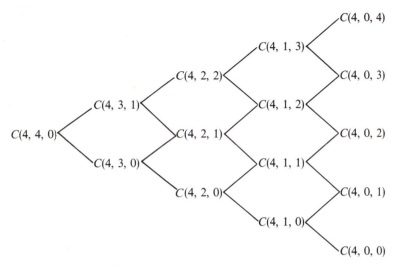

Figure 5-36   Illustration of Binomial Numerical Procedure for Valuing American Options

We could easily expand the analysis to include dividend policies in which the amount paid on any ex-dividend date depends on the stock price at that time in a more general way; the simple case of constant dollar dividends (rather than a constant yield) is especially important.[33] However, this will cause some minor complications. In our present example with a constant dividend yield, the possible stock prices $n - i$ periods from now are completely determined by the total number of upward moves (and ex-dividend dates) occurring during that interval. With other types of dividend policies, the enumeration will be more complicated, since then the terminal stock price will be affected by the timing of the upward moves as well as their total number. But the basic principle remains the same. We go to the expiration date and calculate the call values for all of the possible prices that the stock could have then. Using this information, we step back one period and calculate the call values for all possible stock prices at that time, and so forth.

To illustrate this, consider the case of a constant dollar dividend. Let $n = 3$, $S = 80$, $K = 60$, $r = 1.1$, $u = 1.5$, $d = .5$, and suppose that the stock will pay, when $n = 1$, a dividend of 10 to those who owned the stock during the previous period. Except for the dividend and the different striking price, this is the same as the numerical example given in Section 5-4. Because of the dividend, the stock price when there is one period remaining in the life of the call will be either 170, 50, or 10, rather than 180, 60, or 20 as in the

---

[33] We could also allow the amount to depend on previous stock prices.

earlier example. The following diagram shows the stock prices, call values, and values of Δ for this example. The last trading time before the stock goes ex-dividend occurs when $n = 2$; at that time, the call is worth more than its exercise value even if the stock price is 120, so early exercise would not be optimal. Note that the stock price can now take on six possible values on the expiration date rather than only four. This shows why a constant dollar dividend will require more computation time than a constant dividend yield.

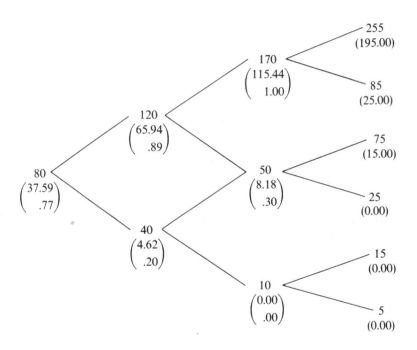

We will now illustrate the use of the binomial numerical procedure in approximating continuous-time call values. In order to have an exact continuous-time formula to use for comparison, we will consider the case with no dividends. Suppose that we are given the inputs required for the Black-Scholes option pricing formula: S, K, t, σ, and r. To convert this information into the inputs d, u, and $\hat{r}$ required for the binomial numerical procedure, we use the relationships

$$d = 1/u, \qquad u = e^{\sigma\sqrt{t/n}}, \qquad \hat{r} = r^{t/n}.$$

Table 5-3 gives us a feeling for how rapidly option values approximated by the binomial method approach the corresponding limiting Black-Scholes values given by $n = \infty$. Since there are no dividends, the American and European values will be the same. At $n = 5$, the values differ by at most $.25, and at $n = 20$, they differ by at most $.07. Although not shown, at $n = 50$ the greatest difference is less than $.03, and at $n = 150$, the values are identical to the penny.[34]

Table 5-3
BINOMIAL APPROXIMATION OF BLACK-SCHOLES CALL VALUES

		$S = 40$			$r = 1.05$				

		$n = 5$			$n = 20$			$n = \infty$		
σ	K	*Expiration Month[a]*								
		JAN	*APR*	*JUL*	*JAN*	*APR*	*JUL*	*JAN*	*APR*	*JUL*
	35	5.14	5.77	6.45	5.15	5.77	6.39	5.15	5.76	6.40
.2	40	1.05	2.26	3.12	.99	2.14	2.97	1.00	2.17	3.00
	45	.02	.54	1.15	.02	.51	1.11	.02	.51	1.10
	35	5.21	6.30	7.15	5.22	6.26	7.19	5.22	6.25	7.17
.3	40	1.53	3.21	4.36	1.44	3.04	4.14	1.46	3.07	4.19
	45	.11	1.28	2.12	.15	1.28	2.23	.16	1.25	2.24
	35	5.40	6.87	7.92	5.39	6.91	8.05	5.39	6.89	8.09
.4	40	2.01	4.16	5.61	1.90	3.93	5.31	1.92	3.98	5.37
	45	.46	1.99	3.30	.42	2.09	3.42	.42	2.10	3.43

NOTE: Assumes no dividends will be paid during the lives of the options.
[a] The January options have one month to expiration; the Aprils, four months; and the Julys, seven months. Both r and σ are expressed in annual terms.

Having checked the accuracy of the binomial numerical procedure on a problem for which we already know the answer, we are prepared to apply it to a new problem—the effect of cash dividends on call values. Now we also need to know δ and the integers k for which $v_k = 1$. Given t and n, these are the integral values of k for which $(k/n)t$ is approximately an ex-dividend date. Consider circumstances identical to those in Table 5-3, except that the stock has a quarterly dividend yield of $\delta = .0125$, which on

---

[34] Since the Black-Scholes values ($n = \infty$) were calculated directly from the Black-Scholes formula, these results demonstrate that our binomial numerical procedure is correct. They also give some indication of its efficiency (that is, accuracy versus computer time). The option values in Tables 5-2 through 5-6 were calculated on an IBM 5100 portable computer, using APL, an interactive computer language.

the basis of the current stock price of $40 would correspond to a quarterly dividend of $.50. Additionally, suppose the first quarterly dividend is due in one-half month from the present. Table 5-4 provides European, pseudo-American, and American call values under these conditions.

Table 5-4
BLACK-SCHOLES CALL VALUES WITH CASH DIVIDENDS

		$S = 40 \quad D = (2, \frac{1}{2})^a \quad r = 1.05$								
		European			Pseudo-American			American ($n = 150$)		
σ	K	*Expiration Month*[b]								
		JAN	*APR*	*JUL*	*JAN*	*APR*	*JUL*	*JAN*	*APR*	*JUL*
.2	35	4.66	4.88	5.16	5.07[c]	5.19[c]	5.44[c]	5.07	5.23	5.51
	40	.76	1.64	2.19	.76	1.73[c]	2.31[c]	.83	1.79	2.36
	45	.01	.33	.72	.01	.33	.74[c]	.01	.36	.78
.3	35	4.75	5.46	6.04	5.08[c]	5.67[c]	6.25[c]	5.10	5.74	6.34
	40	1.21	2.54	3.36	1.21	2.58[c]	3.45[c]	1.27	2.69	3.54
	45	.12	.98	1.71	.12	.98	1.72[c]	.12	1.03	1.80
.4	35	4.95	6.15	7.02	5.13[c]	6.28[c]	7.17[c]	5.22	6.40	7.29
	40	1.67	3.44	4.53	1.67	3.44	4.59[c]	1.72	3.59	4.72
	45	.34	1.76	2.81	.34	1.76	2.81	.34	1.83	2.92

NOTE. The European values are adjusted for dividends by replacing the current stock price (that is, $40) by $S(1 - \delta)^{\bar{v}}$, where $\bar{v}$ is the number of ex-dividend dates prior to an option's expiration date, and δ is the current indicated quarterly dividend yield (that is, .5/40). For each option, the pseudo-American values adjust for the dividend by selecting the highest of at most four European values, one for early exercise just prior to each ex-dividend date prior to expiration, and one assuming exercise at expiration. The American values are adjusted for dividends using the binomial numerical approximation procedure and therefore give full consideration to the impact of early exercise.

[a] $D = (2, \frac{1}{2})$ signifies that the indicated annual dividend, based on the current price and yield, is $2, and that the first quarterly ex-dividend date from the present occurs in half a month. Both r and σ are expressed in annual terms.

[b] The January options have one month to expiration; the Aprils, four months; and the Julys, seven months.

[c] Early exercise is indicated. In every case, this occurs on the last ex-dividend date prior to the call's expiration.

By comparing the limiting Black-Scholes values in Table 5-3 with the European values in Table 5-4, we see that a dividend yield of 5% per year has a significant impact on call values. As we would expect, the effect of dividends is smaller if we allow for the possibility of early exercise. Even the limited flexibility represented in the pseudo-American values gives a sizeable increase for many of the calls, particularly those that are in-the-money.

Early exercise on the last ex-dividend date prior to expiration is indicated for all of the in-the-money calls, as well as some that are now at-the-money or even out-of-the-money. Of course, where early exercise is not indicated, European and pseudo-American values are the same.

As we have previously mentioned, the pseudo-American correction is not complete. Not surprisingly, all American values are somewhat higher, since they reflect the full flexibility to the call buyer from the privilege of early exercise. However, in some cases, the difference is so small that it is eliminated by rounding to the nearest penny, as we have done in the tables. Perhaps the most striking feature shown in Tables 5-3 and 5-4 is the difference between the American call values with and without dividends.[35] One might have thought the possibility of early exercise would mean that dividends would have only a small effect on the value of an American call. However, this opportunity comes only at the cost of voluntarily ending the life of a call that may have many months remaining before expiration and paying the striking price immediately rather than later. Correspondingly, we find that the differences in value are not only significant, but also increase with the length of maturity of the call.

We have used a constant dividend yield in most of our examples only to make the exposition easier. Firms often try to maintain a constant dividend yield in the long run, but not in the short run. Consequently, a constant dividend yield may be a satisfactory way to represent dividends for an option with several years until expiration, while a constant dollar dividend would be more appropriate for the shorter lifetimes of listed options. As we have seen, the binomial numerical method can easily include constant dollar dividends. Calculations with a constant quarterly dividend of $.50 gave values that were virtually identical to those shown in Table 5-4. This suggests that even in those situations where constant dollar dividends are the appropriate choice, a constant dividend yield will still give very useful results if the yield parameter is continually readjusted as the stock price changes in order to keep the implied dividends equal to the constant amount.

American Puts. To derive a method for valuing puts, we again use the binomial formulation. Although it has been convenient to express the argument in terms of a particular security, a call, this is not essential in any way. The same basic analysis can be applied to puts.

---

[35] Since a payout-protected option would have the same value for any dividend policy as it would if the stock pays no dividends, this comparison also shows the value of payout protection. Note that the Black-Scholes model satisfies the conditions for the payout-protection adjustment discussed in Section 4-4. The distribution of the rate of return with reinvestment of cash dividends does not depend on the firm's dividend policy.

Letting P denote the current price of a put, with one period remaining before expiration we have

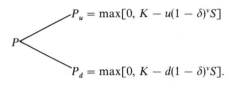

$$P_u = \max[0, K - u(1 - \delta)^v S]$$

$$P$$

$$P_d = \max[0, K - d(1 - \delta)^v S].$$

Once again, we can choose a portfolio of $S\Delta$ in stock and B in bonds which will have the same end-of-period value as the put. By a series of steps which are formally equivalent to the ones we followed in Section 5-3, we can show that

$$P = [pP_u + (1 - p)P_d]/\hat{r},$$

if this is greater than $K - S$, and $P = K - S$ otherwise. As before, $p = (\hat{r} - d)/(u - d)$ and $\Delta = (P_u - P_d)/(u - d)S$. Note that for puts, since $P_u \le P_d$, then $\Delta \le 0$. This means that if we sell an overvalued put, the equivalent portfolio that we buy will involve a short position in the stock.

We might hope that with puts we will be spared the complications caused by optimal exercise before the expiration date. Unfortunately, this is not the case. In fact, the situation is even worse in this regard. Now there are always some possible circumstances in which no one would be willing to hold the put for one more period.

To see this, suppose $K > u(1 - \delta)^v S$. Since $u > d$, then, also, $K > d(1 - \delta)^v S$. In this case, $P_u = K - u(1 - \delta)^v S$ and $P_d = K - d(1 - \delta)^v S$. Therefore, since $(u/\hat{r})p + (d/\hat{r})(1 - p) = 1$,

$$[pP_u + (1 - p)P_d]/\hat{r} = (K/\hat{r}) - (1 - \delta)^v S.$$

If there are no dividends (that is, $v = 0$), then this is certainly less than $K - S$. Even with $v = 1$, it will be less for a sufficiently low stock price.

Thus, there will now be a critical stock price, $\bar{S}$, such that if $S < \bar{S}$, the put should be exercised immediately. By analogy with our discussion for the call, we can see that this is the stock price at which $[pP_u + (1 - p)P_d]/\hat{r} = K - S$. Other things equal, $\bar{S}$ will be higher the lower the dividend yield, the higher the interest rate, and the higher the striking price. Optimal early exercise thus becomes more likely if the put is deep-in-the-money and the interest rate is high. The effect of dividends yet to be paid diminishes the advantages of immediate exercise, since the put buyer will be reluctant to sacrifice the forced declines in the stock price on future ex-dividend dates.

This argument can be extended in the same way as before to value puts with any number of periods to go. However, the chance for optimal exercise before the expiration date once again seems to preclude the possibility of expressing this value in a simple form. But our analysis also indicates that, with slight modification, we can value puts with the same numerical techniques we use for calls. Reversing the difference between the stock price and the striking price at each stage is the only change.[36]

The following diagram shows the stock prices, put values, and values of Δ obtained in this way for the example given in Section 5-4. The values used there were $S = 80$, $K = 80$, $n = 3$, $u = 1.5$, $d = .5$, and $\hat{r} = 1.1$. To include dividends as well, we assume that a cash dividend of 5% ($\delta = .05$)

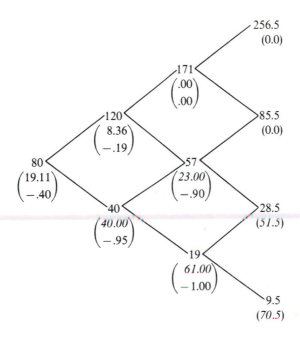

---

[36] Given the theoretical basis for the binomial numerical procedure provided, the numerical method can be generalized to permit $k + 1 \le n$ jumps to new stock prices in each period. We can consider exercise only every k periods, using the binomial formula to leap across intermediate periods. In effect, this means permitting $k + 1$ possible new stock prices before exercise is again considered. That is, instead of considering exercise n times, we would only consider it about n/k times. For fixed t and k, as $n \to \infty$, option values will approach their continuous-time values.

This alternative procedure is interesting, since it may enhance computer efficiency. At one extreme, for calls on stocks that do not pay dividends, setting $k + 1 = n$ gives the most efficient results. However, when the effect of potential early exercise is important and greater accuracy is required, the most efficient results are achieved by setting $k = 1$, as in our description above.

will be paid at the end of the last period before the expiration date. Thus, $(1 - \delta)^{\bar{v}(n, 0)} = .95$, $(1 - \delta)^{\bar{v}(n, 1)} = .95$, and $(1 - \delta)^{\bar{v}(n, 2)} = 1.0$. Put values in italics indicate that immediate exercise is optimal.

Table 5-5 contrasts the values of otherwise identical European and American puts on a stock that does not pay cash dividends prior to the expiration date. For many puts, particularly the low-volatility, long-maturity, deep-in-the-money puts, potential early exercise significantly affects their value. Indeed, since the low-volatility, in-the-money put with one month to expiration is selling at its parity value (that is, $K - S$), immediate exercise is advisable. Incidentally, observe that the low-volatility, in-the-money European puts do not necessarily increase in value as their maturity lengthens.

A comparison of Tables 5-5 and 5-6 shows that dividends increase the value of unprotected European and American puts, just as we would expect. It is interesting to note that the increase is usually larger for a European put than for the corresponding American put. This is because the owner of the European put will get the benefits of the decreases in the stock price on all of the ex-dividend dates, while the owner of the American put may find it advantageous to forego some of these benefits through early exercise in order to receive the striking price sooner. As a result, cash dividends tend to reduce the difference between the values of European and American puts.

Table 5-5
REPRESENTATIVE BLACK-SCHOLES PUT VALUES

		\multicolumn{6}{c}{$S = 40$ \qquad $r = 1.05$}					
		European			American ($n = 150$)		
σ	K	\multicolumn{6}{c}{Expiration Month[a]}				
		JAN	APR	JUL	JAN	APR	JUL
.2	35	.01	.20	.42	.01	.20	.43
	40	.84	1.52	1.88	.85	1.58	1.99
	45	4.84	4.78	4.84	5.00[b]	5.09	5.27
.3	35	.08	.69	1.19	.08	.70	1.22
	40	1.30	2.43	3.06	1.31	2.48	3.17
	45	4.98	5.53	5.97	5.06	5.71	6.24
.4	35	.25	1.33	2.11	.25	1.35	2.16
	40	1.76	3.33	4.25	1.77	3.38	4.35
	45	5.24	6.38	7.17	5.29	6.51	7.39

NOTE: Assumes no dividends will be paid during the lives of the options.
[a] The January options have one month to expiration; the Aprils, four months; and the Julys, seven months. Both r and σ are expressed in annual terms.
[b] Exercise immediately.

Table 5-6

BLACK-SCHOLES PUT VALUES WITH CASH DIVIDENDS

$$S = 40 \quad D = (2, \tfrac{1}{2}) \quad r = 1.05$$

		European			American ($n = 150$)		
σ	K	Expiration Month[a]					
		JAN	APR	JUL	JAN	APR	JUL
.2	35	.01	.30	.65	.01	.31	.66
	40	1.09	1.98	2.54	1.11	2.01	2.58
	45	5.33	5.60	5.93	5.41	5.67	6.02
.3	35	.1 i	.88	1.53	.11	.88	1.55
	40	1.55	2.88	3.71	1.56	2.91	3.74
	45	5.43	6.24	6.92	5.50	6.29	6.99
.4	35	.30	1.57	2.51	.31	1.58	2.52
	40	2.00	3.78	4.88	2.01	3.81	4.92
	45	5.65	7.02	8.02	5.70	7.07	8.10

NOTE: The European values are adjusted for cash dividends by replacing the current stock price (that is, $40) by $S(1 - \delta)^{\bar{\nu}}$, where $\bar{\nu}$ is the number of ex-dividend dates prior to an option's expiration and δ is the current indicated quarterly dividend yield (that is, .5/40). The American values are adjusted for dividends using the binomial numerical approximation procedure and therefore give full consideration to the impact of early exercise.
[a] The January options have one month to expiration; the Aprils, four months; and the Julys, seven months. Both r and σ are expressed in annual terms.

Figure 5-37 is a graph of the optimal exercise boundary with and without dividends for two otherwise identical unprotected American puts. It shows how the boundary changes for a given put as the expiration date comes closer. The upper curve, with no dividends, shows that the boundary steadily increases as time passes. For example, assume that the annualized interest rate is .05, the striking price is $40, and the stock's annual volatility is .3. With nine months to expiration, the current stock price can be as low as $28.80, or 72% of K, without causing immediate exercise to be desirable. However, exercise is optimal at any lower stock price. Eight months later, when the put has one month to expiration, immediate exercise is advisable if the stock is below $34.28, or 85.7% of K. Further calculation shows that the exercise boundary rises with a lower volatility or a higher interest rate. For example, if $\sigma = .2$, other things equal, the optimal exercise boundary is again a smooth convex curve falling from $40 at $t = 0$ to $36 at $t = .75$.

In Section 4-2, we remarked that the optimal exercise boundary for unprotected American puts on stocks which pay dividends may behave in the following way as time passes. The boundary drops to zero just before an ex-dividend date, and then immediately after the ex-dividend date, it jumps

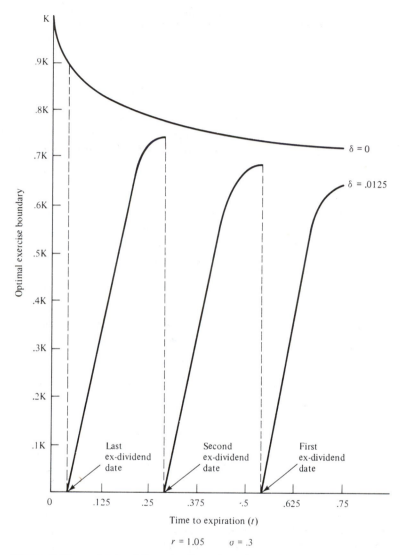

Figure 5-37   Optimal Exercise Boundary for an American Put

upward to a level greater than it had just after the previous ex-dividend date. If this is not the last ex-dividend date, the boundary then starts declining to zero. If it is the last one, the boundary begins to increase and rises to K as the time to expiration goes to zero. Figure 5-37 not only confirms this behavior, but allows us to make two more specific observations for our sample put. First, prior to the last ex-dividend date, the optimal exercise boundary for the put with dividends lies everywhere below the boundary for the otherwise identical put without dividends. Second, between ex-dividend dates the exercise boundary is concave to the origin. The corresponding graph for the case of a constant dollar dividend of $.50 per quarter is very similar to Figure 5-37. The main differences are that after each ex-dividend date the boundary drops much more rapidly to nearly zero and then has a convex segment which reaches zero just before the next ex-dividend date.

It may seem puzzling that the optimal boundary ever goes to zero, but there is an intuitive explanation. Essentially, this says that no matter how low the stock price is, you should never exercise a put immediately before an ex-dividend date. Here is why. Let S be the stock price one second before the ex-dividend date, S^x be the stock price one second afterward, and D be the amount of the dividend. Since other changes in the stock price will be extremely small over so short a period, S^x will be approximately $S - D$. By postponing exercise for two seconds, you get $K - S^x = K - (S - D)$ instead of $K - S$. Of course, you would lose two seconds' worth of interest on $K - S$, but this will be completely insignificant relative to the amount of the dividend. Consequently, even if only a very small dividend will be paid, a put should never be exercised just before an ex-dividend date.

To contrast this with an otherwise identical unprotected American call, calculation confirms that it only pays to consider early exercise just before an ex-dividend date. In effect, the optimal exercise boundary is infinite between these dates. On the first ex-dividend date the stock price must be greater than about $56.80, or 142% of K, for exercise to be optimal. On the second ex-dividend date the critical stock price is $51.60, and on the last it decreases to $42. Additional calculation shows that an increase in the dividend yield decreases these critical values, while an increase in volatility or the interest rate increases them.

Table 5-7 summarizes many of our results about the optimal exercise boundary. Each entry answers the following question. Suppose that in Figure 5-37 we simultaneously draw graphs for two sets of inputs which are the same except for one variable. Will the graph corresponding to the higher value of that variable lie above or below the graph for the lower value of the variable? In the table, an upward arrow means that it will always lie above, while a downward arrow means it will always lie below. Of course, for options with different expiration dates, this comparison would be defined only for the period in which both are outstanding; at the point on the horizontal axis corresponding to the expiration date of the shorter maturity option, the longer one would still have some time remaining. Here is an easy way to remember these results: For a change in any variable except the striking price, the value of an option and its optimal exercise boundary will shift in the same direction for a call and in the opposite direction for a put.

Table 5-7
THE EFFECT OF CHANGES IN THE UNDERLYING VARIABLES ON THE OPTIMAL EXERCISE BOUNDARY

Determining Factors	*Effect of Increase*	
	Put	*Call*
Striking price	↑	↑
Expiration date	↓	↑
Volatility	↓	↑
Interest rate	↑	↑
Cash dividends	↓	↓

Finally, we wish to urge caution in making such statements as "a put with a high volatility is more likely to be exercised during the next month than an otherwise identical put with a low volatility." In the first place, the actual probability that optimal early exercise will occur during any given time period depends on the expected rate of return on the stock, which was not necessary in calculating the optimal boundary or the option value. Furthermore, even if we use the same expected rate of return in each case, the comparison is by no means simple. A higher volatility would indeed make it more likely that the stock price will reach a *fixed* low level, but it will simultaneously lower the level which must be reached. The final result depends on which effect dominates. The same issues arise in comparisons involving different dividend policies. This kind of problem can be solved, but it is relatively complicated, so we will not pursue it further.

how to use the Black-Scholes formula

6

The Black-Scholes formula can be very helpful for investors in the options market. It can be used to measure both the *value* and *risk* of an option in relation to its underlying stock. In conjunction with a more complete model of security price behavior, such as the "capital asset pricing model," it can be used to construct optimal portfolios containing both options and other securities.

In the beginning sections of the chapter, we work through a step-by-step procedure to value a call option on a stock paying no cash dividends using information available in the *Wall Street Journal*. We then discuss how to modify the calculations to include puts and to handle cash dividends and possible early exercise. We also show how to include margin requirements, taxes, and differential borrowing and lending rates. Other complications, such as randomly changing volatilities and interest rates, would force us to reexamine our basic arbitrage approach to option pricing. Although we postpone a formal analysis of these issues until Chapter 7, we will suggest some informal ways to deal with them.

In the latter sections of the chapter, we will show how to use information obtainable from the Black-Scholes formula to assess the risk of option positions involving perhaps many options on the same underlying stock. In particular, the formula can be used to predict how the value of an option position will react to specified changes in the stock price and a reduction in time to expiration. As an illustration, we will consider in detail the problems of implementing a trading strategy designed to take advantage of relative mispricing among options and stock, but at the same time offering maximum protection against incorrect predictions of the direction of stock price movements. In the remainder of the chapter, we look at the more general considerations involved in forming a portfolio of options and other securities which balances portfolio expected return against portfolio risk.[1]

6-1. HOW TO COMPUTE BLACK-SCHOLES VALUES

Table 6-1 contains information taken from the *Wall Street Journal* to value a call option using the Black-Scholes formula. To use the formula, we need to know S (stock price), t (time to expiration), K (striking price), σ (volatility), and r (one plus the interest rate). Clearly, $S = \$40.75$ and $K = \$40$. We determine t by counting the number of calendar days between today's date and the expiration date and dividing by 365. In this case, $t = 133/365 = .3644$ years.

Table 6-1

AN EXAMPLE OF THE BASIC DATA REQUIRED FOR THE FORMULA: THE NATIONAL SEMICONDUCTOR MAY 40 CALL

Today's Date: 1/2/81   Expiration Date: 5/16/81
Striking Price: $40
Today's Price of T-Bill Maturing on 5/14/81: $9,467.23
Today's Stock Price: $40\frac{3}{4}$
Weekly Closing Prices of National Semiconductor Stock Over the Previous
26 Weeks

12/26/80	41	10/24/80	$39\frac{1}{4}$	8/22/80	$38\frac{5}{8}$
12/19/80	$38\frac{5}{8}$	10/17/80	$41\frac{1}{2}$	8/15/80	36
12/12/80	42	10/10/80	$42\frac{1}{4}$	8/8/80	35
12/5/80	$42\frac{3}{4}$	10/3/80	$41\frac{1}{8}$	8/1/80	$32\frac{1}{4}$
11/28/80	$49\frac{3}{4}$	9/26/80	$38\frac{1}{4}$	7/25/80	$29\frac{5}{8}$
11/21/80	44	9/19/80	$41\frac{1}{2}$	7/18/80	$28\frac{7}{8}$
11/14/80	42	9/12/80	$36\frac{1}{4}$	7/11/80	$27\frac{1}{8}$
11/7/80	$37\frac{3}{4}$	9/5/80	$40\frac{1}{4}$	7/3/80	$26\frac{3}{8}$
10/31/80	$37\frac{1}{2}$	8/29/80	$38\frac{1}{4}$		

Interest Rate. We can obtain r directly from the current market price of a Treasury bill maturing at about the same time as the option. In this case, there is a Treasury bill maturing on May 14, 1981, just one day earlier than the last trading day for the option. To determine the current closing price of

---

[1] APL computer programs for producing the output of all tables in this chapter and in Chapter 5 were developed by the authors as part of an integrated APL Option Pricing Library.

this Treasury bill (with $10,000 face value) from the *Wall Street Journal*, define B as the bid discount, A as the asked discount, and n as the number of calendar days to maturity. Then,

$$\text{Current price of T-bill} = \$10,000\left[1 - .01\left(\frac{B+A}{2}\right)\left(\frac{n}{360}\right)\right].$$

Here are the closing quotes for this T-bill for January 2 as reported in the Treasury Issues section of the *Wall Street Journal*:

U.S. Treasury Bills			
Maturity Date	Bid	Asked Discount	Yield
-1981-			
5-14	14.61	14.45	15.44

By applying the formula with $B = 14.61$, $A = 14.45$, and $n = 132$, we find that the current price of the T-bill is, as shown in Table 6-1, $9,467.23. Remember that r^{-t} is the current price of a default-free bond paying one dollar at time t from now and nothing before then. Hence, for our example,

$$r^{-t} = \frac{9,467.23}{10,000}$$

$$r = \left(\frac{9,467.23}{10,000}\right)^{-1/t} = (.9467)^{-365/132} = 1.163448.$$

Volatility. The final and most difficult item to measure is the volatility, σ. Unlike the other variables, we cannot simply look it up in the newspaper. However, we would hope that the information shown in Table 6-1 will give us an estimate of the volatility, and this is indeed the case.

The Black-Scholes formula is based on the assumption that stock prices are lognormally distributed. This means that the natural logarithm of the price relative (final stock price divided by initial stock price) over any period (here, a week) has a normal distribution, with mean and variance proportional to the length of the period. For example, the first four prices in Table 6-1 are 26.375, 27.125, 28.875, and 29.625, so the first three price relatives are $27.125/26.375 = 1.028436$, $28.875/27.125 = 1.064516$, and $29.625/28.875 = 1.025974$. The natural logarithms of these three price relatives are log $1.028436 = .028039$, log $1.065416 = .062520$, and log $1.025974 = .025642$. If the basic assumption underlying the formula is correct, then these are three independent samples from a normal distribution whose standard deviation is the weekly volatility of the stock. By using the rest of our data, we would have twenty-six independent samples from this distribution.

Hence, we can now apply standard statistical techniques for estimating the parameters of a normal distribution with unknown mean μ and variance σ^2. If we did not know these techniques, probably the first thing that would occur to us would be to use the mean, standard deviation, and variance of the sample as our estimates of the unknown actual values. In fact, those are exactly the estimators that we would have obtained from a widely used estimation method known as maximum likelihood, which answers the question, For what values of the unknown actual parameters would we have been most likely to draw this particular sample?

Of course, different samples from the same distribution would give different estimates, and we would like some assurance that our estimators of the standard deviation and variance have desirable properties. In fact, they do, except for one unattractive feature—they are biased. That is, the expected values of our estimators are not equal to the true parameter values. But it is well known that there is an easy way to correct for this; all we have to do is multiply our original estimators by a correction factor which depends on the sample size. In the notation used in Table 6-2, our original estimators, the sample mean and variance, are

$$\hat{\mu} = \frac{1}{n} \sum_{k=1}^{n} \log R_k,$$

$$\hat{\sigma}^2 = \frac{1}{n} \sum_{k=1}^{n} (\log R_k - \hat{\mu})^2,$$

where n is the number of price relatives in the series. The correction factor for the variance is $n/(n-1)$, so our unbiased estimator of σ^2, $\hat{\sigma}_{ub}^2$, is[2]

$$\hat{\sigma}_{ub}^2 = \frac{1}{n-1} \sum_{k=1}^{n} (\log R_k - \hat{\mu})^2$$

$$= \frac{1}{n-1} \sum_{k=1}^{n} [(\log R_k)^2 - \hat{\mu}^2].$$

---

[2] Of course, it is the volatility, the square root of the variance, which appears in the formula; so we might really prefer an unbiased estimate of σ. Unfortunately, the correction factor for the standard deviation is more complicated: $(\frac{1}{2}n)^{1/2}(\frac{1}{2}n - \frac{3}{2})!/(\frac{1}{2}n - 1)!$, where $x!$ is the gamma function (no relation to our gamma), $\int_0^\infty e^{-v} v^x \, dv$. This function is widely used in statistics and is well tabulated; we will meet it again in a completely different context in Chapter 7. Hence, our unbiased estimator of σ is

$$\hat{\sigma}_{ub} = \left[\frac{(\frac{1}{2}n)^{1/2}(\frac{1}{2}n - \frac{3}{2})!}{(\frac{1}{2}n - 1)!} \right] \left[\frac{1}{n} \sum_{k=1}^{n} (\log R_k - \hat{\mu})^2 \right]^{1/2}.$$

Readers who do not like the looks of $\hat{\sigma}_{ub}$ will be relieved to know that $(\hat{\sigma}_{ub}^2)^{1/2}$ will give very similar values for all but very small samples. For example, for the sample shown in Table 6-1, $\hat{\sigma}_{ub}^2 = .005216$, $(\hat{\sigma}_{ub}^2)^{1/2} = .072222$, and $\hat{\sigma}_{ub} = .072949$.

From the information given in Table 6-1, we find that $\hat{\mu} = .016732$ and $\hat{\sigma}_{ub}^2 = .005216$. The worksheet for these calculations is shown in Table 6-2.

Table 6-2
WORKSHEET FOR ESTIMATING σ

S_j	$R_j \equiv S_j/S_{j-1}$	$\log R_j$	$\log R_j - \hat{\mu}$	$(\log R_j - \hat{\mu})^2$
26.375				
27.125	1.028436	.028039	.011307	.000128
28.875	1.064516	.062520	.045788	.002097
29.625	1.025974	.025642	.008910	.000079
32.25	1.088608	.084899	.068167	.004647
35	1.085271	.081830	.065098	.004238
36	1.028571	.028171	.011439	.000131
38.625	1.072917	.070381	.053649	.002878
38.25	.990291	− .009756	− .026488	.000702
40.25	1.052288	.050966	.034234	.001172
36.25	.900621	− .104671	− .121403	.014739
41.5	1.144828	.135254	.118522	.014048
38.25	.921687	− .081550	− .098282	.009659
41.125	1.075163	.072473	.055740	.003107
42.25	1.027356	.026988	.010256	.000105
41.5	.982249	− .017911	− .034643	.001200
39.25	.945783	− .055742	− .072474	.005253
37.5	.955414	− .045611	− .062343	.003887
37.75	1.006667	.000045	− .010088	.000102
42	1.112583	.106684	.089952	.008091
44	1.047619	.046520	.029788	.000887
49.75	1.130682	.122821	.106089	.011255
42.75	.859296	− .151641	− .168374	.028350
42	.982456	− .017700	− .034432	.001186
38.625	.919643	− .083770	− .100502	.010100
41	1.061489	.059672	.042940	.001844
40.75	.993902	− .006117	− .022849	.000522
Total		.435039		.130407

Number of stock prices $(S_j) = 27$ $\hat{\mu} = .435039/26 = .016732$
Number of price relatives $(R_j) = 26$ $\hat{\sigma}_{ub}^2 = (.130407/26)\,(26/25) = .005216$
Estimate of annual variance $= 52(.005216) = .271232$
Estimate of annual volatility $= (.271232)^{1/2} = .52$

We could still not proceed with confidence if we knew that the estimate we calculated from our sample was likely to be wildly different from the true value, σ^2. Intuitively, we know that the more price relatives we have in our sample, the less likely such an unfavorable outcome would be.

In fact, we could find the exact probability distribution of our estimator of $\hat{\sigma}_{ub}^2$; it turns out that it has what is called a gamma distribution with mean σ^2 and variance $2\sigma^4/(n-1)$. We could then answer such questions as, What is the probability that our sample will give an estimate which deviates from the true value by more than 20%? (Interested readers can verify that for the example the answer is .16.) For our purposes now, it is sufficiently reassuring to note that the variance of our estimator steadily decreases as n increases and goes to zero as n goes to infinity. For a large sample, it is very likely that our calculated estimate will be extremely close to the true value.

However, one point may still be troubling you. We have stressed again and again that we did not need to know the expected rate of return on the stock to value an option because it does not appear in the formula. This means that we will be spared the task of predicting the expected rate of return that will prevail in the future. Yet it appears that to estimate and predict the volatility we still must form an opinion about the expected rate of return that prevailed in the past, during the period of our sample. Many readers will be somewhat uncomfortable with this: They may have had prior beliefs that do not accord with the sample mean, or they may be worried that the mean of the lognormal distribution is changing with time, both during the sample and in the future, in a way that is not fully understood. Indeed, this latter possibility, which is completely consistent with the Black-Scholes model,[3] is one reason why we were relieved that we did not have to make predictions about the mean.

Fortunately, these difficulties may not be very important. It turns out that if the time period between our price observations is reasonably small, our estimate of the mean will have only a negligible effect on our estimate of the volatility.

The reason is that the true mean and variance are both proportional to the time period, or at least approximately so if the mean depends on time in any reasonable way, so the squares of the logarithm of the price relatives will tend to be of the same order of magnitude as their mean. Over a week, or a day, both will be small, and the square of the mean will be much smaller still. Now look at the second way of writing $\hat{\sigma}_{ub}^2$:

$$\hat{\sigma}_{ub}^2 = \frac{1}{n-1} \sum_{k=1}^{n} [(\log R_k)^2 - \hat{\mu}^2].$$

Since the sum of the $\hat{\mu}^2$ terms will be small relative to the sum of the $(\log R_k)^2$ terms, their impact on $\hat{\sigma}_{ub}^2$ will be minor. For the example, we find

---

[3] Black and Scholes wrote in terms of lognormality mainly for convenience. They were well aware that the formula is still valid if the mean changes over time, even in an unpredictable way. The critical feature for option pricing is the behavior of the volatility.

that

$$\sum_{k=1}^{n} \frac{\hat{\mu}^2}{n-1} = .000291, \qquad \sum_{k=1}^{n} \frac{(\log R_k)^2}{n-1} = .005507,$$

and

$$\hat{\sigma}^2_{ub} = .005216.$$

This indicates that if we are using daily data, or even weekly data, our estimate of the variance will be insensitive to our estimate of the mean. To illustrate this further, suppose that we decided to ignore the mean altogether by acting as if it were zero. In that case, we would use the sample variance as our estimate of σ^2. According to our hypothesis, this would give an unbiased estimate of σ^2; no correction factor would be necessary because we are not simultaneously estimating the mean. Now suppose that we use this estimator, $\sum_{k=1}^{n} (\log R_k)^2/n$, when the true mean is μ. Then it can be shown that this estimator has mean $\sigma^2 + \mu^2$ and variance $(2\sigma^4 + 4\mu^2\sigma^2)/n$. The distribution of the estimator is σ^2 times a noncentral chi-square distribution. The estimator is biased, but the more closely spaced the fixed number n of observations are, the less important the bias will be. For example, some reasonable values for the annual mean and variance (of the log of the price relatives) of a typical stock are .2 and .1, respectively. Then the corresponding weekly mean and variance would be $.2/52 = .003846$ and $.1/52 = .001923$; since there are approximately 253 business days in a year, the daily figures would be $.2/253 = .0007905$ and $.1/253 = .0003952$. If we used annual observations, the expected value of our estimator would be $.1 + (.2)^2 = .14$, a serious bias of 40%, but if we used weekly observations the expected value would be $.001923 + (.003846)^2 = .001938$, an error of only .78%. If we used daily observations, the expected value would be $.0003952 + (.0007905)^2 = .0003958$; now the bias has dropped to only .15%. To get an estimator of the annual variance from our estimator of the daily variance, we would multiply by 253; so its expected value is $253(.0003958) = .10015$.

As we might expect, we would get essentially the same results even if the mean changes over time. In that case, our observations would be drawings from independent normal distributions with the same variance but with different means, μ_k. In this situation our estimator

$$\sum_{k=1}^{n} \frac{(\log R_k)^2}{n} \quad \text{has expected value } \sigma^2 + \left(\sum_{k=1}^{n} \frac{\mu_k^2}{n} \right).$$

The only difference is that μ^2 is replaced by its average. Of course, our discussion is only meant to be suggestive; it does not provide complete proof of our conclusions. Indeed, special care would be necessary in making all of this precise if the mean is changing randomly. However, we hope that the arguments given will provide sufficient justification for our advice: If you are using daily data, or even weekly data, it is not worthwhile to worry about your estimate of the mean.

One small problem remains: How do we adjust our data for dividends and stock splits? It turns out this can be done very easily. For example, suppose we have the following daily price series:

$$50 \quad 51 \quad 49.5 \quad 48 \quad 25 \quad 27$$

where the stock has gone ex-dividend on day 3 with a dividend of $1.00 and split 2-for-1 on day 5. First, we want to construct a daily series of the total return on the stock; if there were no dividends or splits this would be the same as the series of price relatives. To do this, we would take the price relative series

$$\frac{51}{50} \quad \frac{49.5}{51} \quad \frac{48}{49.5} \quad \frac{25}{48} \quad \frac{27}{25}$$

and adjust it in the following way:

1. Whenever the closing price of an ex-dividend date appears in a numerator, add to it the amount of the dividend.
2. Whenever the closing price of a stock split or stock dividend date appears in a numerator, multiply it by the total number of shares owned after the split for each share owned before the split.

The adjusted series is

$$\frac{51}{50} \quad \frac{49.5 + 1}{51} \quad \frac{48}{49.5} \quad \frac{2(25)}{48} \quad \frac{27}{25}$$

We would then take the natural logarithms of the adjusted series and proceed as before.

Returning to Table 6-2, we note that since there were no dividends or stock splits during this period, no adjustments were necessary. We found that our unbiased estimate of the *weekly* variance is $\hat{\sigma}_{ub}^2 = .130407/25 = .005216$. To annualize this figure, we multiply it by the number of weeks in a year, giving $52(.005216) = .271232$. Thus, our estimate of σ, the annualized standard deviation of the natural logarithms of the price relatives, is $(.271232)^{1/2} = .52$.

Option Value. The basic data have provided all information required for the formula:

$$S = 40.75$$
$$t = .364$$
$$K = 40$$
$$\sigma = .52$$
$$r = 1.163$$

where the call value C is calculated from the Black-Scholes formula

$$C = SN(x) - Kr^{-t}N(x - \sigma\sqrt{t}),$$

where

$$x \equiv \frac{\log(S/Kr^{-t})}{\sigma\sqrt{t}} + \frac{1}{2}\sigma\sqrt{t}.$$

Calculation can be somewhat simplified by rewriting the formula as

$$c = aN\left(\frac{\log a}{b} + \frac{b}{2}\right) - N\left(\frac{\log a}{b} - \frac{b}{2}\right),$$

where $a \equiv S/Kr^{-t}$, $b \equiv \sigma\sqrt{t}$, and $c \equiv C/Kr^{-t}$. The necessary calculations are as follows:

$$Kr^{-t} = 40 \times 1.163^{-.364} = 37.858$$

$$a = S/Kr^{-t} = 40.75/37.858 = 1.0764 \qquad b = \sigma\sqrt{t} = .52 \times \sqrt{.364} = .314$$

$$(b/2) + (\log a)/b = .391 \qquad\qquad -(b/2) + (\log a)/b = .078$$

$$c = aN\left(\frac{\log a}{b} + \frac{b}{2}\right) - N\left(\frac{\log a}{b} - \frac{b}{2}\right) = 1.0764 \times N(.391) - N(.078) = .1711$$

$$C = cKr^{-t} = .1711 \times 37.86 = \$6.48$$

To determine the value of $N(z)$, use tables for the standard normal distribution function, commonly available in most mathematical handbooks or in most introductory books on statistics. The following polynomial approximation, which may have been used to create the tables themselves, can also be used: for z greater than zero,

$$N(z) \approx 1 - (1/\sqrt{2\pi})e^{-z^2/2}(b_1 k + b_2 k^2 + b_3 k^3 + b_4 k^4 + b_5 k^5),$$

where

$$k \equiv 1/(1 + az)$$

and

$$b_1 \equiv .319381530 \qquad b_4 \equiv -1.821255978$$
$$b_2 \equiv -.356563782 \qquad b_5 \equiv 1.330274429$$
$$b_3 \equiv 1.781477937 \qquad a \equiv .2316419$$

For z less than zero, subtract the above calculation for positive z from one. For z equal to zero, $N(z) = \frac{1}{2}$. This approximation produces values of $N(z)$ accurate to within six decimal places.

Since we may wish to calculate the values of several options on the same underlying stock, it is refreshing to realize that the most difficult chore, the computation of σ, need only be done once. However, an active trader may want to use the formula for many different underlying securities over many dates. To facilitate calculation, she can subscribe to an option pricing service that uses the formula, such as the service offered by Fischer Black.[4] Alternatively, or in addition, she may wish to calculate her own values using the computer program listed in the appendix to this chapter. With these, she can input her own estimates of σ, which may differ from the estimate used by the option pricing service.

Lacking computer assistance, she may instead use Tables 6-5 and 6-6, which take advantage of the computational simplification noted above. The numbers in the tables approximate the value of a call normalized with the present value of the striking price, Kr^{-t}, equal to one. Two numbers in the margins determine the call value: the extent to which a call is in- or out-of-the-money (S/Kr^{-t}), which is measured by each row of the table, and the standard deviation of the return of the underlying stock to the expiration date ($\sigma\sqrt{t}$), measured by each column of the table. To determine the value of a call, find the number at the intersection of the appropriate row and column. Then multiply this number by Kr^{-t}. If S/Kr^{-t} and/or $\sigma\sqrt{t}$ fall between the values given in the left column and the top row, approximate the intersecting number by linear interpolation. For example, in our previous numerical example, $S/Kr^{-t} = 1.076$ and $\sigma\sqrt{t} = .314$. Reading across the table, we have

		$\sigma\sqrt{t}$	
		.31	.32
S/Kr^{-t}	1.07	.165	.169
	1.08	.171	.175

---

[4] This was available through printed tables and a time-sharing service. Unlike most other services, Black did not advise the purchase or sale of particular options.

If we start with the intersection (1.07, 1.08), to reach 1.076 we must add about $\frac{6}{10}$ of the distance between .165 and .171 to .165. This gives about .1686. To this we must add $\frac{4}{10}$ of the distance between .165 and .169 or .0016, for a total of .1702 $\approx$ .170. Multiplying .170 by $Kr^{-t} = 37.858$, we derive for the call value $6.44. For $K \leq 50$ the table should produce call values for the formula accurate within $\frac{1}{16}$ of a point; for $K \leq 100$, accuracy should lie within $\frac{1}{8}$ of a point.

The formula values for puts, ignoring the effects of potential early exercise, can also be calculated from the tables. The put-call parity relationship for European options implies that $P = C - S + Kr^{-t}$. Therefore, armed with the value of the corresponding call as computed from the tables, we need only subtract the stock price and add back the present value of the striking price.

Now that we have calculated the value of the National Semiconductor May 40 calls, we have all the information we need to evaluate the May 35, May 45, and May 50 calls as well. On January 2, two other expiration cycles were outstanding: February, with 49 days remaining, and August, with 231 days remaining. Another look at the *Wall Street Journal* and a little calculation gives the T-bill prices corresponding to these expiration dates: $9834.74 and $9159.93, respectively. With this additional information, we can easily compute the formula values for all the striking prices and expiration dates. The results are shown in Table 6-3.

How do these values compare with the actual market prices? Table 6-4 shows the closing prices on January 2 for all of these options as reported in the *Journal*.

Overall, the two sets of figures agree quite closely. Formula values are higher than market prices in six of the twelve cases, while market prices are higher in the remaining six. However, there are some systematic differences: The market prices are uniformly higher for the February calls, while for the August calls it is just the reverse.

Table 6-3

BLACK-SCHOLES VALUES FOR
NATIONAL SEMICONDUCTOR
CALLS ON JANUARY 2, 1981

	February	*May*	*August*
35	7.07	9.38	11.34
40	3.80	6.48	8.67
45	1.77	4.33	6.54
50	.73	2.81	4.89

Table 6-4

CLOSING MARKET PRICES FOR
NATIONAL SEMICONDUCTOR
CALLS ON JANUARY 2, 1981

	February	*May*	*August*
35	$7\frac{1}{4}$	$8\frac{7}{8}$	$11\frac{1}{4}$
40	$4\frac{1}{8}$	$6\frac{5}{8}$	$8\frac{1}{2}$
45	$2\frac{1}{8}$	$4\frac{3}{8}$	6
50	$\frac{13}{16}$	$2\frac{5}{8}$	$4\frac{1}{4}$

TABLE FOR CALCULATING OPTION VALUES FOR $\sigma\sqrt{t} \leq .21$ (LINEAR INTERPOLATIONS ACCURATE WITHIN $\frac{1}{16}$ FOR $K \leq 50$)

Table 6-5

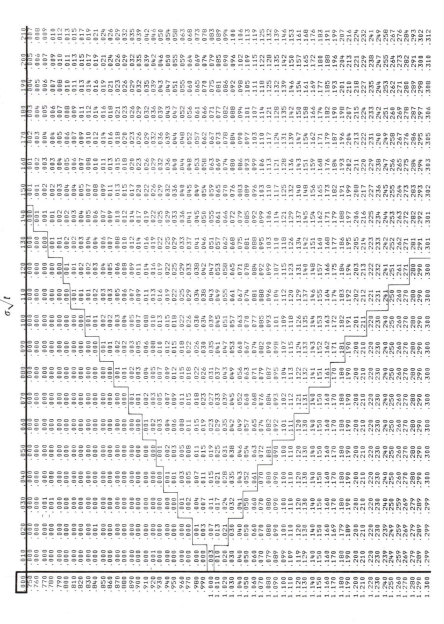

$\sigma\sqrt{t}$

S/Kr^{-t}

Table 6-6

TABLE FOR CALCULATING OPTION VALUES FOR $\sigma\sqrt{t} \geq .22$ (LINEAR INTERPOLATIONS ACCURATE WITHIN $\frac{1}{16}$ FOR $K \leq 50$)

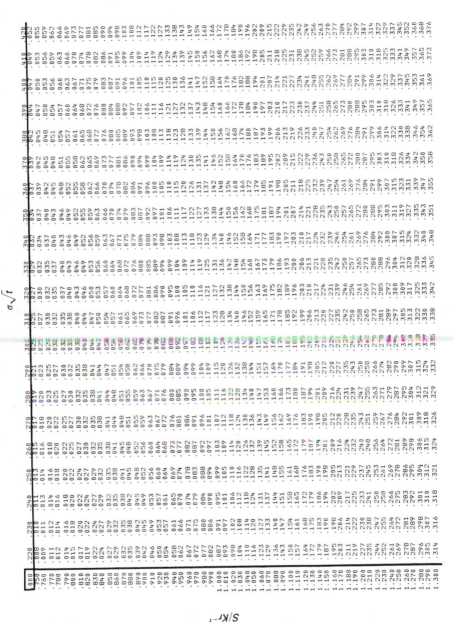

S/Kr^{-t} (rows) vs $\sigma\sqrt{t}$ (columns)

S/Kr^{-t}	000	220	230	240	250	260	270	280	290	300	310	320	330	340	350	360	370	380	390	400	410	420
.750		008	011	011	013	015	017	019	021	025	025	027	030	032	034	037	039	042	044	047	049	052
.760		009	011	012	014	016	018	020	023	025	027	030	032	035	037	040	042	045	048	050	053	055
.770		011	012	014	016	018	020	023	025	027	030	032	035	037	040	043	045	048	051	053	056	059
.780		012	014	016	018	020	022	025	027	030	032	035	038	040	043	046	048	051	054	057	060	062
.790		014	016	018	020	022	025	027	030	032	035	038	040	043	046	049	051	054	057	060	063	066
.800		015	018	018	020	024	027	030	032	035	037	040	043	046	049	052	055	058	061	063	066	069
.810		017	020	020	022	027	030	032	035	038	041	043	046	050	052	055	058	061	064	067	070	073
.820		019	022	022	024	030	032	035	038	041	044	047	050	053	056	059	062	065	068	072	074	077
.830		022	022	024	027	032	035	038	041	044	047	050	053	057	060	063	066	069	072	076	078	081
.840		024	027	029	032	035	038	044	047	050	053	057	061	063	066	070	074	076	080	079	082	085
.850		027	029	032	035	038	041	048	051	054	057	060	064	067	070	074	079	081	085	087	091	090
.860		029	032	035	038	041	044	051	054	057	061	064	068	071	074	078	083	086	089	091	095	094
.870		032	035	038	041	045	048	055	058	061	065	068	072	075	079	083	086	089	093	096	099	098
.880		035	038	042	045	048	051	059	062	066	069	073	076	080	084	087	091	094	098	101	104	103
.890		039	042	045	048	052	056	063	066	070	073	077	081	084	087	092	096	098	103	105	109	108
.900		042	045	049	052	056	060	067	070	074	077	081	085	088	092	097	100	103	108	110	114	112
.910		046	049	053	056	060	064	071	075	079	082	086	090	093	097	101	105	108	111	115	119	117
.920		050	053	057	060	064	068	076	079	083	087	090	094	099	103	106	110	113	116	120	124	122
.930		054	057	061	064	069	072	079	084	087	091	094	099	104	108	111	114	118	123	125	129	127
.940		058	061	065	069	073	076	085	089	092	096	100	105	108	111	115	119	123	127	130	134	133
.950		062	066	070	074	077	081	089	094	096	100	105	110	113	117	122	126	128	133	136	139	143
.960		067	071	075	078	082	086	094	099	101	106	110	116	118	123	127	131	135	139	141	145	149
.970		072	075	079	083	088	091	100	104	106	110	116	121	124	129	133	137	141	144	147	150	154
.980		077	080	084	088	094	098	105	109	113	116	121	127	129	133	138	142	146	150	152	156	160
.990		082	086	090	094	099	103	111	115	118	123	127	132	136	141	144	148	152	156	158	162	166
1.000		087	093	095	099	103	107	115	120	123	128	134	138	142	146	150	154	158	162	164	168	172
1.010		093	097	099	105	109	114	122	126	131	134	140	144	148	152	156	160	164	168	170	174	178
1.020		098	102	105	110	114	118	126	132	136	140	144	150	154	158	162	166	170	174	176	180	184
1.030		104	108	112	116	120	124	132	138	142	146	150	156	160	164	168	172	176	180	182	186	190
1.040		110	114	118	122	127	130	138	144	148	152	158	162	166	171	175	179	183	187	188	192	196
1.050		116	120	124	129	133	136	144	150	154	159	163	167	171	175	181	185	189	193	194	198	202
1.060		123	127	131	135	140	143	151	157	160	165	169	173	177	181	185	191	195	199	201	205	209
1.070		129	133	137	141	147	149	157	163	167	171	175	179	183	189	193	197	203	207	207	211	215
1.080		136	140	144	148	153	156	164	170	174	178	182	186	190	194	198	202	206	210	214	218	222
1.090		143	147	151	155	160	162	170	176	180	185	189	193	197	201	205	209	213	217	221	225	229
1.100		150	154	158	162	166	170	177	184	188	192	196	200	203	207	211	215	219	223	227	231	235
1.110		157	161	165	168	172	176	180	191	196	199	203	206	210	214	218	222	226	230	234	238	242
1.120		164	168	172	176	183	187	194	198	205	206	210	213	217	221	225	229	233	237	241	245	249
1.130		172	175	179	183	190	194	201	205	212	213	217	221	224	228	232	236	240	244	248	252	256
1.140		179	183	187	190	194	198	205	209	216	220	224	228	231	235	239	243	247	251	255	259	263
1.150		187	190	194	198	202	209	216	220	227	227	231	235	239	243	247	250	254	258	262	266	270
1.160		195	198	202	205	212	216	224	227	235	235	239	242	246	250	254	258	262	265	269	273	277
1.170		203	206	209	213	220	224	231	235	243	242	246	250	254	257	261	265	269	273	277	281	284
1.180		211	214	217	221	228	232	239	243	250	250	254	257	261	265	269	272	276	280	284	288	292
1.190		219	222	225	229	235	239	247	251	258	258	261	265	269	272	276	280	284	287	291	295	299
1.200		227	230	233	237	244	247	255	258	265	265	269	273	276	280	284	288	291	295	299	303	307
1.210		235	238	241	245	252	255	263	266	273	273	277	280	284	288	291	295	299	303	306	310	314
1.220		244	247	250	254	256	264	271	274	282	281	285	289	292	296	300	303	307	311	315	318	322
1.230		252	255	258	261	264	272	279	282	290	289	292	296	300	303	307	311	315	319	322	325	329
1.240		261	264	266	269	272	281	287	290	298	297	300	304	307	311	315	319	323	326	329	333	337
1.250		269	272	275	279	281	289	295	299	307	305	309	312	317	319	323	327	330	333	337	341	345
1.260		278	281	283	286	295	298	304	307	315	313	317	320	324	327	331	334	338	341	345	349	352
1.270		287	289	292	295	298	307	313	315	323	322	325	328	332	335	339	342	346	350	353	357	360
1.280		296	298	301	304	307	315	321	324	332	330	333	336	340	343	346	350	354	357	361	365	368
1.290		305	307	310	312	315	324	330	332	340	338	342	345	348	351	355	358	362	365	369	373	376
1.300		314	316	318	321	324	332	338	340?													

S/Kr^{-t} (left axis label)

Managing an Equivalent Portfolio. In Section 5-4, we gave a numerical example of the construction and subsequent revision of an equivalent port-folio. Table 6-7 does the same for the National Semiconductor May 40 call. We estimated the volatility and evaluated the call as of the close of trading on Friday, January 2. Suppose that we set up an equivalent portfolio on the following trading day, Monday, January 5. Using our volatility estimate of .52, we find that with Monday's closing stock price of $40\frac{5}{8}$ and bill price of $.9520, the call value is $6.23 and the call delta is .6419. Hence, to set up the equivalent portfolio, we would buy .6419 shares of stock at $40\frac{5}{8}$ per share for a total value of $26.08. We would finance the stock purchase by invest-ing the formula value, $6.23, and borrowing the remainder, $19.85. These transactions are shown in the first row of the table. To maintain the equiva-lent portfolio we would subsequently sell stock and buy bonds, or buy stock and sell bonds, in the way described in Sections 5-3 and 5-4. For example, on Tuesday, January 6, the closing stock price has dropped to $39\frac{1}{2}$ and the new delta is .6071. The revision strategy then calls for selling .6419–.6071 = .0348 shares of stock and using the proceeds to repay part of the borrowing (that is, buy back some of the bonds that have been sold). These transactions are reported in the second row. After selling the stock and buying the bonds, we have $23.98 worth of stock and owe $18.48 on the borrowing. Hence, the current market value of the equivalent portfolio is $23.98–$18.48 = $5.50, as shown at the end of the row. On Tuesday, the closing market price of the call is $5\frac{3}{4}$ and the Black-Scholes value is $5.50; as judged by the formula, the call went from being overvalued on Friday to undervalued on Monday, then back to overvalued on Tuesday. The remain-ing rows of the table show the results of maintaining the equivalent port-folio in this way over a two-week period.

In the numerical example of Section 5-4, the formula value and the market value of the continually adjusted portfolio of stock and bonds were always equal, but this was no cause for celebration; they were equal by construction. However, if stock prices had not moved in the way that we assumed, their values would not have remained equal. Hence, if the two values remain equal in our current example, with trading at market prices, then this bodes well for the usefulness of the formula. The results are striking: The formula value and the value of the portfolio are always extremely close; the largest discrepancy is $.05 on January 9.

6-2. SOME MODIFICATIONS TO MAKE THE MODEL WORK BETTER

Although we arbitrarily chose the beginning of 1981 for our example in Section 6-1, we did try to pick a stock for which the basic Black-Scholes

Table 6-7

TWO WEEKS IN THE LIFE OF AN EQUIVALENT PORTFOLIO

Date	Stock Price	Call Price	Black-Scholes Value	Delta	Number of Shares Bought or Sold and Their Value	Bill Price (for $1 face value)	Number of Bills Bought or Sold and Their Value	Total Amount Invested In Stock	Total Amount Borrowed	Value of Portfolio
1/5	$40\frac{5}{8}$	$6	$6.23	.6419	buy .6419 = $26.08	$.9520	sell 20.8497 = $19.85	$26.08	$19.85	$6.23
1/6	$39\frac{1}{2}$	$5\frac{3}{4}$	$5.50	.6071	sell .0348 = $1.37	$.9523	buy 1.4433 = $1.37	$23.98	$18.48	$5.50
1/7	$37\frac{3}{4}$	$4\frac{1}{8}$	$4.52	.5531	sell .0540 = $2.04	$.9497	buy 2.1478 = $2.04	$20.88	$16.39	$4.49
1/8	$36\frac{1}{4}$	$3\frac{3}{4}$	$3.70	.4997	sell .0534 = $1.94	$.9501	buy 2.0375 = $1.94	$18.11	$14.46	$3.65
1/9	$36\frac{1}{8}$	$3\frac{7}{8}$	$3.65	.4969	sell .0028 = $.10	$.9486	buy .1081 = $.10	$17.95	$14.34	$3.61
1/12	$35\frac{1}{4}$	$3\frac{1}{8}$	$3.15	.4606	sell .0363 = $1.28	$.9503	buy 1.3470 = $1.28	$16.23	$13.08	$3.15
1/13	$34	$2\frac{3}{4}$	$2.59	.4134	sell .0472 = $1.60	$.9498	buy 1.6888 = $1.60	$14.05	$11.47	$2.58
1/14	$34	$2\frac{1}{2}$	$2.57	.4113	sell .0021 = $.07	$.9507	buy .0746 = $.07	$13.98	$11.41	$2.57
1/15	$34\frac{1}{2}$	$2\frac{5}{8}$	$2.76	.4295	buy .0182 = $.63	$.9508	sell .6600 = $.63	$14.82	$12.04	$2.78
1/16	$35\frac{1}{2}$	$3	$3.19	.4664	buy .0369 = $1.31	$.9510	sell 1.3764 = $1.31	$16.55	$13.35	$3.20

formula would be appropriate. The formula assumes that the stock will not pay cash dividends during the life of the option; this was the case with National Semiconductor. The formula also assumes that the option cannot be exercised before the expiration date, but this did not matter because early exercise of a call is never optimal if there are no dividends. The formula also requires the volatility of the stock to be constant. Historically, the volatility of National Semiconductor has been reasonably stable; the volatility in the first two weeks of January 1981 was not significantly different from that in the last six months of 1980.

In most situations, we will not be so lucky: The basic Black-Scholes formula will no longer be appropriate. Here is a review of the assumptions on which the formula is based:

1. The underlying stock pays no cash dividends during the life of the option.
2. The option can be exercised only on the expiration date.
3. There are no margin requirements, taxes, or transactions costs.
4. The interest rate is constant.
5. The volatility of the stock is constant.
6. Only very small changes in the stock price can occur in a very short period of time.

Usually these assumptions are too restrictive: They rule out factors that are too important to be ignored.

To get useful results, we must make some changes. In doing so, we have two alternatives. First, we can make some informal adjustments to the model that are not completely correct theoretically but will nevertheless give much better results. Second, we can extend the model to include some of the factors that were originally left out. The first approach is easier to apply, while the second gives more accurate answers; the choice between them should depend on your circumstances and objectives. We have already discussed both approaches for handling dividends and early exercise in Chapter 5; in this section, we will briefly review our conclusions and then move on to problems we have not yet considered. The extensions necessary to include situations ruled out by the last three assumptions require fundamental alterations in our option pricing methods; these are presented in Sections 7-1 and 7-8.

Dividends.   If the stock is paying cash dividends, we will want to incorporate them into our previous calculations. First, we need to forecast future dividends and ex-dividend dates. Despite considerable fluctuation in earnings per share, most corporations maintain relatively stable dividends.[5] As a

---

[5] An old but still useful empirical study of corporate dividend policy appears in an article by John Lintner entitled "Distribution of Income of Corporations Among Dividends, Retained Earnings, and Taxes," *American Economic Review*, 46 (May 1956), 97–113.

result, cash dividends over nine months in the future are quite predictable. Typically, the last quarterly dividend or the indicated next quarterly dividend, if one has been announced, is a good prediction of quarterly dividends during the next year. This estimate should be moved slightly upward by the anticipated growth rate in dividends expected over the long term.

Knowing the last or next announced ex-dividend date permits a reliable forecast of future ex-dividend dates. These may be assumed to occur at three-month intervals, although some adjustment may be needed to keep projected ex-dividend dates on business days. Announcements of cash dividends and ex-dividend dates as they occur are routinely available in the *Wall Street Journal's* section entitled "Corporate Dividend News." This same section reports corporate announcements of next quarterly or extra dividends, dates of payment, and dates of record. The ex-dividend date usually precedes the date of record by four business days. Special care in forecasting cash dividends should be taken for firms that occasionally or regularly declare extra dividends, and for firms with a projected ex-dividend date very close to an expiration date of their associated options. In the latter case, a mistake of one or two days could have a significant impact on the value of an option.

The binomial method discussed in Section 5-9 provides a completely correct way to include fully predictable dividends in the Black-Scholes model. An easier, but less accurate, way to adjust for dividends is to use the Black-Scholes formula with the stock price reduced by the present value of the anticipated dividends.

If the firm's future dividend policy is uncertain, then the arbitrage approach to valuation in general breaks down, as we showed in Chapter 5. Extending the model to include uncertain dividends requires the methods discussed in Section 7-8. However, an informal adjustment can be made by using as the final value a weighted average of option values calculated for each possible dividend sequence, with weights equal to the respective probabilities of each sequence occurring. Furthermore, uncertainty about dividends will rarely be an important factor for options with lives of less than one year.

Early Exercise. For most options, the possibility of optimal early exercise cannot be ruled out. Once again, the binomial method of Chapter 5 provides a completely correct way to include this possibility in the Black-Scholes model. As an example, let us return to our calculations for National Semiconductor. To use the binomial method, we need to transform our estimated values for σ and r into the appropriate values u, d, and $\hat{r}$. Suppose that we decide to divide the life of each option into 150 subperiods, so that $n = 150$. Then according to our results in Chapter 5, we want to use the following values for the May options:

$$u = e^{\sigma\sqrt{t/n}} = e^{.52\sqrt{.3644/150}} = 1.025961;$$
$$d = e^{-\sigma\sqrt{t/n}} = e^{-.52\sqrt{.3644/150}} = .974696;$$
$$\hat{r} = r^{t/n} = (1.163448)^{.3644/150} = 1.000368.$$

The values to use for the February and August options will be somewhat different because the values of t and r will be different in each of those cases.

Table 6-8 shows the values given by the binomial method for all of the National Semiconductor puts on January 2, 1981. Table 6-9 shows the corresponding market values. Once again, the market prices and model values are very similar. According to the model, five of the puts are overvalued and four are undervalued.

Table 6-8
BLACK-SCHOLES VALUES FOR NATIONAL SEMICONDUCTOR PUTS ON JANUARY 2, 1981

	February	*May*	*August*
35	.74	1.84	2.73
40	2.43	3.81	4.82
45	5.43	6.62	7.58
50	9.49	10.21	10.97

Table 6-9
CLOSING MARKET PRICES FOR NATIONAL SEMICONDUCTOR PUTS ON JANUARY 2, 1981

	February	*May*	*August*
35	$\frac{13}{16}$	$1\frac{7}{8}$	$2\frac{3}{8}$
40	$2\frac{13}{16}$	$3\frac{3}{4}$	—
45	$5\frac{3}{4}$	7	$7\frac{3}{8}$
50	10	—	—

Unfortunately, the binomial method is really practical only if a computer is available. If not, the informal adjustment suggested in Chapter 5 can be used. We know that early exercise of a call will be optimal only just prior to an ex-dividend date. We can then compute several values for the call, one assuming that it expires on the expiration date, another assuming that it expires just prior to the last ex-dividend date, a third assuming that it expires just before the next-to-last ex-dividend date, and so on. Each of these values is calculated by using the formula with the stock price reduced by the sum of the dividends to be paid during the lives of the options. The value of the call is then taken to be the highest of the computed values.

The corresponding adjustment for puts is not likely to be as effective: In most cases, optimal early exercise can occur at any time. However, we could still calculate values for puts expiring on the expiration date and at several earlier times and then take the highest of these values. Based on our results on optimal early exercise in Section 5-9, a natural choice for these times would be just after each ex-dividend date.

Taxes, Margin Requirements, and Differential Borrowing and Lending Rates. Before concluding that an option offers a superior opportunity, an investor will want to take into account his particular situation with respect to taxes, margin requirements, and differential borrowing and lending rates. Indeed, these three factors provided our second, third, and fourth reasons for using options. Unfortunately, the tax laws and margin requirements are so complex, and circumstances are so widely varied from one individual to another, that it is impossible to give general rules that will be exactly right for all investors. However, we can offer some adjustments to the Black-Scholes model that are correct under idealized conditions. They provide a convenient and practical way to include the main effects of taxes, margin requirements, and differential borrowing and lending rates.

If the following conditions about taxes hold, then no change would be needed in our former analysis:

1. Capital gains, interest, and dividends are all taxed at the same constant rate.
2. Taxes are collected each period (or instant, in the limit) based on realized and accrued gains.
3. Full loss offsets are allowed (that is, capital losses, interest on borrowing, and dividends paid to stock sold short result in a tax rebate at the same rates as the corresponding sources of income).

To keep matters simple, yet deal with the main tax effects, suppose that assumptions (2) and (3) are true, but that different sources of income are taxed at different constant rates:

$$\gamma = \text{tax rate on stock capital gains;}$$
$$\tau = \text{tax rate on option capital gains;}$$
$$\iota = \text{tax rate on interest income;}$$
$$\eta = \text{tax rate on dividend income.}$$

Similarly, if investors received interest on all margin deposits, then (except for differences in borrowing and lending rates) again no change would be needed. But we know that this is not the case for most individual investors: They do not receive interest on the funds generated by the short sale of stock. We mentioned earlier that this restriction should make buying puts and writing calls more attractive relative to shorting the stock; now we will be able to assign an exact value to this advantage.

To see how to include these factors, we return to the binomial model of Chapter 5. There we argued that over one period, the value of a call and the value of a portfolio containing Δ shares of stock and B dollars in bonds would change in the following way:

$$
C
\begin{cases}
C_u \\
C_d
\end{cases}
\qquad
S\Delta + B
\begin{cases}
uS\Delta + rB \\
dS\Delta + rB
\end{cases}
$$

If Δ and B are chosen so that the end-of-period values of the call and the portfolio are equal in each possible outcome, then if the call is to be held for one more period, its current value C must equal $S\Delta + B$. Now we need to make two changes in the argument. First, the before-tax end-of-period values must be replaced by the corresponding after-tax values. Second, if Δ is negative, representing a short sale of stock, then the end-of-period value of the stock and bond portfolio must be reduced by the after-tax value of the forfeited interest on the proceeds of the short sale. Let λ be a variable that equals one if Δ is negative and zero if Δ is positive, and let D stand for the dividend paid at the end of the period to those who owned the stock during the period. Then we could write our revised tree diagram in the following way:

$$
C
\begin{cases}
C_u - \tau(C_u - C) \\
C_d - \tau(C_d - C)
\end{cases}
$$

$$
S\Delta + B
\begin{cases}
(1 - \gamma)(u - D/S)S\Delta + \gamma S\Delta + (1 - \eta)D\Delta \\
\quad + rB - \imath(r - 1)B + \lambda(1 - \imath)(r - 1)S\Delta \\
(1 - \gamma)(d - D/S)S\Delta + \gamma S\Delta + (1 - \eta)D\Delta \\
\quad + rB - \imath(r - 1)B + \lambda(1 - \imath)(r - 1)S\Delta
\end{cases}
$$

By rearranging and using $C = S\Delta + B$, we find that the choices of Δ and B that equate the end-of-period values must satisfy

$$
\left[\frac{(1 - \gamma)(u - D/S) + (1 - \eta)D/S + (\gamma - \tau) + \lambda(1 - \imath)(r - 1)}{1 - \tau} \right] S\Delta
$$

$$
+ \left[\frac{(1 - \imath)r + (\imath - \tau)}{1 - \tau} \right] B = C_u
$$

$$\left[\frac{(1-\gamma)(d-D/S) + (1-\eta)D/S + (\gamma-\tau) + \lambda(1-\iota)(r-1)}{1-\tau} \right] S\Delta$$

$$+ \left[\frac{(1-\iota)r + (\iota-\tau)}{1-\tau} \right] B = C_d.$$

Solving these equations for Δ and B, we find that the form of the solution linking C with C_u and C_d is exactly the same as before; the only change is that the following variables are replaced by the indicated new values:

Variable	Old Value	New Value
Δ	$\dfrac{C_u - C_d}{(u-d)S}$	$\left(\dfrac{1-\tau}{1-\gamma}\right)\left(\dfrac{C_u - C_d}{(u-d)S}\right)$
p	$\dfrac{r-d}{u-d}$	$\dfrac{(1-\iota)r + (\iota-\gamma) - (1-\gamma)d - (\gamma-\eta)(D/S) - \lambda(1-\iota)(r-1)}{(1-\gamma)(u-d)}$
$1-p$	$\dfrac{u-r}{u-d}$	$\dfrac{(1-\gamma)u + (\gamma-\eta)(D/S) + (\gamma-\iota) + \lambda(1-\iota)(r-1) - (1-\iota)r}{(1-\gamma)(u-d)}$
r	r	$\dfrac{(1-\iota)r + (\iota-\tau)}{1-\tau}$

Note that if all tax rates are equal ($\gamma = \tau = \iota = \eta$) and $\lambda = 0$, then the old values and new values are the same. If all tax rates are equal and $\lambda = 1$, then the old and new values of Δ and r are equal; the only change is that p is replaced with $(1-d)/(u-d)$ and $1-p$ is replaced with $(u-1)/(u-d)$.

Although we have referred only to calls, the same steps hold for a put. After making the indicated substitutions, we can proceed exactly as described in Chapter 5 to value any option position. In fact, if margin requirements are an issue, then the analysis should simultaneously consider the entire position in the underlying stock and all options on the stock. The critical issue is whether the Δ of the entire position is positive or negative. For example, if you are considering buying stock and buying a put, you would not want to credit the put for avoiding the loss of interest on a short sale, because that is not the stock-and-bond alternative you would consider; instead of simultaneously having a long and short position in the stock, you would have simply chosen a smaller long position.

Now consider the third factor. Suppose, for whatever reason, that even with full collateral an individual can borrow only at a higher rate than he can lend. This is unlikely to be very important for large professional traders, but it may be significant for some individuals. Here is a simple rule of thumb: Use the borrowing rate in the analysis if your total portfolio involves borrowing; if not, use the lending rate. It is the status of your entire portfolio that matters because if you are lending in one part of the portfolio you would not simultaneously borrow at a higher rate in another part; instead, you would reduce your lending. Of course, this is only a rough rule and it will not always be easy to apply: Sometimes it may not be clear whether you will be borrowing or lending until you have determined your entire investment strategy.

The modifications we have suggested are not perfect. For example, they do not include some of the features of the tax rules, such as limits on loss offsets and interest deduction, that may in turn limit the tax benefits from trading in options. Also, the price changes on which options capital gains and losses are assessed are assumed to be those that would occur in equilibrium when all investors have the tax rates specified. Nevertheless, we believe that these modifications are quite useful. One final point: An investor interested in buying an option would compare it with the alternative of buying the equivalent portfolio; on the other hand, an arbitrageur interested in buying an option would plan to sell the equivalent portfolio. Hence, the implications for short selling, and possibly for borrowing and lending, would be just the opposite in the two cases.

Changing Interest Rates.   Here we must deal with an issue that we glossed over in Section 6-1: Interest rates are definitely not constant. Suppose initially that the one-period interest rate is a known function of time. This implies that the interest rate is changing over time, but in a perfectly predictable way. In applying the binomial method, we would want to use a different interest rate for each period; otherwise, we would proceed exactly as before.

We could obtain the appropriate interest rate for each period from the current market prices of default-free zero-coupon bonds of different maturities. If r_j stands for one plus the interest rate in the jth period, then the current prices of zero-coupon bonds maturing at the ends of periods $k - 1$ and k will be, respectively, $(1/\Pi_{j=1}^{k-1} r_j)$ and $(1/\Pi_{j=1}^{k} r_j)$. Hence, one plus the interest rate prevailing during the kth period, r_k, will be the current price of the k-period bond divided by the current price of the $(k - 1)$-period bond. The interest rates for all other periods could be obtained in a similar way. To see how this would work, consider the January 2 market prices for Treasury bills maturing on May 7 and May 14. We found that the price of the May 14 maturity was \$9467.23; a similar calculation shows that the price of the May 7 maturity was \$9495.49. Hence, one plus the implied one-week interest rate for the period May 7 to May 14 is \$9495.49/\$9467.23 = 1.002985; in annualized terms, the corresponding figure is $(1.002985)^{52} = 1.1676$, or 16.76%.

If we work back through the binomial derivation of the Black-Scholes formula, we will find that the one-period interest rates appear only in the form $(1/\Pi r_j)$. This expression is simply the current value of a zero-coupon bond maturing at the same time as the option.[6] Consequently, if we are using the basic formula, all the information needed about the changing one-period rates will be summarized in a single bond price. The same will be true if we are using the formula combined with the informal adjustments for dividends and early exercise. Hence, the procedure that we used in Section 6-1 would be completely justified if interest rates were changing predictably over time.

However, the calculation of American put values that we made earlier in this section is not entirely appropriate if interest rates are changing. There, in effect, we took the average continuously compounded rate over the life of the option and acted as if this rate would prevail in each period. This neglects the fact that the exact pattern of interest rates will affect the possibility of early exercise. To see why, consider a two-period example in which the interest rate will be 10% in the first period and zero in the second period. We know from Chapter 4 that a put will not be exercised during any period having a zero interest rate. Consequently, early exercise of this put will occur immediately or not at all. Compare this with another two-period example in which the interest rate will be zero in the first period and 10% in the second period. Now an otherwise identical put would never be exercised immediately. The current price of a bond paying $1 on the maturity date, and hence the average interest rate, will be the same in both cases, but the two options will not have the same value. The same issues arise with calls on stocks that pay dividends. In these situations, the full pattern of interest rates is needed. However, in practice there is usually only a small loss of accuracy in ignoring this refinement.

Now let us admit that interest rates not only change over time but do so in a way that is not perfectly predictable. This is another situation in which the arbitrage approach in general breaks down, and we must defer an appropriate extension of the model until Chapter 7.[7] However, in our opinion, uncertainty in interest rates is not an important factor in valuing options with lives of under one year. The best informal adjustment is to ignore the problem altogether and act as if interest rates were a known function of time. However, it should be noted that uncertainty in interest rates may be quite important in the application of option pricing methods to other securities, such as corporate bonds and options on government bonds; we will examine some of these applications in Chapter 7.

---

[6] In the continuous limit, $(1/\Pi r_j)$ becomes the constant e raised to the power $(-\int_0^t \log r(v)\, dv)$. With a constant interest rate, we could have written r^{-t} as the constant e raised to the power $(-(\log r)t)$. As mentioned in Chapter 5, the constant continuously compounded interest rate $\log r$ has, in effect, been replaced by the average continuously compounded interest rate that will prevail over the remaining life of the option, $\int_0^t \log r(v)\,dv/t$.

[7] See Robert C. Merton, "Theory of Rational Option Pricing," *Bell Journal of Economics and Management Science*, 4 (Spring 1973), 141–183 for a special case in which arbitrage methods still apply.

Changing Volatility. If our earlier assumption of constant volatility is correct, then the greater the number of historical stock price observations in our sample, the closer we expect the mean and variance of the sample to approximate the mean and variance of the true distribution of stock return. One way to increase the size of the sample is to use weekly stock prices extending further into the past. Another possibility is to increase the frequency of our sampling to daily rather than weekly observations.[8]

But what if this basic assumption is not completely appropriate? It certainly seems plausible that a host of factors—changes in labor and raw materials costs, changes in selling prices, recapitalizations, mergers, changes in general economic prospects and market sentiment—may alter the probability distribution of stock returns. Indeed, anyone estimating volatility with the procedures described earlier will find that his estimates change over time. If the induced changes in stock volatility could be predicted in advance, then, as shown in Chapter 5, we could reflect this by a minor modification in the Black-Scholes formula. However, to be realistic, many factors that affect volatility are themselves uncertain, so we cannot predict future volatility with certainty. This would be true even if we could measure past volatility without error.

Nonetheless, we may still find it expedient to maintain the assumption of lognormality, since without it we would need to: (1) specify the way the true probability distribution changes over time, (2) forecast future volatility based on this specification, and (3) make a fundamental revision in the Black-Scholes formula. In the next chapter, we discuss the derivation of alternative option pricing formulas which incorporate uncertain volatility. For now, we will consider ways of estimating volatility which minimize the errors created by this complication.

Even though volatilities are not exactly constant, it may still be true that changes in volatility typically evolve slowly over time. The recent past may then serve as an adequate guide to the near future. This implies that the use of closely spaced observations has two important advantages: It allows for a larger sample size without bringing in less relevant data from the more distant past, and, as discussed earlier, it makes the estimates of the volatility insensitive to estimates of the mean. For these reasons, we strongly recommend the use of at least daily data in forecasting volatility over periods of less than one year.[9]

---

[8] Since there is an average of 253 trading days in a year, if we do use daily closing prices, we must remember to annualize a daily standard deviation by multiplying by $\sqrt{253}$, not $\sqrt{365}$. Better yet, adjust for the actual number of trading days within the observation period. If closing bid-ask data are available, the estimated volatility can be further improved by using only bid prices to filter out the extra artificial variation of the last sale price across the bid-ask spread interval.

[9] Unfortunately, as the time interval between observations diminishes, the artificial fluctuation across the bid-ask spread has a greater effect on our estimate of volatility. Thus, there is a kind of "uncertainty principle" at work in financial economics.

A further way to utilize easily accessible data of recent origin, but at the same time have a sufficiently large sample, is to make use of daily high and low stock prices routinely quoted in the financial press. Since the high and low prices are a type of summary of *all* transactions during the day, they should contain more information about the volatility than the closing prices alone. Michael Parkinson,[10] when at the Department of Physics and Astronomy at the University of Florida, showed that, if stock prices are lognormally distributed, a proper use of the high/low daily prices over the past n days provides as good an estimate of the volatility as closing prices over the past $5n$ days. His formula for estimating the volatility based on high and low prices is

$$\sigma = \frac{.627}{n} \sum_{i=1}^{n} \log (H_i/L_i),$$

where $H_i(L_i)$ is the high (low) price for day i.

One problem with this approach arises from discontinuities in trading during the day. This implies, under Parkinson's assumptions, that the reported high (low) will almost certainly be lower (higher) than the high (low) which would have been observed with continuous trading. This means the resulting estimates will be biased downward; they will tend to be systematically lower than the true volatility. To handle this problem, Mark Garman and Michael Klass[11] of the University of California at Berkeley have developed a numerical procedure which can be used to adjust the volatility estimator for the number of trades during the day. They also show how to improve the high/low estimator by simultaneously considering opening and closing prices. Their method could be further improved by modeling different hypothetical price movements for overnight and the daytime trading period. The closing and next-day opening prices can be used as information about hypothetical price movements overnight.

Unfortunately, any method using high and low prices is particularly vulnerable to reporting errors. If any trade during the day is reported incorrectly, there is a good chance that it will appear as the high or low for the day. If good data checks are used and the bias is corrected, and if the lognormality assumption is completely appropriate, then open/high/low/close estimators of volatility will be superior to those based only on closing prices. However, it is conceivable that the open/high/low/close estimators are so sensitive to deviations from lognormality that in other circumstances they will actually perform more poorly than estimators based only on closing prices. More testing is necessary to determine if this potential problem is important.

---

[10] See his paper, "The Random Walk Problem: Extreme Value Method for Estimating the Variance of the Displacement," *Journal of Business*, 53 (January 1980), 61–65.

[11] See their paper, "On the Estimation of Security Price Volatilities from Historical Data," *Journal of Business*, 53 (January 1980), 67–78.

Implicit Volatility. One check on our estimate from historical data is to use the Black-Scholes formula itself to measure the "market's opinion" of the volatility. We already know that, given S, K, t, r, and σ, the formula implies a unique call value C. Similarly, if we insert S, t, K, and r, and the market price of the corresponding call for C, the formula implies a unique volatility σ. That is, knowing C, S, t, K, and r, we then have one equation in one unknown, σ, and can back σ out of the formula. Since we have used the market price for C, the volatility calculated in this manner is the "market's estimate" of σ. We will call this estimate the *implicit volatility*. For example, if $S = 40$, $t = .333$, $K = 40$, $r = 1.05$, and $C = 3.07$, then from Table 5-2 we see that the implicit volatility is .3. Unfortunately, we cannot analytically invert the formula so that σ is alone on the left-hand side and C, S, t, K, and r are on the right. However, there are efficient numerical search procedures[12] which, given S, t, K, and r, find the σ which produces a given C. If our volatility estimate is different from the implicit volatility, an opening purchase or sale of the corresponding option can be interpreted as a bet that our estimate of the volatility is better than the "market's estimate."

In principle, different options on the same underlying stock may have different implicit volatilities. If the volatility is changing over time, then options with different expiration dates would not be expected to have the same implicit volatility. Even for options with the same expiration date, some difference should arise because the possibility of early exercise means that the actual lifetime of the options may not be the same. For example, if a call is deep-in-the-money and the next ex-dividend date is one month away, the implicit volatility will primarily reflect the market's forecast of volatility for only the next month, even though the actual expiration date may be several months away. Consequently, with ideal data, it would be possible to calculate a separate implicit volatility for each option and find the market's forecasted volatility as a function of time. In practice, the true implicit volatilities for different options will be very similar, and apparent differences will be due primarily to the lack of simultaneity in quoted stock and option prices and the inherent coarseness of prices that are quoted in units of 12.5 cents (or 6.7 cents) rather than one cent. One way to reduce these measurement errors is to combine the implicit volatilities from different options into a single volatility figure, σ^*. Suppose $\sigma^* (t_j, K_j)$ represents the implicit volatility for call j with time to expiration t_j and striking price K_j. The simplest procedure is to compute a weighted average,

$$\sigma^* = \sum_{j=1}^{J} \left(\frac{w_j}{\sum_j w_j}\right) \sigma^* (t_j, K_j),$$

---

[12] Particularly efficient is a Newton-Raphson search, which usually locates the implicit volatility in no more than three iterations.

where w_j is the weight given to call j, and J is the total number of calls[13] available on the associated stock.

One choice of weights is $w_j = 1$ for $j = 1, 2, \ldots, J$. This produces an unweighted average which treats each implicit volatility the same. However, since some call prices are more sensitive to σ than others, we may wish to give more weight to those calls. In particular, we know from our sensitivity analysis that the values of near-the-money calls are more sensitive than out-of or in-the-money calls. One way to capture this effect is to set $w_j = \partial C_j / \partial \sigma_j^*$, the sensitivity of a call price with respect to its implicit volatility. Perhaps a better method is to set $w_j = \Omega_j$, the elasticity of a call calculated from its implicit volatility. Moreover, an argument can be made for excluding deep-in and deep-out-of-the-money options entirely because their implicit volatilities are highly sensitive to the minimum allowable price change for options and stock.[14]

Yet another approach searches for the single volatility across all calls on the same underlying stock, which minimizes the sum of the absolute relative deviations of call prices from their corresponding values based on that volatility. That is, if $C(t_j, K_j)$ represents the value of call j with time to expiration t_j and striking price K_j based on volatility σ^*, and $M(t_j, K_j)$ is its corresponding market price, then the problem is to find the σ^* which minimizes the summation

$$\sum_{j=1}^{J} \left| \frac{M(t_j, K_j) - C(t_j, K_j)}{C(t_j, K_j)} \right|.$$

Using a particular weighting scheme, Henry Latané and Richard Rendleman have provided reliable empirical evidence that implicit volatilities are generally a better predictor of actual future stock volatility than historically computed volatilities based on weekly closing stock prices.[15] Although these tests suffer from some of the deficiencies mentioned in Section 6-6, these problems should only serve to bias their results against their conclusions. Therefore, it appears likely that with the availability of options transactions data, measures of implicit volatility should prove helpful in predicting future stock volatility.

---

[13] We can also average implicit volatilities for puts, although here, consideration of the effects of early exercise seriously complicates the numerical search procedure for calculating them.

[14] Stan Beckers has demonstrated that, with implicit volatilities computed from daily closing option and stock prices, using only the implicit volatility of the option nearest the money (that is, the one for which $\partial C / \partial \sigma$ is greatest) appears to produce as good a prediction of future volatility as any of these estimation methods. See his paper, "Standard Deviations Implied in Option Prices as Predictors of Future Stock Price Variability," *Journal of Banking and Finance*, 5 (September 1981), 363–382.

[15] See their paper, "Standard Deviations of Stock Price Ratios Implied in Option Prices," *Journal of Finance*, 31 (May 1976), 369–382.

Fischer Black's Approach to Estimating Volatility.   All the things we have discussed thus far are in themselves useful in predicting volatility. Hence, it seems reasonable that we can do even better by combining them. We can combine information from historical stock price observations with an option's implicit volatility, together with empirical knowledge about how volatilities tend to change over time. Such a method was employed by Fischer Black for his Option Pricing Service.[16] He revised his naive estimate of historical volatility to take into account four observations:

1. Volatilities of different stocks tend to change together in the same direction.

2. Changes in volatilities are often temporary; after a significant change up or down, volatilities seem to revert back toward their previous levels.

3. Changes in stock prices not caused by stock splits or stock dividends are inversely related to changes in their associated volatilities.

4. An option's implicit volatility contains useful information for predicting the true volatility of its associated stock.

Observation 1 implies there is a "market" effect on stock volatilities just as there is a "beta" factor affecting the price of common stocks.

Observation 2 implies volatilities over time on the same stock tend to regress to the mean. This suggests that different volatilities should be associated with options on the same stock with different expiration dates. For example, if the recent volatility of a stock is higher than normal, then higher volatilities should be associated with near-term options and lower volatilities with far-term options.

Observation 3 is not meant to imply that high-priced stocks have low volatilities and low-priced stocks have high volatilities. Rather, it says that stocks that have recently risen in value experience a decline in volatility, and those that have recently fallen in value experience an increase in volatility. Not only does this apply to individual stocks, but also to the behavior over time of the volatility of market indexes. The underlying firm's financial and operating leverage supply a plausible, economic explanation of this effect. When a firm's stock price falls, the percentage decrease in the market value of the equity is usually greater than the percentage decrease in the market value of the firm's debt. This automatically increases a firm's debt-equity ratio in market value terms. In turn, this increases the risk of owning a firm's stock which leads to a rise in the stock's volatility. Even if a firm were purely equity financed, a decline in its stock price might very well be caused by a decline in sales. Profits of firms with high operating leverage (that is, a high ratio of fixed to variable costs) or products with high gross

---

[16] This description of Black's method for estimating volatilities is taken from *Fischer Black on Options*, 1, No. 8 (May 1976).

margin (that is, a large difference between selling price and variable cost per unit) will become proportionately more sensitive to changes in sales. Again, this increases the risk of owning the firm's stock and increases its volatility.

Observation 4 gives recognition to the wisdom of the marketplace. No matter how much we know about the factors affecting a stock's volatility, the market may know something we do not. This missing information will be reflected in the prices of associated options. The higher these prices, other things equal, the higher the "market's estimate" of the volatility.

Black incorporated these observations in his forecast of volatility in the following way. Let

$j = 1, 2, \ldots, J$ index all stocks for which there are listed options,

$S_j =$ the current stock price of stock j,

$S_j^- =$ the price of stock j one month in the past,

$n =$ the number of months to expiration for an option, where $n = 0$ if the current month is an expiration month,

$\bar{\sigma}_j =$ the volatility of stock j estimated from the (about 21) daily closing prices during the previous month, assuming a zero mean stock rate of return,

$\sigma_j^- (n + 1) =$ the final estimated volatility calculated one month in the past for an option on underlying stock j which then had $n + 1$ months to expiration,

$M_j(n) =$ the current market price of the call closest to the money on stock j with n months to expiration,

$C_j(n) =$ the Black-Scholes value of a call with the same terms, based on volatility $\sigma_j^- (n + 1)$,

$\sigma_j(n) =$ the final current estimated volatility for an option with n months to expiration on underlying stock j.

Three further variables are defined in terms of these:

$$S \equiv \frac{1}{J} \sum_{j=1}^{J} S_j, \qquad S^- \equiv \frac{1}{J} \sum_{j=1}^{J} S_j^-, \qquad \text{and} \qquad \bar{\sigma} \equiv \frac{1}{J} \sum_{j=1}^{J} \bar{\sigma}_j.$$

Black first calculated a provisional volatility for options with n months to expiration on each underlying stock:

$$\hat{\sigma}_j(n) \equiv \left[1 - \left(\frac{S - S^-}{S^-} + \frac{S_j - S_j^-}{S_j^-} \right) \div \left(4 + \frac{n}{6} \right) \right]$$

$$\times \left[1 + .15 \frac{M_j(n) - C_j(n)}{C_j(n)} \right] \sigma_j^- (n + 1).$$

This formula makes three adjustments to the volatility estimate $\sigma_j^-(n+1)$ used in the previous month. The first adjustment $[M_j(n) - C_j(n)]/C_j(n)$ moves the estimate up (down) if the market price of the near-the-money call is greater (less) than its formula value based on the old estimate $\sigma_j^-(n+1)$. This reflects Observation 4, and Black only moved his estimate up or down by 15% of this difference. The second adjustment $(S_j - S_j^-)/S_j^-$ reflects Observation 3 and the third adjustment $(S - S^-)/S^-$ reflects Observation 1.

Based on this provisional volatility, Black calculated a "market" volatility for all optioned stocks by averaging options with time to expiration between two and seven months:

$$\hat{\sigma} \equiv \frac{1}{2J} \sum_{j=1}^{J} [\hat{\sigma}_j(2) + \hat{\sigma}_j(7)].$$

Using this, he calculated a revised provisional volatility for options with n months to expiration on each underlying stock:

$$\hat{\sigma}_j(n) \equiv \left[1 + .2 \frac{\bar{\sigma} - \hat{\sigma}}{\hat{\sigma}} \right] \hat{\sigma}_j(n).$$

Again, this revision reflects Observation 1.

Finally, to consider Observation 2, Black averaged this provisional volatility with the volatility calculated solely from the daily stock prices observed during the previous month:

$$\sigma_j(n) = \left(1 - \frac{1}{4 + (n/3)} \right) \hat{\sigma}_j(n) + \left(\frac{1}{4 + (n/3)} \right) \bar{\sigma}_j.$$

This weighting implies that the longer the life of an option the more weight is given to the provisional estimate $\hat{\sigma}_j(n)$. In special situations, especially when unanticipated news has just recently become public relating to an optioned equity, Black adjusted $\sigma_j(n)$ up or down depending on his best judgment.

Tables 6–10(a) and (b) illustrate the ranges that can occur in forecasted volatilities for different stocks. The tables show the four highest and four lowest of the forecasted volatilities Black used to value middle-maturity options during the month of January, 1980. The figures shown give his forecast of the average volatility that would prevail from January 1 to the expiration date of the outstanding option with middle maturity. The first three companies in the table clearly illustrate the possible consequences of high volatility. Their stock prices dropped below the minimum listing requirement, and by August 1980 all three were no longer listed.

Table 6-10(a)
FISCHER BLACK'S HIGHEST FORECASTS OF VOLATILITY FOR JANUARY 1980

Itel (I)	.89
Sambos (SRI)	.68
Braniff International (BNF)	.56
Bally Manufacturing (BLY)	.53

Table 6-10(b)
FISCHER BLACK'S LOWEST FORECASTS OF VOLATILITY FOR JANUARY 1980

American Telephone & Telegraph (T)	.13
Proctor & Gamble (PG)	.14
Consolidated Edison (ED)	.14
General Telephone & Electronics (GTE)	.15

This variation in volatilities for different stocks is also strikingly evident in the figures given in the appendix to this chapter. This appendix shows historical, rather than forecasted, volatilities for the period January 1, 1980 to January 1, 1984 for all stocks having listed options at the end of that period. For each stock, the appendix also gives the historical beta, market weight, and industry group and lists the exchange and expiration cycle on which its options trade.

The forecasted volatilities generated by Black's method may change significantly over time. Table 6-11 illustrates this for eight selected stocks. The table shows the forecasted volatilities at one-year intervals over a nine-year period, January 1975 to January 1984. As before, the figures are for the middle-maturity options. Since all of these stocks are on a January/April/July/October expiration cycle, all of the forecasts would be of the average volatility for the next four months. The table clearly shows how the forecasted volatilities can vary over time—changes of 30% over a one-year interval are not uncommon.

Black's procedure includes the important forces causing change in volatilities and combines them in a sensible way. Just as we would expect, his methods on average produce very good estimates of future volatilities. Although only preliminary results are available, they have confirmed the superiority of Black's forecasts compared to those of several specific alternatives, such as implicit volatility and various statistical techniques which do not account for stock price or market effects on volatility. Of course, Black's judgment sometimes plays an important role in his final predictions, while the alternatives were mechanical procedures that did not have this

Table 6-11

FISCHER BLACK'S FORECASTS OF VOLATILITY FROM JANUARY 1975 TO JANUARY 1984 FOR SELECTED STOCKS

Company	1/75	1/76	1/77	1/78	1/79	1/80	1/81	1/82	1/83	1/84
American Telephone & Telegraph (T)	.21	.14	.12	.09	.12	.13	.14	.15	.22	.20
Atlantic Richfield (ARC)	.30	.25	.21	.22	.25	.21	.25	.31	.41	.35
Eastman Kodak (EK)	.44	.24	.23	.27	.33	.22	.22	.21	.31	.30
International Business Machines (IBM)	.36	.23	.16	.14	.22	.22	.23	.24	.28	.27
Minnesota Mining & Manufacturing (MMM)	.39	.26	.21	.19	.23	.19	.19	.19	.31	.24
Northwest Airlines (NWA)	.54	.39	.29	.33	.41	.32	.32	.33	.45	.38
Polaroid (PRD)	.75	.47	.33	.33	.46	.41	.40	.39	.49	.45
Xerox (XRX)	.46	.40	.27	.24	.30	.24	.25	.29	.35	.31

advantage. And there is still room for improvement; actual realized volatilities can vary significantly from those forecasted. Perhaps introducing information on high and low prices or other intraday prices into Black's methods will give better results. More important, a better understanding of the fundamental economic factors causing changes in volatilities may lead to more powerful formal models and less dependence on judgment. Work in this direction may allow more efficient use of additional sources of information, such as accounting measures of the firm's operations.

Furthermore, we must remember that volatilities that shift in response to changes in stock prices and other variables are inconsistent with the basic assumptions of the Black-Scholes model. However, very good practical results can still be obtained by using the model in combination with volatilities that are frequently revised by a sophisticated procedure such as Black's. One further refinement adjusts option values for the fact that realized volatilities may be substantially different from the best estimate. For example, suppose our best estimate of future volatility is .4, but we also believe that there is a 20% chance the volatility will be .5 and a 20% chance that it will be .3. A convenient way to account for this uncertainty is to use as a final value a weighted average of Black-Scholes values computed with each of the three volatilities, with weights corresponding to the respective probabilities. Statistical studies of the way volatilities change over time can provide help in assessing these probabilities. Typically, this adjustment will lead to higher values for out-of-the-money options and higher values for in-the-money options. These ad hoc modifications of the Black-Scholes model work very well. Nevertheless, we would expect a more general valuation model that formally includes some form of randomly changing volatility to work even better. We will discuss this further in Chapter 7.

Option Prices. After we have measured the inputs needed to apply the Black-Scholes formula (or the binomial numerical recursive procedure to account for early exercise) and calculated the value of an option, it remains to compare this value to the market price. Here, indiscriminate reliance on the newspaper can be very misleading.

Timely measurement of stock and option prices is essential to a proper application of the formula. Mispricings, even to the extent of apparent riskless arbitrage opportunities of the generality of those in Chapter 4, are frequently evident from closing option and stock prices listed in the *Wall Street Journal*. Most of these opportunities do not really exist, as you can verify by trying to take advantage of them the next day. These false signals arise principally from four causes:

1. Nonsimultaneity of the stock and option close
2. The bid-ask spread
3. Commissions
4. Lack of market depth

Even if volume, in terms of share equivalents, may be the same for the stock and its associated options, with several different option series available, the option volume is divided among more securities. In addition, since most of this volume is concentrated in near-the-money, short-term options, other options in an otherwise active class may have very low volume. Since about 50% of the activity on the CBOE is in 10% of the underlying stocks, many other stocks are relatively inactive. Low volume increases the likelihood that the last trade for the day in an option will precede the last trade in its underlying stock by a significant length of time. This means that the stock price at the time the last option trade occurred could be quite different from the closing stock price. Referring to the listed option quotations for January 5, 1977, we find that the CBOE had a relatively active day for that period with 107,022 contracts traded. The breakdown of the volume by expiration is given in Table 6-12.

Table 6-12
PERCENTAGE BREAKDOWN OF CBOE VOLUME
FOR JANUARY 5, 1977

	JAN	*APR*	*JUL*	*FEB*	*MAY*	*AUG*
Total series available	156	152	88	92	88	78
Untraded[a]	12%	3	10	7	7	15
1–5 contracts	8%	5	10	5	15	17
6–20 contracts	8%	12	19	10	14	19
21–100 contracts	25%	26	36	33	39	36
101+ contracts	47%	54	25	45	25	13
Total	100%	100%	100%	100%	100%	100%

[a] Data not available if all options in a given class with the same striking price either did not trade or were not available.

With an expiration date 16 days away, the activity of many of the January options is low, not because of lack of investor interest, but because the out-of-the-moneys may be worth less than $\frac{1}{16}$ of a point. An option-screening process based on closing prices, if applied to all CBOE listed options regardless of their activity, will tend to select options that are only apparently over- or underpriced. One way to overcome this selection bias is to restrict attention only to the most active option series. A better method is to obtain real-time intraday prices.

With only closing prices, the bid-ask spread, particularly for options, poses a difficult problem in a screening process. If you were actually to buy (sell) a small number of options at the close, you will probably get the ask (bid) price quoted by the trading crowd. Just looking at the newspaper, you do not know if the close took place at the bid, at the ask, or in between. For example, if you attempt to sell at the closing price when the closing price was at the ask and the spread was $\frac{1}{4}$, you will probably only be able to sell at $\frac{1}{4}$ lower than the close. More generally, given only closing prices, the band of uncertainty around the close is double the spread. To make matters worse, before taking a position, you should estimate the uncertain bid-ask spread you expect to give up when you close out the position. As if this were not enough, if you try to lock in a profit by covering, the bid-ask spread must be accumulated two times—once for each side of the spread. Particularly, for a neutral spread, because of the many securities involved and the small potential profit, the accumulated bid-ask spreads will, by themselves, destroy most otherwise profitable positions.[17] Unfortunately, selection bias in the screening process favors netting out just those positions you cannot assume at the closing prices. Again, while restriction to the most active option series tends to narrow the band of uncertainty around the closing price, it does not help determine on which side of the bid-ask spread the close occurred. A better method is to obtain access to closing bid-ask spreads or intraday bid-ask spreads.

Commissions, particularly for the public, compound the difficulties created by the bid-ask spread. A simple method for including transactions costs is to deduct (add) the bid-ask spread likely to be sacrificed plus the probable in and out commissions from (to) the formula value of a written (purchased) option. However, since the commission for closing out a position depends on the prices of its constituent securities at that time, this added uncertainty complicates this correction.

6-3. ANALYSIS OF COVERED POSITIONS

Although we have done our best to calculate accurate option values and properly measure their market prices, we are not yet ready to invest. First we must examine the circumstances that will create profits and losses for alternative option positions. In Chapter 1, we used payoff diagrams to perform this function. But they had some unfortunate limitations. They looked only at the profit and loss resulting from holding a position *until its expiration date.* Prior to the recent development of organized option markets, this conventional approach may have been adequate since, for practical purposes, OTC options either had to be exercised or let expire.[18]

---

[17] While neutral spreads will only be occasionally advisable for public investors, they are an ideal strategy for Market Makers who pay low commissions, can earn the bid-ask spread for themselves, and need neutral positions to protect their capital against adverse stock price movements.

[18] Even with OTC options, however, payoff diagrams cannot be used to analyze horizontal spreads, where one option expires subsequent to another, or even vertical spreads for which early exercise is a possibility.

With the introduction of liquid secondary markets for options, a new approach is clearly needed to cope with early closing purchase and sale transactions. In this section, we develop this by using information derivable from the Black-Scholes formula.[19] In so doing, we will be able to classify option positions in a new way. Although this new classification can also be applied to positions involving several options on the same underlying stock, for expositional convenience we will only consider positions consisting of at most two different securities with the same underlying stock. Its extension to more complex positions should be apparent.

Position Delta. The *position value* is the sum of the values of the two associated securities, each weighted by the number bought or sold. Let

V_j = the current value of one unit of security $j = 1, 2$,

n_j = the number of units purchased of security $j = 1, 2$.

Therefore, the value of a position in these two securities is simply

$$\text{Position value} = n_1 V_1 + n_2 V_2.$$

Consistent with earlier notation, $V = S$, C, or P if the security is stock, a call, or a put. Then n is the number of shares, calls, or puts purchased. By convention, $n > 0$ if securities are bought, and $n < 0$ if securities are sold short or written.

The delta of an option tells us how much the option value will change for a small change in the price of the underlying stock, other things equal:

$$\Delta \equiv \frac{\partial V}{\partial S}.$$

For a call, $\Delta = \partial C / \partial S$, always a positive number between zero and positive one, and for a put $\Delta = \partial P / \partial S$, always a negative number between zero and negative one. The stock itself can be regarded as a perpetual payout-protected American call with zero striking price. For it, $\Delta = \partial S / \partial S = 1$.

Similarly, the *position delta* tells us how much the position value will change for a small change in the price of its underlying stock, other things equal. Therefore, for two associated securities,

$$\text{Position delta} = \frac{\partial \text{ position value}}{\partial S} = n_1 \left(\frac{\partial V_1}{\partial S} \right) + n_2 \left(\frac{\partial V_2}{\partial S} \right) = n_1 \Delta_1 + n_2 \Delta_2.$$

---

[19] This section and the next have drawn heavily from *Fischer Black on Options*, 1, Nos. 16–17 (September–October 1976).

The position delta is then the sum of the weighted deltas of its constituent securities.

Figures 6-1 through 6-4 show the Black-Scholes value of a vertical and horizontal spread in calls as a function of the current stock price and time to expiration, where one call is purchased and one call is written.[20] Observe that the vertical spread is bullish throughout the entire range of stock price changes. However, the horizontal spread switches from bullish to bearish as the two calls move in-the-money.

Figures 6-5 through 6-8 show how the position deltas for vertical and horizontal spreads change with the stock price and time to expiration, where again each spread consists of one call bought and one call written.

The position delta measures how exposed our position is to movements in the stock price. If we think the stock price will rise, we want it to be positive; if we think the stock price will fall, we want it to be negative. If we are uncertain about the *direction* of the stock price movement and want to insulate ourselves from this uncertainty, we want our position delta to be zero.

In view of this correspondence, we can refine our earlier definitions of "bearish" and "bullish" positions. In Chapter 1, these were defined in terms of the profit or loss if held to expiration. Here, we redefine these terms to apply to positions which may be liquidated some time prior to expiration. In brief, we adopt the following correspondence:

> Negative delta ⇔ Bearish
> Zero delta ⇔ Neutral
> Positive delta ⇔ Bullish

By definition, a *neutral position* has a zero delta. The neutral position ratio can then be determined by setting the position delta to zero. Since

$$n_1 \Delta_1 + n_2 \Delta_2 = 0,$$

a little algebra shows that, for a neutral position,

$$\frac{n_1}{n_2} = -\frac{\Delta_2}{\Delta_1}.$$

The neutral position ratio is the negative of the inverse of the ratio of the deltas.

---

[20] For the vertical spread, the purchased call has a striking price of 50 and the written call a striking price of 60. For the horizontal spread, the purchased call expires three months after the written call. This description also applies to Figures 6-5 through 6-16.

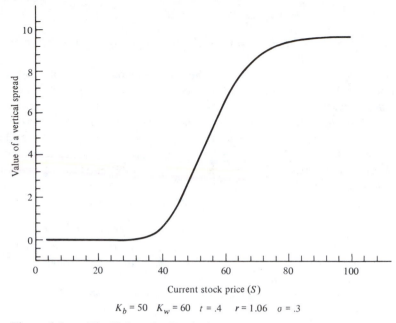

$K_b = 50 \quad K_w = 60 \quad t = .4 \quad r = 1.06 \quad \sigma = .3$

Figure 6-1   The Value of a Vertical Spread as a Function of the
Current Stock Price

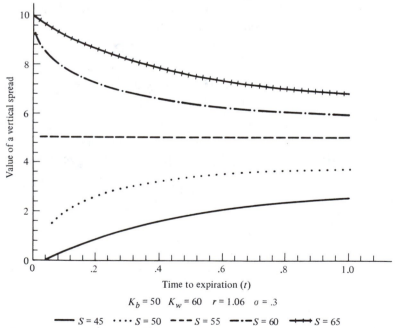

$K_b = 50 \quad K_w = 60 \quad r = 1.06 \quad \sigma = .3$

— $S = 45$ ···· $S = 50$ ‑‑‑ $S = 55$ —·— $S = 60$ ╪╪╪ $S = 65$

Figure 6-2   The Value of a Vertical Spread as a Function of the
Time to Expiration

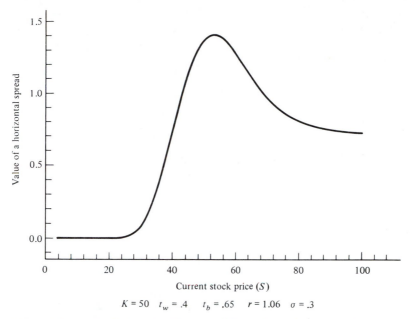

Current stock price (S)

$K = 50$ $t_w = .4$ $t_b = .65$ $r = 1.06$ $\sigma = .3$

Figure 6-3   The Value of a Horizontal Spread as a Function of the Current Stock Price

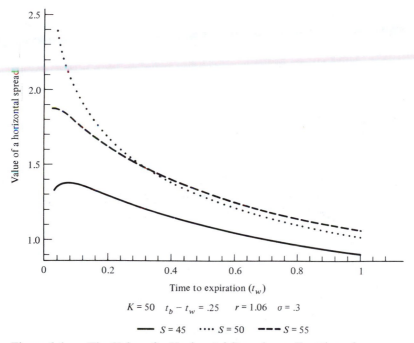

Time to expiration (t_w)

$K = 50$ $t_b - t_w = .25$ $r = 1.06$ $\sigma = .3$

—— $S = 45$ ···· $S = 50$ --- $S = 55$

Figure 6-4   The Value of a Horizontal Spread as a Function of the Time to Expiration

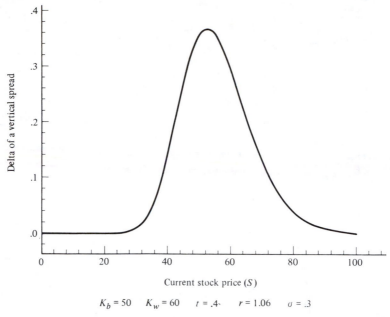

$K_b = 50$ $K_w = 60$ $t = .4$ $r = 1.06$ $\sigma = .3$

Figure 6-5   The Delta of a Vertical Spread as a Function of the
Current Stock Price

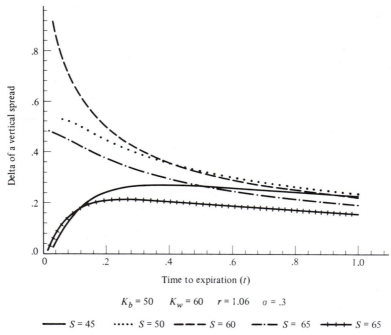

$K_b = 50$ $K_w = 60$ $r = 1.06$ $\sigma = .3$

——— $S = 45$ ····· $S = 50$ ——— $S = 60$ —·— $S = 65$ +++ $S = 65$

Figure 6-6   The Delta of a Vertical Spread as a Function of the
Time to Expiration

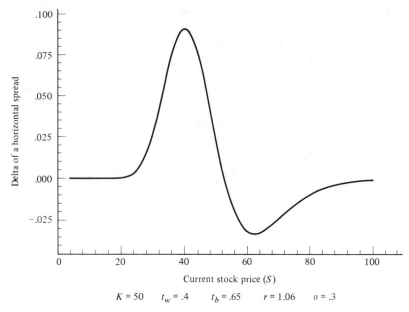

$K = 50 \qquad t_w = .4 \qquad t_b = .65 \qquad r = 1.06 \qquad \sigma = .3$

Figure 6-7   The Delta of a Horizontal Spread as a Function of
the Current Stock Price

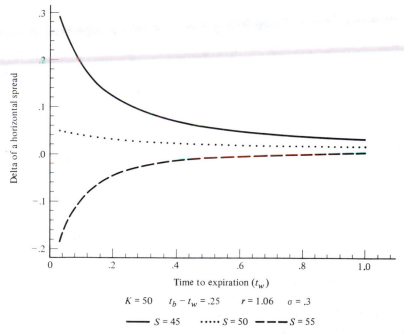

$K = 50 \qquad t_b - t_w = .25 \qquad r = 1.06 \qquad \sigma = .3$

──── $S = 45$ ····· $S = 50$ ─ ─ ─ $S = 55$

Figure 6-8   The Delta of a Horizontal Spread as a Function of
the Time to Expiration

Figures 6-9 through 6-12 show how the neutral position ratio for a vertical and horizontal spread changes with the current stock price and time to expiration.

Knowing the neutral position ratio, we can create a bullish (bearish) position by selecting a higher (lower) position ratio in absolute value than $|-\Delta_w/\Delta_b|$, where Δ_w is the delta of the written or short security, and Δ_b is the delta of the purchased security.

More generally, one way to quantify our desired option strategy is in terms of a *target delta*. We would then choose n_1 and n_2 so that $n_1 \Delta_1 + n_2 \Delta_2$ is equal to a target delta. Maintaining a target delta is related to maintaining a constant beta for an individual's portfolio.

An Example.   Suppose we were considering investing in the 12 puts and calls on XYZ stock on December 21, 1977. Table 6-13 for XYZ is produced using APL program TABLE in conjunction with the APL European option pricing program PC1. Associated with each expiration date (in year/month/ day format) is an interest rate $(r - 1)$ and volatility σ. Although these happen to be the same for each date, in general the interest rate may depend on time if the term structure is not flat, and the volatility may

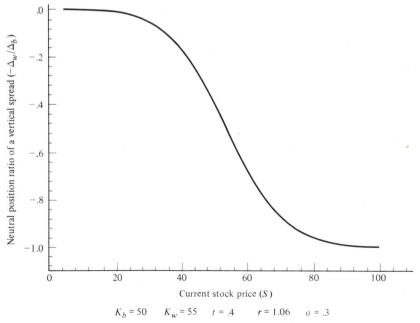

$K_b = 50 \qquad K_w = 55 \qquad t = .4 \qquad r = 1.06 \qquad \sigma = .3$

Figure 6-9   The Neutral Position Ratio of a Vertical Spread as a Function of the Current Stock Price

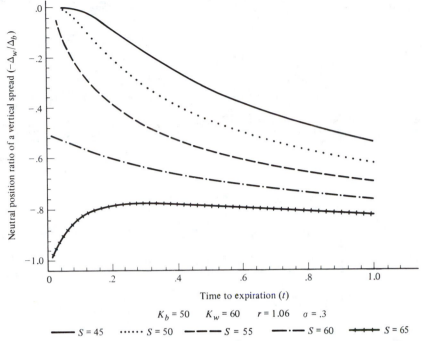

Figure 6-10 The Neutral Position Ratio of a Vertical Spread as a Function of the Time to Expiration

depend on time reflecting its tendency to change predictably over time. Using the most recently announced cash dividend and ex-dividend date, TABLE naively forecasts the forthcoming January, April, and July dividends and ex-dividend dates. From this data, together with the description of each option (its type and series), TABLE calculates Black-Scholes option values and deltas for a range of stock prices centered around the current stock price $S = 40$. The stock prices appear in "eighths notation" above the corresponding call values (CV), call deltas ($C\Delta$), put values (PV), and put deltas ($P\Delta$). For example, a stock price of 403 means $40\frac{3}{8}$. Although Table 6-14 provides Black-Scholes unprotected European values and deltas, TABLE can also output unprotected American option values and deltas by selecting APL option pricing program PC2, and values and deltas based on other formulas developed in Chapter 7 by making other selections.

To put on a *neutral hedge* at the opening in APR/40 calls, when the stock is selling at 40, we can tell from the call delta $\Delta = .5$ that a $1.00 change in the stock price results in roughly a $.50 change in the call price. Therefore, to stay neutral and expect a profit (ignoring transactions costs and margin), we need to write two APR/40 calls at more than $2.52 for

Table 6-13

TRADING SHEET FOR XYZ ON DECEMBER 21, 1977

XYZ 77/12/21

EXPIRATION	ANN INT	ANN VOL	EX-DIV DATE	DIVIDEND
78/01/20	.050	.300	78/01/05	.50
78/04/21	.050	.300	78/04/05	.50
78/07/21	.050	.300	76/07/05	.50

XYZ 77/12/21

390

	CV	CA	PV	PA
JAN35	3.83	.87	.19	-.11
JAN40	.78	.36	2.12	-.63
JAN45	.06	.04	6.38	-.95
APR35	4.67	.73	1.10	-.25
APR40	2.04	.44	3.39	-.53
JUL40	2.84	.46	4.20	-.50

391

	CV	CA	PV	PA
JAN35	3.94	.88	.18	-.11
JAN40	.82	.37	2.04	-.62
JAN45	.06	.05	6.26	-.94
APR35	4.76	.73	1.07	-.24
APR40	2.10	.45	3.32	-.52
JUL40	2.90	.47	4.14	-.49

392

	CV	CA	PV	PA
JAN35	4.06	.89	.17	-.10
JAN40	.87	.38	1.96	-.60
JAN45	.07	.05	6.14	-.94
APR35	4.86	.74	1.04	-.24
APR40	2.16	.46	3.26	-.52
JUL40	2.96	.48	4.07	-.49

393

	CV	CA	PV	PA
JAN35	4.17	.89	.15	-.09
JAN40	.92	.40	1.89	-.59
JAN45	.07	.05	6.02	-.93
APR35	4.95	.74	1.01	-.23
APR40	2.21	.46	3.19	-.51
JUL40	3.02	.48	4.01	-.48

394

	CV	CA	PV	PA
JAN35	4.28	.90	.14	-.09
JAN40	.97	.41	1.81	-.57
JAN45	.08	.06	5.90	-.93
APR35	5.05	.75	.98	-.23
APR40	2.27	.47	3.13	-.50
JUL40	3.08	.49	3.95	-.48

395

	CV	CA	PV	PA
JAN35	4.40	.91	.13	-.08
JAN40	1.03	.43	1.74	-.56
JAN45	.09	.06	5.78	-.93
APR35	5.15	.75	.95	-.22
APR40	2.34	.48	3.06	-.50
JUL40	3.15	.49	3.89	-.47

396

	CV	CA	PV	PA
JAN35	4.51	.91	.12	-.08
JAN40	1.08	.44	1.67	-.54
JAN45	.10	.07	5.67	-.92
APR35	5.24	.76	.92	-.22
APR40	2.40	.49	3.00	-.49
JUL40	3.21	.50	3.83	-.46

397

	CV	CA	PV	PA
JAN35	4.63	.92	.11	-.07
JAN40	1.14	.46	1.60	-.53
JAN45	.11	.07	5.55	-.92
APR35	5.34	.77	.90	-.21
APR40	2.46	.49	2.94	-.48
JUL40	3.28	.50	3.77	-.46

400

	CV	CA	PV	PA
JAN35	4.74	.92	.10	-.07
JAN40	1.20	.47	1.54	-.52
JAN45	.11	.08	5.43	-.91
APR35	5.44	.77	.87	-.20
APR40	2.52	.50	2.88	-.47
JUL40	3.34	.51	3.71	-.45

401

	CV	CA	PV	PA
JAN35	4.86	.93	.10	-.06
JAN40	1.26	.49	1.47	-.50
JAN45	.12	.08	5.32	-.91
APR35	5.54	.78	.84	-.20
APR40	2.59	.51	2.82	-.47
JUL40	3.41	.52	3.65	-.45

402

	CV	CA	PV	PA
JAN35	4.98	.93	.09	-.06
JAN40	1.32	.50	1.41	-.49
JAN45	.13	.09	5.20	-.90
APR35	5.64	.78	.82	-.19
APR40	2.65	.52	2.76	-.46
JUL40	3.48	.52	3.59	-.44

403

	CV	CA	PV	PA
JAN35	5.10	.93	.08	-.05
JAN40	1.38	.51	1.35	-.47
JAN45	.15	.09	5.09	-.89
APR35	5.74	.79	.80	-.19
APR40	2.72	.52	2.70	-.45
JUL40	3.54	.53	3.53	-.44

404

	CV	CA	PV	PA
JAN35	5.21	.94	.07	-.05
JAN40	1.45	.53	1.29	-.46
JAN45	.16	.10	4.98	-.89
APR35	5.84	.79	.77	-.18
APR40	2.79	.53	2.64	-.45
JUL40	3.61	.53	3.48	-.43

405

	CV	CA	PV	PA
JAN35	5.33	.94	.07	-.05
JAN40	1.52	.54	1.23	-.44
JAN45	.17	.11	4.87	-.88
APR35	5.94	.80	.75	-.18
APR40	2.86	.54	2.58	-.44
JUL40	3.68	.54	3.42	-.43

406

	CV	CA	PV	PA
JAN35	5.45	.95	.06	-.04
JAN40	1.59	.56	1.18	-.43
JAN45	.18	.11	4.75	-.88
APR35	6.04	.80	.73	-.18
APR40	2.93	.54	2.53	-.43
JUL40	3.75	.54	3.37	-.42

407

	CV	CA	PV	PA
JAN35	5.57	.95	.06	-.04
JAN40	1.66	.57	1.12	-.42
JAN45	.20	.12	4.64	-.87
APR35	6.15	.81	.70	-.17
APR40	3.00	.55	2.47	-.42
JUL40	3.82	.55	3.31	-.42

410

	CV	CA	PV	PA
JAN35	5.69	.95	.05	-.04
JAN40	1.73	.59	1.07	-.40
JAN45	.21	.13	4.53	-.86
APR35	6.25	.81	.68	-.17
APR40	3.07	.56	2.42	-.42
JUL40	3.89	.55	3.26	-.41

Table 6-14

TRADING SHEET FOR XYZ ON DECEMBER 28, 1977

XYZ 77/12/28

EXPIRATION	ANN INT	ANN VOL	EX-DIV DATE	DIVIDEND
78/01/20	.050	.300	78/01/05	.50
78/04/21	.050	.300	78/04/05	.50
78/07/21	.050	.300	78/07/05	.50

Columns in each block: CV, CA, PV, PA. Rows: JAN35, JAN40, JAN45, APR35, APR40, JUL40.

Left-section column (XYZ 77/12/28):

******** (390) ******** *(390 circled)*
	CV	CA	PV	PA
JAN35	3.73	.90	.12	-.09
JAN40	.61	.33	1.99	-.66
JAN45	.02	.02	6.39	-.96
APR35	4.68	.73	1.05	-.25
APR40	1.95 *(circled)*	.44	3.34	-.54
JUL40	2.77	.46	4.17	-.50

******** 394 ********
	CV	CA	PV	PA
JAN35	4.19	.92	.09	-.06
JAN40	.80	.39	1.67	-.59
JAN45	.04	.03	5.93	-.95
APR35	4.97	.75	.93	-.22
APR40	2.18	.47	3.07	-.51
JUL40	3.01	.48	3.91	-.48

******** (400) ******** *(400 circled)*
	CV	CA	PV	PA
JAN35	4.67	.94	.06	-.05
JAN40	1.01	.46	1.39	-.53
JAN45	.04	.03	5.42	-.94
APR35	5.36	.77	.82	-.20
APR40	2.43 *(circled)*	.50 *(circled)*	2.82	-.48
JUL40	3.27	.51	3.67	-.46

******** 404 ********
	CV	CA	PV	PA
JAN35	5.15	.96	.04	-.03
JAN40	1.26	.52	1.14	-.46
JAN45	.09	.07	4.95	-.92
APR35	5.76	.80	.73	-.18
APR40	2.69	.53	2.58	-.45
JUL40	3.54	.53	3.44	-.43

Right-section grid (XYZ 77/12/28):

Band 1 — 391, 392, 393, 394

******** 391 ********
	CV	CA	PV	PA
JAN35	3.85	.91	.11	-.08
JAN40	.66	.35	1.91	-.64
JAN45	.03	.03	6.26	-.96
APR35	4.73	.73	1.02	-.24
APR40	2.01	.44	3.27	-.53
JUL40	2.83	.47	4.10	-.49

******** 392 ********
	CV	CA	PV	PA
JAN35	3.96	.91	.10	-.08
JAN40	.70	.36	1.83	-.63
JAN45	.03	.03	6.14	-.96
APR35	4.78	.74	.99	-.23
APR40	2.06	.45	3.20	-.52
JUL40	2.89	.47	4.04	-.49

******** 393 ********
	CV	CA	PV	PA
JAN35	4.08	.92	.09	-.07
JAN40	.75	.38	1.75	-.61
JAN45	.04	.03	6.02	-.96
APR35	4.87	.75	.93	-.23
APR40	2.12	.46	3.14	-.52
JUL40	2.95	.48	3.97	-.48

******** 394 ********
	CV	CA	PV	PA
JAN35	4.19	.92	.09	-.06
JAN40	.80	.39	1.67	-.59
JAN45	.04	.03	5.93	-.95
APR35	4.97	.75	.93	-.22
APR40	2.18	.47	3.07	-.51
JUL40	3.01	.48	3.91	-.48

Band 2 — 395, 396, 397, 400

******** 395 ********
	CV	CA	PV	PA
JAN35	4.31	.93	.08	-.06
JAN40	.85	.41	1.60	-.58
JAN45	.04	.03	5.78	-.95
APR35	5.06	.76	.90	-.22
APR40	2.24	.47	3.01	-.50
JUL40	3.08	.49	3.85	-.47

******** 396 ********
	CV	CA	PV	PA
JAN35	4.43	.93	.07	-.05
JAN40	.90	.43	1.53	-.56
JAN45	.05	.04	5.66	-.95
APR35	5.16	.76	.88	-.21
APR40	2.30	.48	2.94	-.49
JUL40	3.14	.50	3.79	-.47

******** 397 ********
	CV	CA	PV	PA
JAN35	4.55	.94	.06	-.05
JAN40	.96	.44	1.46	-.55
JAN45	.05	.04	5.54	-.94
APR35	5.26	.77	.85	-.21
APR40	2.37	.49	2.88	-.49
JUL40	3.20	.50	3.73	-.46

******** (400) ******** *(400 circled)*
	CV	CA	PV	PA
JAN35	4.67	.94	.06	-.05
JAN40	1.01	.46	1.39	-.53
JAN45	.05	.04	5.42	-.94
APR35	5.36	.77	.82	-.20
APR40	2.43 *(circled)*	.50 *(circled)*	2.82	-.48
JUL40	3.27	.51	3.67	-.46

Band 3 — 401, 402, 403, 404

******** 401 ********
	CV	CA	PV	PA
JAN35	4.79	.95	.05	-.04
JAN40	1.07	.48	1.32	-.51
JAN45	.07	.05	5.30	-.93
APR35	5.46	.80	.80	-.20
APR40	2.49	.50	2.76	-.48
JUL40	3.34	.51	3.61	-.45

******** 402 ********
	CV	CA	PV	PA
JAN35	4.90	.95	.05	-.04
JAN40	1.13	.49	1.26	-.50
JAN45	.07	.06	5.18	-.93
APR35	5.56	.79	.77	-.19
APR40	2.56	.51	2.70	-.47
JUL40	3.40	.52	3.55	-.45

******** 403 ********
	CV	CA	PV	PA
JAN35	5.03	.95	.04	-.04
JAN40	1.20	.51	1.20	-.48
JAN45	.08	.06	5.07	-.93
APR35	5.66	.79	.75	-.19
APR40	2.62	.52	2.64	-.46
JUL40	3.47	.52	3.49	-.44

******** 404 ********
	CV	CA	PV	PA
JAN35	5.15	.96	.04	-.03
JAN40	1.26	.52	1.14	-.46
JAN45	.09	.07	4.95	-.92
APR35	5.76	.80	.73	-.18
APR40	2.69	.53	2.58	-.45
JUL40	3.54	.53	3.44	-.43

Band 4 — 405, 406, 407, 410

******** 405 ********
	CV	CA	PV	PA
JAN35	5.27	.96	.03	-.03
JAN40	1.33	.54	1.08	-.45
JAN45	.10	.07	4.83	-.91
APR35	5.86	.80	.70	-.18
APR40	2.76	.53	2.52	-.44
JUL40	3.61	.53	3.38	-.43

******** 406 ********
	CV	CA	PV	PA
JAN35	5.39	.96	.03	-.03
JAN40	1.40	.56	1.03	-.43
JAN45	.11	.08	4.72	-.91
APR35	5.97	.80	.68	-.17
APR40	2.83	.54	2.47	-.43
JUL40	3.68	.54	3.33	-.42

******** 407 ********
	CV	CA	PV	PA
JAN35	5.51	.96	.03	-.02
JAN40	1.47	.57	.97	-.41
JAN45	.12	.09	4.60	-.90
APR35	6.07	.81	.66	-.17
APR40	2.90	.55	2.41	-.43
JUL40	3.75	.55	3.27	-.42

******** (410) ******** *(410 circled)*
	CV	CA	PV	PA
JAN35	5.63	.97	.02	-.02
JAN40	1.54	.59	.92	-.40
JAN45	.13	.09	4.49	-.90
APR35	6.17	.81	.64	-.16
APR40	2.97 *(circled)*	.56 *(circled)*	2.36	-.42
JUL40	3.82	.55	3.22	-.41

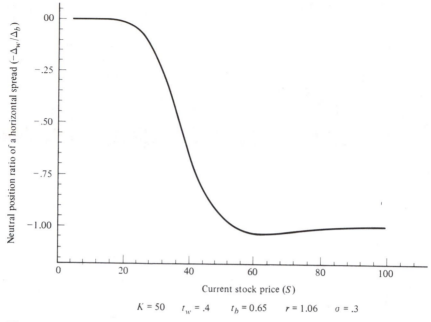

K = 50 t_w = .4 t_b = 0.65   r = 1.06   σ = .3

Figure 6-11   The Neutral Position Ratio of a Horizontal Spread
as a Function of the Current Stock Price

every share purchased at $40. Alternatively, we can use our formula for a
neutral position ratio to reach the same conclusion:

$$\frac{n_1}{n_2} = -\frac{\Delta_2}{\Delta_1} = -\frac{.5}{1} = -\frac{1}{2}.$$

Although our position begins neutral, as the stock price changes and
as the expiration date approaches, if we don't revise our position, its value
will tend to increase or decrease. Referring to Table 6-13, if the stock closes
out the day at 41, the neutral hedge we put on at the opening gains
$(41 - 40) - 2 \times (3.07 - 2.52) = -\$.10$ in *value* per share of stock pur-
chased. The actual profit or loss over the day depends, of course, on
changes in the calls' market prices. On the other hand, had the stock closed
out at 39, the neutral hedge would gain $(40 - 41) - 2 \times (2.04 - 2.52) =$
$-\$.04$ in value per share of stock purchased.

No change in value for a neutral hedge is only promised for a very
small change either way in the stock price. However, even for a dollar
change in the stock price over the day, the value of the hedge changes little.

At first glance, it may seem we lose whether the stock price moves up
or down. However, for a hedge, time works in our favor. Other things

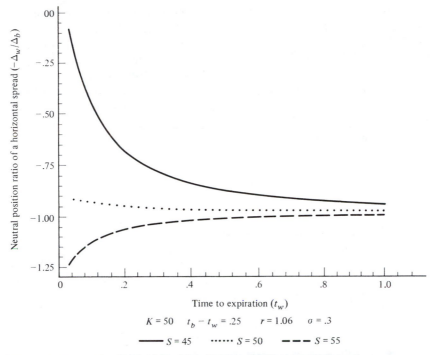

Figure 6-12 The Neutral Position Ratio of a Horizontal Spread as a Function of the Time to Expiration

equal, the call value will decline over time, which is favorable to a writer. Table 6-14 gives the same information for XYZ one week later on December 28, 1977. If the stock price remains unchanged at 40, our hedge gains $(40 - 40) - 2 \times (2.43 - 2.52) = +\$.18$ in value per share. Indeed, even if the stock price moves up to 41 or down to 39, our hedge increases in value. The hedge value will increase as long as the stock price does not change too quickly.

The position delta also changes even if we do not revise the position. On December 21, if the stock moves to 41, the delta becomes $(1 \times 1) - (2 \times .56) = -.12$, and at 39, the delta becomes $(1 \times 1) - (2 \times .44) = +.12$. At 41, the negative delta tells us that the position value will decrease if the stock continues up and increase if it falls back toward 40. Likewise, at 39, the positive position delta gives the opposite conclusion. A comparison of Tables 6-13 and 6-14 shows how the passage of time affects the delta. For example, if the stock remains at 40, one week later the position delta is about the same. Loosely speaking, over short periods of time, changes in the stock price are likely to impact more heavily on deltas than the change in the time to expiration.

Returning to December 21, suppose near midday the stock price falls to $39\frac{5}{8}$, and we see the APR/35 calls are underpriced (that is, priced at less than \$5.15) and the JAN/35 calls are overpriced (priced at more than \$4.40) by the market. An appropriate response would be a bullish horizontal *spread*, where we write the JAN/35s and buy the APR/35s. Since the spread is bullish, to the extent it is one-for-one, our required margin is minimized. To put on a neutral spread, since the APR/35s have the lower delta, we will need to buy more than one APR/35 for each JAN/35. Using the formula for a neutral position ratio:

$$\frac{n_1}{n_2} = -\frac{\Delta_2}{\Delta_1} = -\frac{.91}{.75} \approx -1.2.$$

Were we to buy six APR/35 contracts and write five JAN/35 contracts ($6 \div 5 = 1.2$), we would be virtually neutral.

Near the end of the day, XYZ has recovered at a slight gain and is now selling for $40\frac{1}{4}$. We notice that both the JUL/40 puts and calls are underpriced by the market, so we consider buying a neutral *combination*. Our formula for a neutral position ratio tells us

$$\frac{n_1}{n_2} = -\frac{\Delta_2}{\Delta_1} = -\frac{-.44}{.52} \approx .85.$$

For every put bought, we also buy .85 of a call. Therefore, a position of 100 JUL/40 put contracts and 85 JUL/40 call contracts is neutral.

Position Gamma.   As the underlying stock price moves and the expiration date approaches, the delta of our position changes. To continue to stay at our target delta, we then need to revise our positions carefully over time. Looking at Figures 6-9 and 6-11, we see that the position ratio tends to rise as the calls move more in-the-money. Since deep-in-the-money calls move almost dollar for dollar with the stock, the position ratio should be near one. The sensitivity of the neutral position ratio to movements in the stock price tends to be greatest for vertical spreads when the stock price lies between the striking prices of the calls, and for horizontal spreads when both the calls are deep-out-of-the-money. The more complex influence of time is shown in Figures 6-10 and 6-12.

In practice, transactions costs and occasional jumps in the stock price prevent us from maintaining a particular target delta as the stock price changes. One strategy is to open a position at our desired target delta and revise it only when its delta strays some critical distance from the target. A natural way to measure this is by the difference between the value of the position delta and the value of the target delta.

A reinforcing strategy is to select positions to begin with, that, in addition to coinciding with our target delta, have deltas that are relatively insensitive to movements in the stock price. Recall that an option's gamma measures how much the option delta will change for a small change in the stock price, other things equal. That is,

$$\Gamma \equiv \frac{\partial \Delta}{\partial S}.$$

For both puts and calls, $\Gamma > 0$, and for stock, $\Gamma = 0$. The *position gamma* measures the change in the position delta for small changes in the stock price. By definition, for two associated securities,

$$\text{Position gamma} = \frac{\partial \text{ position delta}}{\partial S}$$

$$= n_1 \left(\frac{\partial \Delta_1}{\partial S} \right) + n_2 \left(\frac{\partial \Delta_2}{\partial S} \right) = n_1 \Gamma_1 + n_2 \Gamma_2.$$

The position gamma is then the sum of the weighted gammas of its constituent securities. *The absolute magnitude of the position gamma, measured at the target delta position ratio, indicates how fast changes in the stock price will push the position delta past the critical distance* and force revision of the position ratio. Figures 6-13 through 6-16 show how the position gamma for a vertical and horizontal spread changes with the stock price and time to expiration, where again each spread consists of one call bought and one call written.

The sign of the position gamma, particularly for delta neutral positions, provides additional information. At zero delta, although the delta indicates the magnitude of our profits or losses should be relatively small due to stock price movements, the delta tells us nothing about the conditions which yield profits and not losses. The position gamma, on the other hand, summarizes just the information we need: If it is negative, we only profit as long as the stock price remains relatively stable; if it is positive, we only profit from large movements in the stock price in either direction. Refining the terminology used in Chapter 1,

> Negative gamma ⇔ Top
> Zero gamma ⇔ Neutral
> Positive gamma ⇔ Bottom

To prevent confusion, we say a zero delta position is "delta-neutral" and a zero gamma position is "gamma-neutral."

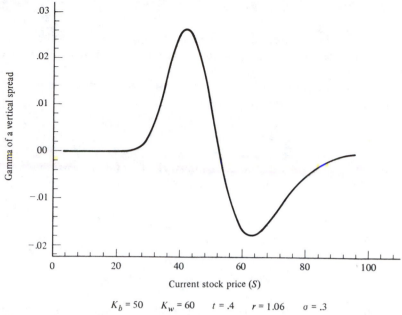

$K_b = 50$ $K_w = 60$ $t = .4$ $r = 1.06$ $\sigma = .3$

Figure 6-13   The Gamma of a Vertical Spread as a Function of the Current Stock Price

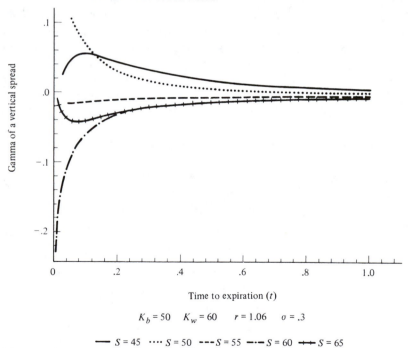

$K_b = 50$ $K_w = 60$ $r = 1.06$ $\sigma = .3$

—— $S = 45$ ···· $S = 50$ --- $S = 55$ —·— $S = 60$ ++ $S = 65$

Figure 6-14   The Gamma of a Vertical Spread as a Function of the Time to Expiration

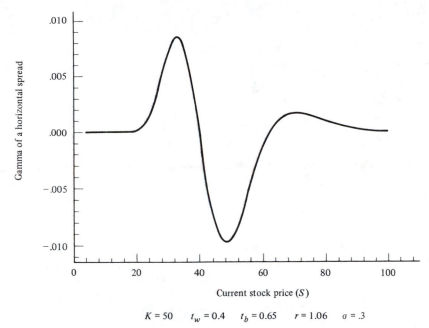

$$K = 50 \qquad t_w = 0.4 \qquad t_b = 0.65 \qquad r = 1.06 \qquad \sigma = .3$$

Figure 6-15   The Gamma of a Horizontal Spread as a Function of the Current Stock Price

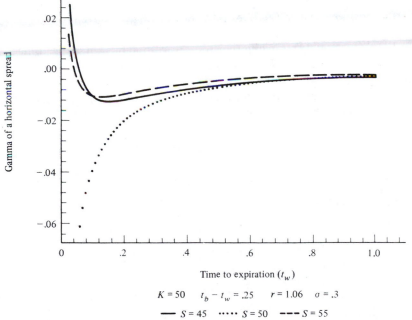

$$K = 50 \qquad t_b - t_w = .25 \qquad r = 1.06 \qquad \sigma = .3$$

—— $S = 45$ ····· $S = 50$ --- $S = 55$

Figure 6-16   The Gamma of a Horizontal Spread as a Function of the Time to Expiration

For a delta-neutral position, we can express the position gamma in terms of the option deltas and the "size" of the position. Since $n_1\Delta_1 + n_2\Delta_2 = 0$, then the

$$\text{Position gamma} = n_1\Delta_1 \left[\frac{\Gamma_1}{\Delta_1} - \frac{\Gamma_2}{\Delta_2} \right].$$

n_1, the number of shares and options that benefit from a rise in the stock price, represents the size of the position. For two securities, while a position delta of zero only determines the ratio in which they are held, an additional fixed gamma target determines the size of the position.

For a hedge of calls written against $n_1 = 1$ share of stock, since $\Delta_1 = 1$ and $\Gamma_1 = 0$, the position gamma is measured simply by $-\Gamma_2/\Delta_2$. In our previous example, the neutral hedge at 40 produced a loss of \$.10 if the stock price rose \$1 and a loss of only \$.04 if the stock price fell \$1. In this case, the position gamma is negative. Indeed, since the position gamma of a hedge in calls is $-\Gamma_2/\Delta_2$ and Γ_2, $\Delta_2 > 0$, this position gamma is always negative.

Position Theta.   Even if the stock price remains unchanged, as the expiration date approaches, the mere passing of time creates profits or losses in option positions. Since the pure influence of time is not captured by delta and gamma, we need a third and final measure to characterize option positions adequately. If, while the stock price remains unchanged, decreasing time to expiration increases (decreases) the value of an option, we say the option has *positive* (negative) *time bias*. For purposes of symmetry, we are tempted to use another greek letter, theta, to describe time bias. Therefore, an option's theta,[21]

$$\Theta \equiv -\frac{\partial V}{\partial t},$$

where we have the following correspondence:

Negative theta $\Leftrightarrow$ Negative time bias
Zero theta $\Leftrightarrow$ Neutral time bias
Positive theta $\Leftrightarrow$ Positive time bias

---

[21] Formulas for evaluating Δ, Γ, and Θ, in terms of S, K, t, r, and σ, have been given in Section 5-8.

For European calls, $\Theta = -\partial C/\partial t < 0$, for European puts $\Theta \equiv -\partial P/\partial t$ is typically negative but can occasionally be positive, and for the stock, $\Theta = -\partial S/\partial t = 0$.

The position theta measures how much the position value will change as time to expiration decreases, other things equal. For two associated securities,

$$\text{Position theta} = -\frac{\partial \text{ position value}}{\partial t}$$

$$= n_1\left(-\frac{\partial V_1}{\partial t}\right) + n_2\left(-\frac{\partial V_2}{\partial t}\right) = n_1\Theta_1 + n_2\Theta_2.$$

Returning again to our example of a delta-neutral hedge, since we experienced a profit a week later, even though the stock price remained unchanged, the hedge had a positive theta. Indeed, it is easy to see the position theta of any hedge in calls must be positive.

Position Delta, Gamma, and Theta Together. The graphs in Table 6-15 describe the 27 logically possible delta-gamma-theta classes of trading strategies. The table indicates the effect on the value of a position (V) of a simultaneous change in the stock price (S) and a reduction in time to expiration (t). For example, for a bullish top position with positive time bias (that is, $\Delta > 0$, $\Gamma < 0$, and $\Theta > 0$), downward movements in the stock price cause the position value to decrease more quickly than upward price movements cause it to increase, and the position value increases even for small downward stock price movements.

All the elementary uncovered positions have direct correspondences:

Long stock:	bullish, gamma-neutral, theta-neutral
Short stock:	bearish, gamma-neutral, theta-neutral
Buy call:	bullish bottom with negative time bias
Write call:	bearish top with positive time bias
Buy put:	bearish bottom with negative time bias
Write put:	bullish top with positive time bias

Since one-for-one hedges and reverse hedges are similar to uncovered option positions, these also have a direct correspondence to the delta-gamma-theta strategy classification. However, spreads and combinations, even if they are one-for-one, have more complex properties and must be examined on a case-by-case basis.

Table 6-15
DELTA-GAMMA-THETA TRADING STRATEGIES

Time Bias	Bearish Δ < 0			Neutral Δ = 0			Bullish Δ > 0		
	Top Γ < 0	Neutral Γ = 0	Bottom Γ > 0	Top Γ < 0	Neutral Γ = 0	Bottom Γ > 0	Top Γ < 0	Neutral Γ = 0	Bottom Γ > 0
Negative Θ < 0	$\partial V/\partial S$	$\partial V/\partial S$	$\partial V/\partial S$	$\partial V/\partial S$	$\partial V/\partial S$	$\partial V/\partial S$	$\partial V/\partial S$	$\partial V/\partial S$	$\partial V/\partial S$
Neutral Θ = 0	$\partial V/\partial S$	$\partial V/\partial S$	$\partial V/\partial S$	$\partial V/\partial S$	$\partial V/\partial S$	$\partial V/\partial S$	$\partial V/\partial S$	$\partial V/\partial S$	$\partial V/\partial S$
Positive Θ > 0	$\partial V/\partial S$	$\partial V/\partial S$	$\partial V/\partial S$	$\partial V/\partial S$	$\partial V/\partial S$	$\partial V/\partial S$	$\partial V/\partial S$	$\partial V/\partial S$	$\partial V/\partial S$

NOTE: This table shows the effect of a change in the stock price on position values for a fixed reduction in the time to expiration. There is an interval around the current stock price S and a reduction in time to expiration for which these descriptions are accurate. *Caution*: They may not apply to sufficiently large movements of the stock price away from its current value, or to sufficiently large reductions in the time to expiration.

Although a delta-neutral, gamma-neutral position cannot generally be constructed from only two associated securities,[22] three or more different options on the same underlying security provide enough flexibility to do so. For example, in a complex vertical "butterfly" spread, the spread ratios for both the otherwise bullish and bearish sides can be chosen so that each side is delta-neutral. Therefore, the overall butterfly will be delta-neutral. Then, since one side will typically have a negative gamma and the other a positive gamma, the sides can be adjusted in size until the sum of the two gammas is zero.

We can look at this butterfly in another way. By appropriately choosing the *spread ratio* of both sides, we can create one delta-neutral top spread and one delta-neutral bottom spread. If our anticipated stock volatility proves too low, we make money on the top spread and lose money on the bottom spread. On the other hand, if it proves too high, we lose money on the top spread and make money on the bottom spread. Therefore, by adjusting the relative *sizes* of the spreads, we set up our position so that the spread profits and losses from errors in predicting volatility are exactly offset.

In general, a position may have negative or positive time bias. However, under certain conditions, we can determine the sign of the bias knowing only the signs of the position value, delta and gamma. For example, positive-value, delta-neutral top positions must have positive theta, while negative-value, delta-neutral bottom positions must have negative theta. While this can be shown from the mathematics,[23] it is easy to see why it must be true. If it were not, a certain loss would accompany the former, while a certain profit would accompany the latter.

6-4. SCREENING NEUTRAL POSITIONS

We are finally prepared to select an option position. If we think a stock is significantly over- or underpriced, it may be better to take an uncovered option position rather than simply buy or short the stock. Depending on our attitudes toward risk, numerous other strategies may be desirable ranging from this extreme to an almost neutral position. Before providing a more general analysis, we will first examine in detail a strategy which takes

---

[22] We can see from our earlier formula for the position gamma of a delta-neutral position, that the position gamma will be zero if and only if, by happenstance, $\Gamma_1/\Delta_1 = \Gamma_2/\Delta_2$.

[23] Recall the continuous-time hedging equation for option valuation developed in Section 5-6, restated here in terms of the position Δ, Γ, and Θ:

$$\Theta = (\log r)V - (\log r)S\Delta - \tfrac{1}{2}\sigma^2 S^2 \Gamma.$$

From this, it is possible to relate Θ to V, Δ, and Γ for any option position. In particular, if $V > 0$, $\Delta \leq 0$, and $\Gamma \leq 0$, then $\Theta > 0$; and if $V < 0$, $\Delta \geq 0$, and $\Gamma \geq 0$, then $\Theta < 0$.

advantage of options that are the most over- and underpriced *relative to the market price of the stock.*

To take advantage of these relative mispricings and, at the same time, minimize risk, delta-neutral positions are a useful strategy. These positions are particularly appropriate if we feel fairly confident about our ability to forecast volatility but wish to avoid the more difficult task of estimating the expected rate of return of the underlying stock. As the derivation of the Black-Scholes formula illustrates, only if our position ratio is delta-neutral will we be able to insulate ourselves from inaccurate predictions of trends in stock prices.

We focus for the moment on the maintenance of delta-neutral positions for two reasons. First, it allows us to isolate the effects of superior ability to value options, apart from the problem of stock valuation. Second, for Market Makers who often take large positions relative to their capital, the simple consideration of avoidance of ruin virtually dictates an interest in delta-neutral positions. Indeed, many Market Makers attempt to adhere quite strictly to a delta-neutral strategy. However, a delta-neutral strategy usually requires relatively frequent trading. As a result, it is not advisable as a consistent practice for investors with significant transactions costs. While public investors fall into this category, Market Makers do not.

We should also mention that the investment procedure detailed in this section is by no means an optimal solution to the general problem of option portfolio selection and revision, even for investors desiring delta-neutral positions. Since this problem is extremely complex, the procedure we describe is designed to accommodate the limited information processing capability of many investors, particularly for decisions which must be made quickly. In the next section, we will discuss more general considerations relating to optimal portfolio construction.

Presuming we can identify mispriced options using the Black-Scholes formula for European options or its associated numerical technique for American options, how do we determine which options are most over- or underpriced? Of all the possible neutral positions—hedges, spreads, and combinations—on the same underlying security, how do we select the most promising? How do we compare neutral positions across different securities? In this section, we provide some answers to these questions.

Screening Options.   An obvious way to identify the most under- or overpriced option on the same underlying security is to measure the *absolute difference between its value and price.* Table 6-16 is produced by the APL program SCREEN. It applies to the same circumstances underlying Table 6-13. By this criterion, the JUL/40 puts are the most underpriced (indeed, the only underpriced) options. Since we will be buying *underpriced* options, we compare their *ask* price to their value. Comparing the *bid* price to value,

Table 6-16
COVERED OPTION POSITION SCREEN

Date: 77/12/21
Formula: PC1

```
********      XYZ XYZ XYZ XYZ XYZ XYZ XYZ XYZ XYZ XYZ      ********
```

	EXPIRATION	ANN INT	ANN VOL	EX-DIV DATE	DIVIDEND
	78/01/20	.050	.300	78/01/05	.50
	78/04/21	.050	.300	78/04/05	.50
	78/07/21	.050	.300	78/07/05	.50

TYPE	SERIES	BID	ASK	**	VALUE	DELTA	GAMMA	THETA	**	ER
STOCK	/00	40.00	40.00		40.00	1.00	.00	.0		.00
CALL	JAN/35	4.63	4.75		4.74	.92	.04	‾4.3		.00
CALL	JAN/40	1.25	1.38		1.20	.47	.11	‾9.1		‾.11
CALL	JAN/45	.06	.13		.11	.08	.04	‾3.1		.00
CALL	APR/35	5.50	5.63		5.44	.77	.04	‾4.2		‾.08
CALL	APR/40	2.50	2.75		2.52	.50	.06	‾4.9		.00
CALL	JUL/40	3.50	3.75		3.34	.51	.04	‾3.8		‾.31
PUT	JAN/35	.13	.19		.10	‾.07	.04	‾2.6		‾.32
PUT	JAN/40	1.50	1.63		1.54	‾.52	.11	‾7.1		.00
PUT	JAN/45	5.38	5.50		5.43	‾.91	.04	‾.9		.00
PUT	APR/35	.75	.88		.87	‾.20	.04	‾2.5		.00
PUT	APR/40	3.00	3.13		2.88	‾.47	.06	‾3.0		‾.26
PUT	JUL/40	3.50	3.63		3.71	‾.45	.04	‾2.0		.18

```
BEST POSITION IN  XYZ:       PROFIT:   2009

  DOLLAR DELTA:     12    DOLLAR GAMMA:    ‾47    THETA:    26

             SELL   96  PUT    APR/40  α  3.00
             BUY   100  PUT    JUL/40  α  3.63


*****************************************************************
```

RANKING OF BEST POSITIONS IN UNDERLYING STOCKS
(FOR EQUAL DOLLAR GAMMA = ‾1 OR 1)

RANK	STOCK	PROFIT
1.	N	73
2.	JCR	58
3.	MN	46
4.	XYZ	43
5.	NSC	37
6.	CK	29
7.	PC	22
8.	LT	15

the JUL/40 calls are the most *overpriced*. This simple measure will tend to favor long-maturity, at-the-money options, and discriminate against short-maturity, out-of-the-money options. Moreover, the absolute difference rule implicitly assumes the number of options we buy or write will be the same for each option.

Instead of the absolute difference, we might measure the *relative difference between value and price*. This is just the absolute difference divided by the price. This will tend to favor out-of-the-money options, such as the JAN/35 put. As before, this rule does not consider the number of options we will buy or write, an important aspect of our strategy.

We really want to compare options, holding fixed the effect of a dollar movement in the stock on the option position. That is, *we want to measure the profit from option positions of equivalent risk*. Ignoring taxes, margin, and commissions, the adjusted position with the greatest or lowest difference between value and price is the one we will select. To standardize for risk, we use the option delta. Recall that the delta measures the expected dollar change in the option price if the stock price increases by a small amount. For example, to neutralize the risk in the JAN/45 and APR/40 calls, for every 12.5 JAN/45 contracts, we must hold 2 APR/40s. These positions have the same dollar risk as one round lot of stock for small changes in the stock price. Therefore, to compare positions of equivalent risk, for each option we calculate its *equalizing ratio*:

$$\mathrm{ER} \equiv \frac{V - M}{|\Delta|},$$

where M represents the market price of the option.[24]

Since the stock has been assumed fairly priced for the purpose of screening, its equalizing ratio is always zero. For an option, let M_b be its bid price and M_a its ask price. Either (1) $V < M_b$, (2) $M_b \leq V \leq M_a$, or (3) $M_a < V$. In the first case, if anything, we plan to sell the option at the bid price, therefore its $\mathrm{ER} = (V - M_b)/|\Delta|$. In the second case, we can neither buy nor sell at an expected profit, so $\mathrm{ER} = 0$. In the third case, since we consider buying the option, $\mathrm{ER} = (V - M_a)/|\Delta|$. As a result, options with negative equalizing ratios are possible sells; those with positive equalizing ratios are possible buys; and those with zero equalizing ratios are considered fairly priced. For XYZ, the best sell is therefore the JAN/35 put and the best buy the JUL/40 put. The ER of −.32 for the JAN/35 put means that selling $1/|\Delta| \approx 14$ puts is *equivalent in expected dollar profit and dollar risk to selling one share of stock at $40.32.*

---

[24] $|\Delta|$ is the absolute value of the delta. It insures that put deltas enter the definition of the equalizing ratio as positive numbers.

Screening Neutral Positions on the Same Stock. For a neutral position (that is, one with a zero position delta that combines only two related securities), the *total equalizing ratio* ($\overline{ER}$) is simply the sum of the absolute values of the two security equalizing ratios. That is,

$$\overline{ER} = |ER_1| + |ER_2|.$$

Because the difference between value and price for each security has been weighted by the inverse of its delta, the total equalizing ratio applies only to covered positions that are neutral.[25]

At first glance, the best delta-neutral position would appear to be the one with the highest total equalizing ratio. On this basis, we would write a combination in JUL/40 calls and JAN/35 puts. To keep it neutral, we must write about $1/.51 \approx 2$ JUL/40 call contracts for every $1/.07 \approx 14$ JAN/35 put contracts written. Indeed, if our values are correct and we can costlessly revise our position with sufficient frequency, a position of exactly these amounts is equivalent in dollar expected profit and dollar risk to buying one round lot of stock at $39.69 and selling one round lot at $40.32. This riskless arbitrage opportunity has a certain profit of $.63.

However, transactions costs and occasional jumps in the stock price make very frequent revision impractical. Not only do we want to initiate positions with a zero delta, but we also prefer positions with deltas as insensitive as possible to the stock price. This will mean that small changes in the stock price will not produce position deltas far from zero. The position gamma provides a natural measure of the delta sensitivity. *To minimize risk, we should compare zero delta positions with the same position gamma in absolute value.* While the zero position delta constraint determines the ratio in which the two covering securities are to be held, the equal position gamma constraint determines the comparable "size" of the position.

As developed in Section 6-3, the formula for the position gamma of a delta-neutral position in two securities is

$$\text{Position gamma} = n_1 \Delta_1 \left[\frac{\Gamma_1}{\Delta_1} - \frac{\Gamma_2}{\Delta_2} \right].$$

To compare positions with equal gamma in absolute value, we can require

$$\left| n_1 \Delta_1 \left[\frac{\Gamma_1}{\Delta_1} - \frac{\Gamma_2}{\Delta_2} \right] \right| = 1. \tag{1}$$

[25] To compare covered positions, we only combine securities with equalizing ratios of opposite sign, unless the position is a combination. For a combination, we only combine securities with equalizing ratios of the same sign. If no options are overpriced or no options are underpriced, then to preserve neutrality, we must either take a hedge or a combination (see Section 5-4).

Since the position is neutral, for a zero delta

$$n_2 = -n_1\left(\frac{\Delta_1}{\Delta_2}\right). \tag{2}$$

The present value of the anticipated profit from a position is simply the difference between position value and cost. That is,

$$\text{Profit} = n_1(V_1 - M_1) + n_2(V_2 - M_2). \tag{3}$$

To measure the profit on a zero delta position with gamma ± 1, n_1 and n_2 must simultaneously satisfy Equations (1), (2), and (3). Substituting for n_1 and n_2 in Equation (3),

$$\text{Profit} = \pm\left(\frac{\Gamma_1}{\Delta_1} - \frac{\Gamma_2}{\Delta_2}\right)^{-1}\left(\frac{V_1 - M_1}{\Delta_1} - \frac{V_2 - M_2}{\Delta_2}\right).$$

If we only consider positions with separately profitable pairs of securities (that is, if we write overpriced options and buy underpriced options[26]), the sign of the profit must be positive. Moreover, we can then replace the second parenthetical term with the total equalizing ratio. As a result, for positions with positive profit,

$$\text{Profit} = k(\overline{\text{ER}})$$

where

$$k \equiv \left|\left(\frac{\Gamma_1}{\Delta_1} - \frac{\Gamma_2}{\Delta_2}\right)^{-1}\right|$$

The positive constant k tells us how much to expand the size of a zero delta position to compare positions with a gamma of ± 1.

SCREEN compares all possible delta-neutral positions in XYZ stock and options. It selects as the "best position" the pair of securities with the highest profit at zero delta and equal gamma.[27] By this criterion, we should buy a horizontal spread in APR/40 and JUL/40 puts. The number bought and sold are standardized so that we buy or sell 100 contracts on the side with the lowest option delta. Depending on available capital and the depth of the market, this position may be scaled up or down accordingly.

---

[26] If either security is not separately profitable, our neutral position will not insure a profit with finite capital, even with continuous revision. See Section 5-4.

[27] This selection does not consider either the equity required to maintain the position (it is not based on rate of return) or the speed with which the market price of an option converges to its proper value. Required equity is not a factor in our selection because its calculation may be quite complex and because it differs substantially among market participants.

Screening Neutral Positions Across Different Stocks. If we are ranking options on different fairly priced stocks, we need to adjust our comparative positions for differences in stock volatility. Since we want to measure risk in dollars, not rates, we multiply the volatility by the current stock price. Thus σS is termed the *stock dollar volatility*. This converts the volatility of the stock's rate of return to the volatility of the *stock price*. The *option dollar volatility* is then the dollar volatility of the stock times the absolute value of the option delta or $|\Delta|\sigma S$.

The greater the dollar volatility of an option on one stock compared to the dollar volatility of an option on another, the more sensitive its value to movements of *equal likelihood* in its underlying stock. Therefore, when comparing options on different stocks, we normalize their equalizing ratios for positions of equal dollar volatility. That is, we compare

$$\frac{V - M}{|\Delta|\sigma S} = \frac{(\text{ER})}{\sigma S}.$$

The option for which this ratio is the highest is considered the best buy, and the option for which this ratio is the lowest the best sell. Just as the inverse of the option delta measures the number of contracts needed to equalize risk across options on the same stock, the inverse of the option dollar volatility measures the number of contracts needed to equalize risk across options to different underlying stocks. This normalized equalizing ratio then measures an option's dollar return per dollar of risk.

For an option position, we define its *dollar delta* as the product of the position delta times the stock's dollar volatility, and its *dollar gamma* or "dollar curvature" as the product of the position gamma times the square of the stock's dollar volatility. Unlike ordinary deltas and gammas, these can be compared across stocks.

The best overall delta-neutral position is the zero delta and equal dollar gamma position with the highest profit. In this case, it is convenient to equalize the dollar gamma by setting it equal to one. For purposes of screening options across different underlying stocks, we calculate

$$\text{Profit} = k(\overline{\text{ER}})$$

where

$$k \equiv \left|\left(\frac{\Gamma_1}{\Delta_1} - \frac{\Gamma_2}{\Delta_2}\right)^{-1}\right| \bigg/ (\sigma S)^2$$

Of course, since $(\sigma S)^2$ is the same for all options to the same stock, this revised measure of profit preserves the ordering within positions related to the same stock. Table 6-17 summarizes the new concepts developed in this and the previous section.

Table 6-17
CONCEPTS FOR ANALYZING OPTION
POSITIONS

1.	Stock price:	S
	Option price:	M
2.	Option value:	V
	Option delta:	$\Delta \equiv \partial V/\partial S$
	Option gamma:	$\Gamma \equiv \partial \Delta/\partial S$
	Option theta:	$\Theta \equiv -\partial V/\partial t$
3.	Position value:	$n_1 V_1 + n_2 V_2$
	Position delta:	$n_1 \Delta_1 + n_2 \Delta_2$
	Position gamma:	$n_1 \Gamma_1 + n_2 \Gamma_2$
	Position theta:	$n_1 \Theta_1 + n_2 \Theta_2$
4.	Stock volatility:	σ
	Stock dollar volatility:	σS
	Option dollar volatility:	$\|\Delta\| \sigma S$
5.	Dollar delta:[a]	$(n_1 \Delta_1 + n_2 \Delta_2) \times \sigma S$
	Dollar gamma:	$(n_1 \Gamma_1 + n_2 \Gamma_2) \times (\sigma S)^2$
6.	Equalizing ratio:	$ER \equiv (V - M)/\|\Delta\|$
	Equalizing ratio: (across stocks)	$ER/\sigma S$
7.	Total equalizing ratio: (for separately profitable pairs of securities)	$\overline{ER} \equiv \|ER_1\| + \|ER_2\|$

[a] We might also define the position dollar volatility as the absolute value of its dollar delta.

For the best delta-neutral position for each stock, SCREEN calculates its dollar delta, dollar gamma, and theta *per day*. In Table 6-16, for XYZ:

$$\text{Dollar delta} = .3 \times 40 \times \{[(-9{,}600) \times (-.47)]$$
$$+ [10{,}000 \times (-.45)]\}/\sqrt{365} = 12,$$
$$\text{Dollar gamma} = (.3 \times 40)^2 \times \{[(-9{,}600) \times .06]$$
$$+ [10{,}000 \times .04]\}/365 = -47,$$
$$\text{Theta} = \{[(-9{,}600) \times (-3)] + [10{,}000 \times (-2)]\}/365 = 26.$$

The dollar delta is not zero due to rounding the number of contracts bought and sold to integers.

SCREEN also calculates the best delta-neutral positions for seven other stocks. To conserve space, a similar format to XYZ has been omitted from Table 6-16. However, SCREEN's overall ranking of these positions is given near the bottom of the table. The put spread in XYZ ranks fourth with a profit of $43 for a position size set so its dollar gamma per day equals -1. Observe that the profit of the full-sized suggested position is $2,009, and its dollar gamma is -47. To calculate the profit at dollar gamma of -1, simply divide 2,009 by $|-47|$.

Analysis in Depth.   Positions, such as the put spread, that hold particular interest, can be subjected to closer scrutiny. Using APL program POSAN, we can generate the output in Table 6-18. For each indicated position and anticipated holding period, POSAN (*position analysis*) calculates the profit or loss in value over the holding period and the dollar delta per day at the end of the holding period, conditional on a range of possible stock prices at the end of the period. The range of stock prices desired is input by the user in terms of the number of standard deviations around the current stock price.

In this case, a coverage of 3 standard deviations was requested. The first position analyzed was the put spread chosen by SCREEN, with an anticipated holding period of seven days. From the calculated current dollar delta, dollar gamma and theta per day, we should have a near-delta-neutral top spread with positive time bias. In other words, we hope the stock price remains stable. Large stock price movements in either direction will create losses—but they must occur fast enough, since time is working in our favor.

In fact, that is just what we observe. If the stock price remains unchanged at 40, the *value*[28] of our position rises by $182 by the end of the week. Observe that by just knowing the position theta per day, we would have guessed $25 \times 7 = \$175$. Our prediction, using theta, is close but not exact. The position theta will not be constant over the holding period, since it depends on the stock price and time. With some interpolation, as long as the stock price stays between $38\frac{1}{8}$ and $41\frac{1}{2}$ by the end of the week, the value of our position increases. From Table 6-16, we know the potential profit from convergence of market prices to values in this position is $2,009. Even in the unlikely event that the stock price rises 3 standard deviations to 46 in one week, the potential profit from convergence is still greater than our anticipated loss in value of $1,883.

By way of contrast, consider the neutral hedge with the APR/40 calls discussed earlier. This is the second position examined in Table 6-18. Scaled

---

[28] *Caution*: The actual profit over the week depends, of course, on changes in the puts' market prices.

Table 6-18
POSITION ANALYSIS

Date: 77/12/21
Formula: PC1

Coverage: 3.0 Sigma

********** XYZ XYZ XYZ XYZ XYZ XYZ XYZ XYZ XYZ XYZ **********

SELL   96 PUT   APR/40
BUY   100 PUT   JUL/40

STOCK PRICE   HOLDING PERIOD   STOCK VOLATILITY
   40.00   7   .300

AVERAGE DOLLAR VOLATILITY: 98

DOLLAR DELTA: 12   DOLLAR GAMMA: ¯48   THETA: 25

STOCK PRICE	35.00	36.00	37.00	38.00	39.00	40.00	41.00	42.00
PROFIT/LOSS	¯1081	¯648	¯283	¯12	147	182	92	¯120
DOLLAR DELTA	297	272	229	169	98	19	¯64	¯143

STOCK PRICE	43.00	44.00	45.00	46.00
PROFIT/LOSS	¯440	¯853	¯1340	¯1883
DOLLAR DELTA	¯218	¯283	¯338	¯380

****

BUY   50 STOCK   /00
SELL 100 CALL   APR/40

STOCK PRICE   HOLDING PERIOD   STOCK VOLATILITY
   40.00   7   .300

AVERAGE DOLLAR VOLATILITY: 449

DOLLAR DELTA: ¯6   DOLLAR GAMMA: ¯222   THETA: 134

STOCK PRICE	35.00	36.00	37.00	38.00	39.00	40.00	41.00	42.00
PROFIT/LOSS	¯6168	¯3570	¯1531	¯86	744	953	554	¯430
DOLLAR DELTA	1607	1357	1066	740	388	19	¯360	¯737

STOCK PRICE	43.00	44.00	45.00	46.00
PROFIT/LOSS	¯1964	¯4005	¯6506	¯9417
DOLLAR DELTA	¯1107	¯1462	¯1798	¯2113

down in size (by a factor of about 5) to be comparable per dollar gamma with the put spread, we see it is roughly similar. Of course, it was not chosen by SCREEN because the APR/40 call value lay within the market bid-ask quote.

6-5. PORTFOLIO CONSIDERATIONS

Neutral trading strategies are only suitable for investors facing very low transactions costs. Investors with higher costs cannot afford to take positions with small potential pre-transactions-costs profits or positions which may require frequent revision. If they want to use options, they should typically take positions which they intend to hold with little revision over several weeks or months.

This brings us squarely against at least two complications which we did not need to consider in the previous section. First, puts and calls on the same underlying security cannot be judged in isolation of the rest of an investor's portfolio. Second, the measures of expected return and risk we have developed thus far (in Sections 5-5 and 6-3) have been based on the expected return and risk of an instantaneously equivalent position in stock and bonds. But positions held over several weeks or months are, as we have shown, equivalent to a stock-bond position *adjusted* in a particular way over time. The instantaneous measures of expected return and risk may be inaccurate for these longer-term positions, or, at best, incomplete.

In this section, we show how to introduce these complications into the choice of an optimal portfolio of stock, options, and default-free bonds. Although we were able to develop option pricing theory without reference to modern portfolio theory, for our current purposes we are forced to draw upon this more complete theory. After all, we can hardly be expected to be able to construct wisely chosen portfolios of stock, bonds, and options if we do not first understand the more elementary considerations involved in forming portfolios containing only stock and bonds.

The Utility Function. Modern portfolio theory begins with the definition of a utility function, which encapsulates the goals of an investor. This can be interpreted as a function which translates the expected return and risk attributes of a portfolio into the return which would leave the investor indifferent between choosing the portfolio or an investment providing that return without risk. This utility-indifferent return is commonly called the portfolio *certainty equivalent return*. An investor can then choose among possibly very different portfolios by comparing their certainty equivalent returns and selecting the portfolio with the highest one.

In the example we will develop, we assume that an investor can summarize the risk attributes of a portfolio by its volatility and *skewness* of return. For a given portfolio, he must weigh the benefits of its expected return against the disadvantage of its volatility. In addition, he may tend to value portfolios with positive skewness more highly or less highly depending on his utility function.

The additional consideration of skewness is a departure from the usual simplifications used in most current applications of portfolio theory. In these applications, an investor is assumed to measure risk solely in terms of volatility. As an empirical observation, unrevised positions in stock and bonds tend to be relatively symmetric in possible outcomes; that is, the probabilities of high and low returns of a given magnitude are roughly equal (provided they are not too extreme). Therefore, their expected return and volatility tend to be a sufficient description of the more likely potential returns.

However, since option positions can be quite skewed, our analysis would be seriously incomplete if we neglected an investor's preference for skewness. If an investor desires skewed rather than symmetric outcomes, either he can revise his stock-bond positions in a particular way over time or, alternatively, he can take a fixed position in options. For example, if he buys puts on shares he owns, he will tend to decrease the probability of large losses at the cost of increased probability of small losses (positive skewness). On the other hand, if he writes calls against shares he owns, he will decrease the probability of large profits and increase the probability of small profits (negative skewness). Depending on his utility function, an investor may not find these tradeoffs offsetting. Indeed, his principal reason for buying or selling options may be to transform what would otherwise be a relatively symmetric outcome from a fixed stock-bond position into a more desirable fixed, but highly skewed, position.

Table 6-19
ILLUSTRATION OF MEASURES OF RETURN AND RISK

	Rate of Return[a]			*Return/Risk Measures*			*Certainty Equivalent[b]*		
	Low	*Medium*	*High*	$m-1$	v	s	$b = .5$	$b = 1$	$b = 1.5$
I	−.49	.50	.59	.20	.49	−.43	.138	.061	−.007
II	−.40	.20	.80	.20	.49	0	.146	.090	.035
III	−.19	−.10	.89	.20	.49	.43	.154	.113	.075

[a] Each rate of return (low, medium, and high) occurs with probability $\frac{1}{3}$.
[b] Exact certainty equivalent rates of return for utility functions with constant proportional risk aversion equal to *b*.

To evaluate a portfolio's certainty equivalent return we will need to measure its expected rate of return, volatility, and skewness. Table 6-19 gives a simple example of how this might be done. It contrasts the returns on three portfolios, I, II, and III, purposely constructed to have the same expected rate of return, $m - 1$, and volatility, v, but different skewness, s. Portfolio I is assumed to have an annual rate of return of $-.49$, $.50$, or $.59$, each with equal probability, $\frac{1}{3}$. Its expected rate of return and standard deviation are then computed by

$$m - 1 = \tfrac{1}{3}(-.49) + \tfrac{1}{3}(.50) + \tfrac{1}{3}(.59) = .20$$
$$v = \sqrt{\tfrac{1}{3}(-.49 - .20)^2 + \tfrac{1}{3}(.50 - .20)^2 + \tfrac{1}{3}(.59 - .20)^2} = .49.$$

By definition, skewness is the cube root of the expected cube of the deviation of the portfolio rate of return from its expected value. Therefore,

$$s = \sqrt[3]{\tfrac{1}{3}(-.49 - .20)^3 + \tfrac{1}{3}(.50 - .20)^3 + \tfrac{1}{3}(.59 - .20)^3} = -.43.$$

Similar calculations lead to the corresponding parameters describing portfolios II and III. We see that skewness can be zero even though the volatility is not (portfolio II) whenever a portfolio has returns symmetrically distributed around its expected value. Also, unlike volatility, skewness can be negative or positive. Among these three candidate portfolios, an investor with a preference for positive skewness would unambiguously prefer portfolio III, and an investor preferring negative skewness would choose portfolio I.

To calculate a portfolio's certainty equivalent return, we next need to know how m, v, and s fit together in an investor's utility function. In our example we will assume that, given unchanged opportunities to invest in securities, an investor does not desire to change the proportionate composition of his portfolio as his current wealth changes. While this assumption may not apply to most investors, there is reason to think it may be approximately true for many others (including the authors, for example), particularly those with relatively large amounts to invest.

As promised, we will now draw upon modern portfolio theory. According to this theory, our assumption considerably narrows the range of candidate utility functions. If $\tilde{R}$, a random variable, is the return (thus, $\tilde{R} - 1$ is the rate of return) on the investor's portfolio, then the investor's utility function *must* take the form

$$\frac{1}{1 - b} \tilde{R}^{1 - b},$$

where b is a positive constant measuring the degree of an investor's risk aversion.[29] It is within the scope of our assumption for the constant b to be quite individualized. For example, for one of the authors b is very close to 1, and for the other, b is about 1.5.

Returning to Table 6-19, if $b = .5$, portfolio I will result in a utility value of $2\sqrt{.51}$, $2\sqrt{1.5}$, or $2\sqrt{1.59}$, depending on whether the portfolio return is low, medium, or high. According to modern portfolio theory, a single number which can be used to rank order candidate portfolio order is the *expected* utility

$$E\left[\frac{1}{1-b}\tilde{R}^{1-b}\right] = \tfrac{1}{3}(2\sqrt{.51}) + \tfrac{1}{3}(2\sqrt{1.5}) + \tfrac{1}{3}(2\sqrt{1.59}) = 2.1332.$$

To give the units of this expected utility greater meaning, we translate it into its certainty equivalent return, $\overline{R}$, by solving the following equation:

$$\frac{1}{1-b}\overline{R}^{1-b} = 2\sqrt{\overline{R}} = 2.1332.$$

That is, we find the certainty equivalent return which provides the investor with the same expected utility as portfolio I. In this case $\overline{R} = 1.138$, and the certainty equivalent rate of return is $\overline{R} - 1 = .138$. An investor with degree of risk aversion $b = .5$ is thus indifferent between an equal chance of earning a rate of return of $-.49$, .50, or .59 and a certain rate of return of .138.

It is clear from the certainty equivalent section of Table 6-19 that an investor's certainty equivalent return depends on his degree of risk aversion,

---

[29] Those familiar with the portfolio theory literature will recognize b as the level of "constant proportional risk aversion." This theory assumes an investor has a utility function $U(\tilde{w})$ over his future wealth. His proportional risk aversion is measured by $-\tilde{w}U''(\tilde{w})/U'(\tilde{w})$.

It is easy to see why $U(\tilde{w}) = [1/(1-b)]\tilde{w}^{1-b}$ implies an investor will not desire to change the proportionate composition of his portfolio as his current wealth w_0 changes. Since $\tilde{w} = w_0\tilde{R}$ and utility is unique up to an increasing linear transformation,

$$\frac{1}{1-b}\tilde{w}^{1-b} = \frac{1}{1-b}(w_0\tilde{R})^{1-b} = w_0^{1-b}\frac{1}{1-b}\tilde{R}^{1-b} \approx \frac{1}{1-b}\tilde{R}^{1-b}.$$

Generally, proportional risk aversion will depend on w_0, but in this case, proportional risk aversion is constant and equal to b since $b = -\tilde{w}U''(\tilde{w})/U'(\tilde{w})$.

If $b = 1$, then it would appear utility is undefined. However, it can be shown for this special case that

$$\lim_{b \to 1} \frac{1}{1-b}\tilde{R}^{1-b} \approx \log \tilde{R}$$

and we can approximate the ordering of portfolios given by logarithmic utility, $\log \tilde{R}$, by regarding b as very close to but not equal to 1.

b, but can also be quite sensitive to portfolio skewness. Positive skewness is always desirable, especially as b increases.

Since most portfolios have not three but almost an infinite number of possible outcomes, it would quickly prove impractical to list each outcome together with its probability. It is often much easier to estimate its parameters, m, v, and s, directly. We would, therefore, like to be able to calculate a portfolio's certainty equivalent return using parameters m, v, and s as inputs (the return/risk measures section of Table 6-19) rather than the possible outcomes (the certainty equivalent section). Unfortunately, knowledge of m, v, and s is usually insufficient to determine $\overline{R}$ exactly. However, it is possible, using the mathematical theory of approximation, to derive a good approximation of $\overline{R}$ based on m, v, and s alone. Application of this theory leads to the following approximation:[30]

$$E\left(\frac{1}{1-b}\tilde{R}^{1-b}\right) \approx \frac{1}{1-b}m^{1-b} - \tfrac{1}{2}bm^{-b-1}v^2 + \tfrac{1}{6}b(b+1)m^{-b-2}s^3.$$

For example, for portfolio I, if $b = .5$ we would approximate

$$E\left(\frac{1}{1-b}\tilde{R}^{1-b}\right)$$

by

$$2\sqrt{m} - \frac{1}{4}\frac{1}{m\sqrt{m}}v^2 + \frac{1}{8}\frac{1}{m^2\sqrt{m}}s^3 =$$

$$2\sqrt{1.2} - \frac{1}{4}\frac{1}{1.2\sqrt{1.2}}(.49)^2 + \frac{1}{8}\frac{1}{(1.2)^2\sqrt{1.2}}(-.43)^3 = 2.1389.$$

which, in turn, implies $\overline{R} = 1.144$. Calculation of other certainty equivalent returns in Table 6-19 using the approximating formula gives a similar degree of accuracy.

In summary, we believe that for portfolios containing options, it is necessary to calculate not only their expected return, m, and volatility, v, but also their skewness, s. Given certain often acceptable assumptions and an investor's degree of risk aversion, we can translate these parameters into an approximation of the certainty equivalent return, $\overline{R}$, of the portfolio. The investor will then select the portfolio with the highest $\overline{R}$.

---

[30] We have approximated the function $(1-b)^{-1}\tilde{R}^{1-b}$ by expanding it in a Taylor series around m, taking its expected value and neglecting terms higher than the third order.

To do all this, we need a way to calculate m, v, and s. We will first discuss how to determine the expected return of a single option, and then extend this to a portfolio expected return. We will show how to break apart these expected returns into components which separately measure different sources of an option or portfolio alpha. It will then be convenient to develop a measure of an option or portfolio beta. Focusing first on a position of several different options to a single underlying stock, we will provide a technique to measure the position volatility and skewness, and then extend this to positions across several underlying stocks. Finally, we will put all this together to calculate certainty equivalent returns.

Expected Return. In Section 5-5, we showed that over a *single* period of binomial stock price movements, the expected return, m_C, of an option properly priced relative to its stock is related to the expected return of the stock, m_S, by

$$m_C - r = \Omega(m_S - r),$$

where the elasticity is $\Omega = (S/C)\Delta$ for a call, or $\Omega = (S/P)\Delta$ for a put. If the stock were mispriced relative to its predicted value according to the capital asset pricing model, then

$$m_S - r = \alpha_S + \beta_S(m_M - r),$$

where m_M is the expected return of the "market portfolio," α_S is the stock alpha reflecting its mispricing, and β_S is the stock beta. If, in addition, the option were mispriced relative to the stock, then we would have a second source for the alpha of an option, $\hat{\alpha}_C$, so that

$$m_C - r = \hat{\alpha}_C + \Omega\alpha_S + \Omega\beta_S(m_M - r).$$

We can raise at least two objections to these formulas. First, as we have already pointed out, they hold only over a single period and may become quite complicated if we anticipate holding an option over several periods. Second, particularly if we plan to close out our option position prior to expiration, it is not clear how we should estimate the portion of the option alpha, $\hat{\alpha}_C$, due to the relative mispricing of the stock and the option.[31] To deal with this difficulty we must have a theory of the option's disequilibrium price behavior.

---

[31] Likewise, we have not explained how to estimate the stock alpha, but this falls outside the scope of this book.

To handle these complications in a reasonable but straightforward manner, we will provisionally assume that:[32]

1. Both the investor and the "market" agree that the interest rate will remain constant and equal to $r - 1$.
2. Both the investor and the "market" agree that the stock return is lognormal with a constant dividend yield δ.
3. The market price of an option at all times through expiration is set equal to the value it would have according to the Black-Scholes formula for European options.
4. The investor's estimates of the annualized discrete expected return and instantaneous volatility of the stock are m and σ; the "market's" estimates are $\bar{m}$ and $\bar{\sigma}$, respectively.

These assumptions[33] isolate a single source of any disagreement between an investor and the market about the *relative* pricing of an option: the stock volatility. In practice, there will be other sources of disagreement (interest rates, dividend yields, the pricing formula itself), but differences in volatility estimates are likely to prove the most important.

Under these conditions, we can derive a surprisingly simple formula for the expected future market price of an option $E(\tilde{V}|h)$ at the end of holding period h, measured as a fraction of a year.[34]

---

[32] We speak here as though the "market" had a mind of its own. This is a device for deriving inferences from security market prices. For example, the "market's" estimate of stock volatility $\bar{\sigma}$ can be inferred, given the Black-Scholes formula, from the implicit volatility contained in the current market price of an associated option.

[33] An unstated, but implicit, assumption requires that the investor knows that he and the market agree about r and δ, knows that the market uses the Black-Scholes formula to price options, and knows the market's estimates $\bar{m}$ and $\bar{\sigma}$.

[34] To see how this formula is derived, consider a call with no dividends remaining until expiration. Our problem is to integrate

$$E(\tilde{C}|h) = \int_{-\infty}^{\infty} [Se^y N(\tilde{x}) - Kr^{h-t} N(\tilde{x} - \bar{\sigma}\sqrt{t - h})] \frac{1}{\sigma\sqrt{2\pi h}} e^{-(y - \mu h)^2/2\sigma^2 h} dy,$$

where y is the natural logarithm of the return of the stock over holding period h, $\mu \equiv (1/h)E(y) = \log m - \frac{1}{2}\sigma^2$, and

$$\tilde{x} \equiv \frac{\log (Se^y/Kr^{h-t})}{\bar{\sigma}\sqrt{t - h}} + \frac{1}{2}\bar{\sigma}\sqrt{t - h}.$$

It helps to use the integral

$$\int_{-\infty}^{\infty} N(A + Bz) \frac{1}{\sqrt{2\pi}} e^{-z^2/2} dz = N\left(\frac{A}{\sqrt{1 + B^2}}\right)$$

for constants A and B.

> $E(\tilde{V}\mid h)$ is equal to the Black-Scholes European option value $V(S, K, t, r, \sigma, \delta)$, except that V is evaluated at $V(Sm_S^h, Kr^h, t, r, \sqrt{a\sigma^2 + (1 - a)\bar{\sigma}^2}, \delta)$, where $a \equiv h/t$.

In other words, the expected future market price of an option at the end of holding period h is equal to the price that option would have today if the current stock price were Sm_S^h, the striking price Kr^h, the time to expiration t, and the market's estimate of the volatility $\sqrt{a\sigma^2 + (1 - a)\bar{\sigma}^2}$, where a is the fraction of the option's time to expiration taken up by the holding period. When the holding period is very short relative to t, the volatility in this formula is almost entirely determined by the market $[\sqrt{a\sigma^2 + (1 - a)\bar{\sigma}^2} = \bar{\sigma}]$. On the other hand, if the option is to be held to expiration, then the volatility is completely determined by the investor $[\sqrt{a\sigma^2 + (1 - a)\bar{\sigma}^2} = \sigma]$.

The option's *annualized* expected return is

$$m_C = \left[\frac{E(\tilde{V}\mid h)}{V}\right]^{1/h},$$

where V is its current market price. Raising $E(\tilde{V}\mid h)/V$ to the $1/h$ power annualizes this expectation.

Consider, now, a universe of options, stock, and bonds,[35] where we index securities by $j = 1, 2, \ldots, J$. If a security were an option, its expected future value after holding period h would be $E(\tilde{V}_j\mid h)$, and this would be determined by applying the above formula. If it were a stock, then $E(\tilde{V}_j\mid h) = S_j m_j^h$; if it were a default-free bond with a current price of \$1, then $E(\tilde{V}_j\mid h) = r^h$. We can think of a portfolio as containing n_j units of each security j. Its current market value is $\Sigma_j n_j V_j$ and its expected future market value at the end of holding period h is $\Sigma_j n_j E(\tilde{V}_j\mid h)$. The portfolio's annualized expected return is then

$$m = \left[\frac{\Sigma_j n_j E(\tilde{V}_j\mid h)}{\Sigma_j n_j V_j}\right]^{1/h}.$$

Here we have presumed each security will be held at least h fraction of a year. To evaluate m over a period during which some positions were closed would require that we knew in advance under what conditions positions would be closed and how the proceeds, if any, would be reinvested.

Despite the two objections we raised earlier to the single period formula for the expected option returns, we might still hope that this

---

[35] We exclude bonds subject to default. These pose special problems which will be considered in Chapter 7.

simpler formula would provide a useful approximation of the exact expected return over a specified holding period. This would save us the trouble of using the more complex formula. Table 6-20 lists the exact expected returns to call options with various striking prices and maturities. If the investor and the market agree about the stock volatility, the table indicates that annualized expected returns will tend to be insensitive to the holding period. Indeed, in this case the value of $m_C - 1$ derived from the instantaneous approximation

$$\log m_C - \log r = \Omega(\log m_S - \log r),$$

where

$$\Omega = \frac{S}{C} N(x)$$

is, to the nearest percent, the same as the exact discrete value over a one-day holding period. However, when an investor believes an option is over- or undervalued relative to its underlying stock, then the option expected return can become quite sensitive to the holding period and an instantaneous approximation may be misleading for sufficiently long holding periods.

Table 6-20

REPRESENTATIVE BLACK-SCHOLES CALL EXPECTED RATES OF RETURN

		$m = 1.10$			$\sigma = .3$			$S = 40$		$r = 1.05$	

		Expiration Month										
		JAN[a]			*APR*				*JUL*			
$\bar{\sigma}$	K											
		Holding Period (Days)										
		1	15	30	1	15	60	120	1	15	60	210
.25	35	.63	.64	.64	.58	.57	.55	.53	.47	.47	.45	.42
	40	25.89	19.39	15.11	1.79	1.72	1.55	1.38	.95	.93	.89	.77
	45	b	b	b	6.84	6.35	5.14	4.11	1.98	1.93	1.77	1.42
.3	35	.47	.47	.47	.34	.34	.34	.34	.29	.29	.29	.28
	40	1.08	1.07	1.06	.48	.48	.48	.48	.37	.37	.37	.36
	45	2.38	2.37	2.36	.66	.66	.65	.65	.45	.45	.45	.44
.35	35	.21	.22	.24	.15	.15	.15	.16	.15	.15	.15	.16
	40	−.58	−.61	−.64	−.01	−.01	−.01	−.02	.09	.09	.09	.08
	45	−.98	−.99	−.99	−.24	−.25	−.27	−.30	−.01	−.01	−.02	−.03

NOTE: No adjustment is made for dividends.
[a] The January options have one month to expiration; the Aprils, four months; and the Julys, seven months. The option expected rates of return and r, m, σ, and $\bar{\sigma}$ are expressed in annual terms.
[b] Greater than 10,000.

Alpha.   For some applications we would like to know what portion of an option or portfolio expected return, based on our opinions, can be attributed to mispricing in the market. We can identify two sources of mispricing for stocks:

1. The expected return of the market portfolio relative to the interest rate (*market alpha*);
2. The expected stock return relative to the expected return of the market portfolio (*pure stock alpha*);

and a third additional source for options:

3. The expected option return relative to the expected return of its underlying stock (*pure option alpha*).

The market alpha might derive from our feeling that stocks as a group are over- or underpriced, the pure stock alpha from special information we have about the expected return of an individual stock, and the pure option alpha from different forecasts of stock volatility.

To isolate the market alpha, we need a theory about how the market goes about relating its expectation of the return of the market portfolio to the interest rate. Naturally, this will depend on the degree of risk aversion of the society as a whole. Other things equal, the more risk-averse the society, the greater the difference between the expected market portfolio return, m_M, and the interest rate, $r - 1$. The capital asset pricing model provides just such a theory. Unfortunately, this model, as it is usually described, is not consistent with multiperiod portfolio choice among securities that tend to have lognormal distributions. However, a modified model, discussed in Section 5-7, offers a way around these difficulties. According to this theory, the market sets prices so that its opinion of the expected market portfolio return, $\bar{m}_M$, is related to the degree of market risk aversion, b_M, and the volatility of the market portfolio, σ_M, by

$$\log \bar{m}_M = \log r + b_M \sigma_M^2 .$$

An investor's forecast of the expected market portfolio return, m_M, will generally be different from $\bar{m}_M$. For example, if he thinks most securities are generally underpriced relative to default-free bonds, then $m_M > \bar{m}_M$ and he will have a positive market alpha, α_M, defined by $m_M = \alpha_M + \bar{m}_M$.

A second source of mispricing is the pure stock alpha,[36] $\hat{\alpha}_S$. This can be determined by comparing the investor's and market's expected returns for a stock. According to the same theory, the market sets the stock price so that its opinion of the expected stock return is

$$\log \bar{m}_S = \log r + b_M \rho \sigma \sigma_M.$$

Here σ is the instantaneous volatility of the stock and ρ is the correlation of the stock's instantaneous rate of return with the rate of return of the market portfolio. Substituting for b_M from the previous equation and exponentiating, we can rewrite this as

$$\bar{m}_S = re^{(\rho\sigma/\sigma_M)\log(\bar{m}_M/r)}.$$

The investor's own estimate m_S may differ from $\bar{m}_S$ for two reasons: He believes this stock is mispriced relative to other stocks ($\hat{\alpha}_S \neq 0$), or he believes stocks as a group are mispriced ($\alpha_M \neq 0$). Combining these, his estimated expected stock return is

$$m_S = \hat{\alpha}_S + re^{(\rho\sigma/\sigma_M)\log(m_M/r)}.$$

Putting this together with the previous equation, we can relate m_S and $\bar{m}_S$ by

$$m_S = \hat{\alpha}_S + \hat{\hat{\alpha}}_S + \bar{m}_S,$$

where $\hat{\hat{\alpha}}_S \equiv re^{(\rho\sigma/\sigma_M)\log(m_M/r)} - re^{(\rho\sigma/\sigma_M)\log(\bar{m}_M/r)}$. We derive $\hat{\hat{\alpha}}_S$ solely from the market alpha and it quantifies the effect of α_M on the investor's expected return of the stock. The sum of $\hat{\alpha}_S$ and $\hat{\hat{\alpha}}_S$ is the *total stock alpha*, α_S.

An option has yet another source of mispricing: the relation between its price and the price of its underlying stock. According to our formula for expected option return, this expectation depends on three types of estimates:

1. The stock expected return (x);
2. The stock volatility (y);
3. The stock volatility used by the market to price an option (z).

---

[36] The size of α_M and $\hat{\alpha}_S$ will depend on how quickly the disequilibrium is corrected in the market. Here we assume that an abnormal annualized expected rate of return of $\log(1 + \alpha_M)$ on the market portfolio can be earned continuously over the next year. We make a similar assumption with regard to $\hat{\alpha}_S$.

Let us denote this dependence by $m_C(x, y, z)$. For example, the market's estimate $\bar{m}_C = m_C(\bar{m}_S, \bar{\sigma}, \bar{\sigma})$, and the investor's estimate $m_C = m_C(m_S, \sigma, \bar{\sigma})$. The total option alpha, $\alpha_C = m_C - \bar{m}_C$, can then be broken down into three components[37]:

1. Pure option alpha

$$\hat{\alpha}_C = m_C(\bar{m}_S, \sigma, \bar{\sigma}) - m_C(\bar{m}_S, \bar{\sigma}, \bar{\sigma})$$

2. Additional alpha deriving from pure stock alpha

$$\hat{\hat{\alpha}}_C = m_C(\bar{m}_S + \hat{\alpha}_S, \bar{\sigma}, \bar{\sigma}) - m_C(\bar{m}_S, \bar{\sigma}, \bar{\sigma})$$

3. Additional alpha deriving from market alpha

$$\hat{\hat{\hat{\alpha}}}_C = m_C(\bar{m}_S + \hat{\hat{\alpha}}_S, \bar{\sigma}, \bar{\sigma}) - m_C(\bar{m}_S, \bar{\sigma}, \bar{\sigma})$$

To extend this to portfolio alphas, since an alpha is a *rate* of return, we need to add 1 to each security alpha before annualizing the units. We can then treat it similarly to an expected return. For example, if α_j is the total alpha for security j, then the annualized portfolio alpha is

$$[\Sigma_j w_j(1 + \alpha_j)^h]^{1/h} - 1 ,$$

where $w_j \equiv n_j V_j / \Sigma_j n_j V_j$ is the portfolio weight of security j.

Most of the ideas in this section are illustrated in Table 6-21, a sample of computer output of PORTAN (*portfolio analysis*) for December 21, 1977. All calculations are based on the Black-Scholes European option pricing formula adjusted for a constant dividend yield (PC1). A portfolio of investments in three underlying stocks (ABC, LMN, and XYZ) and government bonds ($\Delta\Delta\Delta$) is analyzed over a three-month holding period.

The user has input some basic parameters describing the market environment: the interest rate, $r - 1 = .05$, the market portfolio alpha, $\alpha_M = .01$, the market portfolio volatility, $\sigma_M = .18$, and the degree of market risk aversion, $b_M = 1.3$. PORTAN then calculates the market excess return $\bar{m}_M - r = r(e^{b_M \sigma_M^2} - 1) = .045$. This implies the investor forecasts $m_M - 1 = .05 + .01 + .045 = .105$. He is bullish about the market as a whole, in the sense that the market's expectation $\bar{m}_M = .95$.

ABC stock has a current market price $S = 40$ and the user has forecast for ABC a pure stock alpha $\hat{\alpha}_S = .025$, a volatility $\sigma = .3$, and a correlation with the market portfolio $\rho = .5$. The total stock alpha $\alpha_S = .033$, of which .008 is the contribution of the market alpha as it is filtered through ABC stock. The overpriced LMN/APR/40 calls have a pure option alpha

---

[37] Because of partial effects, the total option alpha will usually be approximately, but not exactly, equal to the sum of its three component alphas.

Table 6-21
PORTFOLIO ANALYSIS

```
DATE:  77/12/21
FORMULA:  PC1

HOLDING PERIOD:  90 DAYS
```

INTEREST RATE	MARKET EXCESS RETURN	MARKET ALPHA	MARKET VOLATILITY	MARKET RISK AVERSION
.050	.045	.010	.180	1.3

```
*********************************************************************
**********    ABC ABC ABC ABC ABC ABC ABC ABC ABC ABC ABC ABC    **********
```

	PRICE	ALPHA	VOLATILITY	CORRELATION
	40.00	.025	.300	.500

				MARKET			ALPHA		
--------POSITION--------				PRICE	BETA	MARKET	STOCK	OPTION	TOTAL
BUY	100	STOCK	/00	α	40.00	.84	.008	.025	.000	.033

```
*********************************************************************
**********    LMN LMN LMN LMN LMN LMN LMN LMN LMN LMN LMN LMN    *********◄◄◄◄
```

	PRICE	ALPHA	VOLATILITY	CORRELATION
	40.00	.000	.300	.300

				MARKET			ALPHA		
--------POSITION--------				PRICE	BETA	MARKET	STOCK	OPTION	TOTAL
BUY	100	STOCK	/00	α	40.00	.50	.005	.000	.000	.005
SELL	100	CALL	APR/40	α	2.75	‾3.79	‾.043	.000	.268	.232

```
*********************************************************************
**********    XYZ XYZ XYZ XYZ XYZ XYZ XYZ XYZ XYZ XYZ XYZ XYZ    **********
```

	PRICE	ALPHA	VOLATILITY	CORRELATION
	40.00	.040	.300	.700

				MARKET			ALPHA		
--------POSITION--------				PRICE	BETA	MARKET	STOCK	OPTION	TOTAL
BUY	100	STOCK	/00	α	40.00	1.18	.012	.040	.000	.052
BUY	100	PUT	APR/40	α	2.63	‾8.04	‾.057	‾.175	.261	‾.016

```
*********************************************************************
**********    ΔΔΔ ΔΔΔ ΔΔΔ ΔΔΔ ΔΔΔ ΔΔΔ ΔΔΔ ΔΔΔ ΔΔΔ ΔΔΔ ΔΔΔ ΔΔΔ    **********
```

BUY	10	BOND	78/ 6.50	α	101.43
BUY	10	BOND	80/ 7.00	α	103.72

```
*********************************************************************
**************************************  PORTFOLIO SUMMARY  *********************************
```

	EXPECTED RETURN	VOLATILITY	SKEWNESS	BETA	ALPHA MARKET	STOCK	OPTION	TOTAL	PORTFOLIO WEIGHT
ABC	.121	.309	.296	.84	.008	.025	.000	.033	.28
LMN	.082	.167	‾.230	.26	.002	.000	.019	.022	.27
XYZ	.121	.188	.292	.61	.006	.020	.020	.046	.30
ΔΔΔ	.050	.000	.000	.00	.000	.000	.000	.000	.15
TOTAL	.100	.137	.115	.49	.005	.013	.011	.029	1.00

```
CERTAINTY EQUIVALENT COMPARISIONS
(INVESTOR RISK AVERSION:   1.0)
```

BOND PORTFOLIO	.050
MARKET PORTFOLIO	.085
MARKET-BOND EQUIVALENT PORTFOLIO	.072
STOCK-BOND EQUIVALENT PORTFOLIO	.079
OPTION PORTFOLIO	.090

when written of $\hat{\alpha}_C = .268$, which more than offsets the negative contribution of the filtered market alpha $-.043$, leaving a total option alpha $\alpha_C = .232$.

The portfolio summary near the bottom of Table 6-21 gives the expected rates of return for each position. ABC stock has an expected return of

$$\hat{\alpha}_S + re^{\rho\sigma/\sigma_M(\log m_M/r)} - 1 = .025 + 1.05^{.833(\log 1.105/1.05)} - 1 = .121.$$

Even though XYZ stock has a higher expected rate of return, because of the presence of the purchased puts, the XYZ put hedge has about the same expected rate of return as ABC stock. The total alpha for the put hedge is .046, which roughly equals contributions being made by the pure stock alpha (.02) and the pure option alpha (.02). The default-free investment in government bonds has a .05 rate of return. Taken together,[38] considering the portfolio weights, the portfolio expected rate of return is .10 and the total portfolio alpha is .029. Stocks rank ahead of options, and options rank ahead of the market portfolio, in terms of their contribution.

Beta.   In Section 5-5, we showed that over a *single* period of binomial stock price movements, the beta, β_C, of an option properly priced relative to its stock can be inferred from the stock beta, β_S, by the formula $\beta_C = \Omega\beta_S$. The same objections we raised with respect to an option's expected return apply here with equal force. If we adopt the same assumptions used to derive our formula for expected return and use our modified capital asset pricing model, we can derive a formula for the beta of an option $\beta_C(h)$ over holding period h:

$$\beta_C(h) = \frac{m_C^h - (V'/V)}{m_M^h - r^h}$$

where V' is equal to the Black-Scholes European option value $V(S, K, t, r, \sigma, \delta)$ except that V' is evaluated at

$$V\left(Sr^h\left[\frac{m_S^h}{(m_S - \alpha_S)^h}\right], Kr^h, t, r, \sqrt{a\sigma^2 + (1-a)\bar{\sigma}^2}, \delta\right)$$

where $a \equiv h/t$.

---

[38] Since all numbers are annualized, the *deannualized* expected returns of each position are averaged, then the resulting average is reannualized.

If there were no pure stock or option alphas ($\hat{\alpha}_C = \hat{\alpha}_S = 0$), then V'/V simplifies to r^h. We would then have the usual interpretation of beta as the ratio of the excess (over the riskless rate) return of a security to the excess return of the market portfolio. Note also that, other things equal, as we alter the holding period, not only do we change the annualized expected option return, m_C, but we also change the option's beta, $\beta_C(h)$.

The portfolio beta is simply a weighted average of the betas of the individual securities in the portfolio where the weights are the proportionate values of the holdings of each security:

$$\beta(h) = \Sigma_j w_j \beta_j(h).$$

In Table 6-21, the beta on XYZ stock over a three-month holding period is .84, approximately equal to the instantaneous beta $\rho\sigma/\sigma_M = (.3)(.5)/.18 = .83$. The betas of the written calls (-3.79) and purchased puts (-8.04) are both negative and comparatively large in magnitude. The overall portfolio beta is only .49, due to the hedging influence of the options and the purchased bonds.

Position Volatility and Skewness. To determine a certainty-equivalent rate of return, in addition to the portfolio expected return, we need to know its volatility and skewness. We begin by asking an easier question: Considering only a position of options to a *single* underlying stock, how do we measure its volatility and skewness?

Through holding period h, the volatility and skewness of this position are, respectively,

$$\frac{1}{\Sigma_j n_j V_j} \sqrt{E[(\Sigma_j n_j \tilde{V}_j - \bar{E})^2]} \quad \text{and} \quad \frac{1}{\Sigma_j n_j V_j} \sqrt[3]{E[(\Sigma_j n_j \tilde{V}_j - \bar{E})^3]},$$

where $\bar{E} \equiv \Sigma_j n_j E(\tilde{V}_j \mid h)$. We already know how to calculate $E(\tilde{V}_j \mid h)$ and we know the value of $\tilde{V}_j$ of each option at the end of the holding period conditional on the stock price $\tilde{S}$ at that time. The remaining problem is to calculate the expectations $E[(\Sigma_j n_j \tilde{V}_j(\tilde{S}) - \bar{E})^2]$ and $E[(\Sigma_j n_j \tilde{V}_j(\tilde{S}) - \bar{E})^3]$. Writing these expectations this way makes it clear that they are taken over a single random variable—the future stock price $\tilde{S}$, which we have assumed to have a lognormal return with parameters m_S and σ. This is a problem in numerical integration which is easily solved by computer.

Unlike the expected return, there is no clear way to annualize the volatility and skewness. With the hope of making these parameters relatively insensitive to the pure effect of the holding period, we will annualize the volatility[39] by dividing by $\sqrt{h}$ and annualize the skewness by dividing by $\sqrt[3]{h^2}$.

The portfolio summary section of Table 6-21 shows that the annualized volatility of the hedge in LMN is .167, which is, as we would expect, less than the volatility of the underlying stock. Again, as expected, the skewness of the hedge in calls is negative, while the skewness of the XYZ hedge in puts is positive.

Table 6-22 gives us some idea about how sensitive the annualized position volatility is to the length of the holding period. Neutral hedges in calls exhibit very great sensitivity.[40] For example, a neutral hedge in APR/40 calls requires the purchase of .572 shares for each written option. The position volatility rises from .01 for a one-day holding period to .18 if held unrevised to expiration. In contrast, the 1 : 1 hedges show relatively little variation in volatility as the holding period lengthens. For these, the instantaneous approximation

$$\text{Position volatility} \approx \frac{\text{position dollar delta}}{\text{position current value}}$$

is quite accurate and, for most practical purposes, we can be spared our problem in numerical integration. In the case of the APR/40 call, since $S = 40$, $C = 3.07$, $\Delta_S = 1$, and $\Delta_C = .572$, the position dollar delta is

$$(\Sigma_j n_j \Delta_j)\sigma S = (1 - .572)(.3)(.40) = 5.14$$

and the position current value is

$$\Sigma_j n_j V_j = 40 - 3.07 = 36.93.$$

As a result, the instantaneous (first-order) approximation to the position volatility is $5.14/36.93 = .14$.

---

[39] If the position return were *lognormal*, our method would be unambiguously correct for annualizing its instantaneous volatility.

[40] Despite this, computer simulation indicates that the hedge ratio which minimizes the hedge position *dollar* volatility for the options in Table 6-22 is typically very close to the option delta (that is, the neutral hedge ratio), regardless of the holding period.

REPRESENTATIVE BLACK-SCHOLES VOLATILITIES OF CALL POSITIONS: EXACT AND SECOND-ORDER APPROXIMATIONS

$m = 1.10 \qquad \sigma = \bar{\sigma} = .3 \qquad S = 40 \qquad r = 1.05$

Expiration Month

Holding Period (Days)

Position	K	JAN[a] 1	JAN 15	JAN 30	APR 1	APR 15	APR 60	APR 120	JUL 1	JUL 15	JUL 60	JUL 210
Uncovered	35	2.18 (2.18)	2.20 (2.19)	2.23 (2.19)	1.59 (1.59)	1.61 (1.60)	1.68 (1.61)	1.77 (1.63)	1.33 (1.33)	1.34 (1.33)	1.39 (1.34)	1.56 (1.38)
	40	4.42 (4.42)	4.83 (4.74)	5.30 (5.05)	2.23 (2.23)	2.30 (2.27)	2.52 (2.38)	2.82 (2.52)	1.70 (1.70)	1.74 (1.72)	1.85 (1.76)	2.23 (1.90)
	45	7.74 (7.57)	11.07 (10.34)	15.73 (12.53)	2.96 (2.96)	3.14 (3.09)	3.75 (3.46)	4.64 (3.90)	2.10 (2.10)	2.17 (2.14)	2.40 (2.26)	3.23 (2.62)
1:1 Hedge	35	.02 (.02)	.03 (.03)	.04 (.03)	.06 (.06)	.06 (.07)	.07 (.08)	.08 (.09)	.08 (.08)	.08 (.08)	.08 (.09)	.09 (.11)
	40	.14 (.15)	.15 (.16)	.16 (.17)	.14 (.14)	.14 (.14)	.15 (.16)	.15 (.17)	.14 (.14)	.14 (.14)	.14 (.15)	.15 (.17)
	45	.27 (.27)	.27 (.27)	.27 (.27)	.21 (.21)	.21 (.22)	.22 (.22)	.22 (.23)	.19 (.19)	.19 (.19)	.19 (.20)	.20 (.21)
Neutral Hedge	35	— (—)	.02 (.02)	.04 (.03)	— (—)	.03 (.03)	.06 (.06)	.09 (.09)	— (—)	.03 (.03)	.05 (.06)	.10 (.11)
	40	.03 (.03)	.12 (.13)	.18 (.18)	.01 (.02)	.06 (.06)	.12 (.13)	.18 (.18)	.01 (.01)	.04 (.05)	.09 (.10)	.19 (.18)
	45	.07 (.08)	.32 (.29)	.54 (.41)	.02 (.03)	.10 (.10)	.21 (.20)	.33 (.29)	.02 (.02)	.06 (.07)	.13 (.14)	.30 (.26)

NOTE: No adjustment is made for dividends. Approximations are in parentheses.

[a] The January options have one month to expiration; the Aprils, four months; and the Julys, seven months. r, σ, and m are expressed in annual terms.

A better (second-order) approximation takes some account of the holding period:[41]

$$\text{Position volatility} \approx \frac{\sqrt{(\text{position \$ delta})^2 + .584\,(\text{position \$ gamma})^2 \times \text{holding period}}}{\text{position current value}}$$

The neutral hedge in APR/40 calls has a position dollar delta of

$$(\Sigma_j n_j \Delta_j)\sigma S = [(.572 \times 1) - (1 \times .572)](.3)(40) = 0,$$

as it must have to be neutral. Since $\Gamma_S = 0$ and $\Gamma_C = .0567$, its position dollar gamma is

$$(\Sigma_j n_j \Gamma_j)\sigma^2 S^2 = (0 - .0567)(.3^2)(40^2) = -8.16$$

and its position current value is

$$\Sigma_j n_j V_j = (.572 \times 40) - (1 \times 3.07) = 19.81.$$

Therefore, over holding period $h = 120/365 = .3288$ years, the approximate position volatility is $\sqrt{.584 \times (8.16)^2 \times .3288/19.81} = .18$. Although this method of approximation may give satisfactory results for neutral positions, it can be quite misleading for uncovered positions.

Portfolio Volatility and Skewness. Calculation of the exact volatility and skewness for a portfolio containing several stocks and options quickly becomes impractical, even on a large computer. To see what is involved,

---

[41] To derive this approximation, let $\tilde{V}$ be the uncertain value of the position at the end of holding period h, and let Δ and Γ be the current position delta and gamma. Expanding $\tilde{V}$ in a Taylor series around the current stock price S,

$$\tilde{V} = V + \Delta(\tilde{S} - S) + \tfrac{1}{2}\Gamma(\tilde{S} - S)^2 + \cdots,$$

where all terms involving time to expiration and higher-order terms involving the stock price are omitted. Taking the variance of both sides,

$$\text{Var } \tilde{V} \approx \Delta^2 \text{ Var}(\tilde{S} - S) + \tfrac{1}{4}\Gamma^2 \text{ Var}[(\tilde{S} - S)^2].$$

Since $\text{Var}(\tilde{S} - S) \approx \sigma^2 S^2 h$ and $\text{Var}[(\tilde{S} - S)^2] \approx 2\sigma^4 S^4 h^2$, then

$$\sqrt{\frac{\text{Var } \tilde{V}}{h}} \approx \sqrt{(\Delta\sigma S)^2 + .5(\Gamma\sigma^2 S^2)^2 h}.$$

Computer simulation shows this to be downward-biased for neutral positions. Changing the dollar gamma weighting coefficient from .5 to .584 tends to eliminate this bias.

consider a portfolio containing n_j units of each security j. In general,[42]

$$v = \frac{1}{h(\Sigma_j n_j V_j)} \sqrt{\Sigma_j \Sigma_k n_j n_k [E(\tilde{V}_j \tilde{V}_k | h) - E(\tilde{V}_j | h) E(\tilde{V}_k | h)]}.$$

Since we can easily estimate $E(\tilde{V}_j | h)$ for each security, the only difficulty lies in calculating $E(\tilde{V}_j \tilde{V}_k | h)$. Again, this is a problem in numerical integration, but it has the complication that the prices of two stocks, not one, may be involved. Compared to an integration over one stock price, this roughly squares the number of calculations.

We might hope that, like $E(\tilde{V}_j | h)$, we could express the expectation $E(\tilde{V}_j \tilde{V}_k | h)$ as the sum of more easily calculable terms. Indeed, some progress in this direction is possible; but even this simplification leaves a costly expression to solve by computer.[43]

---

[42] The covariance of $\tilde{V}_j$ and $\tilde{V}_k$ is $E[(\tilde{V}_j - E[\tilde{V}_j])(\tilde{V}_k - E[\tilde{V}_k])]$ which simplifies to $E(\tilde{V}_j \tilde{V}_k) - E(\tilde{V}_j)E(\tilde{V}_k)$.

[43] For the pair of calls $j = 1, 2$ with no dividends remaining until expiration, we need to calculate

$$E(\tilde{C}_1 \tilde{C}_2) = \int_{-\infty}^{\infty} \int_{-\infty}^{\infty} \Pi_{j=1}^2 [S_j e^{y_j} N(\tilde{x}_j) - K_j r^{h-t_j} N(\tilde{x}_j - \bar{\sigma}_j \sqrt{t_j - h})]$$
$$f(y_1, y_2; \mu_1, \mu_2, \sigma_1, \sigma_2, \rho_{12}) dy_1 dy_2$$

where

$$x_j \equiv \frac{\log(S_j e^{y_j} / K_j r^{h-t_j})}{\bar{\sigma}_j \sqrt{t_j - h}} + \tfrac{1}{2} \bar{\sigma}_j \sqrt{t_j - h}, \ y_j \equiv \log(\tilde{S}_j / S_j),$$

and $f(y_1, y_2)$ is a bivariate normal density function with parameters $\mu_j h \equiv E(\log \tilde{S}_j / S_j) = m_j h - \tfrac{1}{2} \sigma_j^2 h$, $\sigma_j^2 h \equiv \text{Var}(\log \tilde{S}_j / S_j)$, and ρ_{12}, the correlation between $\log(\tilde{S}_1 / S_1)$ and $\log(\tilde{S}_2 / S_2)$. Integration of successive terms yields:

$$E(\tilde{C}_1 \tilde{C}_2) = (S_1 m_1^h)(S_2 m_2^h) e^{\sigma_{12} h} N_2\left(x_1 + \frac{\sigma_{12} h}{\sigma_1^* \sqrt{t_1}}, x_2 + \frac{\sigma_{12} h}{\sigma_2^* \sqrt{t_2}}; \rho_{12}^*\right)$$
$$- (S_2 m_2^h)(K_1 r^{h-t_1}) N_2(x_1 - \sigma_1^* \sqrt{t_1} + \frac{\sigma_{12} h}{\sigma_1^* \sqrt{t_1}}, x_2; \rho_{12}^*)$$
$$- (S_1 m_1^h)(K_2 r^{h-t_2}) N_2\left(x_1, x_2 - \sigma_2^* \sqrt{t_2} + \frac{\sigma_{12} h}{\sigma_2^* \sqrt{t_2}}; \rho_{12}^*\right)$$
$$+ (K_1 r^{h-t_1})(K_2 r^{h-t_2}) N_2(x_1 - \sigma_1^* \sqrt{t_1}, x_2 - \sigma_2^* \sqrt{t_2}; \rho_{12}^*)$$

where

$$x_j \equiv \frac{\log(S_j m_j^h / K_j r^{h-t_j})}{\sigma_j^* \sqrt{t_j}} + \tfrac{1}{2} \sigma_j^* \sqrt{t_j},$$

$$\sigma_j^* \equiv \sqrt{\frac{h}{t_j} \sigma_j^2 + \left(1 - \frac{h}{t_j}\right) \bar{\sigma}_j^2}, \quad \rho_{12}^* \equiv \frac{\sigma_{12} h}{\sigma_1^* \sigma_2^* \sqrt{t_1 t_2}}, \quad \sigma_{12} \equiv \rho_{12} \sigma_1 \sigma_2.$$

$N_2(x, y; \rho)$ is the standard bivariate normal distribution function with correlation parameter ρ.

This second expression for $E(\tilde{C}_1 \tilde{C}_2)$ is easier to calculate than the first because there are well-developed routines for estimating bivariate normal probabilities. Nonetheless, we still must calculate four bivariate normal probabilities for each pair of securities in the portfolio. With just 30 securities in the portfolio, this amounts to 1,740 nonredundant calculations of bivariate normal probabilities.

For this reason, we suggest using an approximation. The general expression for portfolio volatility can be rewritten

$$v = \sqrt{\Sigma_j w_j^2 v_j^2 + \Sigma_j \Sigma_{k \neq j} w_j w_k \rho_{jk} v_j v_k},$$

where w_j is the portfolio weight of security j, v_j its annualized discrete volatility, and ρ_{jk} is the correlation between the rate of return of security j and the rate of return of security k. To make this easier to calculate, it is frequently assumed in modern portfolio theory that for every pair of different securities j and k, $\rho_{jk} = \rho_j \rho_k$ where ρ_j is the correlation of the rate of return of security j with the rate of return of the market portfolio, and ρ_k has a similar interpretation for security k.[44] This "diagonal" assumption allows us to write the portfolio volatility in terms of single summations:

$$v = \sqrt{[\Sigma_j w_j^2 (1 - \rho_j^2) v_j^2] + [\Sigma_j w_j \rho_j v_j]^2}.$$

A similar interpretation follows for portfolio skewness:

$$s = \sqrt[3]{[\Sigma_j w_j^3 (1 - \bar{\rho}_j^3) s_j^3] + [\Sigma_j w_j \bar{\rho}_j s_j]^3},$$

where

$$\bar{\rho}_j \equiv \rho_j \left(\frac{v_j}{v_M}\right)\left(\frac{s_M}{s_j}\right).$$

Here, v_M and s_M are the discrete volatility and skewness of the return of the market portfolio.[45]

In this case, as we see from Table 6-21, for the entire portfolio $m = .100$, $v = .137$, and $s = .115$.

---

[44] This assumption is motivated by the following hypothesis governing security price behavior: All securities j have random returns r_j which are linearly related to the market return by

$$r_j = a_j + b_j r_M + \varepsilon_j.$$

We define a_j and b_j as constants specific to each security, r_M and ε_j are uncorrelated, and ε_j and ε_k, for any two different securities, are uncorrelated. This divides the source of the risk of any security into two components: a single factor common to all securities, r_M, which is responsible for any correlation of returns of different securities, and a residual component, ε_j, specific only to security j.

By definition, the covariance $\mathrm{Cov}(r_j, r_M) = \rho_j v_j v_M$, and our hypothesis implies $\mathrm{Cov}(r_j, r_M) = b_j v_M^2$. Thus, $b_j = \rho_j v_j / v_M$, which is the same as the security beta. Similarly, $\mathrm{Cov}(r_j, r_k) = \rho_{jk} v_j v_k$, and our hypothesis implies $\mathrm{Cov}(r_j, r_k) = b_j b_k v_M^2$. Thus, $\rho_{jk} = b_j b_k v_M^2 / v_j v_k$. Substituting for b_j, we have $\rho_{jk} = \rho_j \rho_k$.

[45] Since we assume the return on the market portfolio is lognormal, we can calculate v_M and s_M in terms of m_M and σ_M:

$$v_M = m_M \sqrt{e^{\sigma_M^2} - 1}, \qquad s_M = m_M \sqrt[3]{(e^{\sigma_M^2} - 1)^2 (e^{\sigma_M^2} + 2)}.$$

In this case, since $m_M = 1.105$ and $\sigma_M = .18$, $v_M = .201$ and $s_M = .164$. We infer ρ_j from our previous estimate of β_j. That is, $\rho_j \approx \beta_j v_M / v_j$.

Certainty Equivalents. We can summarize the net effect of all holdings by the investor's certainty equivalent return. This depends not only on the securities held but also on the investor's degree of risk aversion. In Table 6-21, the user has set this at $b = 1.0$, which contrasts with the market $b_M = 1.3$. The last portion of the table compares the certainty equivalents of successively more complex portfolios.

The simplest strategy is to invest only in default-free bonds. In this case, $m = r = 1.05$, $v = s = 0$, and its certainty equivalent rate of return is obviously .05.

Suppose, instead, the user had invested only in the market portfolio; then, although his position would be risky ($v = v_M = .201$), its expected return ($m = m_M = 1.105$) and skewness ($s_M = .164$) more than compensate, raising the certainty equivalent rate of return to .085.

Consider the somewhat more complex strategy of dividing his investment between the market portfolio and bonds so that the instantaneous beta of this investment is the same as the instantaneous beta of the actual position. Then, since the portfolio instantaneous[46] $\beta = .50$,

$$m = r(1 - \beta) + m_M \beta = 1.05(1 - .5) + 1.105(.5) = 1.078,$$
$$v = |\beta| v_M = .5(.201) = .101,$$
$$s = \beta s_M = .5(.164) = .082.$$

and the certainty equivalent rate of return is reduced to .072. This suggests that the user may be better off borrowing (selling bonds) instead of lending (buying bonds) to push his portfolio beta closer to or greater than 1, the beta of the market portfolio.

Although this strategy can take advantage of the user's market alpha, it does not benefit from pure stock alphas. To capture this additional effect, but at the same time leave the risk comparable, we ask, What is the certainty equivalent return on a fixed portfolio of stock and bonds selected to duplicate the instantaneous properties of the actual portfolio as closely as possible? To do this, we replace each actual position with an instantaneously equivalent portfolio of bonds and the underlying stock. For example, the delta of LMN/APR/40 calls is .5. We would substitute for the actual position in LMN: $100(1 - .5) = 50$ round lots of stock, and $100(40 - 2.75) - 100(40)(1 - .5) = \$1,725$ in bonds. Had we made a similar replacement for every position, the portfolio certainty equivalent rate of return would have been .079.

While such a strategy captures benefits from stock alphas, it does not reflect the additional advantages from the relative mispricing of stock and

---

[46] The instantaneous portfolio beta is usually a good approximation of the actual beta over the holding period. In this case, they differ by .01.

options, or from portfolio skewness caused by options. These, of course, are captured in the certainty equivalent return of the actual portfolio ($m = .100$, $v = .137$, and $s = .115$), which is .090. The difference ($.090 - .079$) measures the benefit from using the options market.

Some Remaining Difficulties.   Although we will not pursue our portfolio analysis of options any further, we realize that it has not been fully satisfactory. Some things, like transactions costs, margin requirements, differential borrowing and lending rates, and taxes are relatively easy to introduce. It would be considerably more difficult to provide a good rule for choosing the best holding period. Also, while we have provided a means of deciding between candidate portfolios, we have not shown how to search efficiently for the best portfolio for an investor. We have left this problem at the stage of comparisons among certainty equivalent returns by trial and error.

6-6. EMPIRICAL EVIDENCE

In view of the strong theoretical models of option pricing and the extraordinary growth of organized option markets, as of the time of this writing surprisingly little empirical academic research has been completed on option prices. Prior to listed option trading in the United States, a few empirical tests of the put-call parity relationship, arbitrage conditions, the Black-Scholes formula, and other earlier option pricing models were done using over-the-counter data. We will not review the results of this work here since most of it either suffers from severe data deficiencies or has been outdated by more recent but still limited tests of listed option prices.

The first tests using listed option prices are found in two articles by Dan Galai.[47] Using his sample of 16,000 option/days covering the first seven months of CBOE activity, Galai calculates the rate of return, for each option for each day, of a neutral hedged position with the associated stock. In particular, if, according to the Black-Scholes formula, an option is underpriced, he buys one option and shorts a neutrally hedged fraction of the associated stock at their closing market prices. If an option is overpriced, he writes an option and buys a neutrally hedged fraction of one share at their closing market prices. Revising positions daily, Galai calculates the average dollar return for each option over his sample period. Returns are calculated before taxes, and transactions costs (both commissions and bid-ask spread) were ignored.

---

[47] See "Tests of Market Efficiency of the Chicago Board Options Exchange," *Journal of Business*, 50 (April 1977), 167–197; and "Empirical Tests of Boundary Conditions for CBOE Options," *Journal of Financial Economics*, 6 (June–September 1978), 187–211. Galai is currently a Professor of Finance at Hebrew University, Jerusalem, Israel.

The return averaged over all options was $10 per option contract per day. These results are consistent across subsamples by expiration date. Moreover, only 13 out of 201 options recorded a negative average return, and the return of each of these 13 was not significantly different (in a statistical sense) from zero. Seventy-one of the 188 options registering positive returns were statistically significant. Galai also shows that performance increased substantially when he could revise daily rather than just buy and hold until an option's expiration or the end of his sample period.

If the hedged positions, as revised daily, created risk that an investor could not easily diversify away by simultaneously holding other securities, then the high option returns might not be excessive. The returns would merely be adequate compensation for the risks borne. However, Galai shows that the nondiversifiable risk of the hedge position was virtually zero. Of course, this is precisely what we would expect from neutral hedges, where the position ratio is changed daily. For options to be efficiently priced, the hedges should then return the default-free rate of interest on the funds required to maintain them. However, the observed returns were considerably above opportunity costs.

Measurement error in data inputs is another possible explanation. Galai found that correcting the formula for dividends only served to increase the average return to $15 per option day. His results were little changed by other reasonable estimates of the interest rate and stock volatility.

However, the imposition of a 1% one-way transaction cost on day-to-day changes in option and stock positions virtually eliminated the excess returns. Even if transaction costs per day were reduced by revising the hedges less frequently, no excess profits were earned because the before-transaction-costs returns were also reduced by this strategy. Nonetheless, for Market Makers, whose transaction costs are considerably less than 1%, significant excess returns would evidently have been possible.

As a final modification, Galai assumes a single-day lag (longer on weekends) between the time of the decision to form a hedge and the actual execution of the hedge. Galai argues that it may be misleading to suppose an investor can trade at the same prices he uses to decide whether to initiate the trade. There is a lag between decision and execution. Working with daily closing prices, Galai set the lag at one day. This more strenuous test of the Black-Scholes formula reduced average dollar returns per option day to $5 before transaction costs. Of the 37 options with negative returns, none were statistically significant, and of the 164 options with positive returns, 12 were statistically significant. Correcting the Black-Scholes formula for dividends made little difference in these results.

Galai also tests certain spreading strategies which confirm his hedging results. He concludes:

To what extent the hedge return is going to be affected by the accuracy of closing prices is an empirical question that will be left for future research. Until new results are available and ignoring transaction costs and taxes, I have to conclude that, with respect to the closing prices and for the period investigated and assuming the validity of the Black-Scholes model, the CBOE displayed opportunities to make above-normal dollar returns. [p. 189]

This conclusion is carefully and justifiably hedged. Even for Market Makers whose apparent transaction costs are quite small, there are the hidden costs of the price of a seat, monthly dues to the exchange, and the opportunity cost of lost time. However, substantially less capital is required for Market Makers than for the public to assume the same option positions.

More recent empirical tests have appeared in three articles by Robert Trippi, by Donald Chiras and Steven Manaster, and by James MacBeth and Larry Merville.[48] All three adopt a similar testing methodology. For each class of options in the sample, the market price of each option is compared to its value based on a weighted average implicit standard deviation for the class, using the Black-Scholes formula. In the first paper, based on weekly closing prices from August, 1974, through March, 1975, an option is considered purchased (sold) if its market price is 15% less (more) than its value. In the second paper, using monthly data from June, 1973, through April, 1975, an option is considered purchased (sold) if its market price is 10% less (more) than its value. Both studies conclude that above average abnormal returns were available in the options market.

The third article uses daily closing prices for the year 1976 for six very active option classes. Rather than follow the results of a trading strategy, MacBeth and Merville attempt to identify common characteristics of those options which are overpriced relative to their weighted average implicit standard deviations, and those which are underpriced. For their sample, they find out-of-the-money options tend to be underpriced and in-the-money options tend to be overpriced. To put it another way, relative to their market prices, the Black-Scholes formula overvalues out-of-the-money options and undervalues in-the-money options. The authors note that this finding is inconsistent with market folklore, particularly for out-of-the-money options. Indeed it is quite possible that their results are an artifact of a small sample of options and a short time period covered.

This work is only the beginning of a series of empirical studies about to be published on listed option prices. These will attempt to provide indi-

---

[48] See their respective articles, "A Test of Option Market Efficiency Using a Random-Walk Valuation Model," *Journal of Economics and Business*, 29 (Winter 1977), 93–98; "The Information Content of Option Prices and a Test of Market Efficiency," *Journal of Financial Economics*, 6 (June–September 1978), 213–234; "An Empirical Examination of the Black-Scholes Call Option Pricing Model," *Journal of Finance*, 34 (December 1979), 1173–1186.

vidual tests of the three hypotheses that Galai tested jointly: the mathematical structure of the Black-Scholes formula, the methodology for measurement of its inputs (particularly volatility), and the efficiency of the options market in pricing options. Moreover, several alternative formulas to be developed in Chapter 7 are also being examined.

Galai's principal caveat—the questionable accuracy of daily closing prices—is critical. In contrast to stock, where empirical research often makes do with monthly—or, at best, weekly—prices, use of even daily prices for options poses several significant difficulties. First, since an option's value depends on the contemporaneous price of its underlying stock, it is very important to know the stock price at the time of the closing option transaction. However, as we have already emphasized, since the stock and option often close at different times, the stock close, in many cases, is an inadequate approximation of the stock price at the time of the option close. Second, knowing only the option close, we cannot tell whether the close is at the bid, at the ask, or in between, so we cannot actually know at what price options could have been bought or sold. There remains a band of uncertainty around the close equal to twice the spread, and the magnitude of the spread—though usually within one-fourth—is also uncertain. In contrast to stock, this is particularly important for options, since the spread is apt to be a relatively large percentage of the option price. Third, with only closing prices, we have no information about the depth of the market at that price—how many contracts could have been bought or sold at that price. Fourth, for certain other reasons relating to Market Maker behavior, closing prices may not be representative of the actual trades that could have been made near the end of the day. Fifth, because the underlying conditions that determine an option's value change over time, efficient statistical procedures necessitate use of a large sample of data over small periods of time. For many purposes, daily data do not occur with sufficient frequency.[49]

There are also a number of restrictions on realistic trading opportunities that have not been fully appreciated in empirical studies. For example, the short sale up-tick rule prohibits short sales immediately following a down-tick in the stock. For option strategies requiring short selling, it may be that excess profits can only be demonstrated during periods where the assumed short sales could not have been executed. Care must also be taken that opening transactions in restricted options have not been assumed.[50] In hedging or spreading tests, it must be remembered that

---

[49] Realizing the problems inherent in daily data, Galai used a small sample of CBOE transactions for his tests of general arbitrage conditions. Again he discovers some instances during the day when boundary violations appear of sufficient magnitude to provide opportunities for riskless arbitrage.

[50] Prior to October 31, 1980, opening transactions for public customers were prohibited in options which were both $5.00 out-of-the-money and priced less than $0.50.

it is either impossible or impractical to initiate both sides of the position simultaneously. In practice, even a Market Maker, who tries to maintain neutral spreads, must "leg" into a position one side at a time, exposing himself to interim adverse stock price movements.

These trading restrictions, as well as problems of reliability of reported stock and option prices, are critically damaging to existing empirical tests of options market efficiency. That is not to say that the market is therefore efficient, but rather that the existing empirical evidence is inconclusive. However, in a promising development for future research, the CBOE has recently taken the unprecedented step of making transaction data available for academic research. Dating from August 1976, the exchange has virtually complete records in computer-readable form of all reported CBOE transactions. In particular, for each transaction, the records provide the option identification (underlying stock, type, series), date, time of day, number of contracts traded, price of contract, and the underlying stock price at the time the option transaction is recorded. In addition, for each revision in the bid-ask spread (that is, market quote) during the day, the records provide the option identification, date, time of day, and the new bid-ask quote[51] The availability of these data represents an invaluable contribution to academic work in finance and should permit virtually definitive studies of several questions relating to options markets.

---

[51] This is the CBOE's MDR data base described in Section 3-4. For obvious reasons, the identification symbols of the floor traders were excised before release of the data. To our knowledge, no major U.S. securities exchange has ever released such an extensive and detailed data base, including bid-ask quotes, for open academic investigation. Moreover, because of the data-entry procedures described in Section 3-3, the data are of exceptionally high quality.

APPENDIX 6A
Valuation with Programmable Calculators

One program is provided for programmable pocket calculators. Although it is written specifically for the HP-67, its program steps can be converted for other calculators with sufficient memory.

Program Description

Program Title Black-Scholes European Option Values and Deltas	
Name Robert Geske	**Date** 6/30/78
Address Graduate School of Management, University of California	
City Los Angeles	**State** California **Zip Code** 90024

Program Description, Equations, Variables, etc. This program calculates Black-Scholes European put and call values and deltas by using the Black-Scholes Formula for calls, the put-call parity relationship, and a three-term polynomial approximation to the normal distribution function. No adjustment is made for cash dividends, although the user can make a European correction by inputting, in place of the stock price, the stock price minus the present value of the cash dividends prior to the expiration of the option. Typical execution time is 10 seconds, and output is accurate to the penny.

Equations used are:

(1) Black-Scholes call formula:

$$C = SN(v) - Kr^{-t}N(v - \sigma\sqrt{t}), \text{ where } v = \frac{\log(S/Kr^{-t})}{\sigma\sqrt{t}} + \frac{1}{2}\sigma\sqrt{t}$$

(2) Put-call parity relationship: $P = C - S + Kr^{-t}$

(3) Polynomial approximation to the normal distribution

$$N(z) = 1 - \frac{1}{\sqrt{2\pi}} e^{-z^2/2}(b_1k + b_2k^2 + b_3k^3), \text{ where } k = \frac{1}{1 + pz}$$

$$b_1 \equiv .4361836, \quad b_2 \equiv -.1201676, \quad b_3 \equiv .9372980, \quad p \equiv .33267$$

Operating Limits and Warnings

User Instructions

Black-Scholes European Option Values and Deltas

| 1 | stock price S | striking price K | time to expiration t | 1 + interest rate r | volatility σ | 2 |

STEP	INSTRUCTIONS	INPUT DATA/UNITS	KEYS		OUTPUT DATA/UNITS
1	Load program on/from side 1				
2	Load data constants on/from side 2	.4361836	sto	01	
	used for polynomial approximation	.1201676	sto	02	
	of normal distribution function	.937298	sto	03	
		.33267	sto	04	
3	Interchange primary/secondary registers		f	p⩾s	
4	Enter: stock price	S	sto	A	
5	Enter: striking price (negative for puts)	K	sto	B	
6	Enter: time to expiration	t	sto	C	
7	Enter: one plus interest rate	r	sto	D	
8	Enter: volatility	σ	sto	E	
9	Press A (for call or put value)		a		value
10	Press R/S (for call or put delta)		r/s		delta
	Δ and (C or P) can be recalled				
	from registers 7 and 8, respectively				
	For a new option change the appropriate				
	inputs (steps 4-8) and proceed to step 9.				
	The only inputs which must be entered				
	are those which differ from the previous				
	case.				
	Example:				
	Load side 1 (program) and side 2 (data)				
	Interchange primary/secondary registers		f	p⩾s	
	Enter: stock price	40	sto	A	
	Enter: striking price	40/-40	sto	B	
	Enter: time to expiration	.333	sto	C	
	Enter: 1 plus interest rate	1.05	sto	D	
	Enter: volatility	.3	sto	E	
	Press A		a		3.07/2.42
	Press R/S		r/s		.57/-.43

STEP	KEY ENTRY	KEY CODE	COMMENTS	STEP	KEY ENTRY	KEY CODE	COMMENTS
001	31 25 11	f lbl a			71	x	
	34 12	rcl b			34 02	rcl 2	
	35 64	h abs			61	+	
	34 14	rcl d		060	34 09	rcl 9	
	34 13	rcl c			71	x	
	42	chs			34 01	rcl 1	
	35 63	h y^x			61	+	
	71	x			34 09	rcl 9	
	33 06	sto 6			71	x	
010	34 11	rcl a			34 07	rcl 7	
	35 52	h x≷y			32 54	q x^2	
	81	÷			02	2	
	31 52	f ln			81	÷	
	34 15	rcl e		070	42	chs	
	34 13	rcl c			32 52	q e^x	
	31 54	f √x			35 73	h π	
	71	x			02	2	
	33 00	sto 0			71	x	
	81	÷			31 54	f √x	
020	34 00	rcl 0			81	÷	
	02	2			71	x	
	81	÷			34 05	rcl 5	
	61	+			31 42	f p≷s	
	33 09	sto 9		080	31 71	f x<0	
	31 22 01	f gsb 1			22 03	gto 3	
	33 07	sto 7			35 52	h x≷y	
	34 11	rcl a			01	1	
	71	x			35 52	h x≷y	
	33 08	sto 8			51	-	
030	34 09	rcl 9			35 22	h rtn	
	34 00	rcl 0			31 25 03	f lbl 3	
	51	-			35 52	h x≷y	
	31 22 01	f gsb 1			35 22	h rtn	
	34 06	rcl 6		090	31 25 02	f lbl 2	
	71	x			34 11	rcl a	
	42	chs			33 51 08	sto - 8	
	33 61 08	sto + 8			34 06	rcl 6	
	34 12	rcl b			33 61 08	sto + 8	
	31 71	f x<0			01	1	
040	31 22 02	f gsb 2			33 51 07	sto - 7	
	34 08	rcl 8			35 22	h rtn	
	84	r/s					
	34 07	rcl 7		100			
	35 22	h rtn					
	31 25 01	f lbl 1					
	31 42	f p≷s					
	33 05	sto 5					
	35 64	h abs					
	33 07	sto 7					
050	34 04	rcl 4					
	71	x					
	01	1					
	61	+					
	35 62	h 1/x		110			
	33 09	sto 9					
	34 03	rcl 3					

REGISTERS									
0 $\sigma\sqrt{t}$	1	2	3	4	5	6 Kr^{-t}	7 $N(v)$	8 C, P	9 v
S0	S1 b_1	S2 b_2	S3 b_3	S4 p	S5 z	S6	S7 $|z|$	S8	S9 k
A S	B K	C t	D r	E σ	I				

APPENDIX 6B

Stocks with Exchange-Traded Options

Company Name (Ticker Symbol)	Historical Volatility[b] 1/1/80– 1/1/84	Historical Beta[b] 1/1/80– 1/1/84	Market Weight[b] 1/1/80– 1/1/84	Industry Group	Exchange[c]	Expiration Cycle[d]
Abbott Labs (ABT)	.26	.89	.35	Health Care/Hosptl. Supp.	PH	2
Advanced Micro Devices (AMD)	.55	2.15	.11	Electronics	P	1
Aetna Life & Casualty (AET)	.26	.98	.23	Insurance	A	1
Air Products & Chemicals (APD)	.31	1.05	.09	Chemicals (specialized)	PH	3
Alcan Aluminum (AL)	.31	1.26	.24	Aluminum	A	3
Allied Corp. (ALD)	.30	1.17	.19	Chemicals (diversified)	PH	1
Allis-Chalmers (AH)	.37	.97	.01	Machinery	PH	1
Aluminum Co. of America (AA)	.31	1.01	.23	Aluminum	C	1
Amax (AMX)	.48	1.38	.10	Metals & Mining	A	3
Amdahl (AMH)	.55	2.18	.05	Computers/Data Processing	C	2
Amerada-Hess (AHC)	.45	1.61	.15	Petroleum	PH	2
American Brands (AMB)	.21	.58	.21	Multi-industry	A	3
American Broadcasting (ABC)	.30	.95	.10	Broadcasting	P	2
American Can (AC)	.26	.69	.06	Packaging & Containers	A	2
American Cyanamid (ACY)	.36	1.04	.16	Chemicals (specialized)	A	1
American Electric Power (AEP)	.17	.48	.19	Electric Utility	C	2
American Express (AXP)	.33	1.33	.41	Financial Services	A, C	1
American Home Products (AHP)	.22	.74	.49	Drugs	A	1
American Hospital Supply (AHS)	.26	.97	.19	Health Care/Hosptl. Supp.	C	2
American Medical International (AMI)	.36	1.25	.07	Medical Services	P	3
American Tel. & Tel. (T)	.17	.58	3.75	Telecommunications	C	1
AMF, Inc. (AMF)	.36	1.18	.03	Recreation	A	2
AMP, Inc. (AMP)	.27	.98	.26	Electronics	C	2
AMR Corp. (AMR)	.48	1.52	.11	Airline	A	2

Company				Industry		
Anacomp (AAC)	.58	1.31	.01	Computers/Data Processing	PH	1
Anheuser-Busch (BUD)	.24	.73	.19	Beverages	PH	3
Apache (APA)	.48	1.58	.02	Petroleum Producing	C	3
Archer Daniels Midland (ADM)	.38	1.13	.11	Food Processing	PH	3
Armco (AS)	.31	.89	.09	Steel	PH	2
ASA Ltd. (ASA)	.43	1.09	.03	Investment Company	A	2
Asarco (AR)	.46	1.52	.05	Metals & Mining	A	3
Ashland Oil (ASH)	.34	.78	.05	Petroleum (integrated)	PH	1
Atlantic Richfield (ARC)	.35	1.52	.68	Petroleum (integrated)	C	1
Automatic Data Processing (AUD)	.31	.93	.08	Data Processing	PH	2
Avco (AV)	.38	1.49	.05	Financial Services	A	3
Avnet (AVT)	.35	1.32	.10	Electronics	A	2
Avon Products (AVP)	.27	.84	.12	Toiletries/Cosmetics	C	1
Baker International (BKO)	.39	1.58	.08	Machinery	P	3
Baldwin-United (BDW)	.66	1.15	.01	Insurance/Financial Services	P	1
Bally Manufacturing (BLY)	.42	1.28	.03	Hotels/Gaming	A,C	2
Bankamerica (BAC)	.29	.99	.20	Banking	C	1
Bard (C.R.) (BCR)	.40	1.17	.03	Health Care/Hosptl. Supp.	PH	1
Bausch & Lomb (BOL)	.32	.91	.04	Health Care/Hosptl. Supp.	A	1
Baxter Travenol Labs (BAX)	.27	.92	.21	Health Care/Hosptl. Supp.	C	2
Beatrice Foods (BRY)	.24	.69	.20	Food Processing	A	3
Becton Dickinson (BDX)	.24	.69	.05	Health Care/Hosptl. Supp.	PH	3
Bethlehem Steel (BS)	.31	1.01	.08	Steel (integrated)	C	1
Beverly Enterprises (BEV)	.44	1.24	.04	Medical Services	P	3
Black & Decker Manufacturing (BDK)	.31	.81	.08	Machine Tools	C	2
Blue Bell (BBL)	.27	.59	.03	Apparel	PH	1
Boeing (BA)	.35	1.25	.27	Aerospace	C	2
Boise Cascade (BCC)	.32	1.08	.07	Paper & Forest Products	C	2
Bristol-Myers (BMY)	.24	.92	.36	Drugs/Toiletries/Cosmetics	C	3
Browning-Ferris Industries (BFI)	.36	1.17	.09	Industrial Services	A	3
Brunswick (BC)	.40	1.14	.04	Recreation	C	3
Bucyrus-Erie (BY)	.37	.94	.02	Machinery (const. & mining)	A	3
Burlington Northern (BNI)	.34	1.44	.23	Railroad/Resources	C	1

(continued)

Table notes *a–h* appear on page 358.

APPENDIX 6B (continued)

Company Name (Ticker Symbol)	Historical Volatility[b] 1/1/80– 1/1/84	Historical Beta[b] 1/1/80– 1/1/84	Market Weight[b] 1/1/80– 1/1/84	Industry Group	Exchange[c]	Expiration Cycle[d]
Burroughs (BGH)	.31	1.15	.14	Computers/Data Processing	A, C	1
Campbell Red Lake (CRK)	.51	1.36	.08	Gold	PH	1
Capital Cities Comm. (CCB)	.25	.78	.12	Broadcasting/Publishing	C	2
Caterpillar Tractor (CAT)	.27	.90	.28	Machinery (const. & mining)	A	2
CBS Inc. (CBS)	.25	.75	.12	Broadcasting	C	2
Celanese (CZ)	.23	.69	.07	Chemicals (diversified)	C	3
Cessna Aircraft (CEA)	.43	1.18	.03	Aerospace	C	2
Champion International (CHA)	.33	1.10	.10	Paper & Forest Products	C	3
Charter (CHR)	.54	1.32	.01	Petroleum (integrated)	PH	3
Chase Manhatten (CMB)	.26	.87	.10	Banking	A	3
Chicago and North Western Trans. (CNW)	.59	1.35	.04	Railroad	C	1
Church's Fried Chicken (CHU)	.33	.76	.03	Restaurants	PH	3
CIGNA Corp. (CI)[e]	.32	1.12	.20	Insurance (diversified)	C	1
Cincinnati Milacron (CMZ)	.36	.96	.05	Machine Tools	PH	2
Citicorp (FNC)	.32	1.24	.29	Banking	C	1
City Investing (CNV)	.35	1.01	.09	Multi-industry	PH	1
Clorox (CLX)	.35	.92	.04	Household Products	PH	1
Coastal Corp. (CGP)	.50	1.71	.04	Petroleum (integrated)	A, C	3
Coca-Cola (KO)	.25	.82	.46	Beverages	C	2
Coleco (CLO)	.66	1.43	.02	Toys & School Supplies	PH	1
Colgate-Palmolive (CL)	.29	.85	.11	Household Products	C	2
Colt Industries (COT)	.38	.76	.08	Steel (specialty)	PH	2
Combustion Engineering (CSP)	.32	1.05	.07	Machinery (specialty)	P	3
Comdisco (CDO)	.55	1.50	.03	Financial Services	P	1
Commodore International (CBU)	.59	1.81	.08	Computers/Data Processing	PH	2
Commonwealth Edison (CWE)	.18	.46	.27	Electric Utility	C	2
Communication Satellite (CQ)	.33	1.02	.04	Telecommunications	PH	1
Community Psych. Center (CMY)	.38	1.20	.04	Health Care/Hosptl. Supp.	PH	1
Computer Sciences (CSC)	.43	1.19	.02	Computers/Data Processing	C	3

Computervision (CVN)	.50	1.94	Computers/Data Processing	PH	2
Consol. Edison (ED)	.19	.54	Electric Utility	A	2
Continental Illinois (CIL)	.31	.85	Banking	C	2
Continental Telecom (CTC)	.23	.56	Telecommunications	A	1
Control Data (CDA)	.37	1.68	Computers/Data Processing	C	2
Cooper Industries (CBE)	.33	1.01	Machinery (specialty)	A	1
Corning Glass Works (GLW)	.26	.87	Electrical Equipment	C	3
Cray Research (CYR)	.50	1.84	Computers/Data Processing	P	3
Crown Zellerbach (ZB)	.33	1.04	Paper & Forest Products	A	1
CSX (CSX)^e	.29	1.08	Railroad	P	2
Cullinet Software (CUL)	.51	1.64	Computers/Data Processing	C	1
Dart & Kraft (DKI)^e	.20	.67	Food Processing	A	1
Data General (DGN)	.46	1.60	Computers/Data Processing	P	3
Datapoint (DPT)	.55	1.51	Computers/Data Processing	C	2
Dataproducts (DPC)	.48	1.62	Computers/Data Processing	P	1
Dayton-Hudson (DH)	.27	.80	Retail Stores	P	1
Deere (DE)	.29	1.01	Agricultural Equipment	A	3
Delta Airlines (DAL)	.35	1.24	Airline	C	1
Denny's (DEN)	.35	.96	Restaurants	P	3
Diamond Shamrock (DIA)	.38	1.15	Chemicals (diversified)	P	1
Diebold (DBD)	.32	.94	Office Services	C	2
Digital Equipment (DEC)	.35	1.43	Computers/Data Processing	A, C	1
Disney (Walt) Productions (DIS)	.29	.85	Entertainment	A, C	1
Dome Mines (DM)	.56	1.64	Gold	PH	2
Dominion Resources (D)	.22	.40	Electric Utility	PH	1
Donaldson Lufkin (DLJ)	.50	1.82	Securities Brokerage	PH	3
Dorchester Gas (DGS)	.53	1.60	Petroleum (integrated)	P	2
Dow Chemical (DOW)	.32	1.32	Chemicals (diversified)	C	3
Dresser Industries (DI)	.37	1.39	Oilfield Services	PH	1
Dr Pepper (DOC)	.36	.81	Beverages	A	2
Duke Power (DUK)	.20	.45	Electric Utility	PH	1
Du Pont (DD)	.28	1.15	Chemicals (diversified)	A, C	1
Eastern Gas & Fuel (EFU)	.37	1.15	Coal	PH	1

(continued)

Table notes *a–h* appear on page 358.

APPENDIX 6B (continued)

Company Name (Ticker Symbol)	Historical Volatility[b] 1/1/80–1/1/84	Historical Beta[b] 1/1/80–1/1/84	Market Weight[b] 1/1/80–1/1/84	Industry Group	Exchange[c]	Expiration Cycle[d]
Eastman Kodak (EK)	.25	.97	.80	Photographic Equipment	C	1
Eckerd (Jack) (ECK)	.33	.83	.07	Retail Stores (specialty)	C	1
Edwards, A.G. (AGE)	.44	1.69	.02	Securities Brokerage	C	2
EG & G, Inc. (EGG)	.36	1.23	.06	Precision Instruments	PH	3
Electronic Data Systems (EDS)	.35	1.08	.12	Office Equipment	PH	3
Emerson Electric (EMR)	.22	.68	.29	Electrical Equipment	A	3
Emery Air Freight (EAF)	.41	1.01	.03	Air Freight	PH	3
Engelhard (EC)[e]	.36	.96	.07	Metals & Mining	C	1
ENSERCH Corp. (ENS)	.31	.89	.08	Natural Gas	P	2
Esmark (ESM)	.28	.74	.11	Food Processing	C	3
E-Systems (ESY)	.37	1.01	.06	Aerospace	P	2
Exxon (XON)	.21	.94	2.03	Petroleum	C	1
Federal Express (FDX)	.39	1.49	.13	Air Freight	C	1
Fin'l. Corp. of America (FIN)	.53	1.47	.06	Savings & Loan	PH	3
Firestone Tire (FIR)	.33	.89	.07	Tire & Rubber	A	2
First Boston (FBC)	.48	1.87	.03	Securities Brokerage	C	3
First Chicago (FNB)	.34	1.02	.07	Banking	C	1
First Mississippi (FRM)	.50	1.63	.02	Chemicals (diversified)	A	2
Fleetwood Enterprises (FLE)	.45	1.43	.04	Recreation	A	2
Flow General (FGN)	.61	1.75	.01	Health Care/Hosptl. Supp.	A	2
Fluor (FLR)	.39	1.49	.09	Building (construction)	C	1
Ford Motor (F)	.36	1.28	.49	Autos & Trucks	C	3
Foster Wheeler (FWC)	.42	1.28	.03	Machinery (specialty)	P	1
Freeport McMoRan (FTX)[e]	.49	1.91	.09	Metals & Mining	C	3
GAF Corp. (GAF)	.45	.99	.02	Multi-industry	PH	1
GCA Corp. (GCA)	.58	2.02	.03	Precision Instruments	A	2
General Dynamics (GD)	.37	1.33	.20	Aerospace	C	2
General Electric (GE)	.22	1.01	1.69	Electrical Equipment	C	3
General Foods (GF)	.21	.64	.17	Food Processing	C	2

Company				Industry		
General Instrument (GRL)	.40	1.54	.06	Electronics	PH	3
General Motors (GM)	.28	1.12	1.48	Autos & Trucks	C	3
Genuine Parts (GPC)	.28	.67	.10	Auto Parts	P	2
GEO International (GX)e	.50	1.53	.01	Oilfield Services	A	2
Georgia-Pacific (GP)	.36	1.43	.16	Paper & Forest Products	PH	1
Getty Oil (GET)	.36	1.37	.49	Petroleum (integrated)	PH	3
Gillette (GS)	.26	.77	.09	Toiletries/Cosmetics	A	3
Global Marine (GLM)	.51	1.81	.02	Oilfield Drilling	A	3
Golden Nugget (GNG)	.48	1.32	.03	Hotels/Gaming	A	2
Goodyear Tire & Rubber (GT)	.29	.93	.20	Tire & Rubber	A	1
Gould (GLD)	.35	.94	.08	Electrical Equipment	A	1
Grace (W. R.) (GRA)	.27	.98	.14	Chemicals (diversified)	C	2
Great Western Financial (GWF)	.44	1.44	.05	Savings & Loan	C	1
Greyhound (G)	.29	.92	.08	Multi-industry	C	1
GTE Corp. (GTE)	.22	.76	.53	Telecommunications	A	3
Gulf & Western Industries (GW)	.31	1.05	.15	Multi-industry	C	3
Gulf Canada (GOC)	.46	1.56	.20	Petroleum (integrated)	PH	2
Gulf Oil (GO)	.34	1.27	.45	Petroleum (integrated)	A	1
Hall, Frank B. (FBH)	.38	.48	.02	Insurance	A	2
Halliburton (HAL)	.38	1.70	.30	Oilfield Drilling	C	1
Harris (HRS)	.33	1.09	.10	Electronics	C	2
Hecla Mining (HL)	.63	1.64	.02	Metals & Mining	A	3
Hercules (HPC)	.30	.96	.12	Chemicals (diversified)	A	3
Hewlett-Packard (HWP)	.33	1.45	.67	Precision Instruments	C	2
Hilton Hotels (HLT)	.31	1.03	.10	Hotels/Gaming	P	2
Hitachi (HIT)	.37	.58	.64	Multi-industry	C	1
Holiday Inns (HIA)	.35	1.32	.11	Hotels/Gaming	C	2
Homestake Mining (HM)	.49	1.28	.07	Gold	C	1
Honeywell (HON)	.31	1.24	.19	Computers/Data Processing	C	2
Hospital Corporation of America (HCA)	.33	1.11	.22	Medical Services	P	1
Household International (HI)	.28	.83	.10	Financial Services	A	1
Houston Natural Gas (HNG)	.27	.79	.11	Natural Gas	P	1
Hughes Tool (HT)	.41	1.79	.07	Machinery (drilling)	C	3

(continued)

Table notes a–h appear on page 358.

351

APPENDIX 6B (continued)

Company Name (Ticker Symbol)	Historical Volatility[b] 1/1/80– 1/1/84	Historical Beta[b] 1/1/80– 1/1/84	Market Weight[b] 1/1/80– 1/1/84	Industry Group	Exchange[c]	Expiration Cycle[d]
Humana (HUM)	.35	1.24	.13	Medical Services	C	2
Hutton (E. F.) Group (EFH)	.48	2.10	.06	Securities Brokerage	A	1
Inexco Oil (INX)	.46	1.65	.02	Petroleum Producing	PH	2
International Business Machines (IBM)	.24	1.12	4.71	Computers/Data Processing	C	1
International Flavors & Fragrances (IFF)	.33	.87	.06	Chemicals (specialized)	C	2
International Minerals (IGL)	.29	.84	.07	Chemicals (specialized)	C	1
International Paper (IP)	.28	1.09	.19	Paper & Forest Products	C	1
ITT Corp. (ITT)	.24	.91	.39	Multi-industry	C	3
Johnson & Johnson (JNJ)	.26	.95	.49	Health Care/Hosptl. Supp.	C	1
Joy Manufacturing (JOY)	.31	.88	.04	Machinery (const. & mining)	PH	2
K-Mart (KM)	.33	1.14	.26	Retail Stores	C	3
Kaneb Services (KAB)	.42	1.39	.02	Coal, Oilfield Drilling	A	3
Kerr-McGee (KMG)	.40	1.19	.10	Petroleum (integrated)	C	1
Key Pharmaceuticals (KPH)	.50	1.25	.04	Drugs	P	3
Lear Siegler (LSI)	.35	1.19	.05	Aerospace	PH	3
Lehman (LEM)	.22	.53	.05	Investment Company	PH	2
Levi Strauss (LVI)	.33	.93	.11	Apparel	P	1
Lifemark (LMK)	.42	1.26	.05	Medical Services	C	3
Lilly, Eli (LLY)	.23	.73	.27	Drugs	C	1
Litton Industries (LIT)	.33	1.42	.19	Multi-industry	C	3
Lockheed (LK)	.43	1.47	.16	Aerospace	P	3
Loral (LOR)	.38	1.05	.04	Electronics	C	1
Louisiana Land & Expl. (LLX)	.43	1.58	.05	Petroleum Producing	PH	2
Louisiana-Pacific (LPX)	.36	1.22	.05	Paper & Forest Products	A	2
LTV Corp. (LTV)	.49	1.76	.06	Steel (integrated)	A	3
M/A-COM Inc. (MAI)	.49	1.70	.05	Precision Instruments	A	2
Mapco (MDA)	.33	.93	.04	Coal	P	1
Marriott (MHS)	.28	.90	.12	Hotels/Gaming	PH	1
Martin Marietta (ML)	.34	.83	.08	Aerospace	PH	3

Company				Industry		
Mary Kay Cosmetics (MKY)	.48	1.32	.03	Toiletries/Cosmetics	C	3
Mattel (MAT)	.60	1.55	.01	Toys & School Supplies	A	2
MCA Inc. (MCA)	.29	.81	.13	Entertainment	PH	2
McDermott (MDR)	.38	1.27	.06	Oilfield Services	PH	2
McDonald's (MCD)	.26	.94	.27	Restaurants	C	3
McDonnell Douglas (MD)	.36	1.22	.15	Aerospace	P	2
Medtronic (MDT)	.36	.94	.04	Health Care/Hosptl. Supp.	C	2
Merck (MRK)	.23	.80	.42	Drugs	C	1
Merrill Lynch (MER)	.44	2.14	.18	Securities Brokerage	A, C	1
Mesa Petroleum (MSA)	.48	1.58	.06	Petroleum Producing	A	1
Metromedia (MET)	.34	.53	.06	Broadcasting	A	2
MGM/UA Entertainment (MGM)e	.52	1.39	.05	Entertainment	P	2
Middle South Utilities (MSU)	.22	.45	.14	Electric Utility	C	3
Minnesota Mining & Manufacturing (MMM)	.23	.96	.61	Multi-industry	C	1
Mitchell Energy & Development (MND)	.51	1.59	.07	Petroleum (integrated)	P	3
Mitel (MLT)e	.52	1.37	.03	Telecommunications	A	3
Mobil (MOB)	.34	1.32	.74	Petroleum (integrated)	C	2
Mohawk Data Sciences (MDS)	.52	1.99	.01	Computers/Data Processing	P	3
Monsanto (MTC)	.26	.88	.27	Chemicals (diversified)	C	1
Morgan (J. P.) (JPM)	.20	.70	.17	Banking	PH	3
Motorola (MOT)	.33	1.42	.34	Electronics	A	1
Murphy Oil (MUR)	.45	1.62	.07	Petroleum (integrated)	P	2
National Distillers (DR)	.25	.77	.06	Chemicals (specialized)	A	2
National Medical Care (NMD)	.54	1.22	.02	Medical Services	PH	3
National Medical Enterp. (NME)	.41	1.53	.10	Medical Services	A	2
National Patent Dev. (NPD)	.58	1.43	.02	Health Care/Hosptl. Supp.	P	3
National Semiconductor (NSM)	.52	2.09	.08	Electronics	A, C	2
NCR Corp. (NCR)	.31	1.25	.22	Computers/Data Processing	C	3
Newmont Mining (NEM)	.40	1.30	.10	Metals & Mining	PH	3
NL Ind. (NL)	.43	1.73	.06	Oilfield Services	PH	2
Noble Affiliates (NBL)	.46	1.64	.05	Oilfield Drilling	A	2
Norfolk Southern (NSC)	.24	.74	.25	Railroad	C	3

(continued)

Table notes a–h appear on page 358.

APPENDIX 6B (continued)

Company Name (Ticker Symbol)	Historical Volatility[b] 1/1/80– 1/1/84	Historical Beta[b] 1/1/80– 1/1/84	Market Weight[b] 1/1/80– 1/1/84	Industry Group	Exchange[c]	Expiration Cycle[d]
Northern Telecom (NT)	.32	1.03	.28	Telecommunications	C	3
Northrop (NOC)	.34	.93	.08	Aerospace	C	2
Northwest Airlines (NWA)	.38	1.24	.06	Airline	C	1
Northwest Industries (NWT)	.36	.91	.06	Multi-industry	C	3
Novo Industries (NVO)[e]	.32	1.13	.08	Drugs	A	2
Oak Industries (OAK)	.50	1.19	.01	Electronics; Cable TV	PH	1
Occidental Petroleum (OXY)	.31	1.24	.15	Petroleum (integrated)	C	2
Ocean Drilling & Expl. (ODR)	.43	1.42	.09	Oilfield Drilling	A	2
Owens-Corning (OCF)	.36	1.02	.07	Building (materials)	PH	3
Owens-Illinois (OI)	.30	.87	.07	Packaging & Containers	C	3
Paine-Webber (PWJ)	.55	2.11	.03	Securities Brokerage	C	1
Paradyne (PDN)	.57	1.84	.02	Data Processing	C	3
Parker Drilling (PKD)	.47	1.63	.02	Oilfield Drilling	P	3
Penn Central (PC)	.46	1.40	.07	Multi-industry	PH	3
Penney (J. C.) (JCP)	.31	1.01	.26	Retail Stores	A	2
Pennzoil (PZL)	.44	1.48	.11	Petroleum (integrated)	C	1
Pepsico (PEP)	.27	.83	.23	Beverages	C	1
Perkin-Elmer (PKN)	.42	1.53	.08	Precision Instruments	P	3
Petrolane (PTO)	.42	1.06	.05	Oilfield Services	PH	1
Pfizer (PFE)	.28	.99	.36	Drugs; Health Care	A	3
Phelps Dodge (PD)	.38	1.14	.04	Copper	A	1
Phibro-Salomon (PSB)	.45	1.80	.29	Commodities Trading; Financial Serv.	PH	1
Philip Morris (MO)	.26	.94	.57	Beverages; Tobacco	A	3
Phillips Petroleum (P)	.38	1.43	.33	Petroleum (integrated)	A	2
Pitney Bowes (PBI)	.29	.83	.07	Office Equipment	A	1
Pittston (PCO)	.40	1.17	.03	Coal	PH	2
Pogo Producing (PPP)	.46	1.34	.02	Petroleum Producing	P	1
Polaroid (PRD)	.39	1.19	.07	Photographic Equipment	C, P	1
PPG Industries (PPG)	.29	.71	.15	Building (materials)	PH	2

Company			Industry		
Prime Computer (PRM)	.57	2.20	.05	Computers/Data Processing	A	3
Procter & Gamble (PG)	.20	.68	.60	Household Products	A	1
Ralston Purina (RAL)	.29	.76	.17	Food Processing	C	3
Raychem (RYC)	.33	1.02	.05	Chemicals (specialized)	P	1
Raytheon (RTN)	.31	1.23	.23	Aerospace	C	2
RCA Corp. (RCA)	.33	1.04	.18	Multi-industry	C	3
Reading & Bates (RB)	.46	1.74	.02	Oilfield Drilling	P	2
Resorts International "A" (RTA)	.44	1.33	.02	Hotels/Gaming	P	1
Revlon (REV)	.29	.89	.07	Toiletries/Cosmetics	C	3
Reynolds Industries (RJR)	.25	.89	.44	Tobacco	C	2
Reynolds Metals (RLM)	.27	.82	.05	Aluminum	P	2
Rockwell International (ROK)	.34	1.20	.32	Aerospace	C	3
ROLM Corp. (RM)	.44	1.47	.08	Telecommunications	C	3
Rowan (RDC)	.48	1.60	.04	Oilfield Drilling	PH	2
Royal Dutch Petroleum (RD)	.26	.99	.76	Petroleum (integrated)	A	2
Ryder System (RDR)	.31	.81	.08	Trucking/Trans. Leasing	P	2
Sabine (SAB)	.39	1.04	.02	Oilfield Services	C	1
Safeway Stores (SA)	.24	.60	.09	Grocery Stores	C	3
Schering-Plough (SGP)	.29	.94	.12	Drugs	C	2
Schlumberger (SLB)	.37	1.60	.92	Oilfield Services	C	2
Scientific Atlanta (SFA)	.48	1.40	.02	Electronics	P	3
Scott Paper (SPP)	.33	.91	.10	Paper & Forest Products	PH	1
Seagram (VO)	.31	.86	.21	Beverages	P	2
Searle (G.D.) (SRL)	.36	1.06	.14	Drugs	A	2
Sears, Roebuck (S)	.29	1.16	.83	Retail Stores	C	3
Sedco (SED)	.44	1.38	.05	Oilfield Drilling	A	3
Shaklee (SHC)	.45	1.11	.02	Food Processing	A	1
Shell Oil (SUO)	.37	1.32	.78	Petroleum (integrated)	P	2
Signal Companies (SGN)	.36	1.19	.23	Autos & Trucks	A	2
Singer (SMF)	.44	1.17	.03	Multi-industry	A	2
Skyline (SKY)	.40	1.27	.01	Mobile Homes	C	2
Smith International (SII)	.38	1.03	.03	Machinery (drilling)	P	1
Smithkline Beckman (SKB)	.28	.89	.30	Drugs	P	3

(continued)

Table notes *a–h* appear on page 358.

APPENDIX 6B (continued)

Company Name (Ticker Symbol)	Historical Volatility[b] 1/1/80–1/1/84	Historical Beta[b] 1/1/80–1/1/84	Market Weight[b] 1/1/80–1/1/84	Industry Group	Exchange[c]	Expiration Cycle[d]
Sony (SNE)	.40	1.12	.23	Electronics	P	2
Southern (SO)	.19	.39	.23	Electric Utility	C	2
Southland Royalty (SRO)	.52	1.22	.05	Petroleum (integrated)	P	1
Southwest Airlines (LUV)	.39	1.02	.05	Airline	C	3
Sperry (SY)	.32	1.37	.15	Computers/Data Processing	C	1
Squibb (SQB)	.29	.85	.15	Drugs	C	1
Standard Oil (Cal.) (SD)	.34	1.44	.75	Petroleum (integrated)	A	3
Standard Oil (Ind.) (SN)	.35	1.55	.94	Petroleum (integrated)	C	2
Standard Oil (Ohio) (SOH)	.37	1.47	.70	Petroleum (integrated)	A	3
Sterling Drug (STY)	.33	.89	.10	Drugs	A	2
Storage Technology (STK)	.51	1.83	.03	Computers/Data Processing	C	1
Storer Communications (SCI)	.39	1.28	.04	Broadcasting/Cable TV	A	2
Sun (SUN)	.35	1.26	.32	Petroleum (integrated)	PH	2
Superior Oil (SOC)	.46	1.58	.30	Petroleum Producing	C	3
Sybron (SYB)	.39	.93	.01	Health Care/Hosptl. Supp.	A	1
Syntex (SYN)	.31	1.10	.11	Drugs	C	3
Tandy (TAN)	.44	1.72	.29	Retail Stores (specialized)	A, C	1
Tektronix (TEK)	.30	.99	.09	Precision Instruments	C	3
Teledyne (TDY)	.33	1.20	.22	Electrical Equipment	C, P	1
Telex (TC)	.60	1.92	.02	Computers/Data Processing	A	3
Tenneco (TGT)	.27	1.00	.36	Natural Gas	A	2
Tesoro Petroleum (TSO)	.49	1.37	.01	Petroleum (integrated)	PH	2
Texaco (TX)	.28	1.12	.58	Petroleum (integrated)	A	1
Texas Instruments (TXN)	.37	1.25	.21	Electronics	C	1
Texas International (TEI)	.66	1.66	.01	Petroleum Producing	A	2
Texas Oil & Gas (TXO)	.42	1.36	.32	Petroleum Producing	PH	3
Textron (TXT)	.29	.60	.07	Machinery	PH	3
Thrifty Corp. (TFO)	.41	1.05	.02	Retail Stores (specialized)	A	1
Tidewater (TDW)	.42	1.37	.02	Oilfield Services	C	2

Company				Industry		
TIE Communications (TIE)	.56	1.81	.06	Telecommunications	P	1
Time (TL)	.28	.89	.23	Publishing	PH	3
Tosco (TOS)	.60	1.74	.01	Petroleum (integrated)	A	2
Toys 'R' Us (TOY)	.39	1.17	.12	Retail Stores (specialized)	C	3
Transamerica (TA)	.28	.87	.13	Insurance (diversified)	PH	2
Trans World (TW)	.47	1.58	.07	Airline	P	3
Travelers (TIC)	.29	.95	.17	Insurance (diversified)	P	2
Tri-Continental (TY)	.20	.66	.05	Investment Company	PH	3
TRW Inc. (TRW)	.24	.85	.18	Multi-industry	A	1
Tymshare Inc. (TYM)	.53	1.10	.02	Computers/Data Processing	PH	2
UAL Inc. (UAL)	.46	1.50	.08	Airline	C	2
Union Carbide (UK)	.25	1.01	.28	Chemicals (diversified)	A	1
Union Pacific (UNP)	.35	1.45	.37	Railroad/Resources	PH	2
U.S. Air (U)	.45	1.50	.05	Airline	P	3
U.S. Home (UH)	.50	1.64	.03	Building (construction)	A	1
U.S. Steel (X)	.34	.98	.20	Steel (integrated)	A	2
United Technologies (UTX)	.28	1.22	.27	Multi-industry	C	1
Unocal (UCL)	.40	1.58	.35	Petroleum (integrated)	P	1
Upjohn (UPJ)	.25	.81	.11	Drugs	C	3
Valero Energy (VLO)	.49	1.74	.03	Natural Gas	A	3
Varian Associates (VAR)	.37	1.19	.07	Electronics	A	2
Veeco Instruments (VEE)	.52	1.84	.02	Precision Instruments	P	3
Verbatim (VRB)	.51	1.65	.02	Computers/Data Processing	P	1
Viacom International (VIA)	.39	1.12	.03	Broadcasting/Cable TV	C	3
Wal-Mart Stores (WMT)	.32	.77	.34	Retail Stores	C	3
Walter (Jim) Corp. (JWC)	.37	.86	.04	Building (materials)	C	2
Wang Labs (WAN)	.46	1.89	.30	Computers/Data Processing	P	1
Warner Communications (WCI)	.43	1.20	.11	Entertainment	C	2
Warner-Lambert (WLA)	.31	1.08	.15	Drugs	A	1
Waste Management (WMX)	.38	1.16	.14	Industrial Services	PH	2
Wendy's International (WEN)	.41	1.31	.05	Restaurants	P	3
Western Co. of North America (WSN)	.49	1.49	.03	Oilfield Services	A	1
Western Union (WU)	.40	1.21	.06	Telecommunications	PH	1

Table notes *a–h* appear on page 358.

(continued)

357

APPENDIX 6B (continued)

Company Name (Ticker Symbol)	Historical Volatility[b] 1/1/80–1/1/84	Historical Beta[b] 1/1/80–1/1/84	Market Weight[b] 1/1/80–1/1/84	Industry Group	Exchange[c]	Expiration Cycle[d]
Westinghouse Electric (WX)	.31	1.39	.30	Electrical Equipment	A	1
Weyerhaeuser (WY)	.29	1.07	.28	Paper & Forest Products	C	1
Whittaker (WKR)	.42	1.42	.02	Multi-industry	A	3
Williams Companies (WMB)	.43	1.31	.06	Chemicals (specialized)	C	2
Williams Electronics (WMS)[e]	.63	1.28	.01	Electronics	PH	3
Winnebago (WGO)	.68	1.41	.02	Recreational Vehicles	C	1
Woolworth (F. W.) (Z)	.30	.86	.07	Retail Stores	PH	2
Xerox (XRX)	.28	1.11	.30	Office Equipment	C, P	1
Zapata (ZOS)	.50	1.95	.02	Oilfield Services	P	3
Zenith Radio (ZE)	.45	1.33	.05	Electronics	A	2

[a] The table includes all stocks for which both the stock itself and listed options on that stock were available for trading on 12/31/83.

[b] The historical volatilities and betas are estimates computed from daily data for the period 1/1/80 to 1/1/84. A value-weighted portfolio of all stocks traded on the New York and American Stock Exchanges was used as the market portfolio in computing the betas. The market weights give the ratio of the total market value of the stock of the company on 12/31/83 to the total market value of the stocks of all companies on the New York and American Stock Exchanges on that date.

[c] The options exchanges are: A, AMEX; C, CBOE; P, Pacific; PH, Philadelphia.

[d] The expiration cycles are: 1, January/April/July/October; 2, February/May/August/November; 3, March/June/September/December.

[e] For each of the following companies, the statistics given cover less than the full four-year period and begin on the following dates: CIGNA, 4/20/82; CSX, 11/13/80; Dart and Kraft, 9/26/80; Engelhard Corporation, 5/27/81; Freeport-McMoRan, 4/08/81; GEO International, 2/19/81; MGM/UA Entertainment, 6/17/80; Mitel, 5/18/81; Novo Industries, 4/30/81; Williams Electronics, 2/26/81. The shorter periods are due mainly to the creation of new firms during the period through mergers and spinoffs; generally, a new firm was considered to have been created whenever a new CUSIP number was assigned for standard identification purposes.

[f] The stocks with the five highest volatilities over the entire period 1/1/80 to 1/1/84 are: Winnebago, .68; Baldwin-United, .66; Texas International, .66; Coleco, .66; Hecla Mining, .63.

[g] The stocks with the five lowest volatilities over the entire period 1/1/80 to 1/1/84 are: American Electric Power, .17; American Telephone and Telegraph, .17; Commonwealth Edison, .18; Consolidated Edison, .18; Southern Company, .19.

[h] The distribution of the stocks in the table by volatility interval is: .10–.19, 5; .20–.29, 93; .30–.39, 145; .40–.49, 82; .50–.59, 42; .60–.69, 10.

generalizations
and applications

7

In this chapter, we extend our results on option valuation in several ways. In Section 7-1, we examine option valuation for more general types of stock price movements than were considered in Chapter 5. In Section 7-2, we discuss how to value contingent claims whose payoffs are more complex than those of ordinary options. This leads naturally to a very important application: Section 7-3 shows that most corporate securities can be valued by option pricing methods. In the course of this section, we give a number of examples for specific kinds of corporate securities. One of these examples in turn leads, in Section 7-4, to a discussion of down-and-out options, which are like ordinary options but with the additional provision that the contract is cancelled if the stock price reaches a designated level. The application to corporate securities then allows us to return to option valuation with a different perspective. If common stock is like an option on the firm that issued it, then a listed option can be viewed as an option on an option. This observation has some interesting implications for valuation, which we examine in Section 7-5. In Sections 7-6 and 7-7, we examine the valuation of options on more than one stock and options on futures. In the concluding section, we discuss some further generalizations and offer some opinions about their relative importance.

7-1. ALTERNATIVE DESCRIPTIONS OF STOCK PRICE MOVEMENTS

The stock price movements that led to the Black-Scholes formula had three important properties:

(a) The possible percentage changes in the stock price over any period did not depend on the level of the stock price at the beginning of the period.

(b) Over a very small interval of time, the size of the change in stock prices was also *small*; roughly speaking, although we were certain a change would occur, not much could happen before we could do something about it.

(c) Over a single period, only *two* stock price outcomes were possible.

We will now ask what happens to our option pricing approach if

1. (a) is false but (b) and (c) are true.
2. (b) is false but (a) and (c) are true.
3. (c) is false but (a) and (b) are true.
4. (b) and (c) are false but (a) is true.

Before proceeding, it will be useful to consider what we are doing and what we hope to gain. We are not advancing an argument about why stock prices must or should have particular probabilistic properties. The actual properties of stock price movements are the result of the interaction of many different economic forces. Fortunately, for our purposes we do not need to sort out and understand all of these interactions. All we need to know is the probabilistic description determined by their cumulative effects. What we would like to do, then, is have available option pricing models for a variety of possible types of stock price behavior. If, for whatever reasons, price movements of a stock seem to have a particular probabilistic structure, we can then select the appropriate option pricing model.

In pursuing this goal, we should not necessarily be disturbed if we have not refined every detail of a stock's price movement. Indeed, we will have gained nothing if we make the description so complicated that we cannot obtain any results. Our objective will always be to make simplifications that make the model tractable yet still capture all of the essential features. The ultimate test of this must be whether or not a new model works better than alternative older ones in the particular goals we are trying to achieve.

In any case, we would certainly argue that having alternative or more general models available could not possibly make us worse off, since we could always refrain from using them until we are sure they are better. If, in addition, a new model includes the older one as a special case and still requires only inputs that are readily obtainable, then we can be optimistic that it will turn out to be an improvement.

Alternative 1. Stock Price Movements with Volatility Dependent on the Level of the Stock Price. As we mentioned in Section 5-6, we could certainly have allowed the u and d movements of our binomial process to differ *predictably* from period to period. This would be relevant, for example, if a firm's investment policy were changing systematically over time. As an extreme illustration, suppose a firm which now holds only government bonds announces that at time τ in the future it will sell the bonds and use the proceeds to enter the stock market and buy some of the shares of another firm with step sizes u' and d'. Then, for our firm, $u = d = r$ before time τ, and $u = u'$ and $d = d'$ after time τ.

This line of argument suggests an even more fundamental generalization. Suppose that we allowed the step sizes to depend on the beginning-of-the-period stock price, as well as the date. Once we specify this dependence, giving the step sizes and probabilities for every possible stock price and time, we will have again said everything necessary to determine the probability distribution of the stock price at any future date. But this distribution will no longer be lognormal, since successive relative stock price changes are no longer independent.[1]

More explicitly, suppose we now represent the up-and-down movements of our binomial process as $u(S, t)$ and $d(S, t)$ to indicate their dependence on the stock price and time. Similarly, we represent the probability of an up movement by $q(S, t)$. For example, suppose we let

$$u(S, t) = 1 + \frac{1}{2\sqrt{S}}, \qquad d(S, t) = 1 - \frac{1}{2\sqrt{S}}, \qquad \text{and} \qquad q(S, t) = \frac{1}{2}.$$

Figure 7-1 illustrates the path the stock would then follow over two periods if its initial value were 100.

In this example, u and d depend only on the beginning stock price in each period and not separately on time. Although it is still possible to value an option by an arbitrage analysis, the distribution of stock price changes in each period is no longer independent of changes in previous periods. In particular, an up movement followed by a down movement no longer yields the same final stock price as a down movement followed by an up movement.

---

[1] Moreover, to fully specify the distribution, we would also have to add the requirement that if the stock price reaches zero, the firm is bankrupt and its value can never again become positive.

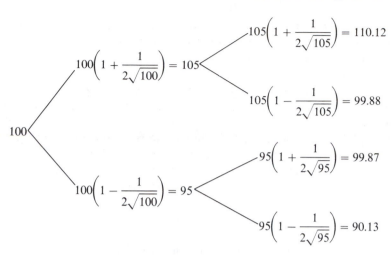

Figure 7-1   Illustration of Square Root Process

Suppose, now, motivated in part by our earlier limiting arguments in Section 5-6, that we require the absolute magnitude of an up or down move in any period to be the same. That is,

$$u(S,\ t) - 1 = 1 - d(S,\ t).$$

Let $\mu(S,\ t)$ and $\sigma(S,\ t)$ denote the limiting instantaneous mean and volatility of the stock rate of return at time t when the stock price is S. If we then set

$$u(S,\ t) = 1 + \sigma(S,\ t)\sqrt{t/n} \qquad \text{and} \qquad q = \frac{1}{2} + \frac{1}{2}\left[\frac{\mu(S,\ t)}{\sigma(S,\ t)}\right]\sqrt{t/n},$$

we can follow an argument similar to that in Section 5-6 to show that, as $n \to \infty$, the mean and variance of the binomial process approach the correct limiting values. If $\sigma(S,\ t) = \sigma$, independent of S and t, we could again derive the Black-Scholes formula, as a check on our generalization.

This gives us a general procedure, well suited for computational purposes, for valuing options when the variance of the stock rate of return depends on the price of the underlying stock, or on time as well. For certain types of dependence, we can find an explicit expression for the value of European calls that will be analogous to the Black-Scholes formula. An important illustration of this occurs when the instantaneous volatility $\sigma(S,\ t)$ has the form

$$\sigma(S,\ t)S = \hat{\sigma}S^p,$$

where $\rho < 1$. This family of processes has the property that the elasticity of the variance is constant,[2] and they can be labeled in this way as *constant elasticity of variance diffusions*. The Black-Scholes case corresponds to $\rho = 1$.

For these processes, if ρ is less than 1, the variance of the rate of return, $\sigma^2(S, t)$, will vary inversely with the stock price, a feature which several studies have found to be characteristic of actual stock price movements. In Section 6-2, we briefly indicated a plausible economic rationale for this behavior in terms of the effects of financial and operating leverage. Financial leverage, as we shall see, can be treated in a different way. However, it is not in itself sufficient to explain the magnitude of the dependence that these tentative studies have found.

For the constant elasticity of variance processes, the value of a payout-protected American call can be represented by an explicit formula. Let $(n - 1)! \equiv \int_0^\infty e^{-v}v^{n-1} \, dv$ represent the gamma function. Here n can have any positive real values greater than or equal to one. If n is an integer, then this function simplifies to $(n - 1)! = (n - 1)(n - 2) \cdots 2 \cdot 1$. Now define the gamma density function:

$$g(n, z) \equiv \frac{e^{-z}z^{n-1}}{(n - 1)!},$$

CONSTANT ELASTICITY OF VARIANCE OPTION PRICING FORMULA[3]

$$C = S \sum_{n=1}^{\infty} g(n, x)G(n + \lambda, y) - Kr^{-t} \sum_{n=1}^{\infty} g(n + \lambda, x)G(n, y)$$

where

$$\lambda \equiv \frac{1}{2(1 - \rho)}$$

$$x \equiv \frac{2\lambda \log r}{\hat{\sigma}^2(r^{t/\lambda} - 1)} S^{1/\lambda}r^{t/\lambda}$$

$$y \equiv \frac{2\lambda \log r}{\hat{\sigma}^2(r^{t/\lambda} - 1)} K^{1/\lambda}$$

---

[2] In particular, $(\partial\sigma/\partial S) \cdot (S/\sigma) = \rho - 1$.

[3] Simplified formulas for two special cases, $\rho = \frac{1}{2}$ (square root process) and $\rho = 0$ (absolute process) can be found in John Cox and Stephen Ross, "The Valuation of Options for Alternative Stochastic Processes," *Journal of Financial Economics*, 3 (January–March 1976), 145–166.

and complementary gamma distribution function:

$$G(n, w) \equiv \int_w^\infty g(n, z)\, dz\,.$$

These functions are widely used in statistics and are well tabulated. The formula is obtained by the procedure we mention earlier, taking the discounted expected value of the call in a risk-neutral world.

The sums in the formula can be easily evaluated with a computer. Table 7-1 shows representative call values for several values of ρ. The

Table 7-1
REPRESENTATIVE CONSTANT ELASTICITY OF VARIANCE DIFFUSION CALL VALUES

| | | $S = 40$ | $r = 1.05$ | | | | | | | |

		$\rho = 1$ (*Black-Scholes*)			$\rho = \frac{1}{2}$ (*Square Root*)			$\rho = 0$ (*Absolute*)		
σ	K	JAN^a	APR	JUL	JAN	APR	JUL	JAN	APR	JUL
.2	35	5.15	5.76	6.40	5.15	5.79	6.44	5.15	5.81	6.49
	40	1.00	2.17	3.00	1.00	2.17	3.00	1.00	2.17	3.00
	45	.02	.51	1.10	.02	.47	1.04	.02	.43	.98
.3	35	5.22	6.25	7.17	5.23	6.31	7.26	5.25	6.38	7.36
	40	1.46	3.07	4.19	1.46	3.07	4.19	1.46	3.08	4.19
	45	.16	1.25	2.24	.14	1.18	2.13	.13	1.12	2.04
.4	35	5.39	6.89	8.09	5.42	6.99	8.23	5.45	7.09	8.38
	40	1.92	3.98	5.37	1.92	3.98	5.37	1.92	3.99	5.39
	45	.42	2.10	3.43	.38	2.00	3.29	.35	1.91	3.17

NOTE: Assumes that no dividends will be paid during the lives of the options. For each level of ρ, the value of $\hat{\sigma}$ has been standardized so that the current volatility is the same in each case.

[a] The January options have one month to expiration; the Aprils, four months; and the Julys, seven months. Both r and σ are in annualized units.

values of $\hat{\sigma}$ are standardized so that the *current* volatility is the same in each case. In other words, as ρ is changed, $\hat{\sigma}$ is also changed so that $\hat{\sigma}S^\rho = \sigma S = 40\sigma$. Differences in the option values are thus solely due to differences in the way the volatility will subsequently change as the stock price changes.

Alternative 2. Jump Stock Price Movements. Turning now to the second alternative,[4] there are indeed situations where the stock price can have a large change over a very small time period, yet our arbitrage-type valuation arguments will still apply. These situations, as in the Black-Scholes case, are obtained as limiting cases of a binomial process. Previously, as h became small, each of the step sizes, u and d, also became small, and each of the probabilities, q and $1 - q$, became close to $\frac{1}{2}$. Had we instead assumed u and d were both fixed as h became small, then the stock price over the time to expiration would either have exploded to infinity or vanished to zero with certainty.

However, this was not the only alternative. Suppose, instead, that as h becomes small, one of the step sizes (say, for the upward move) remains constant, but the probability q it will occur becomes very small. At the same time, the size of the other move becomes very small, but its probability becomes very close to 1. Such a situation need not be explosive or vanishing.

As an illustration, suppose, in place of our former correspondence for u, d, and q, we instead set

$$u = u, \qquad d = e^{\xi(t/n)}, \qquad \text{and} \qquad q = \lambda(t/n).$$

This correspondence captures the essence of a *pure jump process* in which each successive stock price is almost always close to the previous price ($S \to dS$), but occasionally, with low but continuing probability, significantly different ($S \to uS$). Observe that as $n \to \infty$, the probability of a change by d becomes larger and larger, while the probability of a change by u approaches zero.

With these specifications, the initial condition of the central limit theorem that we used in Section 5-6 is no longer satisfied. It can be shown that the stock price movements converge to a log-Poisson, rather than to a lognormal distribution as $n \to \infty$.

Since this situation is included as a special case of our original binomial analysis, we can find the corresponding option price by taking the appropriate limits of the binomial formula. Let us define

$$\Psi[x; y] = \sum_{i=x}^{\infty} \frac{e^{-y}y^i}{i!}$$

---

[4] This alternative was first developed by John Cox and Stephen Ross in their paper, "The Pricing of Options for Jump Processes," Working Paper No. 2-75, Rodney L. White Center for Financial Research, University of Pennsylvania, April 1975.

as the complementary Poisson distribution function with argument x and parameter y. The limiting option pricing formula for the above specification[5] of u, d, and q turns out to be

JUMP PROCESS OPTION PRICING FORMULA

$$C = S\Psi[x; y] - Kr^{-t}\Psi[x; y/u]$$

where

$$y \equiv \frac{(\log r - \xi)ut}{u - 1}$$

and x is the smallest nonnegative integer greater than or equal to

$$\frac{\log(K/S) - \xi t}{\log u}$$

A very similar formula applies if d stays constant while $u - 1$ becomes small. Of course, q must also become large to prevent the stock price from vanishing with certainty.

Alternative 3. Multinomial Stock Price Movements. Suppose that the period-by-period stock price movements follow a trinomial instead of a binomial process, as we have thus far assumed. The simplest example would be one where the stock price either went up, stayed the same, or went down. Each period we would then have three possible outcomes:

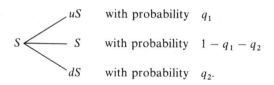

Now we can no longer create a riskless portfolio with a hedge, since a hedge ratio that would equate the returns under two outcomes could not in the third. Thus we could not exactly replicate the payoff to an option with a controlled portfolio of stock and bonds. We no longer have a way of linking the option price and the stock price that does not depend on investors'

---

[5] Of course, we continue to set $\hat{r} = r^{t/n}$.

attitudes toward risk or on the characteristics of other assets. Now the equilibrium option price will, in general, depend on these variables, as well as on those appearing previously.

We might now suspect that binomial stock price movements must be in some sense necessary, as well as sufficient, to derive option pricing formulas based solely on arbitrage considerations. To value an option by arbitrage methods, there must exist a portfolio of other assets which exactly replicates in every circumstance the payoff received by an optimally exercised option. Our basic proposition is the following: Suppose, as we have, that markets are perfect, that changes in the interest rate are never random, and that changes in the stock price are always random. In a model with *discrete* periods, a necessary and sufficient condition for options of all striking prices and times to expiration to be valued by arbitrage using only stock and bonds in the portfolio is that in each period

a. The stock price can change from its beginning-of-period value to only two ex-dividend values at the end of the period.

b. The dividends and the size of each of the two possible changes are presently known functions depending on (i) current and past stock prices, (ii) current and past values of random variables whose changes in each period are perfectly correlated with the change in the stock price, and (iii) calendar time.

The sufficiency of the condition can be established by a straightforward generalization of Alternatives 1 and 2. Its necessity is implied by the discussion at the beginning of Alternative 3.

On the other hand, there are discrete-period multiple state processes that will converge as the length of the periods becomes smaller and smaller to the same limit as a given two-state process meeting the above conditions. For instance, suppose that in the three-state example given above we let

$$u = e^{\sigma\sqrt{2t/n}}, \qquad d = 1/u,$$
$$q_1 = \tfrac{1}{4} + \tfrac{1}{4}\,(\mu/\sigma)\sqrt{2t/n},$$
$$q_2 = \tfrac{1}{4} - \tfrac{1}{4}\,(\mu/\sigma)\sqrt{2t/n}.$$

It can be verified that as $n \to \infty$ (that is, $h \to 0$), this process will converge to the same lognormal process that was obtained in Chapter 5 as the limit of a multiplicative binomial process. Since the resulting descriptions of stock price movements would be the same in the continuous-time limit, it seems reasonable to think that the corresponding option values would also be the same, even though over discrete periods one value will depend on attitudes toward risk and the other will not. Intuitively, it seems that as the length of the period becomes small (that is, as $h \to 0$), this dependence must also become small more rapidly than h. This is essentially true, although we will not attempt to justify it properly.

Alternative 4. Diffusion-Jump Stock Price Movements. The type of stock price movements in Alternative 2 captures the phenomenon of a discontinuous jump in the stock price, as might be caused by the sudden and unexpected arrival of important information. Such jumps may be important, and the ability to represent them for option pricing may be very useful. At the same time, stock price movements may be better described by multinomial instead of binomial movements. For example, if a jump occurs, we would want the resulting price change to be itself random, rather than constant. We might also want to combine this type of behavior with the type discussed earlier, so that we would have rare and possibly large changes superimposed on very frequent small changes.

This brings us to Alternative 4.[6] Now, for the first time, we will not be able to value all options by arbitrage methods, even in the continuous-time limit. This is caused both by the combination of continuous and discontinuous changes and by the random nature of the discontinuous changes. This stands in sharp contrast to the earlier cases, where either the changes became continuous in the continuous-time limit or else there was only a deterministic discontinuous change.

It might be useful to pause and depict the alternative types of stock price movements we are considering. Figure 7-2 contrasts the types of stock price behavior governing Alternatives 1, 2 and 4, respectively. Although (a) is jagged (that is, nondifferentiable), it is nonetheless continuous throughout. In (b) and (c), the dashed vertical lines indicate discontinuities. Observe that in (b) the jumps are of the same relative (to S) magnitude and all in the same direction, while this is not true for (c). Moreover, unlike (b), the movement in (c) follows an uncertain path between jumps.

In certain cases, despite the impossibility of constructing riskless arbitrage positions, we can still derive an option valuation formula that does not depend on attitudes toward risk. Suppose that there is a very large number of securities available, so that each security will make up only a very small fraction of a well-diversified portfolio. Suppose, also, that the rare events that cause sudden discontinuous changes in the price of a stock affect only that stock or, at most, the stock of a few other firms (such as the other party in a litigation or in a merger). The risk of these sudden changes will be diversifiable, and the market will consequently pay no risk premium over the riskless rate for bearing this risk. The equilibrium expected rate of

---

[6] This alternative was first developed by Robert Merton in his article, "Option Pricing When Underlying Stock Returns Are Discontinuous," *Journal of Financial Economics*, 3 (January–March 1976), 125–144.

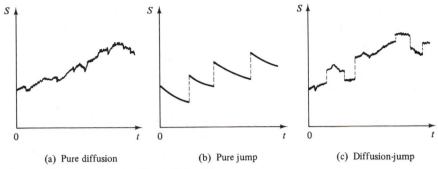

(a) Pure diffusion   (b) Pure jump   (c) Diffusion-jump

Figure 7-2   Alternative Stock Price Movements

return on the stock, and on an option, would thus not be affected by the presence of this diversifiable jump risk.

Although these arguments are only intuitive, they can be completely justified. They give us a way to link the equilibrium price of an option with the price of the underlying stock. Let us recall our original valuation arguments. There we constructed a portfolio containing a long position in Δ shares of stock and the amount B in bonds to replicate the returns of a call. We then argued that in equilibrium the current value of the stock-bond portfolio must equal the current value of the call. Suppose that in the present case we create a similar portfolio and choose the number of shares of stock to again replicate the call for the small continuous movements. The portfolio would, in equilibrium, replicate the call if a jump did not occur but not if one did occur. But when a jump did occur, the risk would be completely diversifiable, so, in equilibrium, the expected return (but not necessarily the realized return) must be the riskless rate times the amount invested.

The linkage again gives us a valuation equation that must be satisfied by the equilibrium option price. Notice that even though the diversifiability of the jump risk meant that attitudes toward risk and the characteristics of other assets will not matter, this is still not an arbitrage theory in the same sense as before. One could again realize sure profits if market prices deviated from formula values, but only by holding a portfolio that was not only continually adjusted but also well diversified.

A specific pricing formula is available for one particularly interesting case. Suppose that the stock price at the end of the period can take on these values with the corresponding possibilities:

Ending Value	Probability
uS	$q[1 - \lambda(t/n)]$
dS	$(1 - q)[1 - \lambda(t/n)]$
uzS	$q\lambda(t/n)$
dzS	$(1 - q)\lambda(t/n)$

where $\log z$ is a normally distributed random variable with mean $-\frac{1}{2}\delta^2$ and variance δ^2. This implies z itself is lognormally distributed with an expected value of one.[7]

Let us now fix t and let n approach infinity and specify u, d, and q in the same way we did for the Black-Scholes formula.[8] We would then obtain a continuous-time, continuous-state lognormal process upon which are superimposed infrequent jumps that are themselves lognormally distributed. The parameter λ determines the frequency of the jumps. When the jumps are perfectly diversifiable, we can employ the procedure outlined above to price the call in terms of the underlying stock. The resulting formula for the value of a call is

DIFFUSION-JUMP PROCESS OPTION PRICING FORMULA

$$C = \sum_{i=0}^{\infty} \frac{e^{-\lambda t}(\lambda t)^i}{i!} \, C_i(S, K, t, \sqrt{\hat{\sigma}^2 + \delta^2(i/t)}, r)$$

where C_i is the Black-Scholes value of a call with time to expiration t and striking price K on a stock with current price S and volatility

$$\sigma_i = \sqrt{\hat{\sigma}^2 + \delta^2(i/t)}$$

Table 7-2 shows how diffusion-jump call values depend on the importance of the jump component of their underlying stock price movement. This component is measured by (1) the percentage γ of the total stock volatility σ^2 explained by the jump, and (2) the expected number of jumps per year λ. As before in Table 7-1, to facilitate comparison with the corresponding Black-Scholes values (middle panel of Table 5-2), the parameters of the diffusion-jump stock price process have been chosen so that the current volatility of the stock is the same in both formulas ($\sigma^2 = \hat{\sigma}^2 + \lambda\delta^2$). Since the volatility does not depend on the stock price in either model, this equality will continue to hold as the stock price subsequently changes, unlike the case with the constant elasticity of variance formula.

For a given λ and σ, as the magnitude of a typical jump increases, γ increases, and the call departs further from its corresponding Black-Scholes

---

[7] We are assuming here that the expected rate of return of the stock, given that a jump has occurred, is zero. See Merton's paper for a more general formula that allows for an arbitrary expected rate of return.

[8] In particular, $d = 1/u$ and $u = \exp(\hat{\sigma}\sqrt{t/n})$. $\hat{\sigma}$ is the volatility of the diffusion component and σ will continue to represent the overall stock volatility, considering both diffusion and jump components. Of course, we continue to set $\hat{r} = r^{t/n}$.

Table 7-2
REPRESENTATIVE DIFFUSION-JUMP CALL VALUES

		$S = 40$		$\sigma = .3$		$r = 1.05$			
		$\lambda = 1$			$\lambda = 3$			$\lambda = 5$	
γ	K	JAN^a	APR	JUL	JAN	APR	JUL	JAN	APR	JUL
	35	5.23	6.24	7.16	5.23	6.25	7.17	5.22	6.25	7.17
.2	40	1.42	3.04	4.16	1.44	3.06	4.18	1.45	3.07	4.18
	45	.17	1.23	2.21	.17	1.25	2.23	.17	1.25	2.23
	35	5.26	6.21	7.11	5.26	6.24	7.15	5.25	6.24	7.16
.5	40	1.27	2.88	4.02	1.35	2.99	4.12	1.38	3.02	4.15
	45	.18	1.14	2.10	.19	1.21	2.18	.18	1.23	2.20
	35	5.30	6.20	7.05	5.30	6.24	7.12	5.29	6.24	7.14
.8	40	1.00	2.55	3.72	1.15	2.84	4.01	1.23	2.93	4.08
	45	.21	.99	1.87	.23	1.15	2.10	.23	1.19	2.15

NOTE: Assumes no dividends during the lives of the options. $\sigma^2 \equiv \hat{\sigma}^2 + \lambda\delta^2$ is the total volatility squared of the continuous and jump components. $\gamma \equiv \lambda\delta^2/\sigma^2$ is then the percentage of the total volatility squared due to the jump component. Given σ, γ, and λ, the remaining variables $\hat{\sigma}$ and δ are then chosen to satisfy these equalities.

[a] The January options have one month to expiration; the Aprils, four months; and the Julys, seven months. Both r and σ are in annualized units.

value. Similarly, for a given γ, as λ increases, the expected frequency of the jump increases, and the jump component looks more like a diffusion. As a result, the call value begins to approximate its corresponding Black-Scholes value. In brief, a comparison of the middle panel of Table 5-2 shows that when $\gamma = .2$ and $\lambda = 5$, there is almost no difference between diffusion-jump and Black-Scholes call values. However, as the jump component becomes more significant in terms of γ and λ, some interesting differences arise. When $\gamma = .8$ and $\lambda = 1$, the jump component produces significantly higher values for near-expiration, out-of-the-money calls, but significantly lower values otherwise.

7-2. GENERALIZED OPTIONS

To this point, we have been exclusively concerned with ordinary puts and calls. One reason why we have examined puts and calls in such detail is that they can be used as "building blocks" for constructing much more general options. With just a little more effort, we will be able to value and compare the characteristics of many other types of securities.

From this broader perspective, we can think of a European call as a security whose payoff is a particularly simple function of the stock price at the expiration date, namely, max[0, $S^* - K$]. We now wish to consider securities whose payoffs depend on the stock price in a more general way. We will be interested in the following question: How can we use ordinary puts and calls to value these generalized options? In this chapter, we proceed by showing that there is a portfolio of ordinary European options whose payoffs duplicate the payoffs received from the generalized option. In the next chapter, in a different context, we follow an alternative approach that infers from ordinary options sufficient information to value the generalized option.

There are a number of reasons why we should be interested in the former representation. First of all, it gives us an immediate restriction on relative equilibrium prices. If there are no arbitrage opportunities, then two portfolios with identical payoffs must have identical current market values. This is true even in circumstances where it might be difficult to value the constituent options in the equivalent portfolio. Of course, if we do have a procedure to value the ordinary options, then this gives an immediate way to apply this procedure to value the generalized option. Furthermore, our approach of valuing a generalized option indirectly, by valuing an equivalent portfolio of ordinary options, applies to many corporate securities.

Let us first suppose that the only payoff F^* to the generalized option is received after elapsed time T, and that this payoff is an arbitrary continuous function of the stock price at that time, S^*. Thus, the payoff can be written as $F^*(S^*)$. For example, $F^*(S^*)$ might equal $\sqrt{S^*}$. In the case of a call, $F^*(S^*) = C^* = \max[0, S^* - K]$.

For the moment, assume $F^*(S^*)$ is a continuous piecewise linear function passing through the origin (that is, $F^*(0) = 0$). Figure 7-3 shows how such a function might appear. The "break points" (kinks) of the function have been labeled K_0, K_1, and K_2. The slopes of each segment have been labeled, consecutively, λ_0, λ_1, and λ_2. That is, the values of F^* at each break point are, respectively,

$$F^*(K_0) = 0,$$
$$F^*(K_1) = \lambda_0(K_1 - K_0),$$
$$F^*(K_2) = \lambda_0(K_1 - K_0) + \lambda_1(K_2 - K_1).$$

It is easy to show that *any such payoff function $F^*(S^*)$ can be exactly duplicated by an appropriately chosen portfolio of calls.* We only need to use calls with time to expiration T. To illustrate the recipe, we continue with the above example. Table 7-3 provides an arbitrage analysis of this problem. To construct a perfect hedge, we start by writing λ_0 options with striking price K_0 (zero). This will coincide with F^* up to K_1. Then add the

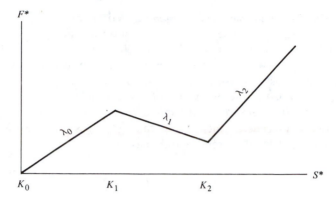

Figure 7-3   Continuous Piecewise Linear Function

number of options with striking price K_1 which will make the slope of the payoffs to the option portfolio coincide with F^* between K_1 and K_2. This requires that we not only write λ_1 options with striking price K_1, but that we buy back λ_0 options with striking price K_1 to nullify the effect over the range $K_1 \leq S^* < K_2$ of the λ_0 options we have written previously. We then repeat this procedure with options with striking price K_2. From the arbitrage table, it is apparent that the current value of the generalized option is

$$F = \lambda_0 C(K_0) + (\lambda_1 - \lambda_0)C(K_1) + (\lambda_2 - \lambda_1)C(K_2).$$

Table 7-3
ARBITRAGE TABLE ILLUSTRATING GENERALIZED OPTION

	Current Date	Expiration Date		
		$K_0 \leq S^* < K_1$	$K_1 \leq S^* < K_2$	$K_2 \leq S^*$
Write λ_0 calls at K_0	$\lambda_0 C(K_0)$	$\lambda_0(K_0 - S^*)$	$\lambda_0(K_0 - S^*)$	$\lambda_0(K_0 - S^*)$
Write $\lambda_1 - \lambda_0$ calls at K_1	$(\lambda_1 - \lambda_0)C(K_1)$	—	$(\lambda_1 - \lambda_0)(K_1 - S^*)$	$(\lambda_1 - \lambda_0)(K_1 - S^*)$
Write $\lambda_2 - \lambda_1$ calls at K_2	$(\lambda_2 - \lambda_1)C(K_2)$	—	—	$(\lambda_2 - \lambda_1)(K_2 - S^*)$
Buy generalized option	$-F$	$\lambda_0(S^* - K_0)$	$\lambda_0(K_1 - K_0)$ $+$ $\lambda_1(S^* - K_1)$	$\lambda_0(K_1 - K_0)$ $+$ $\lambda_1(K_2 - K_1)$ $+$ $\lambda_2(S^* - K_2)$
Total		—	—	—

Clearly, this example may be generalized to any number of break points. Furthermore, suppose the payoff function did not pass through the origin but had an intercept at $F^*(K_0) = I$. Then we can simply add to the portfolio of calls I unit zero-coupon bonds with time to maturity T. Alternatively, if we insist on using only ordinary options to reconstruct the generalized option, the present value of these bonds could be written as $P(I) + C(0) - C(I)$, where $P(I)$ is the current value of a European put with striking price I. In general, then, given that $F^*(S^*)$ is piecewise linear, the present value, F, of $F^*(S^*)$ is representable as

$$F = [P(I) + C(0) - C(I)] + \lambda_0 C(K_0) + \sum_{i=1}^{n} (\lambda_i - \lambda_{i-1}) C(K_i),$$

where there are $n + 1$ break points $K_0, K_1, K_2, \ldots, K_n$.

Now suppose that F^* is not piecewise linear. The natural suggestion would be to value F^* by finding a piecewise linear function $G^*(S^*)$ that is closest to $F^*(S^*)$. This is the right track, but to give it meaning, we need to decide how we are going to measure closeness. We might first think of minimizing the sum of the squared errors of F^* from G^*, since this is a tractable measure familiar from regression analysis.[9] Or we might consider using the sum of the absolute values of the errors.[10]

But here we are losing sight of our purpose. We are not interested, per se, in having the payoffs close. What we want is the current values of the generalized option and the approximate call portfolio to be close. To guarantee this *under all circumstances*, we need to use as a standard the maximum absolute difference between G^* and F^*, $\max_x |G^*(x) - F^*(x)|$. We can then say definitely that to prevent arbitrage, the absolute difference between the current values must be less than or equal to the present value of this maximum absolute difference. We could, of course, refine this by considering $\max_x [G^*(x) - F^*(x)]$ and $\min_x [G^*(x) - F^*(x)]$, separately. This would produce lower and upper bounds around the value of F.

Now it seems intuitively reasonable that, as we admit more and more calls with different striking prices, we get a better and better approximation. For any level of tolerance we choose, no matter how small, we should be able to find an assortment of options that will make the difference in current values even smaller. This is in fact true, but we will not go into the technical details.

In each case, our problem is to identify the portfolio of calls, by specifying their striking prices and the number of calls of each striking

---

[9] That is, find the piecewise linear function G^* that minimizes the integral

$$\int_0^\infty [G^*(x) - F^*(x)]^2 \, dx.$$

[10] That is, $\int_0^\infty |G^*(x) - F^*(x)| \, dx$.

price, which is equivalent in payoff to the generalized option. If we know how to value the constituent calls, or market prices exist for these calls, we can then value exactly or, at worst, place lower and upper bounds on the current value of the generalized option.

7-3. CORPORATE SECURITIES[11]

Corporate securities are very similar to the generalized options discussed in the previous section, although now the underlying asset is the *total value of the firm* rather than the value of the stock. The result is an unexpected bonus: We can value corporate securities by the same methods we use to value options. For the simplest cases, it is only a matter of reinterpreting the variables. Of course, things will usually not be that easy; options were intentionally designed with streamlined terms, while corporate securities often have quite complex contractual provisions. When all of the relevant complications are brought in, the analysis is more difficult, but the same basic principles still apply.

This approach has many potential benefits. It provides a way to determine the relative value, risk, and expected return of any corporate security. It also shows how these quantities will be affected by changes in the underlying variables or in the contractual provisions. Furthermore, it gives a way to find the optimal conversion and call strategies for corporate securities. Consequently, the results will be useful to both investment analysts and managers of firms.

We will illustrate the correspondence between corporate securities and options with seven examples for firms which have these securities, in addition to their common stock, outstanding:

1. A single issue of zero-coupon bonds
2. An issue of senior zero-coupon bonds and an issue of subordinated (junior) zero-coupon bonds
3. Warrants
4. Convertible bonds
5. Callable bonds
6. Callable convertible bonds
7. Bonds with safety covenants

The examples are chosen to show a number of important features of corporate securities in as simple a setting as possible.

Options are issued as well as purchased by individuals. Corporate securities are, of course, issued by firms (and, in particular, the owners of the

---

[11] Fischer Black, Myron Scholes, and Robert Merton, in their 1973 articles on option pricing, suggested the correspondence between corporate securities and options.

firm, the stockholders). This leads to several important differences between option valuation and corporate security valuation.

We will present the first two examples and use them as a context for explaining three of the differences. Next we will discuss four additional differences and use examples 3, 4, 5, and 6 to illustrate them. We will then discuss three final differences. The last example will be considered in Section 7-4.

In discussing corporate securities, we will assume that all agents act optimally in their own best interests and that all transactions costs, margin requirements, and taxes can be ignored. We also assume, unless explicitly stated otherwise, that (1) the firm is allowed to finance payouts by the sale of assets; and (2) if a payment to a claim other than stock is not made, the firm is declared bankrupt and reorganized, the ownership of the firm passes to the nonstock claim-holders, and the holders of the common stock receive nothing. Finally, (3) we assume that no further securities will be issued while the ones we are currently considering (excluding the stock) are still outstanding.

When corporate securities are expressed in terms of options, it is always understood that the options are unprotected options on the value of a firm making the prescribed payouts. These representations are completely general and hold for uncertain interest rates and arbitrary stock price processes. Paradoxically, these representations are the most difficult in situations that seem to be the most like options—warrants and convertible bonds—and are the easiest and least restrictive in situations involving only stock and bonds, which are apparently not like options at all.

Example 1. Zero-Coupon Bonds.   The easiest way to begin is with a specific example.[12] Suppose that a holding company, Berkeford Holdings, has all its funds invested in Teledyne common stock. Berkeford Holdings owns 1,000 shares of Teledyne, which, at the close of trading on January 2, 1980, was worth $127 per share. Berkeford has two classes of securities outstanding: 1,000 shares of its own common stock and 120 zero-coupon bonds. Each of these bonds promises to pay $1,000 on its maturity date, July 18, 1980; hence, the total amount due will be $120,000. Since they are zero-coupon bonds, no coupon payments are due in the meantime. Teledyne has a standing policy against paying cash dividends, so as a result there will be no cash payments going into or coming from Berkeford until the maturity date.

On the maturity date, the Berkeford stockholders plan to pay off the bonds by floating a new debt issue. However, if at that time Teledyne is worth less than $120 per share, they will be unable to do so. No one is

---

[12] This example was first developed by Robert Merton in his article, "On the Pricing of Corporate Debt," *Journal of Finance*, 29 (May 1974), 449–470.

going to pay $120,000 for a new debt issue giving only a partial claim to assets worth less than $120,000. For the same reason, the firm could not raise enough to pay off the bondholders by selling more stock.

Of course, the stockholders could make up the difference out of their own pockets. But since Berkeford is a corporation with limited liability, they are under no obligation to do so, nor would this be in their best interests. In effect, they would be throwing good money after bad, when they could instead use it to form a completely new company on which the old bondholders would have no claim. Consequently, the stockholders will be either unable or unwilling to keep the firm from bankruptcy, and the ownership of the Teledyne stock will pass to the bondholders.

Naturally, the bondholders could keep the firm in operation by agreeing to renegotiate the terms of the debt, but at this point, why should they? The argument that the Teledyne stock might soon be worth enough to pay off the bonds in full is hardly persuasive. That would be a "heads you win, tails I lose" gamble for the bondholders. If they obtain full ownership of the Teledyne by way of bankruptcy, they would have the full benefit of subsequent gains and bear the full burden of subsequent losses; if they renegotiate, they would still bear the full burden of subsequent losses, but now they would have to share the gains with the stockholders. Consequently, it would be in the bondholders' interest to enforce their claim and receive full ownership of the Teledyne stock, and, as a result, the Berkeford stock would then be worthless.

Of course, this sad state of affairs may never come about. If Teledyne is worth more than $120 per share on the maturity date, then the stockholders should be able to sell enough new securities to pay off the old bondholders and avoid bankruptcy. In summary, Table 7-4 shows the value of each class of Berkeford securities on the maturity date in terms of the total value of the 1,000 shares of Teledyne at that time, denoted as V^*.

Now we turn to the question we really want to answer: How much should the Berkeford securities be worth on January 2? Clearly, the current total value of all the securities must be $127,000, the current value of the firm's assets, but how would we expect this total to be divided between the stock and the bonds? A second look at Table 7-4 shows how options can

Table 7-4

PAYOFFS TO BERKEFORD SECURITIES ON THE
MATURITY DATE

	$V^* \leq 120{,}000$	$V^* > 120{,}000$
Berkeford bonds	V^*	120,000
Berkeford stock	0	$V^* - 120{,}000$

provide the answer. Each share of Berkeford stock has exactly the same payoff as a call option on one share of Teledyne stock with a striking price of 120 and an expiration date of July 18. Similarly, the bondholders as a group are in exactly the same position as a covered writer who owns 1,000 shares of Teledyne and has written 1,000 such calls against them; each single bond represents 1/120 of this position. Consequently, everything we have said about calls and covered writing positions will also be valid for the Berkeford stock and bonds.

Table 7-5 is an excerpt from the closing option prices for January 2 as reported in the *Wall Street Journal*. By pure coincidence, it turns out that one of the options listed there is a Teledyne call with a striking price of 120 and an expiration date of July 18. Its closing market price is $21. Consequently, the closing price of Berkeford stock should be exactly the same, $21 per share. The entire bond issue should then be worth $127,000 − $21,000 = $106,000, or $883.33 per bond. In fact, Table 7-5 gives us the information we would need to say how much the Berkeford securities would be worth if the firm had a somewhat different capital structure. For example, suppose the firm had issued 130 bonds instead of 120. Then each share of Berkeford stock would be a call with a striking price of 130 rather than 120, and its market price would be $16. Table 7-6 shows the total current market value that the stock and bonds would have for several alternative amounts of outstanding total debt.

If we look again at Table 7-4, we can see that the payoff to the bondholders can be interpreted in another way. It is exactly the same as that received by someone who owns a *default-free* zero-coupon bond paying $120,000 on July 18 and who has written 1,000 European puts on Teledyne, each with a striking price of 120 and an expiration date of July 18. Since the

Table 7-5
SOME CLOSING CALL OPTION PRICES ON JANUARY 2, 1980

Stock	Striking Price	Jan	Apr	Jul	N.Y. Close
Stor Tec	10	6	7	$7\frac{3}{4}$	$16\frac{1}{4}$
Stor Tec	15	$1\frac{3}{8}$	$2\frac{1}{2}$	$3\frac{3}{8}$	$16\frac{1}{4}$
Stor Tec	20	$\frac{1}{16}$	$\frac{13}{16}$	$1\frac{1}{2}$	$16\frac{1}{4}$
Tandy	20	$10\frac{3}{4}$	—	—	$29\frac{3}{8}$
Tandy	25	6	—	—	$29\frac{3}{8}$
Tandy	30	$\frac{1}{4}$	$2\frac{7}{8}$	$3\frac{3}{4}$	$29\frac{3}{8}$
Teldyn	110	18	—	—	127
Teldyn	120	$8\frac{7}{8}$	16	21	127
Teldyn	130	$2\frac{13}{16}$	$10\frac{3}{8}$	16	127
Teldyn	140	$\frac{3}{8}$	$6\frac{1}{8}$	$11\frac{3}{8}$	127
Teldyn	150	$\frac{3}{16}$	3	$7\frac{1}{2}$	127

Table 7-6

THE MARKET VALUE OF BERKEFORD STOCK AND BONDS FOR ALTERNATIVE CAPITAL STRUCTURES

Promised Payment to Bondholders	*Current Market Value of Bonds*	*Current Market Value of Stock*	*Current Market Value of Stock and Bonds*
120,000	106,000	21,000	127,000
130,000	111,000	16,000	127,000
140,000	115,625	11,375	127,000
150,000	119,500	7,500	127,000

Berkeford bonds have some possibility of default, they sell for less than an otherwise similar default-free bond (which, at prevailing rates, would be worth about \$111,830). The difference is exactly the value of the European puts.

Table 7-7 summarizes our conclusions. There, K stands for the promised payment to the bondholders, S is the value of one share of stock, n is the number of shares outstanding, and B is the total value of the bonds. Figure 7-4 shows a graph of the payoffs and gives a preview of coming attractions.

Bond traders and financial managers often speak in terms of the yield on a bond rather than the price of a bond. The *yield-to-maturity* on a bond is the discount rate which would make the present value of the promised coupon and principal payments equal to the current price of the bond. Readers familiar with the literature on capital budgeting will recognize this as the bond's internal rate of return. A related measure is the *default premium*, which tells by how much the yield-to-maturity of a given bond exceeds that of a default-free bond with the same promised payments.

The discount bonds we are considering now provide a particularly convenient setting for examining yields. In this case the (continuously compounded) yield-to-maturity, denoted as $\log R$, is simply $[\log(K/B)]/T$, where T is the time remaining until the maturity date. In other words, it is

Table 7-7

ZERO-COUPON BONDS

	Value on Current Date	*Value on Maturity Date*		*Representation in Terms of Calls*
		$V^* \leq K$	$K < V^*$	
Bonds	B	V^*	K	$V - C(V; K)$
Stock	nS	–	$V^* - K$	$C(V; K)$

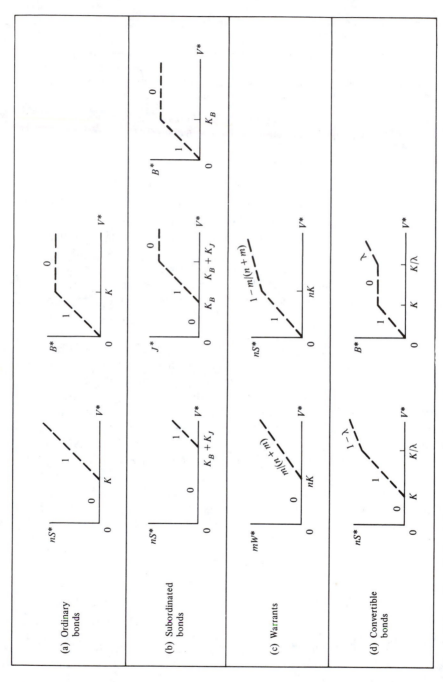

Figure 7-4 Payoffs from Corporate Securities at Maturity

the compounded rate of return which will be earned on the bonds if the bonds are paid in full. Table 7-8 shows the current yields that would prevail on Berkeford bonds for the alternative capital structures shown in Table 7-6. By using Table 7-5, we can find the market values that the bonds would have if they matured on January 18 or April 18, rather than July 18. For calls with striking prices of 100 and 110 which are not shown in Table 7-4, we have estimated the market value they would have had if traded, and calculated the corresponding values for the bonds.[13] Table 7-8 also shows the yields-to-maturity for all of these bonds.

Table 7-8
YIELDS-TO-MATURITY FOR BERKEFORD BONDS
(IN PERCENT PER YEAR)

	Maturity Date		
Promised Payment to Bondholders	*January 18*	*April 18*	*July 18*
100,000	13.18	15.26	16.11
110,000	20.83	19.26	19.20
120,000	33.81	26.59	22.87
130,000	104.35	37.04	29.13
140,000	233.57	50.11	35.26
150,000	383.08	64.93	41.90

Just as we would expect, for any given maturity date, the yield-to-maturity increases as the debt-equity ratio increases. Its behavior as the maturity date changes is a little more complicated. For a promised payment significantly lower than the current value of the assets, it increases with time to maturity; for higher promised payments, it decreases. It is often said that this is because the probability of default increases in the former case and decreases in the latter case. Unfortunately, as we will see shortly, this argument is, at best, very misleading.

Since Berkeford is a holding company, we would have no trouble determining the market value of its assets. All we have to do is look up the market price of Teledyne stock. If, instead, Berkeford had been, say, a manufacturing company with a complex array of plant and equipment, the market value of the assets would no longer be directly observable. However, it would still be observable indirectly, because it would by definition be

---

[13] This was done with the Black-Scholes formula using, for each expiration date, the implicit volatility calculated from the at-the-money calls. The continuously compounded riskless rate used was 13%.

equal to the total market value of all of the firm's securities. We could then think of the Berkeford stock as a call on the total value of the firm's securities, or more briefly, the value of the firm.

When a firm issues new securities, both the firm and the buyers naturally want to make sure they are getting a fair price. They can hardly expect to find out by looking up the value of an equivalent security in the newspaper as we did for Berkeford. Even if they could, they would have no way to judge whether this equivalent security was itself correctly priced. This is where option valuation theory comes in. If we have a way to find the exact value of an option on V, then we can find the fair value of the firm's securities for any capital structure that it might wish to consider.

Here is a concrete example. If the value of the firm follows a continuous process with a constant volatility σ, and r is constant through time, then we know that the Black-Scholes formula provides the correct current value of the stock. All we would have to do is relabel the variables in our derivation for puts and calls to obtain the value of the stock and bonds as:

$$nS = VN(z) - Kr^{-T}N(z - \sigma\sqrt{T}),$$
$$B = VN(-z) + Kr^{-T}N(z - \sigma\sqrt{T}),$$

where

$$z \equiv \frac{\log(V/Kr^{-T})}{\sigma\sqrt{T}} + \tfrac{1}{2}\sigma\sqrt{T}.$$

These formulas show the relationship that must hold between the value of the stock S, the value of the bonds B, and the value of the firm V to prevent opportunities for riskless profitable arbitrage. If the assets of the firm are not directly tradable, how would this arbitrage operation work? Since $V \equiv B + nS$, the above formulas can also be interpreted as implicit relationships between the stock price S and the current value of the bonds B. These marketed securities could be traded to set up the appropriate hedged positions.

These exact formulas can be used to examine the yield-to-maturity, $\log R$, and the default premium, $g = \log R - \log r$, in greater detail than we did earlier. It is straightforward to show that:

$$g = -\frac{1}{T}\log N(-z) + \frac{1}{w}N(z - \sigma\sqrt{T})$$

where

$$w \equiv Kr^{-T}/V$$
$$z \equiv \frac{\log w}{\sigma\sqrt{T}} + \tfrac{1}{2}\sigma\sqrt{T}$$

The default premium g which gives sufficient compensation to a lender for default risk can consequently be expressed as an exact function of w, σ, and T. w is the debt-to-total-value ratio where the debt is valued at the present value (assuming no default) of its face value. σ, the volatility of the value of the firm, can be thought of as a measure of operating risk. T is the time to maturity for the debt. Thus, the *default premium depends solely on capital structure, operating risk, and debt maturity.*

Since the default premium does not depend on the expected rate of change in the value of the firm, the bonds of one company may have a lower default premium than those of another company, yet actually have a higher variance of rate of return. Also, the bonds of the first company may be more risky than those of the second in the sense of having a higher variance of rate of return. Hence, although yield-to-maturity is a commonly used measure, it must be interpreted very carefully.

A sensitivity analysis of the default premium using the Black-Scholes formula is provided in Table 7-9. As the operating risk σ increases, or the debt-to-value ratio w increases, the default premium always increases. This is as we would predict. However, as we saw before, the time to maturity has no such simple effect.

Table 7-9
REPRESENTATIVE DEFAULT
PREMIUMS

σ	w	Maturity (in Years) 3	6	9
.2	.2	—	—	—
	.5	.1	.4	.6
	.8	2.1	2.0	1.9
.3	.2	—	.1	.3
	.5	1.0	1.6	1.8
	.8	4.5	4.0	3.6
.4	.2	.2	.7	1.2
	.5	2.7	3.4	3.5
	.8	7.2	6.1	5.5

In Chapter 5, we showed how to find the expected rate of return of a call in terms of the expected rate of return of the underlying stock. The assumptions we made in this example allow us to apply an identical analysis to find the expected rate of return of the stock, μ_S, or bonds, μ_B, in terms of the expected rate of return on the total firm, μ_V. The latter will be determined by the firm's investment policy. For a given μ_V, we can then answer a traditional question in finance: How do the firm's "cost of equity"

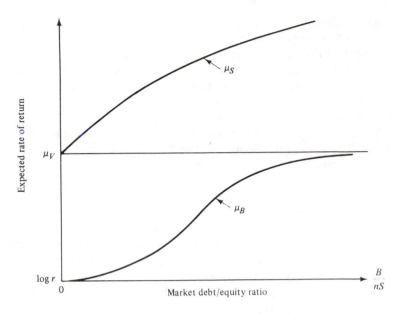

Figure 7-5   The Expected Rate of Return of Stock and
Bonds As a Function of the Market Debt/Equity
Ratio

(μ_S) and "cost of debt" (μ_B) depend on the debt-equity ratio? Figure 7-5
shows μ_S and μ_B as a function of the ratio of the market value of the debt to
the market value of the equity.

Of course, Table 7-9 and Figure 7-5 apply only to a very simplified
and unrealistic corporate capital structure. Many firms have several types of
debt outstanding, with a complex set of rules governing priority in the event
of bankruptcy. Corporate bonds usually have coupon payments and may
be convertible into common stock at the discretion of the owner or callable
at a fixed price at the discretion of the corporation. Debt comes equipped
with complex restrictive covenants circumscribing the firm's operating, dividend, and refinancing policies. We will now investigate several of these
complications.

Example 2. Subordinated Zero-Coupon Bonds.[14]   Suppose now that Berkeford has three classes of securities outstanding. As before, there are 1,000
shares of common stock and 120 senior zero-coupon bonds, each of which
promises to pay $1,000 on its maturity date, July 18. The third security is an

---

[14] This example was first developed by Fischer Black and John Cox in their article, "Valuing
Corporate Securities: Some Effects of Bond Indenture Provisions," *Journal of Finance*, 31
(May 1976), 351–368.

issue of 30 junior zero-coupon bonds, each of which also promises to pay $1,000 on the same maturity date, July 18. According to the indentures, the junior bondholders can only be paid after the senior bondholders have been paid in full.

Now let us see what will happen on the maturity date of the bonds. If the assets are then worth less than $120,000, they will all go to the senior bondholders, and neither the junior bondholders nor the stockholders will receive anything. If they are worth somewhere between $120,000 and $150,000, the senior bondholders will be paid in full and the junior bondholders will get what is left; once again, the stockholders will get nothing. If things work out well and the Teledyne stock is worth more than $150,000, then Berkeford will avoid bankruptcy, both sets of bondholders will be paid in full, and the stock will have some residual value. All of this is summarized in Table 7-10.

Table 7-10
PAYOFFS TO BERKEFORD SECURITIES ON THE MATURITY DATE

	$V^* \leq 120,000$	$120,000 < V^* \leq 150,000$	$V^* > 150,000$
Senior bonds	V^*	120,000	120,000
Junior bonds	0	$V^* - 120,000$	30,000
Stock	0	0	$V^* - 150,000$

No second look is necessary this time; we immediately see that the owners of the senior bonds are once again exactly like a covered writer who owns 1,000 shares of Teledyne and has written 1,000 calls, each with a striking price of 120 and an expiration date of July 18. The fact that the stockholders and the junior bondholders have now divided the remaining slice of the pie has not affected the senior bondholders in any way. Similarly, we find that each share of stock is again like a call on Teledyne stock, only now the striking price is 150 rather than 120.

What about the junior bondholders? A little reflection shows that their position is exactly the same as the owner of a bullish vertical spread in Teledyne which is long 1,000 July 120s and short 1,000 July 150s. Consequently, everything we know about vertical spreads can be applied directly to the junior bonds.

By turning back to Tables 7-5 and 7-6, we can find the current market values of all of these securities. The senior bonds are worth the same as before, $106,000. Each share of stock is worth $7.50, so the total market value of the stock is $7,500. We can now find the market value of the Berkeford junior bonds in two ways. We can calculate the value of the vertical spread directly, or we can subtract the value of the stock and senior bonds from the total value of the assets. Either way, we get the market value of the remaining slice of the pie, $13,500.

Table 7-11 summarizes these results. There, J stands for the current value of the junior bonds, K_B is the promised payment to the senior bond-holders, and K_J is the promised payment to the junior bondholders. Figure 7-4(b) graphs the payoffs shown in the table.

Table 7-11
SUBORDINATED ZERO-COUPON BONDS

	Value on Current Date	*Value on Maturity Date*			*Representation in Terms of Calls*
		$V^* \leq K_B$	$K_B < V^* \leq K_B + K_J$	$K_B + K_J < V^*$	
Senior bonds	B	V^*	K_B	K_B	$V - C(V; K_B)$
Junior bonds	J	—	$V^* - K_B$	K_J	$C(V; K_B) - C(V; K_B + K_J)$
Stocks	nS	—	—	$V^* - K_B - K_J$	$C(V; K_B + K_J)$

Again, given proper specification of the stochastic process followed by the value of the firm and a constant riskless interest rate, we could derive exact valuation formulas for B, J, and S. One interesting implication of such an analysis is that, unlike the senior bonds, the value of the junior bonds may be an increasing function of the interest rate, the time to maturity, and volatility of the value of the firm. In addition, the junior bonds may be more volatile than the firm as a whole. All of these things would occur when V is low relative to $K_B + K_J$. In other words, in some circumstances, the junior bonds can behave more like a stock than a bond. This is not completely surprising, because for low values of V both the stockholders and the junior bondholders are contemplating the same fate; they are both likely to end up with nothing.

Just as our example of a single issue of zero-coupon bonds can be generalized to consider junior zero-coupon bonds, our second example can be greatly expanded with little conceptual difficulty. We can easily allow for an arbitrary number of bond issues maturing at different dates, each of which receives an arbitrary stream of payments. Each of these can depend on the value of the firm at time of payment. Of course, this is essential even if the promised payment is constant, since the amount actually received may be less than that and depend on the value of the firm. Moreover, the stock may be receiving an arbitrary stream of dividend payments, each of which also depends on the value of the firm. Note that if several payments are to be paid at the same time, the contract must specify a system of priorities among them in case they cannot all be fully paid.

Each payment at the end of time $t < T$ can be valued by exactly the same procedure we applied to the payment at maturity. The only difference is that we will express the payment after time t in terms of options with time to expiration t rather than T. All of the corporate securities are then packages of options on the value of the firm, given that the firm will be paying out the promised stream. Of course, if the payments up to a given date reduce the value of the firm to zero, then the subsequent payments become worthless, just as would be the case for any option on a bankrupt stock. The recipes discussed earlier could be used to express any given payment in terms of options. The representation for any of the bonds (or the stock) would just be the sum of the representations of each of its promised payments. Note that only European options will be used.

It might seem that in using only European options we have overlooked something. Since the stockholders do have a choice at each coupon payment date—namely, not making the payment—then American options apparently would be required. But the assumptions we made earlier guarantee that this is not the case. If the stockholders can make payments by selling assets, and will receive nothing if a payment is missed, it will always be in their interests to make the payments until there are no assets left in the firm.

None of the results would be changed if, when a payment is missed, the bondholders receive the minimum of (1) the total value of the firm, or (2) the market price of a package of riskless bonds whose payments are the same as the remaining promised payments on the corporate bonds. Again, it will always be in the stockholders' interests to make the payments.

Suppose instead that the contract, or court rulings, provide that when a payment is missed, the bondholders receive the minimum of (1) the total value of the firm, or (2) the promised final payment (the face value of the bond). Then, neglecting transactions costs, the stockholders may find it in their interests to miss a payment purposely. In this case the situation is more complicated, and a general representation in terms of European options is not possible. We will return to this briefly in Example 5.

Options versus Corporate Securities.   Examples 1 and 2 and the subsequent discussion highlight three important differences between options and corporate securities:

A. **The underlying asset for corporate securities is the total market value of all the equities and liabilities of the firm.**

B. **The owners of corporate securities receive the payouts being made by the firm.**

C. **The issuers of corporate securities may have the power to alter the firm's decisions with respect to investment, dividend, and financing policy.**

For an option, the underlying value of the stock was clearly defined and easily observable. For a corporate security, the required variables may be more difficult to obtain. Our theory, which is one of relative valuation, requires us to use the total value of the firm's equities and liabilities as V. This means that for a specific valuation formula, we must specify the stochastic process followed by the total market value of all of the firm's securities. Unlike an option, the value of any corporate security is itself part of this total value. Earlier, we did not need to place any restrictions on the possible disequilibrium behavior of option prices, but now we do for corporate securities. If any corporate security is undervalued (relative to V), then at least one of the other securities must be overvalued. Furthermore, some of the liabilities may be privately held and hence not traded, so we would have to estimate their current values to get the input V needed in the valuation formula.

The second difference is self-evident. The owner of an option never receives any part of the payouts being made by the firm. In contrast, the owners of the corporate securities receive, as a group, all of the payouts. Common and preferred stockholders receive dividends, and bondholders receive coupon payments. This means that the value of any one of these securities will usually not be derived solely from a single payment, as would be the case with an option. Instead, its total value will be the sum of the current values of all of the payments it will receive. Often, these payments can be valued as separate options, so a corporate security will then be equivalent to a package of options, rather than a single option, on the value of the firm.

We mentioned both of the first two differences while discussing the examples. However, we glossed over another important way in which Berkeford stock is different from a call option on the assets of the firm. Call options are owned by individuals who presumably have no influence on the firm's decisions about investment, dividend, and financing policies. In contrast, the Berkeford shareholders, in principle, have the power to alter Berkeford's policies on all these things. Hence, several of the fundamental determinants of option value, such as the volatility, dividend rate, and the striking price, may be under the control of the owner of the option. The volatility could be changed by changing the firm's investment policy, and the striking price could be changed by issuing more bonds with equal priority and using the proceeds to retire stock.

When the bonds were first issued, the stockholders were undoubtedly thinking of the firm as a going concern and had only honorable intentions. However, if things subsequently go wrong, the contemplation of disaster may be sufficient to bring out the worst in them. If the bonds were initially priced on the assumption of particular values for the determining variables, and the stockholders could later change them in a way helpful to them–

selves (increasing the value of their call option), they may succumb to the temptation to do so. In this way, the total value of the firm could be redistributed from the bondholders to the stockholders. But the bondholders will foresee this possibility and insist on contractual covenants that will keep the shareholders from acting against their interests. Stockholders will realize that they will not be able to sell bonds without some such assurances, and will accordingly include them in the terms of the bonds they offer for sale.

We can use our first example to illustrate why the bondholders must be protected and how they could be hurt if the stockholders suddenly find some completely unexpected way to get around the restrictions. Here are the effects of some one-time changes in Berkeford's financing, dividend, and investment policies.

1. Financing policy.   Suppose the Berkeford stockholders suddenly issue 20 more bonds having equal priority with the ones now outstanding, and use the proceeds of the sale to buy back stock. The promised payment to the bondholders is now $140,000. Table 7-6 shows that the total market value of the bonds will be $115,625. The new bondholders will own 20/140 of the total issue, for which they will have paid (20/140)($115,625) = $16,518, which in turn was used to buy back part of the stock. The remaining stock is worth $11,375. The stockholders thus have $16,518 in cash and $11,375 in stock, for a total gain of $6,893 over the stock's former value of $21,000. Of course, this has come directly out of the pockets of the hapless original bondholders, who have watched the value of their securities drop from $106,000 to (120/140)($115,625) = $99,107.

2. Dividend policy.   Suppose now that the Berkeford stockholders suddenly declare an immediate cash dividend of $25.40 per share. To raise the cash, they sell 200 shares of the Teledyne stock. Now the stockholders as a group have the dividend, $25,400, and they have a call on 800 shares of Teledyne stock with a total striking price of $120,000. This call is equivalent to owning 80% of a call on 1,000 shares of Teledyne stock with a total striking price of $150,000. We know that the market price of this latter call is $7,500, so the market price of the Berkeford stock after the dividend is paid would be .8($7,500) = $6,000. Consequently, the market value of the bonds will then be 800($127) − $6,000 = $95,600. The stockholders now have $25,400 in their pockets and stock worth $6,000, for a total gain of $10,400 over the stock's former value of $21,000. Correspondingly, the bondholders have lost the $10,400; the value of their bonds has dropped from $106,000 to $95,600.

3. Investment policy.   Now suppose that the Berkeford stockholders pull a third possible trick, a substitution of assets. They announce that they have traded the firm's 1,000 shares of Teledyne for 8,000 shares of Storage Technology. Like Teledyne, Storage Technology pays no cash dividends. At first this looks more promising for the bondholders. Table 7-5 shows that the current price of Storage Technology is $16.25 per share, so the firm now has $130,000 in assets backing up its bonds instead of $127,000. Unfortunately for the bondholders, this is not the only difference; Storage Technology is much more volatile than Teledyne. Each share of Berkeford stock is now the same as a call on eight shares of Storage Technology with a striking price of 120. This is equivalent to eight calls, each on one share with a striking price of 15. According to Table 7-5, each of these calls is worth $3.375, so each Berkeford share is worth $27. The total market value of the stock is now $27,000. The stockholders have gained $6,000 by switching into riskier assets. Even though the firm as a whole gained $3,000 in the swap, the stockholders gained even more, so the bondholders have ended up losing $3,000. If the swap had been made on even terms, they would have lost even more.

Although this sort of asset switch was blatantly obvious, the same effects can cause trouble in more insidious ways. The stockholders can be guilty of sins of omission as well as commission. Without proper incentives, they may forego opportunities which would increase the total value of the firm but simultaneously lower its volatility. Although it would not arise with a holding company, this underinvestment phenomenon can also appear in another subtle form. If the stockholders of a failing firm can pay more dividends by avoiding proper maintenance of the physical assets, they will certainly have an incentive to do so.

Of course, we do not observe this sort of thing happening regularly, and for good reasons. Over time, bondholders have learned what to watch out for and have insisted on effective protection. Also, the value of the assets of most firms is much greater than the amount promised to the bondholders. In effect, their stockholders have deep-in-the-money calls. In these cases, even if the covenants could be circumvented, the gains to the stockholders from even large changes in the dividend, financing, or investment policies will be negligible, so they have very little temptation to try such tactics. In addition, both managers and stockholders may be concerned about their long-term reputations, and properly so; if an attempted redistribution destroys future opportunities, the anticipated gains may prove illusory. Nevertheless, attempts at all of the things we have mentioned have happened many times when firms have been close to bankruptcy, and bondholders must always be aware of this possibility.

Naturally, if a firm with debt outstanding wishes to make a major change in its operations which would violate one or more bond covenants, it can try to renegotiate the terms of the debt. Option valuation can be particularly helpful in determining which tradeoffs are acceptable. Here is a simple example. Suppose that the Berkeford bonds were maturing on April 18 instead of July 18. The stockholders are looking at the calendar and having trouble sleeping, so they propose that the maturity date be extended to July 18. In return, they offer to raise the total promised payment to the bonds. How large an increase would be necessary? Each share of stock is now a call on Teledyne with a striking price of 120 and an expiration date of April 18. From Table 7-5 we find that the market value of this call is $16. Hence, the current market value of the bonds is $127,000 − 1,000 ($16) = $111,000. As it happens, that is exactly the value the bonds would have with a July maturity date and a total promised payment of $130,000, so that is the answer. The bondholders should be willing to make the switch as long as they are promised at least $130,000.

In the previous examples, the claimholders did not have the right to exchange their claims for other corporate liabilities. Many corporate securities do have this right, and although this feature seems immediately analogous to an American option, there are several important differences:

D. **When a corporate security is exercised and converted into common stock, new shares are issued.**

E. **If a corporate security requires payment of a striking price upon conversion, it is paid to the firm and increases the total level of funds in the firm.**

F. **For corporate securities that can be converted any time before maturity, because of differences D and E, it is not always optimal to exercise all corporate securities with identical terms at the same time.**

Each of these contrasts with an option, which, upon exercise, neither increases the number of outstanding shares nor alters the scale of the firm. Moreover, since the exercise of options has no effect on the firm, it is always optimal to exercise all American options with identical terms at the same time.

We will first illustrate differences D and E by Example 3, where the firm has outstanding common stock and a single issue of European warrants. Here the problems of difference F do not occur. Then we will give a specific numerical example of American warrants that demonstrates the possibility of the following circumstances:

1. The optimal exercise policy for a monopolist owning all of the warrants may involve sequential rather than simultaneous exercise.

2. Individual competing warrant holders can be led to take actions that will make all of them worse off than if they had worked together.

Finally, after a related example, Example 4, we use Examples 5 and 6 to illustrate a seventh difference between options and corporate securities:

G.   With corporate securities, it is possible for the issuer alone, or both the issuer and the owner simultaneously, to have discretionary rights about the disposition of the securities.

Of course, with options, these rights are only vested with the owner.

Example 3. Warrants.   A warrant is similar to a call. Its owner has the right to buy a fixed number of shares of a specified common stock at a specified price at any time until a given date.[15] However, they are not exactly the same. Warrants are issued by corporations rather than by individuals. When a warrant is exercised, new shares are created, and the exercise price (striking price) paid for them becomes part of the assets of the firm. Warrants are typically protected against stock splits and stock dividends in the same way as options; occasionally, partial protection against cash dividends is also provided. Unlike options, warrants sometimes have exercise prices which change over time.[16] In addition, some warrants may have unusual specific provisions; in any case, the contractual terms will be provided in the warrant agreement.[17]

To study the valuation of warrants, we will start with another example, Stanley Investments. Stanley is a lot like Berkeford: It also has all its funds invested in 1,000 shares of Teledyne stock. But the two firms are not identical: The original Stanley stockholders chose to issue warrants rather than bonds. With a little luck, we should be able to find the value of the Stanley stock and warrants in the same way we did for the Berkeford stock and bonds.

---

[15] Executive stock options and preemptive rights are corporate securities very similar to warrants, except the former are issued to employees and have restricted marketability, and the latter are issued to existing stockholders and have a very short life.

[16] For example, the exercise price of Textron warrants increased from $10.00 to $11.25 on May 1, 1979. Such changes can have an important effect on the optimal exercise strategy. Remember that a call should be exercised early only just before an ex-dividend date *or* just before an increase in the striking price.

[17] Readers who agree that a warrant is similar to a call may now be wondering about a puzzling observation: Often firms have voluntarily reduced the exercise price or lengthened the maturity of their warrants. How can this be in the best interest of the stockholders (the writers of the warrants)? The answer lies in a peculiar quirk of the tax law. Formerly, if warrants expired unexercised, the entire amount the firm originally received from the sale of the warrants was taxed as ordinary income on the expiration date, a procedure quite inconsistent with the taxation of other corporate securities. Firms thus had an incentive to change things so that a warrant about to expire worthless would be exercised, but with as little value as possible.

Here are the details about Stanley's capital structure. Currently out-standing are 1,000 shares of common stock and 250 warrants, each of which can be exchanged for one share of newly issued common stock upon payment of an exercise price of $120. The maturity date of the warrants is July 18, 1980 (today is still January 2); unlike most other warrants, their contract states that they cannot be exercised before the maturity date.

Now think about what the warrant holders will do on the maturity date. If it pays for any one warrant holder to exercise, then it will pay for all of them to exercise. Each will do so if the securities he receives by convert-ing are worth more than $120; otherwise, he will keep his money. If the 1,000 shares of Teledyne are worth V^* on the maturity date and the warrant holders convert, the value of Stanley's assets will increase to $V^* + \$120(250) = V^* + \$30,000$. The warrant holders will receive 250 newly issued shares, so they will then own $250/(1,000 + 250) = 20\%$ of the outstanding stock. Hence, they will be willing to make the exchange when-ever 20% of $V^* + \$30,000$ is greater than $30,000. This will be true when-ever V^* is greater than $120,000; if V^* is less than or equal to $120,000, the warrant holders will prefer to let their warrants expire unexercised. Table 7-12 summarizes these payoffs; the entries account for the fact that warrant holders will have to part with the exercise price if they convert and that this money will become part of the assets of the firm.

Table 7-12
PAYOFFS TO STANLEY SECURITIES ON THE MATURITY DATE

	$V^* \leq 120,000$	$V^* > 120,000$
Stanley stock	V^*	$.8(V^* + 30,000)$ $= V^* - .2(V^* - 120,000)$ $= 120,000 + .8(V^* - 120,000)$
Stanley warrants	0	$.2(V^* + 30,000) - 30,000$ $= .2(V^* - 120,000)$

As a group, the warrant holders own 20% of 1,000 call options on Teledyne, each on one share with a striking price of 120. We know that the current market price of one of these calls is $21. Hence, the total market value of the warrants should be $.2(1,000)(\$21) = \$4,200$; each individual warrant should be worth $\$4,200/250 = \$16.80$. Since the current total market value of all of the securities must be $127,000, the total value of the stock should be $\$127,000 - \$4,200 = \$122,800$, or $122.80 per share.

Now compare the Stanley and Berkeford securities. Were the original Stanley stockholders more adventuresome than those of Berkeford in issuing an exotic security like a warrant? No, quite the contrary. Another look at Table 7-12 shows that the Stanley stockholders will get exactly the same payoff as for a package containing all of the Berkeford bonds and 80% of the Berkeford stock. The Berkeford stockholders, on the other hand, have a package containing all of the stock and none of the bonds. One share of Stanley stock is thus a much more conservative investment than one share of Berkeford stock.

To study all this in more general terms, consider a corporation that has outstanding only two classes of obligations: n shares of common stock and m European warrants, each of which can be converted into one share of newly issued common stock upon payment of the exercise price K. If we label the current value of each warrant as W, then $V = nS + mW$. If it pays to exercise the warrants at expiration, their aggregate value will be:

$$mW^* = \left(\frac{m}{n + m}\right)(V^* + mK) - mK = \left(\frac{m}{n + m}\right)(V^* - nK)$$

and the value of an individual warrant will be:

$$W^* = \left(\frac{1}{n + m}\right)(V^* - nK).$$

Clearly, it will be optimal to exercise the warrants if and only if $V^* > nK$. Figure 7-4(c) and Table 7-13 summarize the payoff functions of the stock and warrants.

This analysis shows how to reconstruct warrants as call options on the *total value* of the firm. Yet warrants are commonly interpreted as otherwise identical call options on the *stock* of the firm. A European call option has payoff $\max[0, S^* - K]$. With only European warrants and stock in the

Table 7-13
EUROPEAN WARRANTS

	Current Date	Expiration Date		Representation in Terms of European Calls
		$V^* \leq nK$	$nK < V^*$	
Stock	nS	V^*	$\left(\frac{n}{n + m}\right)(V^* + mK)$	$V - \left(\frac{m}{n + m}\right)C(V; nK)$
Warrants	mW	—	$\left(\frac{m}{n + m}\right)(V^* - nK)$	$\left(\frac{m}{n + m}\right)C(V; nK)$

capital structure, we see from Table 7-13 that a single share of stock will be worth $S^* = (V^* + mK)/(n + m)$ if $S^* > K$. Therefore, the call will be worth $\max[0, (V^* + mK)/(n + m) - K]$. But this is equivalent to the payoff of a single European warrant on the stock. As a result, an otherwise identical European call and warrant must have the same current value to prevent arbitrage.

Despite this equivalence, the presence of warrants in the capital structure may affect the applicability of the Black-Scholes formula, where a call or warrant is valued relative to its underlying stock. If the value of the firm follows a continuous process with constant volatility, the stock itself will not do so if warrants are also present in the capital structure. Thus, a condition for applying the Black-Scholes formula to the warrant (or the call) as an option on the *stock* will not be met.

Suppose we ask a somewhat different question. Let us compare the value of a call on a firm *without warrants* to the value of a warrant on an "otherwise identical" firm with warrants. This is the comparison that would be relevant if we had some procedure for valuing calls and wanted to apply that same procedure for valuing warrants. To satisfy the "otherwise identical" requirement, consider a firm with just one class of obligations outstanding: n shares of common stock. In this case, $V = nS$. Let C represent the value of a call on a share of the firm's stock.

Now suppose the firm issues m warrants with a value of W for each warrant. This brings us squarely against a difficulty: What does the firm do with the proceeds from the sale of the warrants? To make a useful comparison, we will assume the warrant proceeds are handled in a way that leaves the current stock price unchanged. One possibility is for the firm to distribute the proceeds as dividends to the shareholders and leave its real investment decisions unchanged. If the present value of the firm were independent of its capital structure, then after this distribution, $V = n\hat{S} + mW$, where $\hat{S}$ is now the new, ex-dividend value of the stock. But since the stockholders received mW in dividends, they are just as well off as before.

Let S^* be the price per share of the stock on the expiration date if no warrants had been issued. Therefore, if it pays to exercise the warrant, the *value of the stock cum exercise* will be

$$\hat{S}^* = \frac{nS^* + mK}{n + m} = \frac{S^* + \lambda K}{1 + \lambda},$$

where $\lambda \equiv m/n$ is the dilution factor. The numerator is the total value of the now outstanding stock, and the denominator is the corresponding number of shares. It will pay to exercise the warrant only if the value of the warrant cum exercise is greater than the exercise price, that is, $\hat{S}^* > K$.

Therefore, on its expiration date, the value of the warrant $W*$ is $\max[0, \hat{S}* - K]$, or, equivalently,

$$W* = \begin{cases} \dfrac{S* - K}{1 + \lambda} & \text{if} \quad S* > K \\ 0 & \text{if} \quad S* \leq K. \end{cases}$$

In contrast, the value of a European call with the same striking price and expiration date, written on the same stock (except where warrants have not also been issued) will be on its expiration date

$$C* = \begin{cases} S* - K & \text{if} \quad S* > K \\ 0 & \text{if} \quad S* \leq K. \end{cases}$$

Observe that a portfolio of $1 + \lambda$ warrants will have the same dollar value at expiration as one call. Therefore, to avoid riskless profitable arbitrage, $1 + \lambda$ warrants and one call must have the same current price. As a result,

$$W = \left(\frac{1}{1 + \lambda}\right)C.$$

More generally, the firm might have invested the warrant proceeds instead of distributing them to its shareholders. Again, to make the correct comparison, we would then assume the firm invested the proceeds to leave the stock price the same. In either case, we will reach the same conclusion.

The dilution effect causes an otherwise identical European warrant to sell for less than the corresponding European call. Just how much less depends on the ratio λ of the number of outstanding warrants to the number of outstanding shares prior to exercise. As an empirical matter, the dilution factor can be of significant size. For example, the AT&T warrants, the first listed on the New York Stock Exchange, which expired on May 15, 1975, had a dilution factor of about 6%.

However, suppose warrants comprise a very small fraction of the capital structure, and we are willing to approximate the value of a European warrant by using the Black-Scholes formula relative to the stock price. What special aspects of warrants, compared with listed calls, might create practical valuation problems?

A warrant typically has a longer time to expiration, so the riskless rate of interest is a more significant determinant of its value. For example, consider a payout-protected warrant to one share with exercise price of 40 and time to expiration of ten years, written on common stock with a current price of 40 and an annualized volatility of .3. If the Black-Scholes formula were used to value this warrant, a change in the annualized interest rate from .05 to .06 would change the value of the warrant from $20.87 to $22.06. The value of a similar nine-month call would change from $4.82 to $4.96. In percentage terms, this difference in interest rates is twice as important for the warrant as for the call.

If, like a call, a warrant carries no protection against cash dividends, the value of the warrant will be very sensitive to corporate dividend policy. In the above example, with a .05 interest rate and a constant annual dividend yield of 2.5%, the value of a European call would fall from $4.82 to $4.38. However, the European warrant value would decline from $20.87 to $13.73. The longer time to expiration of the warrant increases the impact of the anticipated dividend yield, and any uncertainty in the dividend yield, on the value of a warrant.

Over the longer time to expiration of a warrant, the stock volatility is not likely to remain stable, as required by the Black-Scholes formula. Models with fluctuating volatility are therefore likely to be important for valuing warrants.

If the warrants may be exercised before maturity, then it may seem that we can simply reinterpret the European calls as American calls. However, this is not necessarily true, and the points raised in differences D, E, and F may become critically important. The issues involved are complicated and not yet fully resolved. A complete discussion would be quite lengthy; we will, instead, give an example that illustrates the types of things that may occur.[18]

The example is set in the context of our two-point discrete time process, with one period remaining in the life of the warrants. Suppose that the firm has n shares of common stock and two warrants outstanding. All markets are now open for trading, and any warrant holder may, if he wishes, exercise now. If he does so, he receives one newly issued share of common stock in return for the exercise price, which immediately becomes part of the assets of the firm. Then one period passes, and the value of the assets in the firm is multiplied by either u or d. Trading is then reopened, and the warrant holders again have the opportunity to exercise or else let the warrants expire, since this is now the expiration date. Each warrant holder thus has the choice of converting now or of waiting. Because of the points mentioned above, the value of each strategy will depend on the strategy followed for the other warrant.

Table 7-14 introduces the notation for the present value of each warrant conditional on the policy followed by both warrants.

---

[18] For a detailed discussion of these issues, see David C. Emanuel, "Warrant Valuation and Exercise Strategy," *Journal of Financial Economics*, 12 (August 1983), 211–236 and George M. Constantinides and Robert W. Rosenthal, "Strategic Analysis of the Competitive Exercise of Certain Financial Options," *Journal of Economic Theory*, 32 (February 1984), 128–138.

Table 7-14
NOTATION FOR VALUE OF WARRANT

	Both Convert	Only One Converts	Both Do Not Convert
Converted	A	B	not possible
Unconverted	not possible	C	D

Now we can easily apply the earlier analysis of warrants and our basic binomial valuation procedure to find the values of warrants A, B, C, and D. These will be

$$A = \left(\frac{1}{n+2}\right)V - \left(\frac{n}{n+2}\right)K,$$

$$B = \left(\frac{1}{n+1}\right)V - \left(\frac{n}{n+1}\right)K - \left(\frac{1}{n+1}\right)C,$$

$$C = \left(\frac{p}{r}\right)\max\left[u\left(\frac{1}{n+2}\right)(V+K) - \left(\frac{n+1}{n+2}\right)K, 0\right]$$
$$+ \left(\frac{1-p}{r}\right)\max\left[d\left(\frac{1}{n+2}\right)(V+K) - \left(\frac{n+1}{n+2}\right)K, 0\right],$$

$$D = \left(\frac{p}{r}\right)\max\left[u\left(\frac{1}{n+2}\right)V - \left(\frac{n}{n+2}\right)K, 0\right]$$
$$+ \left(\frac{1-p}{r}\right)\max\left[d\left(\frac{1}{n+2}\right)V - \left(\frac{n}{n+2}\right)K, 0\right],$$

where p is, as before, $(r-d)/(u-d)$. The payoffs in each instance are described in Table 7-15. In each pair, the payoff received by I is given first and that of II is given second.

Table 7-15
POSSIBLE WARRANT PAYOFFS

Warrant Holder II

		Convert	Do Not Convert
Warrant Holder I	Convert	(A, A)	(B, C)
	Do Not Convert	(C, B)	(D, D)

Suppose that $C > D > A > B$. If the market structure is such that warrant holders act as competing individuals who cannot communicate and form binding agreements, the outcome is clear. The equilibrium point for this game will be for neither warrant holder to convert, since neither would then have an incentive to make a unilateral change in his policy. Furthermore, suppose that $B + C > 2D$. Then if the market structure is such that the warrant holders can communicate and enter into binding agreements with side payments, they could realize a further gain from the following sequential policy: One warrant holder will convert now, the other will wait, and the gain will be divided between them. This, of course, is the strategy that would be followed by a monopolist who owned both warrants. A monopolist could thus find it advantageous to exercise one of the warrants before maturity even though the stock is not paying dividends. Similar arguments apply when there are more than two warrants outstanding.

The following numerical example shows that all of these conditions may occur. It is constructed for convenience in showing several things simultaneously, rather than for empirical realism or for emphasis on the magnitude of the effects considered. Let

$$n = 4, \quad V = 1,000, \quad K = 26, \quad u = 1.8, \quad d = .1, \quad \text{and} \quad r = 1.05.$$

We then find that $A = 149.33$, $B = 148.74$, $C = 152.28$, and $D = 150.44$. Therefore, $C > D > A > B$ and $B + C > 2D$.

In this example, the value of the warrants when warrant holders act as competing individuals is the same as the value the warrants would have if they were held by a single individual who was constrained to exercise all of the warrants at the same time. It turns out that this property remains true under fairly general conditions, including situations in which the warrants held by competing individuals would not necessarily all be exercised simultaneously. Consequently, valuation results obtained under the very convenient assumption that all warrants must be exercised at the same time can be valid for widely held warrants in which exercise occurs sequentially. A number of interesting questions remain to be resolved about the many intermediate situations in which some individuals have large holdings of warrants and other individuals have small holdings. All of these issues may be relevant for other corporate securities as well.

Example 4. Convertible Bonds. Convertible bonds combine many of the features of warrants and ordinary bonds. Like ordinary bonds, they are entitled to receive fixed coupon and principal payments and have priority over the stock in the event of bankruptcy or reorganization. Like warrants, they can be surrendered to the firm at the discretion of their owner in return for a specified number of shares of newly issued common stock. Of course, warrants also require the payment of an exercise price when this exchange is made, while convertible bonds rarely do. For them, the exercise price is in effect the future coupon and principal payments which are foregone when they are exchanged for stock. Consequently, a convertible is like a package of an ordinary bond and a warrant with a changing exercise price equal to the value of the bond.[19]

Convertible bonds thus provide one response to some of the conflicts of interest between stockholders and bondholders mentioned earlier. Here the approach is to reduce the conflicts by giving the bondholders the right to become stockholders on specified terms. Another approach is to provide the bondholders with additional protective restrictions. This is illustrated in Example 7, bonds with safety covenants.

Convertibles are normally protected against stock splits and stock dividends in the same way as options. This and the other terms of the contract are contained in their indenture agreements; sometimes, special provisions will be included. One very important provision is not at all special, for it is found with nearly every convertible—the firm has the right to buy back the issue at any time for a specified price. As one might expect, this considerably complicates the valuation of convertibles, so we will take things one step at a time. We will first discuss convertibles that do not have this provision, and then discuss bonds with this provision in Example 5.[20]

Suppose that Stanley Investments has issued convertible bonds instead of warrants. Specifically, suppose the firm has outstanding 1,000 shares of common stock and 120 bonds, each of which promises to pay $1,000 on the maturity date, July 18, and nothing before then. So far this is identical to the Berkeford bonds, but the Stanley bonds have an additional feature: On the maturity date, but not before then, each bond can be exchanged for $33\frac{1}{3}$ shares of newly issued common stock.

Under what circumstances would this exchange take place? If the bondholders convert, they will own $120(33\frac{1}{3})/(1,000 + 120(33\frac{1}{3})) = 80\%$ of V^*. If they do not convert, they will receive $120,000 or V^*, whichever is smaller. Hence, the bondholders will choose to convert whenever 80% of V^* is greater than $120,000, which will be true whenever V^* is greater than $150,000. Table 7-16 summarizes the payoffs to the Stanley securities on the maturity date.

Do these payoffs look familiar? Think of the second Berkeford example with both junior and senior bonds. The Stanley bondholders will receive exactly the same payoff as someone who owns 80% of the Berkeford

---

[19] Some warrants allow a designated bond to be used at par value in place of cash to pay the exercise price.

[20] Examples 4, 5, and 6 were first developed in Jonathan E. Ingersoll, Jr., "A Contingent-Claims Valuation of Convertible Securities," *Journal of Financial Economics*, 4 (May 1977), 289–322 and Michael J. Brennan and Eduardo S. Schwartz, "Convertible Bonds: Valuation and Optimal Strategies for Call and Conversion," *Journal of Finance*, 32 (December 1977), 1699–1716.

Table 7-16

PAYOFFS TO STANLEY SECURITIES ON THE MATURITY DATE

	$V^* \leq 120{,}000$	$120{,}000 < V^* \leq 150{,}000$	$V^* > 150{,}000$
Stanley convertible bonds	V^*	120,000	$.8V^* = 120{,}000$ $+ .8(V^* - 150{,}000)$
Stanley stock	0	$V^* - 120{,}000$	$.2V^* = 30{,}000$ $+ .2(V^* - 150{,}000)$

stock and all of the Berkeford senior bonds. Accordingly, the current market value of their claim should be $.8(\$7{,}500) + \$106{,}000 = \$112{,}000$. The Stanley stockholders will, in turn, receive exactly the same payoff as someone who owns the remaining 20% of the Berkeford stock and all of the Berkeford *junior* bonds. Hence, the current total market value of the stock should be $\$127{,}000 - 112{,}000 = .2(\$7{,}500) + \$13{,}500 = \$15{,}000$, or \$15 per share. We thus see that the stock of a firm with convertible bonds outstanding can itself behave much like a junior bond. We know from our earlier discussion that when the value of the firm is low, the value of the junior bonds can increase when the volatility of the firm increases. Hence, the conversion feature reduces, but does not eliminate, the incentives for stockholders to undertake riskier projects if the firm gets into trouble.

To state this in more general terms, consider a corporation that has outstanding only two classes of securities: n shares of common stock and m convertible bonds, each of which can be converted into k newly issued shares immediately after time to maturity T. As long as they are not converted, the bonds are to receive specified coupon payments and a final payment of K/m per bond. Again, for simplicity, we assume the stock pays no dividends. If conversion is chosen, then the bondholders would own the fraction

$$\lambda \equiv \frac{mk}{n + mk}$$

of the firm. It will thus be in the bondholders' interest to convert only if $V^* > K/\lambda$. Figure 7-4(d) and Table 7-17 describe the payoff functions of the convertible bonds and the stock.

Of course, virtually all convertible bonds are of the American type and can be converted at the bondholder's discretion any time on or before the maturity date. As long as the stock receives no dividends, it is easy to show that early conversion would never be optimal. The representation in terms of European calls would then remain valid for an American convertible. However, with arbitrary payments *both* to bondholders and stock-

Table 7-17
CONVERTIBLE BONDS

	Current Date	Maturity Date			Representation in Terms of European Calls
		$V^* \leq K$	$K < V^* \leq K/\lambda$	$K/\lambda < V^*$	
Bonds	B	V^*	K	λV^*	$V - C(V; K) + \lambda C(V; K/\lambda)$
Stock	nS	—	$V^* - K$	$(1 - \lambda)V^*$	$C(V; K) - \lambda C(V; K/\lambda)$

holders, and with *American* convertibles, early exercise may be desirable, and no representation is possible in terms of ordinary options. Nonetheless, it can be shown that it is never optimal to convert the bonds prior to maturity if the value of the coupons exceeds λ times the sum of the value of the coupons and the value of the dividends for all dates before maturity. This condition says that bondholders should never convert as long as the value of the payouts they receive is a greater fraction of total payouts before conversion than it would be after conversion. In this case, American and European convertibles will have the same value. In any event, as we will illustrate in Example 6, convertible bonds can be readily valued by option pricing methods even when no direct representation in terms of options is possible.

Example 5. Callable Bonds. Most ordinary bonds, as well as convertibles, have a provision that allows the firm to repurchase ("call") the issue at any time for a specified amount (the call price) plus the accrued interest since the last coupon date. Typically, the initial call price will be somewhat above the par value of the bonds and will decline gradually over time. Sometimes the call privilege will be deferred until the bonds have been outstanding for some length of time.

Why are call provisions so prevalent? A common answer is that they give firms the opportunity to refinance on more favorable terms if interest rates fall or the fortunes of the firm improve. But of course investors are aware of this and will accordingly be willing to pay less for a callable bond than for a corresponding noncallable one. Unless firms are convinced that investors systematically overvalue callable bonds relative to noncallable ones, this answer would still not give a convincing reason for the firms always to use callable bonds.

A more cogent explanation is that bondholders who have quite properly protected themselves with various indenture restrictions may have the potential to make a nuisance of themselves by blocking certain mergers, acquisitions, or major investments. Even when the proposed change would benefit the bondholders, they might find it advantageous to use their position to extract even greater benefits. Of course, all of this could be taken into account in the initial pricing of noncallable bonds, but their existence might then lead the firm to avoid certain policies that would otherwise be attractive. Firms can minimize or avoid the whole problem by using a call provision that places an upper limit on what the firm will have to pay to eliminate the bonds from its capital structure.

Another explanation concerns the effects of unanticipated decreases in the inflation rate. A decrease in inflation will not decrease the dollar amount of the coupon payments of outstanding bonds, but it probably will reduce the future dollar profits of the firm and therefore its ability to meet these payments. If inflation, and therefore interest rates, decrease too suddenly for the firm to buy back the bonds as interest rates fall, then lack of a call provision could lead to a costly reorganization.

Furthermore, it may be the case that court rulings would provide that in the event of default the bondholders receive either the total value of the firm or the promised final payment plus accrued interest, whichever is lower. Then a firm with "noncallable" bonds in effect has the right to call them anyway for a price of the final payment plus the coupon due by voluntarily defaulting. Of course, the resulting reorganization would be costly in many ways, but it still could be to the stockholders' advantage if interest rates become sufficiently low. Bondholders will realize the possibility of this implicit call and take it into account in the price they are willing to pay for the bonds. According to this argument, bonds will be effectively callable in any case, so it will be beneficial to everyone to use an explicit call provision rather than drain off resources with a costly implicit call.[21, 22]

Once again, we will use the simplest possible setting to illustrate the analogy with options. Consider a corporation with two classes of obligations: n shares of common stock and a single issue of callable bonds, with time to maturity T and promised payments consisting of specified coupon payments and a final payment of K. The stockholders have the right to buy back the bond issue *at any time* τ for an aggregate call price of K_τ, which may vary with time. Again, we assume the stock receives no dividends prior to the maturity date.

Under these conditions, the stock is equivalent to an American call on the value of the firm, with striking price of K_τ prior to the maturity date and K on the maturity date. Table 7-18 describes the payoff function of the callable bonds and the stock.

---

[21] This was first noted by Scott Mason.

[22] One further argument for using callable bonds is based on a feature of the tax laws: The calling of a bond gives the bondholder a capital gain and the firm an ordinary loss.

Table 7-18
CALLABLE BONDS

	Current Date	Date τ (If Called)	Maturity Date (If Not Called)		Representation in Terms of American Calls
			$V^* \le K$	$K < V^*$	
Bonds	B	K_τ	V^*	K	$V - C(V; K_\tau, K)$
Stock	nS	$V_\tau - K_\tau$	—	$V^* - K$	$C(V; K_\tau, K)$

In Chapter 4, we gave a sufficient condition for there to be no advantage to exercising an American call before expiration when the striking price K was constant. For a callable bond (where the "striking price" now depends on time), the corresponding condition is that the call price must always be greater than the present value of the principal payment plus the present value of the remaining coupons.

Example 6. Callable Convertible Bonds. Just as convertible bonds combine features of both warrants and ordinary bonds, callable convertible bonds combine features of both callable bonds and convertible bonds. In effect, they are convertible bonds with one additional provision: At any time the stockholders have the right to call the bonds for a designated amount (the call price plus interest). If a call does occur, the bondholders have a fixed length of time in which to convert their bonds. If they choose not to convert, then they must allow the stockholders to buy back the bonds for the designated amount.

Callable convertible bonds thus illustrate the seventh difference between options and corporate securities: Both the issuer and the owner simultaneously have discretionary rights about the disposition of the security. This typically makes callable convertible bonds more complicated than our previous examples. Various conditions can be given in which a call, or early conversion, would never occur, and in these situations a callable convertible would be equivalent to Example 4 or 5. In general, however, no representation in terms of ordinary options will be possible. Consequently, callable convertibles provide a natural setting for demonstrating that option valuation methods can still be applied.

As a specific example, consider a firm with two types of securities outstanding, 150 shares of common stock, and 100 callable convertible bonds maturing two periods from now. Each of the bonds is entitled to receive a coupon payment of $100 each period, plus a promised payment of $1000 on the maturity date. At any time on or before the maturity date, the stockholders have the right to call the bonds for a call price of $1100 each, and the bondholders have the right to exchange each of their bonds for one newly issued share of common stock. If the bondholders choose to convert, they will thus own $100/(150 + 100) = 40\%$ of the firm. If a call occurs, the bondholders must make their choice immediately. To focus on the main issues, and avoid the questions of sequential conversion considered at the end of Example 3, assume that all of the bonds are required to be converted simultaneously.

Suppose that the interest rate is 8% per period, and that the current total value of the firm after the current coupon has been paid is $200,000. Over each period, this value will, before coupon payments, either increase by 50% or decrease by 50%. The following table shows the possible circumstances for the firm over the next two periods and the possible values of the bonds on the maturity date; all values in the diagram are in thousands of dollars.

Value of the Firm		Value of Bonds on the Maturity Date	
		If converted	If not converted
	$435 - 10 = 425$	170	100
$300 - 10 = 290$			
	$145 - 10 = 135$	54	100
200			
	$135 - 10 = 125$	50	100
$100 - 10 = 90$			
	$45 - 10 = \ 35$	14	35

By comparing the converted and unconverted values of the bonds on the maturity date, we see that the bondholders would choose to convert at that time if the ex-coupon total value is $425,000; otherwise, they would be better off receiving the full promised payment or whatever part of that payment the firm is able to make.

Now we can use our familiar recursive technique to move backward one period and find the value of the bonds when there is one period remaining; here $p = (1.08 - .5)/(1.5 - .5)$. If the ex-coupon value of the firm at that time is $290,000, then the ex-coupon value of the entire issue of bonds if held for one more period would be

$$\frac{.58(\$170,000) + .42(\$100,000)}{1.08} + \frac{\$10,000}{1.08} = \$139,444.$$

The last term on the left-hand side, $10,000/1.08, is the present value of the coupon payment to be received on the maturity date. If the bondholders convert at this time, their holding will be worth only .4($290,000) = $116,000; so they would prefer to continue holding the bonds rather than convert. Of course, the stockholders are looking at things from the opposite point of view. The larger the slice of the pie that is going to the bondholders, the smaller is the slice left for them. They wish to use their call privilege to maximize the value of the stock and minimize the value of the bonds. In the current situation, they can in effect force the bondholders to convert by calling the bonds. If the bonds are called, the bondholders would no longer have the opportunity to hold them one more period as they preferred. Instead, their choice would then be to convert immediately or receive the total call price of $110,000. Since the conversion value of their claim is $116,000, they would choose to convert. (Note that if the call price had been somewhat higher—for example, $1200 per bond— the bondholders would have preferred to accept the call price instead of converting.)

If the ex-coupon value of the firm with one period to go were $90,000 instead of $290,000, then the value of the bonds if held one more period would be

$$\frac{.58(\$100,000) + .42(\$35,000)}{1.08} + \frac{\$10,000}{1.08} = \$76,574,$$

and their value if converted would be .4($90,000) = $36,000. Clearly, the stockholders would not want to call and the bondholders would not want to convert; so here the bonds would in fact be held for one more period.

Now we have all the information needed to find the value of the bonds when there are two periods remaining. If the bonds are held over the next period, their current value would be

$$\frac{.58(\$116,000) + .42(\$76,574)}{1.08} + \frac{\$10,000}{1.08} = \$101,334.$$

The last term on the left-hand side is the present value of the coupon that will be received when there is one period remaining; the value of the coupon to be received on the maturity date is already included in the values in the first term on the left-hand side. Since $101,334 is less than the total call price of $110,000, the stockholders would not wish to call the bonds. On the other hand, $101,334 is greater than the immediate total conversion value of $80,000; so the bondholders would not want to convert. Consequently, the bonds will in fact be held one more period, and their total current value is $101,334, or $1,013.34 per bond.

A very similar calculation can be done to show that the current value of an otherwise identical issue of nonconvertible bonds is $93,734; so here the conversion feature is worth $7600 to the bondholders. It can also be shown that the current value of an otherwise identical issue of noncallable bonds is $113,924.63; so the call feature decreases the value of the bonds by $12,590.63.

At this point, it is worthwhile to mention several further differences between options and corporate securities, even though they do not play a role in our examples. Again, they arise from the fact that corporate securities are issued by firms rather than individuals. Each will prevent the relative valuation of corporate securities from being identical to that for options on the stock of an all-equity firm. However, *none are sufficient to keep the general principles of option valuation from being applicable.*

H. The value of an option sold by an individual is unaffected by any other options he or she may have sold; this is not true for a firm.

Each option issued by an individual is a separate asset supported by sufficient collateral. In contrast, securities of a firm are all claims to the same set of assets and must be valued as a group. To focus on specific points, we assumed in our examples that the firm had only two classes of securities outstanding. Most have more than this, sometimes many more. If these multiple issues involve callable or convertible securities, as is usually the case, it will not be possible to represent them in terms of ordinary options.

I. The payoffs to an option depend only on the value of the underlying asset; the payoffs to corporate securities may depend on other variables as well.

As an example, some corporate securities have provisions that require a reorganization of the firm if certain accounting variables reach specified levels. The following section discusses a situation where the same type of provision depends on the underlying asset, the value of the firm, rather than accounting variables.

J. With corporate securities, the act of issuance may itself convey information.

The buyer of an option does not know the identity of the seller. He cannot tell if it is someone who is likely to have special information. Neither does he know the total position of the seller, nor whether the seller is simultaneously engaging in offsetting trades. The fact that someone is willing to write a particular option conveys very little information. On the other hand, the potential buyer of a prospective corporate security knows all of these things. The outstanding securities of a company are a matter of public record, and the decision to issue has been made by the firm's management, presumably a well-informed group. Consequently, the fact that a firm is willing to issue a particular type of security may contain information.

7-4. DOWN-AND-OUT OPTIONS

Our final example is bonds with safety covenants. Safety covenants are contractual provisions that give the bondholders the right to force bankruptcy or reorganization of the firm if it is doing poorly according to some standard. A common standard is omission of interest payments on the bonds. However, if the stockholders are allowed to sell the assets of the firm to meet the interest payments, then this criterion may not provide the desired security for the bondholders; additional provisions will be necessary. A convenient way to specify such a provision and examine its effects is to consider a safety covenant of the following form: If the value of the firm falls to a specified level, which may change over time, then the bondholders are entitled to force the firm into bankruptcy and obtain the ownership of the assets.

In all of our previous examples, we have used European and American options to value corporate securities. Again, it might seem that American options will offer the flexibility needed to value bonds with safety covenants, but this is not the case. The reason is that American options, in effect, have an upper (for calls) or lower (for puts) boundary which is determined by the optimal exercise policy; it cannot be specified arbitrarily. Moreover, otherwise identical American options with different striking prices will have different optimal exercise boundaries. Therefore, even if we knew the optimal exercise boundary in advance (and we do not), we could not construct a portfolio with a finite number of American options that would be equivalent to bonds with a safety covenant.

To value a bond with a safety covenant, American options are not only inadequate but are also a more complex form of option than we need. Yet European options are clearly too simple. However, there is another type of option which has just the right features.

> A *down-and-out call* is identical to a European call with
> the additional feature that the contract is cancelled if the
> stock price reaches or goes below a prespecified *lower*
> boundary, which may be a function of time. The contract

also specifies the rebate received, if any, if cancellation occurs. The amount of the rebate is received when the "knock-out" boundary is first reached, and it may depend on the time this occurs.

An *up-and-out put* (or up-and-away put) is the same, except the contract is cancelled when the stock price reaches or goes above a prespecified *upper* boundary.

Down-and-out calls and up-and-out puts differ in an important way from American and European options. Like American options, their value depends not only on the stock price at expiration, but also on the path it may follow in getting there. Unlike the American option, the critical boundary at which its value is determined is specified in advance by the contract. As a result, these options provide an important building block for valuing complex securities with features similar to bonds with safety covenants.

What is more, down-and-out options have been available in the U.S. over-the-counter market since 1967, and may someday be traded on listed exchanges. In the days before listed options, the secondary market for calls was virtually nonexistent. Then, as now, covered call writers might be forced to liquidate their stock position if the price dropped sharply. Since they could not easily liquidate the option position simultaneously, they could be whipsawed badly if the stock rose again. Down-and-out calls eliminate this unwanted risk by automatically liquidating the option position (and would save transaction costs for public writers who followed this policy). Even after the development of the options exchanges, some investment banking firms have occasionally received and met requests from clients to write down-and-out calls.

It should be immediately clear that if the assumptions we made in Chapter 5 hold, then we can apply our binomial valuation approach to down-and-out options. The only difference in the numerical procedure used with American options is the following. Instead of checking at each point to see if exercise is optimal and assigning the exercise value if it is, we now check to see if the knock-out boundary has been reached and assign the rebate value if it has. We can again lock in sure profits from mispricing by using an equivalent portfolio of stocks and bonds.

As an illustration, reconsider the numerical example discussed in Section 5-4. Suppose that the knock-out price is $H = 70$, and the rebate is $R = 2$, there are two periods remaining, and the current stock price is 120. Let $D(S, n)$ be the value of a down-and-out call with n periods remaining. Again we work backward from the expiration date. Clearly, $D(180, 1) = C(180, 1) = 107.26$. Now, however, $D(60, 1) = 2$, since 60 is below the knock-out boundary. Thus,

$$D(120, 2) = [pD(180, 1) + (1 - p)D(60, 1)]/r = 59.23.$$

We can compare this with $C(120, 2) = 60.46$. The value of a down-and-out call with no rebate is obviously less than or equal to the value of a corresponding regular call.

Unlike the case of American options for which early exercise may be optimal, it is possible to develop a simple binomial formula to value down-and-out options. This simplification arises because the knock-out boundary for down-and-out options is known in advance, while the optimal exercise boundary for an American option is not. The approach begins by dividing the total value of a down-and-out call into two mutually exclusive parts:

1. The present value of the final payment $\max[0, S^* - K]$ to be received only if the contract is not previously cancelled.
2. The present value of the rebate to be received only if the knock-out boundary is reached.

In deriving (1), we only consider stock price paths that do not cross the boundary. Derivation of (2) is complicated by the need to know not only *if* the rebate will be received, but also *when* it will be received, since its timing affects its present value. However, the two portions of the option's value are, to some extent, separable, since (1) is unaffected by the size of the rebate and (2) is unaffected by the striking price.

To conserve space, we will bypass the full development of the binomial formula and simply state the limiting result when both the knock-out boundary H and the rebate R are constant (assuming $S, K \geq H$):

DOWN-AND-OUT OPTION PRICING FORMULA

$$D = SN(x) - Kr^{-t}N(x - \sigma\sqrt{t})$$
$$- [S(S/H)^{-2\xi}N(y) - Kr^{-t}(S/H)^{-2\xi+2}N(y - \sigma\sqrt{t})]$$
$$+ R[(S/H)^{-2\xi+1}N(z) + (S/H)N(z - 2\xi\sigma\sqrt{t})]$$

where

$$\xi \equiv \frac{\log r}{\sigma^2} + \tfrac{1}{2}$$

$$x \equiv \frac{\log(S/K)}{\sigma\sqrt{t}} + \xi\sigma\sqrt{t}$$

$$y \equiv \frac{\log(H^2/SK)}{\sigma\sqrt{t}} + \xi\sigma\sqrt{t}$$

$$z \equiv \frac{\log(H/S)}{\sigma\sqrt{t}} + \xi\sigma\sqrt{t}$$

Note that the value D of the down-and-out call has been written as the sum of three terms: (1) the value of an otherwise identical ordinary European call, (2) minus the reduction in value due to the early cancellation feature of the down-and-out call, (3) plus the value of the rebate.

An up-and-out put has a similar formula, except that we replace S, K, and H by $-S$, $-K$, and $-H$, respectively, and all terms of the form $N(z)$ are replaced with $N(-z)$. Of course, now S and K must be less than or equal to H.

These formulas can be easily generalized to incorporate a knockout boundary H which depends exponentially on time to expiration, as in $He^{-\gamma t}$, and to incorporate a rebate R which depends exponentially and/or linearly on time to expiration, as in $(R + \alpha t)e^{-\beta t}$, where α, β, and γ are fixed parameters.[23]

Down-and-out options thus provide the building blocks we need to value bonds with safety covenants. Suppose that a firm has only two classes of securities outstanding: n shares of common stock and a single issue of bonds with a safety covenant and a promised final payment of K. The safety covenant specifies that the firm will be reorganized, with the bondholders receiving ownership of the assets, if the value of the firm drops to H_τ (which may depend on time). The bonds receive coupon payments, but the stock pays no dividends. Then the value of the stock and bonds can be written in terms of a down-and-out call as shown in Table 7-19.

Table 7-19
BONDS WITH SAFETY COVENANTS

	Current Date	First Date τ that $V_\tau \le H_\tau$	Maturity Date If $V_\tau > H_\tau$ for All τ		Representation in Terms of Down-and-Out Calls
			$V^* \le K$	$K < V^*$	
Bonds	B	V_τ	V^*	K	$V - D(V; K)$
Stock	nS	$-$	$-$	$V^* - K$	$D(V; K)$

Here $D(V; K)$ is the value of a down-and-out call with exercise price K and knock-out boundary H_τ expiring at the same time as the bonds. If the stock pays dividends, then the value of each of the dividends it may receive during the life of the bonds can also be written in terms of down-and-out calls; the

---

[23] If a European down-and-out option is not protected against cash dividends, we might think we could simply replace the stock price with the stock price reduced by the present value of the dividends. This would be similar to our treatment of non-payout-protected European calls. However, the different contractual provisions of the down-and-out call imply that this correction will be inappropriate.

value of the stock will be $D(V; K)$ plus the value of the dividends. Furthermore, if we make the same assumptions as in Example 2, with the addition of a safety covenant which is constant over time, then the formula given above can be used to value the stock and bonds. In fact, Example 2 would then correspond to the special case of no safety covenant (that is, $H_\tau = 0$).

7-5. COMPOUND OPTIONS

Coming full circle, we return to the valuation of ordinary puts and calls. But with the foregoing analysis of corporate securities, we can approach ordinary option valuation from a different perspective.

Thus far, in our discussion of ordinary options, we have regarded the stochastic movement of the stock price as given or primitive to the problem. Even with the more general processes discussed in Section 7-1, we did not depart from this context. Yet, of the two variables—the total value of the firm V, or its stock price S—the former would seem to be the more fundamental. In Example 1, with zero-coupon bonds, we saw how the capital structure of the firm mediates between V and S as the fortunes of the firm evolve through time. In that case, we took V as primitive and deduced the characteristics of S from it. Of course, we could have worked in reverse and assumed the stock price followed a stationary random process to deduce an exact formula for V in terms of S. But such an approach would have seemed unnatural, since the debt-equity ratio, which (in perfect markets) leaves the equilibrium value of the firm unaffected, clearly affects the stochastic properties of the stock price. In particular, increases in financial leverage will lead to increases in the stock volatility.

Robert Geske, a Professor of Finance at UCLA, has developed a new model for pricing puts and calls that takes this observation into account.[24] His approach views the stock as an option on the value of the firm, where the value of the firm follows a stationary random walk. Moreover, he assumes the Black-Scholes formula gives the relationship between the value of the stock and the value of the firm. As we have seen, this implies the stock price itself follows a *nonstationary* random walk with a volatility that increases as the stock price decreases. From this perspective, a call option on the stock is then an option on an option, which we term a *compound option*. We thus need a modified formula for the value of the call that takes account of the influence of the capital structure of the firm on the stock return distribution. As we would expect from the implied inverse relation between stock volatility and stock price, the resulting formula has many of the same properties as the constant elasticity model with $\rho < 1$.

[24] See his article, "The Valuation of Compound Options," *Journal of Financial Economics*, 7 (March 1979), 63–81.

We can think of the call as valued through a two-stage binomial process. First, the value of the firm V determines the stock price S at each point in time prior to the maturity of the bonds. With two periods remaining,

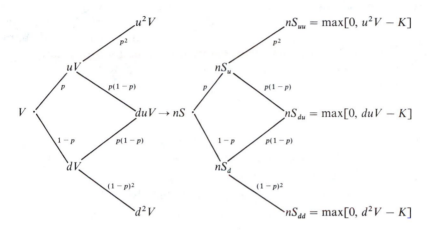

From our analysis in Chapter 5, to eliminate profitable riskless arbitrage, $p \equiv (r - d)/(u - d)$ and

$$S_d = [pS_{du} + (1 - p)S_{dd}]/r, \qquad S_u = [pS_{uu} + (1 - p)S_{ud}]/r,$$

and

$$S = [pS_u + (1 - p)S_d]/r.$$

Second, suppose we want to value a call option on the stock with one period to go (that is, it expires one period before the bond matures). Representing its striking price by k,

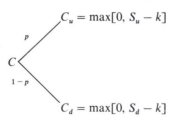

Since the call can only have two possible values at the end of the period, as before we can set up a riskless hedge with the stock. From previous analysis, we know

$$C = [pC_u + (1 - p)C_d]/r.$$

However, this result is different from the binomial model developed in Chapter 5, because $S_u \neq uS$ and $S_d \neq dS$. Instead, the distribution of the stock price is more complicated, but can nevertheless be deduced from the stationary binomial distribution of the value of the firm. In particular, by successive substitutions, we can relate the call value C directly to V, K, k, u, d, and r. Thus, the call value is related to V and K, which determine the capital structure of the firm. More generally, the number of periods until the expiration of the call and the number of periods until the maturity of the bonds also enter the relationship.

With this motivation, we will simply state the resulting limiting valuation formula (proof can be found in Geske's paper). Letting

$$V = \text{the current value of the firm,}$$
$$K = \text{the face value of the bonds,}$$
$$k = \text{the striking price of the call,}$$
$$T = \text{the time to maturity of the bonds,}$$
$$t = \text{the time to expiration of the call } (t \leq T),$$
$$\sigma = \text{the volatility of the } \textit{value of the firm,}$$
$$r = \text{one plus the default-free interest rate, and}$$
$$n = \text{the number of outstanding shares,}$$

the current value of the call is the sum of three terms:

COMPOUND OPTION PRICING FORMULA

$$nC = VN_2(x, y; \sqrt{t/T}) - Kr^{-T}N_2(x - \sigma\sqrt{t}, y - \sigma\sqrt{T}; \sqrt{t/T}) - nkr^{-t}N(x - \sigma\sqrt{t})$$

where

$$x \equiv \frac{\log(V/\bar{V}r^{-t})}{\sigma\sqrt{t}} + \tfrac{1}{2}\sigma\sqrt{t} \qquad y \equiv \frac{\log(V/Kr^{-T})}{\sigma\sqrt{T}} + \tfrac{1}{2}\sigma\sqrt{T}$$

and $\bar{V}$ satisfies

$$\bar{V}N(z) - Kr^{-(T-t)}N(z - \sigma\sqrt{T-t}) - nk = 0$$

where

$$z \equiv \frac{\log(\bar{V}/Kr^{-(T-t)})}{\sigma\sqrt{T-t}} + \tfrac{1}{2}\sigma\sqrt{T-t}$$

$N_2(z_1, z_2; \rho)$ is the probability that, for two random variables having a *bivariate* normal distribution with correlation coefficient ρ, the first variable takes on a value less than or equal to z_1 and the second variable takes on a value less than or equal to z_2. $N(z)$ is, as before, the univariate normal distribution function.

By breaking this formula into components, its seeming complication is easily unraveled. From its definition, $\bar{V}$ is the value of the firm on the expiration date of the call for which the stock price at that date equals the striking price. Then $\bar{V}$ is the value of the firm for which we are indifferent between exercising or not exercising the call. Therefore, if $V > \bar{V}$, the call is currently in-the-money. Similarly, if $V > K$, the debt is also "in-the-money." When both $V > \bar{V}$ and $V > K$, then as $\sigma \to 0$, $nC \to V - Kr^{-T} - nkr^{-t}$. $V - Kr^{-T}$ ($\equiv nS$) is the value of the stock when the firm is certain not to default. If the call is certain to finish in-the-money, then S minus the present value kr^{-t} of its striking price is the value of the call. To consider the possibility of default and the call finishing out-of-the-money, these three terms, V, Kr^{-T}, and nkr^{-t}, are each weighted by a probability.

The compound option formula generalizes the Black-Scholes formula to consider the effects of firm capital structure on the volatility of its stock. Instead of regarding the stock volatility as fixed, the formula moves one step backward and regards the firm value volatility as fixed. The Black-Scholes formula emerges as a special case if either $K = 0$ or $T = \infty$. In either case, the firm effectively has no debt and $V = nS$. The difference between the compound and Black-Scholes call value and delta[25] becomes significant the greater the likelihood of default on the debt. Default is more likely the higher the debt-equity ratio, $w \equiv Kr^{-T}/V$, and the higher the volatility of the firm, σ. Potential default on debt becomes more important for an option the closer its time to maturity, t, is to the time to maturity of the debt, T.

7-6. OPTIONS ON MORE THAN ONE STOCK

We saw in Chapter 5 that most of the apparent limitations in the binomial approach disappear when the model is interpreted and implemented in an appropriately realistic way, but an important question remains: How can the method be used to value securities whose payoffs depend on more than one stock? At first glance, the binomial approach does not seem to apply in this situation. However, the advanced mathematics used in the original Black and Scholes and Merton formulations can be easily extended to

---

[25] The compound option delta $\partial C/\partial S$ can be shown to be

$$\Delta = N_2(x, y; \sqrt{t/T})/N(y).$$

include payoffs depending on many stocks, and fortunately the same is true for the binomial approach as well.[26]

To see how this would work, first consider securities whose payoffs depend on the price of two uncorrelated stocks. Imagine that price movements and trading opportunities occur in the following way. Each stock is affected by a separate source of uncertainty, and new information about these sources arrives sequentially. In the first period only the first stock changes randomly, in the second period only the second stock changes randomly, and then in the third period the process starts over again. When a stock price changes, it takes on one of only two possible values. In the first period, the second stock grows at the riskless rate and in the second period the first stock grows at the riskless rate. As the length of the periods and the size of the price movements become smaller and smaller in an appropriate way, the probability distribution of the stock prices approaches a bivariate lognormal distribution, which is the natural generalization of the univariate lognormal distribution underlying the Black-Scholes model. In other words, in the limiting case the continuously compounded rates of return of the stocks have a bivariate normal distribution.

As a specific example, suppose that the price of the first stock will increase or decrease by 20% in the first period and that the price of the second stock will increase or decrease by 50% in the second period. The current price of each stock is 100, and the riskless interest rate is 10% per period. Consider an option with two periods until expiration that gives its owner the right to buy *either*, but not both, of the stocks for a striking price of 90. If the option is exercised, the owner will of course choose to buy the stock with the higher price.

The diagrams given below show the possible stock prices and the corresponding option values.

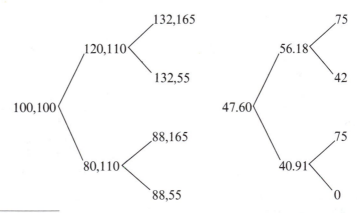

---

[26] This extension of the binomial approach was developed in Jeremy Evnine, "Three Essays in the Use of Options Pricing Theory," Ph.D. dissertation, University of California at Berkeley, June 1983.

These option values are obtained by working backward period by period from the expiration date in just the same way as in Chapter 5. The main difference is that in each period a different value of p would apply, depending on which stock is changing randomly. In the first period, when only the first stock is changing randomly, we would have $p_1 = (1.1 - .8)/(1.2 - .8) = .75$, and in the second period, when only the second stock is changing randomly, we would have $p_2 = (1.1 - .5)/(1.5 - .5) = .6$. For example, calculating $[.6(75) + .4(42)]/1.1$ gives 56.18, and calculating $[.75(56.18) + .25(40.91)]/1.1$ gives 47.60.

The value of delta for the stock that is changing randomly is derived in the same way as in Chapter 5, while the delta for the other stock can be specified arbitrarily. Analogous to the single variable case, it can be shown that the values of the deltas can be chosen to converge in the limiting case to the first partial derivatives of the value of the claim with respect to the stock prices. One final caveat should be remembered in applying this model. If the empirically measured volatility of one of the stocks is σ and if the calendar time before expiration is divided into n periods, then the value of u for that stock should be chosen to be exp $(\sigma\sqrt{t/.5n})$ rather than exp $(\sigma\sqrt{t/n})$ as before. This is because in the two-variable model the stock will be changing randomly in only one-half of the periods.

Although some pairs of stocks are uncorrelated, this is rarely the case. To have a useful procedure, we would want to be able to include stocks whose returns are correlated. This can be accomplished with a simple extension of the setup just described. Imagine now that there is a third separate source of uncertainty that affects both stocks. As before, information about the sources arrives sequentially, but now a complete cycle takes three periods before starting over again. In the third period, either both stocks will move up or both stocks will move down. In this way, one can obtain in the limiting case a bivariate lognormal distribution with any desired degree of correlation. Furthermore, the valuation principles of Chapter 5 can still be applied in a straightforward way. This framework can be easily generalized to include cash dividends and an arbitrary number of stocks.

Options on stock indexes in principle provide an important application of these methods. Most such indexes are weighted averages of the prices of their constituent stocks. It might seem that the index itself could be treated as a single security, but that would be strictly correct only if the volatility of the index depended only on the value of the index and not on the separate prices of the underlying stocks. Consequently, options on stock indexes are in general examples of securities whose payoffs depend on the prices of a number of stocks; the most likely exception may be options on an index comprising all marketed securities. We hasten to add, however, that in practice very good approximate results can be obtained by considering an index to be a single security, especially when sophisticated methods similar to those described in Chapter 6 are used to generate estimates of the volatility of the index. In Chapter 8, we discuss options on indexes and portfolios in more detail and give some further results on their valuation.

7-7. OPTIONS ON STOCK FUTURES

In this section, we discuss an application that draws on several of our previous results: options on stock futures.[27] In return for payment of the striking price, an individual who exercises a call option of this kind receives a long position in a futures contract at a recorded price equal to the striking price. The net value of this position is the futures price minus the striking price. The individual is entitled to withdraw this amount in cash immediately, and it would be to his advantage to do so in order to earn interest on the proceeds. The remaining part of the account would then be a long position in a futures contract at a recorded price equal to the futures price. This remaining part would in itself have no current value and could be costlessly closed out by taking an offsetting short position in the futures contract. Consequently, this call option is equivalent to one giving upon exercise a cash payment equal to the difference between the futures price and the striking price. A put option works in a completely analogous way.

As discussed in Appendix 2A, a futures price is not itself the price of a traded asset. As a result, options on stock futures differ in some fundamental ways from options on stocks. Nevertheless, a slight modification of the binomial method can be used to value these options. Suppose that if the current futures price is F, then the futures price at the end of the period will be either uF or dF. Suppose furthermore that the interest rate is constant. Consider first a call option with one period until expiration. Proceeding in the same way as in Chapter 5, we would wish to find a portfolio containing Δ futures contracts and B dollars in bonds whose payoff would exactly duplicate the payoff to the option. Here we come to a critical difference between stock options and futures options: The position in Δ futures contracts would require no current investment and at the end of one period would have a value equal to Δ times the change in the futures price. Consequently, the total investment required in the portfolio is B, and we would wish to choose Δ and B so that

$$(uF - F)\Delta + rB = C_u$$

$$(dF - F)\Delta + rB = C_d,$$

where C_u is the call value at the end of the period if the futures price moves

---

[27] The first application of the Black-Scholes methodology to options on futures was Fischer Black, "The Pricing of Commodity Options," *Journal of Financial Economics*, 3 (January–March 1976), 167–179.

to uF and C_d is the call value at the end of the period if the futures price moves to dF. Solving these equations gives

$$\Delta = \frac{C_u - C_d}{(u - d)F}$$

$$B = \left[\left(\frac{1 - d}{u - d}\right)C_u + \left(\frac{u - 1}{u - d}\right)C_d\right]\bigg/r.$$

Just as before, the value of the call is the larger of its exercise value and the current value of the equivalent portfolio. In other words, the value of the call is given by

$$C = \left[\left(\frac{1 - d}{u - d}\right)C_u + \left(\frac{u - 1}{u - d}\right)C_d\right]\bigg/r \tag{1}$$

if this value is greater than $F - K$, and if not, $C = F - K$. The standard recursive procedure can then be used to value a call with any number of periods remaining by working backward one period at a time. By comparing formula (1) with the corresponding formula for an option on a stock, we see that the only change is in the coefficients of C_u and C_d.

Before proceeding, it will be useful to recall some of the results of Appendix 2A. There we showed that if interest rates are constant, as we assumed above, then forward prices and futures prices are equal. Furthermore, if there are no arbitrage opportunities, their common value F is given by

$$F = \frac{S - D}{r^{-t}},$$

where S is the current stock price, D is the present value of the dividends to be paid during the life of the contract, and r^{-t} is current price of a zero-coupon bond maturing at the same time as the contract.

Several additional points are now worth mentioning. First, it turns out that it may be optimal to exercise a call on a stock futures price even though the stock itself is not paying dividends. Intuitively, this is because, other things equal, the futures price will decline over time as the zero-coupon bond increases in value. This decline will affect the futures option in the same way that a continual constant dividend yield would affect a stock option. This same effect would tend to discourage, but not preclude, the early exercise of a put option on a stock futures price. On the other hand, the current futures price will already include the effect of all cash dividends to be paid during the life of the futures contract. Consequently, unlike the stock price, the futures price will not drop on an ex-dividend date and cash dividends will not affect a futures option in the same way as a stock option.

The fact that the futures price depends on the dividends to be paid leads to a second important point: One would not necessarily expect a stock with constant volatility to have a futures price with constant volatility. As a simple example, suppose a stock will pay with certainty a single dividend of $10 on the maturity date of the futures contract. The present value of the dividends is then $D = 10r^{-t}$, and the futures price is $F = (S/r^{-t}) - 10$. If the stock price has constant percentage moves in each period, the futures price will not. Consequently, the generalization of the binomial method given in Alternative 1 of Section 7-1, where the values of u and d can depend on price levels and time, will be especially relevant for futures options.

Finally, it is important to remember that unanticipated changes in interest rates will directly affect the futures price even if stock prices and dividends remain the same. As a result, options on futures will be more sensitive to randomness in interest rates than will options on stocks.

7-8. AN OUTLINE OF SOME FURTHER EXTENSIONS

In Alternatives 3 and 4 of Section 7-1, we examined some cases in which options could not be valued by arbitrage methods: It was no longer possible to construct a portfolio of stock and bonds that would duplicate the payoff to an option. This same situation can arise for other reasons. For example, the volatility may depend on random variables other than the stock price, or interest rates may fluctuate randomly over time. How can we value an option when these factors are too important to be ignored? Here we are reaching a point where option pricing theory ceases to be a separate area and becomes part of a general theory of asset valuation. Complete coverage of this would require a monograph in itself. Instead, we will give an informal presentation of some of the results.

The best way to approach the conclusions of the more general theory is to return to our results of Chapter 5 and view them from a different perspective. There we found that in equilibrium,

$$
\begin{aligned}
\text{(expected rate of return on a call} & \\
- \text{ riskless interest rate)} & \\
= \Omega \text{(expected rate of return on stock} & \\
- \text{ riskless interest rate)}, &
\end{aligned}
\tag{1}
$$

where $\Omega = S\Delta/C$ and $\Delta = C_S$, the partial derivative of C with respect to S.

The expected rate of return on the stock includes both an expected price change component and a cash dividend component. Since the owner of an option is not entitled to receive any dividends, the expected rate of return on the call consists only of an expected price change component. By multiplying (1) through by the value of the call, C, and rearranging, we have

$$\text{expected change in the call price}$$
$$= (\text{riskless interest rate}) (\text{call price})$$
$$+ (\text{risk premium}). \tag{2}$$

Under the assumptions made in Chapter 5, the only random variable on which the call price depends is the price of the underlying stock. Hence, the only type of risk rewarded in the risk premium is stock price risk. Furthermore, we know from Chapter 5 that we can break the risk premium into two parts:

$$\text{risk premium} = (\text{partial derivative of the call price}$$
$$\text{with respect to the stock price})$$
$$\times (\text{premium for stock price risk}). \tag{3}$$

The first term on the right-hand side is a measure of the call's sensitivity to stock price risk; the second term is the market risk premium for stock price risk. The premium for stock price risk can, in turn, be expressed as

$$(\text{expected change in the stock price})$$
$$+ (\text{cash dividend})$$
$$- (\text{riskless interest rate}) (\text{stock price}). \tag{4}$$

Note also that if we already knew the risk premium as a function of the stock price from some independent argument, we would have all the information necessary to value a call. From the results described in Chapter 5, we know that as a purely mathematical proposition, the expected change in the call price can be written as

$$\text{expected change in the call price}$$
$$= \tfrac{1}{2} (\text{variance of stock price}) \, C_{SS}$$
$$+ (\text{expected change in stock price}) \, C_S + C_t. \tag{5}$$

By substituting (3), (4), and (5) into (2), we have

$\frac{1}{2}$ (variance of stock price) C_{SS}
        + (expected change in stock price) $C_S + C_t$
   = (riskless interest rate) C
        + C_S[expected change in stock price
        + cash dividend
        − (riskless interest rate) S]C_S.   (6)

This gives a partial differential equation that the value of a call must satisfy; by solving this equation, we can find the value of a call. Of course, given the assumptions of Chapter 5, (6) is simply the Black-Scholes equation with dividends. However, the same argument applies if the volatility depends on the stock price, as described in Alternative 1.

    Now suppose that the total risk premium depends not only on the stock price but also on another random variable, factor X. For example, factor X may affect the stock's volatility. Suppose also that, like the stock price, factor X can change by only a small amount in a very short period of time. It turns out that the basic forms of (3) and (5) still apply. There are only three differences. First, the total risk premium will contain a second component accounting for factor X risk:

risk premium = [(partial derivative of the call price
        with respect to the stock price)
      × (premium for stock price risk)]
    + [(partial derivative of the call price
        with respect to factor X)
      × (premium for factor X risk)].   (7)

Second, the premium for factor X risk will not have the same general form as (4) unless factor X is itself the market value of some asset. Third, the expected change in the call price will include the effect of the random changes in factor X:

(expected change in call price)
   = $\frac{1}{2}$ (variance of stock price) C_{SS}
      + (covariance of stock price and factor X) C_{SX}
      + $\frac{1}{2}$ (variance of factor X) C_{XX}
      + (expected change in the stock price) C_S
      + (expected change in factor X) $C_X + C_t$.   (8)

By equating the expected change in the call price to the riskless interest rate times the call price plus the total risk premium, we once again have a partial differential equation that can be solved, at least numerically, to give the call price in terms of the stock price, factor X, and time. Although a generalization of the binomial method can be used to generate this numerical solution, it will usually not be the most efficient approach to use when there are multiple sources of risk; the great strength of the binomial method lies in its ability to simultaneously illustrate the fundamental principles of option valuation and provide numerical solutions when there is only a single relevant source of risk.

The solution of the equation will also give the sensitivity of the call price to changes in each source of risk. In Chapter 6, we showed how to use C_S to construct a portfolio of calls having any desired level of stock price risk. Just as was the case for stock price risk, the sensitivity of a portfolio to factor X risk will be a weighted average of the sensitivities of its individual components, with weights corresponding to the portfolio proportions. Consequently, we can use C_X to construct a portfolio having any desired level of factor X risk, or we can use C_S and C_X together to control both sources of risk simultaneously.

If additional factors are important, they can be included in the same way. To make all this operational, we would have to identify the factors, estimate their expected changes, variances, and covariances, and measure their risk premiums. Identification of the factors in principle requires a complete description of the economic environment in which the firm operates, but in practice all but a few of the possible candidates will be unimportant. In our opinion, only variables capturing random changes in volatility, interest rates, and dividends will be worth including. For simplicity, we might take factor X to be the volatility itself, factor Y to be the short-term interest rate, and factor Z to be the dividend yield. We could then use historical data to estimate their expected changes, variances, and covariances. Measuring the risk premiums on the factors is more difficult, but a good approximation may be to assume that they are close to zero and can be ignored. For interest rate risk, this assumption would correspond to what is commonly called the *expectations hypothesis* of the term structure of interest rates.

This approach can be extended in several ways. If the stock price or the additional factors can take sudden jumps, then the right-hand side of (8) is augmented by a term which is the likelihood of a jump occurring times the expected change in the call price if a jump does occur. If the possibility of a jump does not in itself command an extra risk premium, then the right-hand side of (7) will be unaffected. An example of this, the case of perfectly diversifiable jumps in the stock price, was given in Alternative 4 of Section 7-1. If the risk premium term is affected, then the story becomes too complicated to consider further here, but once again the general theory of asset valuation can provide specific and useful results. One further generalization is relevant for some applications of option pricing to other areas. If the owner of a call were entitled to receive periodic payments from the issuer of a call, then these payments would be part of the expected rate of return on a call and hence would be added to the left-hand side of (2), (5), (6), and (8).

Although the discussion has been in terms of a call, exactly the same

Table 7-20
ADJUSTMENTS TO THE BLACK-SCHOLES FORMULA

Change in Assumptions	Ad-hoc Adjustment	Complete Adjustment
(1) Stock pays cash dividends.	Use B-S formula with present value of dividends subtracted from stock price.	Binomial method.
(2) Option can be exercised before the expiration date.	Calculate B-S value for different expiration dates after adjusting for dividends as in (1); choose highest value.	Binomial method.
(3) Volatility is a known function of time.	Use B-S formula adjusted as in (1) and (2) with $\sigma^2 t$ replaced by $\int_0^t \sigma^2(v)dv$.	Binomial method with u and d depending on time.
(4) Volatility depends on stock price and time.	Act as if volatility does not depend on stock price in binomial model or B-S formula adjusted as in (1), (2), (3), but use continually updated estimate of volatility.	See Section 7-1, Alternative 1, and Section 7-5.
(5) Volatility depends on time, stock price, and other random variables.	Calculate option prices from binomial method or adjusted B-S formula as in (1) and (2) for a number of values of the volatility parameter; take a weighted average of these prices, with each weight corresponding to the probability of obtaining that average volatility; probabilities may be different for different maturities; update probabilities regularly.	See Section 7-8.

Table 7-20 (*Continued*)

Change in Assumptions	Ad-hoc Adjustment	Complete Adjustment
(6) Stock price can make sudden jumps.	Consider the occurrence of a jump as a very brief period of very high volatility and use (5).	If all other assumptions of B-S formula are satisfied, and jump risk is diversifiable, see Section 7-1, Alternative 4; if not, see Section 7-8.
(7) Interest rate is a known function of time.	Use adjusted B-S formula with a single interest rate obtained from a zero-coupon bond with same maturity as option.	Use complete term structure of default-free bonds to infer interest rate to use in each period of binomial model.
(8) Interest rate changes randomly over time.	Act as if interest rate is a known function of time, but continually update interest rates used.	See Section 7-8.
(9) Margin requirements and taxes.	See Section 6-2.	See Section 6-2.

arguments would apply for a put. The only change would be in the boundary conditions of the partial differential equation. In fact, the arguments are equally applicable to many other kinds of securities. Options on U.S. Treasury bonds or Government National Mortgage Association securities can be valued using the general approach outlined above. The same methods can be applied to corporate securities, which we discussed in Section 7-3.

This brings our discussion of stock option valuation techniques to a close. Table 7-20 summarizes our conclusions. If the assumptions underlying the Black-Scholes model were exactly met in reality, then Chapter 5 would tell the whole story. Unfortunately, that is not the case. Chapter 6 outlined a number of ad hoc, but very effective, ways of dealing with important issues that were excluded by the basic assumptions. It also gave theoretically correct ways of handling some of the potential problems; this section has discussed theoretically correct ways of approaching most of the remaining problems.

Some of the modifications listed in Table 7-20 are of major importance; others are minor improvements that are needed only in very refined trading operations. In our opinion, it is essential to include dividends and the possibility of early exercise in any use of the model for investment purposes. However, going one step further and allowing for the possibility that dividends may differ somewhat from their most likely levels typically has little effect on option values. Similarly, for the relatively short maturities of listed options, there is not much to be gained from explicitly including interest rate risk. It is very important, however, to continually update the interest rate information being used.

Although margin requirements, transactions costs, and tax considerations can be quite important for individual investment decisions, there are good reasons for believing that their effect on option prices is relatively small. As we have mentioned earlier, professional traders have much more favorable margin requirements and transactions costs than do individual investors. For pricing relations that can be enforced by arbitrage, it will be the minimal margin requirements and transactions costs of professional traders that are reflected in market prices. Furthermore, to the extent that this arbitrage involves transactions that are all taxed at the same rate, the effect of taxes will be minimal as well.

Potentially, the most important factors of all concern the description of stock price movements: The dependence of volatility on the stock price, the dependence of volatility on other random variables, and the possibility of sudden jumps. As compared to the Black-Scholes model, the typical effect of including each of these factors separately is as follows:

1. Volatility varies inversely with the stock price—lower values for out-of-the-money calls, higher values for in-the-money calls.
2. Volatility depends on other random variables—higher values for out-of-the-money calls, higher or lower values for in-the-money calls.
3. Possibility of sudden jumps—higher values for out-of-the-money calls, lower values for in-the-money calls.

For puts, the words "higher" and "lower" should be interchanged. Although each of these factors alone can have a major impact on option value, they tend to offset one another. The first factor works in the opposite direction from the others, so the overall effect of simultaneously including all three factors can be relatively small for most stocks. All this leads us to conclude that the Black-Scholes model adjusted only for dividends and early exercise will work surprisingly well on average, even though the environment is rich enough to allow all our reasons for using options to be valid.[28]

---

[28] For further information on the generalizations described in this section, see John C. Cox, Jonathan E. Ingersoll, Jr., and Stephen A. Ross, "An Intertemporal General Equilibrium Model of Asset Prices," *Econometrica*, 53 (March 1985) and the references cited there.

innovations
in options markets

8

8-1. THE ECONOMIC FUNCTION
OF SECURITIES MARKETS

From the perspective of an economist, though possibly not that of an investor, a book on options markets would be incomplete unless it gave at least passing consideration to the social function of these markets. In particular, what benefits does the existence of an organized options market confer upon society? And how can this market be improved? At the present time, these questions are especially relevant. Organized options markets for puts and calls on common stock are quite new in the United States, and their ultimate scope and form is by no means a settled issue. Furthermore, opponents of options markets can readily make a plausible-sounding argument that such markets promote unnecessary speculation with little compensating benefit; those who disagree with this conclusion must be able to defend their position. In Chapter 2, we gave a number of reasons why an individual investor might find options useful. These reasons suggested, but did not imply, that the existence of options markets could improve the welfare of all investors. In this chapter we will examine this more closely. We will also see how an options market may be beneficial even to individuals who never trade in options. However, before we can adequately discuss these issues, we first need to develop a general perspective for the assessment of innovations in securities markets.

Basic Functions. A securities market performs three basic economic functions:

1. *Individual wealth allocation.* By issuing and purchasing securities, possibly indirectly through financial institutions, individuals (that is, consuming units) are able to affect the timing of their consumption of real goods and services over their lifetimes and are able to pool and redistribute among themselves the risks of fluctuation in the value of the economy's real assets.

2. *Firm resource allocation.* By issuing securities, firms (that is, producing units) are able to raise capital from diverse sources. The securities market, by implicitly charging firms different prices, allocates scarce capital among competing uses.

3. *Source of information.* The securities market provides information in the form of prices, which can be useful for making a variety of important economic decisions.

By borrowing or lending, an individual can choose to postpone or accelerate the personal consumption of her wealth. By investing in relatively low-risk securities, such as bonds, an individual can shift the bearing of higher risks to other individuals. However, since investors are, on balance, risk averse—they can only be induced to bear greater risk if their investment promises greater average or expected return—low return will typically accompany investments of low risk. Thus, the securities market provides flexibility in matching the risk of investments with the preferences and opinions of different individuals. Not only are risks *redistributed* through the securities market, with greater expected return as the compensation for bearing risk, but, to some extent, risk can be *pooled* through diversification to achieve reduced risk without sacrificing expected return. This occurs whenever two investments with the same expected return counterbalance each other—when one does well and the other does poorly or vice versa. In this case, combining them in a portfolio leaves expected return the same but reduces overall risk.

Stock prices that properly reflect available information about corporate prospects play an important role in allocating resources among them. Higher equity prices encourage firms to raise equity capital. Perhaps more important, equity prices provide early signals to firms of the market's approval or disapproval of their actions. By these means, the preferences of investors and the aggregate wisdom of the marketplace are indirectly made available to corporate managers.

It is a basic principle of economics that prices produced in competitive markets provide participants in the economy with useful information for making a variety of economic decisions. In particular, an organized and active securities market brings to bear on security prices the pooled knowledge of all participants in the market. According to much of the evidence on "efficient markets," this pooled knowledge contains better predictions of future events than any participant or small group of participants can consistently discover on their own. Thus, the securities market performs an extremely useful economic function by making these superior predictions generally available.

These predictions improve current economic decision making. For example, current spot prices on commodity exchanges contain information about future spot prices that can guide current decisions to produce and inventory commodities. Empirical analysis indicates that the near-term anticipated rate of inflation can be deduced from T-bill discounts. It has been confirmed that recent past changes in stock market prices tend to be a leading indicator of general economic activity. The yield curve, showing the relationship at the current time among yields of bonds of differing maturity, can be used to estimate future spot interest rates. The yield curve itself can be directly used to determine discount rates in present-value calculations for corporate investment decisions, where alternative projects have cash flows with different time profiles. Furthermore, differences in yields of corporate bonds of the same maturity contain information about the likelihood of future bankruptcy. One of the key problems of a financial economist is to learn how to unravel these predictions from current security prices.

In general, the greater the variety of securities provided by the market, the better the three functions we have given will be performed. At one extreme, with no securities market, a decentralized economy—such as in the United States—might be seriously impaired. At the other extreme, we can imagine a securities market providing so many securities that no additional security could be created whose returns could not be duplicated by a portfolio of already existing securities. In the jargon of finance theory, the securities market would then be "complete."

Unfortunately, a number of practical matters prohibit the creation of our idealized complete market. Chief among these are the difficulty of writing specific and enforceable contracts to cover certain contingencies (such as options on future labor income), the costs of exchanging securities (transactions costs), and government regulation. Since it is neither practical nor desirable to create securities for every possible contingency, an important question is which few of all possible securities should be provided by the market.

Complete Markets. We can illustrate the role of securities in a complete market by a simple example. Suppose we are concerned with investing to receive a return at some future date. In the future, only three *states* can occur: depression, normalcy, and prosperity. Suppose the securities market makes available just one security, one share of which returns $1 if depression occurs, $2 under normalcy, and $3 under prosperity. We represent this situation by the following tableau:

$$S = \begin{bmatrix} 1 \\ 2 \\ 3 \end{bmatrix}.$$

By purchasing x shares of this security, we can buy a pattern of returns across states of $(x \quad 2x \quad 3x)$. For example, by purchasing three shares, the pattern would be $(3 \quad 6 \quad 9)$ or by short selling two shares, we would have $(-2 \quad -4 \quad -6)$.

However, suppose we really wanted to purchase a position with returns $(0 \quad 1 \quad 2)$. Unfortunately, with just this one security available, it is impossible to purchase this pattern of returns. All possible patterns of returns are scalar multiples of $(1 \quad 2 \quad 3)$. However, if the market makes available an additional "riskless" security, then this pattern of returns can be achieved. A riskless security has the same return for every state. In this case, the augmented tableau becomes

$$[S_1 \quad S_2] = \begin{bmatrix} 1 & 1 \\ 2 & 1 \\ 3 & 1 \end{bmatrix}.$$

By purchasing one share of S_1 and short selling (or, if you prefer, "borrowing") one share of S_2, the position yields

$$\begin{bmatrix} 1 \\ 2 \\ 3 \end{bmatrix} - \begin{bmatrix} 1 \\ 1 \\ 1 \end{bmatrix} = \begin{bmatrix} 0 \\ 1 \\ 2 \end{bmatrix}.$$

More generally, with these two securities it is possible to achieve patterns of returns across states of $(x + y \quad 2x + y \quad 3x + y)$. In the above case, $x = 1$ and $y = -1$.

However, even with these two securities, some patterns of returns across states can still not be purchased—for example, $(0 \quad 0 \quad 1)$. This follows, since there are no values of x and y which simultaneously satisfy the three equations

$$x + y = 0,$$
$$2x + y = 0,$$
$$3x + y = 1.$$

Indeed, this should not be surprising, since *three* simultaneous linear equations in *two* unknowns generally have no solution. The market can correct this deficiency by making available a third security. Not just any third security will solve the problem, however. For example, suppose the third security had a pattern of returns of (0   1   2). It is easy to see this would not be an improvement, since its pattern of returns can already be constructed from a portfolio of the two already existing securities. To solve the problem, the market must create a wholly new security—that is, one whose pattern of returns cannot be constructed by forming a portfolio of the already existing securities. Toward this end, consider a third security with returns (1   0   0). Clearly, this security cannot be duplicated by a portfolio of the two existing securities. This augments the tableau to

$$[S_1 \quad S_2 \quad S_3] = \begin{bmatrix} 1 & 1 & 1 \\ 2 & 1 & 0 \\ 3 & 1 & 0 \end{bmatrix}.$$

The following portfolio shows that we can achieve the desired pattern of returns with these three securities:

$$\begin{bmatrix} 1 \\ 2 \\ 3 \end{bmatrix} - 2 \begin{bmatrix} 1 \\ 1 \\ 1 \end{bmatrix} + \begin{bmatrix} 1 \\ 0 \\ 0 \end{bmatrix} = \begin{bmatrix} 0 \\ 0 \\ 1 \end{bmatrix}.$$

With these three securities, we can illustrate something quite important: By forming an appropriate portfolio, it is possible to achieve *any* pattern of returns across the three states. To see this, first observe that we can also use these three securities to yield

$$- \begin{bmatrix} 1 \\ 2 \\ 3 \end{bmatrix} + 3 \begin{bmatrix} 1 \\ 1 \\ 1 \end{bmatrix} - 2 \begin{bmatrix} 1 \\ 0 \\ 0 \end{bmatrix} = \begin{bmatrix} 0 \\ 1 \\ 0 \end{bmatrix}.$$

This implies, for the purpose of constructing patterns of returns across states, we could just as well regard the initial tableau as

$$\begin{bmatrix} 1 & 0 & 0 \\ 0 & 1 & 0 \\ 0 & 0 & 1 \end{bmatrix}.$$

This is permissible since each pattern of returns in the tableau can be constructed from a portfolio of the three original securities. To see that any pattern of returns (x y z) can be constructed, observe that we simply purchase x shares of the first security (1 0 0), y shares of the second (0 1 0), and z shares of the third (0 0 1).

In brief, *whenever the number of different securities equals the number of possible states, portfolios of those securities can be constructed which yield any pattern of returns across the states.* By "different" we mean securities whose pattern of returns across states cannot be duplicated by a portfolio of the other existing securities. In this case, we say the existing securities *span* all states and the financial market is said to be *complete*. It is complete because no other "different" security can be created; that is, the patterns of returns of all additional securities are spanned by the existing securities.

More generally, the set of all possible patterns of returns constructable by forming portfolios of an existing set of securities is said to be the *space spanned* by those securities. For example, the space spanned by the tableau

$$\begin{bmatrix} 1 & 1 \\ 2 & 1 \\ 3 & 1 \end{bmatrix}$$

is described by

$$\begin{bmatrix} x + y \\ 2x + y \\ 3x + y \end{bmatrix}$$

for all values of x and y. Clearly, this space is smaller than the space spanned by complete markets.

A security yielding \$1 if a single state occurs, and nothing otherwise, is called a *state-contingent claim*. As we have seen, if the market is complete, the space spanned by the actual securities is also spanned by a set of state-contingent claims, one for each state.

In a complete market, working only from the arbitrage principle, it is possible to infer the prices of state-contingent claims from the prices of actual securities. Consider the tableau

$$[S_1 \quad S_2 \quad S_3] = \begin{bmatrix} 1 & 1 & 1 \\ 2 & 1 & 0 \\ 3 & 1 & 0 \end{bmatrix},$$

where S_1, S_2, and S_3 are interpreted as the current prices of three securities with future payoffs across states as described by the tableau. From our previous analysis we know that a portfolio of one unit each of security 1 and 3, held long against two short of security 2 has the same payoff for every state as a state-contingent claim paying off only in prosperity. Therefore, if π_3 represents the current price of this state-contingent claim, to prevent arbitrage

$$\pi_3 = S_1 - 2S_2 + S_3.$$

Similarly, if π_2 is the price of a state-contingent claim corresponding to normalcy, then

$$\pi_2 = -S_1 + 3S_2 - 2S_3,$$

and if π_1 corresponds to depression, $\pi_1 = S_3$.

We can also use the state-contingent prices to reconstruct the prices of the actual securities. Since each actual security can be interpreted as a portfolio of state-contingent securities, to prevent arbitrage, its current price must be equal to the sum of the prices of its constituent state-contingent securities. Therefore,

$$S_1 = \pi_1 + 2\pi_2 + 3\pi_3,$$
$$S_2 = \pi_1 + \pi_2 + \pi_3,$$
$$S_3 = \pi_1.$$

Each actual security is analogous to a ticket book containing tickets of three colors—red, green, and blue. If depression occurs, for example, each red ticket may be exchanged for $1, and the green and blue tickets are worthless. In the example above, S_1 represents a book containing one red, two green, and three blue tickets.

The above three equations suggest a standard procedure for calculating state-contingent prices from known prices of actual securities. Given the prices of the actual securities and their state-contingent payoffs, we have three simultaneous equations in three unknowns π_1, π_2, and π_3. The reader should convince himself or herself that the solution for these unknowns is consistent with our previous analysis.

If arbitrage is not to be possible, knowing the three state-contingent prices allows us to value any other security from its pattern of payoffs across states. For example, consider a fourth security described by the tableau

$$S_4 = \begin{bmatrix} 1 \\ 2 \\ 1 \end{bmatrix}.$$

To prevent arbitrage, $S_4 = \pi_1 + 2\pi_2 + \pi_3$. To see this, suppose, to the contrary, that $S_4 > \pi_1 + 2\pi_2 + \pi_3$. Then we should be able to form a portfolio of the three actual securities S_1, S_2, and S_3 which duplicates the pattern of payoffs of S_4 but has a lower value. To identify this portfolio, substitute our solutions for π_1, π_2, and π_3 in this inequality:

$$S_4 > (S_3) + 2(-S_1 + 3S_2 - 2S_3) + (S_1 - 2S_2 + S_3) = -S_1 + 4S_2 - 2S_3.$$

Consulting the previous tableau, it is easy to verify this portfolio has the same payoffs across states as S_4. To earn a sure profit on zero investment, simply sell S_4 short, use part of the proceeds to purchase this portfolio, and pocket the difference. No matter what state occurs, the future gain on the portfolio will exactly offset the future loss on S_4.

Generalizing, suppose there are N possible states denoted by $n = 1, 2, \ldots, N$ and J actual securities denoted by $j = 1, 2, \ldots, J$. If all the actual securities are different and $N = J$, then the market is complete. If arbitrage is not possible, the prices of actual securities will then imply a unique set of state-contingent prices π_n, one for each state. Likewise, if arbitrage is not possible, knowing the state-contingent prices π_n, we can value any pattern of payoffs across states. For example, the price of a riskless security yielding $1, no matter what state occurs, is equivalent to the value of a portfolio of state-contingent claims, one for each state. That is, the price of a riskless security is simply $\sum_{n=1}^{N} \pi_n$ and the riskless one plus rate of interest

$$r \equiv \frac{1}{\sum\limits_{n=1}^{N} \pi_n}.$$

Finally, investors will be able to achieve the same allocation across states whether we confine them to trading actual securities or, instead, we replace the actual securities with the full set of state-contingent claims.

Why, ignoring transactions costs, are complete markets desirable? We will give two answers, a simple one and a more complex one. The simple answer is that complete markets are desirable because they provide the maximum flexibility for investors. Most people would agree that more choice is better than less. But this does not mean that *everyone* in the society is made better off by more opportunities. It is possible that the creation of new "different" securities in an incomplete market would not offer some investors any new patterns of returns that they would prefer to the preexisting patterns. At the same time, these new securities, through the altered demands of other investors, could cause a realignment of the current market prices of securities, reducing the present value of these investors' portfolios.

This motivates the more complex answer. *Given the social totals of return in each state*, we say a financial market is *Pareto-efficient* if no other set of securities can make some investors better off without making at least one other investor worse off. In a Pareto-efficient financial market, no change in the market would be unanimously approved by investors. An important theorem of financial economics is that *a complete market is always Pareto-efficient irrespective of the nature of investors, while an incomplete market must be Pareto-inefficient in some circumstances.*

Nevertheless, an incomplete market may be Pareto-efficient. For example, consider the extreme case where all investors are economically identical (that is, they have the same opportunities, preferences, and expectations). In this case, no trading can occur, since identical investors must hold identical positions. Prices on whatever securities exist are set such that each investor is content with his own endowed pattern of returns across states. No desired trading implies that the financial market is Pareto-efficient, even if *no securities* exist. However, if investors were economically different, some trading would generally be desirable. For example, investors very averse to risk may desire to exchange their endowed highly uncertain pattern of returns for a relatively riskless pattern. In this case, a condition of no existing securities would probably be Pareto-inefficient. The unique feature of complete markets is its property of Pareto-efficiency irrespective of the economic identities of investors.

As we have mentioned, the costs of exchanging securities, the difficulty of writing specific and enforceable contracts to cover certain contingencies, and government regulation prevent the creation of a complete financial market. Given the practical impossibility of complete markets, we need to ask two questions:

1. Given the traditional securities issued by firms, what other securities can be created that would move the financial market toward completeness without excessive transactions costs?

2. Are investors sufficiently similar that maximum welfare can be approximated closely with only a few securities in addition to the basic set of securities issued by firms? If so, which securities are they?

These questions are central to the formation of efficient security exchanges and financial intermediaries. The remainder of this chapter provides some interesting answers demonstrating the efficacy of options.

8-2. THE CONTRIBUTION OF OPTIONS

Gambling usually refers to the purchase of a future monetary reward that may

1. Be unproductive from a social point of view.
2. Have a negative expected future value.
3. Be highly uncertain.
4. Have a short time before payoff.
5. Arise from uninformed differences of opinion among several participants who bet against each other.

All five characteristics typify horse race betting. If options did not make it possible to obtain new patterns of returns or reduce the cost of obtaining existing patterns, could not affect corporate production decisions, or did not lead to a wider dissemination of useful information, then they too would, in aggregate, have all of the characteristics of gambles and none of the features of useful investments.

It is easy to dismiss options as mere gambling opportunities; it is harder to demonstrate that options perform a useful social function. We will now advance this more difficult and more interesting argument. First, we will consider options as an aid to individual wealth allocation; second, as an aid to firm resource allocation; and third, as a source of information.

Individual Wealth Allocation.   Stephen Ross, Professor of Economics and Finance at Yale University, has developed a careful justification for options as an aid to individual wealth allocation.[1] Given that complete markets, since they provide individuals with a wide range of opportunities, are desired from a social point of view, how best can the financial market achieve something approaching completeness? Underlying his analysis is the plausible presumption that it may be cheaper, in terms of transaction costs, to expand the number of opportunities through options on existing basic securities, rather than through the creation of new basic securities.

The power of options to complete the market is illustrated by Example 1. Suppose there are three possible states and only one basic security available with returns

$$S = \begin{bmatrix} 1 \\ 2 \\ 3 \end{bmatrix}.$$

---

[1] See his article, "Options and Efficiency," *Quarterly Journal of Economics*, 90 (February 1976), 75–89.

Although S cannot itself span the states, by creating calls on S with striking prices $K = 1$ and $K = 2$, we have

$$C(S, 1) = \begin{bmatrix} 0 \\ 1 \\ 2 \end{bmatrix} \quad \text{and} \quad C(S, 2) = \begin{bmatrix} 0 \\ 0 \\ 1 \end{bmatrix}.$$

If these three securities are taken together, we have the augmented tableau

$$[S \quad C(S, 1) \quad C(S, 2)] = \begin{bmatrix} 1 & 0 & 0 \\ 2 & 1 & 0 \\ 3 & 2 & 1 \end{bmatrix}.$$

It is easy to see that the three securities span the three states. Creating options from the single basic security has completed the market.[2]

Will this always be possible? To see why not, consider Example 2:

$$S = \begin{bmatrix} 2 \\ 2 \\ 3 \end{bmatrix}.$$

All call options written on this basic security must have the following payoff at expiration: $C = \max[0, S - K]$. Clearly, it will be impossible to write options that will distinguish between the first two states. Whatever options we create, the first two rows of the augmented tableau must be the same. Therefore, the power of options to complete the market is restricted to situations where the list of basic securities has returns that can distinguish between each state.

What about the more general situation, where there is more than one basic security and no one basic security, taken by itself, can distinguish between each state? For Example 3 suppose the tableau formed by available basic securities is

$$[S_1 \quad S_2] = \begin{bmatrix} 1 & 1 \\ 1 & 2 \\ 2 & 1 \\ 2 & 2 \end{bmatrix}.$$

---

[2] Indeed, there is a simple recipe for using call options to manufacture a state-contingent claim for any state except the one with the highest payoff—the formation of a "butterfly" spread. For example, to create a state-contingent claim that pays off in depression, form the following portfolio of calls:

$$C(S, 0) - 2C(S, 1) + C(S, 2).$$

The market is incomplete, since we have four states and only two basic securities. First, consider augmenting the tableau with puts and calls. Since each row is different, a *necessary* condition is satisfied to span the states with puts and calls. Unfortunately, this condition is *not sufficient*. Augmenting the tableau with the only "nontrivial" calls[3] (that is, calls with some 0 and some positive returns) on S_1 and S_2, we have

$$[S_1 \quad C(S_1, 1) \quad S_2 \quad C(S_2, 1)] = \begin{bmatrix} 1 & 0 & 1 & 0 \\ 1 & 0 & 2 & 1 \\ 2 & 1 & 1 & 0 \\ 2 & 1 & 2 & 1 \end{bmatrix}.$$

Since the sum of the first and fourth rows equals the sum of the second and third rows, the four states are not spanned by these securities. It is easy to show that trying puts, or puts in combination with calls, will also not complete the market.

If ordinary puts and calls will not complete the market, even though every row of the basic securities is different, what about more general forms of options? In the preface to this book, we defined an option contract quite broadly as *any security whose payoffs are contractually dependent on the values of some other underlying security (or securities)*. Let us use the term *simple options* to refer to options whose payoff is a deterministic function of the value of a *single underlying security*.[4] Puts and calls are familiar examples of simple options. Another example would be an option with payoff S^2 or one with a payoff $\max[\log S, (S - K)^2]$. Knowing the value of S at expiration fully determines the payoff from these two simple options.

An even more general class of options are *complex options*. These options have payoff that are a deterministic function of the values of a *given set of underlying securities*. For example, a complex option written on basic securities S_1 and S_2 might have a payoff at expiration of $S_1^2 + kS_2^3$, where k is a positive constant. Knowing the values of S_1 and S_2 at expiration fully determines the payoff from the complex option. An *option on a portfolio* of underlying securities is a special case of a complex option. A portfolio is defined with a payoff equal to a convex combination of its constituent elements. That is, if $S_1, S_2, \ldots, S_m$ are the values of the underlying securities,

---

[3] Since trivial calls have either zero payoff in all states or positive payoffs in all states, they will not help to complete the market.

[4] In Section 7-2, we referred to these as generalized options to emphasize the fact that their payoffs are more general than those of ordinary options, even though they still depend only on the price of a single security.

and $w_1, w_2, \ldots, w_m$ are constants such that $0 < w_j < 1$ and $\Sigma_j w_j = 1$, then the value of a portfolio of the underlying securities is

$$\sum_{j=1}^{m} w_j S_j.$$

The w_j are the relative weights of the securities in the portfolio. An option with payoff $(\Sigma_j w_j S_j)^2 + \log(\Sigma_j w_j S_j)$ is an example of an option on a portfolio. Its payoff is a deterministic function of the value of the portfolio. In particular, in two states, where the individual underlying securities have different values, an option on a portfolio may have the same payoff. Finally, special cases of an option on a portfolio are *puts and calls on a portfolio*. A call on a portfolio has payoff $\max[0, (\Sigma_j w_j S_j) - K]$ and a put on a portfolio has payoff $\max[0, K - (\Sigma_j w_j S_j)]$.

We can summarize this discussion by listing the categories of options we have defined:

1. Simple options
    —ordinary calls
    —ordinary puts
    —other simple options

2. Complex options
    —calls on a portfolio
    —puts on a portfolio
    —other options on a portfolio
    —other complex options

Now we are prepared to return to our original question: If ordinary puts and calls will not complete the market, what about more general forms of options? This is an important question, because its answer will tell us if it is easy to improve on the performance of ordinary puts and calls. Ross proves two elegant and important results, one related to simple options and the other to complex options:

---

1. Simple options: For a given set of basic securities, ordinary puts and calls span the same space as all simple options.
2. Complex options: For a given set of basic securities, there exists an "efficient" portfolio such that puts and calls on this portfolio span the same space as all complex options.

Since these propositions are proved in Ross's article, we will not repeat their proof here.

However, these results are striking and deserve further comment. The first proposition says that ordinary puts and calls are at least as powerful as any set of simple options. Nothing is lost, compared to simple options, in the simplicity of ordinary puts and calls. Perhaps this proposition explains their popularity. Moreover, if a riskless security does not exist, it is noteworthy that calls are not sufficient; generally, puts will be needed to span the space of all simple options. For Example 4, consider the tableau

$$[S_1 \quad S_2 \quad S_3] = \begin{bmatrix} 0 & 1 & 0 \\ 0 & 1 & 1 \\ 0 & 0 & 1 \\ 1 & 1 & 1 \end{bmatrix}.$$

All rows are different, so we might hope to complete the market with ordinary calls. Since calls must have a positive striking price, all nontrivial call options on S_1, S_2, and S_3 have payoffs directly proportional to the values of the securities on which they are written. For example,

$$C(S_2, \tfrac{1}{2}) = \begin{bmatrix} \frac{1}{2} \\ \frac{1}{2} \\ 0 \\ \frac{1}{2} \end{bmatrix},$$

which is a multiple of $\frac{1}{2}$ of the payoffs of S_2. As such, ordinary calls cannot complete the market. But writing a put on S_1, with the striking price of 1, augments the tableau to

$$[S_1 \quad P(S_1, 1) \quad S_2 \quad S_3] = \begin{bmatrix} 0 & 1 & 1 & 0 \\ 0 & 1 & 1 & 1 \\ 0 & 1 & 0 & 1 \\ 1 & 0 & 1 & 1 \end{bmatrix}$$

and completes the market. Puts are generally needed to equal or better the power of arbitrary simple options.

Example 3 demonstrated that, even if the rows of returns of basic securities were all different, ordinary puts and calls might not span the entire space. From the first proposition, we also know that all simple options could do no better. However, complex options can complete the market. To see this in Example 3, consider calls written on a portfolio containing two units of S_1 for each unit of S_2:

$$2\begin{bmatrix} 1 \\ 1 \\ 2 \\ 2 \end{bmatrix} + \begin{bmatrix} 1 \\ 2 \\ 1 \\ 2 \end{bmatrix} = \begin{bmatrix} 3 \\ 4 \\ 5 \\ 6 \end{bmatrix}.$$

Since the payoffs of this portfolio distinguish between each state, we know from Example 1 that calls written on it with striking prices 3, 4, and 5 will complete the market. Therefore, complex options are more powerful than simple options. Indeed, Ross proves that *complex options will complete the market whenever no two rows of the values of basic securities are identical.* For simple options, this condition was necessary but not sufficient; for complex options, it is both necessary and sufficient.

To compensate for the weakness of ordinary puts and calls, we need complex options. However, options written on multiple contingencies are apt to prove costly in terms of transaction costs. It is here that the significance of Proposition 2, Ross's most surprising conclusion, becomes evident. Existing options markets consist of a profusion of puts and calls written on an expanding list of underlying securities. According to Proposition 2, from the point of view of completing the market, we can scrap the chaos of existing contracts and replace them with puts and calls written on a *single* portfolio. Of course, this portfolio cannot be chosen arbitrarily. But Proposition 2 assures us that a portfolio can be found such that puts and calls written on it are at least as powerful as any set of complex options, and, in particular, probably more powerful than all ordinary puts and calls. What constitutes this "efficient" portfolio depends on the tableau of the returns of all basic securities. Whatever its composition, it must distinguish between states as well as the entire tableau. Although there is generally no simple way to define it, as Sections 8-3 and 8-4 suggest, for practical purposes, the "market portfolio," containing all basic securities in proportion to their market values, may be a good approximation.

Our analysis in this section has, for purposes of simplicity, considered only a single period. In Sections 5-1 and 5-3 we looked at the problem of valuing an option in this context when the stock price could take on only two possible values at the end of the period. There we found an illustration of the principle stated earlier in this section: Whenever the number of different securities equals the number of possible states, portfolios of those securities can be constructed which yield any pattern of returns across the states. We can restate the results developed in Section 5-3 in our current terms, and it is worthwhile to make a brief digression to do so.

We have two securities: the stock, S_1, and a riskless bond, S_2. Their tableau of payoffs in the two states, u and d, is

$$[S_1 \quad S_2] = \begin{bmatrix} uS_1 & 1 \\ dS_1 & 1 \end{bmatrix}.$$

If we again let r denote one plus the interest rate, then $S_2 = 1/r$. Let π_u and π_d represent the state-contingent prices for the two states, u and d, respectively. Therefore, π_u is the current price of one dollar to be received at the end of the period if and only if state u occurs. Since the current price of each of the securities must be equal to the sum of the prices of its constituent state-contingent claims, we have

$$S_1 = \pi_u(uS_1) + \pi_d(dS_1)$$
$$S_2 = \pi_u + \pi_d.$$

By solving these two equations and using the fact that $S_2 = 1/r$, we find that

$$\pi_u = \left(\frac{r-d}{u-d}\right)\frac{1}{r} \text{ and } \pi_d = \left(\frac{u-r}{u-d}\right)\frac{1}{r}.$$

A call has a payoff of C_u in state u and C_d in state d, so its current value C must be

$$C = \pi_u C_u + \pi_d C_d$$
$$= \left[\left(\frac{r-d}{u-d}\right)C_u + \left(\frac{u-r}{u-d}\right)C_d\right]\Big/ r,$$

which coincides with Equation (3) of Section 5-3.

However, as we saw in Section 7-1, if the stock price can take on three or more values at the end of the period, we cannot create a stock and bond portfolio that will duplicate the payoff of an option in every circumstance. In our current terms, those two securities are not sufficient to span the possible states; their current prices do not contain enough information to uniquely determine the prices of state-contingent claims. In that case, as we found earlier in this section, options can play an important role in completing the market.

The basic results that we developed in this section in a one-period setting remain valid in a multi-period setting. Moreover, our analysis in Section 5-3 alerts us to an important feature of the completion of markets that is evident only in a multi-period context: The possibility of sequential trading may, to some extent, serve as a substitute for a full set of state-contingent claims. To see how this might work, consider the two-period model derived in Section 5-3. At the end of the second period, three distinct returns were possible from a buy-and-hold investment in the stock: u^2, ud, and d^2. The corresponding tableau of payoffs is

$$[S_1 \quad S_2] = \begin{bmatrix} u^2 S_1 & 1 \\ ud S_1 & 1 \\ d^2 S_1 & 1 \end{bmatrix}.$$

Apparently we would need to add another security, such as an option, to complete the market.[5] Alternatively, we would need trading in three different state-contingent claims. However, the opportunity to readjust the amount of stock and bonds held at the end of the first period means that a dynamically revised portfolio of these two securities *can* span the state space, even though a static portfolio with fixed amounts of the securities *cannot*. Indeed, it is this principle that underlies our entire development of option valuation in Chapter 5. As a result, trading in only the two basic securities is, in this case, sufficient to complete the market.[6] Consequently, option theory has provided us with two important insights: It has shown how a full set of options can be equivalent to a full set of state-contingent claims, and it has shown that, in certain circumstances, a full set of state-contingent claims is unnecessary.

Firm Resource Allocation.   In Section 8-1, we argued that stock prices that properly reflect available information about corporate prospects assist the efficient allocation of real resources. Puts and calls, through a type of arbitrage with their underlying stocks, can increase the number and diversity of individual preferences and expectations that come to bear on equity prices. For example, if the prices of calls were to become too high, relative

---

[5] Note that if *ud* and *du* were regarded as separate states, then an ordinary option would not be sufficient to complete the market: Our requirement that the list of basic securities have returns that can distinguish between each state would not be satisfied. However, it can be shown that in this case the down-and-out calls (or up-and-out puts) discussed in Section 7-4 will be sufficient to complete the market.

[6] However, if the full weight of transactions costs is considered, it will be impractical for many individuals to attempt to duplicate state-contingent claims by sequential trading. Again, it is here that options prove useful, since they substitute a fixed position for one that must be frequently revised.

to the underlying stock, arbitrageurs could sell calls against a long position in the stock. By this means, the stock price would tend to rise, and the preferences and expectations of option investors would be reflected in the price. The options market reduces transaction costs to assume particular positions. Thus, investors, with certain types of information who might otherwise have remained out of the stock market, may find options a superior vehicle for taking advantage of this information. In so doing, their information would be rapidly and effectively impounded in the stock price. Furthermore, the managers of a firm may be able to infer from option prices exactly what effect the adoption of a contemplated investment project will have on the firm's market value; we will discuss this further in Section 8-4.

Source of Information.   The prices of options, like those of other securities, contain implicit predictions about future events. An option's price will depend on and contain information about anticipated future volatility, cash dividends, and interest rates. For example, as we discussed in Section 6-2, one can use the market price of an option to determine its "implicit volatility"—the market's prediction of the volatility of the underlying stock during the remaining life of the option. This information may be useful for a variety of investment decisions having nothing to do with options. Consequently, individuals who have no confidence in their ability to predict volatility directly will benefit from having the market consensus available to them.[7]

Possible Objections to Options.   Other than the gambling argument with which we began this section, the most common objection to options is that they attract "risk capital" out of the equities market. In its naive form, this argument has little to recommend it. Proponents of the equity shortage point of view overlook a basic economic identity. Puts and calls are issued by individuals and financial intermediaries, not by nonfinancial corporations. On the aggregate national balance sheet, stocks, warrants, and corporate bonds appear as offsetting items to real assets. Like any form of debt between individuals and/or financial intermediaries, options do not appear. The liabilities of writers are cancelled by the claims of buyers. We have seen that a long position in a call is similar to a levered long position in the stock itself. Hence, the buyer of a call is indeed someone who potentially

---

[7] Among option investors, one occasionally hears that it is a good time to buy options because option prices are low relative to the past. If interest rates and dividends had not changed, a believer in "efficient markets" would instead conclude that the volatilities of optioned stocks are low relative to the past.

would have bought the stock but instead did not. But the seller of the call has, in effect, reduced his position in the stock; he is someone who would have sold the stock but did not. Consequently, it is completely incorrect to conclude that the purchase of an option necessarily represents a reduction in the total net demand for the stock. A more sophisticated argument might claim that the establishment of an options market will lead to a new equilibrium in which the total level of investment in productive resources could just as easily be lower than before, rather than higher. This is true, but it does not imply that such a change would make people worse off; physical investment can be too high as well as too low. Indeed, if options serve to complete the market, we have seen that the new state of affairs cannot be Pareto-inefficient compared to the old one.

A somewhat different point of view maintains that the composition of equity investment will be adversely affected, even if its total level is unchanged. Here is the argument. Many individuals who wish to bear a high degree of risk in hope of a high return cannot do so directly with a highly levered diversified equity portfolio because of limited borrowing opportunities. Before the existence of an options market, these individuals invested in very risky stocks, which were often new and small companies. Now they are buying calls instead, thus making it more expensive for these companies to raise equity capital. The argument has some validity, because such an outcome is certainly possible; but it is misleading, because this outcome could be socially beneficial. Indeed, it could be maintained that in the past these companies improperly benefited from regulations inhibiting borrowing. In any case, several studies commissioned by the CBOE have found no conclusive evidence that options affect either the total level or the composition of equity investment. It has also been said that options lower the total volume of trading in the underlying stock and therefore reduce the "liquidity" of the market. In fact, our earlier reasoning suggested that this certainly could happen. However, these same studies found no definite evidence of such an effect.

A completely different argument against options trading concedes that its overall effects are beneficial but maintains that it should nevertheless be limited or banned because it may tempt some individuals into making foolish or inappropriate investments. Implicit in this is the belief that it would be infeasible to provide compensation for those who were truly misled because it would be impossible to separate them from well-informed but unscrupulous investors who were merely unlucky. This issue basically involves a moral judgment, not an economic argument. In our opinion, a minimal amount of prudent regulation can give irrational or poorly informed investors a proper degree of protection without inhibiting the growth of options markets.

8-3. OPTIONS ON THE MARKET PORTFOLIO*

At the time of this writing, no organized market exists in the United States for options on a portfolio of securities.[8] However, financial theory suggests that such securities, if properly structured, are potentially of greater social usefulness than conventional puts and calls on single equity securities.

Proposal. Before outlining this argument, we will first provide a specific proposal[9] for put and call contracts on the New York Stock Exchange Composite Index.[10] These contracts would be quite similar to ordinary options. Each contract would have an opening date, an expiration date, and a striking price. All contracts would be immediately settled in cash following the closing date. To illustrate, assume an Index call is listed as follows:

Opening date	June 23, 1980
Expiration date	June 19, 1981
Striking price	50

If the Index is 55 at the close of trading on the expiration date, the buyer of the call is entitled to 100 times the difference between 50 and 55—that is, $500—and the writer would be obligated to pay $500. Early exercise would not be allowed.

As with ordinary options, a clearing corporation would guarantee performance of the obligations of all Index options and would be considered the issuer of all Index options. Index options would be issued by the

---

* See the addendum on pages 457–458 for a comparison of the proposal of this section with the subsequent development of listed index options.

[8] However, during the 1970s, two U.S. companies offered mutual fund insurance. This is equivalent to selling a put on a fund's portfolio. In 1979 both companies announced that they were discontinuing the sale of new policies. Equity-linked life insurance policies available in the United Kingdom and Canada provide benefits dependent on the performance of a portfolio of equities subject to a minimum guaranteed benefit. From the point of view of the insured, she has purchased an equity portfolio hedged by a purchased put against it. In 1980, CDA Securities, Inc. created an over-the-counter market in call options on First Index Investment Trust, a mutual fund in the Vanguard Group.

[9] This proposal draws heavily on a statement prepared by Mark Rubinstein at the request of the Philadelphia Stock Exchange for presentation to the Securities and Exchange Commission, entitled *An Economic Justification of an Organized Market for Trading Options on a Stock Market Index* (May 1977), as well as on a statement prepared by the Philadelphia Stock Exchange for presentation to the Securities and Exchange Commission, entitled *A Proposal for an Index Type Option Trading Unit* (May 1977).

[10] This index is a weighted average of the prices of all stocks on the NYSE, with the corresponding weights proportional to the total market values of their outstanding shares. For a description of this index, both its construction and past daily behavior, see the pamphlet entitled *Common Stock Indices* available from the Research Department of the New York Stock Exchange.

clearing corporation only to its own clearing member firms, which, in turn, would guarantee performance to the clearing corporation by writers of those options that finish in-the-money. A secondary market would be made in the normal manner on the floor of an exchange.

As long as the Index remains below 100, the exchange would list options with striking prices at 2-point intervals surrounding the current level of the Index. For example, if the Index is at 51, the exchange would open puts and calls at 50 and 52. If, subsequently, the Index has a daily close above 52, the exchange would open puts and calls at 54 on the following business day.

Index options would be listed on a March/June/September/December expiration cycle. As for ordinary options, the expiration date would be the third Friday of the expiration month. Due to anticipated demand for long-term contracts, the exchange would open 3-, 6-, 12-, and 24-month contracts. Subsequently, options would be opened so that one maturity is available in each of the four time intervals: zero to 3 months, 3 to 6 months, 6 to 12 months, and 12 to 24 months. For example, if the exchange opens 3-, 6-, 12-, and 24-month contracts in June 1980, it would open new 6-month contracts in September, 12-month contracts in December, 6-month contracts in March 1981, and 24-month contracts in June 1981. The maturity profile during the year would then be described by Table 8-1.

Table 8-1
MATURITY PROFILE OF INDEX OPTIONS

Month	*Maturity Profile*						
June 1980	③	⑥	⑫	㉔			
July	1	5	11	23			
Aug.	1	4	10	22			
Sep.		3	9	21	⑥		
Oct.		2	8	20	5		
Nov.		1	7	19	4		
Dec.			6	18	3	⑫	
Jan. 1981			5	17	2	11	
Feb.			4	16	1	10	
Mar.			3	15		9	6
Apr.			2	14		8	5
May			1	13		7	4
June				12		6	3	㉔

NOTE: Circled numbers represent newly opened options.

Similar to the treatment of stock splits on stocks underlying ordinary options, Index options would be protected against revisions in the Index to new base values.[11] Like ordinary options, Index options would not be protected against cash dividends on stocks comprising the Index. Except insofar as the Index is adjusted by the New York Stock Exchange for new stock issues, listings, and delistings, Index options would also not be protected against changes in the composition of the Index.

At the outset, customer margin rules for Index options would parallel rules for ordinary options.[12] However, there is considerable reason to believe these requirements should be weakened for Index options. In particular, in comparison with the high volatilities of stocks on which ordinary options are listed, it seems that these margin requirements are unnecessarily severe. The dangers of short squeezes or incentives for price manipulation of the underlying asset are considerably reduced for Index options. Unlike with ordinary options, position and exercise limits do not seem necessary.

Since the NYSE updates the Index only at half-hour intervals during the day, the exchange would use its own computer facilities to provide continuously updated calculations of the Index during the day to the public and to floor traders.

One may wonder why, in view of its greater visibility, we have not suggested the Dow Jones Industrial Average as the underlying aggregate for Index options. First, the NYSE index is a much more broadly based index of equities, compared to the Dow Jones 30 Industrials. Second, the stocks in the DJIA are arbitrarily weighted by their stock price levels so that a stock split in a Dow Jones stock, for example, will affect the future volatility of the DJIA and thereby the value of an option written on it. In contrast, the NYSE index is value-weighted and more nearly corresponds to the ideal index suggested by financial theory. Third, options on the much broader NYSE index are less vulnerable to changes in the composition of the index caused by adding or deleting securities. Fourth, manipulation of option prices by trading in the underlying assets is even more unlikely with the NYSE index. Fifth, the level of the NYSE index corresponds closely to the value of a typical share, and the NYSE intends to revise the index from time to time to maintain this correspondence. Finally, by focusing investor attention on the NYSE Composite Index, we would hope to popularize a more inclusive and representative index of market performance.

---

[11] The Index was set equal to 50 on December 31, 1965, and has not been revised since to a new base value, although the New York Stock Exchange intends to do so if the market value of an "average share" departs sufficiently far from the level of the Index.

[12] Since there is probably no practical collateral for written Index options, they would require margin as if held uncovered. This could significantly reduce the appeal of the proposed securities. This would not be a problem if options could be bought or sold on a diversified closed-end fund, managed to mimic a stock index (a previous CBOE proposal), or a no-load open-end index fund.

Principal Innovations. In addition to the longer maturities of some Index options, there are three other essential differences between this proposal and ordinary option trading.

1. NO NEED TO SELECT INDIVIDUAL SECURITIES. Index options are primarily designed to assist investors in adopting an appropriate portfolio posture toward market or economywide risk. The empirical observation that marketwide risk accounts for roughly 40% of the variation in returns of typical equity securities, the development during the past 15 years of increasing empirical support for the "efficient market" or "random walk" theory of stock price behavior, the nature of optimal individual portfolios that arise in theoretical models of financial equilibrium, as well as recent investor interest in the diversification service offered by index funds—all indicate there are many investors who wish to invest in the market as a whole. Index options are particularly useful for investors who wish to invest in equity securities but who lack the expertise—or otherwise wish to avoid the need—to select individual securities.

2. NO UNDERLYING SECURITY TO DELIVER. In ordinary option trading, the writer must deliver the security upon exercise of a call, unless she offsets her option by a closing purchase transaction—in effect, she settles her obligation in cash. Likewise, the buyer of a call that finishes in-the-money must exercise her option and take delivery of the stock to realize her profit, unless she enters into a closing sale transaction—in effect, realizes her benefits in cash. The proposed Index option *requires* the writer and buyer to settle in cash if it finishes in-the-money.

This difference between ordinary option trading and Index options is more apparent than real. When options are about to terminate in-the-money, most option writers do, in fact, settle their obligations in cash by a closing purchase transaction. Typically, there are savings in transaction costs that make a cash settlement preferable for both buyers and writers.

This proposal, therefore, results in considerable simplification of the trading and settlement procedure that can be expected to reduce transactions costs. The mechanical step of delivery of securities is completely eliminated in all cases. To realize her profit, a buyer whose call finishes in-the-money would not have to follow either of the procedures with related transaction costs currently in use: (a) entering into a closing purchase transaction, or (b) taking delivery of and then selling the underlying security. Indeed, the argument for cash settlement is so strong, even ordinary puts and calls should be listed with this provision.

3. ELIMINATION OF RANDOM ASSIGNMENT OF EXERCISE NOTICES. There is an uncontrolled element in the ordinary options market that can materially affect the profit and loss of a writer. Exercise notices are assigned to writers,

based on random selection. If an option is in-the-money, the writer cannot completely control the time when her loss will be realized. To illustrate, several uncovered writers may write identical options simultaneously and may all realize different results due to factors beyond their control. Indeed, if an option temporarily in-the-money expires out-of-the-money, any writer who had not been assigned a notice of exercise would retain the option sale price and would sustain no loss at all on her position.

This uncontrolled and random effect on the investment results of a writer is completely eliminated by this proposal. All writers who simultaneously write identical contracts in the proposed options will realize an identical level of profit or loss if they do not themselves enter into a closing transaction.

General Economic Justification.   What types of securities should be made available in the financial market? Sections 8-1 and 8-2 suggest a surprising simplification of this complicated issue. A market can perform much of its three functions—individual wealth allocation, firm resource allocation, and source of information—by creating, in addition to the basic securities issued by firms, the following two types of instruments:

1. Default-free securities of varying maturities that permit individual borrowing and lending at the same rates of interest.
2. Puts and calls of varying maturities and striking prices on the portfolio containing all real assets in the economy (that is, the "market portfolio").

To demonstrate this contention, we first discuss the conditions for the market portfolio to approximate Ross's efficient portfolio. It will be recalled that puts and calls available on this single "efficient" portfolio provide at least the same investment flexibility as all available basic securities and options on these basic securities. To take the most elementary case, suppose all the uncertainty surrounding the returns of all securities were completely resolved by knowing the returns on the market portfolio. Then, the coincidence between the market and efficient portfolios would be exact, since the return of the market portfolio would distinguish between all states.

Admittedly, it is a strong presumption to suppose that all uncertainty in the securities market is resolved by the market portfolio. This would imply, for example, that the returns of GM and AT&T stock were certain, given the level of a comprehensive market index. A more general requirement for the approximation to be exact is that *the return of the market portfolio describes the relevant aspect of each state.* If all investors held options on the market and nothing else, they would then be indifferent to the returns of its constituent securities, given the return for the market as a whole. An important theorem of financial economics is that the portfolio needs of all economically rational and risk-averse investors, who are only concerned with their level of wealth, will be fully satisfied by options on the market portfolio *if all investors agree on the probabilities of individual security returns conditional on the market return.*[13] Under these more general circumstances for each level of future market return, investors may still be uncertain about the returns from GM and AT&T, but they must attach the same subjective probabilities to these conditional returns. Investors may, of course, disagree about the probable market return as well as about the unconditional returns of GM and AT&T. However, all disagreement (though not all uncertainty) must be resolved, given the future market return. The logic underlying this theorem derives from the desire for diversification by risk-averse investors. Since all investors have the same conditional beliefs about all security returns, none chooses to slant her portfolio more than the market portfolio in the direction of one security than another. This avoids unnecessary assumption of risk.

While the conditions for the coincidence of Ross's efficient portfolio and the market portfolio are not exactly met in real life, they may be a reasonable approximation. Disagreements among investors about the returns on specific securities often boil down primarily to disagreement about the market return. Much of the volume of trading in basic securities and ordinary options derives not from disagreement about returns conditional on the market, but from disagreement about the market return itself. Substantial reductions in unnecessary transactions costs could then be expected from the introduction of Index options, since desired portfolios could be formed with fewer transactions using Index options with high liquidity.

Specific Applications. With this rather abstract justification of Index options behind us, we now examine some specific ways of using them to achieve socially desirable objectives. If we *at first ignore individual differences in endowed income and expectations,* even with the complications created by transactions costs and taxes, there should be considerable interest in opportunities for default-free borrowing and lending and investment in the market portfolio.

How will Index options foster this type of investment? The purchase of a deep-in-the-money Index call comes close to duplicating the performance of the Index itself. For example, if the Index is currently at 50 and an investor purchases a six-month call with a 35 striking price for approximately $15, as long as the Index value on the closing date is above 35, she will have the same dollar return as if she had been able to purchase the

---

[13] For details, see Nils Hakansson, "Welfare Aspects of Options and Supershares," *Journal of Finance*, 33 (June 1978), 759–776.

Index itself. As a matter of record, on only 21 trading dates, out of a total of 2,892 days, from July 1, 1965 to January 26, 1977, would such an investment have failed to duplicate the returns from the Index itself.[14]

Alternatively, as shown in Section 2-2, neglecting dividends, commissions, and margin, an investment in the Index is *exactly* the same as a portfolio containing (1) a purchased Index call and (2) a written Index put with the same expiration date and striking price, together with (3) lending an amount equal to the striking price divided by one plus the rate of interest on the loan.[15]

In summary, proper use of Index options permits an investor virtually to duplicate the performance of the underlying Index, even though it is not practical to invest in the Index itself. She has done so without paying the load fees, management fees, and turnover transactions costs of mutual funds and without bearing the additional risks of discount fluctuations of closed-end funds. Moreover, she has, in effect, purchased a market value weighted share of every common stock listed on the New York Stock Exchange—a more broadly based set of assets than is currently offered even by index funds.[16] This adds up to more diversification at less cost.

Although default-free instruments—U.S. government bills, notes, and bonds, savings deposits, certificates of deposit, federal agency securities— exist in profusion, few individuals can borrow at the same rate they can lend. For example, investors who purchase stock on margin must pay their brokerage house a minimum of $\frac{1}{2}\%$ to 1% over the call loan rate (that is, the rate brokers can borrow from banks), a rate higher than they receive on lending opportunities of similar risk. This borrowing-lending rate differential increases to 2% for small accounts. This differential, in addition to directly penalizing individual investors, also acts to discourage beneficial economywide risk-taking when the impact across all investors is jointly considered. Those individuals who wish to bear more of society's risk are discouraged from doing so and, since they borrow less, others who would prefer to lend more find fewer willing borrowers.

Index options help to reduce the deleterious effects of the differential between individual borrowing and lending rates. Recall that an investment in the Index itself is virtually the same as a portfolio of a purchased Index

---

[14] These dates all occurred in March and April of 1974, just prior to the historical low in the Index during September and October of 1974. However, over no six-month interval (that is, 126 trading days), even during this period, did the Index fall by more than 36%.

[15] If the same minimum margin requirements on ordinary options also apply to Index options, then public investors who wish to duplicate the performance of the Index may hope to minimize the margin deposit on the written put. This margin deposit is minimized by writing a deep-out-of-the-money Index call. In particular, if the striking price of the put and call is seven-tenths of the value of the Index, the margin deposit will be negligible.

[16] For example, Vanguard Index Trust holds a portfolio with the same market value weights as Standard and Poor's Composite Index of 500 stocks.

call, a written Index put with the same expiration date and striking price, and lending an amount equal to the striking price divided by one plus the rate of interest. Consider an investor who wishes to borrow on margin to purchase a large diversified portfolio of equity securities. She is therefore implicitly lending when she buys the portfolio and is offsetting this by borrowing on margin, thus sacrificing the borrowing-lending rate differential. If, instead, she could purchase an Index call, possibly combined with an Index put, she might save this differential. In effect, proper use of Index options provides a means of borrowing without giving up the borrowing-lending rate differential.[17]

In brief, considering only the implications of differences in individual preferences, Index options make two important contributions to the menu of securities currently available. First, under some circumstances, they provide a less costly instrument for obtaining large-scale diversification and, second, they allow individuals to borrow to purchase a diversified portfolio of equity securities on terms more compatible with those on which they can lend.

Considering now *individual differences in endowed income and expectations*, we can distinguish at least four more sources of demand for Index options:

1. Use by individuals with undiversified earned income.
2. Use by institutional investors as insurance against their equity positions.
3. Use by investors to hedge their exposure to market-wide risk.
4. Use by investors with differences in opinion about future market-wide events.

First, many individuals, from the nature of their wage or salary income, are more vulnerable than others to a downturn in the general economic activity. Adequate protection against this eventuality is difficult to purchase through existing listed securities. Other individuals may find their wage or salary income excessively tied to the fortunes of a particular firm or industry. According to relevant empirical research, there is a correlation between individual securities and the market portfolio, such that the variation in the return to a large diversified portfolio of equity securities accounts for about 40% of the variation in return to a typical equity security. Index options—in particular, purchased Index puts—provide a useful means of acquiring the desired protection.

Second, many institutions, such as pension, endowment, and trust funds, hold portfolios with returns highly correlated with the Index. Many would like to provide their beneficiaries with additional income by writing

---

[17] By now this should be a familiar argument. See Sections 2-3 and 6-2.

calls against their portfolios, or they would like to protect their beneficiaries against a substantial decline in value by purchasing puts against the portfolio of securities they hold.

One strategy is to write calls or buy puts against many of the securities in their portfolios. As an alternative, Index options not only avoid the awkwardness of investing in options on many underlying stocks, but also provide more adequate protection. Even ignoring transactions costs, *an investment in a portfolio of calls (or puts) on all stocks in the Index is not equivalent to a call (or put) on the Index itself.*[18]

Compare the returns of a portfolio of two calls, each written on a different underlying stock, to the returns of one call written on a portfolio of the two stocks. Suppose the current prices of stocks ABC and XYZ both equal 50. Consider the returns from a portfolio of two six-month calls, one written on ABC and the other on XYZ, both with striking price of 50. Six months later we can have four possibilities.

1. Both calls on ABC and XYZ finish in-the-money.
2. Only the call on ABC finishes in-the-money.
3. Only the call on XYZ finishes in-the-money.
4. Both calls on ABC and XYZ finish out-of-the-money.

In Case 1, suppose ABC and XYZ are both 60, then the portfolio of calls would be worth $(60 - 50) + (60 - 50) = 20$. In Case 2, while ABC would be 60, suppose XYZ is worth 40. The portfolio would then be worth $(60 - 50) + 0 = 10$. In Case 3, we would have just the opposite result, so that the portfolio would be worth $0 + (60 - 50) = 10$. Finally, in Case 4, with both stocks at 40, the portfolio of calls is worth $0 + 0 = 0$. Summarizing, for a portfolio of calls, corresponding to each possibility, we have a portfolio valued at expiration of:

1. 20
2. 10
3. 10
4. 0

On the other hand, consider one six-month call written on a portfolio containing one share of ABC and one share of XYZ, with a striking price of $50 + 50 = 100$.[19] Six months later, in Case 1, the call is worth

---

[18] Recall our earlier discussion in Section 4-4.

[19] Equivalently, we could consider two six-month calls, each with 50 striking price, written on an equally weighted index of ABC and XYZ, where the index is initially set equal to the sum of the stock prices, $50 + 50$, divided by 2, or 50.

$(60 + 60) - 100 = 20$. In Cases 2 and 3, since the stock portfolio is worth $60 + 40 = 100$, it does not pay to exercise the call. Similarly, in Case 4, since the stock portfolio is worth only $40 + 40 = 80$, the call is worthless. Summarizing, for a call on a portfolio, corresponding to each possibility, we have a value at expiration of:

1. 20
2. 0
3. 0
4. 0

The returns of the portfolio of calls and the call on the portfolio differ whenever ABC and XYZ have sufficiently different performances such that one call in the portfolio of calls finishes in-the-money, while the other does not. Moreover, since the portfolio of calls always does as well—and often does better—than a call on a portfolio, the former will be more expensive to purchase. This example easily generalizes to put options and to portfolios of many underlying securities. In general, the greater the extent to which the returns of the underlying securities do not move together, the greater the difference between a portfolio of calls and a call on a portfolio.

Consider the position of an investor who writes calls against each security in her equity portfolio. The example illustrates that it is possible for the total position (for example, written calls plus equities) to lose money even though the equity portfolio remains the same in value (that is, outcomes 2 and 3, above). Had she instead been able to write an at-the-money *call on her portfolio*, the call would only be exercised against her if her equity portfolio increased in value. Alternatively, consider an investor who tries to insure that the value of her position will not fall below a given level by buying puts on each equity security in her portfolio. In this case, it is possible for the total position (that is, purchased puts plus equities) to increase in value even though her equity portfolio decreases or remains the same in value. The portfolio of puts therefore provides more protection than required. Had she instead purchased an at-the-money *put on her portfolio*, she would only exercise the put if her portfolio fell in value. Unlike a portfolio of puts, a put on her portfolio provides exactly the protection desired and no more.

Index options, therefore, provide protection better matched than a portfolio of options to the risk of most institutional portfolios. In addition, this protection will cost less. Suppose we assume a typical optioned equity has a volatility of .3. In contrast, the volatility of the Index calculated from daily observations, from 1965 through 1977, was .16. Using the Black-Scholes option pricing formula, if the annual interest rate is 8% and the striking price is 50, two at-the-money, six-month calls with volatilities of .16

and .3 should cost $3.28 and $5.16, respectively. Therefore, we can expect an Index option to be roughly 60% of the cost of a corresponding portfolio of options. Ideally, institutions should deal in options on the exact portfolios they hold. However, the profusion of options that would then need to be created exceeds the bounds of practicality. For most institutions, we suspect that Index options are the most practical vehicle. In addition to a possibly longer menu of maturities, a further advantage of Index options over a portfolio of options is the probable reduction in transactions costs through a reduction in the bid-ask spread.[20]

Third, many investors may feel that though they have expertise in gauging the fortunes of individual firms, they have no special knowledge about the market as a whole. Though they may be correct about the relative performance of specific firms, they may still not realize a profit due to unfavorable market-wide events. Index options provide an easy way to hedge against these market-wide events while retaining the desired exposure to the specific risks of individual firms. For example, an investor who believes a particular stock is underpriced may want to combine a long position in this stock with written in-the-money Index calls.

Fourth, an important reason for departing from the levered market portfolio strategy discussed previously is differences in investor expectations. At present, it is difficult for investors who are optimistic about prospects for the economy as a whole to take a fully appropriate investment position. Again, one possibility is to purchase a large diversified portfolio of calls. Transaction costs might make the investment quite costly. Moreover, as we have seen, such a portfolio does not give adequate consideration to return dependencies among the underlying securities. The appropriate and direct way of involvement is the purchase of an Index call.

As with ordinary options, investors can also use Index options through spreads and combinations to take more complex positions, whose success depends in large part on their estimates of future volatility of the Index. For example, buying an Index call and a put insures profits as long as the Index moves either up or down sufficiently to cover the option prices plus commissions.

As a source of information, Index options should prove similar to ordinary options. Given the current level of the Index, interest rates, the striking price, and expiration date of an Index call or put, its price will primarily depend on the "market's" anticipated volatility of the Index. Index option prices provide important, otherwise unobtainable, information to the economy. For example, the financial press frequently speculates, from questionable sources, that the "investment outlook" is uncertain. With

---

[20] Market Makers will be able to use Index options to balance their positions, permitting them to quote tighter spreads on ordinary options as well.

Index options, a believer in "efficient markets" can easily check this statement by examining their prices. Unlike ordinary options, Index options consider return dependencies among different stocks, relevant to the economy as a whole. For example, it is quite possible that during a period when prices of ordinary options are high, prices of Index options may be low or at normal levels. This indicates that although there is considerable uncertainty in the returns of individual stocks, because of offsetting effects, the stock market as a whole is anticipated to be relatively stable.[21]

Any clarification of the risks of diversified investment in the corporate sector should improve the allocation of capital between aggregate current consumption and investment. The market will be better informed and less likely to over- or underinvest, thereby reducing economic instability. Moreover, better aware of the risks of diversified equity investment, individuals can adjust the leverage of their personal portfolios to reflect more accurately the risk they are willing to bear. For instance, in the current practices of several institutional portfolio managers, the anticipated volatility of the market is a critical input into their decision-making processes. The natural vehicles for obtaining this information are Index options.

Predictions of the business cycle frequently form a basis for government economic policy, and although the stock market is one of the best leading indicators, it can give false signals. Although we have not carefully examined this possibility, the additional information on anticipated market volatility provided by Index options may refine the usefulness of this indicator.

Finally, Index options may well provide valuable information for real investment decisions. Corporations acting in the interests of their shareholders make investments whose discounted cash flows have positive present value. Being uncertain, these cash flows should be discounted for risk as well as time. If the Black-Scholes option pricing formula holds for Index options, the existence of just one Index option would permit inference of the implicit volatility of the Index itself. This, combined with the methodology developed in the next section, would provide a technique for estimating the appropriate risk discount factors.

Addendum. Since this was written, listed markets in index futures and index options have been developed in the United States. Some, but not most, of the uses of index options discussed here will be better met by index futures. As anticipated here, these markets have become very active, with

---

[21] A good example is provided by the six-month period from June 30, 1973 to December 31, 1973. Although the Dow Jones Industrial Average showed little change over this period, the stocks comprising the Average exhibited considerable cross-sectional variability: 13 of the 30 stocks comprising the Average had price changes 20% or greater in absolute magnitude.

trading volume (measured in share equivalents) exceeding trading volume in the underlying instruments.

Nonetheless, there still remain two critical differences between the proposal in this chapter and current exchange-traded securities: The proposal advocates the use of long-term (more than one year) European options, while the exchange-traded options that are now available are all short-term (less than one year) American options. This, together with the desire of many financial institutions to create options on their own portfolios rather than on a standardized index, has created an interest in dynamic asset allocation strategies. Following the principles outlined in Section 2-3 and more fully developed in Chapter 5, these institutions pursue a systematic policy of revising their asset mix through time (such as revising the proportions of their portfolio devoted to stock and Treasury bills) to achieve the effect of having taken an option position with their entire portfolio as the underlying asset.

8-4. THE SUPERFUND

Description. A more radical innovation—the "superfund"—has recently been proposed by Nils Hakansson, Professor of Accounting and Finance at the University of California, Berkeley.[22] Given the basic securities (that is, stocks and bonds) issued by corporations, what other financial instruments should be created? Although stocks and bonds identified with particular corporations may provide the most efficient way to raise capital, it does not follow that most investors are directly interested in these basic securities. With this in mind, Hakansson suggests the formation of a financial intermediary called a superfund, similar to an ordinary mutual fund with respect to its assets, but quite different from a mutual fund with respect to its liabilities. The assets of a superfund would consist of a portfolio of basic securities, and against these assets, the superfund would issue "supershares."

> A *supershare* is a security, which on its expiration date
> entitles its owner to a given dollar value proportion of the
> assets of the superfund, provided the value of those assets
> on that date *lies between a lower and an upper value.*
> Otherwise, the supershare expires worthless.

For example, suppose the portfolio of assets purchased by the superfund were, in fact, the New York Stock Exchange Composite Index—that

---

[22] See his article, "The Purchasing Power Fund: A New Kind of Financial Intermediary," *Financial Analysts Journal*, 32 (November-December 1976), 49–59.

is, a portfolio of all the stocks on the New York Stock Exchange purchased in proportion to their market values. A "level 50" supershare would entitle its owner to receive the level of the Index divided by 50, if the index finished between 50 and 51 on the expiration date. Otherwise, the supershare would expire worthless. Therefore, if the Index did finish between 50 and 51, the supershare would return between $1.00 and $1.02. Similarly, a level 47 supershare would return between $1.00 and about $1.02 if the Index finished between 47 and 48. More generally, if $Q*$ represents the value of a K_1 level supershare on its expiration date, K_1 and K_2 are its lower and upper payoff boundaries, and $S*$ is the level of the Index on the expiration date, then

$$Q* = \begin{cases} 0 & \text{if } S* < K_1 \\ S*/K_1 & \text{if } K_1 \leq S* < K_2. \\ 0 & \text{if } K_2 \leq S* \end{cases}$$

The concept of "state-contingent claim," developed in Section 8-1, is the theoretical model motivating the supershare. It will be recalled that a state-contingent claim to state n pays $1 if, and only if, state n occurs. Otherwise, it expires worthless. A supershare takes as the relevant state-of-the-world the value of the portfolio of basic securities on which it is written. Since this portfolio can assume a continuous number of values between any two boundaries, the return of a supershare, given that it pays off, is to some extent uncertain. However, this uncertainty can be made as small as one would like by setting the lower and upper boundaries sufficiently close.

Taking first things first, how could a superfund guarantee its obligations as an issuer of supershares? Suppose the superfund invested $50 million in the Index when the Index was at 50 on January 2, 1985. Ignoring commissions, the superfund would then have purchased 1 million "shares" in the Index. On January 2, 1985, it would simultaneously sell

25,000,000 level 25 supershares
26,000,000 level 26 supershares
⋮
50,000,000 level 50 supershares
51,000,000 level 51 supershares
⋮
74,000,000 level 74 supershares
75,000,000 level 75 supershares

all of which would expire January 2, 1986. The proceeds from this sale would finance the $50 million investment in the Index. We will show later that arbitrageurs would assure that, ignoring commissions, $50 million would be raised from this sale of supershares. If we suppose the probability is small that the Index at the end of the year would be less than 25 or greater than 75, to round off the list, a single series of supershares would be sold, based on lower and upper boundaries of 0 and 25, and a single series based on a lower boundary of 76 with no upper boundary. This latter supershare would be equivalent to an ordinary European call with a striking price of 76.

Since it has issued just the right number of supershares for each level of the Index, no matter what the value of the Index on January 2, 1986, the superfund is guaranteed to meet all its obligations. For example, if the Index finished at 55.40, the superfund would hold assets worth $55.40 \times 1,000,000 = \$55,400,000$. All supershares, except level 55, would have expired worthless. For each level 55 supershare, the superfund would be obligated to deliver $\$55.40 \div 55 \approx \$1.0078$. But since it issued exactly 55,000,000 of these supershares and $\$1.0078 \times 55,000,000 \approx \$55,400,000$, the superfund has just enough funds after selling its portfolio to meet its obligations.

Pricing.   Using the Black-Scholes option pricing formula, we can estimate the likely values of supershares. Recall that, according to the formula, the value of a payout-protected European call is

$$C = SN(x) - Kr^{-t}N(x - \sigma\sqrt{t}),$$

where

$$x \equiv \frac{\log(S/Kr^{-t})}{\sigma\sqrt{t}} + \tfrac{1}{2}\sigma\sqrt{t}.$$

Following the logic used in Section 5-6, for our current purposes, $SN(x)$ can be interpreted as the benefits from holding the call, and $Kr^{-t}N(x - \sigma\sqrt{t})$ as the costs of holding the call.

What would then be the value of an "incomplete call," $\hat{C}$, which gave the right to buy the stock for *nothing* if and only if $S^* \geq K$ on the expiration date? It would have the same value as C, except no future costs would be incurred; that is,

$$\hat{C} = SN(x),$$

where

$$x \equiv \frac{\log(S/Kr^{-t})}{\sigma\sqrt{t}} + \tfrac{1}{2}\sigma\sqrt{t}.$$

A supershare can be constructed from a portfolio of just two of these incomplete calls. Table 8-2 provides the arbitrage analysis.

Table 8-2
CONSTRUCTING A SUPERSHARE

	Current Date	Expiration Date		
		$S^* < K$	$K \le S^* < K + 1$	$K + 1 \le S^*$
Buy $1/K$ incomplete calls at K	$\dfrac{-\hat{C}(K)}{K}$	—	$\dfrac{S^*}{K}$	$\dfrac{S^*}{K}$
Write $1/K$ incomplete calls at $K + 1$	$\dfrac{\hat{C}(K+1)}{K}$	—	—	$\dfrac{-S^*}{K}$
Total		—	$\dfrac{S^*}{K}$	—

Therefore, a supershare is equivalent to a portfolio of incomplete calls $[\hat{C}(K) - \hat{C}(K + 1)]/K$.

In other words, the present value $Q(K)$ of a K-level supershare is:

$$Q(K) = (S/K)[N(x_1) - N(x_2)]$$

where

$$x_1 \equiv \frac{\log(S/Kr^{-t})}{\sigma\sqrt{t}} + \tfrac{1}{2}\sigma\sqrt{t}$$

$$x_2 \equiv \frac{\log(S/(K + 1)r^{-t})}{\sigma\sqrt{t}} + \tfrac{1}{2}\sigma\sqrt{t}$$

Suppose the volatility of the Index is $\sigma = .12$, the interest rate is $r - 1 = .05$, and the Index is currently at $S = 50$. Using our formula, Table 8-3 lists the values of supershares on the Index with one year to expiration. Other things equal, had the volatility been .2 instead of .12, the deep-in- and out-of-the-money supershares would become more valuable and the at-the-money supershares less valuable. For example, the "level 40," "level 50," and "level 70" supershares are then valued at 2.60, 3.72, and .78 cents, respectively.

Application. The power and versatility of a superfund only become evident if we consider portfolios of supershares. Table 8-4 shows how to use super-

Table 8-3
VALUE OF SUPERSHARES ON THE INDEX

Index level = 50			*Interest rate* = .05		
Volatility = .12			*Time to expiration* = 1		

K	Value (in cents)	K	Value (in cents)	K	Value (in cents)
25	a	42	1.78	59	2.92
26	a	43	2.37	60	2.44
27	a	44	3.02	61	2.01
28	a	45	3.71	62	1.63
29	a	46	4.38	63	1.30
30	a	47	5.00	64	1.02
31	a	48	5.50	65	.80
32	a	49	5.88	66	.61
33	.01	50	6.11	67	.47
34	.03	51	6.17	68	.35
35	.06	52	6.07	69	.26
36	.11	53	5.83	70	.19
37	.20	54	5.47	71	.14
38	.35	55	5.02	72	.10
39	.57	56	4.51	73	.07
40	.87	57	3.97	74	.05
41	1.28	58	3.44	75	.04

[a] Less than .005 cent.

shares to construct a number of illustrative positions. A $50 one-year maturity default-free zero-coupon bond is purchased by buying 52 supershares at each level from 25 to 75. This insures a return of 52 to 53, irrespective of the future level of the Index. In terms of rate of return, this position guarantees 4%–6%; this compares to the 5% interest rate used in the formula. We can buy the Index itself, by purchasing at each level the number of supershares equal to the level itself. If profitable riskless arbitrage is not to exist, then, ignoring commissions, this portfolio of supershares must cost exactly the initial level of the Index. If it did not, a sure profit could be made on no investment by buying or selling the stock in the Index against an offsetting position in supershares. This also explains why the superfund is guaranteed to meet its obligations.

By purchasing Position 3 through supershares, we have taken a levered position *without margin*. As securities markets are currently structured, (1) we would need our broker's approval for this transaction, (2) our stock would be held as collateral backing the loan, (3) we would be subject

Table 8-4
ILLUSTRATIVE SUPERSHARE POSITIONS

Position	*Equivalent in Supershares*	*Cost*[a] *(in dollars)*	*Gross Return if Index is:* 45	53	60
1. Buy default-free bond	52 "level 25," ... 52 "level 50," ... 52 "level 75"	50	52	52	52
2. Buy Index	25 "level 25," ... 50 "level 50," ... 75 "level 75"	50	45	53	60
3. Buy Index with 50% leverage	2 "level 27," ... 48 "level 50," ... 98 "level 75"	50	38	54	68
4. Short Index	79 "level 25," ... 54 "level 50," ... 29 "level 75"	50	59	51	44
5. Fixed return if Index goes up; nothing otherwise	91 "level 51," ... 91 "level 63," ... 91 "level 75"	50	0	91	91
6. Bet on Index going up exactly to 60–61	2047 "level 60"	50	0	0	2047
7. Buy at-the-money call on Index	1 "level 51," ... 13 "level 63," ... 25 "level 75"	3.42	0	3	10
8. Buy at-the-money put on Index	25 "level 25," ... 13 "level 37," ... 1 "level 49"	1.53	5	0	0

[a] Based on the Black-Scholes option pricing formula, with the Index initially at 50, annualized volatility of .12, annualized interest rate of .05, and a one-year maturity for supershares. Commissions are ignored.

to a possible margin call if the stock fell enough in value, and (4) we would sacrifice to the broker a $\frac{1}{2}$% to 2% differential between the interest rate at which we can borrow and the rate at which we can lend. Supershares make all this unnecessary. Indeed, since no supershare equivalent position requires that we *sell* supershares, all problems created by potential default are nonexistent. This advantage of supershares is particularly significant for Position 4. In existing securities markets, in addition to the four features mentioned above, short sales entail loss of interest on the proceeds from the sale. This creates a considerable bias against short sales and may partially explain why short selling is relatively unpopular.[23] However, by using supershares to create a short position, we can receive all the benefits of a conventional short position plus, in effect, interest on the proceeds from the sale. For example, in a conventional short sale, if the stock remains unchanged, we break even. In an equivalent supershare position, if the Index stays at 50, our gross return is 54, for an 8% rate of return on our $50 investment.

Not only can supershares be used to duplicate purchased positions in puts and calls (that is, Positions 7 and 8), they can also be used to create positions currently unavailable in existing markets, such as Positions 5 and 6. Not only do supershares considerably enlarge the variety of investment opportunities available, but also they reduce positions to their natural elements.

The superfund concept admits of several variants. Financial theory suggests that investor demands for the fund may be greater if it held a diversified portfolio of corporate bonds, as well as stock. The fund may want to offer supershares of several maturities. It may also want to provide protection against unanticipated inflation. This could easily be accomplished if the condition for payment were the future value of the Index deflated by the Consumer Price Index. Through an appropriate portfolio of these supershares, the superfund could make a purchasing power bond available to the public.

The prices of supershares also contain useful economic information. Corporations acting in the interests of their shareholders make real investments whose discounted cash flows have positive present value. Being uncertain, these cash flows should be discounted for risk, as well as time. As we have mentioned, the yield curve can be used to determine the time discount factors. Of much greater difficulty is the calculation of the risk discount factors. Indeed, this is of sufficient difficulty that most large corporations only consider risk in very crude ways. However, the prices of supershares are themselves the natural risk discount factors. For a given maturity, they are approximately what the market would pay today for a future $1 received if and only if the Index is at a given level.

To take a simple example, suppose a firm considered undertaking a project with an uncertain return one year from now. To discount for risk, the firm would first identify the *expected* future cash inflow from the project, *conditional* on each possible future level of the Index. Table 8-5 lists possible expected returns for the project. Second, the firm would multiply (that is, discount) each return per dollar for the project times the value of the corresponding supershare (see Table 8-3). Third, these products would

---

[23] Other rational reasons for the unpopularity of short selling include tax disadvantages (see Chapter 3) and the "tick rule" which requires that a short sale can only be executed following an up-tick in the stock price or after one or more zero ticks preceded by an up-tick.

Table 8-5

EXPECTED PROJECT RETURNS, CONDITIONAL ON INDEX

| *Index level* = 50 | | | *Interest rate* = .05 | |
| *Volatility* = .12 | | | *Time to expiration* = 1 | |

K	*Return per Dollar*	K	*Return per Dollar*	K	*Return per Dollar*
25	.400	42	.876	59	1.244
26	.428	43	.904	60	1.260
27	.456	44	.932	61	1.276
28	.484	45	.960	62	1.292
29	.512	46	.988	63	1.308
30	.540	47	1.016	64	1.324
31	.568	48	1.044	65	1.340
32	.596	49	1.072	66	1.356
33	.624	50	1.100	67	1.372
34	.652	51	1.116	68	1.388
35	.680	52	1.132	69	1.404
36	.708	53	1.148	70	1.420
37	.736	54	1.164	71	1.436
38	.764	55	1.180	72	1.452
39	.792	56	1.196	73	1.468
40	.820	57	1.212	74	1.484
41	.848	58	1.228	75	1.500

be summed and the sum compared to the number 1. If the sum exceeds 1, then the present value per dollar invested exceeds $1, and the project should be accepted.[24] Otherwise, the project is rejected. In this example, the present value per dollar of the project is 1.069, so the project should be accepted if the firm wants to act in the interests of its shareholders.

In practice, it is not necessary to identify a return per dollar with each supershare. Indeed, the above table was generated by separately measuring the return per dollar for supershare levels 25, 50, and 75. The intermediate returns were interpolated.

It should be emphasized that even given the future level of the Index, the return from the project is typically uncertain. However, financial theory suggests (see Section 8-3) that the risk of a project that is independent of the level of the Index will be costlessly diversified away by investors. Therefore,

---

[24] Stating this symbolically, if $X(K)$ is the expected future cash inflow per dollar invested conditional on the future level of the index between K and $K + 1$, then the project should be accepted if and only if

$$\sum_{K=25}^{75} Q(K) \cdot X(K) > 1.$$

in the discounting process, we can replace the random project returns conditional on the level of the Index with their expected values. This has the further virtue of placing the responsibility for estimating the probabilities of future events with those best qualified. A firm that uses supershare prices as discount rates effectively settles the difficult question of gauging the future course of the market portfolio on the consensus of investor opinion. Instead, the firm can focus on estimating the expected cash flows from its potential projects, given the future levels of the Index.

If supershares of different maturities are available, then their prices can be used to value projects with cash flows received over many future periods. Each expected cash flow conditional on the market can be discounted by the price of the appropriate supershare expiring at the corresponding date. Moreover, even if no supershares existed, under certain conditions the values of all supershares could be determined from the price of just one Index option. In particular, if the conditions for the Black-Scholes option pricing formula were met, given the term structure of interest rates inferable from government bonds, all supershare prices over market states and dates could be calculated knowing the Index volatility. This volatility, in turn, could be derived implicitly from the Black-Scholes formula knowing the market price of just one Index option and the concurrent level of the Index. If this procedure proved useful, financial economics could claim considerable success toward solving one of its most important problems: how to unravel informed predictions of future economic events from security prices. Its success would be all the more remarkable in view of the very few securities needed to make the relevant prediction.

Criticism. The superfund is an exciting financial concept. Its successful introduction might dramatically alter and streamline existing financial markets. We would be delivered from the chaos of existing securities to their natural building blocks. Hakansson has compared the investment positions in supershares to chemical formulas relating molecules to their constituent elements.

The hard questions of eventual implementation fall into three categories: (1) operation, (2) regulation, and (3) liquidity. What institutions would first experiment with the concept? How would newly issued supershares initially be sold? How would the secondary market be organized? What would be the exercise procedure? Would the concept be approved by the Securities and Exchange Commission? What special regulation of superfunds would be required to prevent fraud? And, most important, how high would and could transaction costs be to maintain the market? How would the viability of other sectors of the securities industry be affected? Since the supershare concept remains untested, these questions have not been answered. However, in his article, Hakansson provides some useful speculation.

Supershares and Index options offer alternative means of accomplishing similar goals. In fact, as should be clear from Section 8-2, if puts and calls on the Index existed with a sufficient variety of striking prices, supershares could virtually be created from appropriate portfolios of Index options.[25] The principal advantage of Index options is their immunity to the "knife-edge effect." For example, consider the buyer of a large number of "level 60" supershares. If the Index finishes at 59.99, her position is worthless, while if it finishes at 60.00, she will realize an enormous profit. Her incentive to manipulate the Index during the week of maturity may be considerable. Of course, it would take substantial capital to affect the level of such a broadly based aggregate as the Index, particularly since there would no doubt be some buyers of "level 59" supershares with an opposite motivation.

Like moving to the metric system, Index options would require some adjustment in the habits of thought of practitioners. However, the recent immediate success of the organized market for puts and calls, T-bill futures, and other new securities suggests that the financial community is very

---

[25] The payoffs to supershares can be approximated by "butterfly" spreads of Index options. As we shorten the distance covered by a single supershare (that is, let adjoining levels get closer and closer), this approximation becomes exact.

This relationship between Index options and supershares has been clarified by Douglas Breeden and Robert Litzenberger in their article, "Prices of State-Contingent Claims Implicit in Option Prices," *Journal of Business*, 51 (October 1978), 621–651. In the limit, our valuation formula of uncertain income, in terms of supershares, becomes exactly expressible in terms of Index options. In particular, suppose we let the distance between adjoining supershares be k. Then we can rewrite our previous formula as

$$\lim_{k \to 0} \sum_{n=0}^{\infty} Q(nk) \cdot X(nk) = \int \frac{\partial^2 C}{\partial K^2} X(K) \, dK.$$

$\partial^2 C/\partial K^2$ is the second derivative of an Index call with striking price K and an expiration date coinciding with the receipt of the cash flows.

Breeden and Litzenberger show this representation is quite general, requiring only that $C(K)$ be twice differentiable. If, less generally, the conditions for the Black-Scholes formula obtain, then

$$\frac{\partial^2 C}{\partial K^2} = \frac{r^{-t}}{K\sigma\sqrt{t}} N'(x - \sigma\sqrt{t}),$$

so that the valuation formula becomes

$$\frac{r^{-t}}{\sigma\sqrt{t}} \int \frac{N'(x - \sigma\sqrt{t})}{K} X(K) \, dK.$$

If the expected cash flows $X(K)$ can be conveniently expressed as a continuous function of K, this alternative representation should prove more attractive.

adaptive. It is possible, though unlikely, that the overwhelming application of supershares would be to construct puts and calls on the Index. If this proved true, transaction costs might be minimized by marketing Index options directly. Finally, although supershares do not require margin, they only escape its attendant problems at the price of setting up a primary market to originate them. Even supershares, if originated similarly to ordinary puts and calls by investors, would require margin.

APPENDIX 8A

An Index of Option Prices

The Chicago Board Options Exchange now calculates and publishes a weekly index of CBOE call and put option prices. In comparison with common stock indices, the construction of a useful index of option prices is a more challenging task. In the case of common stock, most economists and investors are interested in the same thing: the return of a typical dollar invested in the stock market. The New York Stock Exchange computes this for NYSE stocks by calculating the total market value of all stocks on the exchange. Except for some changes that need not concern us here, this is divided by a fixed divisor to produce an index value centered at 50 for December 31, 1965. One amendment to the index that might improve its usefulness would be a correction for cash dividends on the appropriate ex-dividend dates. As currently calculated, the index understates the pretax return to an investor by the amount of the dividends.

Unfortunately, for options, there is less agreement over how to construct a useful index. Since there are so many ways options can and are used, it is not possible to develop an index (or even a few different indices) that would reflect a relevant standard of realized returns to most investors. Moreover, a sensible index of option prices should be designed to convey the additional information about economic activity not already supplied by indices taken from other securities markets.

In the context of the Black-Scholes formula, as well as its generalizations, the key piece of information contained in option prices, which is not easy to infer from other securities, is forecasts of stock volatility.[1] This suggests that an index of call option prices should be constructed in the following way:

NOTE: The subject of this appendix should not be confused with options on an index discussed in Section 8-3.

[1] The Black-Scholes formula, generalized for cash dividends, also contains an implicit forecast of dividends over the life of the option.

Step 1. Calculate the implicit volatility of all or at least a few calls on each underlying stock.

Step 2. Through some weighting procedure, determine a single implicit volatility for each underlying stock.

Step 3. For each underlying stock, convert this implicit volatility into the price of a call with a standardized time to expiration and striking price.[2]

Step 4. Average these option prices across all underlying stocks to create a single option price for the market.

A similar approach could be used to construct a put option index.

We will illustrate these steps by example. Suppose we consider standardizing our index to represent the price of a six-month at-the-money call. Since no call with exactly these terms typically exists on a given day, we will need to infer from those that do exist what its price would be.

For *Step 1*, for each underlying stock, we select the four calls whose terms most nearly bracket a six-month at-the-money call: $C(K_1, t_1)$, $C(K_2, t_1)$, $C(K_1, t_2)$, and $C(K_2, t_2)$ where $K_2 > S > K_1$, and $t_2 > \frac{1}{2} > t_1$. Using the Black-Scholes formula, the six-month T-bill rate, and an appropriate dividend adjustment, we calculate their respective implicit volatilities $\sigma(K_1, t_1)$, $\sigma(K_2, t_1)$, $\sigma(K_1, t_2)$, and $\sigma(K_2, t_2)$.

For *Step 2*, first define $\lambda \equiv (K_2 - S)/(K_2 - K_1)$ and compute

$$\sigma(S, t_1) \equiv \lambda\sigma(K_1, t_1) + (1 - \lambda)\sigma(K_2, t_1)$$

and

$$\sigma(S, t_2) \equiv \lambda\sigma(K_1, t_2) + (1 - \lambda)\sigma(K_2, t_2).$$

Now define $\lambda \equiv (t_2 - \frac{1}{2})/(t_2 - t_1)$ and compute

$$\sigma(S, \tfrac{1}{2}) \equiv \lambda\sigma(S, t_1) + (1 - \lambda)\sigma(S, t_2).$$

$\sigma(S, \frac{1}{2})$ is our estimate of the implicit volatility for a six-month at-the-money call. Observe that our estimation procedure gives more weight to the implicit volatility of a call option, the closer its terms are to a six-month at-the-money option. Indeed, if by coincidence such an option existed on a given day, all the weight would be given to it and none to the other three.

Since we want our index to convey an unalloyed reading of stock volatility, we need to standardize the call price in *Step 3* to eliminate interest rate effects. This can be done by choosing a striking price K such

---

[2] Dividend effects could be removed from the index by first calculating the implicit volatility considering dividends in Step 2 and then setting dividends equal to zero in Step 3.

that $K = S\sqrt{r}$. Such an option will actually be somewhat out-of-the-money. Under these circumstances, the Black-Scholes formula reduces to

$$\frac{C}{S} = 2N\left[\frac{\sigma}{\sqrt{8}}\right] - 1.$$

For each underlying stock j, using the implicit volatility $\sigma_j(S_j, \frac{1}{2})$ from *Step 2* above, we then use this formula to calculate the *relative* price $C_j(S_j\sqrt{r}, \frac{1}{2})/S_j$.

To eliminate the pure stock price level effect on the index, in *Step 4* we average these relative prices, not the call prices themselves. The index is then a simple average of the relative prices across all underlying stocks:

$$\text{Index} = \frac{1}{J} \sum_{j=1}^{J} \frac{C_j(S_j\sqrt{r}, \frac{1}{2})}{S_j}.$$

Although the index is quoted in terms of an average of relative prices, it is nonetheless possible to deduce from it the average implicit volatility

$$\frac{1}{J} \sum_{j=1}^{J} \sigma_j(S_j, \frac{1}{2})$$

of underlying stocks. This follows from a property of the Black-Scholes formula that over realistic parameter values for any $0 \le \lambda \le 1$ to a very close approximation[3]

$$\lambda C(\sigma_1) + (1 - \lambda)C(\sigma_2) \approx C[\lambda\sigma_1 + (1 - \lambda)\sigma_2].$$

For at-the-money calls, this property is apparent from Figure 5-6.

The CBOE uses a similar but more complex procedure for computing its index.[4] The exchange selects the same four call options for each underlying stock and calculates their implicit volatilities as in *Step 1*. In *Step 2*, it computes a simple average of these

$$\sigma^* \equiv [\sigma(K_1, t_1) + \sigma(K_2, t_1) + \sigma(K_1, t_2) + \sigma(K_2, t_2)]/4.$$

---

[3] Of course, by suitably permuting Steps 3 and 4, the index could be made to represent exactly this average implicit volatility. That is, for Step 3 we would average the implicit volatilities across all stocks and for Step 4 convert this single average volatility into a single relative price.

[4] This procedure is described in detail in "The CBOE Call Option Index: Methodology and Technical Considerations" prepared by the Research Department of the Chicago Board Options Exchange, March 1979.

In *Step 3*, this volatility is used via the Black-Scholes formula to calculate the theoretical value of a six-month at-the-money call, $C^*(S, \frac{1}{2})$. However, the CBOE does not regard this as its final estimate of a standardized call price. Again it uses σ^* to calculate the four Black-Scholes call values $C^*(K_1, t_1)$, $C^*(K_2, t_1)$, $C^*(K_1, t_2)$, and $C^*(K_2, t_2)$. These five theoretical values are then used to construct weights to average the four actual call prices.

Specifically the CBOE computes its estimate of $C(S, \frac{1}{2})$ according to

$$C(S, \tfrac{1}{2}) = \lambda_1 C(K_1, t_1) + \lambda_2 C(K_2, t_1) + \lambda_3 C(K_1, t_2) + \lambda_4 C(K_2, t_2),$$

where

$$y \equiv \text{sign}[C^*(K_1, t_1) - C^*(K_2, t_2)], \qquad \Sigma \equiv \lambda_1 + \lambda_2 + \lambda_3 + \lambda_4,$$

and

$$\lambda_1 \equiv y[C^*(S, \tfrac{1}{2}) - C^*(K_2, t_2)]/\Sigma, \qquad \lambda_3 \equiv [C^*(S, \tfrac{1}{2}) - C^*(K_2, t_1)]/\Sigma,$$
$$\lambda_2 \equiv [C^*(K_1, t_2) - C^*(S, \tfrac{1}{2})]/\Sigma, \qquad \lambda_4 \equiv y[C^*(K_1, t_1) - C^*(S, \tfrac{1}{2})]/\Sigma.$$

This procedure tends to give most weight to the prices of options whose theoretical values are closest to the theoretical value of a six-month at-the-money call.

In *Step 4*, the index is calculated by a simple average of these relative prices across all underlying CBOE stocks:

$$\text{CBOE Index} = \frac{1}{J} \sum_{j=1}^{J} \frac{C_j(S_j, \tfrac{1}{2})}{S_j}.$$

There are two differences between our suggested index and the CBOE index, only one of which is empirically significant. Clearly, we use a different weighting procedure to obtain the value of a standardized option for each underlying stock. Ours at least has the property that all the weight is placed on the price of a six-month at-the-money call, if it exists, while this is not typically true for the CBOE procedure.[5] Moreover, our weighting procedure is less complicated. However, preliminary simulations indicate that any difference between the two indices due to weighting is empirically negligible.

Of greater significance is the fact that the CBOE index standardizes its relative price to an at-the-money call (that is, $K = S$), while ours standardizes to a somewhat out-of-the-money call (that is, $K = S\sqrt{r}$). This difference causes changes in the CBOE index to reflect both volatility and

---

[5] Evidently, to surmount this objection, if such an option exists, the CBOE substitutes the price of this option for its weighted average price. This induces a discontinuity that our procedure does not require.

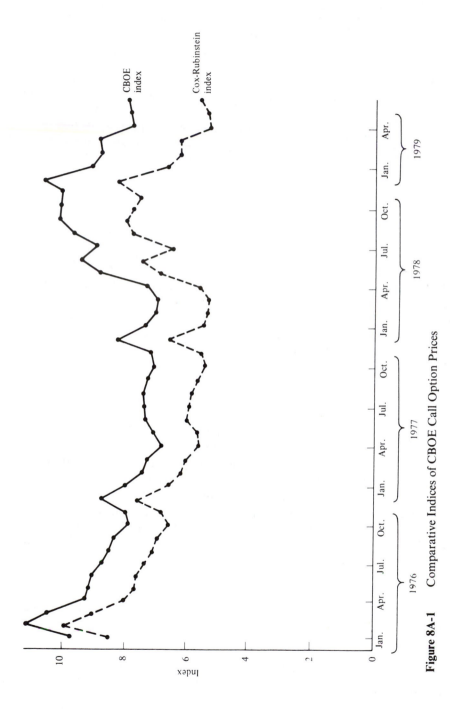

Figure 8A-1   Comparative Indices of CBOE Call Option Prices

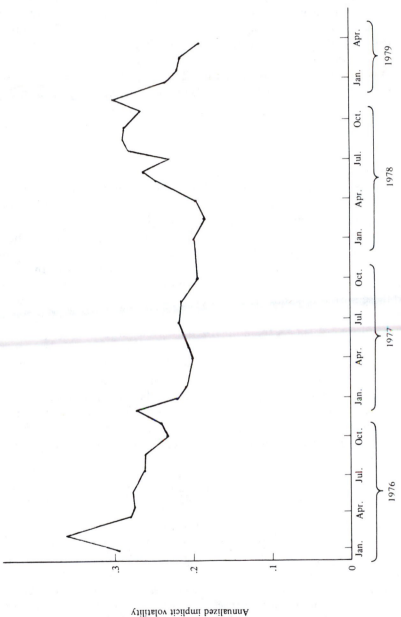

Figure 8A-2   Implicit Volatility in CBOE Call Option Index

interest rate changes, while ours is a pure reflection of changes in volatility.[6] This accords with our principle that a sensible index of option prices should be designed to convey only the additional information not already supplied by indices taken from other securities markets.[7] Adapting the CBOE index for this purpose requires using the appropriate interest rate to back out the implicit volatility of the index, then using this implicit volatility to calculate the relative price for a call with $K = S\sqrt{r}$.

Figure 8A-1 does precisely this. The upper line shows the CBOE Index as of the final Thursday for each month from January 1976 through June 1979. One way to see the effects of changes in interest rates is to ask at what level the Index would be had the interest rate remained constant at its level at the end of January 1976, while letting the implicit volatility follow its actual pattern over time. In that case, by June 28, 1979 the Index would have been at 6.89 instead of its actual level 7.97. This difference was caused by an increase in the interest rate over the period from 5.26% to 9.56%.[8]

The lower line in Figure 8A-1 shows our index over the period. Since this index removes interest rate effects, it is a pure reflection of the implicit volatility of the CBOE Index at each date.[9] Of course, it is systematically lower because it measures the relative price of a six-month call which is somewhat out-of-the-money. Our index shows more change over the period because, while the implicit volatility tended to decline, interest rates rose.[10] Had these moved together instead of in opposition, the CBOE Index would have exhibited greater change over the period.

Figure 8A-2 shows the annualized volatility from six-month options implicit in the CBOE Call Option Index. Since the CBOE procedure does not separate out the effects of cash dividends, our calculation of volatilities implicit in the index will tend to be downward biased: If it were not for dividends, call prices would be higher causing the estimated implied volatilities to be higher. It may be possible to overcome this defect by a simple correction, but we will not pursue it here. Potentially of equal significance is the use of an incorrect interest rate, which could bias our estimates in either direction.

---

[6] It should be remembered from earlier chapters that at least in the context of the Black-Scholes formula, neither index will reflect changes in the expected *direction* of stock price movements.

[7] To be fair, we should mention that the CBOE Index has the advantage of relating to an option with which more investors can readily identify. However, setting $K = S\sqrt{r}$ to construct a put option index will mean that (except for their American aspects) both call and put indices will have the same value whenever puts and calls have the same implicit volatilities. This would facilitate comparison of these indices.

[8] We use the average rate on total bids accepted in the weekly auction for 26-week T-bills.

[9] Since we have made no dividend adjustments, our index will also reflect a forecast of future dividends. Even if an adjustment is made, our index will depend somewhat on our ability to forecast near-term dividends.

[10] Recall that declining volatility, other things equal, decreases Black-Scholes call prices, while rising interest rates increase these prices.

glossary of symbols

a	In the binomial model, the minimum number of up moves in the underlying stock price for a call option to finish in-the-money.
d	In the binomial model, one plus the rate of return of a stock if the stock price moves *down* over the next period.
g	Bond default premium.
$g(n, z)$	Gamma density function evaluated at n and z.
h	In the binomial model, the elapsed time between successive price changes.
j	In the binomial model, the (random) number of up moves in the underlying stock price during the life of an option.
k	The number of shares that can be purchased by a single convertible bond; call or put striking price in a compound option context.
m	The expected return of a security over a single period; the number of outstanding warrants of a firm, each to one share; the number of convertible bonds of a firm, each convertible into k shares.
n	In the binomial model, the number of periods remaining in the life of an option; the number of units purchased of a security; the number of outstanding common shares of a firm.
p	In the binomial model, the risk-neutral probability defined as $[(r - d)/(u - d)]$.
p'	In the binomial model, a probability defined as $(u/r)p$.
q	In the binomial model, the subjective probability that the stock price will move up over the next period.
r	One plus the interest rate on a default-free loan over a fixed length of calendar time.
$\hat{r}$	In the binomial model, one plus the interest rate over a period of length h.
t	Time to expiration of an option.
u	In the binomial model, one plus the rate of return of the stock if the stock price moves *up* over the next period.
v	The standard deviation of return of a security over a single period.
w	A firm's debt-to-total-value ratio, where the debt is valued at the present value, assuming no default, of its face value.
B	In the binomial model, the dollar amount invested in bonds in the hedging portfolio.

C	Current value of a call option to one share.
C^*	Value of a call option to one share on its expiration date.
D	Present value of the cash dividends per share that will be paid with certainty during the remaining life of an option.
D^+	Present value of the *maximum* cash dividends per share that will be paid during the remaining life of an option.
D^-	Present value of the *minimum* cash dividends per share that will be paid during the remaining life of an option.
ER	The equalizing ratio of an option.
F	The forward price of a forward contract; the futures price of a futures contract; the current value of a generalized option.
F^*	Value of a generalized option on its expiration date.
$G(w; n)$	Complementary gamma distribution function with parameter n evaluated at w.
H	Knock-out price for a down-and-out option.
K	Option striking price; lower payoff boundary of a supershare.
K_B	Total face value of a firm's senior bonds.
K_J	Total face value of a firm's junior bonds.
$N(z)$	Standard normal distribution function evaluated at z.
$N'(z)$	Standard normal density function evaluated at z.
$N_2(z_1, z_2; \rho)$	Standard bivariate normal distribution with correlation parameter ρ evaluated at z_1 and z_2.
P	Current value of a put option to one share.
P^*	Value of a put option to one share on its expiration date.
Q	Current value of a supershare.
Q^*	Value of a supershare on its expiration date.
R	Yield-to-maturity of a bond; rebate from a down-and-out option.
S	Current market price of one share of stock.
S^*	Market price of one share of stock on an option's expiration date.
$\overline{S}$	The *maximum* stock price at which a put is optimally exercised.
$\underline{S}$	The *minimum* stock price at which a call is optimally exercised.
T	Time to expiration of a generalized option; time to maturity of a bond.
V	Current total value of a firm.
V^*	Total value of a firm on the maturity date of its bonds.
W	Current value of a warrant to one share.
W^*	Value of a warrant to one share on its expiration date.
α	Alpha of a security—the excess expected rate of return of a security over and above that justified by its level of risk.
β	Beta of a security—the covariance of the security's rate of return with that of the market portfolio, divided by the variance of rate of return of the market portfolio.

γ	The percentage of total volatility explained by the jump component in a diffusion-jump model.
Γ	Gamma of an option—the sensitivity of the option delta to small changes in the underlying stock price.
δ	The dividend yield of a stock; the volatility of the jump component in a diffusion-jump process model.
Δ	In the binomial model, the number of shares in the hedging portfolio, reinterpreted as the delta of an option—the sensitivity of the option value to small changes in the underlying stock price.
ζ	The parameter determining the size of a jump in a jump process model.
Θ	Theta of an option—the sensitivity of the option value to a small reduction in the time to expiration.
λ	The parameter determining the probability of a jump in a pure-jump or diffusion-jump process model.
μ	The expected continuously compounded rate of return of a security per unit of time.
$\hat{\mu}$	The expected continuously compounded rate of return of a security over a single interval of length h.
$\hat{\hat{\mu}}$	Statistical estimate of the expected continuously compounded rate of return of a security per unit of time.
ν	Zero/one variable indicating the occurrence of an ex-dividend date.
$\bar{\nu}(n, i)$	In the binomial model, the number of ex-dividend dates occurring during the next $n - i$ periods.
π	The current price of a state-contingent claim.
ρ	The elasticity of the standard deviation of the stock rate of return.
σ	The standard deviation of the continuously compounded rate of return of a security per unit of time.
$\hat{\sigma}$	The standard deviation of the continuously compounded rate of return of a security over a single interval of length h; a parameter determining the volatility in a constant elasticity of variance diffusion model; the volatility of the diffusion component in a diffusion-jump process model.
$\hat{\hat{\sigma}}$	Statistical estimate of the standard deviation of the continuously compounded rate of return of a security per unit of time.
$\Phi[a; n, p]$	Complementary binomial distribution function with parameters n and p, evaluated at a.
$\Psi[x; y]$	Complementary Poisson distribution function with parameter y evaluated at x.
Ω	Elasticity of an option—the ratio of the percentage change in the option value to a small percentage change in the underlying stock price.

bibliography

The bibliography includes references on options and some important related subjects. References are grouped under the following nine headings:

1. Option Pricing: Theory
2. Option Pricing: Numerical Analysis
3. Option Pricing: Empirical Analysis
4. Option Trading Strategies
5. Distribution of Stock Price Changes
6. Options on Financial Instruments Other than Common Stocks
7. Valuation of Corporate Securities
8. Valuation of Other Financial Contracts
9. Innovations in Options Markets

References that fall in more than one category are classified under their primary subject.

Section 1 includes basic articles on option valuation. Most of these articles are concerned exclusively with options on common stocks, but many of their conclusions are applicable to other kinds of options as well. Section 2 lists works that discuss numerical methods for implementing some of the theoretical results cited in Section 1. The articles in Section 3 present some empirical tests of the theoretical results on valuation and give additional statistical information about the behavior of option prices. The papers cited in Section 4 provide evidence on the consequences of following a wide variety of option-trading strategies. Section 5 lists the voluminous literature on an important ingredient of stock option value, the distribution of stock price changes. Articles examining the effect of options trading on the behavior of stock prices are included in this section. In Section 6, we cite articles that concentrate on various aspects of options on financial instruments other than common stocks, including U.S. Treasury bills and bonds, foreign currency, and commodity futures. As we discuss in Chapter 7, option pricing theory has important implications for the valuation of corporate securities; Section 7 gives some references in this area. Section 8, in turn, lists articles showing how option pricing methods can be applied to many other kinds of financial contracts. A few articles discussing corporate or other securities are listed in Section 1 instead, because they represent contributions to, rather than applications of, the theory of stock option valuation. Finally, Section 9 gives references to topics covered in Chapter 8. These include the role of options markets in improving social welfare and the proposed development of new securities with option-like features.

Most articles on option pricing and its applications written after 1973 are based on the articles by Fischer Black and Myron Scholes, "The Pricing of Options and

Corporate Liabilities," *Journal of Political Economy,* 81 (May–June 1973), 637–659, and Robert C. Merton, "Theory of Rational Option Pricing," *Bell Journal of Economics and Management Science,* 4 (Spring 1973), 141–183. For articles written before that time, we have included only those that had an especially important role in the development of the subject; for subsequent articles, we have tried to be reasonably comprehensive. Additional references for works published before 1973 can be found in Richard Brealey and Connie Pyle, *A Bibliography of Finance and Investment* (Cambridge, Mass.: M.I.T. Press, 1973). The distribution of stock price changes is an area separate from option pricing, so here most earlier references are of continuing relevance and have been included.

The options exchanges provide another valuable source of information. They publish and distribute a wide variety of helpful brochures and pamphlets on options. Topics covered include contractual terms, elementary trading strategies, margin requirements, tax considerations, and statistical summaries. The titles available change frequently, but current lists can be obtained from the exchanges.

There are also dozens of general reference books available on options. Of these, the three whose approaches are most consistent with that taken in our book are Gary L. Gastineau, *The Stock Options Manual,* 2nd ed. (New York, NY: McGraw-Hill, 1979); Richard M. Bookstaber, *Option Pricing and Strategies in Investing* (Reading, Mass.: Addison-Wesley, 1981); and Robert A. Jarrow and Andrew T. Rudd, *Option Pricing* (Homewood, Ill.: Irwin, 1983). The annotated bibliography in the book by Gastineau provides a detailed description of most of the other books on options. Additional references to a few specialized books are given in the appropriate sections to follow.

1. OPTION PRICING: THEORY

Bachelier, Louis, "Theorie de la Speculation," *Annales de l'Ecole Normale Superieure,* 17 (1900), 21–86. English translation by A. J. Boness in *The Random Character of Stock Market Prices,* ed. Paul H. Cootner, pp. 17–78. Cambridge, Mass.: M.I.T. Press, 1967.

Bhattacharya, Sudipto, "Notes on Multiperiod Valuation and the Pricing of Options," *Journal of Finance,* 36 (March 1981), 163–180.

Black, Fischer, "Fact and Fantasy in the Use of Options," *Financial Analysts Journal,* 31 (July–August 1975), 36–41 and 61–72.

Black, Fischer, and Myron Scholes, "The Pricing of Options and Corporate Liabilities," *Journal of Political Economy,* 81 (May–June 1973), 637–659.

Boness, A. James, "Elements of a Theory of Stock-Option Value," *Journal of Political Economy,* 72 (April 1964), 163–175.

Boyle, Phelim P., and David Emanuel, "Discretely Adjusted Option Hedges," *Journal of Financial Economics,* 8 (September 1980), 259–282.

Brennan, Michael J., "The Pricing of Contingent Claims in Discrete Time Models," *Journal of Finance,* 34 (March 1979), 53–68.

Brown, David, and Chi-fu Huang, "Option Pricing in a Lognormal Securities Market with Discrete Trading," *Journal of Financial Economics,* 12 (August 1983), 285–286.

Chen, Andrew H. Y., "A Model of Warrant Pricing in a Dynamic Market," *Journal of Finance,* 25 (December 1970), 1041–1060.

Cox, John C., and Stephen A. Ross, "The Valuation of Options for Alternative Stochastic Processes," *Journal of Financial Economics,* 3 (January–March 1976), 145–166.

―――, "A Survey of Some New Results in Financial Option Pricing Theory," *Journal of Finance,* 31 (May 1976), 383–402.

Cox, John C., Stephen A. Ross, and Mark Rubinstein, "Option Pricing: A Simplified Approach," *Journal of Financial Economics,* 7 (September 1979), 229–263.

Cox, John C., and Mark Rubinstein, "A Survey of Alternative Option Pricing Models," in *Option Pricing,* ed. Menachem Brenner, pp. 3–33. Lexington, Mass.: D. C. Heath, 1983.

Galai, Dan, "Characterization of Options," *Journal of Banking and Finance,* 1 (December 1977), 373–385.

Garman, Mark B., "An Algebra for Evaluating Hedge Portfolios," *Journal of Financial Economics,* 3 (October 1976), 403–427.

Geske, Robert, "Pricing of Options with Stochastic Dividend Yield," *Journal of Finance,* 33 (May 1978), 617–625.

———, "The Valuation of Compound Options," *Journal of Financial Economics,* 7 (March 1979), 63–81.

———, "A Note on an Analytical Formula for Unprotected American Call Options on Stocks with Known Dividends," *Journal of Financial Economics,* 7 (December 1979), 375–380.

Geske, Robert, and Richard Roll, "On Valuing American Call Options with the Black-Scholes European Formula," *Journal of Finance,* 39 (June 1984), 443–455.

Geske, Robert, Richard Roll, and Kuldeep Shastri, "Over-the-Counter Option Market Dividend Protection and Biases in the Black-Scholes Model: A Note," *Journal of Finance,* 38 (September 1983), 1271–1278.

Gleit, Alan, "Valuation of General Contingent Claims: Existence, Uniqueness, and Comparisons of Solutions," *Journal of Financial Economics,* 6 (March 1978), 71–88.

Harrison, J. Michael, and David M. Kreps, "Martingales and Arbitrage in Multiperiod Securities Markets," *Journal of Economic Theory,* 20 (July 1979), 381–408.

Harrison, J. Michael, Richard Pitbladdo, and Stephen M. Schaefer, "Continuous Price Processes in Frictionless Markets Have Infinite Variation," *Journal of Business,* 57 (July 1984), 353–365.

Harrison, J. Michael, and Stanley R. Pliska, "Martingales and Stochastic Integrals in the Theory of Continuous Trading," *Stochastic Processes and their Applications,* 11 (1981), 261–271.

Hsia, Chi-Cheng, "On Binomial Option Pricing," *Journal of Financial Research,* 6 (Spring 1983), 41–50.

Kreps, David M., "Arbitrage and Equilibrium in Economies with Infinitely Many Commodities," *Journal of Mathematical Economics,* 8 (March 1981), 15–35.

———, "Multiperiod Securities and the Efficient Allocation of Risk: A Comment on the Black-Scholes Option Pricing Model," in *The Economics of Information and Uncertainty,* ed. John J. McCall, pp. 203–232. Chicago, Ill.: University of Chicago Press, 1982.

Kruizenga, Richard J., "Put and Call Options: A Theoretical Market Analysis." Doctoral dissertation, Massachusetts Institute of Technology, 1956. Excerpts reprinted in *The Random Character of Stock Market Prices,* ed. Paul H. Cootner, pp. 377–411. Cambridge, Mass.: M.I.T. Press, 1967.

Lee, Wayne Y., Ramesh K. S. Rao, and J. F. G. Auchmuty, "Option Pricing in a Lognormal Securities Market with Discrete Trading," *Journal of Financial Economics,* 9 (March 1981), 75–101.

McDonald, Robert, and Daniel Siegel, "Option Pricing When the Underlying Asset Earns a Below-Equilibrium Rate of Return: A Note," *Journal of Finance,* 39 (March 1984), 261–265.

McKean, Henry P., Jr., "Appendix: A Free Boundary Problem for the Heat Equation Arising from a Problem in Mathematical Economics," *Industrial Management Review,* 6 (Spring 1967), 32–39.

Merton, Robert C., "The Relationship Between Put and Call Option Prices: Comment," *Journal of Finance,* 28 (March 1973), 183–184.

———, "Theory of Rational Option Pricing," *Bell Journal of Economics and Management Science,* 4 (Spring 1973), 141–183.

———, "Option Pricing When Underlying Stock Returns are Discontinuous," *Journal of Financial Economics,* 3 (January–March 1976), 125–144.

———, "The Impact on Option Pricing of Specification Error in the Underlying Stock Price Returns," *Journal of Finance,* 31 (May 1976), 333–350.

———, "On the Pricing of Contingent Claims and the Modigliani-Miller Theorem," *Journal of Financial Economics,* 5 (November 1977), 241–250.

Perrakis, Stylianos, and Peter J. Ryan, "Option Pricing Bounds in Discrete Time," *Journal of Finance,* 39 (June 1984), 519–525.

Rao, Ramesh K. S., "Modern Option Pricing Models: A Dichotomous Classification," *Journal of Financial Research,* 4 (Spring 1981), 33–44.

Rendleman, Richard J., Jr., and Brit J. Bartter, "Two-State Option Pricing," *Journal of Finance,* 34 (December 1979), 1093–1110.

Roll, Richard, "An Analytic Valuation Formula for Unprotected American Call Options on Stocks with Known Dividends," *Journal of Financial Economics,* 5 (November 1977), 251–258.

Rubinstein, Mark, "The Valuation of Uncertain Income Streams and the Pricing of Options," *Bell Journal of Economics,* 7 (Autumn 1976), 407–425.

———, "Displaced Diffusion Option Pricing," *Journal of Finance,* 38 (March 1983), 213–217.

Rubinstein, Mark, and Hayne E. Leland, "Replicating Options with Positions in Stock and Cash," *Financial Analysts Journal,* 37 (July–August 1981), 63–72.

Samuelson, Paul A., "Rational Theory of Warrant Pricing," *Industrial Management Review,* 6 (Spring 1967), 13–31.

Samuelson, Paul A., and Robert C. Merton, "A Complete Model of Warrant Pricing that Maximizes Utility," *Industrial Management Review,* 10 (Winter 1969), 17–46.

Scholes, Myron, "Taxes and the Pricing of Options," *Journal of Finance,* 31 (May 1976), 319–332.

Smith, Clifford W., Jr., "Option Pricing: A Review," *Journal of Financial Economics,* 3 (January-March 1976), 3–51.

Sprenkle, Case M., "Warrant Prices as Indicators of Expectations and Preferences," *Yale Economic Essays,* 1 (1962), 172–231.

Stoll, Hans R., "The Relationship Between Put and Call Options Prices," *Journal of Finance,* 24 (December 1969), 802–824.

Thorp, Edward O., "Extensions of the Black-Scholes Option Model," *Proceedings of the 39th Session of the International Statistical Institute,* (August 1973), 1029–1036.

Whaley, Robert E., "A Note on an Analytical Formula for Unprotected American Call Options on Stocks with Known Dividends," *Journal of Financial Economics,* 7 (October 1979), 375–380.

———, "On the Valuation of American Call Options on Stocks with Known Dividends," *Journal of Financial Economics,* 9 (June 1981), 207–212.

2. OPTION PRICING: NUMERICAL ANALYSIS

Boyle, Phelim P., "Options: A Monte Carlo Approach," *Journal of Financial Economics,* 4 (May 1977), 323–338.

Brennan, Michael J., and Eduardo S. Schwartz, "The Valuation of American Put Options," *Journal of Finance,* 32 (May 1977), 449–462.

———, "Finite Difference Methods and Jump Processes Arising in the Pricing of Contingent Claims: A Synthesis," *Journal of Financial and Quantitative Analysis,* 13 (September 1978), 461–474.

Courtadon, Georges, "A More Accurate Finite Difference Approximation for the Valuation of Options," *Journal of Financial and Quantitative Analysis,* 17 (December 1982), 697–703.

Jarrow, Robert, and Andrew Rudd, "Approximate Option Valuation for Arbitrary Stochastic Processes," *Journal of Financial Economics,* 10 (November 1982), 347–369.

Johnson, H. E., "An Analytic Approximation of the American Put Price," *Journal of Financial and Quantitative Analysis,* 18 (March 1983), 141–148.

Manaster, Steven, and Gary Koehler, "The Calculation of Implied Variances from the Black-Scholes Model: A Note," *Journal of Finance,* 37 (March 1982), 227–230.

Parkinson, Michael, "Option Pricing: The American Put," *Journal of Business*, 50 (January 1977), 21–36.

3. OPTION PRICING: EMPIRICAL ANALYSIS

Beckers, Stan, "The Constant Elasticity of Variance Model and Its Implications for Option Pricing," *Journal of Finance,* 35 (June 1980), 661–673.

_____, "Standard Deviations Implied in Option Prices as Predictors of Future Stock Price Variability," *Journal of Banking and Finance,* 5 (September 1981), 363–382.

Bhattacharya, Mihir, "Empirical Properties of the Black-Scholes Formula Under Ideal Conditions," *Journal of Financial and Quantitative Analysis,* 15 (December 1980), 1081–1095.

Black, Fischer, and Myron Scholes, "The Valuation of Option Contracts and a Test of Market Efficiency," *Journal of Finance,* 27 (May 1972), 399–418.

Blomeyer, Edward C., and Robert C. Klemkosky, "Tests of Market Efficiency for American Call Options," in *Option Pricing*, ed. Menachem Brenner, pp. 101–121. Lexington, Mass.: D.C. Heath, 1983.

Boness, A. James, "Some Evidence on the Profitability of Trading in Put and Call Options," in *The Random Character of Stock Market Prices,* ed. Paul H. Cootner, pp. 475–496. Cambridge, Mass.: M.I.T. Press, 1967.

Bookstaber, Richard M., "Observed Option Mispricing and the Nonsimultaneity of Stock and Option Quotations," *Journal of Business*, 54 (January 1981), 141–155.

Boyle, Phelim, and A. L. Ananthanarayanan, "The Impact of Variance Estimation in Option Valuation Models," *Journal of Financial Economics,* 5 (December 1977), 375–388.

Castagna, A. D., and Z. P. Matolcsy, "A Two Stage Experimental Design to Test the Efficiency of the Market for Traded Stock Options and the Australian Evidence," *Journal of Banking and Finance,* 6 (December 1982), 521–532.

Chiras, Donald P., and Steven Manaster, "The Information Content of Option Prices and a Test of Market Efficiency," *Journal of Financial Economics,* 6 (June–September 1978), 213–234.

Cornell, Bradford, "Using the Option Pricing Model to Measure the Uncertainty Producing Effect of Major Announcements," *Financial Management*, 7 (Spring 1978), 54–59.

Cornell, Bradford, and Dhafrallah Hammani, "Option Pricing in Bear and Bull Markets,"*Journal of Portfolio Management,* 5 (Summer 1979), 30–32.

Emanuel, David C., and James D. MacBeth, "Further Results on the Constant Elasticity of Variance Call Option Pricing Model," *Journal of Financial and Quantitative Analysis,* 17 (November 1982), 533–554.

Farkas, Karen L., and Robert E. Hoskin, "Testing a Valuation Model for American Puts," *Financial Management*, 8 (Autumn 1979), 51–56.

Finnerty, Joseph E., "The CBOE and Market Efficiency," *Journal of Financial and Quantitative Analysis,* 13 (March 1978), 29–38.

French, Dan W., and Glenn V. Henderson, Jr., "Substitute Hedged Options Portfolios: Theory and Evidence," *Journal of Financial Research*, 4 (Spring 1981), 21–69.

Fuller, Russell J., "Factors Which Influence Listed Call Option Prices," *Review of Business and Economic Research,* 13 (Winter 1977–78), 21–34.

Galai, Dan, "Tests of Market Efficiency of the Chicago Board Option Exchange," *Journal of Business,* 50 (April 1977), 167–197.

_____, "Empirical Tests of Boundary Conditions for CBOE Options," *Journal of Financial Economics,* 6 (June–September 1978), 187–211.

_____, "A Convexity Test for Traded Options," *Quarterly Review of Economics and Business,* 19 (Summer 1979), 83–90.

_____, "The Components of the Return from Hedging Options Against Stock," *Journal of Business,* 56 (January 1983), 45–54.

_____, "A Survey of Empirical Tests of Option Pricing Models," in *Option Pricing*, ed. Menachem Brenner, pp. 45–80. Lexington, Mass.: D.C. Heath, 1983.

Gould, John P., and Dan Galai, "Transactions Costs and the Relationship Between Put and Call Prices," *Journal of Financial Economics*, 1 (June 1974), 105–129.

Gultekin, N. Bulent, Richard J. Rogalski, and Seha M. Tinic, "Option Pricing Model Estimates: Some Empirical Results," *Financial Management*, 12 (Spring 1982), 58–69.

Ho, Thomas S. Y., and Richard G. Macris, "Dealer Bid-Ask Quotes and Transaction Prices: An Empirical Study of Some AMEX Options," *Journal of Finance*, 39 (March 1984), 23–45.

Jarrow, Robert, and Andrew Rudd, "Tests of an Approximate Option-Valuation Formula," in *Option Pricing*, ed. Menachem Brenner, pp. 81–100. Lexington, Mass.: D.C. Heath, 1983.

Kalay, Avner, and Marti G. Subrahmanyam, "The Ex-Dividend Day Behavior of Option Prices," *Journal of Business*, 57 (January 1984), 113–128.

Kassouf, Sheen T., "An Econometric Model for Option Price with Implications for Investors' Expectations and Audacity," *Econometrica*, 37 (October 1969), 685–694.

_____, "The Lag Structure of Option Price," *Journal of Econometrics*, 4 (November 1976), 303–310.

Klemkosky, Robert C., and Bruce G. Resnick, "Put-Call Parity and Market Efficiency," *Journal of Finance*, 34 (December 1979), 1141–1155.

_____, "An Ex Ante Analysis of Put-Call Parity," *Journal of Financial Economics*, 8 (December 1980), 363–378.

Latané, Henry A., and Richard J. Rendleman, Jr., "Standard Deviations of Stock Price Ratios Implied in Option Prices," *Journal of Finance*, 31 (May 1976), 369–382.

Leabo, Dick A., and Richard J. Rogalski, "Warrant Price Movements and the Efficient Market Model," *Journal of Finance*, 30 (March 1975), 163–177.

MacBeth, James D., and Larry J. Merville, "An Empirical Examination of the Black-Scholes Call Option Pricing Model," *Journal of Finance*, 34 (December 1979), 1173–1186.

_____, "Tests of the Black-Scholes and Cox Call Option Valuation Models," *Journal of Finance*, 35 (May 1980), 285–300.

Manaster, Steven, and Richard J. Rendleman, Jr., "Option Prices as Predictors of Equilibrium Stock Prices," *Journal of Finance*, 37 (September 1982), 1043–1058.

Panton, D., "Chicago Board Call Options as Predictors of Common Stock Price Changes," *Journal of Econometrics*, 4 (1976), 101–113.

Patell, James M., and Mark A. Wolfson, "Anticipated Information Releases Reflected in Call Option Prices," *Journal of Accounting and Economics*, 1 (August 1979), 117–140.

_____, "The Ex Ante and Ex Post Effects of Quarterly Earnings Announcements Reflected in Option and Stock Prices," *Journal of Accounting Research*, 19 (Autumn 1981), 434–458.

Phillips, Susan M., and Clifford W. Smith, Jr., "Trading Costs for Listed Options: The Implications for Market Efficiency," *Journal of Financial Economics*, 8 (June 1980), 179–201.

Puglisi, Donald J., "A Rationale for Option Buying Behavior: Theory and Evidence," *Quarterly Review of Economics and Business*, (Spring 1974), 55–66.

Rogalski, Richard J., "Variances and Option Prices in Theory and Practice," *Journal of Portfolio Management*, 4 (Winter 1978), 43–51.

Rush, David F., and Ronald W. Melicher, "An Empirical Examination of Factors Which Influence Warrant Prices," *Journal of Finance*, 29 (December 1974), 1449–1466.

Schmalensee, Richard, and Robert R. Trippi, "Common Stock Volatility Expectations Implied by Option Premia," *Journal of Finance*, 33 (March 1978), 129–147.

Shelton, John P., "The Relation of the Pricing of a Warrant to the Price of Its Associated Common Stock," *Financial Analysts Journal*, 23 (May–June and July–August 1967), 88–99.

Sterk, William E., "Tests of Two Models for Valuing Call Options on Stocks with Dividends," *Journal of Finance*, 37 (December 1982), 1229–1238.

_____, "Comparative Performance of the Black-Scholes and Roll-Geske-Whaley Option Pricing Models," *Journal of Financial and Quantitative Analysis*, 18 (September 1983), 345–354.

Trennepohl, Gary, "A Comparison of Listed Option Premiums and Black and Scholes Model Prices: 1973–1979," *Journal of Financial Research,* 4 (Spring 1981), 11–20.

Trennepohl, Gary, and William P. Dukes, "An Empirical Test of Option Writing Strategies," *Review of Business and Economic Research,* 13 (Fall 1977), 48–58.

———, "Return and Risk from Listed Option Investment," *Journal of Financial Research,* 2 (Spring 1979), 37–49.

Trippi, Robert R., "A Test of Option Market Efficiency Using a Random-Walk Valuation Model," *Journal of Economics and Business,* 29 (Winter 1977), 93–98.

Van Horne, James C., "Warrant Valuation in Relation to Volatility and Opportunity Costs," *Industrial Management Review,* 10 (Spring 1969), 19–32.

Whaley, Robert E., "Valuation of American Call Options on Dividend Paying Stocks: Empirical Tests," *Journal of Financial Economics,* 10 (March 1982), 29–58.

4. OPTION TRADING STRATEGIES

Arnott, Robert D., "Modeling Portfolios with Options: Risks and Returns," *Journal of Portfolio Management,* 7 (Fall 1980), 66–73.

Asay, Michael R., "Implied Margin Requirements on Options and Stocks," *Journal of Portfolio Management,* 7 (Spring 1981), 55–62.

Block, Alan J., "An Option for the Art of Stability," *Journal of Portfolio Management,* 4 (Winter 1978), 27–30.

Bookstaber, Richard M., and Roger G. Clarke, "Options Can Alter Portfolio Return Distributions," *Journal of Portfolio Management,* 7 (Spring 1981), 63–70.

———, "An Algorithm to Calculate the Return Distribution of Portfolios with Option Positions," *Management Science,* 29 (April 1983), 419–429.

———, *Option Strategies for Institutional Investment Management.* Reading, Mass.: Addison-Wesley, 1983.

Boyle, Phelim P., and David Emanuel, "Discretely Adjusted Option Hedges," *Journal of Financial Economics,* 8 (September 1980), 255–282.

Brody, Eugene D., "Options and the Mathematics of Defense," *Journal of Portfolio Management,* 1 (Winter 1975), 2–6.

Dawson, Frederic A., "Risks and Returns in Continuous Option Writing," *Journal of Portfolio Management,* 5 (Winter 1979), 58–63.

Evnine, Jeremy, and Andrew Rudd, "Option Portfolio Risk Analysis," *Journal of Portfolio Management,* 10 (Winter 1984), 23–27.

Galai, Dan, and Robert Geske, "Option Performance Measurement," *Journal of Portfolio Management,* 10 (Spring 1984), 42–46.

Gastineau, Gary L., and Albert Madansky, "Why Simulations Are an Unreliable Test of Option Strategies," *Financial Analysts Journal,* 35 (September–October 1979), 61–76.

Gombala, Michael J., Rodney L. Roenfeldt, and Philip L. Cooley, "Spreading Strategies in CBOE Options: Evidence on Market Performance," *Journal of Financial Research,* 1 (Winter 1978), 33–44.

Grube, R. Corwin, and Don B. Panton, "How Well Do Filter-Rule Strategies Work for Options?" *Journal of Portfolio Management,* 4 (Winter 1978), 52–57.

Grube, R. Corwin, and J. Michael Terrell, "Risks and Rewards in Covered Call Positions," *Journal of Portfolio Management,* 5 (Winter 1979), 64–68.

Hart, James F., "The Riskless Option Hedge: An Incomplete Guide," *Journal of Portfolio Management,* 4 (Winter 1978), 58–63.

Hettenhouse, George W., and Donald J. Puglisi, "Investor Experience with Put and Call Options," *Financial Analysts Journal,* 3 (July–August 1975), 53–58.

Katz, Richard C., "The Profitability of Put and Call Option Writing," *Industrial Management Review,* (Fall 1963), 55–69.

Malkiel, Burton G., and Richard E. Quandt, *Strategies and Rational Decisions in the Securities Options Market.* Cambridge, Mass.: M.I.T. Press, 1969.

Merton, Robert C., Myron S. Scholes, and Mathew L. Gladstein, "The Returns and Risks of Alternative Call-Option Portfolio Investment Strategies," *Journal of Business,* 51 (April 1978), 183–242.

_____, "The Returns and Risks of Alternative Put-Option Portfolio Investment Strategies," *Journal of Business,* 55 (January 1982), 1–55.

Moriarty, Eugene, Susan Phillips, and Paula Tosini, "A Comparison of Options and Futures in the Management of Portfolio Risk," *Financial Analysts Journal,* 37 (January–February 1981), 61–67.

Mueller, Paul A., "Covered Options: An Alternative Investment Strategy," *Financial Management,* 10 (Autumn 1981), 64–71.

Phillips, Susan M., and Paula A. Tosini, "A Comparison of Margin Requirements for Options and Futures," *Financial Analysts Journal,* 38 (November–December 1982), 54–59.

Pounds, Henry M., "Covered Call Option Writing: Strategies and Results," *Journal of Portfolio Management,* 4 (Winter 1978), 31–42.

Pozen, Robert C., "The Purchase of Protective Puts by Financial Institutions," *Financial Analysts Journal,* 34 (July–August 1978), 47–60.

Reback, Robert, "Risk and Return in CBOE and AMEX Option Trading," *Financial Analysts Journal,* 31 (July–August 1975), 42–52.

Rendleman, Richard J., Jr., "Optimal Long-Run Option Investment Strategies," *Financial Management,* 10 (Spring 1981), 61–76.

Sears, R. Stephen, and Gary L. Trennepohl, "Measuring Portfolio Risk in Options," *Journal of Financial and Quantitative Analysis,* 17 (September 1982), 391–409.

_____, "Diversification and Skewness in Option Portfolios," *Journal of Financial Research,* 6 (Fall 1983), 199–212.

Slivka, Ronald R., "Risk and Return for Option Investment Strategies," *Financial Analysts Journal,* 36 (September–October 1980), 67–73.

_____, "Call Options Spreading," *Journal of Portfolio Management,* 7 (Spring 1981), 71–76.

Yates, Jr., James W., and Robert W. Kopprasch, Jr., "Writing Covered Call Options: Profits and Risks," *Journal of Portfolio Management,* 7 (Fall 1980), 74–79.

5. DISTRIBUTION OF STOCK PRICE CHANGES

Ali, Mukhtar M., and Carmelo Giacotto, "The Identical Distribution Hypothesis for Stock Market Prices—Location- and Scale-Shift Alternatives," *Journal of the American Statistical Association,* 77 (March 1982), 19–28.

Ball, Clifford A., and Walter N. Torous, "A Simplified Jump Process for Common Stock Returns," *Journal of Financial and Quantitative Analysis,* 18 (March 1983), 53–66.

_____, "The Maximum Likelihood Estimation of Security Price Volatility: Theory, Evidence, and Application to Option Pricing," *Journal of Business,* 57 (January 1984), 97–112.

Barnea, Amir, and David H. Downes, "A Re-examination of the Empirical Distribution of Stock Price Changes," *Journal of the American Statistical Association,* 68 (June 1973), 348–356.

Beckers, Stan, "A Note on Estimating the Parameters of a Diffusion-Jump Model of Stock Returns," *Journal of Financial and Quantitative Analysis,* 36 (March 1981), 127–140.

_____, "Variances of Security Price Returns Based on High, Low, and Closing Prices," *Journal of Business,* 56 (January 1983), 97–112.

Beranek, William, and Cyrus J. Mehta, "Tracking Asset Volatility by Means of a Bayesian Switching Regression," *Journal of Financial and Quantitative Analysis,* 17 (June 1982), 241–263.

Black, Fischer, "Studies of Stock Price Volatility Changes," *Proceedings of the 1976 Meetings of the American Statistical Association, Business and Economic Statistics Section,* (August 1976), 177–181.

Blattberg, Robert C., and Nicholas J. Gonedes, "A Comparison of the Stable and Student Distribution of Statistical Models for Stock Prices," *Journal of Business,* 47 (April 1974), 244–280.

Boness, A. James, Andrew H. Chen, and S. Jatusipitak, "Investigations of Nonstationarity in Prices," *Journal of Business,* 47 (October 1974), 518–537.

Christie, Andrew A., "The Stochastic Behavior of Common Stock Variances," *Journal of Financial Economics,* 10 (December 1982), 407–432.

Clark, Peter K., "A Subordinated Stochastic Process Model with Finite Variance for Speculative Prices," *Econometrica,* 41 (January 1973), 135–156.

Dowell, C. Dwayne, and R. Corbin Grube, "Common Stock Returns During Homogeneous Activity Periods," *Journal of Financial and Quantitative Analysis,* 13 (March 1978), 79–92.

Epps, Thomas W., "Security Price Changes and Transaction Volumes: Theory and Evidence," *American Economic Review* (September 1975), 586–597.

_____, "The Stochastic Dependence of Security Price Changes and Transactions Volume in a Model with Temporally Dependent Price Changes," *Journal of the American Statistical Association,* 71 (December 1976), 830–834.

_____, "Security Price Changes and Transaction Volume: Some Additional Evidence," *Journal of Financial and Quantitative Analysis,* 12 (March 1977), 141–146.

_____, "Co-movements in Stock Prices in the Very Short Run," *Journal of the American Statistical Association,* 74 (June 1979), 291–298.

Epps, Thomas W., and Mary L. Epps, "The Stochastic Dependence of Security Price Changes and Transactions Volume: Implications for the Mixture-of-Distribution Hypothesis," *Econometrica,* 44 (March 1976), 305–321.

Fama, Eugene F., "Mandelbrot and the Stable Paretian Hypothesis," *Journal of Business,* 36 (October 1963), 420–429.

_____, "The Behavior of Stock Market Prices," *Journal of Business,* 38 (January 1965), 34–105.

Fama, Eugene F., and Marshall E. Blume, "Filter Rules and Stock-Market Trading," *Journal of Business,* 39 (January 1966), 226–241.

Fielitz, Bruce D., "Stationarity of Random Data: Some Implications for the Distribution of Stock Price Changes," *Journal of Financial and Quantitative Analysis,* 6 (June 1971), 1025–1034.

Fielitz, Bruce D., and James P. Rozelle, "Stable Distributions and the Mixtures of Distribution Hypotheses for Common Stock Returns," *Journal of the American Statistical Association,* 78 (March 1983), 28–36.

Fielitz, Bruce D., and E. W. Smith, "Asymmetric Stable Distributions of Stock Price Changes," *Journal of the American Statistical Association,* 67 (December 1972), 813–814.

French, Kenneth R., "Stock Returns and the Weekend Effect," *Journal of Financial Economics,* 8 (March 1980), 55–69.

Garbade, Kenneth D., and Zvi Lieber, "On the Independence of Transactions on the New York Stock Exchange," *Journal of Banking and Finance,* 1 (October 1977), 151–172.

Garbade, Kenneth D., and Chandra P. Sekaran, "Opening Prices on the New York Stock Exchange," *Journal of Banking and Finance,* 5 (September 1981), 345–355.

Garman, Mark B., and Michael J. Klass, "On the Estimation of Security Price Volatilities from Historical Data," *Journal of Business,* 53 (January 1980), 67–78.

Gibbons, Michael R., and Patrick Hess, "Day of the Week Effects and Asset Returns," *Journal of Business,* 54 (October 1981), 579–596.

Greene, Myron T., and Bruce D. Fielitz, "Long-Term Dependence in Common Stock Returns," *Journal of Financial Economics,* 4 (May 1977), 339–349.

Hagerman, Robert L., "More Evidence on the Distribution of Security Returns," *Journal of Finance,* 33 (September 1978), 1213–1221.

Hayes, Samuel L., III, and Michael E. Tennenbaum, "The Impact of Listed Options on the Underlying Shares," *Financial Management,* 8 (Winter 1979), 72–77.

Hsu, Der-Ann, "Tests for Variance Shift at an Unknown Time Point," *Journal of the Royal Statistical Society, Series C,* 26 (1977), 279–284.

_____, "Detecting Shifts of Parameter in Gamma Sequences with Applications to Stock Price and Air Traffic Flow Analysis," *Journal of the American Statistical Association,* 74 (March 1979), 31–40.

_____, "A Bayesian Robust Detection of Shift in the Risk Structure of Stock Market Returns," *Journal of the American Statistical Association,* 77 (March 1982), 29–39.

Hsu, Der-Ann, Robert B. Miller, and Dean W. Wichern, "On the Stable Paretian Behavior of Stock Market Prices," *Journal of the American Statistical Association,* 69 (March 1974), 108–113.

Klemkosky, Robert C., and Terry S. Maness, "The Impact of Options on the Underlying Securities," *Journal of Portfolio Management,* 6 (Winter 1980), 12–17.

Kon, Stanley J., "Models of Stock Returns—A Comparison," *Journal of Finance,* 39 (March 1984), 147–165.

Mandelbrot, Benoit, "The Variation of Certain Speculative Prices," *Journal of Business,* 36 (October 1963), 394–419.

Mandelbrot, Benoit, and Howard M. Taylor, "On the Distribution of Stock Price Differences," *Operations Research,* 15 (November 1967), 1057–1062.

Moore, Arnold B., "Some Characteristics of Changes in Common Stock Prices," in *The Random Character of Stock Market Prices,* ed. Paul H. Cootner, pp. 139–161. Cambridge, Mass.: M.I.T. Press, 1967.

Morgan, I., "Stock Prices and Heteroscedasticity," *Journal of Business,* 49 (October 1976), 496–508.

Neiderhoffer, Victor, "Clustering of Stock Prices," *Operations Research,* 13 (March–April 1965), 258–265.

_____, "A New Look at Clustering of Stock Prices," *Journal of Business,* 39 (April 1966), 309–313.

Neiderhoffer, Victor, and M. F. M. Osborne, "Market Making and Reversal on the Stock Exchange," *Journal of the American Statistical Association,* 61 (December 1966), 897–916.

Officer, Dennis T., and Gary L. Trennepohl, "Price Behavior of Corporate Equities Near Option Expiration Dates," *Financial Management,* 10 (Summer 1981), 75–80.

Officer, R. R., "The Distribution of Stock Returns," *Journal of the American Statistical Association,* 67 (December 1972), 807–812.

Ohlson, James A., "On Financial Disclosure and the Behavior of Security Prices," *Journal of Accounting and Economics,* 1 (December 1979), 211–232.

Oldfield, George S., Jr., Richard J. Rogalski, and Robert A. Jarrow, "An Autoregressive Jump Process for Common Stock Return," *Journal of Financial Economics,* 5 (December 1977), 389–418.

Osborne, M. F. M., "Brownian Motion in the Stock Market," *Operations Research,* 7 (March–April 1959), 145–173.

_____, "Periodic Structure in the Brownian Motion of Stock Prices," *Operations Research,* 10 (May–June 1962), 345–379.

Parkinson, Michael, "The Extreme Value Method for Estimating the Variance of the Rate of Return," *Journal of Business,* 53 (January 1980), 61–65.

Patell, James M., and Mark A. Wolfson, "The Intraday Speed of Adjustment of Stock Prices to Earnings and Dividend Announcements," *Journal of Financial Economics,* 13 (June 1984), 223–252.

Perry, Philip R., "The Time-Variance Relationship of Security Returns: Implications for the Return-Generating Stochastic Process," *Journal of Finance,* 37 (June 1982), 857–870.

Piccini, Raymond, "Stock Market Behavior Around Business Cycle Peaks," *Financial Analysts Journal,* 36 (July–August 1980), 55–57.

Praetz, Peter D., "The Distribution of Share Price Changes," *Journal of Business,* 45 (January 1972), 49–55.

Press, S. James, "A Compound Events Model for Security Prices," *Journal of Business,* 40 (July 1967), 317–335.

Rozelle, James P., and Bruce P. Fielitz, "Stationarity of Common Stock Returns," *Journal of Financial Research,* 3 (Fall 1980), 229–242.

Scholes, Myron, and Joseph Williams, "Estimating Betas from Nonsynchronous Data," *Journal of Financial Economics,* 5 (December 1977), 309–328.

Schwartz, Robert A., and David K. Whitcomb, "The Time-Variance Relationship: Evidence on Autocorrelation in Common Stock Returns," *Journal of Finance*, 32 (March 1977), 41–56.

Simkowitz, Michael A., and William L. Beedles, "Asymmetric Stable Distributed Security Returns," *Journal of the American Statistical Association*, 75 (June 1980), 306–312.

Smidt, Seymour, "A New Look at the Random Walk Hypothesis," *Journal of Financial and Quantitative Analysis*, 3 (September 1968), 235–261.

Teichmoeller, John, "A Note on the Distribution of Stock Price Changes," *Journal of the American Statistical Association*, 66 (June 1971), 282–284.

Trennepohl, Gary L., and William P. Dukes, "CBOE Options and Stock Volatility," *Review of Business and Economic Research*, 14 (Spring 1979), 49–60.

Upton, David E., and Donald S. Shannon, "The Stable Paretian Distribution, Subordinated Stochastic Processes, and Asymptotic Lognormality: An Empirical Investigation," *Journal of Finance*, 34 (September 1979), 1031–1039.

Westerfield, Randolph, "The Distribution of Common Stock Price Changes: An Application of Transactions Time and Subordinated Stochastic Models," *Journal of Financial and Quantitative Analysis*, 12 (December 1977), 743–765.

Whiteside, Mary M., William P. Dukes, and Patrick M. Dunne, "Short Term Impact of Option Trading on Underlying Securities," *Journal of Financial Research*, 6 (Winter 1983), 313–321.

Wichern, Dean W., Robert B. Miller, and D. A. Hsu, "Changes of Variance in First-Order Autoregressive Time Series Models—With an Application," *Journal of the Royal Statistical Society, Series C*, 25 (1976), 248–256.

Young, William E., "Random Walk of Stock Prices: A Test of the Variance-Time Function," *Econometrica*, 39 (September 1971), 797–812.

6. OPTIONS ON FINANCIAL INSTRUMENTS OTHER THAN COMMON STOCKS

Asay, Michael R., "A Note on the Design of Commodity Option Contracts," *Journal of Futures Markets*, 2 (Spring 1982), 1–7.

——— "A Note on the Design of Commodity Option Contracts: A Reply," *Journal of Futures Markets*, 3 (Fall 1983), 335–338.

Ball, Clifford A., and Walter N. Torous, "Bond Price Dynamics and Options," *Journal of Financial and Quantitative Analysis*, 18 (December 1983), 517–531.

Biger, Nahum, and John Hall, "The Valuation of Currency Options," *Financial Management*, 12 (Spring 1983), 24–28.

Black, Fischer, "The Pricing of Commodity Contracts," *Journal of Financial Economics*, 3 (January–March 1976), 167–179.

Burton, T. Edwin, "Observations on the Theory of Option Pricing on Debt Instruments," in *Option Pricing*, ed. Menachem Brenner, pp. 35–44. Lexington, Mass.: D.C. Heath, 1983.

Camerer, Colin, "The Pricing and Social Value of Commodity Options," *Financial Analysts Journal*, 38 (January–February 1982), 62–67.

Courtadon, Georges, "The Pricing of Options on Default-Free Bonds," *Journal of Financial and Quantitative Analysis*, 17 (March 1982), 75–100.

Cox, John C., Jonathan E. Ingersoll, Jr., and Stephen A. Ross, "A Theory of the Term Structure of Interest Rates," *Econometrica*, 53 (March 1985).

Eckardt, Walter L., Jr., "Equivalent Delivery Procedures for GNMA Futures Contracts and Options," *Journal of Futures Markets*, 4 (Spring 1984), 75–85.

Feiger, George, and Bertrand Jacquillat, "Currency Option Bonds, Puts and Calls on Spot Exchange and Hedging of Contingent Foreign Earnings," *Journal of Finance*, 34 (December 1979), 1129–1143.

Figlewski, Stephen, and M. Desmond Fitzgerald, "Options on Commodity Futures: Recent Experience in the London Market," in *Option Pricing*, ed. Menachem Brenner, pp. 223–235. Lexington, Mass.: D.C. Heath, 1983.

Garman, Mark B., and Steven W. Kohlhagen, "Foreign Currency Option Values," *Journal of International Money and Finance,* 2 (December 1983), 231–237.

Giddy, Ian H., "Foreign Exchange Options," *Journal of Futures Markets,* 3 (Summer 1983), 143–166.

Grabbe, J. Orlin, "The Pricing of Call and Put Options on Foreign Exchange," *Journal of International Money and Finance,* 2 (December 1983), 239–253.

Hoag, James W., "The Valuation of Commodity Options," in *Option Pricing,* ed., Menachem Brenner, pp. 183–221. Lexington, Mass.: D.C. Heath, 1983.

McDonald, Robert, and Daniel Siegel, "A Note on the Design of Commodity Option Contracts: A Comment," *Journal of Futures Markets,* 3 (Spring 1983), 43–46.

Parkinson, Michael, "The Valuation of GNMA Options," *Financial Analysts Journal,* 38 (September–October 1982), 66–76.

Rendelman, Richard J., Jr., and Brit J. Bartter, "The Pricing of Options on Debt Securities," *Journal of Financial and Quantitative Analysis,* 15 (March 1980), 11–24.

7. VALUATION OF CORPORATE SECURITIES

Black, Fischer, and John C. Cox, "Valuing Corporate Securities: Some Effects of Bond Indenture Provisions," *Journal of Finance,* 31 (May 1976), 351–368.

Brennan, Michael J., and Eduardo S. Schwartz, "Convertible Bonds: Valuation and Optimal Strategies for Call and Conversion," *Journal of Finance,* 32 (December 1977), 1699–1716.

_____, "Corporate Income Taxes, Valuation, and the Problem of Optimal Capital Structure," *Journal of Business,* 51 (January 1978), 103–114.

_____, "Analyzing Convertible Bonds," *Journal of Financial and Quantitative Analysis,* 15 (November 1980), 907–929.

Constantinides, George M., and Robert W. Rosenthal, "Strategic Analysis of the Competitive Exercise of Certain Financial Options," *Journal of Economic Theory,* 32 (February 1984), 128–138.

Emanuel, David C., "Warrant Valuation and Exercise Strategy," *Journal of Financial Economics,* 12 (August 1983), 211–236.

_____, "A Theoretical Model for Valuing Preferred Stock," *Journal of Finance,* 38 (September 1983), 1133–1155.

Galai, Dan, and Ronald W. Masulis, "The Option Pricing Model and the Risk Factor of Stock," *Journal of Financial Economics,* 3 (January–March 1976), 53–81.

Galai, Dan, and Mier I. Schneller, "Pricing Warrants and the Value of the Firm," *Journal of Finance,* 33 (December 1978), 1333–1342.

Geske, Robert, "The Valuation of Corporate Liabilities as Compound Options," *Journal of Financial and Quantitative Analysis,* 12 (November 1977), 541–552.

Geske, Robert, and H. E. Johnson, "The Valuation of Corporate Liabilities as Compound Options: A Correction," *Journal of Financial and Quantitative Analysis,* 19 (June 1984), 231–232.

Ho, Thomas S. Y., and Ronald F. Singer, "Bond Indenture Provisions and the Risk of Corporate Debt," *Journal of Financial Economics,* 10 (December 1982), 375–406.

_____, "The Value of Corporate Debt with a Sinking-Fund Provision," *Journal of Business,* 57 (July 1984), 315–336.

Hsia, Chi-Cheng, "Optimal Debt of a Firm: An Option Pricing Approach," *Journal of Financial Research,* 4 (Fall 1981), 221–231.

Ingersoll, Jonathan E., Jr., "A Contingent-Claims Valuation of Convertible Securities," *Journal of Financial Economics,* 4 (May 1977), 289–322.

_____, "An Examination of Corporate Call Policies on Convertible Securities," *Journal of Finance,* 32 (May 1977), 463–478.

Kassouf, Sheen T., *Evaluation of Convertible Securities.* New York: Analytic Publishers, 1969.

Lee, C. Jevons, "The Pricing of Corporate Debt: A Note," *Journal of Finance,* 36 (December 1981), 1187–1189.

Mason, Scott P., and Sudipto Bhattacharya, "Risky Debt, Jump Processes, and Safety Covenants," *Journal of Financial Economics,* 9 (September 1981), 281–307.

Merton, Robert C., "On the Pricing of Corporate Debt: The Risk Structure of Interest Rates," *Journal of Finance,* 29 (May 1974), 449–470.

Noreen, Eric, and Mark Wolfson, "Equilibrium Warrant Pricing Models and Accounting for Executive Stock Options," *Journal of Accounting Research,* 19 (Autumn 1981), 384–398.

Schwartz, Eduardo S., "The Valuation of Warrants: Implementing a New Approach," *Journal of Financial Economics,* 4 (January 1977), 79–93.

_____, "The Pricing of Commodity-Linked Bonds," *Journal of Finance,* 37 (May 1982), 525–539.

Smith, Clifford W., Jr., and Jerold L. Zimmerman, "Valuing Employee Stock Option Plans Using Option Pricing Models," *Journal of Accounting Research,* 14 (Autumn 1976), 357–364.

Thorp, Edward O., and Sheen T. Kassouf, *Beat the Market: A Scientific Stock Market System.* New York: Random House, 1967.

8. VALUATION OF OTHER FINANCIAL CONTRACTS

Ananthanarayanan, A. L., and Eduardo S. Schwartz, "Retractable and Extendible Bonds: The Canadian Experience," *Journal of Finance,* 35 (March 1980), 31–47.

Bartter, Brit J., and Richard J. Rendleman, Jr., "Fee-Based Pricing of Fixed-Rate Bank Loan Commitments," *Financial Management,* 8 (Spring 1979), 13–20.

Boyle, Phelim P., and Eduardo S. Schwartz, "Equilibrium Prices of Guarantees Under Equity-Linked Contracts," *Journal of Risk and Insurance,* 44 (December 1977), 639–680.

Brealey, Richard A., Stewart D. Hodges, and Michael J. P. Selby, "The Risk of Bank-Loan Portfolios," in *Option Pricing,* ed. Menachem Brenner, pp. 153–182. Lexington, Mass.: D.C. Heath, 1983.

Brennan, Michael J., and Eduardo S. Schwartz, "The Pricing of Equity-Linked Life Insurance Policies with an Asset Value Guarantee," *Journal of Financial Economics,* 3 (June 1976), 195–213.

_____, "Savings Bonds, Retractable Bonds, and Callable Bonds," *Journal of Financial Economics,* 5 (August 1977), 67–88.

_____, "Alternative Investment Strategies for the Issuers of Equity-Linked Life Insurance Policies with an Asset Value Guarantee," *Journal of Business,* 52 (January 1979), 63–93.

_____, "Savings Bonds: Valuation and Optimal Redemption Strategies," in *Financial Economics: Essays in Honor of Paul Cootner,* ed. William F. Sharpe and Cathryn M. Cootner, pp. 202–215. Englewood Cliffs, N.J.: Prentice-Hall, 1982.

Courtadon, Georges, "A Note on the Premium Market of the Paris Stock Exchange," *Journal of Banking and Finance,* 6 (December 1982), 561–564.

Cox, John C., Jonathan E. Ingersoll, Jr., and Stephen A. Ross, "An Analysis of Variable Rate Loan Contracts," *Journal of Finance,* 35 (May 1980), 389–404.

Dunn, Kenneth B., and John J. McConnell, "A Comparison of Alternative Models for Pricing GNMA Mortgage-Backed Securities," *Journal of Finance,* 36 (May 1981), 471–484.

_____, "Valuation of GNMA Mortgage-Backed Securities," *Journal of Finance,* 35 (June 1981), 599–616.

Fischer, Stanley, "Call Option Pricing When the Exercise Price is Uncertain, and the Valuation of Index Bonds," *Journal of Finance,* 33 (March 1978), 169–176.

Galai, Dan, "Pricing of Optional Bonds," *Journal of Banking and Finance,* 7 (September 1983), 323–337.

Haugen, Robert A., and Lemma W. Senbet, "Resolving the Agency Problems of External Capital Through Options," *Journal of Finance,* 35 (June 1981), 629–648.

Hawkins, Gregory D., "An Analysis of Revolving Credit Agreements," *Journal of Financial Economics,* 10 (March 1982), 59–82.

Ingersoll, Jonathan E., Jr., "A Theoretical Model and Empirical Investigation of the Dual

Purpose Funds: An Application of Contingent-Claims Analysis," *Journal of Financial Economics,* 3 (January–March 1976), 83–123.

Jones, E. Phillip, and Scott P. Mason, "Valuation of Loan Guarantees," *Journal of Banking and Finance,* 4 (March 1980), 89–107.

Margrabe, William, "The Value of an Option to Exchange One Asset for Another," *Journal of Finance,* 33 (March 1978), 177–186.

Merton, Robert C., "An Analytic Derivation of the Cost of Deposit Insurance and Loan Guarantees: An Application of Modern Option Pricing Theory," *Journal of Banking and Finance,* 1 (June 1977), 3–11.

_____, "On the Cost of Deposit Insurance When There Are Surveillance Costs," *Journal of Business,* 51 (July 1978), 439–452.

Sharpe, William F., "Corporate Pension Funding Policy," *Journal of Financial Economics,* 3 (June 1976), 183–193.

Smith, Clifford W., Jr., "Applications of Option Pricing Analysis," in *Handbook of Financial Economics,* ed. James L. Bicksler, pp. 79–121. New York: North-Holland Publishing Company, 1979.

_____, "On the Theory of Financial Contracting: The Personal Loan Market," *Journal of Monetary Economics,* 6 (July 1980), 333–357.

Sosin, Howard W., "On the Valuation of Federal Loan Guarantees to Corporations," *Journal of Finance,* 35 (December 1980), 1209–1221.

Stapleton, R. C., and M. G. Subrahmanyam, "The Valuation of Multivariate Contingent Claims in Discrete Time Models," *Journal of Finance,* 39 (March 1984), 207–228.

Stulz, Rene M., "Options on the Minimum or the Maximum of Two Risky Assets: Analysis and Applications," *Journal of Financial Economics,* 10 (July 1982), 161–185.

9. INNOVATIONS IN OPTIONS MARKETS

Arditti, Fred D., and Kose John, "Spanning the State Space with Options," *Journal of Financial and Quantitative Analysis,* 15 (March 1980), 1–9.

Banz, Rolf W., and Merton H. Miller, "Prices for State-Contingent Claims: Some Estimates and Applications," *Journal of Business,* 51 (October 1978), 653–672.

Bick, Avi, "Comments on the Valuation of Derivative Assets," *Journal of Financial Economics,* 10 (November 1982), 331–345.

Breeden, Douglas T., and Robert H. Litzenberger, "Prices of State-Contingent Claims Implicit in Option Prices," *Journal of Business,* 51 (October 1978), 621–651.

Brennan, Michael J., and R. Solanki, "Optimal Portfolio Insurance," *Journal of Financial and Quantitative Analysis,* 16 (September 1981), 279–300.

Ederington, Louis H., "Living With Inflation: A Proposal for New Futures and Options Markets," *Financial Analysts Journal,* 36 (January–February 1980), 42–48.

Friesen, Peter H., "The Arrow-Debreu Model Extended to Financial Markets," *Econometrica,* 47 (May 1979), 689–707.

Galai, Dan, "A Proposal for Indexes for Traded Call Options," *Journal of Finance,* 34 (December 1979), 1157–1172.

Garman, Mark B., "The Pricing of Supershares," *Journal of Financial Economics,* 6 (March 1978), 3–10.

Gastineau, Gary L., "An Index of Listed Option Premiums," *Financial Analysts Journal,* 33 (May–June 1977), 70–75.

Gatto, Mary Ann, Robert Geske, Robert Litzenberger, and Howard Sosin, "Mutual Fund Insurance," *Journal of Financial Economics,* 8 (September 1980), 283–317.

Goldman, M. Barry, Howard B. Sosin, and Mary Ann Gatto, "Path Dependent Options: Buy at the Low, Sell at the High," *Journal of Finance,* 34 (December 1979), 1111–1128.

Goldman, M. Barry, Howard B. Sosin, and Lawrence A. Shepp, "On Contingent Claims that Insure Ex-Post Optimal Stock Market Timing," *Journal of Finance,* 34 (May 1979), 401–413.

Hakansson, Nils H., "The Purchasing Power Fund: A New Kind of Financial Intermediary," *Financial Analysts Journal,* 32 (November–December 1976), 49–59.

———, "The Superfund: Efficient Paths toward Efficient Capital Markets in Large and Small Countries," in *Financial Decision Making under Uncertainty,* ed., Haim Levy and Marshall Sarnat, pp. 165–201. New York: Academic Press, 1977.

———, "Welfare Aspects of Options and Supershares," *Journal of Finance,* 33 (June 1978), 754–776.

John, Kose, "Efficient Funds in Financial Markets with Options: A New Irrelevance Proposition," *Journal of Finance,* 37 (June 1981), 685–695.

———, "Market Resolution and Valuation in Incomplete Markets," *Journal of Financial and Quantitative Analysis,* 19 (March 1984), 29–44.

Leland, Hayne E., "Who Should Buy Portfolio Insurance?" *Journal of Finance,* 35 (May 1980), 581–594.

Ross, Stephen A., "Options and Efficiency," *Quarterly Journal of Economics,* 90 (February 1976), 75–89.

Rubinstein, Mark, "An Economic Evaluation of Organized Options Markets," *Journal of Comparative Corporate Law and Securities Regulation,* 2 (June 1979), 49–64.

Singleton, J. Clay, and Robin Grieves, "Synthetic Puts and Portfolio Insurance Strategies," *Journal of Portfolio Management,* 10 (Spring 1984), 63–69.

index

t denotes table; n denotes footnote.